Microsoft®

SQL Server™ 7.0

by Sharon Bjeletich and Greg Mable et al.

SAMS

Unleashed

Microsoft® SQL Server™ 7.0 Unleashed

Copyright ©1999 by Sams Publishing

International Standard Book Number: 0-672-31227-1

Library of Congress Catalog Card Number: 97-69133

Printed in the United States of America

First Printing: May 1999

02   01   00   99   4   3   2   1

Trademarks

Warning and Disclaimer

EXECUTIVE EDITOR
Rosemarie Graham

ACQUISITIONS EDITOR
Neil Rowe

DEVELOPMENT EDITORS
Marla Reece-Hall
Matt Larson
Rosemarie Graham

MANAGING EDITOR
Jodi Jensen

PROJECT EDITOR
Dana Rhodes Lesh

COPY EDITORS
Kris Simmons
Alice Martina Smith

INDEXER
Rebecca Salerno

PROOFREADERS
Mona Brown
Jill Mazurczyk

TECHNICAL EDITORS
Sakhr Youness
Chris Hoke
Patrick Thurman
Ivan Oss

SOFTWARE DEVELOPMENT SPECIALIST
Todd Pfeffer

INTERIOR DESIGNER
Gary Adair

COVER DESIGNER
Aren Howell

COPY WRITER
Eric Borgert

LAYOUT TECHNICIANS
Brandon Allen
Stacey Richwine-DeRome
Timothy Osborn
Staci Somers

Overview

Contents

PART IV   SQL SERVER ADMINISTRATION TASKS AND TOOLS   211

9   THE SQL SERVER ENTERPRISE MANAGER   213

PART V   TRANSACT-SQL   447

21   USING TRANSACT-SQL IN SQL SERVER 7.0   449

About the Authors

Sharon Bjeletich is an independent consultant for her company Meta Technical Services, Inc., based in the Pacific Northwest. She has worked in the microcomputer industry since 1981, becoming an independent consultant in 1984. Since then she has served as an analyst, architect, developer, and trainer. Ms. Bjeletich has consulted for many companies in the Pacific Northwest and served as a principal engineer at Corbis Corporation. In addition, she worked as a technical officer for Information Systems for the World Health Organization in Geneva, Switzerland, for eight years, where her duties included presenting seminars on microcomputers and research management for the People's Republic of China. She is also one of the authors of the Designing and Implementing Databases with Microsoft SQL Server 7.0 Microsoft Certified Professional certification exam. Sharon can be reached at `sharon@metatechnical.com`.

Greg Mable is president of .exe Software, Inc., a consulting company located in Michigan that specializes in network site support, Web design, and SQL Server development. He is an MCSE and MCSD with more than 15 years of computing experience, and he has worked with SQL Server since its inception, when it was comarketed with the Ashton-Tate label (and he has the manuals and disks to prove it!). He has served as a SQL Server database administrator for such companies as Ameritech and Metropolitan Life.

Irfan Chaudhry has been working as a consultant for the past several years with various sized clients, including Fortune 500 companies and legal firms, mainly on NT-based projects. He has his MCSE and is currently working on his MCSD. Irfan has written and been published previously on the topics of Windows NT Server and Microsoft Internet Information Server. Currently, he is working as a senior network engineer at Affiliated Distributors, based in King of Prussia, PA.

Ted Daley brings more than 10 years of experience in the computer industry and the business world. Ted is currently the lead consultant and teacher for MB Consulting, a firm specializing in providing database expertise to a variety of federal, state, educational, and commercial clients throughout the United States. His consulting and training efforts focus on Microsoft SQL Server on the Windows NT platform. His expertise spans enterprisewide reporting, decision support, and data warehousing systems. He can be reached at `teddaley@cizer.com`.

John Del Buono began programming small routines using a Commodore 64, which has grown into a career of what makes computers tick. Studying various computing platforms, he began to acquire a growing interest in how they store, process, and communicate data. A break came when a position opened up in IBM for a technician that had a background not only in computer hardware, but also in network and database administration. From that point, John moved to Florida, where at Office Depot Corporate he was positioned as a systems analyst/DBA for a call-tracking application. This application used Microsoft SQL server as a back end and was customized using Visual Basic for Applications. Currently, John is employed with Isogon Corporation in New York City as lead developer for a database intensive management tool.

Simon Gallagher graduated in 1991 from the University of Kent at Canterbury, England, with a first-class bachelor of science with honors degree in computer science. He is currently a senior consultant and part-time instructor for the Indianapolis office of NewMedia, Inc. Simon is also a Microsoft Certified Professional and Microsoft Certified Trainer in SQL Server, and he just recently attained his Microsoft System Engineer status. He is also a Certified PowerBuilder Associate since version 3.0. Simon has been programming in PowerBuilder since version 2.0 and has successfully fielded a number of different applications, ranging from a property tax reporting system to an order entry system. He has been involved with a number of different hardware platforms and operating systems, and has a broad knowledge of databases and development languages. He has also coauthored a number of books, including *PowerBuilder 4 Unleashed, PowerBuilder 5 Unleashed, and PowerBuilder 6 Unleashed*, and has contributed with chapters and technical editing to other development language and database books. You can reach Simon on the Internet at raven@iquest.net. You can also explore his Web pages at http://members.iquest.net/~raven/raven.html.

Joe Giordano is currently employed as a senior network/software engineer at a growing consulting firm in Raleigh, NC. His 12 years of experience in the field have led him to provide solutions for pharmaceutical, manufacturing, technical, and government firms, to name a few. In addition to consulting, he uses his extensive knowledge to train other professionals in the field. Aside from his busy work schedule, he enjoys spending time with his wife and two children in the Raleigh area.

Tibor Karaszi is a SQL Server trainer for Cornerstone, based in Sweden. He has been working with SQL Server for nearly 10 years as a DBA, application developer, database designer, consultant, and instructor. Tibor has also been involved in internal Microsoft education throughout Europe. In addition to certification as a Microsoft Certified Trainer, Tibor also holds the Microsoft Certified Systems Engineer (MCSE) and Microsoft Certified Solution Developer (MCSD) titles and has been recognized by Microsoft as a SQL Server MVP. Tibor can be reached at tibor@cornerstone.se.

Matt Larson is a database manager in the J.D. Edwards software development team located in Denver, CO. Matt holds a bachelor of science in business administration (emphasis on Information Systems) from the University of Colorado, where he graduated first in his class. He has also written and/or edited for *Microsoft SQL Server 7.0 DBA Survival Guide, Sams Teach Yourself Microsoft SQL Server 7.0 in 21 Days, Oracle8 Server Unleashed*, and *Oracle Unleashed* (Second and Third Editions). Matt can be reached at mattlarson@usa.net.

Vipul Minocha is vice president of technology development with CareTools. He is one of the original authors of *Microsoft BackOffice Unleashed* and contributing author for *SQL Server Unleashed, Third Edition*. He can be reached at minochav@yahoo.com.

Mark Nippert is a software consultant for Fulcrum Software Corporation in Raleigh, NC. Mark is a Microsoft Certified Solution Developer, and he specializes in new technologies such as Microsoft Transaction Server. He has developed software for companies in many industries: finance, sales, education, pharmaceuticals, real estate, and so on. Mark enjoys hearing from peers, so please feel free to send an idea, a story, or just a hello to markn@FulcrumCorp.com.

Bob Pfeiff is a Microsoft Certified Solution Developer (MCSD) and Certified Trainer (MCT) whose experience includes mainframe operations management, client/server application design, development and project management, data warehouse design, implementation and project management, and SQL Server application performance tuning and optimization. He is also a Microsoft Most Valuable Professional (MVP) for SQL Server. He can be reached at rpfeiff@erols.com.

Matthew Shepker is a SQL Server consultant and network integrator in Overland Park, KS. Matthew has been working with SQL Server for more than four years in a variety of business applications, including online transaction processing, decision support systems, and other custom software. He has coauthored two other books and has written one book. Matthew is an MCSE and MCT and is now one test away from his MCSD. Matthew currently lives in Overland Park, KS, with his wife, Misty.

Kevin Viers is manager of the Enterprise Technologies Group at Keiter, Stephens Computer Services, Inc., and a graduate of James Madison University. He has more than five years of consulting experience, specializing in designing, developing, and implementing enterprise solutions. Kevin cut his programming teeth on PowerBuilder and has since developed a broad development background including SAP, Active Server Pages, and Visual Basic. Kevin lives with his wife, Pam, and his boxer, Alli, in Richmond, VA. He can be reached via the internet at kviers@kscsinc.com.

Dedication

I would like to dedicate this book to my parents, Robert and Joan Bjeletich, and to my daughter, Melina Bjeletich Miller.

—Sharon Bjeletich

This book is dedicated to Ron Soukop, one of the original members of the SQL Server development team, who is considered the father of SQL Server. We, your many children, salute you!

—Greg Mable

Acknowledgments

Unleashed books are the result of the efforts of many people: writers, editors, technical reviewers, and others. This book benefited from the diligence and talent of all the authors, and it would not have been completed without the patience and guidance of the Sams staff, especially Rosemarie Graham, Neil Rowe, Corrine Wire, Marla Reece-Hall, and Dana Lesh.

Technical guidance, input, and review were also provided by Dan Michaud, Shirley Kloss, Sharon Dooley (from all her good advice on the www.swynk.com SQL Server list), Kevin O'Halloran, Heather Kautzky, Steven Martin, and Naser Ghaddah. Musimbi Kanyoro provided her usual inspiration, and Rob and Caryl Bjeletich provided personal guidance. As always, I have to acknowledge the patience and understanding of my daughter, Melina, during all those weekends when I wasn't available and she didn't complain.

—Sharon Bjeletich

No one person can do it all (except for maybe Bill Gates himself). I would like to express my thanks and appreciation for all the support that I have received from Sams Publishing, including Rosemarie Graham, Marla Reece-Hall, Neil Rowe, Corrine Wire, Dana Lesh, and Kris Simmons. I also want to thank my wife, Linda, and my son, Joseph, for their patience with me while I buried myself in my home office to work on the many beta releases.

I also would like to thank Richard Waymire, Kalen Delaney, all the Microsoft Most Valuable Players who tirelessly monitor the SQL Server newsgroups, and the people who put together the Sphinx workshop in Los Angeles, especially Roger Doherty.

—Greg Mable

Tell Us What You Think!

As the reader of this book, *you* are our most important critic and commentator. We value your opinion and want to know what we're doing right, what we could do better, what areas you'd like to see us publish in, and any other words of wisdom you're willing to pass our way.

As an associate publisher for Sams Publishing, I welcome your comments. You can fax, email, or write me directly to let me know what you did or didn't like about this book—as well as what we can do to make our books stronger.

Please note that I cannot help you with technical problems related to the topic of this book, and that due to the high volume of mail I receive, I might not be able to reply to every message.

When you write, please be sure to include this book's title and author as well as your name and phone or fax number. I will carefully review your comments and share them with the author and editors who worked on the book.

Fax:	(317) 581-4770
Email:	mstephens@mcp.com
Mail:	Michael Stephens
	Associate Publisher
	Sams Publishing
	201 West 103rd Street
	Indianapolis, IN 46290 USA

Introduction

The release of newest version of Microsoft SQL Server, version 7.0, has been a much-anticipated event. With this release, SQL Server completely breaks its ties from Sybase SQL Server and begins to stand on its own as a corporate database product. It has been targeted to support not only the small- to medium-sized businesses that have been SQL Server's traditional market, but also the larger organization tasked with implementing both transactional systems, very large databases, and data warehousing.

SQL Server 7.0 has been completely rewritten, including the relational engine and the query engine, many of the familiar tools are gone or have a new look, and new tools have been introduced. This brings many new challenges to the database professional tasked with understanding, implementing, and supporting this product. One of the goals of this new *Unleashed* book is to help you understand the new product, not only from an academic point of view, but also from an implementation point of view. In other words, you will learn how this new product will affect your existing databases and applications and how you can best take advantage of its new features.

Because SQL Server 7.0 is completely rewritten and can almost be considered a version 1.0 release, there is still much to be learned and understood about how the product will actually perform in a production environment. It takes a good year of use by a wide community of database users to truly appreciate and understand a new product's features (and pitfalls). The writers of this edition have been using the product for many months before the actual product release, and much of the information comes from this actual experience. The approach of this *Unleashed* book is to compile the expertise of many experts from many areas of business and the world, creating a compendium of practical advice. The intent is to provide you with a daily tool to help in the upgrading of your existing systems to the new version and the creation of new systems and to optimize your use and understanding of the new features.

Who Is This Book's Intended Audience?

This *Unleashed* book is intended for an intermediate-to-advanced level of user. However, because SQL Server 7.0 is a new product, new features and tools are covered more in-depth to ensure that they're fully understood. Concepts that are well understood in the SQL Server 6.5 environment will not be covered at an introductory level in this book.

If you are responsible for analysis, design, implementation, support, administration, or troubleshooting of SQL Server 7.0, this book should provide an excellent source of experiential information. You can think of this as a book of "applied technology." The emphasis is on the more complex aspects of the product, including using the new tools, writing Transact-SQL, server administration, query analysis and optimization, data warehousing, managing very large databases, and performance tuning.

The book is divided into the following eight parts:

- Part I, "SQL Server in the Corporate Enterprise"—The use of SQL Server 7.0 and the Internet, including three-tier architecture, thick and thin architecture, and universal data access are covered, as well as how Windows NT 5.0, clustering, and OLE DB partner with SQL Server 7.0.

- Part II, "Installation and Upgrade"—The chapters in this part include coverage of how to install a new server and client utilities, how to upgrade from a previous version, and backward-compatibility issues.

- Part III, "SQL Server Database Architecture"—This part covers in-depth the physical and logical database architecture, including the new database filegroup system and new datatypes. Performance improvements and the use of stored procedures, triggers, constraints, rules, and cursors are covered. The system tables and stored procedures provided by the server are detailed as well as SQL Server 7.0's new information schema views.

- Part IV, "SQL Server Administration Tasks and Tools"—All the tools and tasks required to administer SQL Server 7.0 are covered in-depth in this section. This includes the use of SQL Enterprise Manager, security and user management, roles, permissions, replication, the SQL Server Agent, email integration, and setting up alerts. Backup, restore, recovery, maintenance, remote and linked server management, and BCP (bulk copy program) are also covered. The command-line utilities available for SQL Server 7.0 are included, and a chapter on administering very large databases provides expert advice.

- Part V, "Transact-SQL"—This part covers in-depth all the Transact-SQL statements and includes expert tips and advice on optimizing their use. A chapter on transactions offers resources on the correct use and management of transactions in client applications, as well as troubleshooting their use on the server.

- Part VI, "Performance and Tuning"—Database design and performance, query analysis, and optimization are covered in-depth in this section, as well as the SQL Server Profiler, parallel and distributed queries, and optimizing and tuning the configuration options. A comprehensive chapter on understanding SQL Server 7.0 locking behavior and its performance implications can also be found in this section.

- Part VII, "BackOffice Integration"—This part provides detailed information on how SQL Server 7.0 integrates with SMS Server, SQL Mail and Exchange Server, Internet Information Server (IIS), and Index Server. A chapter on the new OLAP Server that is delivered with SQL Server 7.0 can be found here, as well as chapters on using the new Data Transformation Services (DTS) to populate data warehouses and perform distributed transactions and on the use of Microsoft Transaction Server (MTS). A chapter on serving SQL Server data on the Internet/intranet is also included.
- Part VIII, "Appendixes"—This part includes appendixes on troubleshooting and standards, as well as programming tools such as ADO, SQL-DMO, and VBScript.

Conventions Used in This Book

Names of commands and stored procedures are presented in a special monospaced computer typeface. Because SQL Server doesn't make a distinction between upper- and lowercase for SQL keywords in actual SQL code, many code examples show SQL keywords in lowercase, and the text of this book has followed that convention.

We have assumed that you installed with case sensitivity on (that is, you have chosen the *binary* sort order). We have purposely not capitalized the names of objects, databases, or logins/users where that would be incorrect. That has left sentences starting like this: "sysdatabases includes…" with an initial lowercase character.

Code and output examples are presented separately from regular paragraphs and also are in a monospaced computer typeface. Here's an example:

```
select id, name, audflags
from sysobjects
where type != "S"

id          name                            audflags
----------- ------------------------------- -----------
144003544   marketing_table                 130
```

> **NOTE**
>
> Perhaps the most controversial convention in the book is to use lowercase to spell dbcc, the database consistency checker, in code.

When we provide the syntax for a command, we've attempted to follow these conventions:

Key	*Definition*
`command`	Command names, options, and other keywords.
`placeholder`	Monospaced italic indicates values you provide.
`{}`	Indicates that you must choose at least one of the enclosed options.
`[]`	Means the value/keyword is optional.
`()`	Parentheses are part of the command.
¦	Indicates that you can select only one of the options shown.
,	Indicates that you can select any of the options shown separated by commas.
`[...]`	Indicates that the previous option can be repeated.

Consider the following example:

```
grant {all ¦ permission_list} on object [(column_list)]
     to {public ¦ user_or_group_name [, [...]]}
```

In this case, the *`object`* value is required, but the *`column_list`* is optional. Note also that items shown in plain computer type, such as `grant`, `public`, or `all`, should be entered literally as shown. Placeholders are presented in italics, such as *`permission_list`* and *`user_or_group_name`*; a placeholder is a generic term for which you must supply a specific value or values. The ellipsis in the square brackets following *`user_or_group_name`* indicates that multiple user or group names can be specified, separated by commas. You can specify either the keyword `public` or one or more user or group names, but not both.

Good Luck!

You are in good shape now. You have chosen a fine platform for building database applications, one that can provide outstanding performance and rock-solid reliability at a reasonable cost. And you now have the information you need to make the best of it.

I wish you all the best with SQL Server.

SQL Server in the Corporate Enterprise

PART

I

IN THIS PART

Evolution of the Client/Server Environment

by Kevin Viers

IN THIS CHAPTER

CHAPTER 1

This chapter will provide you with a basic foundation of knowledge about the client/server computing architecture. I think it is safe to assume that if you are reading this book, you are at least familiar with client/server technology and you understand that a database management system (DBMS), such as Microsoft SQL Server 7.0, usually plays a key role in that architecture. Nevertheless, this chapter examines the evolution of the architecture and discusses the concepts that are most relevant in today's enterprise computing environment.

The chapter is divided into the following sections:

- The foundations of client/server computing
- The traditional two-tier client/server architecture
- The evolution of three-tier and n-tier client/server architectures
- The role of the Internet in client/server computing

Before Client/Server Existed

Regardless of the physical architecture, every computer application consists of at least three functional tiers. Those tiers follow:

- Presentation tier—This tier deals with the interface between the user and the system. The presentation tier is responsible for collecting user input and displaying information to the user.
- Business logic tier—This tier is what actually adds meaning or value to the underlying data. This is where data is validated, calculations are performed, and various other processing of information takes place.
- Data access tier—This tier is responsible for the physical storage and servicing of the underlying data.

The way that these functional tiers are distributed across the physical hardware helps to define the architecture. Even before the term *client/server* was used to describe a specific computer architecture, clients and servers existed. If you think about it, in every transaction, there is a client and a server. The client is the entity that requests some information or service, and the server is the entity that provides the information or service to the client.

Mainframe or Host-Based Computing

The original computing architecture was the mainframe or host-based architecture. In this environment, virtually all the processing power exists on a central host machine. The business logic tier and the data access tier reside centrally on the host. The user of the

application interfaces with the data through a *dumb* terminal. The terminal is referred to as dumb simply because it has no inherent processing power of its own. The only processing provided by the terminal is sending keystrokes to the host and displaying data to the user. Technically speaking, the presentation tier also resides on the host in this environment. Although data is displayed on the dumb terminal, the host computer makes all the decisions on how the data is to be presented.

Because these host machines were extremely expensive and maintenance costs were equally high, it made sense for an organization to centralize as much of its data and application logic as possible. Over time, however, many organizations began to find that this centralized environment caused severe backlogs both in application processing and development. The answer to this problem was the PC.

PC LAN Computing

As the PC became affordable, it made sense to use the inherent processing power of the PC to offload work from the host. Many departmental users began using their PCs to perform various operations that used to rely on the host. Probably the first power PC applications were spreadsheets that could perform much of the number crunching and calculations that used to be performed on the host. Eventually, file system databases such as dBASE and FoxPro became prevalent. Users were able to create their own database-driven applications.

In this architecture, the presentation tier and the business logic tier typically reside on a local PC. The data access tier resides on another machine within the local area network, perhaps a network file server.

The file system databases work well for individual applications and local PC use. They are not, however, ideally suited for multiuser environments where many users need access to the same information. Using these file system databases over a LAN for shared data access began to cause increasing stress on network traffic and proved incapable of scaling to the large enterprise-type applications that are needed to run a business. Again, the answer to this problem lies in technological advance.

Client/Server

The advent of the relational database management system (RDBMS) was really the key technology that drove the client/server computing architecture. The RDBMS served as a central storage location for an organization's data. The RDBMS was designed to handle multiuser access to a shared set of data. All the locking and connection management is handled by the RDBMS along with security. Structured Query Language (SQL) was created to be a universal programming language to request specific data from an RDBMS.

The client/server architecture was really a marriage of the best features of both the host-based environment and the PC LAN environment. This architecture utilizes the power of the PC to perform the presentation of data along with the complicated business processing that adds value to that data. The RDBMS provides a centralized storage area for data and provides the services to manage shared, concurrent access to that data. The client/server architecture can take many forms, depending on how you choose to separate the presentation, business logic, and data tiers. The following sections examine each predominant client/server architecture in more detail.

Traditional Client/Server

When you hear the term client/server, the inclination is to think of only the two sides of the transaction, the client and the server. Most of us are familiar with this traditional two-tiered view of client/server, which involves a client application running on a workstation and a database management system running on a server.

In a typical two-tier client/server system, the client application must connect directly to an RDBMS, such as SQL Server. This means that each client workstation must be loaded with vendor-specific libraries and drivers to establish connections with the database. Client applications are also responsible for logging onto the RDBMS and maintaining connections, along with handling error messages and the like returned from the RDBMS.

The business logic layer can reside on the client, the server, or both in a two-tier system. Figure 1.1 illustrates this principle.

FIGURE 1.1

A two-tier client/server architecture.

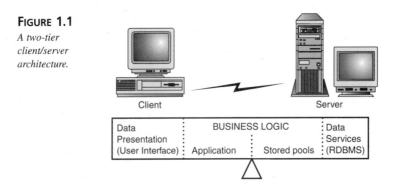

Some inherent problems arise from the two-tier client/server model. Those problems differ depending on the location of the business logic layer.

As businesses grow, they change. This change usually takes the form of changes to the business logic applied in computer applications. When the business logic layer resides in the client application, it is difficult to implement these changes. Every time business logic changes, the client application must be rebuilt and redistributed to every client workstation. In an organization where there are hundreds or thousands of client workstations, this process can present quite a problem.

The advent of stored procedures solved some of these problems. Stored procedures allowed programmers to place the business logic layer on the server. If you let stored procedures perform the business logic, the client applications don't have to change with changing business rules. Stored procedures, however, might not provide you with the level of sophistication you require in your business logic. Stored procedure languages typically do not provide the same capabilities that appear in an application programming language.

The problems with two-tier client/server architectures were addressed by adding a third tier and creating, you guessed it, the three-tier or n-tier client/server architecture.

N-tier Architecture

Some people use the term *three-tier*, and others use *n-tier*. N-tier simply means that a system has at least three tiers. The n-tier client/server architecture involves separating the three functional tiers across three logical tiers. This does not mean that you need three physical machines to implement an n-tier architecture. In fact, you could conceivably run an n-tier client/server system on one machine. The point to remember is that the three functional tiers are separated into three separate entities, each running as a separate application or process. Figure 1.2 illustrates this principle.

The primary goal of the n-tier architecture is to separate the business logic from both the presentation and data access layers into a set of reusable objects, sometimes called business objects. Business objects are like stored procedures in that they allow you to centralize your business logic and keep it separate from your client applications. Unlike stored procedures, however, you can write your business objects in languages such as Visual Basic, C++, or Java and take advantage of the capabilities of those languages.

This type of architecture has many obvious advantages. Once an n-tier architecture is put in place, applications are much easier to develop and maintain. You can bring new applications online relatively easily by reusing existing business objects. Database changes and business logic changes can be made without redistributing client applications. Programmers can concentrate on developing business rules without having to worry about user interface issues.

FIGURE 1.2

An n-tier client/server architecture.

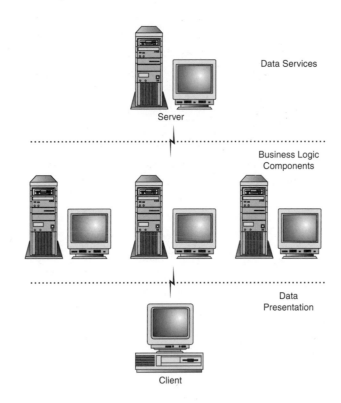

These advantages do not come without a cost. Implementing a successful n-tier architecture requires a complex infrastructure to handle low-level services such as connection pooling, thread maintenance, and transaction monitoring. Some products, however, such as Microsoft Transaction Server (MTS), handle many of these complex infrastructure issues and reduce the complexity of implementing an n-tier solution.

The Internet as a Client/Server Platform

Of course, the Internet is making a profound impact on the way we develop systems. We used to think of client/server computing as relying on the existence of a local area network to communicate between client applications and database servers. The Internet has enabled developers to create complex client/server applications that are accessible from anywhere in the world via an Internet connection.

The basic building blocks of an Internet-based client/server architecture are a Web browser, an Internet server, and a set of data transmission and presentation protocols (TCP/IP, HTTP, and HTML). The Web browser acts as the client and is responsible, at a minimum, for accepting user input and displaying information to the user. The Internet server responds to client requests for information and processes those requests accordingly. The TCP/IP, HTTP, and HTML protocols define a universal standard for transmitting and displaying information over the Internet.

The Internet can be a key component in implementing any of the basic computing architectures discussed so far. In its simplest form, Internet-based client/server applications can resemble the mainframe or host-based architecture with the Internet browser providing dumb terminal capabilities and all business logic and data access being provided by a central server. Figure 1.3 illustrates this principle.

FIGURE 1.3

An Internet client/server architecture.

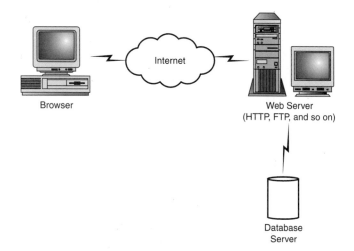

Browser

Internet

Web Server
(HTTP, FTP, and so on)

Database
Server

The Internet can also provide the platform for complex n-tier client/server architectures. In an n-tier architecture, the Internet server simply acts as a gateway that directs client requests to the appropriate business objects and transmits those responses back to the Web browsers. This setup is just like any n-tier architecture in that the business logic of the application is separated into a set of business objects that are reusable across applications. Figure 1.4 illustrates this principle.

The Internet provides a platform that truly allows you to customize the physical architecture of your systems to meet your organizational needs.

Thick and Thin Clients

There are many variations in how to establish an Internet-based client/server architecture. One of the biggest debates within the development community is the debate between *thick* clients and *thin* clients. The root of this issue is how much of the processing power or business logic layer resides on the client side of the application.

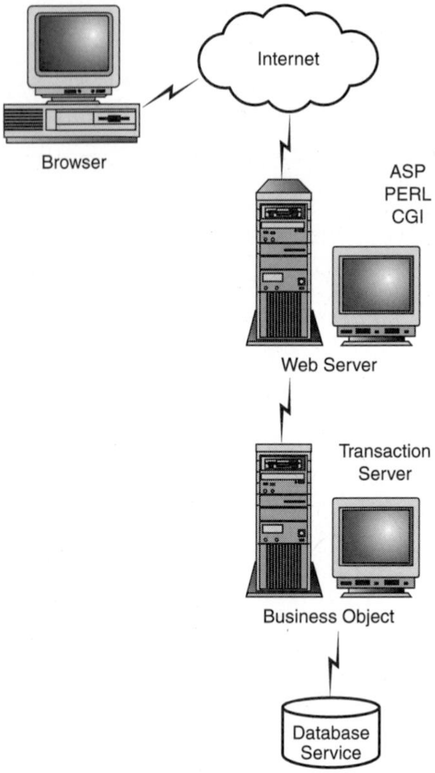

FIGURE 1.4

An n-tier Internet client/server architecture.

Browser

Internet

ASP
PERL
CGI

Web Server

Transaction
Server

Business Object

Database
Service

Remember that in the early days of client/server computing, most of the business logic was coded within a client application that was running on a workstation. This arrangement is considered a *thick* client architecture. As its name implies, the client side of the application is responsible for a greater portion of the overall processing of the application.

Once you move the business logic out of the client side of the equation, you begin to move toward a thin client architecture. In a thin client scenario, very little, if any, processing occurs on the client side. This type of architecture is common in an Internet scenario when a user interfaces with an Internet server application through a Web browser. In this case, the Web browser is the client and does nothing more than accept user input and transfer information to an Internet server to process the request.

Which architecture is correct? The answer to this question depends largely on your individual situation. There are advantages and disadvantages to each. The point to remember is that you should not assume one architecture is correct for all situations.

Summary

This chapter provided a high-level view of the evolution of the client/server architecture, from its roots in host-based computing to today's Internet-based n-tier distributed architecture. As you are well aware, each of the different architectures mentioned in this chapter are in existence today. You don't have to look far to find a mainframe system or a traditional two-tier client/server system.

Whether you are developing in a traditional two-tier environment or in a distributed n-tier environment, Microsoft SQL Server 7.0 can play a key role in your architecture. The focus of the remainder of this book is SQL Server 7.0 and the role it can play in your organization.

Microsoft SQL Server and the Windows NT Enterprise

by Kevin Viers

IN THIS CHAPTER

You probably have a pretty good understanding of client/server computing and how it evolved. The next step is to understand the enterprise and how you can leverage SQL Server 7.0 within the enterprise. This chapter will provide you with a base level of understanding about what enterprise computing means and the role that SQL Server plays.

What Is the Enterprise?

The first thing you need to do is understand what I mean by enterprise computing. It seems that enterprise has become quite a buzzword these days. This term probably means different things to different people; however, I would like to share with you how the enterprise is defined in this book.

Stated simply, enterprise computing defines the entire set of technologies required to develop the mission-critical business applications of today's organizations. These technologies include the network operating systems, the application development environments, the database management systems, the servers, the desktops, and everything in between. When you think of enterprise development, you probably think of n-tier, distributed, and Web-based application development. Although these are certainly types of enterprise development, they are just pieces of a bigger puzzle.

Rather than focus on a concrete definition of enterprise computing, I suggest that you understand the characteristics of enterprise computing to understand the role that SQL Server 7.0 plays in the enterprise. The following are the primary characteristics of an enterprise:

- Scalability—As organizations grow, so does the need for more computing power. The systems in place must enable an organization to leverage existing hardware and to quickly and easily add computing power as needs demand.

- Availability—As organizations rely more on information, it is more critical that the information is available at all times and under all circumstances. Downtime is not acceptable.

- Interoperability—As organizations grow and evolve, so do their information systems. It is impractical to think that an organization will not have many heterogeneous sources of information. The ability for applications to get to all the information, regardless of its location, is becoming increasingly important.

- Reliability—An organization is only as good as its data and information. It is critical that the systems providing that information are bulletproof.

The remainder of this chapter discusses some of the products on which Microsoft is basing its enterprise computing strategy. Although some of these products are not covered in this book, I think it is important to understand the role that they play in the enterprise and how SQL Server 7.0 fits into the bigger picture.

Windows NT Enterprise Edition

Most of us are familiar with Windows NT Server. It is at the core of many of today's organizational computing infrastructures. In years past, many large organizations relied solely on UNIX or on mainframe-based operating systems to provide their mission-critical application services. This was due in large part to the inherent scalability and reliability in both of those operating environments. Microsoft has recognized the need to provide the same level of performance, reliability, and scalability in its Windows NT Server product. As a result of this initiative, it has developed Windows NT Server Enterprise Edition (NTSEE).

NTSEE is based on the original Windows NT 4.0 Server engine with several enhancements and bundled services to provide the high availability, enhanced performance, and comprehensive services required in the largest enterprises. Two primary performance enhancing benefits have been added to NTSEE:

- 4GB RAM tuning—This enhancement enables NTSEE to address up to 3GB of RAM. The standard NT Server can only address up to 2GB of RAM per process. This addition can provide a major performance boost for applications' large databases on machines with more than 2GB of physical RAM.

- Eight-processor symmetric multiprocessor (SMP) support—NTSEE is licensed for use on up to eight processor SMP servers.

In addition to these performance enhancing features, NTSEE is bundled with several services that are designed to enhance your ability to develop the large-scale distributed applications that are necessary within your enterprise. The following sections briefly describe each of these services.

Transaction Server

One of the primary characteristics of enterprise computing is scalability. This implies not only scalable computing power, but also scalable application development. As an organization grows, the need for rapid development and easy modification of mission-critical applications intensifies. This need has resulted in an explosion of component-based distributed application development. This type of application development is commonly referred to as *n-tier application development*. It is characterized by the separation of business logic from presentation and data logic. By creating a set of independent, reusable components that can encapsulate an organization's business logic, you can create a scalable application development architecture. This type of architecture enables you to quickly bring new applications online and to change business logic without having to recompile and redistribute client applications.

This distributed application development architecture is not without its difficulties. The components that encapsulate your business logic rely on a complex infrastructure to enable them to reside on servers and effectively service all of your client applications. In the early days of distributed computing, creating and maintaining this infrastructure was more complicated than creating the business logic itself. Programmers were forced to focus on putting in the "plumbing" required to manage the distributed environment instead of focusing on programming the business logic, which we all know is the real value.

In an effort to make the development and deployment of distributed applications easier, Microsoft introduced the Microsoft Transaction Server (MTS). MTS defines an application programming model for developing component-based distributed systems. MTS provides the application infrastructure so that programmers can focus on developing business logic. MTS provides the thread- and process-management capabilities to allow components to operate in a multiuser environment. Additionally, MTS provides the database connection pooling and state management functionality necessary in a distributed enterprise development environment.

Message Queue Server

Two other important characteristics of enterprise computing are availability and interoperability. An enterprise usually consists of many heterogeneous entities that must function together as a logical whole. For example, your enterprise might have both a Windows NT Server network and a legacy mainframe system. Likewise, you might have remote or disconnected users who need access to enterprise application resources. In any event, the enterprise systems must be available and interoperable.

The Message Queue Server (MSMQ) enables availability and interoperability by allowing applications to easily communicate with one another. You may be thinking, "Applications communicate with each other all the time, so why do I need MSMQ?" The answer is that MSMQ allows applications to communicate with one another asynchronously. In other words, an application can send a request to a receiving application and continue with another task even if the receiving application is unusable or disconnected from the network.

The MSMQ is based on a store-and-forward model. Applications send messages to MSMQ, and those messages are stored in queues. Each application involved in the communication sends messages to MSMQ and receives messages from MSMQ. MSMQ is effective in situations where sending and receiving applications run at different times or where the cost of message loss or interruption is extremely high.

Cluster Server

Probably the most important feature of NTSEE—the one that truly makes it an enterprise-class operating system—is the Cluster Server (MSCS). This is the feature of NTSEE that provides the availability and reliability that your enterprise will demand.

Reliability and availability are two of the characteristics that are inherent in enterprise computing. When your systems are reliable and available, you are able to minimize downtime. It has been estimated that system downtime costs U.S. businesses as much as $4 billion annually. Clustering enables you to minimize system downtime by allowing you to create systems that continue to run, even in the event of a system failure.

MSCS lets you create a cluster of two computers or nodes, each running NTSEE and MSCS, that function as one logical NT Server. All the client applications that access a clustered server only see one entity. This single entity is referred to as a "virtual server." MSCS is capable of detecting hardware or software failures and automatically shifting control of the server to the healthy node. Not only do clusters provide the capability to fail-over due to hardware or software failure, but also you can manually switch control from one node to the other to perform routine maintenance or even replacement. Because the users see only one virtual server, they are never aware that a failure has occurred and their applications continue to be serviced.

Clustering should not be confused with fault tolerance. In a fault-tolerant solution, generally one server is kept idle and contains a mirror image of the primary server. The backup server is only utilized in case of a failure. In a clustering solution, both systems are active, meaning that each processor can service clients. When one node fails, the other node simply picks up the slack. Later, I discuss how SQL Server 7.0 can use a clustered NT Server to provide highly available and reliable database service to the enterprise.

Universal Data Access

Within the enterprise, managing data and information is the primary purpose of virtually every computer system. It is this information, and its efficient use, that defines the strategic advantage of most businesses. Universal Data Access (UDA) is a term coined by Microsoft to represent its overall strategy for providing access to data across an organization, from the desktop to the enterprise.

Businesses today require ever more complex access to their mission-critical data. It used to be that all the data in an organization was stored on a mainframe or on a few dedicated DBMSs. In today's environment, important data can be distributed virtually anywhere throughout the organization, from file systems to a mail store to Web-based content.

Microsoft defines UDA as "a platform, application, and tools initiative that defines and delivers both standards and technologies." At the core of UDA is a component object model (COM) technology called OLE DB. OLE DB is a collection of COM interfaces that encapsulate various database management services. The interfaces provide published standards with which vendors can create their own components to utilize these services. Vendors can use OLE DB to create both *data providers* and *data consumers*. In this way, any OLE DB consumer can get access to data from any OLE DB provider. SQL Server 7.0 functions as both an OLE DB consumer and provider.

Leveraging SQL Server in the Enterprise

By now, you have seen that there are many pieces to the enterprise puzzle. SQL Server 7.0 is simply one of those pieces; however, it is the focus of this book, so it is important to understand the enterprise features that have been built into the product and will help you fully leverage SQL Server in your enterprise.

At the beginning of this chapter, I said that you should focus on the characteristics of enterprise computing. The remaining sections focus on certain features of the product and how those features support the enterprise. The following features are discussed:

- OLE DB support—interoperability
- Parallel query execution—scalability
- Distributed queries—interoperability
- Clustering and fail-over support—availability and reliability

OLE DB Support

SQL Server 7.0 provides direct support for OLE DB applications, such as those using ActiveX Data Objects (ADO). In fact, SQL Server 7.0 ships with several OLE DB providers for use with heterogeneous data sources, such as Oracle and JET databases. As mentioned previously, the OLE DB specification is the cornerstone of the Universal Data Access strategy and is the primary component of SQL Server's interoperability.

SQL Server 7.0 is both an OLE DB consumer and an OLE DB provider. This enables SQL Server 7.0 to expose its data to any OLE DB–compliant consumer application and to consume data from any OLE DB–compliant data source. Currently, OLE DB is a widely accepted data access standard and virtually all major data sources have OLE DB providers available. These data sources include Oracle, JET, DB2, VSAM, and even Excel spreadsheets. As a result, SQL Server can interoperate with all of these data sources and function effectively within the enterprise.

Parallel Query Execution

To provide enhanced performance capabilities and additional scalability to very large databases, SQL Server 7.0 is capable of executing a single query in parallel across multiple CPUs. This enables SQL Server to complete complex queries with large amounts of data very quickly. To use the parallel query processing capability of SQL Server, your system must be running on an SMP machine with more than one CPU.

If you are running SQL Server on an SMP machine with multiple processors, SQL Server will automatically look for those queries it feels will benefit from a parallel execution plan. If you execute a query that is selected for parallel query processing, SQL Server determines the best execution plan and distributes the query across different threads to different processors. In most instances, you do not know whether SQL Server used parallel query processing for a query. You can somewhat control the behavior of the parallel processing by setting a *cost threshold for parallelism* option. This option specifies that SQL Server should only use parallel query processing when the cost of executing the query on a single processor exceeds the threshold. More than likely, you will want to allow SQL Server to use its own determination.

Parallel query processing enables SQL Server 7.0 to effectively scale to meet the large database requirements commonly found in complex enterprises without a resulting performance degradation. It also allows you to utilize the full capabilities of high-end multiprocessor hardware within the enterprise.

Distributed Queries

Wouldn't it be nice if all the data in the world was kept in a set of replicated SQL Server databases? Many of us have had that thought at one time or another. The reality, however, is that most mission-critical information within the enterprise is scattered across many different, or heterogeneous, data sources.

For many years, one of the biggest challenges facing information technology (IT) has been how to get to all the enterprise data, regardless of its source, and present that data to users as one homogenous entity. Typical users couldn't care less that one set of data is in

Oracle, another is in SQL Server, a third is in DB2, and yet another set of data is in an Excel spreadsheet. They want to see data as it should be seen, as one interrelated grouping of information.

A *distributed query* within SQL Server enables you to access data from multiple data sources within the context of a single Transact-SQL statement. In other words, a distributed query enables you to issue a single SELECT statement that pulls data from not only SQL Server, but also from Oracle, Access, DB2, and other data sources. Distributed queries allow objects from other data sources (on the same or remote machines) to appear as any other table or view within SQL Server; Figure 2.1 illustrates this concept.

FIGURE 2.1

A distributed query scenario.

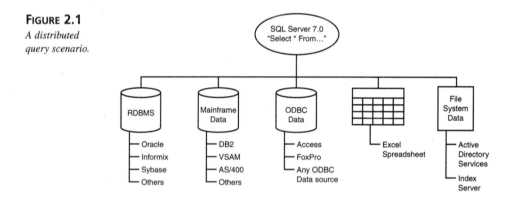

The distributed query capability of SQL Server 7.0 can play a key role in enabling you to achieve the interoperability that is critical within the enterprise by seamlessly accessing many heterogeneous data sources.

Clustering and Fail-Over Support

SQL Server 7.0 provides support for Windows NT Server Enterprise Edition and Cluster Server. By taking advantage of the clustering capabilities of NTSEE, SQL Server 7.0 provides the high availability and reliability required of an enterprise class database management system.

SQL Server 7.0 can use a clustered NT environment to provide fail-over support. When you install SQL Server on a clustered virtual server, there are two nodes available to run SQL Server. This allows either node to take over in the event of a hardware or network failure. If a failure does occur, the MSCS automatically handles the fail-over process. In the event of a fail-over, any transactions in process at the time of the fail-over are rolled back, and the clients must reconnect to SQL Server.

Don't confuse fail-over support in a clustering scenario with a standby server. SQL Server 7.0 also supports the concept of a standby server. In this scenario, two physical servers each have a duplicate copy of your database. The database must be kept in sync via routing database and transaction log backups. In the event of a failure, the standby server will be brought online as the primary server. The databases must be synched via transaction log backups. Unlike the clustered scenario, this is not a foolproof mechanism for providing fail-over support.

In either case, SQL Server 7.0 is capable of providing both the availability and reliability that is required within the enterprise.

Summary

Providing a clear definition of enterprise computing is not an easy task. The technologies involved are complex and span many areas of computing, including architecture, programming, networking, and platform integration. The important thing to remember is that any enterprise solution must be scalable, available, reliable, and interoperable. SQL Server 7.0 has many features built-in to help develop just such a solution and to effectively leverage it in your enterprise.

Installation and Upgrade

PART

II

IN THIS PART

SQL Server Installation

by Greg Mable

IN THIS CHAPTER

CHAPTER 3

Those of you who have been running SQL Server version 6.*x* or earlier, get ready (you might want to sit down first): SQL Server 7.0 runs on a laptop! Under Windows 95/98! Those of you new to SQL Server might be impressed that the same code base used to generate the version that runs on an Alpha AXP server is the same code base used to execute on an Intel Pentium laptop. One code base, one setup program. The arrangement is simple and easy—and supports the philosophy of overall reduced cost of ownership. You might ask then, how easy is it to install SQL Server? How about this answer: Insert the CD-ROM, run setup, and select the default options, and in a few minutes, you have a fully functional, extremely powerful relational database system.

Now, this single code base is a distinction you won't find in any other major competitor's product. Those products might be able to compete in other areas, but not when it comes to a single code base from which the product is built. Multiplatform code bases have been written to the lowest common denominator because not all operating systems are created equal. Consequently, the code must compensate for the discrepancies.

Let's look beneath the hood. SQL Server is built upon a set of services, each of which provides a distinct set of features. The MSSQLServer service is the database engine, the guts behind the product. The SQLServerAgent, the equivalent of a task scheduler, controls automated job processing. The DTC is the Distributed Transaction Coordinator and acts as a facilitator in a distributed system involving multiple servers. The MSSearch service provides full-text search capabilities.

Unite these services under the control of an intuitive GUI, the SQL Server Enterprise Manager running as a snap-in to the Microsoft Management Console (MMC), to form a scalable, easy-to-use product. The MMC provides a single, consistent interface for administrators to manage not only SQL Server and its related services, but also other products (see Figure 3.1). The Enterprise Manager features a task pad to group many of the commonly run administrative tasks into categories and offers numerous wizards to assist in completing the tasks.

FIGURE 3.1

SQL Server task pads in the Microsoft Management Console.

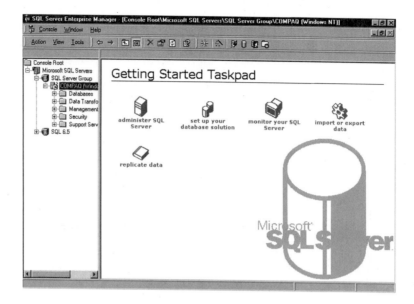

Before you can play with any of these new features, you have to install the product. You don't really expect me to tell you to simply run setup, do you? Well, I could, but let's first find out what you need to run SQL Server.

Hardware and Software Requirements

As with any product you install, you need to know its hardware and software requirements before you can install it. For SQL Server, a general rule of thumb is that if the computer runs Windows 95, Windows 98, or Windows NT, then SQL Server will run on it. That is a general statement and not a hard-and-fast rule. SQL Server is scalable and can run on a laptop configured with Windows 95/98 or on a DEC Alpha AXP server. However, it will run poorly on a computer configured with a slow disk drive and meager amount of RAM.

TIP

If you are planning to install SQL Server on a Windows 95/98 computer, then 32MB RAM is the minimum requirement. If you are planning to install SQL Server on a Windows NT workstation or server, then 64MB RAM is the minimum requirement. I do not recommend, although it is certainly possible, installing SQL Server on a Windows NT server that is configured to be the primary or backup domain controller. Unless you have a small network, a PDC or BDC is periodically busy validating user access, which slices some of the processor and disk time away from SQL Server. You want to provide a constant, steady environment for SQL Server, not one in which the server is constantly interrupted. I suggest installing it on either an NT workstation or an NT member server. What is the difference between installing it on an NT workstation and installing it on an NT server? Simply put, it's performance. NT Workstation targets a single user, and its resource sharing is limited. NT Server is optimized for resource sharing and concurrent user access. Use the NT Workstation version for development. Remember, you're managing a database system, so the faster the disk drives, the better. Use SCSI controllers if possible.

You can install SQL Server on the following platforms:

- DEC Alpha AXP and compatible systems
- Intel or compatible, Pentium 166 MHz or higher, Pentium Pro, or Pentium II
- 32MB RAM (minimum) (64MB RAM for Enterprise edition)
- CD-ROM drive
- 180MB (full installation), 170MB (typical), 65MB (minimum), 90MB (management tools only); add an additional 50MB for OLAP Services and an additional 12MB for the English Query

Strictly speaking, a CD-ROM drive is not required; you can install SQL Server from a network share point. For more information about the specific supported hardware, visit the Windows NT hardware compatibility list at
`www.microsoft.com/ntserver/info/hwcompatibility.htm`.

Software Requirements

SQL Server's software is simple: It will run under Microsoft Windows 95, Windows 95 OSR2, Windows 98, Windows NT Server 4.0 or later with Service Pack 4.

SQL Server also requires that you install Internet Explorer 4.01 with Service Pack 1 or later. By default, IE 4.01 is installed under Windows 98 and Windows NT 5.0. If you do not have IE 4.01 installed, you can also install it from the SQL Server CD-ROM.

Step-by-Step Server Installation

In this section, I walk you step-by-step through a typical installation of SQL Server and offer you some tips regarding the various options that you may select. You can simply select all of the default options to be up and running in no time. However, I outline the various options available and discuss what would work best in your particular situation.

Figure 3.2 shows the first screen you see when you insert the CD-ROM.

FIGURE 3.2

SQL Server installation.

From the SQL Server setup main menu, you can choose to review the README.TXT file (which you should always review prior to setting up any product) and the installation prerequisites, install the server components, click a hyperlink to SQL Server on the Web where you can review some of the white papers and reviewer's guides on SQL Server, or view the online documentation. Proceed to the main installation screen for installing SQL Server's components.

SQL Server consists of four main components (see Figure 3.3).

FIGURE 3.3

SQL Server component installation.

In this section, I cover the installation of the Database Server - Full Product component. The Database Server - Desktop Edition component installation follows the same steps but is aimed at desktop computers such as a laptop or workstation. The installation of the OLAP Services and the English Query components is covered later in this chapter.

Installation Editions

You basically have two options for installation: a desktop installation or a full product installation (which can be either the standard product or the Enterprise edition, depending on the hardware and operating system).

Table 3.1 describes the operating system and the features supported by each edition.

TABLE 3.1 FEATURES SUPPORTED BY THE INSTALLATION EDITION

	Desktop	*Standard*	*Enterprise*
Operating system	Windows 95, Windows 98, Windows NT Workstation, Windows NT Server, Windows NT Server Enterprise Edition	Windows NT Server, Windows NT Server Enterprise Edition	Windows NT Server Enterprise Edition

	Desktop	*Standard*	*Enterprise*
Extended (> 2GB) memory support	No	No	Yes
Failover support	No	No	Yes
Replication support	Full merge Subscriber only for transaction replication; no publishing for transaction replication	Full	Full replication
Maximum CPUs	2	4	32
Database size limit	4GB per database	No limit	No limit
Full-text search	No (except for full-text index administration)	Yes	Yes
OLAP Services support	Client pivot table only	Yes (except for no user-defined cube partitions)	Yes

Based on the type of installation you want, you should select the appropriate edition. As you can see from the table, if you will be installing SQL Server on a laptop or workstation, you should select the desktop edition. If you are installing SQL Server on an NT Server, choose either the standard or enterprise editions (depending upon your hardware and operating system configuration).

Upgrading an Existing Database

Before you even begin installation, one of the first questions you might ask is whether SQL Server 7.0 can be installed on a computer that already has SQL Server 6.5 installed. Yes, you can install SQL Server 7.0 alongside an installation of SQL Server 6.5. Chapter 5, "Upgrading from Previous Versions," contains a discussion of this process. SQL Server 7.0 can upgrade SQL Server 6.0 and 6.5 installations; however, versions prior to 6.0 cannot be upgraded by the Upgrade Wizard.

The new version of SQL Server makes many enhancements to the system. One of the changes is the format of the database files. Databases created under SQL Server versions 6.5 and earlier must be upgraded to the new file format. If you are installing SQL Server 7.0 on a computer that already has SQL Server 6.5 installed, you are prompted during the installation process to run the Upgrade Wizard upon completion, as shown in Figure 3.4. You can either run it after setup has completed or at a later time.

FIGURE 3.4

Upgrading existing data.

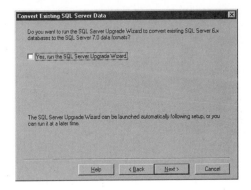

Installation Types

The next step is to decide which type of installation you want (see Figure 3.5).

FIGURE 3.5

Choosing the SQL Server setup type.

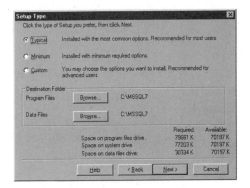

Your choices are Typical, Minimal, and Custom. The Typical installation option is appropriate for most users. I first describe the minimal installation.

Minimal

The Minimal option installs the following programs:

- SQL Server Service Manager, a program used to start, pause, and stop the various SQL Server services

- SQL Server Network Utility, which allows you to configure the various network libraries that SQL Server will communicate on
- The SQL Server uninstall program

The minimal installation is appropriate for a server you will not use to directly administer the network or perform any prolonged work. An example is a rack-mounted server or a server to which you do not have physical access. The Minimal option is appropriate if you will be administering the server from another computer, such as your workstation. That way, you keep the components installed on the server to a minimum—just those you need to start, stop, and minimally configure SQL Server.

Typical

The next choice, Typical, installs SQL Server with all the management tools described in the preceding section and also includes the following:

- Client Network Utility, which configures the network libraries that the client will use to communicate with the server. (See Chapter 4, "Client Installation," for more information.)
- Enterprise Manager, which is a snap-in to the Microsoft Management Console. (See Chapter 9, "The SQL Server Enterprise Manager," for more information.)
- MSDTC Administrative Console, a tool to manage and monitor distributed transactions running on the server. (See Chapter 22, "Transaction Management and Distributed Transactions," for more information.)
- Query Analyzer, which is an interactive query tool. (See Chapter 24, "Query Analysis," for more information.)
- Profiler, which is a trace tool for capturing SQL commands sent to the server and result sets returned from the server. (See Chapter 27, "Using the SQL Server Profiler," for more information.)
- Performance Monitor, which contains counters for SQL Server. (See Chapter 28, "Monitoring SQL Server Performance," for more information.)
- Books Online, the electronic version of the documentation.

3

SQL SERVER
INSTALLATION

Custom

The third choice, Custom, allows you to control exactly what services to install. You can specify Full-Text Search (Microsoft Search Service), which provides support for full-text searching of SQL Server data. You can also choose to install the development libraries. These are the various libraries and header files that you need to develop SQL Server applications using Open Data Services, SQL-DMO, ODBC, DB-Library, Embedded

SQL, and MS DTC. See Appendix D, "Programming Tools and Interfaces," for a discussion of the various programming interfaces to SQL Server. You can also choose to install the necessary DLLs for use with the virtual device interface. This allows you to back up and restore from a virtual device. See Chapter 12, "SQL Server Backup, Restore, and Recovery," for a discussion of SQL Server's backup capabilities.

SQL Server Programs and Data Location

Once you have decided which type of setup you want to install, you need to decide where to install the program and data files. The program files are the executables, DLLs, and other related files used by SQL Server and its associated programs. The default location is C:\MSSQL7. The data files are the database and log files used by SQL Server. SQL Server creates several databases during setup, such as the following:

- The master database, which is used to store information about all the databases defined on the server.
- The MSDB database, which is used by the SQL Server Agent to store the various tasks defined on a database.
- The model database, which is a template database—that is, any changes made to this database are inherited by any new databases created.
- The tempdb database, which is exactly that—a temporary database used by SQL Server as a working scratch area.
- The two sample databases, Pubs and Northwind, which are referenced in the online documentation and sample programs.

You can specify a location for these databases. I suggest specifying a local drive for both the program files and the data files, although you can specify a network drive for either. If SQL Server is unable to locate the network drive for whatever reason at startup (the network is down or the computer on which the files are located has failed), then the server will fail to start.

A new feature of SQL Server 7.0 is its ability to dynamically grow and shrink the size of its database files. You do not need to specify a maximum limit for your database; the system will automatically increase it as well as shrink it when appropriate. This feature, called on-demand disk management, is part of the overall reduced cost-of-ownership philosophy. See Chapter 7, "Physical Database Architecture," for more discussion of the new disk formats.

> **TIP**
>
> It is customary to place the data files on a drive separate from the program files. For best performance, place the database files on a separate physical drive dedicated to SQL Server. This will allow SQL Server's on-demand disk management to freely grow and shrink the database files as necessary without the concern that its growth will interfere with other files.

The next set of options, as shown in Figure 3.6, contains the most important choices that you will make during installation. You cannot change these choices later unless you reinstall SQL Server. Let's carefully review them.

FIGURE 3.6

*Character set,
sort order, and
Unicode collation.*

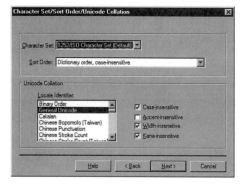

Character Set

SQL Server employs a single character set, which is the set of all characters that can be represented in the database. Character sets are based on a single byte that translates into 256 different characters. Because of this limitation, they cannot represent all the different languages in the world. You must select a character set that contains the characters you most need to represent. The default character set is the ISO character set, also referred to as ISO 8859-1, Latin-1, or the ANSI character set. You may also see it referenced as Code Page 1252. This character set works best for Western Hemisphere and Western Europe installations.

> **TIP**
>
> Select the default character set, ISO, unless you have a specific need to select another set. If you decide to choose a character set other than the default one, you may encounter difficulty when working with other systems' SQL Server databases. For example, you will not be able to restore a database from a backup that was performed on a SQL Server system configured with a different character set. In short, keep the default unless you absolutely must choose another character set.

If you decide to use a character set other than the default, you need to configure the client computer to use the same character set. Windows 95/98 and Windows NT clients can be configured using Control Panel settings. DOS and Windows 3.*x* clients need to change code pages in the CONFIG.SYS and AUTOEXEC.BAT file. Refer to the SQL Server online documentation for details.

When choosing a character set, you are selecting a single character set to be used for all databases created in the system. You cannot choose one character set for one database and another character set for another. The same restriction applies to sort orders. Whatever sort order you choose at installation is the sort order used for all databases defined in the system. Let's examine the sort order choices more closely.

Sort Order

As a database administrator or developer, you might wonder, does the name Employees refer to the same table that the name employees refers to? In other words, is the database case sensitive? Well, the answer is that it depends. The default, which is the best choice for the majority of installations, does not distinguish between lowercase and uppercase letters. The characters A and a are treated equally. That means table names, field names, and so on are not case sensitive by default. The default sort order is dictionary order, not case sensitive. Dictionary order refers to handling characters with diacritical marks. With dictionary order, diacritical marks are distinguishable by the system.

If you are concerned about performance, you might think you want to choose the fastest sort order, which is the binary sort order. It arranges characters by their order in the installed character set. As a general rule, you should have a good reason for choosing an option other than the default. Choosing a sort order other than the default means the you might not be able to restore a database backup from another system unless that system has the same sort order. Choosing a sort order based solely on its performance is not a good idea because the difference in performance between the default sort order and binary sort order is negligible.

Unicode

The Unicode standard was developed to overcome the limitation of character sets. This standard uses two bytes to store a character's value. With two bytes, all the many symbols of every language can be represented. Because Unicode uses two bytes instead of one byte to represent a character, a set of datatypes is available. The nchar, nvarchar, and ntext datatypes are equivalent to their corresponding non-Unicode counterparts; the difference is the extra byte for each character stored. (They require twice the space as their non-Unicode counterparts.) The prefix n stands for national.

A Unicode collation is separate from the collation used for the character set. A Unicode collation consists of a locale and a sorting style. The default Unicode collation works best for most installations, especially Western and European. The Unicode comparison style is used for the locale specified. For example, the width-insensitive and Kana-insensitive comparison styles are applicable only to the East Asian locales.

As with the character set and sort order options, you must reinstall SQL Server if you need to change the Unicode locale and comparison style after installation.

Network Libraries

SQL Server can communicate over a wide variety of network protocols through its use of network libraries. Network libraries are a set of DLLs that separate SQL Server's networking functions from its database kernel and other services. These network libraries use various interprocess communication mechanisms (IPCs) to transmit data. For example, the TCP/IP library uses Windows sockets as its IPC mechanism.

SQL Server can also communicate over different network libraries simultaneously, as shown in Figure 3.7.

FIGURE 3.7

SQL Server network libraries.

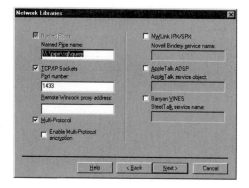

You can configure some clients to communicate using one network library and other clients to communicate using a different one. Let's take a closer look at each network library.

Named Pipes

The default network library for Windows NT installations is named pipes. SQL Server does not support named pipes on Windows 95/98 installations because the underlying operating system does not fully support the server side of the named pipes API. Named pipes is fully supported only on Windows NT installations. Client computers must communicate using a network library other than named pipes when connecting to SQL Server on a Windows 95/98 computer.

TCP/IP

The TCP/IP network library allows SQL Server to communicate using Windows Sockets as its underlying IPC mechanism with the TCP/IP protocol.

The default TCP/IP port number where SQL Server listens is 1433. Because Microsoft Windows 95/98 cannot support the named pipes API, these platforms use the TCP/IP sockets network library by default.

Multiprotocol

The multiprotocol network library uses remote procedure calls (RPCs), which allow clients to connect to SQL Server using a variety of network protocols. An RPC works by determining which network protocols are available and then using each one until it establishes a connection. NWLink IPX/SPX, TCP/IP sockets, and named pipes are currently supported.

The multiprotocol network library allows clients to be authenticated using Windows NT Authentication and supports encryption of passwords and data. It also offers performance comparable to that of native IPC network libraries.

TIP

When communicating over a data channel that you want to secure, choose the multiprotocol library and enable multiprotocol encryption to encrypt all user data and passwords. This consideration is especially important for systems on the Internet or an intranet.

Other Protocols

With a minimal amount of configuration, SQL Server can communicate over other network protocols. They include NWLink IPX/SPX, Banyan Vines, and AppleTalk. Refer to the online documentation for further details.

Once you have selected which network libraries that SQL Server will communicate on, your next step is to configure which accounts SQL Server and its related SQL Server Agent will use.

SQL Server and SQL Server Agent User Accounts

Windows NT services can run under the context of either the local system or an NT user account that you assign to it. During the SQL Server installation process, you must make this choice, as shown in Figure 3.8.

FIGURE 3.8
SQL Server services account setup.

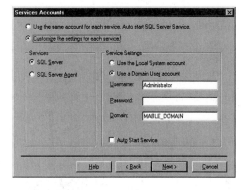

When you install SQL Server under Windows NT, several NT services are installed by SQL Server—namely, MSSQLServer, the database engine; SQLServerAgent, the task scheduler; MSDTC, the distributed transaction coordinator; and, if selected, the Microsoft Search service. These services appear in the list of services in the Services applet of the Control Panel.

If you elect to run a service under the local system account, the service is restricted to the machine on which it is running; it cannot access any resource on the network. If you choose to run the service under an account from an NT domain, the account must be part of the local administrator's group and must have the run-as-service privilege granted to it. During the setup process, you have a chance to select an account from the NT domain, and this right is automatically granted to the account. For example, if you are installing SQL Server to include replication, you will need to specify a Windows NT domain account for the MSSQLServer and SQLServerAgent services.

> ### TIP
>
> If you are installing SQL Server for the first time and you are not fully comfortable with selecting an NT user account, choose the option to run the SQL Server services under the local system account. That way, you do not need to determine which user account to select or worry about its security access on the network. If, however, you want to choose a user account, choose a single account for all the services. For example, you can create an NT domain account called SQLAdministrator. Ensure that the account is a member of the computer's local administrator's group, that the account has the logon-as-service right, and that its password has no expiration date. Then, at a later time, you can change the account assigned to a particular service by running the Services applet from Control Panel.

Starting SQL Server and SQL Agent Automatically

During the installation process, you can elect to have the SQL Server, SQL Server Agent, and the DTC service start automatically at boot time. This feature is useful for environments where you need SQL Server to automatically start without user intervention if the server is rebooted. This option is part of the reduced cost-of-ownership philosophy. You can also configure this option from the Services applet in Control Panel. This option is not available under Windows 95/98. However, you can add to the startup folder a batch file that contains a reference to the SQL Server executable file SQLSRV.EXE.

Verifying Installation

During the course of installation, setup starts SQL Server and connects to it several times. When the installation is complete, you can test the installation yourself in several ways. Perhaps the easiest way is to start SQL Server using the SQL Server Service Manager. Once the server is running, you can connect to it using the command-line utility OSQL. From a command prompt, type the following command-line options:

```
OSQL -Usa -P
```

The option -U specifies a username (which in this case is sa [the system administrator]), and -P specifies the password option (which in this case is null). By default, the sa password is null. If successful, the OSQL prompt will appear:

```
1>
```

You can enter commands to the server, and you might want to enter a command such as

```
1>select @@servername
2>go
```

This returns the name of the server on which SQL Server is running. At this point, you can exit by typing exit.

Installation Using SMS

You can use Microsoft Systems Management Server (SMS) version 1.2 to automatically install SQL Server. The SQL Server CD-ROM contains a Package Definition Format (PDF) file, SMSSQL70.PDF, which automates the generation of a SQL Server package in SMS. It includes instructions for running the three setup command files also provided on the CD-ROM. To run your own custom command file, use the SMSSQL70.PDF file as a template, and modify a copy of it to run your command file.

Unattended Installation

All the options I have discussed are accessible from a setup initialization file. This allows you to run the setup program without responding to any of the prompts from the program. Instead, all the responses are taken from the setup initialization file. The SQL Server CD-ROM includes some setup initialization files you can use. If you want to include initialization options other than the ones specified in these files, you should create a new setup initialization file rather than edit an existing one.

You can create a new setup initialization file by running setup and selecting the options you need. The setup initialization file SETUP.ISS is created in the \Windows or \WinNT directory.

Microsoft English Query

As part of the effort to make SQL Server an easier product for the average user, Microsoft developed a set of progressive technologies packaged together as English Query. English Query is a tool you can use to develop applications that let a user query the database using English statements rather than SQL. It consists of two components:

3

SQL SERVER
INSTALLATION

- The domain editor, which is the tool used to teach the system about your database
- The query engine, which translates the English statements into SQL

When you run setup, you can elect to install the full product, or you can choose the custom option, as shown in Figure 3.9.

FIGURE 3.9

English Query custom installation options.

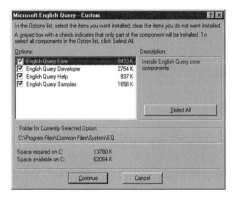

You can install just the Query Core if you already have an application built, or you can select the Query Core, Developer tool, and related help files and sample applications.

OLAP Services

In its effort to offer a scalable, robust server product, Microsoft added the OLAP Services to SQL Server. This gives SQL Server the ability to handle multidimensional data in an online analytical processing (OLAP) environment.

SQL-based engines are not ideally suited to working with large sets of data involving aggregate functions, cross tabulations, and the like. OLAP services fits into this need for a middle-tier database server.

OLAP Services requires an NT workstation or server running Windows NT 4.0 with Service Pack 4 at a minimum. It will not run under Windows 95/98. It also requires 64MB of RAM.

Clients that connect to OLAP Services must support DCOM, which includes Windows 95 with DCOM95 installed and Windows 98. TCP/IP must be installed as the network protocol.

You can elect to install the following OLAP components, as shown in Figure 3.10. A full installation of OLAP Services takes approximately 50MB of disk space and installs four separate components:

- The OLAP Server
- The OLAP Manager
- Client components
- Sample applications

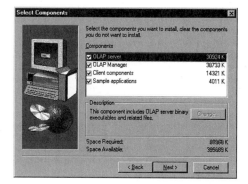

FIGURE 3.10

OLAP Services custom installation options.

Once OLAP Services is installed, you can begin to work with some of the sample databases. See Chapter 34, "Using the OLAP Server," for a discussion of OLAP.

Summary

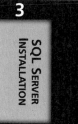

Microsoft SQL Server 7.0 is a highly scalable product and can run a Windows 95 laptop as well as a DEC Alpha multiprocessor computer. It offers a robust set of services, including support for OLAP environments. This chapter reviewed its hardware and software requirements. I then described the installation process step-by-step, covering all the major options.

SQL Server offers a desktop, standard, and enterprise edition of the product. You simply select the edition that is appropriate for your environment. It provides minimal, typical, and custom installation options. Typical works best for most installations. The character set, sort order, and Unicode collation options must be selected with care because you can change them only by reinstalling the product. I covered the various network libraries that SQL Server supports. They include support for many non-Microsoft platforms such as Banyan Vines. I covered the various services that are installed with SQL Server and discussed the difference between running the services under the local system account and one of your own choosing. I also examined how to start these services automatically upon bootup. Finally, you learned how to verify an installation of SQL Server once setup is complete and how to install SQL Server automatically using SMS and an initialization file.

The last two sections covered the installation of the other SQL Server components: the OLAP Services and the English Query. OLAP Services provides support for online analytical processing environments, and English Query is an advanced tool for querying a database using plain English statements.

Client Installation

by Simon Gallagher

CHAPTER 4

When the server piece of your database solution is operational, it is ready to respond to client applications. You can set up a client machine to interact with SQL Server in one of two ways: by running the Setup program to install the client tools or by copying the database library and named pipes network library files to the client's system directory for use with custom applications.

This chapter looks at how and what can be installed for a client, describes the configuration choices that can be made, and looks at each of the available network libraries.

Client Setup

Clients can be set up to access SQL Server using the native database library, using ODBC, or through OLE DB. The following sections look at how these connectivity options are set up, along with the available network protocols.

In the simplest client setup, you copy the database library file, NTWDBLIB.DLL, along with the named pipes network library file, DBNMPNTW.DLL, to the client's system directory. This approach works only for the named pipes protocol because this is the default network library used by SQL Server. For any other protocol, you must install the client tools and make the change using the Client Configuration utility.

The client software can be configured in three different ways:

- Choice of network protocols used by client software to connect to SQL Server. You define the names of the servers available on your network, which are used by both DB-Library and ODBC-based applications.
- The creation of ODBC data sources, which allow access to a specific server using data source names (DSN).
- Default DB-Library option settings.

TIP

The first item in the preceding list illustrates a point that most ODBC application developers do not understand about their connections to the server: Client installation can require more than just making sure that the ODBC drivers are installed; it also may require the correct selection and configuration of a network library.

Microsoft SQL Server can communicate with a client using a number of different methods (see Figure 4.1). If the client is on the same machine as the server, Windows InterProcess Communication (IPC) components are used; this arrangement includes local named pipes and shared memory. If the client is remote, a network IPC is used.

FIGURE 4.1

IPC communication architecture.

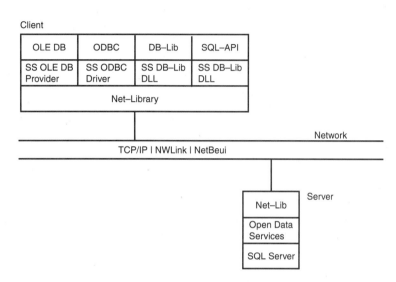

Some network APIs can be used over many different network protocols. For example, named pipes can be used over both NetBEUI and TCP/IP.

Communication between a client application and SQL Server occurs at the application level using a protocol called Tabular Data Stream (TDS). Information is contained in TDS packets for transmission; the packets themselves are contained within the protocol stack used by the Net-Library being used. For example, if the network library is TCP/IP Sockets, then the TDS packets are encapsulated in TCP/IP packets. A TDS packet has a default size of 4KB, which can be changed to a value in the range of 512 bytes through 32KB.

> **TIP**
>
> Unless you really, *really* know what you are doing and have a good reason to change the packet size for the network protocol configuration you are running, leave the default value as is.

4

CLIENT INSTALLATION

Table 4.1 identifies the client and server side Net-Libraries for each supported IPC.

TABLE 4.1   CLIENT AND SERVER NET-LIBRARIES

Net-Library	Client	Server	Supported Protocols
Shared Memory	DBMSSHRN.DLL	SSMSSH70.DLL	Local memory copy
Multiprotocol	DBMSRPCN.DLL	SSMSRP70.DLL	TCP/IP, NetBEUI, NWLink
Named Pipes	DBNMPNTW.DLL	SSNMPN70.DLL	TCP/IP, NetBEUI, NWLink
Windows Sockets	DBMSSOCN.DLL	SSMSSO70.DLL	TCP/IP
Novell SPX/IPX	DBMSSPXN.DLL	SSMSSP70.DLL	NWLink
AppleTalk	DBMSADSN.DLL	SSMSAD70.DLL	AppleTalk
Banyan Vines	DBMSVINN.DLL	SSMSVI70.DLL	Banyan Vines

NOTE

The support for DECNet sockets has been dropped with SQL Server version 7.0.

You can open up a SQL Server to interact with a wide variety of clients at the same time—even if those clients use different protocols. Following is a list of the Net-Library installations to which SQL Server listens:

Windows NT	Windows 9x
TCP/IP	TCP/IP (default)
Multiprotocol	Multiprotocol
N/A	Shared Memory
Named Pipes (default)	N/A

The Shared Memory network library is only used when the client and server are on the same Windows 95/98 computer. Clients that have the client tools installed receive all the Net-Libraries; the default is named pipes. The client can connect only to servers that are listening on the same protocol as the client is trying to use. See "Multiprotocol," later in this chapter, for more information on this topic.

NOTE

Because the named pipes Net-Library is installed by default on both Windows NT and Windows 9x clients, these clients can immediately connect to NT-based SQL Servers. Clients to Windows 9x-based servers must use the Client Configuration utility to change the default protocol to TCP/IP or Multiprotocol.

When running an application on the same computer as SQL Server, you can use the following names to reference the SQL Server:

Windows NT	*Windows 95 or Later*
Computer name	Computer name
(local)	(local)

Connections are made through either the shared memory (Windows 9x) or named pipes (Windows NT) Net-Library.

TIP

If you are installing SQL Server on a standalone machine, you have two options: You can either install the Microsoft Loopback adapter and NetBEUI, or you can use the period as the server name to cause the client tool to try to connect to a local pipe rather than to a named pipe.

The SQL Server Client Configuration Utility

The SQL Server Client Configuration utility (`CLICONFG.EXE`) is launched from the SQL Server program group and allows you to do the following:

- Change the default network protocol
- Create network protocol connections to specific servers with special configuration requirements (specific Net-Library choices, ports, names, and so on)
- Search for and display information about all the network libraries currently installed on a system
- Display the DB-Library version currently installed on the system and set defaults for DB-Library options

4

CLIENT INSTALLATION

To use anything other than the default Net-Library, you must use the Client Configuration utility. This utility creates Registry entries for each network protocol configuration you choose.

> **NOTE**
>
> The Client Configuration utility does not install the Net-Libraries; this task is done using SQL Setup. The Client Configuration utility also does not install the network protocols; these are installed through the Network applet in the Control Panel.

Configuring ODBC Data Sources

To configure ODBC data sources, you must use the ODBC Data Source Administrator by selecting the ODBC applet in the Control Panel. With this tool, you can check driver versions and add and modify data sources to use the SQL Server ODBC driver. When you create or modify a SQL Server data source, the Microsoft SQL Server DSN Configuration Wizard opens to help step you through the configuration.

Client Requirements

Before you can install the SQL Server client management tools and various library files, make sure that the computer meets the following requirements:

- Processor—DEC Alpha AXP or Intel (486/33 MHz or higher) or compatible systems
- Memory—32MB of RAM (minimum)
- Hard disk space—73MB of available disk space (for client management utilities only)
- Operating system—Windows NT Server 4.0 with Service Pack 4 or later, Windows NT Workstation 4.0 with Service Pack 4 or later, or Windows 95 or later
- Network software—Windows NT or Windows 95 built-in networking software (if you are using Banyan Vines or AppleTalk ADSP, you need additional network software)

> **NOTE**
>
> Client utility support has changed from previous SQL Server versions (6.5 and earlier). Client tools are now available for installation only under Windows 9x and Windows NT.

Network Protocol Support

To facilitate client-to-server communication in a variety of network architectures, Microsoft provides a choice of network libraries for use based on your network protocols. The next sections examine the different protocols available and how we can customize their use.

Network Protocols

Using the Client Configuration utility, you can choose the specific network library you want to use to make connections to your SQL Servers. All the network libraries are implemented as dynamic link libraries (DLLs) and are used during network communication using specific InterProcess Communication mechanisms.

> **NOTE**
>
> With distributed computing—of which a client connection to a server is the most fundamental—a connection is made at a process-to-process level to allow communication in both directions. The foundation for this approach is an InterProcess Communication mechanism—of which Windows Sockets, Remote Procedure Calls (RPCs), NetBIOS, named pipes, and mailslots are all examples.

> **TIP**
>
> If you have any problems with the protocols on which SQL Server is listening—as I did while dealing with the beta version of the software—you can examine and modify the Registry key \HKEY_LOCAL_MACHINE\SOFTWARE\Microsoft\ MSSQLServer\MSSQLServer\ListenOn. Of course, it goes without saying that you make modifications to the Registry at your own risk!

The following sections detail each of the available network libraries.

Named Pipes

Named pipes is the default network library used by SQL Server running on NT, listening on a standard pipe of \\.\pipe\sql\query. This pipe name can be changed after installation to make it more difficult for malicious attacks against publicly accessible SQL Servers.

If you do change the server's default pipe, you must use the General tab in the Client Configuration dialog box to connect to the new pipe name. To set up the new pipe, click the Add button and enter the server's name and the new pipe name (see Figure 4.2). The dialog box in Figure 4.2 shows that we are going to connect to the machine named RAVEN that is listening on the pipe \nmi_secure_sql.

FIGURE 4.2

Configuring an alternative named pipe.

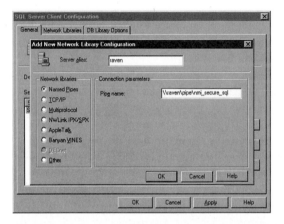

> **NOTE**
>
> Under Windows 95, the 32-bit named pipe network library does not support server enumeration; this is the mechanism used to create the list of available servers for each of the Microsoft tools.

TCP/IP Sockets

TCP/IP Sockets allow communication over the TCP/IP protocol using standard Windows Sockets as the IPC mechanism. Using TCP/IP, the SQL Server service is assigned to port 1433; this is the official Internet Assigned Number Authority (IANA) socket number. If this value is changed on the server, you must set up a specific entry using the Client Configuration utility to indicate the modified port number.

For information on connecting to a SQL Server hidden behind a proxy server, see "Connecting to SQL Server through Microsoft Proxy Server," later in this chapter.

> **NOTE**
>
> For SQL Server 7.0, TCP/IP Sockets is the default network library with Windows 9x servers.

Multiprotocol

The Multiprotocol network library allows communication over supported Windows NT IPC mechanisms. Currently, Microsoft considers only named pipes, TCP/IP Sockets, and NWLink IPX/SPX to be tested and supported. The remote procedure call (RPC) service receives the server's name from the Multiprotocol network library; based on the network protocols available on the client, RPC attempts to use each protocol in turn until a connection is successfully made. The client must be using a Net-Library and protocol stack that corresponds to one the SQL Server is listening on. A client connecting with the Multiprotocol Net-Library over TCP/IP can connect to a SQL Server running the TCP/IP protocol. If the server were running the SPX/IPX protocol stack, no connection could be made.

Among the protocols that RPC supports are Windows-based Novell clients using SPX or IPXODI.

Multiprotocol allows authentication by Windows NT over all supported RPC protocols. It can also be configured to encrypt the user's password and data during all client-to-server communication. Multiprotocol's ability to encrypt and authenticate is a large advantage over the other protocols, and outweighs this protocol's slightly lower performance.

> **NOTE**
>
> To use multiprotocol encryption for passwords and data for *all* clients, you must turn on the Enable Multiprotocol Encryption option for the SQL Server; this is *not* a client setting.

4

CLIENT INSTALLATION

The server's address is determined in the same manner as it is for named pipes: by the server's name. Multiprotocol does not support server enumeration from the client side; servers listening on just Multiprotocol do not appear in such browse lists on clients able to enumerate available servers.

To map a computer name to a physical node, the RPC service makes use of the network protocol's naming service: WINS for TCP/IP, SAP for NWLink IPX/SPX, and NetBIOS broadcasts for named pipes.

NWLink IPX/SPX

Novell SPX-based clients require the NWLink IPX/SPX protocol. In a default installation of SQL Server, the service name is that of the computer. Should this default be changed, you must make a customized entry for that server for each client.

The Client Configuration utility allows the specification of the following items:

- Service Name
- Network Address, consisting of the following:
    - Address
    - Port
    - Network

Your network administrator can provide this information for you.

AppleTalk ADSP

To allow Apple Macintosh clients to use their native AppleTalk network protocol, the AppleTalk ADSP is the network library of choice.

> **NOTE**
>
> Macintosh clients can also communicate using TCP/IP.

Custom AppleTalk entries allow you to specify the object name and zone of the SQL Server within the AppleTalk network.

Banyan Vines

The network library used to communicate over Banyan Vines IP network protocol is the Banyan Vines Sequenced Packet Protocol (SPP).

When a SQL Server listening on Banyan Vines is installed, it is assigned an address of the form *servicename@group@org*. This address is what you must specify when setting up the client.

> **NOTE**
>
> Banyan Vines is currently only available on Intel-based machines.

Troubleshooting Client Connections

Setting up your clients to connect to your SQL Servers is not always as simple as installing the protocols on the machine. You may have to make modifications to the default settings for a protocol (as detailed in the previous sections). You may also have some additional steps or problems to overcome.

You should troubleshoot client connection problems in the same way you tackle any other problem: methodically and carefully. You must first consider the different elements involved and then isolate them, test them, and eliminate them as the source of the problem. So what elements do we need to consider?

- Client hardware—Network interface card (NIC), network cable
- Network hardware—Routers, bridges, WAN links
- Server hardware—Network interface card, network cable
- Client software—Operating system, other applications, network protocol, network library, database library, SQL application, login, password
- Server software—Operating system, network protocol, network libraries, SQL Server configuration

Some of these items are obvious and easily identified: *Is* the cable plugged into the card/wall? Others require more work and other tools. Some hardware problems such as troublesome network architecture components require other steps.

The first step is to determine whether you can see the server's name in a network browse list (look in the Network Neighborhood in Windows NT/9x or use the `net view` command). If you cannot see the server, you may have a router or incompatible network protocol problem.

The next step is to try to make a network connection to a share on the SQL Server and attempt to read and write a file to that location.

Finally, you can try a different protocol from the client. If you can connect with one protocol but not another, you have eliminated at least some of the potential problem areas.

Troubleshooting Named Pipes

You can test a network connection over named pipes with a couple different approaches. The first approach checks whether you can see a server and its resources and makes use of the `net view` command. To check the connection, enter the following statement in a command window:

```
net view \\servername
```

4

CLIENT
INSTALLATION

If this command is successful, you will see a list of resources. The next thing to try is to connect to the server's named pipe using the `net use` command:

```
net use \\servername\IPC$
```

If you can open a connection in this way but still get a failure when trying to connect a SQL tool, you can use the `makepipe` and `readpipe` command-line utilities. On the server, enter the following command:

```
makepipe
```

On the client, enter this command:

```
readpipe /Sservername /Dstring
```

In this syntax, *string* is anything you want; if the string contains a space, the string must be enclosed in quotation marks. The server process creates and manages the pipe; the client uses `DosOpen` to connect and then executes `DosWrite` to the pipe; the server hopefully does a `DosRead` to receive the value sent. If the connection is a success, you should see results similar to these:

```
SvrName:\\raven
PIPE    :\\raven\pipe\abc
DATA    :test
Data Sent: 1 : test
Data Read: 1 : test
```

The server also reacts to the `readpipe` call with the `makepipe` utility, showing something like this:

```
Waiting for client to send... 1
Data Read:       test
Waiting for client to send... 2
Pipe closed
Waiting for Client to Connect...
```

If you do not get this result, network named pipe services are probably not loaded. You must install them before clients can make named pipe connections.

Troubleshooting TCP/IP Connections

The simplest way to check the visibility of a server is to use the `ping` utility, which has this form:

```
ping IPAddress¦ServerName
```

You can use the name of the server if it can be identified by a DNS, WINS, or HOSTS file. If `ping` is successful, you should receive some feedback on the time it takes for a packet to bounce back from the server. If the server cannot be found, you receive an error message.

Installing ODBC

The ODBC Administration tool and SQL Server driver are installed from the SQL Server CD-ROM. After it is installed, you can use the ODBC Administrator, accessed from the Control Panel, to create user, system, or file data sources:

- User DSNs are local to a computer and may only be used by the current user.

- System DSNs are local to a computer, rather than dedicated to a user. This arrangement allows the system—or any user with the correct privileges—to use the data source.

- File DSNs are file-based data sources that can be shared by any user having the same driver installed. They can be stored on a file server for common access.

Troubleshooting ODBC Connections

Most of the same steps described in the "Troubleshooting Client Connections," earlier in this chapter, also apply to investigating ODBC connection problems. However, there is one additional tool in your ODBC repertoire: `odbcping`, which allows you to test the visibility of a server through a data source and to check whether ODBC is correctly installed. This 32-bit utility can be found in the BINN directory under the SQL Server installation directory. The syntax for `odbcping` is shown here:

odbcping { **-S**servername ¦ **-D**datasource } **-U**login **-P**password

In this syntax, *servername* is the name of the server you want to test the connection to, *datasource* is the ODBC data source name on the local machine, and *login* and *password* are valid values for that server. `odbcping` returns either the version of the SQL Server ODBC driver and the server name if successful, or an error message as specified by the ODBC driver.

Here is an example verifying a connection through a data source:

```
odbcping /DRavenDSN /Usimon /Psecret
```

Here is an example of connecting directly to a server:

```
odbcping /SRaven /Usimon /Psecret
```

4

CLIENT
INSTALLATION

OLE DB

There is some misunderstanding about where the OLE DB interface from Microsoft fits in the grand scheme of client connectivity. OLE DB is actually a specification *for* a data access interface rather than *an* interface. It is intended to provide the basis for client access to a wide range of data storage systems.

Microsoft has provided a guide, available from its Web site, shown in Table 4.2, for which technology should be used for a given situation.

TABLE 4.2   ODBC VERSUS OLE DB

Situation	*Technology*
Accessing standard relational	ODBC is the best choice databases from a non-OLE environment
Exposing a data interface	OLE DB is the best choice to non-SQL data
Programming in an OLE environment	OLE DB is the best choice
Building interoperable	OLE DB is the only choice database components

> **NOTE**
>
> An integral part of OLE DB is a driver manager that enables OLE DB clients to talk to ODBC providers.

Table 4.3 shows the actual technical differences between the ODBC and OLE DB interfaces.

TABLE 4.3   TECHNICAL DIFFERENCES BETWEEN ODBC AND OLE DB

ODBC	*OLE DB*
Data Access API	Database Component API
C-Level API	COM API
SQL-based data	All tabular data
SQL-based standard	COM-based standard
Native providers	Component architecture

Connecting to SQL Server over the Internet

By making your SQL Server accessible over the Internet, you can allow worldwide client access to your data. Although this permits a large degree of information sharing, it comes with the added burden of securing the access and modification of that data. The following sections explain how to secure access to your SQL Server using a variety of approaches.

To connect your client application to a Microsoft SQL Server over the Internet, the server must be running either TCP/IP Sockets or the Multiprotocol Net-Library. The client can then connect to a specific IP address; if the computer is registered with a domain name sever (DNS), it can connect with its registered name using TCP/IP or named pipes.

> ### TIP
>
> Named pipes can be a little less than reliable in a WAN environment, so it is strongly recommended that you make use of TCP/IP or Multiprotocol (which uses TCP/IP.)

Securing Connections over the Internet

Making your SQL Server visible on the Internet should make you think very carefully about the security of the server and the data it contains. One way to protect your data is to hide the server behind a firewall (as described in the next section); another way is to make connections encrypted.

Rather than setting up your SQL Server to accept only encrypted multiprotocol connections, you can configure individual clients to request that their connection be encrypted. This approach allows intranet clients to connect without the added burden of encryption, while still allowing less secure Internet clients to individually ask for encryption.

The single step required on each client is to modify a Registry key. This new key can be captured and merged into each new client's own Registry during client installation. Here is the key in question:

```
HKEY_LOCAL_MACHINE\SOFTWARE\Microsoft\MSSQLServer\Client\RPCNetlib
```

This key must be created by you; under this key, you must add a value called Security with a datatype of REG_SZ and a value of Encrypt.

Configuring SQL Server for a Specific Port

If you are using the Multiprotocol network library on SQL Server, be aware that the TCP/IP port number (and the SPX socket) on which it listens is dynamically chosen each time the SQL Server service is started.

To allow clients to connect over the Internet without having to reset their configuration every time the server is restarted, you must modify the SQL Server to listen on a specific port.

Using `regedit`, modify the Registry key
`HKEY_LOCAL_MACHINE\SOFTWARE\MICROSOFT\MSSQLSERVER\MSSQLSERVER\RPCNetlib`.

You will find this key only if you have the Multiprotocol Net-Library installed. Under this key, create a new value with the name `RPCprotocols` with a value type of `REG_MULTI_SZ`.

Then enter a string for each protocol on which the server is listening and specify the port, name, or socket it is to use:

- `ncacn_ip_tcp[,port]`
- `ncacn_np[,name]`
- `ncacn_spx[,socket]`

Connecting to SQL Server through Microsoft Proxy Server

If SQL Server is to be hidden behind Microsoft Proxy Server, you must specify the Remote WinSock proxy address when you set up the TCP/IP Sockets Net-Library. This is done through SQL Setup and the Change Network Support option. You must enter the port number and the proxy server address (the DNS name or the IP address) in the Port Number box for the TCP/IP Sockets protocol. Then enter the DNS name or the IP address of the proxy server in the Remote WinSock Proxy Address box.

> **NOTE**
>
> If you are using Remote WinSock (RWS), you must define the local address table (LAT) for the proxy server such that the listening node address does not appear in the LAT.

On the client side, you follow the same configuration steps as you do for connecting directly over the Internet (see the preceding section). You connect to the specified port of the proxy, which carries out the redirection to the actual port on which the SQL Server is listening.

Summary

This chapter explains the requirements and the options available when installing the SQL Server client software. The chapter also looks at each of the available protocols and explains how to modify their default settings to reach SQL Servers listening on modified protocol settings.

Upgrading from Previous Versions

by Kevin Viers

CHAPTER 5

If you are like most people, you are probably installing SQL Server 7.0 with the ultimate intention of upgrading and replacing an existing SQL Server 6.*x* installation. Of course, it is possible that SQL Server 7.0 will be your first database implementation or that you are switching from a competing database vendor; however, this chapter addresses those who are planning to upgrade an existing installation of SQL Server.

Microsoft provided a utility called the SQL Server Upgrade Wizard to perform the upgrade of a single installation of SQL Server 6.*x* to SQL Server 7.0. You as a DBA have many choices that determine how to perform your upgrade, and the bulk of this chapter is dedicated to covering the Upgrade Wizard and how to use it effectively. Additionally, I discuss various configuration and compatibility issues that you should keep in mind both before and after an upgrade.

Before You Upgrade

Upgrading from a previous version of SQL Server is a major software upgrade, and you should take great care in the planning stages of the upgrade. More than likely, you currently have several databases running under one or more implementations of SQL Server. Likewise, you probably have many end-user applications accessing that data. It is imperative that end-user applications not suffer any loss of functionality or significant downtime and that none of your data is lost while you upgrade your SQL Server installation.

For your upgrade to go as smoothly as possible, you should invest a significant amount of time up front in planning your upgrade. The old saying "an ounce of prevention is worth a pound of cure" is an extremely prescient statement when you upgrade a SQL Server database. You should take the time to understand how the SQL Server upgrade process works and make sure that you know the answers to key configuration questions before you begin. Some of those questions follow:

- Are you going to upgrade on a single machine, or is your SQL Server 7.0 installation going to reside on a separate machine?
- Are you going to upgrade all the databases from a particular SQL Server 6.*x* installation or only some of them?
- Do you plan to consolidate multiple SQL Server 6.*x* installations into one SQL Server 7.0 installation?
- Does your SQL Server 6.*x* participate in replication?
- Does your SQL Server 6.*x* rely on any custom sort orders for applications to function properly?

- How do your stored procedures use the `ANSI_NULLS` and `QUOTED_IDENTIFIER` settings?
- How are your SQL Server 6.*x* logons defined?

These items are by no means an exhaustive list of questions to answer during the upgrade process. They do, however, represent some of the major considerations that you must clarify before you begin. The SQL Server Upgrade Wizard walks you through the process of upgrading a SQL Server 6.*x* installation. As you step through the wizard, you are prompted for several configuration choices. The answers to the questions here will help you decide which options to choose while you run the Upgrade Wizard. The following section discusses the entire upgrade process and examines each option in detail.

I strongly recommend that you read the entire chapter and get a good feel for how the upgrade process works. You should then be able to examine your current SQL Server 6.*x* implementation and determine the most effective and efficient upgrade scenario for your individual situation.

One Computer or Two?

Probably the first thing you need to decide is whether you are going to upgrade to SQL Server 7.0 on the same machine as an existing SQL Server 6.*x* installation or on a different machine. SQL Server 7.0 supports both one-computer and two-computer upgrades.

One-Computer Upgrade

In a one-computer upgrade, you will actually install SQL Server 7.0 on the same machine as the 6.*x* installation you want to upgrade. If you know that you want to upgrade every database on your 6.*x* installation or if your 6.*x* server is involved in replication, this is an appropriate choice. It is important to note that the one-computer upgrade is the only method that you can use to upgrade a server involved with replication.

> **CAUTION**
>
> Only one version of SQL Server can be active at one time on a single machine. As a result, when you install SQL Server 7.0 on a machine that already has SQL Server 6.*x* installed, the 6.*x* will be shut down. If you plan to keep some SQL Server 6.*x* databases active after the upgrade, you might not want to use a single computer upgrade. If you want to have both versions running on a single machine, you can use Microsoft's SQL Server Switch utility to switch between active versions.

A one-computer upgrade will also require you to analyze how much disk space you have available. As a general rule, you need 1.5 times the disk space currently occupied by your 6.*x* databases to perform the upgrade. Depending on the data transfer method you choose, you might require significant available disk space to perform an upgrade. I discuss the available data transfer options later in this chapter.

Two-Computer Upgrade

In a two-computer upgrade, you can upgrade the SQL Server 6.*x* installation from one server to a SQL Server 7.0 installation running on a separate machine. This is probably an appropriate decision if you plan to keep your SQL Server 6.*x* installation active for any time after the upgrade.

If you want to perform a two-computer upgrade, both computers must belong to the same Windows NT domain or to two domains with appropriate trust relationships, and both servers should be running under the same security context. This is required because the Upgrade Wizard must be able to shut down and start up SQL Server 6.*x*. To ensure that your two-computer upgrade will not have any security-related issues, perform the following steps:

1. Ensure that both computers are in the same domain or that appropriate trust relationships exist.

2. Create an NT domain user and add that user to the Administrators group of each server.

3. On each server, set the domain user you just created as the startup account for the MSSQL (6.*x*) or MSSQLServer (7.0) service. You do this through the Services applet in the Control Panel.

> **NOTE**
>
> If the SQL Server 6.*x* that you want to upgrade is involved in a replication scenario, you cannot use the two-computer upgrade method.

Data Transfer Method

The other major decision facing you before you upgrade is whether to use named pipes for data transfer or to use a tape drive. Either method will work equally well; however, there are advantages and disadvantages to each. These two options are discussed in more detail in the following sections.

> **NOTE**
>
> Both data transfer methods require that the named pipes network protocol be installed. Both the SQL Server 6.x installation and the SQL Server 7.0 installation must be set to listen to the default named pipe \\.\pipe\sql\query.

Named Pipes Transfer

The named pipes data transfer method uses named pipes to transfer data in memory from your 6.x installation to the 7.0 installation. This is the most reliable method and will certainly provide the best performance. Using this data transfer method in a one-computer upgrade scenario requires that you have sufficient free disk space. The SQL Server 6.x data and log devices must remain on the computer until the upgrade is complete. As a result, you are actually storing your databases twice on the same machine.

If you have sufficient disk space, the named pipes transfer is the method to use.

Tape Transfer

As mentioned previously, having enough available disk space can be a real issue if you decide to perform a one-computer upgrade. In addition to the space required to install SQL Server 7.0, you need approximately 1.5 times the disk space currently occupied by your 6.x databases. If you must do a one-computer upgrade and you do not have sufficient free disk space, you can choose to use tape transfer.

To use this data transfer method, you must have a tape backup device installed on your server. When using tape transfer, you can choose to have the SQL Server Upgrade Wizard delete the 6.x database devices before creating the 7.0 data files. It can do this because the 6.x data is transferred to tape before the devices are deleted.

> **CAUTION**
>
> If you choose to have the 6.x devices deleted, be careful. All devices are deleted even if you are only upgrading one database. You should only use this option if you are planning to upgrade all the databases in a particular 6.x installation.

Upgrade Checklist

So far, I have discussed some general things that you should consider before upgrading your SQL Server 6.x installation. All these decisions are important and will help you to formulate a sound upgrade plan and to use the SQL Server Upgrade Wizard as effective-ly as possible for your individual situation.

There are, however, some generic "check list" items that you should perform before any upgrade, regardless of your particular situation. The following is a list of actions that you should perform on your SQL Server 6.*x* installation before you run the SQL Server Upgrade Wizard:

- Back up all your data and log device files (.DAT files). This will enable you to restore your databases if the upgrade should encounter any problems.
- Set tempdb to a minimum of 10MB. Microsoft actually recommends that you set this to 25MB.
- Make sure that all your database users have logons in the master database.
- Disable startup stored procedures. This is necessary because the Upgrade Wizard will automatically start and stop the 6.*x* services. If your startup stored procedures begin executing, the Upgrade Wizard can hang.
- If your 6.*x* server is involved in replication, stop replication and clear the log.
- Shut down any applications or services that are dependent on SQL Server 6.*x*.
- Run DBCC on your SQL Server 6.*x* databases to ensure the consistency of the databases.

Once you have prepared your SQL Server 6.*x* installation and decided how you want to perform the upgrade, you will use the SQL Server Upgrade Wizard to actually perform the upgrade. As previously mentioned, several other configuration issues will dictate the choices you make as the Upgrade Wizard prompts you. Make sure you read the entire section about the Upgrade Wizard and understand all the configuration options before you actually begin an upgrade.

Running the SQL Server Upgrade Wizard

The actual upgrade of a database is quite straightforward. SQL Server 7.0 ships with a utility called the SQL Server 7.0 Upgrade Wizard. This wizard automates the task of upgrading one or more databases from a single installation of SQL Server 6.5 to a single installation of SQL Server 7.0. Like every other wizard you have ever used, the Upgrade Wizard walks you through the process and prompts you for configuration information along the way.

The remainder of this section covers each step in running the Upgrade Wizard and outlines the options you have in performing your upgrade. As mentioned previously, you should understand the entire upgrade process and all of the configuration choices you will have to make before you actually attempt to upgrade a database.

The SQL Server Upgrade Wizard is located in the Start Menu Programs folder in a program group called Microsoft SQL Server - Switch. Figure 5.1 shows the introductory dialog box. After you click past the introductory screen, you have to begin making the configuration choices for your particular upgrade scenario.

FIGURE 5.1

The SQL Server Upgrade Wizard Welcome dialog box.

Choosing Data Transfer Options

The dialog box shown in Figure 5.2 lets you choose several options about how your data is transferred from your 6.*x* installation to your new SQL Server 7.0 database.

FIGURE 5.2

The Data and Object Transfer dialog box.

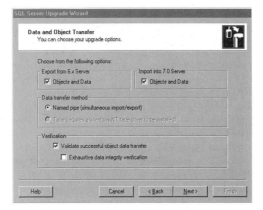

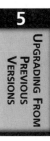

5

UPGRADING FROM PREVIOUS VERSIONS

The first set of options are to enable the Upgrade Wizard to export objects and data from SQL Server 6.*x* and to import objects and data into SQL Server 7.0. By default, both options are checked.

The second set of options allow you to choose which data transfer method you want to use to move the objects and data. The available options are named pipes and tape. Refer to the section "Before You Upgrade" to learn more about when to use each method.

> **NOTE**
>
> If you choose to use the tape data transfer method, then you can run the Upgrade Wizard in two phases. You can choose either to export the SQL Server 6.*x* objects and data to tape or to import data from tape into the new SQL Server 7.0 database. You can choose to export and import the data in one session; however, the Upgrade Wizard will export the 6.*x* data to tape first and then import the data into the 7.0 database.

The final set of options on this dialog allows you to choose the level of verification performed after the upgrade has occurred:

- No Verification—If you leave the options unchecked, no data verification will be performed. You will need to manually compare data via row counts or other methods once the upgrade has completed. This is not a recommended approach to performing your upgrade.

- Validate Successful Object Transfer—If you check this option, the Upgrade Wizard will examine the SQL Server 6.*x* databases (including the security, schema, stored procedures, and number of rows in each table) and store this information. Once the upgrade is complete, the Upgrade Wizard will compile the same list from the SQL Server 7.0 databases. The lists are compared and any discrepancies are reported.

- Exhaustive Data Integrity Verification—This option is only available if you check the Validate Successful Object Transfer option. If you check this option, the Upgrade Wizard will perform check sum operations on each column in each table both before and after the upgrade. The check sums are compared and any discrepancies are reported.

You might wonder how to determine the level of verification that you should use during an upgrade. My opinion has always been "better safe than sorry." The only real drawback to having the Upgrade Wizard perform the highest level of verification is that the upgrade will take longer and will use more disk space. The disk space issue might be a concern if you are doing a one-computer upgrade and using named pipes; however, the peace of knowing that your data has been upgraded successfully is well worth the wait.

Setting Logon Information

The dialog box shown in Figure 5.3 allows you to enter logon information about the export and import servers.

FIGURE 5.3

The Logon dialog box.

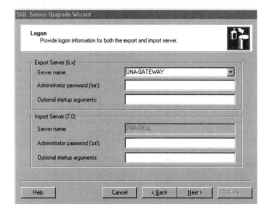

The export server is the machine where the 6.*x* database is running. By default, the Upgrade Wizard enters the name of the machine on which the wizard is running. If you are performing a one-computer upgrade, you can accept the default. If you are performing a two-computer upgrade, however, you need to enter the machine name where the 6.*x* database is running. Refer to the section "Before You Upgrade" for more information about two-computer upgrade requirements.

> **NOTE**
>
> The SQL Server Upgrade Wizard can only upgrade from one installation of SQL Server 6.*x*. If you need to upgrade databases from several 6.*x* machines, you need to consolidate those databases onto one server before you perform the upgrade.

The Upgrade Wizard has to shut down and start up both the 6.*x* and 7.0 servers in order to perform the upgrade. Don't worry—the Upgrade Wizard will present a dialog box that warns you before the databases are actually shut down. You need to provide the sa password for each server along with any trace flags or other startup options that you require when starting the SQL Server.

5

UPGRADING FROM PREVIOUS VERSIONS

> **CAUTION**
>
> If any users are accessing databases involved in the upgrade, they will be disconnected and will not be able to access the database during the upgrade.

Choosing Code Page

The code page defines how SQL Server interprets the bit patterns used to store character data. The default code page is 1252, which is the ISO character set. This character set is made up of the characters found in most languages that originated in Western Europe. In most instances, you should accept the default. It is possible, however, that the actual code page in use for your 6.x installation is different from the code page recorded in the master database. If you know for sure that this is the case, you should choose the actual code page.

The dialog box shown in Figure 5.4 allows you to assign the code page to use when creating the new databases.

FIGURE 5.4

The Code Page Selection dialog box.

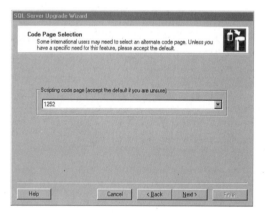

Choosing Databases to Upgrade

When upgrading to SQL Server 7.0, you can choose to upgrade one or more databases running on a single SQL Server 6.x installation. The dialog box shown in Figure 5.5 lets you choose which databases you want to upgrade.

FIGURE 5.5

Database selection.

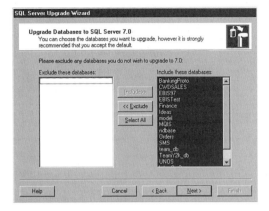

By default, all the databases found on the export server are included for upgrade. If you want to exclude any databases from the upgrade, simply highlight the desired database and click Exclude. You can run the Upgrade Wizard at a later time to upgrade any databases that have not already been updated.

> **CAUTION**
>
> If you choose not to upgrade all the databases from a 6.*x* server, be aware of cross-database dependencies. The Upgrade Wizard will not create a logon in 7.0 if the default database of that logon is not being upgraded. This can cause serious problems if a logon is listed as the owner of objects in a database that is being upgraded while the logon's default database is not being upgraded. In this case, the objects are not created and the upgrade will fail. Make sure to thoroughly examine any such dependencies if you are not going to upgrade all the databases at the same time.

Creating the New Databases

The SQL Server Upgrade Wizard will create the new databases in 7.0 before transferring any database objects or data. The dialog box shown in Figure 5.6 allows you to choose how the Upgrade Wizard will create these databases.

5

UPGRADING FROM PREVIOUS VERSIONS

FIGURE 5.6

*The Database
Creation
dialog box.*

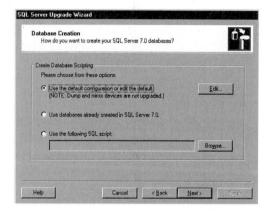

The Upgrade Wizard gives you the following options for creating the new databases on your 7.0 server:

- Use the default configuration.
- Use databases already created on SQL Server 7.0.
- Use a SQL script file.

Each of these options is discussed in more detail in the following sections.

Using the Default Configuration

If you choose the default configuration option, the Upgrade Wizard estimates the storage space required for the creation of the database and log files and creates those files for you. The log file created by the Upgrade Wizard will be twice the size of the total log segments allocated for each SQL Server 6.x database. By default, the Upgrade Wizard will create the database file and log file in the same location as the existing SQL Server 6.x database and log devices.

You can edit the default configuration of each database file and log file by clicking the Edit button shown in Figure 5.6. The dialog box shown in Figure 5.7 lets you edit configuration information about each database file and log file.

To edit configuration information, highlight the file you want to edit and double-click. You can change the name and path of the file along with its initial size and autogrow characteristics. Figure 5.8 shows the dialog box used to edit the configuration of each file.

FIGURE 5.7

The Database Layout dialog box.

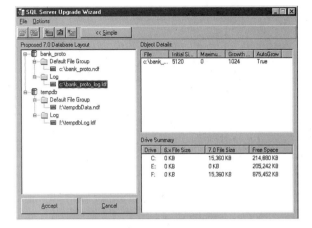

FIGURE 5.8

The Data File Properties dialog box.

> **NOTE**
>
> The SQL Server Upgrade Wizard calculates the size of the new database file based only on loaded data in the 6.*x* database. If you are not planning to allow the database file to autogrow, you need to make allowances for this by increasing the initial size of your database file. It is highly recommended, however, that you allow the database file to autogrow.

Using Databases Already Created

If you choose the option to use databases already created, the Upgrade Wizard does not create any databases for you on 7.0. You must manually create all the databases on the import server before running the upgrade. You must name the databases exactly as they are named in 6.*x*.

> **CAUTION**
>
> If you choose to manually create databases, be careful how you size your database files. The database might require more disk space on 7.0 than it did on 6.*x*. In fact, Microsoft recommends that you allow 1.5 times the disk space for a database in 7.0 after it has been upgraded.

Using a SQL Script

If you choose to use a SQL script, the Upgrade Wizard will use a SQL script file to create databases on the import server. Specify the desired script file in the box shown earlier in Figure 5.6. The caution in the previous section about sizing your database files is applicable to this option as well.

Setting System Configuration Options

The dialog box shown in Figure 5.9 allows you to set various system configuration options.

FIGURE 5.9

The System Configuration dialog box.

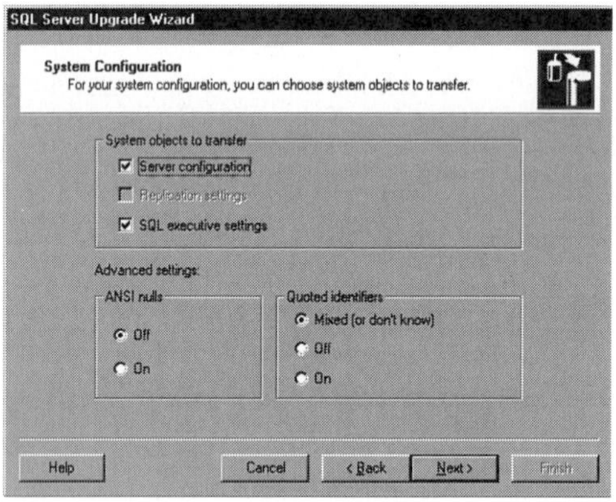

The Upgrade Wizard allows you to set the following system configuration options:

- System objects to transfer
- ANSI nulls
- Quoted identifier

Each of these options is discussed in more detail in the following sections.

System Objects to Transfer

The System objects to transfer option lets you check which system-level objects you want to transfer during the upgrade:

- Server Configuration—The Upgrade Wizard will transfer and upgrade any server configuration options, such as remote server registrations and remote logon registrations. Any configuration option that is no longer supported in 7.0 will not be transferred.

- Replication Settings—If any of the databases you are upgrading are involved in a replication scenario, then any articles, subscriptions, and publications of each database will be transferred and upgraded.

- SQL Executive Settings—Any task scheduled by the 6.*x* SQL Executive will be transferred and upgraded. All tasks will be set up to run through SQL Server Agent on the 7.0 server.

ANSI Nulls

The ANSI nulls option controls how the Upgrade Wizard sets the `ANSI_NULLS` database option when creating database objects in SQL Server 7.0. The `ANSI_NULLS` setting controls default nullability and the behavior of comparisons against null values. It is important to understand how your SQL Server 6.*x* database objects use the `ANSI_NULLS` options. The Upgrade Wizard will create all database objects with the `ANSI_NULLS` setting that you choose in this dialog box. In other words, all objects will be created with `ANSI_NULLS` set to either ON or OFF.

If your 6.*x* database contains objects, such as stored procedures, that use different `ANSI_NULLS` settings, you need to run the upgrade and then re-create those objects that need a different `ANSI_NULLS` setting. This is necessary because SQL Server 7.0 resolves the `ANSI_NULLS` setting at the time the object is created, whereas SQL Server 6.*x* resolves the `ANSI_NULLS` setting during query execution.

Quoted Identifier

The Quoted identifier option controls how the Upgrade Wizard sets the `QUOTED_IDENTIFIER` database option when creating database objects in SQL Server 7.0. The `QUOTED_IDENTIFIER` setting determines how SQL Server treats double quotation marks ("). You can choose to set the `QUOTED_IDENTIFIER` to ON, OFF, or Mixed. Again, it is important that you understand how your 6.*x* databases use this setting before you attempt an upgrade.

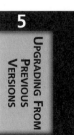

If you know that all the database objects in your 6.*x* database use the same QUOTED_IDENTIFIER setting, then you should select either ON or OFF in the Upgrade Wizard, depending on the setting used in the 6.*x* database. If your 6.*x* database objects use a mix of the two settings, or if you are unsure of which settings are used, you should choose the Mixed option. When the Mixed option is selected, the Upgrade Wizard attempts to upgrade all database objects with QUOTED_IDENTIFIER set to ON. If any objects fail to upgrade, the Upgrade Wizard attempts to upgrade those objects with QUOT-ED_IDENTIFIER set to OFF.

Completing the Upgrade Wizard

The dialog box shown in Figure 5.10 indicates that the Upgrade Wizard has finished gathering configuration information and is ready to begin transferring database objects and data.

FIGURE 5.10

The Completing the SQL Server Upgrade Wizard dialog box.

If the Upgrade Wizard has encountered any warning conditions while gathering configuration information and examining the 6.*x* databases, you will see a list of warnings and possible choices in the dialog box. Most of the warnings listed will not be severe and should not stop you from successfully upgrading a database.

When you click Finish, the Upgrade Wizard will begin the process of transferring and upgrading the database objects and data from the databases you selected to upgrade. Depending on the size of the databases you are upgrading, this could be a lengthy process. Figure 5.11 shows a status meter that continually updates you on the progress of the upgrade.

Figure 5.11

The Script Interpreter dialog box.

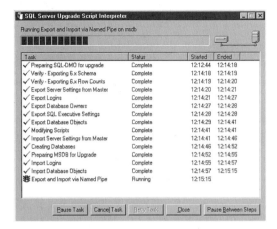

While the upgrade is processing, you have the option of pausing any of the steps that are being performed or canceling the upgrade. If any of the steps fail, you are notified with a red stoplight.

Under the Hood

I hope you will not encounter any problems with the upgrade of your database. In the event that problems do arise and your upgrade does not complete successfully, you can turn to several troubleshooting mechanisms. The Upgrade Wizard does an excellent job of maintaining an audit trail of activities as they are performed. This audit trail is stored as a set of detailed log files.

If errors are encountered during the upgrade, you will see a dialog box like the one shown in Figure 5.12 that highlights informational files you can view for more details about the problems that occurred.

Figure 5.12

The Informational Files Found dialog box.

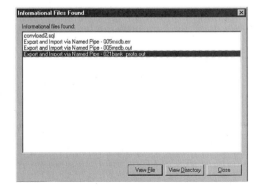

5

UPGRADING FROM PREVIOUS VERSIONS

Every time you run the Upgrade Wizard, a folder is created in the \\mssql7\upgrade directory with a standard naming convention. The folder is named with the machine name of the export server followed by a date and time. Inside this folder, you will find a tremendous number of files that you can use to track down problems. Any file with an .ERR extension indicates that an error occurred. All of the files are standard text files that can be read with Notepad or any other text editor. You can refer to the SQL Server 7.0 Books Online for a detailed description of each file that is created and what is contained in each.

If the Upgrade Wizard completes successfully, you will see the dialog box shown in Figure 5.13.

FIGURE 5.13

The successful completion dialog box.

After You Upgrade

After you have upgraded your databases, you might decide that you want to remove your 6.x installation. I suggest leaving your 6.x server installed until you are completely sure that the upgrade was successful. Don't assume that because the Upgrade Wizard indicated success, the upgrade was definitely successful. It is a good idea to wait until your client applications have run against the new database for some period of time before you remove the old database.

> **CAUTION**
>
> If you have run a one-computer upgrade and you decide to remove the 6.*x* server, make sure that you set the 6.*x* server as the active server before running the uninstall program. If you have the 7.0 server active when you attempt to uninstall 6.*x*, you will remove parts of each and corrupt the Registry!

Summary

The SQL Server Upgrade Wizard is a great tool that makes upgrading from a previous version of SQL Server a straightforward and intuitive task. It is important that you have a clear upgrade plan and that you are aware of all the relevant configuration issues before you begin an upgrade.

Maintaining Backward Compatibility

by Sharon Bjeletich

IN THIS CHAPTER

Why Backward Compatibility Is Important

One of the challenges of rewriting a database engine is ensuring that existing applications and data are supported and that these applications will function in the expected manner. Most applications written to run against an enterprise database are complex, and rewriting or modifying them to run as expected against a new server engine, no matter how powerful or feature-rich it is, is a daunting prospect—one not easily undertaken. Microsoft helps you accomplish the goal with backward compatibility levels, which on a user database level, support either SQL Server 7.0 or pre-SQL Server 7.0 functionality. Bringing a database to a backward compatibility level is an interim migration solution because you should upgrade all your databases to a 7.0 level to support enhancements.

Compatibility levels for databases upgraded by the Upgrade Wizard (part of SQL Server 7.0) are automatically set to the matching level of the previous installation version. The compatibility level settings are 60, 65, and 70. The model database is created at setup time with a compatibility level for SQL Server 7.0, so new databases that are created support all the new features of 7.0—but you can change this setting. Then, you can change compatibility levels on the upgraded databases to support new functionality or set new databases to a pre-7.0 level to support legacy applications.

> **NOTE**
>
> Throughout this chapter, the term *application* applies to anything that is written by a user and can include client applications, scripts, triggers, stored procedures, and so on.

Although most applications should work as expected when upgraded, sophisticated administration tasks, utilities, and scripts probably won't. You must evaluate such areas for modification. Basically, because the engine changes, system tables, functions, procedures, and utilities that are part of SQL Server 7.0 also change. Although there are views supplied for pre-7.0 system tables, the direct access of system catalogs is strongly discouraged by Microsoft in this version. Also, some system stored procedures are no longer available. Microsoft indicates that all Transact-SQL statements should work properly, both in user and administrative applications. However, the behavior may not be exactly what you expect.

NOTE

Although it isn't common, administrative functions, stored procedures, and statements are sometimes used within user applications. You cannot modify only administrative applications and assume that you will not need to change user applications.

Although most administrative functions, stored procedures, and statements are not commonly part of user applications, we all know that the real world has forced this to occur at times. Unfortunately, we can't make the simple assumption that only administrative applications will need to be modified or that user applications can remain unchanged.

You should perform an impact analysis on all applications and scripts that run against SQL Server to determine the presence of unsupported features or features with different behavior.

Upgrading from previous versions is covered in depth in Chapter 5, "Upgrading from Previous Versions," and isn't discussed here other than how it pertains to maintaining backward compatibility.

Backward Compatibility Level Details

Microsoft organized the new functions and behaviors of SQL Server 7.0 into four groups, which in Books Online are also call levels, leading to confusion for some users over what constitutes a backward compatibility level. You can set a backward compatibility level only to a corresponding SQL Server version number: 60, 65, or 70. The levels used to group different functions and behaviors in Books Online (currently indicated as Levels 1, 2, 3, and 4) subset this information according to the potential impact on applications. Therefore, you can use these groups to perform impact analyses against existing applications and scripts. For clarity in this chapter, the groups are referred to as backward compatibility level impact groups. Only changes considered high impact to existing applications are included here; for the specific features of each group, refer to Books Online.

> **TIP**
>
> Organizations that keep all application code on central servers and follow for-
> mal administrative and naming standards have a distinct advantage in impact
> analyses. This is where all that hard work pays off.
>
> An easy and effective way to perform an impact analysis is to use a tool (such as
> one of the many flavors of grep) that can search all files in a subdirectory,
> reporting the location or line number of each instance. You can then evaluate
> the code for upgrade impact. If you have followed the standards outlined in
> Appendix C, "Defining System Administration and Naming Standards," you can
> include all SQL Server stored procedures, rules, constraints, triggers, and so on
> in the analysis.

Backward Compatibility Level Impact Group 1

Group 1 consists of features that are no longer supported in SQL Server 7.0 and, as such,
have the highest impact on existing applications. Although the features mostly pertain to
administrative functions, you should evaluate all code for their presence before upgrading.

You should assume that you must rewrite administrative programs and relearn and even
rethink approaches to optimizing databases. This process has the highest impact of any
of the changes made to SQL Server as far as determining when an organization can make
an upgrade. Although existing applications might run unchanged against a database with
a backward compatibility level set to the previous version, you still have to maintain,
optimize, and back up that database server. Most large organizations invest many hours
in developing administrative programs to perform these functions.

> **CAUTION**
>
> I cannot emphasize enough how critical it is to evaluate the impact on adminis-
> trative tools and operations before upgrading to SQL Server 7.0. This area was
> not the major concern in previous version upgrades, and it holds the largest
> potential for upgrade work for production systems. Not performing this evalua-
> tion can lead to unexpected upgrade delays, as well as the possibility of
> unpleasant surprises after the upgrade.

Some of the more significant changes include the following:

- The backup history tracking tables have been replaced with new system tables, including backupfile, backupmediafamily, backupmediaset, and backupset. These tables are still in the msdb database and can be considered to be supersets of the old tracking tables, including much more information about a backup.

- Because device usage has changed completely, disk refit and disk reinit are no longer available. They have been replaced by the create database and alter database statements, which now create the operating system files and databases in one step.

- The different flavors of the sorted_index option of the create index statement are gone.

- The allow_dup_row and ignore_dup_row options of the create index statement are no longer available.

- Segments, as well as all related stored procedures, are no longer supported.

- The set_disable_def_cnst_chk setting has been removed.

- set showplan has been replaced with set showplan_all and set showplan_text and no longer executes the query.

- SQL_DMO has changed significantly, and Microsoft recommends that all applications be rewritten.

- Because many system stored procedures and system tables have changed, database administrators should evaluate them for each application.

- Because databases and logs have changed, all applications that refer to them and their supporting system tables and stored procedures must be changed.

- The probe login has been removed. The Windows NT Performance Monitor used this login; it now uses integrated security to access the SQL Server, so you must be sure that the NT logon has the appropriate privileges.

Backward Compatibility Level Impact Group 2

Compatibility level impact Group 2 contains major changes in behavior for existing features. These changes appear more often in user applications than Group 1 changes, so you should fully understand them before upgrading.

Some of the more significant changes include the following:

- The skip and init options of the backup statement used together may no longer overwrite backup device contents in some situations.

- The truncate_only option of the dump statement behaves exactly the same as the no_log option.

- You must use different syntax with the `restore` command to load multiple transaction logs, requiring all but the last `restore` statement to include the `with norecovery` option.

- Some organizations have used a system of applying transaction logs with the `no chkpt. on recovery` option of `sp_dboption` enabled for warm standby servers or manual replication; it is now recommended that you use the `standby` option of the `restore` command.

- Because the `bcp` utility has a flag for 6.*x* behavior, it is recommended that you use the same version for both `bcp out` and `bcp in`—something that is not obvious from the data file itself. You might find that you will want to use the new Data Transformation Services (DTS) to perform these data migration jobs. It is a very powerful tool that, although it might be slower than `bcp` in some instances, is well worth using because of its flexibility and ease of use. DTS is covered in Chapter 35, "Data Transformation Services."

- The `open objects` and `user connections` configuration options have default values of `0` for automatic growth.

- Direct date value addition and subtraction (using the + and – operators) are now supported for `datetime` and `smalldatetime` datatypes.

- Databases with compatibility level settings of 60 or 65 interpret each empty string as a single space; a setting of 70 causes an interpretation of an empty string as an empty string.

- Dropping a clustered index requires all nonclustered indexes to be rebuilt, making a larger impact than in previous versions.

- A `rollback` statement inside a stored procedure used in an `insert .. exec ...` statement causes the entire transaction to be rolled back and the batch to stop execution.

- Applications using the ODBC API must handle the `SQL_SUCCESS_WITH_INFO` error code in a different manner.

- `grant` and `revoke` behave differently because `revoke` is now used to remove a previously granted permission with the new `deny` statement for blocking permission.

- All cursors should be reopened after issuing a `rollback` statement when `close_cursor_on_commit` is set to `off`. Cursors can now be declared as local or global. In previous versions, cursors were always global, with the scope of the cursor being global to the connection. Local cursors now are scoped for the batch, stored procedure, or trigger they are created in.

- Multiple event triggers, as well as multiple recursive triggers, are allowed for each table.

- The `master` database is searched before user databases for stored procedures with a prefix of `sp_`.

- You must preface table hints (`holdlock`, `index`, `nolock`, and so on) using the `with` clause and use parentheses for all but the `holdlock` hint.

- The `repeatable read` and `serializable` options of the `set transaction isolation level` statement no longer behave in the same way. These used to effectively have the same result. `serializable` is considered to have the same effect as using the `HOLDLOCK` hint on all tables, whereas `repeatable read` can allow the insert of phantom rows and can appear in later reads in a transaction.

- You can make modifications against more than one table in an updateable view.

Backward Compatibility Level Impact Group 3

Group 3 consists of features that are supported only for backward compatibility and should be replaced as soon as possible because there is no guarantee they will be supported in future releases.

Some of the more significant changes include the following:

- You should replace `dump` and `load` statements with the new `backup` and `restore` statements.

- `dbcc newalloc` is identical to `dbcc checkalloc` and should be replaced with the new syntax; `dbcc textall` and `dbcc textalloc` functionality is included in `dbcc checkdb` and `dbcc checktable`.

- Using `suids` causes a performance penalty and should be replaced with the appropriate new system ID.

- You should replace the `fastfirstrow` query hint with `option (fast n)`.

- `xp_grantlogin` and `xp_revokelogin` should be replaced with `sp_grantlogin` and `sp_revokelogin`.

Backward Compatibility Level Impact Group 4

Group 4 consists of minor changes. Obviously, the impact on existing applications is negligible, except for user aliases, which have been replaced with roles. This replacement can have a large impact on organizations that extensively use aliases.

> **NOTE**
>
> It is a common practice to alias users to dbo for development and administration users who need dbo privileges. Tables created in this manner had dbo as the owner and could be referenced as *dbo.tablename*. Now, a table created with a user aliased to dbo will have an owner with that user's name, as in *username.tablename*, rather than *dbo.tablename*.

Some of the more significant changes include the following:

- Although user aliases are still supported, they have replaced by roles because it is no longer necessary to assume the identity of another users.

- dbcc output formats have changed.

- You can no longer use Enterprise Manager to subscribe to one or more replication articles.

- Microsoft indicated that the SQL-92 syntax for outer joins will be the only syntax supported in future releases. There are a number of books, including those by the renowned SQL author Joe Celko, which fully explain how to write SQL-92 statements correctly.

> **NOTE**
>
> A common mistake made in converting the older style Transact-SQL statements to ANSI SQL-92 is in the correct specification of query conditions or arguments in outer joins that restrict the inner table. In the older syntax, criteria could be specified in the WHERE clause. This could be ambiguous. In the ANSI SQL-92 syntax, this criteria should always be specified for outer joins in the FROM clause. For example, the following query is written in the older style Transact-SQL:
>
> ```
> SELECT titles. title, qty
> FROM titles, sales
> WHERE titles.title_id *= sales.title_id
> AND stor_id = '7066'
> ```
>
> This query would be written in ANSI SQL-92 with the criteria in the FROM clause as follows:
>
> ```
> SELECT titles.title, qty
> FROM titles LEFT OUTER JOIN sales
> ON titles.title_id = sales.title_id
> AND stor_id = '7066'
> ```

This syntax causes the restriction on the inner table to be performed at the time of the join, rather than applied to the results of the outer join. The problem with writing this query incorrectly in the new syntax (by using a WHERE clause) is that results will be returned, just not the complete set of results, making it difficult to catch the error.

Summary

Setting the backward compatibility level lets legacy SQL Server 6.*x* applications and data co-exist with new systems designed using the 7.0 feature set. However, because you can set the compatibility level only for user databases, it is important to fully understand and appreciate the modifications and analyses that you must make to migrate these systems, with an emphasis on administrative tasks.

SQL Server Database Architecture

PART

III

IN THIS PART

Physical Database Architecture

by Tibor Karaszi

IN THIS CHAPTER

CHAPTER 7

If you have worked with earlier versions of SQL Server, you will notice that the physical database architecture in SQL Server 7.0 has been almost completely re-architectured. The basic architecture did not change from version 1.0 to version 6.5. The reason for the new architecture is to provide increased performance, better scalability, and improved stability. The new architecture also provides a foundation for features that might be introduced in future versions (for example, table partitioning, intertable clustering, and so on).

Why bother learning about the internal structure at all? Although there is less to tune and fewer knobs to turn in version 7.0 than in previous versions, you can always perform a better tuning job if you have a basic knowledge of the internal architecture. In addition, some system messages refer to internal structures.

This chapter looks at the storage structures in SQL Server and how those structures are maintained and managed. This information can help you understand various issues raised in many of the subsequent chapters.

SQL Server Storage Structures

A DBA does not see data and storage the same way SQL Server does. A DBA or end user sees these things:

- Databases, physically stored in files
- Tables and indexes, placed in filegroups
- Rows, stored in tables

SQL Server sees these things:

- Databases, physically stored in files
- Pages, allocated to tables and indexes
- Information, stored on pages

Data Pages and Extents

The *page* is the smallest level of I/O in SQL Server and is the fundamental storage unit. Pages contain the data itself or information about the physical layout of the data. The page size is the same for all page types: 8KB (before version 7.0, the page size was 2KB).

Page Types

There are six page types in SQL Server, as listed in Table 7.1.

TABLE 7.1 PAGE TYPES

Page Type	Stores
Data	The actual rows, found in the tables
Index	Index entries and pointers
Text and Image	Textual and image data
Global Allocation Map	Information about allocated (used) extents
Page Free Space	Information about free space on pages
Index Allocation Map	Information about extents used by a table or an index

All pages have a similar layout. They all have a page header, which is 96 bytes, and a body, which consequently is 8096 bytes. The page layout is shown in Figure 7.1.

FIGURE 7.1

The page layout.

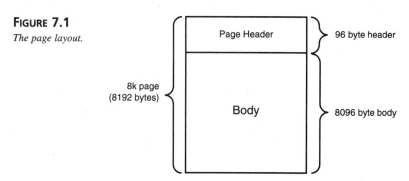

The information stored in the page header and body depends on the page type. You can examine a page by using the DBCC PAGE command. You must be logged in with sysadmin privileges to run the DBCC PAGE command. The syntax for the DBCC PAGE command is as follows:

```
DBCC PAGE ('dbname' ¦ dbid, file_no, page_no [, 0 ¦ 1 ¦ 2]
```

The last parameter, the print option, determines how the page contents will be returned. 0, the default, returns only the page header. 2 returns the page header and a hexdump of the page, formatted row by row. 1 returns the same information as does 2, but the body is returned as a single block of data. You must first run DBCC TRACEON (3604) if you want to get the results from DBCC PAGE returned to an application.

> ### TIP
>
> Built-in help is available for some of these undocumented DBCC commands. If you want help on DBCC PAGE, for instance, run these commands:
>
> ```
> DBCC TRACEON (3604)
> DBCC HELP (page)
> ```
>
> You should note, however, that undocumented commands are not supported. Because the command may not be available in a later release, or the syntax or result may change, you use these commands at your own risk.

We will have a closer look at the page contents as we describe the different page types.

Data Pages

The actual data rows in tables are stored on data pages. Figure 7.2 shows the basic structure of a data page.

FIGURE 7.2

The structure of a SQL Server data page.

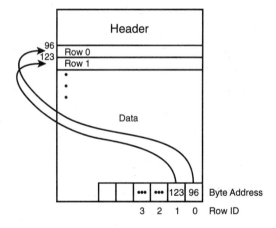

A data row in SQL Server cannot cross page boundaries. The maximum row size is 8060 bytes. Because each row also incurs some overhead, the maximum usable row size is slightly lower than 8060 bytes. The data row size does not take into account columns of text or ntext and image datatypes because these are handled differently.

The following example shows the error returned from SQL Server when trying to create a table with a too-large row size:

```
CREATE TABLE customer_info
(cust_no INT, cust_address NCHAR(200), info NCHAR(4000))
```

```
Server: Msg 1701, Level 16, State 2
Creation of table 'customer_info' failed because the row size
 would be 8425, including internal overhead.
This exceeds the maximum allowable table row size, 8060.
```

You can create a table with data rows that could conceivably exceed 8060 bytes if the table contains variable-length columns. Although the table will be created, the following message will be returned:

```
CREATE TABLE customer_info
(cust_no INT, cust_address NCHAR(200), info NVARCHAR(4000))
```

```
The total row size (8427) for table 'customer_info' exceeds
 the maximum number of bytes per row (8060). Rows
 that exceed the maximum number of bytes will not be added.
```

Note that this is technically no warning message because no error number is returned.

If you then try to insert a row that exceeds 8060 bytes of data and overhead, the insert fails with the following error message:

```
Server: Msg 511, Level 16, State 1
Cannot create a row of size 8405 which is greater than the
 allowable maximum of 8060.
The statement has been aborted.
```

Header

The *page header* contains control information. Some fields assist when SQL Server checks for consistency among its storage structures and some fields are used when navigating among the pages that constitute a table. Here is a list of some of the fields in the page header:

- Page ID is the identification of the page. It consists of two parts: the file ID number and the page number.

- Next Page and Previous Page are the next and previous pages in the page chain. These are always zero for a heap table. See "Heaps and Indexes," later in this chapter, for examples.

- Type is an internal code that describes the page type.

- Index ID describes the ID of an index. 0 means that it is a data page for a heap table. 1 means that the page is a data page for a clustered table. A value greater than 1 is the ID of a nonclustered index; the value 255 indicates a text or image page.

The Row Offset Table

The location of a row within a page is determined by the *row offset table*, which is located at the end of the page. To find a specific row within a page, SQL Server finds the starting byte address for a given row ID.

When you insert a row into a heap table, the row goes at the end of the page as long as the page will fit there. When you delete a row from a heap table, the byte address is set to 0, indicating that there is a "hole," or some available space, at that address. When you delete a row, the rows are not shuffled to keep the free space at the end of the page, as they were with previous versions of SQL Server. If you insert data on a page where there is free space, but the free space is fragmented across the page because there have been deletions, the rows will be compacted before the row is inserted. Figure 7.3 shows how the free space and the offset table are handled when you insert and delete data on a heap table. The example uses a fixed row length of 10 bytes (the same algorithms are used for other or variable row lengths). Note that more rows fit on the page than are drawn in Figure 7.3.

FIGURE 7.3

Inserting and deleting rows on a heap table data page.

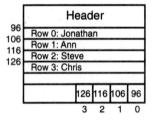
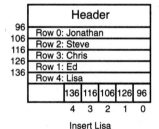

Note that deleting Ann does not remove the information physically stored on the page; the only modification is that the byte address for Row ID 1 is changed to 0 (unused). When Ed is inserted, he goes to the end of the page because there is space available there. However, when Lisa is to be inserted, there is no space available at the end of the page, so the rows are compacted to make available space at the end of the page. Row IDs do not change for existing rows, so index entries for those rows do not have to be updated.

The algorithm for managing the insertion and deletion of rows on a clustered table is very similar to that for a heap table. The difference is that when a page is compacted to reclaim free space, the row-offset table is adjusted to keep the rows in the clustered key order, by row number.

Index Pages

Index information is stored on index pages. An *index page* has the same layout as a data page. The difference is the type of information stored on the page. Generally, a row in an index page contains the index key and a pointer to the page at the next (lower) level.

The actual information stored in an index page depends on the index type and whether it is a leaf-level page or not.

- Clustered indexes, nonleaf pages—Each index row contains the index key and a pointer (the fileId and a page address) to the next (lower) page in the index tree. The *leaf level* of a clustered index is the actual data page; therefore, it has the exact same layout as a data page.

- Nonclustered index, nonleaf pages—Each index row contains the index key and a pointer (the fileId and a page address) to the next (lower) page in the index tree. Each row also contains a reference to the data row the index row refers to. This reference for a heap table is a RowId (the fileId, a page address, and a row offset address). For a clustered table, the reference is the clustered key. This arrangement allows the corresponding row (if any) in the index tree to be deleted when the data row is deleted.

- Nonclustered index, leaf pages—Rows on this level do not include a separate field with the page address for the next (lower) page because that information is available in the RowId or clustered key value.

Extents

If SQL Server allocated one page at a time as pages are needed for a table (or an index), the data would be scattered around the disk. Scanning such a table would not be very efficient. Therefore, pages for each object are grouped together into *extents*; one extent consists of eight pages.

Earlier versions of SQL Server reserved one extent for a table or index at time of creation. No other objects could be stored on this extent. In version 7.0, this algorithm has changed a bit: Version 7.0 introduces *mixed extents*.

When a table or index is created, a page on a mixed extent is allocated. If no mixed extent exists for the database, such an extent is allocated. A mixed extent can contain pages from several tables or indexes. A mixed extent can contain pages from a maximum of eight tables or indexes (because an extent is eight pages).

As the table grows beyond the mixed extent, *uniform extents* are reserved for the table.

Figure 7.4 shows the use of mixed and uniform extents.

FIGURE 7.4

Mixed and uniform extents.

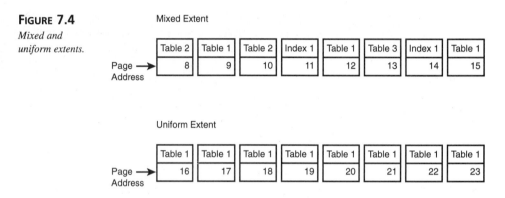

Log Data

The transaction log is stored in a physically separate location from the data. It is no longer stored on a system table, as it was in previous versions, which means that the log does not compete with data pages for memory resources. The allocation of space as log records are inserted is also simplified. The transaction log is physically stored in one or several log files, which SQL Server handles as a series of records.

Text and Image Data

If you want to store large amount of text or binary data, you can use the text, ntext, and image datatypes. (For information about how to use these datatypes, see Chapter 8, "Logical Database Architecture.") Each column for a row of these datatypes can store up to 2GB (minus 2 bytes) of data. Version 7.0 has done some re-architecting for these datatypes; these datatypes wasted quite a lot of data storage (in some circumstances) in earlier versions because each column and row with any data in it was allocated one page (2KB).

The text and image values are not stored as part of the data row but as a collection of pages on their own. For each value of these columns, all that is stored on the data page is a 16 byte pointer, which points to the location of the text or image data. A row with several text and image columns has one pointer for each column.

A table has one collection of pages to hold the text and image pages. The anchor for this collection is stored in sysindexes for the table, indid 255. One enhancement in version 7.0 is that one page can hold text and image data from several columns and several rows. This wastes a lot less storage if smaller amounts of data are stored in these columns.

Text and image information is presented externally (to the user) as a long string of bytes. Internally, however, the information is stored in a set of pages, organized as a B-tree structure. If an operation addresses some information in the middle of the data, SQL Server can navigate through the B-tree to find the data. In previous versions, SQL Server had to follow the page chain to find the desired information.

Physically, text and image data is stored on a set of pages. Logically, it is handled as a B-tree. The data row points to a 64 byte root structure. This root structure points to the pages on which the actual text or image data is stored. Note that columns within the same row—and even rows within the same table—can share space on the same page.

If the amount of text or image data exceeds 32KB, SQL Server allocates intermediate B-tree index nodes that point to the text and image pages. In this situation, the intermediate node pages and the text/image pages are not shared between columns and rows.

Global Allocation Map Pages

The Global Allocation Map (GAM) pages track whether extents have been allocated to objects and indexes and whether the allocation is for mixed extents or uniform extents. There are two types of GAMs:

- Global Allocation Map—The GAM keeps track of allocated extents, regardless of whether the allocation is for a mixed extent or a uniform extent. The structure of the GAM is straightforward: Each bit in the page (except for the page header) represents one extent, where 1 means that the extent is not allocated and 0 means that the extent is allocated. A single GAM covers 64,000 extents, or 4GB of data. Page number 2 on each file is a GAM page, and there is another GAM every 64,000 extents (512,000 pages) after the first GAM.

- Shared Global Allocation Map (SGAM)—The SGAM keeps track of mixed extents that have free space available. An SGAM has a structure similar to a GAM, with each bit representing an extent. A value of 1 means that the extent is a mixed extent and there is free space (at least one unused page) available on the extent. A value of 0 means that the page is not allocated, that the extent is a uniform extent, or that the extent is a mixed extent with no free pages.

Table 7.2 summarizes the meaning of the bit in GAMs and SGAMs.

TABLE 7.2   MEANING OF THE GAM AND SGAM

Extent Usage	GAM Bit	SGAM Bit
Free	1	0
Uniform	0	0
Mixed, with no free pages	0	0
Mixed, with free pages	0	1

When SQL Server needs to allocate a uniform extent, it simply searches the GAM for a bit with 1 and sets it to 0. To find a mixed extent with free pages, it searches the SGAM for a bit with 1. When a mixed extent is allocated, a GAM with 1 is searched, the bit is set to 0, and the corresponding SGAM bit is set to 1. There is some more processing involved as well—such as spreading the data evenly across database files—but the allocation algorithms are still very simple.

Page number 3 on each database file is an SGAM page; there is another SGAM each 64,000 extents (512,000 pages) after the first SGAM.

Index Allocation Map Pages

Index Allocation Map (IAM) pages keep track of extents used by a certain heap or index. IAM pages are allocated as needed and are spread randomly throughout the database files. An IAM does not span database files; if the heap or index spreads to a new database file, a new IAM for the heap or index is created in that file.

The IAM has a bitmap, indicating the extents used by the heap or index (just as do GAMs and SGAMs). The `FirstIAM` column in the `sysindexes` table points to the first IAM page for a table or an index.

Page Free Space Pages

A Page Free Space (PFS) page records whether or not each page is allocated and the amount of free space on the page. The PFS covers 8,000 pages. The PFS has a bitmap for each page that indicates whether the page is empty, 1 to 50 percent full, 51 to 80 percent full, 81 to 95 percent full, or more than 95 percent full. The PFS page is page number 1 on each file; there is another PFS page for each 8,000 pages. SQL Server uses PFS pages to find free pages on extents and to find pages with space available on extents.

Figure 7.5 shows the layout of GAM, SGAM, and PFS pages on a database file.

FIGURE 7.5
The layout of GAM, SGAM, and PFS pages.

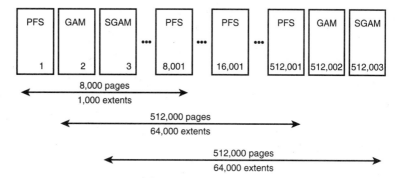

Database Files and Filegroups

The way a database allocates physical storage is much simplified in SQL Server version 7.0 as compared to earlier versions.

A database is created over a set of operating system files. These files are created at the same time as the database is created or expanded. The minimum number of operating system files for each database is two because the transaction log is always separated from the data and index pages. The maximum size for a database file is 32TB; the maximum size for a log file is 4TB.

> **NOTE**
>
> In versions of SQL Server before version 7.0, a database was created over a number of *database devices*. These devices had to be created before the creation of the database by using the DISK INIT command. The transaction log could be mixed with data and index pages, limiting the options for backup and recovery. One database device could also contain fragments from several databases.
>
> This concept originated from the early versions of Sybase, in which a database device was mapped to a physical disk or a disk partition.

All databases have a default filegroup that contains the primary data file (described later in this section) and all other data files that are not put into other filegroups. The default filegroup contains all system tables and all tables and indexes that are not explicitly created in another filegroup. You can add one or more filegroups to the database. A database file can be put into a filegroup. A database file can be a member of one and only one filegroup. This functionality allows you to map a table or index to a certain database file or set of files, thus controlling the placement of data. A typical installation recommends the use of RAID to spread I/O across disks; more advanced installations or installations with large databases can also benefit from this level of control.

Each database has a table called `sysfiles`, which contains information about the database files. Table 7.3 lists the columns in the `sysfiles` table.

TABLE 7.3 THE `sysfiles` TABLE

Column Name	Description
fileid	The database identification number. Unique for each database.
groupid	Identification of the filegroup to which the file belongs.
size	Size of the file (in pages).
maxsize	The maximum size of the file. `0` means that the file does not auto grow; `-1` means that the file can auto grow until the disk is full. The auto grow feature is described in the following section.
growth	Auto growth increment in either pages or percentage of the file size.
status	Indicates whether the growth is in pages or in percentage of file size.
perf	Reserved for future use.
name	The logical name of the file.
filename	The physical name of the file, including path.

The `sysfilegroups` table contains information about the database filegroups, as shown in Table 7.4.

TABLE 7.4 THE `sysfilegroups` TABLE

Column Name	Description
groupid	The filegroup identification number. Unique within the database.
allocpolicy	Reserved for future use.
status	`0x8` indicates read-only; `0x10` indicates the default filegroup.
groupname	Name of the filegroup.

The following statement returns the filename, size in MB (not including auto grow), and the name of the filegroup to which each file belongs:

```
SELECT name, size/128, groupname
 FROM sysfiles sf INNER JOIN sysfilegroups sfg
               ON sf.groupid = sfg.groupid
```

On-Demand Disk Management

A feature that is very much welcomed by SQL Server DBAs is the auto grow feature. In earlier releases, the size of a database and database device was expandable, but not automatically. One of the more common error messages from SQL Server was error 1105, which means that SQL Server ran out of space in the database.

In version 7.0, you can specify that a database file should grow automatically as space is needed. SQL Server can also shrink the size of the database if the space is not needed. You can control whether or not you use this feature along with the increment by which the file is to be expanded. Listing 7.1 gives an example of a database with a 10MB growth increment for the first database file, 20MB for the second, and 20 percent growth increment for the log file.

LISTING 7.1 CREATING A DATABASE WITH AUTO GROWTH

```
CREATE DATABASE Customer
ON ( NAME='Customer_Data',
    FILENAME='D:\SQL_data\Customer_Data1.mdf',
    SIZE=50,
    MAXSIZE=100,
    FILEGROWTH=10),
   ( NAME='Customer_Data2',
    FILENAME='E:\SQL_data\Customer_Data2.ndf',
    SIZE=100,
    FILEGROWTH=20)
LOG ON ( NAME='Customer_Log',
    FILENAME='F:\SQL_data\Customer_Log.ldf',
    SIZE=50,
    FILEGROWTH=20%)
GO
```

The Customer_Data file has an initial size of 50MB, a maximum size of 100MB, and a file increment of 10MB.

The Customer_Data2 file has an initial size of 100MB, a file growth of 20MB, and can grow until the E: disk partition is full.

7

PHYSICAL DATABASE ARCHITECTURE

The transaction log has an initial size of 50MB; the file increases by 20 percent with each file growth. The increment is based on the *current* file size, not the size originally specified.

Primary Data File

Every database has one and only one primary database file. The primary database file contains pointers to all other database files for the database. Enterprise Manager defaults the file extension for the primary database file to .mdf. It is often sufficient to use only one database file for tables and indexes (the primary database file). The file can, of course, be created on a RAID partition.

> ### CAUTION
>
> If you lose the primary data file, you cannot back up an isolated transaction log. This is because SQL Server will not be able to find the transaction log files (because the primary data file is lost).
>
> So make sure that you always have redundancy for the primary data file. You might want to create a small primary data file, which you put on a mirrored drive, and a larger secondary data file, which holds the main part of your data.

The primary database file always belongs to the default filegroup.

Secondary Data File

A database can have any number of secondary files (well, the maximum numbers of files per database is 32,767). You can put a secondary file in the default filegroup or in some other filegroup. Here are three situations in which the use of secondary database files might be beneficial:

- Disk partition size—Suppose that you have to create a database with a size of 8GB (log excluded). You have two 4GB disks for this purpose. You can create the database over two database files, 4GB each.

- Partial backup—A backup can be done over the entire database or a subset of the database. The subset is a set of files or filegroups. The partial backup feature is useful for large databases, where it is impractical to back up the entire database. When recovering with partial backups, a transaction log backup must also be available. For more information about backups, see Chapter 12, "SQL Server Backup, Restore, and Recovery."

Physical Database Architecture

CHAPTER 7

113

7

PHYSICAL
DATABASE
ARCHITECTURE

- Control over placement of database objects—When you create a table or index, you can specify the filegroup in which the object is created.

Listing 7.2 shows the use of a secondary database file and a filegroup that controls the placement of database objects.

LISTING 7.2   USING A FILEGROUP TO CONTROL PLACEMENT FOR A TABLE

```
CREATE DATABASE Customer
ON ( NAME='Customer_Data',
    FILENAME='D:\SQL_data\Customer_Data1.mdf',
    SIZE=50,
    MAXSIZE=100,
    FILEGROWTH=10)
LOG ON ( NAME='Customer_Log',
    FILENAME='F:\SQL_data\Customer_Log.ldf',
    SIZE=50,
    FILEGROWTH=20%)
GO

ALTER DATABASE Customer
 ADD FILEGROUP Cust_table
GO

ALTER DATABASE Customer
 ADD FILE
   ( NAME='Customer_Data2',
    FILENAME='E:\SQL_data\Customer_Data2.ndf',
    SIZE=100,
    FILEGROWTH=20)
 TO FILEGROUP Cust_Table
GO

USE Customer
CREATE TABLE customer_info
(cust_no INT, cust_address NCHAR(200), info NVARCHAR(3000))
 ON Cust_Table
GO
```

The CREATE DATABASE statement creates a database with a primary database file and a log file. The first ALTER DATABASE statement adds a filegroup.

A secondary database file is added with the second ALTER DATABASE command. This file is added to the Cust_Table filegroup.

The CREATE TABLE statement creates a table; the ON Cust_Table clause places the table in the Cust_Table filegroup (the Customer_Data2 file on the E: disk partition).

Log File

Each database has at least one log file. In version 7.0, the transaction log is no longer a system table as it was in previous versions (`syslogs`). The log is quite simply a series of log records. This means that the log can no longer be mixed with data pages.

A database can have several log files, and each log file can have a maximum size of 4TB. A log file cannot be part of a filegroup.

> **NOTE**
>
> You can think of this arrangement as if all log files are implicitly part of a "log" filegroup. All log records go to this filegroup, and no other pages will be placed there.
>
> This view is similar to the way previous releases of SQL Server handled the separation of the transaction log—through the predefined `logsegment` segment.

Tables

A cornerstone of the relational database model is that there is only one structure that carries information in a relational database: the table.

A table is defined as a set of columns with certain properties, such as the datatype, nullability, constraints, and so on. Information about datatypes, constraints, and the like can be found in Chapter 8.

Relaxed Limitations on Table Size and Dimensions

Many limitations have been relaxed in version 7.0 of SQL Server. One limitation in earlier versions was the maximum row length of 1962 bytes. This limitation sometimes caused a somewhat convoluted table structure: A large row size would have to be decomposed into several rows or several tables. Both of these solutions were hard to work with. In version 7.0, the limitation for a row size is 8060 bytes.

Another limitation of the earlier versions of SQL Server—which was very often encountered—was the maximum size of 255 bytes for CHAR, VARCHAR, BINARY, and VARBINARY columns. The solution to this limitation involved repeating columns, using several columns for one logical column, using several rows (as in the `syscomments` table), or using the TEXT or IMAGE datatype. Version 7.0 enlarges the maximum size for these datatypes to 8000 bytes. For instance, you can now store text up to a few KB without using the somewhat cumbersome TEXT and IMAGE datatypes. Note, however, that the new Unicode datatypes require twice the amount of storage space, thus limiting NCHAR and NVARCHAR datatypes to 4000 characters.

A restriction not too frequently encountered was the limit of 255 columns per table; in version 7.0, the number of columns per table has been expanded to 1024.

Clustered Tables

A *clustered table* is a table for which a clustered index has been created. When you create a clustered index, the rows are sorted in the order of the columns in the index key. The data pages are chained together in a doubly linked list (each page points to the next page and to the previous page). The page pointers are stored in the page header. Figure 7.6 shows an example of a clustered table. (Note that the figure shows only the data pages.)

FIGURE 7.6

A clustered table.

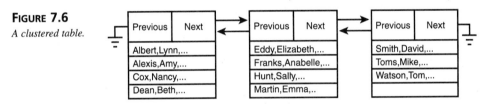

Heap Tables

A table without a clustered index is a *heap table*. There is no imposed row ordering for a heap table.

How does SQL Server find the rows when it has to perform a table scan on a heap table? In earlier releases of SQL Server, the data pages were doubly linked in a manner similar to that of a clustered table. SQL Server looked up the first page in the sysindexes table and then scanned each page, following the page chain. Unfortunately, the table could become fragmented over time. As rows were deleted, a whole page could be deallocated and reused. This meant that SQL Server might have to go back and forth within the physical file when scanning the table. In fact, there was no way to reorganize the data pages for a table without a clustered index (with the exception of creating a clustered index and then dropping it).

In version 7.0, there is no page ordering between the data pages on a heap table. Instead of registering page usage on the data pages, a higher level of page maps the used pages. Each heap table has at least one IAM (Index Allocation Map) page. The address of the first IAM page is stored in the sysindexes table (sysindexes.FirstIAM). The IAM page registers which extents are used by the table. SQL Server can then quite simply scan the extents pointed out by the IAM page, in physical order.

Each IAM can map 1,000 extents (64MB). More IAM pages are created for the heap table as needed. A heap table has at least one IAM page for each file on which the heap table has extents. Figure 7.7 shows the structure of a heap table.

FIGURE 7.7

The structure of a heap table.

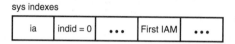

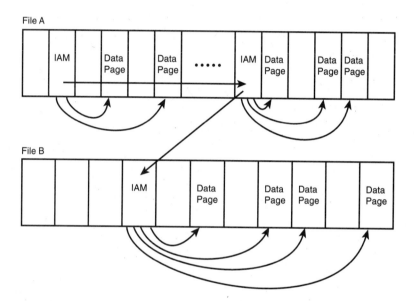

Indexes

If a table has no indexes, SQL Server has to retrieve every page, looking at every row to find out whether the row satisfies the search arguments. SQL Server has to scan all the pages because there's no way of knowing whether the rows found are the only rows that satisfies the search arguments. This search method is referred to as a *table scan*. Needless to say, this is not a very efficient way to retrieve data. The optimizer in SQL Server always calculates the cost of performing a table scan and uses that as a base line when evaluating other access methods. Access methods and the optimizer are discussed in Chapter 24, "Query Analysis."

Suppose that the table is stored on 10,000 pages; even if only one row is to be returned or modified, all the pages must be searched, resulting in a scan of almost 80MB of data.

We need a mechanism to identify specific rows within a table quickly and easily. This functionality is provided through two types of indexes: clustered and nonclustered.

Indexes are stored structures that are separate from the actual data pages. Indexes are used to speed up access to the data; they can also be used to enforce the uniqueness of the data rows.

Indexes in SQL Server are *binary trees* (B-trees) (see Figure 7.8). There is a single root page at the top of the tree, which branches out into N pages at each intermediate level until it reaches the bottom (leaf level) of the index. The leaf level has one row stored for each row in the table. The index tree is traversed by following pointers from the upper-level pages down through the lower-level pages. Each level of the index is linked as a doubly linked list.

FIGURE 7.8

The structure of a B-tree.

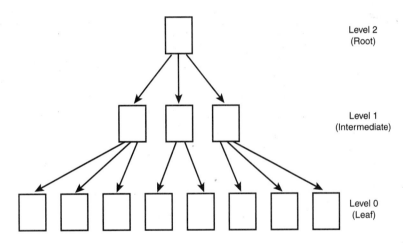

Level 2 (Root)

Level 1 (Intermediate)

Level 0 (Leaf)

An index can have many intermediate levels depending on the number of rows in the table, the index type, and the index key width. The maximum number of columns in an index is 16; the maximum row width is 900 bytes.

Clustered Indexes

When you create a *clustered index*, all rows in the table are sorted and stored in the clustered index key order. Because the rows are physically sorted by the index key, you can have only one clustered index per table. You can compare a clustered index to a filing cabinet: The data pages are like folders in a file drawer in alphabetical order, and the data rows are like the records in the file folder, also in sorted order.

You can think of the intermediate levels of the index tree as file drawers, also in alphabetical order, that assist you in finding the appropriate file folder. Figure 7.9 shows an example of a clustered index.

FIGURE 7.9

The structure of a clustered index.

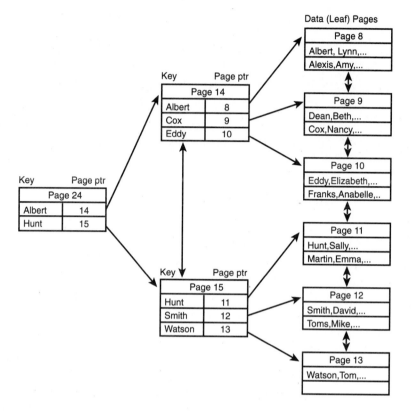

In Figure 7.9, note that the data page chain is in clustered index order. The rows on each page are not necessarily in clustered index order, but the row IDs within the page are in order. A clustered index is useful for range-retrieval queries because the rows within the page are physically located in the same page or on adjacent pages.

The leaf level of a clustered index contains all the columns in the table, so the data pages are the leaf level of a clustered index. To find all instances of a clustered index key value, SQL Server must eventually scan all data pages.

SQL Server performs the following steps when searching for a value using a clustered index:

1. Queries sysindexes for the table where indid = 1. The sysindexes.root column contains the fileId and page address for the root page of the index.

2. Compares the search value against the values on the root page.

3. Finds the highest key value on the page where the key value is less than or equal to the search value.

4. Follows the page pointer to the next level down in the index.

5. Continues following page pointers (that is, it repeats steps 3 and 4) until the data page is reached.

6. Searches the rows on the data page to locate a match for the search value. If a matching row is not found on that data page, the table contains no matching values.

Because clustered indexes contain only page pointers, the size and number of levels in a clustered index depends on the width of the index key and the number of pages in the table.

Nonclustered Indexes

A *nonclustered index* is a separate index structure, independent of the physical sort order of the data in the table. You can have up to 249 nonclustered indexes per table.

You can think of a nonclustered index as the index in the back of a book. To find the pages on which a specific subject is discussed, you look up the subject in the index and then go to the pages referenced in the index. This is an efficient method as long as the subject is discussed on only a few pages. If the subject is discussed on many pages, or if you want to read about many subjects, it can be more efficient to read the entire book.

A nonclustered index works in a similar fashion to the book index. From the index's perspective, the data rows are randomly spread throughout the table. The nonclustered index tree contains the index key in sorted order. There is a row at the leaf level for each data row in the table.

If there is no clustered index created for the table, the leaf level of the index will contain a pointer to the data page and the row number within the page where the row is located (see Figure 7.10).

If there is a clustered index created for the table, the leaf level will contain the clustered index key for the row. If the clustered index is not a unique index, a unique identifier will be automatically added to the duplicate values for the clustered key (see Figure 7.11). The advantage of pointing out the clustered key value is that if a row is moved (for example, as a result of an update), the nonclustered indexes stay stable—they don't have to be updated.

7

PHYSICAL
DATABASE
ARCHITECTURE

FIGURE 7.10

A nonclustered index on a heap table.

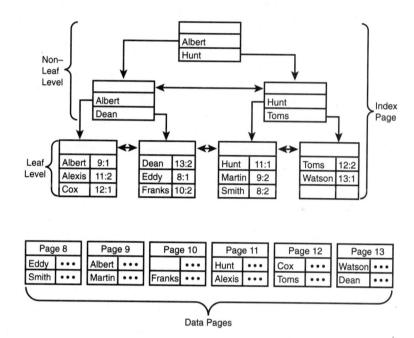

SQL Server performs the following steps when searching for a value using a nonclustered index:

1. Queries `sysindexes` for the table where `indid > 1` and `indid <= 250`. The `sysindexes.root` column contains the `fileId` and page address for the root page of the index.

2. Compares the search value against the values on the root page.

3. Finds the highest key value on the page where the key value is less than or equal to the search value.

4. Follows the page pointer to the next level down in the index.

5. Continues following page pointers (that is, it repeats steps 3 and 4) until the leaf page is reached.

6. Searches the rows on the leaf page to locate a match for the search value. If a matching row is not found on the leaf page, the table contains no matching values.

7. If a match is found on the leaf page, SQL Server either follows the pointer to the data page or searches through the clustered index for the value, if such exists.

Because clustered indexes contain page and row pointers, the size and number of levels in a nonclustered index depends on the width of the index key and the number of rows in the table.

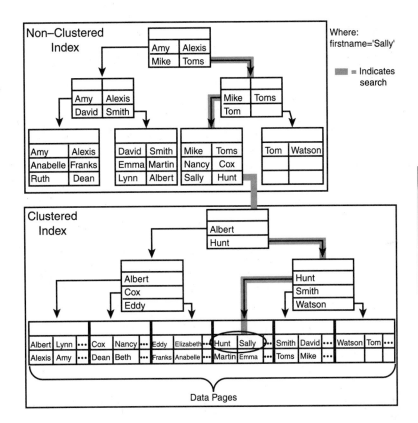

FIGURE 7.11

A nonclustered index on a clustered table.

Improved Design Using Row Locators

Earlier versions of SQL Server stored row locators (the RowId) in nonclustered indexes to identify the data row. If the table had a clustered index and a page split occurred (as a result of an INSERT or UPDATE), many rows were moved to another page. All corresponding rows in nonclustered indexes had to be modified to reflect the new RowId. This made page splits costly.

In version 7.0, nonclustered indexes on clustered tables no longer include the RowId. Instead, the nonclustered index points to the clustered key. When SQL Server searches through a nonclustered index, it starts searching through the clustered index, using the clustered key, to find a row. This adds a few pages to the search. The good thing is that if a page split occurs in a clustered table, the nonclustered indexes stay stable.

If the table is a heap table, no page splits occur. What happens is that each new row basically goes to the end of the table.

Summary

A database is created on a set of database files. A database file can be configured to grow automatically, if desired. The smallest unit of I/O and the basic storage construct is a page, which is 8KB. Pages from a table or index are clustered together eight by eight, in extents. Extents can be shared among tables, resulting in less storage waste for small tables. By using filegroups, you can control the file (or set of files) in which a table or index should be stored.

A clustered index sorts the table according to the index key. Clustered indexes are very efficient when you are searching for a range of values. Nonclustered indexes (also called B-trees) point to the data row, either the clustered key or the RowId.

The physical database architecture has been simplified and enhanced in version 7.0 of SQL Server. A larger page size means more efficient I/O—it also means that more data fits on a page. The use of a clustered key on nonclustered indexes means fewer page splits when you are inserting and updating.

Addressable storage has been extended as well. The maximum size of a single database file is 32TB, and the maximum size of a database is 1,048,516TB—probably more than we can afford to administer in the near (or distant?) future!

Logical Database Architecture

by Tibor Karaszi

In This Chapter

In this chapter, we will take a look at features in SQL Server available for you when you define and develop the back end of your database application. This includes knowing the datatypes, defining integrity rules, and using stored procedures to encapsulate business functions. We will also take a look at how SQL Server keeps track of metadata (data about your data).

Datatypes

The most basic type of integrity feature is defining the datatype that each column can hold. Not only does it limit the "characters" that you can store, but it also gives SQL Server some basic understanding about the semantics of your data. For instance, SQL Server can distinguish between adding string and numeric information. Each column in your tables is based on a datatype. The following example creates a table to hold information about orders:

```
CREATE TABLE orders
(order_id INT NOT NULL,
customer_id INT NOT NULL,
order_date DATETIME NOT NULL)
```

The `order_id` and `customer_id` columns can hold integers, and `order_date` can hold date and time information. `CREATE TABLE` and the concept of `NULL` is discussed Chapter 21, "Using Transact-SQL in SQL Server 7.0." SQL Enterprise Manager has a graphical interface for creating tables where you pick the datatype for each column from a drop-down box, as shown in Figure 8.1.

FIGURE 8.1

Choosing the datatype when creating a table in SQL Enterprise Manager.

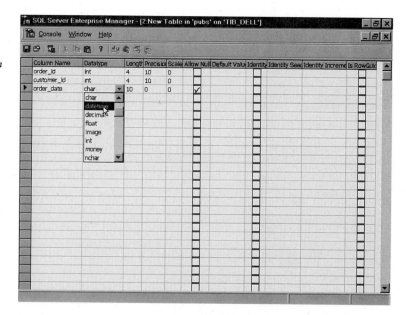

Datatypes are also used when defining views and declaring variables, with parameters to stored procedures, and so on.

> **NOTE**
>
> You should choose the datatype carefully. The datatype that you choose has ramifications in the space utilization, performance, and so on of your system. Choosing the proper datatype can also make it easier for the application developer—for instance, storing date information in a datetime datatype instead of as a character string.
>
> SQL Server 7.0 allows you to change the datatype for existing tables as long as an implicit conversion is possible. Nevertheless, you might have to modify existing applications, scripts, batches, and so on to reflect the change.

Character and Binary Datatypes

Strings are stored in character datatypes. There are six different character datatypes available and the differences between them concern code page, fixed or variable length, and the maximum length that you can store. The character datatypes are char, nchar, varchar, nvarchar, text, and ntext.

Binary datatypes store *binary* strings, strings consisting of binary values instead of characters. The available binary datatypes are binary, varbinary, image, and timestamp.

char, nchar, varchar, and nvarchar

The most common string datatypes are fixed length (char) and variable length (varchar) character types. Version 7.0 introduces Unicode datatypes, which can store virtually all known characters. The Unicode variable name counterparts start with the letter n (nchar and nvarchar).

If your installation will support users from several countries, it is a good idea to use Unicode datatypes. Two bytes are used to store a character instead of one byte, as with char and varchar. Your installation is still, somewhat, language-dependent because Unicode collation is chosen at installation time and applies to all tables stored within the server. The Unicode collation determines the sort order for all characters in the Unicode standard. For more information about sort orders and collation, refer to Chapter 3, "SQL Server Installation."

8

LOGICAL
DATABASE
ARCHITECTURE

For columns defined as char or nchar, SQL Server will fill out the string to the specified number of bytes. Columns defined as varchar and nvarchar will store only the length actually entered, possibly truncating trailing spaces.

How SQL Server handles trailing spaces is determined through SET ANSI_PADDING and whether the column is fixed length or variable length. Table 8.1 outlines of the settings for trailing spaces.

TABLE 8.1 HANDLING TRAILING SPACES BASED ON WHETHER SET ANSI_PADDING IS ON OR OFF

ANSI_PADDING *Setting*	char *and* nchar	varchar *and* nvarchar
ON	String is padded with spaces to the length of the column.	String is not padded with spaces to the length of the column. Trailing spaces are preserved.
OFF	String is padded with spaces to the length of the column.	Trailing spaces are trimmed.

The behavior is determined when the table is created, not when queries are executed against the table.

The maximum number of characters that you can store for char and varchar columns is 8,000 bytes. Because Unicode columns require two bytes per character, the maximum number of characters for nchar and nvarchar columns is 4,000.

NOTE

Before version 7.0, the maximum length was 255 bytes. If you are involved in porting an application to take advantage of the new features in SQL Server version 7.0, you might want to verify that tables are not using several columns, several rows, or the text datatype to store strings with a maximum length between 255 and 8,000 bytes.

How do you decide whether you should use fixed- or variable-length columns? The storage structure is simpler for fixed-length datatypes than for variable length, so variable-length datatypes require some extra processing overhead when reading and modifying data. If you expect the stored column length to vary considerably, you probably want to use variable-length datatypes instead of fixed-length datatypes.

If you try to insert a longer string than the column definition allows, SQL Server will truncate the string. No error message is returned.

To express character data with Transact-SQL, always encapsulate the character string within single or double quotes. (Single quotes are generally recommended because it adheres to the ANSI standard.) Problems can arise if the string expression contains the same character as you use to encapsulate the string with:

```
CREATE TABLE strings (string CHAR(30))
GO
INSERT strings (string) VALUES ('The car is owned by Lisa.')
GO
INSERT strings (string) VALUES ('Lisa's car is red.')
```

The following error message was returned from the second INSERT statement:

```
Server: Msg 170, Level 15, State 1
Line 1: Incorrect syntax near 's'.
Server: Msg 105, Level 15, State 1
Unclosed quote before the character string ')
'.
```

SQL Server's parser cannot differentiate between the quote within your data and the quote that terminated the string. If you double the quote sign, the first quote will act as an escape character to SQL Server. Such a function can be written in the host language and can be called for each string to be inserted into SQL Server:

```
INSERT strings (string) VALUES ('Lisa''s car is red.')
```

binary and varbinary

The binary datatypes are similar to their character counterparts; the difference is that they are designed to hold binary information. SQL Server interprets character data based on the sort order, whereas binary data is simply a stream of bits. Use the binary datatypes to store hexadecimal values.

To express binary information, precede the hexadecimal value with 0X:

```
CREATE TABLE binary_data (bin_info binary(10))
INSERT binary_data (bin_info) VALUES (0x4F)
SELECT * FROM binary_data

bin_info
--------------------
0x4F
```

SQL Server will truncate binary values that are too long. The same rule applies for binary data regarding padding values as it does for character datatypes, with the difference that binary data is padded with zeroes.

uniqueidentifier

The uniqueidentifier datatype was added to version 7.0, and it is used to generate values that are guaranteed to be unique. Uniqueness is not achieved through the datatype itself; the unique value is generated through the NEWID() function. uniqueidentifier is a 16-byte binary datatype, and it is seldom used for other purposes than comparison between values.

Listing 8.1 creates a table with a globally unique value for an order ID and a column for the customer ID:

LISTING 8.1   USING THE uniqueidentifier DATATYPE

```
CREATE TABLE orders
(order_id uniqueidentifier ROWGUIDCOL DEFAULT NEWID()
 PRIMARY KEY NOT NULL,
customer_id INT)
INSERT orders (customer_id) VALUES(1)
SELECT * FROM orders

order_id                                customer_id
------------------------------------    -----------
0C85DE72-0A03-11D2-B279-00104B47FB8D 1
```

The order_id column is defined as a uniqueidentifier datatype. A default (the NEWID() function) is also assigned to the column so that SQL Server generates unique values for each inserted row. The ROWGUIDCOL property can only be defined for one column in a table. This property acts as information: "This is the unique column within the table." You can reference the column defined with the ROWGUIDCOL property using the ROWGUIDCOL keyword:

```
SELECT ROWGUIDCOL FROM orders

order_id
-----------------------------------
0C85DE74-0A03-11D2-B279-00104B47FB8D
```

SQL Server uses the same algorithms to generate a unique value as when a GUID is assigned to a COM object. The generated value is unique across all networked computers in the world. One use for `uniqueidentifier` is merge replication so SQL Server can identify rows when it synchronizes updates performed at several sites.

timestamp

The `timestamp` datatype is a `binary(8)` column with some special behavior. The use of a `timestamp` column is uniquely identifying versions of each row in a table.

There are three important steps involving timestamps:

1. Create a table with a timestamp column.
2. Automatically update a timestamp column.
3. Provide optimistic concurrency using the timestamp value.

To create a table with a timestamp column, use the `timestamp` datatype in the CREATE TABLE statement. The following example creates a customer contact table with a `timestamp` column named `ts`. You can use any legal name for the timestamp column:

```
CREATE TABLE contacts
(cont_id int IDENTITY,
f_name char(20),
l_name char(25),
tel char(14),
ts timestamp)
```

You can have only one timestamp column per table. If you want to add a timestamp column to a table, just add the column with the `timestamp` datatype. SQL Server will automatically generate timestamp values for existing rows, as shown in Listing 8.2.

LISTING 8.2 ADDING A TIMESTAMP COLUMN TO A TABLE WITH EXISTING DATA

```
CREATE TABLE contacts
(cont_id int IDENTITY PRIMARY KEY,
f_name char(20),
l_name char(25),
tel char(14))
INSERT contacts (f_name, l_name, tel)
 VALUES ('Steve', 'Johnsson', '408 496-7223')
```

continues

8

LOGICAL
DATABASE
ARCHITECTURE

LISTING 8.2   CONTINUED

```
INSERT contacts (f_name, l_name, tel)
 VALUES ('Cheryl', 'Carson', '415 548-7723')
ALTER TABLE contacts  ADD ts timestamp
SELECT * FROM contacts

cont_id  f_name   l_name     tel            ts
-------- -------- ---------- -------------- ------------------
1        Steve    Johnsson   408 496-7223   0x000000000000012D
2        Cheryl   Carson     415 548-7723   0x000000000000012E
```

If you don't name the column (yes, you can leave out the column name for timestamp columns), SQL Server will name the column timestamp for you. Although this name is the default, leaving it is not a good idea. timestamp is an ANSI SQL-92 reserved word, so it might become a keyword in some future version of SQL Server.

You never specify a timestamp value explicitly for the timestamp column. SQL Server will generate a value for each inserted row and a new value each time the row is updated.

> **NOTE**
>
> How does SQL Server come up with a new, database-unique value for each row? For each modification, SQL Server generates a timestamp value in the transaction log, and this is the value used for the timestamp column. If you insert several rows consecutively, you will see how the value increases steadily. If SQL Server performs some system activity between two inserts, you will see a "jump" in the timestamp values because some values are consumed by the logging done due to the system activities.
>
> The timestamp values will increase steadily with each record written to the transaction log. SQL Server will not reuse timestamp values. Error 935 is generated when you have 1,000,000 values left (based on possible values for a binary(8) column). I would be surprised if you ever see this value; even with a steady 100 transactions per second, you will not reach maximum for well over 100 years.

The third step in the use of the `timestamp` column is providing *optimistic concurrency*. To avoid having two users editing customer information for the same customer, you have two approaches:

1. Lock the customer when displaying the form. This leads to blocking if several users want to edit the same customer at the same time. If one user opens the form and goes to lunch, the customer rows are locked until a timeout happens. Timeouts do not happen unless a client application defines them or they are set at the server level.

2. Read and store the timestamp value when loading the form that displays the customer information. When the change is written, the application checks the timestamp value in the database. If the value is different, someone else has changed the information since you read it. Now you can handle the situation—for instance, display a message to the user and ask the user to re-enter the changes. You take an optimistic approach and do not expect to have conflicts. If conflicts occur, you handle them.

The same concept applies to cursor handling as well.

SQL Server uses the function `TSEQUAL` to compare timestamp values. Consider two users, Len and Maria, each attempting to change the telephone number for Steve Johnsson in the `customers` table. Each displays the customer form, and the application submits the following SQL statement:

```
SELECT cont_id, f_name, ts FROM contacts WHERE cont_id = 1
```

Both users retrieve the same timestamp value for Steve Johnsson, and the application stores it in an variable. Maria changes the telephone number and presses the Change button in the form. The application submits the following SQL statement:

```
UPDATE contacts
  SET tel = '408 496-7224'
  WHERE cont_id = 1
  AND TSEQUAL(ts,0x000000000000013F)
```

To use the `TSEQUAL` function, the rest of the `WHERE` clause must uniquely identify a row. The `cont_id` column is the primary key for the table, so it has a unique index. You can be sure that the `UPDATE` statement only modifies one row.

SQL Server evaluates the `TSEQUAL` function for the row. It retrieves the timestamp value in the table and compares it to the expression passed with the function. If the value is the same, the update is allowed; no one has changed the value in the meantime.

8

LOGICAL DATABASE ARCHITECTURE

SQL Server has now modified the timestamp value for Steve Johnsson. Therefore, if Len tries to perform an UPDATE passing the same timestamp value as Maria did, it will no longer match against the stored value within the table:

```
UPDATE contacts
 SET tel = '408 496-7724'
  WHERE cont_id = 1
  AND TSEQUAL(ts,0x000000000000013F)
```

SQL Server will return an error to the client application, stating that the timestamp values don't match:

```
Server: Msg 532, Level 16, State 1
The timestamp (changed to 0x0000000000000143)
  shows that the row has been updated by another user.
Server: Msg 3621, Level 16, State 1
The statement has been aborted.
```

> **CAUTION**
>
> TSEQUAL is an undocumented function. It is used internally by the Application Programming Interfaces (API) available for SQL Server. These APIs have their own way for the user to ask for optimistic concurrency.
>
> You should not use the TSEQUAL function yourself. Always use the function call, property, and so on defined by the API to achieve optimistic concurrency.
>
> The reason that TSEQUAL was used in the preceding example is to show the use of the timestamp datatype without having to introduce some 3GL-language syntax.

Text and Image Data

Many applications need to store more than 8,000 bytes of data. Long comments, detailed descriptions, digitized photographs, pictures, and so on might need more capacity than 8,000 bytes. SQL Server provides a mechanism for storing binary large objects (BLOBs) as large as 2GB per row, using the text, ntext, and image datatypes.

> **NOTE**
>
> Prior to version 7.0, the maximum length for character datatypes and binary datatypes was 255 bytes. In many cases, text or image datatypes were used to store more information. If 8,000 bytes are enough, and you are involved in porting an application to version 7.0, you might want to consider using the

character or binary datatypes instead. They are easier to work with and generally provide better performance (although massive performance improvements have been made to text and image data handling in version 7.0).

The text and ntext (Unicode) datatypes store character strings. ntext uses two bytes per character, so you are limited to 1GB Unicode characters per record. The image datatype is used for binary information.

The following table has a Unicode text column called longstring:

```
CREATE TABLE texts
(id int IDENTITY,
longstring ntext NULL)
```

First, insert three rows into the table. For now, use the INSERT statement to insert textual data:

```
INSERT texts (longstring)
 VALUES(NULL)
INSERT texts (longstring)
 VALUES(N'Robert K served in the Peace Corps.')
INSERT texts (longstring)
 VALUES(REPLICATE(N'Robert K served in the Peace Corps.', 100))
```

The first row's text value is NULL; the following two rows have string values. The last row uses the REPLICATE function to generate a longer string. The INSERT statement will not insert more than a little less than 8,000 bytes.

Let's take a look at some functions that can be used against text and image data. First, you want to find the length of the string for each row:

```
SELECT id, DATALENGTH(longstring), LEN(longstring) FROM texts

id
----------- ----------- -----------
1           NULL        NULL
2           70          35
3           7000        3500
```

Note that DATALENGTH returns bytes, whereas LEN returns the number of characters:

```
SELECT PATINDEX('%Peace%', longstring),
       SUBSTRING(longstring, 500, 20)
  FROM texts

----------- --------------------
NULL        NULL
24
24          served in the Peace
```

8

The PATINDEX function returns the starting position of the *first* occurrence of a pattern for the column. SUBSTRING returns the specified number bytes from the starting position.

WRITETEXT, READTEXT, and UPDATETEXT

So far, the text and image datatypes haven't really given any advantage over the character and varchar datatypes because INSERT won't insert more than 8,000 bytes. With the use of WRITETEXT, READTEXT, and UPDATETEXT, you can manipulate up to 2GB of data per row.

To use these statements, you first need a pointer to your data, a page pointer(a varbinary(16) datatype). This is returned by the TEXTPTR function. Logically, you can view the data as a chain of pages, and TEXTPTR returns a pointer to the first page in this chain. For information on the physical structure of text and image data, refer to Chapter 7, "Physical Database Architecture."

```
SELECT id, textptr(longstring) as textpointer
 FROM texts
```

```
id           textpointer
----------   -----------------------------------
1            NULL
2            0xFFFF724C0F0000007C00000001000100
3            0xFFFF734C0F0000007C00000001000200
```

The text pointer for the first row is NULL. Before you can use any of the three text or image statements, you have to update the column with data or NULL.

To replace a string (or image value), you use the WRITETEXT statement, which has the following syntax:

```
WRITETEXT table.column textpointer [WITH LOG] data
```

> **NOTE**
>
> By default, the modification is not logged. Use WITH LOG to make the modification logged. You achieve better performance by using nonlogged operations, and the transaction log is used less as well.
>
> To run the statements as nonlogged statements, you must set the database option select into/bulkcopy. After a nonlogged operation has occurred, you cannot perform transaction log backup. If you have a backup scenario that relies on transaction log backup, you should perform a database backup after any nonlogged operations have occurred.

In Listing 8.3, you replace the string for the row with ID 2.

LISTING 8.3   REPLACING A STRING WITH THE WRITETEXT STATEMENT

```
DECLARE @pageptr varbinary(16)
SELECT  @pageptr = textptr(longstring)-- as textpointer
 FROM texts
 WHERE id = 2
WRITETEXT texts.longstring @pageptr WITH LOG
    N"He reads and writes French."
```

You can update a part of the string with UPDATETEXT. The syntax for UPDATETEXT is

```
UPDATETEXT {dest_table.column dest_textpointer}
{NULL ¦ insert_offset} {NULL ¦ delete_length}
[WITH LOG]
[inserted_data ¦ [{source_table.column source_textpointer}]
```

To replace existing text, specify the starting position with insert_offset and how many characters (or bytes for image data) to replace. In Listing 8.4, you change French to English.

LISTING 8.4   REPLACING A PART OF A STRING WITH THE UPDATETEXT STATEMENT

```
DECLARE @pageptr varbinary(16)
SELECT  @pageptr = textptr(longstring)-- as textpointer
 FROM texts
 WHERE id = 2
UPDATETEXT texts.longstring @pageptr
 20 6 WITH LOG N"English"
```

If you want to append data, you specify NULL for insert_offset:

```
UPDATETEXT texts.longstring @pageptr
 NULL 0  WITH LOG N" He is fluent in French."
```

You can also specify another column (possibly from another table) as the source of the text data. In Listing 8.5, you insert the text from the row with id = 3 into the row with id = 1. First, you need to update the column to get a textpointer.

LISTING 8.5   UPDATING THE VALUE OF A TEXT COLUMN BASED ON INFORMATION IN ANOTHER COLUMN

```
UPDATE texts
 SET longstring = NULL
 WHERE id = 1
```

continues

8

LOGICAL
DATABASE
ARCHITECTURE

LISTING 8.5 CONTINUED

```
DECLARE @ptr_from VARBINARY(16), @ptr_to VARBINARY(16)
SELECT @ptr_from = TEXTPTR(longstring)
 FROM texts
 WHERE id = 3
SELECT @ptr_to = TEXTPTR(longstring)
 FROM texts
 WHERE id = 1

UPDATETEXT texts.longstring @ptr_to
 0 NULL WITH LOG texts.longstring @ptr_from
```

To read text and image data, you can use the ordinary SELECT statement. Prior to version 7.0, ISQL/w would only return 255 bytes of data. This is configurable in Query Analyzer (select Query, Current Connection Options, Advanced). How you have SET TEXTSIZE also limits the number of bytes to be returned by a SELECT statement.

To handle a large amount of data, you might consider reading it in chunks with the READ-TEXT command. The following example reads 50 characters beginning at position 400:

```
DECLARE @ptr VARBINARY(16)
SELECT @ptr = TEXTPTR(longstring)
 FROM texts WHERE id = 3
READTEXT texts.longstring @ptr 400 50

longstring
--------------------------------------------------
rt K served in the Peace Corps.Robert served in t
```

> **NOTE**
>
> If you are using text and image data from a programming language, such as Visual Basic or C++, check out the special functions for long datatypes available in the API that you are using.
>
> For instance, ADO uses the GetChunk and AppendChunk methods to read and write chunks of data.
>
> OLE DB uses the ISequentialStream interface for text and image data. The ISequentialStream::Read method reads chunks of data, and ISequentialStream::Write writes chunks of data.
>
> ODBC uses the SQLGetData and SQLPutData functions to read and write chunks of data.

`datetime` Datatypes

To store date and time information, use the `datetime` and `smalldatetime` datatypes. These datatypes store both a date part and a time part. There are no separate time and date datatypes for storing only times or only dates.

`smalldatetime` is less precise and covers a smaller range of dates, but it occupies half the space, as shown in Table 8.2.

TABLE 8.2   `datetime` AND `smalldatetime` ATTRIBUTES

	datetime	smalldatetime
Storage size	8 bytes	4 bytes
Precision	3/100 second	1 minute
Minimum value	Jan. 1, 1753	Jan. 1, 1900
Maximum value	Dec. 31, 9999	June 6, 2079

> **NOTE**
>
> The reason for the minimum value for `datetime` is that the Gregorian and Julian calendars were 13 days apart until they were synchronized in September, 1752. SQL Server has no separate datatypes for Gregorian and Julian datatypes.

8

LOGICAL
DATABASE
ARCHITECTURE

Expressing Datetime Values

The following statement creates a table with an integer and a datetime column:

```
CREATE TABLE dates
 (id int IDENTITY,
  datevalue datetime)
```

You pass datetime data as a string to SQL Server. SQL Server tries to parse the string to a datetime value; if it doesn't succeed, an error message (421) is returned:

```
INSERT dates(datevalue)
VALUES('June 30, 1998 9:39AM')
```

SQL Server accepts many ways of expressing the date and time part. If any part is missing, SQL Server will provide a default value for that part. The default value for the date part is `Jan 1, 1900`, and the default value for the time part is `12:00:00:000AM`. The order in which you specify the date and time part does not matter. The date and time parts must be separated by a space.

If you exclude the century and the year is 0-49, SQL Server assumes the 21st century (20xx). If the value is 50-99, SQL Server assumes 20th (19xx).

There are three ways to express the date part and two ways to express the time part. The date part can be expressed using the alphabetic date format. The month is specified as the full month name or as an abbreviation. Commas are optional and capitalization is ignored. Table 8.3 provides some examples of the alphabetic date format.

TABLE 8.3   ALPHABETIC DATE FORMAT

Insert Format	datetime *Value*
'Jun 30 1998'	1998-06-30 00:00:00.000
'Jun 30 98'	1998-06-30 00:00:00.000
'Jun 06 15'	2015-06-06 00:00:00.000
'June 1998 30'	1998-06-30 00:00:00.000
'30 June 1998'	1998-06-30 00:00:00.000
'1998 jun'	1998-06-01 00:00:00.000
'1998 JUNE 30'	1998-06-30 00:00:00.000

If there is ambiguity regarding the year and the day parts, the first numeric value is assigned to the day. If the day is excluded, the century part must be included, and the day is assigned as the first day of month.

You can also use the numeric date format, where you specify the month with a numeric value. You separate the parts with either a slash (/), hyphen (-), or period (.). The setting of SET DATEFORMAT determines how SQL Server parses the year, month, and day parts of the string. The parsing of date parts can also be determined through a language, activated through SET LANGUAGE, or assignment to a login ID. The dateformat is specified as mdy (month, day, year), ymd, and so on.

Table 8.4 gives some examples of date expressions with the numeric date format.

TABLE 8.4   NUMERIC DATE FORMAT

Insert Format	dateformat *Setting*	datetime *Value*
'6/30/1998'	mdy	1998-06-30 00:00:00.000
'06-30-98'	mdy	1998-06-30 00:00:00.000
'06.1998.30'	myd	1998-06-30 00:00:00.000
'30/6/49'	dmy	2049-06-30 00:00:00.000
'30/6/50'	dmy	1950-06-30 00:00:00.000

The third way of expressing a date is the unseparated string format. The format is `yyyymmdd` or `yymmdd`.

The time part can be specified in 12-hour format or 24-hour format. To specify midnight, specify `12:00 AM` or `00:00`. For date and time, you can precede the millisecond part by a period (`.`) or a colon (`:`). If you precede the millisecond part with a period, a single digit means tenths of a second, two digits mean hundredths of a second, and three digits mean thousandths of a second.

Table 8.5 outlines some examples of expressing the time part (and some express both date and time format).

TABLE 8.5   EXPRESSING TIME PART AND BOTH DATE AND TIME

Insert Format	`datetime` *Value*
`'14:30'`	`1900-01-01 14:30:00.000`
`'14:30:20:2'`	`1900-01-01 14:30:20.003`
`'14:30:20.2'`	`1900-01-01 14:30:20.200`
`'2pm'`	`1900-01-01 14:00:00.000`
`'2 PM'`	`1900-01-01 14:00:00.000`
`'19980630 2PM'`	`1998-06-30 14:00:00.000`
`'14:30 30 Jun 1998'`	`1998-06-30 14:30:00.000`

8

LOGICAL
DATABASE
ARCHITECTURE

To change the way that SQL Server returns datetime data, you can use the `CONVERT` function, which is discussed in Chapter 21.

Logical Datatype: `bit`

To store on/off or true/false values, you can use the `bit` datatype. This datatype can hold 1, 0, or NULL. In Listing 8.6, you create a table that includes a bit column, inserts a row into the table, and updates that row.

LISTING 8.6   USING THE `bit` DATATYPE TO STORE BOOLEAN VALUES

```
CREATE TABLE customer_info
(cust_id int IDENTITY,
 cust_name varchar(100),
 status bit)
INSERT customer_info (cust_name, status)
 VALUES('The Bookstore', 1)
UPDATE customer_info
 SET status = 0
 WHERE cust_id = 1
```

> **NOTE**
>
> Prior to version 7.0, the bit column was not nullable. You might come across tables using tinyint or char(1) where the bit datatype is more appropriate.

Several bit columns (up to eight) can occupy a single byte. SQL Server "collects" up to eight bits into a single byte of physical storage.

Numeric Datatypes

SQL Server has several datatypes that can hold numeric values. The differences between these are range of values, data storage size, and the precision they allow. There are four basic categories for numeric datatypes:

- Integers—int, smallint, and tinyint
- Approximate numeric datatypes—float and real
- Exact numeric datatypes—numeric and decimal
- Money datatypes—money and smallmoney

Integer Datatypes

SQL Server provides three basic datatypes that can hold integer values: int, smallint, and tinyint. Table 8.6 lists the difference between these three datatypes.

TABLE 8.6   INTEGER DATATYPES

Datatype	tinyint	smallint	int
Storage size	1 byte	2 bytes	4 bytes
Minimum value	0	$-32,768$ (-2^{15})	$-2,147,483,648$ (-2^{31})
Maximum value	255	$32,767$ $(2^{15}-1)$	$2,147,483,647$ $(2^{31}-1)$

Integer datatypes are often a good choice for keys because they allow a large number of unique values but require few bytes of storage space. They can also be used with the IDENTITY property. SQL Server generates a new value for each inserted row for the column that has the IDENTITY property. IDENTITY is further described in Chapter 21.

Listing 8.7 creates a table with an identity column over a smallint datatype, a customer name column, and a discount column.

LISTING 8.7 USING THE smallint DATATYPE TO STORE INTEGER VALUES

```
CREATE TABLE customer_info
(cust_id smallint IDENTITY,
 cust_name varchar(100),
 discount tinyint)
INSERT customer_info (cust_name, discount)
 VALUES('The Bookstore', 30)
INSERT customer_info (cust_name, discount)
 VALUES('The New Bookstore', 25)
SELECT * FROM customer_info

cust_id cust_name                                   discount
------- ---------------------------------------- --------
1       The Bookstore                               30
2       The New Bookstore                           25
```

What if you come to the point when 32,767 is not enough for cust_id? Prior to version 7.0, you had to copy the information to another table with the new structure and rename the tables. In version 7.0, you can change the datatype for a column with the ALTER TABLE statement.

Approximate Numeric Datatypes

The approximate datatypes are useful if you want to be able to store values within a very large range and have the same precision for each value, regardless of how small or large the number is. Table 8.7 outlines the difference between the approximate numeric datatypes.

TABLE 8.7 THE float AND real DATATYPES

	float	real
Storage size	4 or 8 bytes	4 bytes
Precision	Up to 15 digits	7 digits
Minimum value	−1.79E+308	−3.40E+38
Maximum value	1.79E+308	3.40E+38

The storage size for float depends on the precision chosen. float(1) to float(24) uses 4 bytes, and float(25) to float(53) uses 8 bytes.

float and real are useful for scientific and statistical data where absolute accuracy is not required and where the data in a column may vary from a very small value to a very large value.

8

LOGICAL DATABASE ARCHITECTURE

Note, however, that not all numbers can be represented by `float` and `real`. Therefore, what you insert might not be what you get later as shown in Listing 8.8.

LISTING 8.8   USING THE `float` DATATYPE TO HOLD APPROXIMATE NUMERICAL INFORMATION

```
CREATE TABLE floats
(id int IDENTITY,
 f_value real)
INSERT floats (f_value) VALUES(0.33)
SELECT * FROM floats


id             f_value
-----------    ----------------------
1                  0.33000001
UPDATE floats SET f_value = f_value * 2 WHERE id = 1
SELECT * FROM floats


id             f_value
-----------    ----------------------
1                  0.66000003

--What if we use float with maximum precision instead?
DROP TABLE floats
GO
CREATE TABLE floats
(id int IDENTITY,
 f_value float(53))
INSERT floats (f_value) VALUES(0.33)
SELECT * FROM floats


id             f_value
-----------    -------------------------------------
1                  0.33000000000000002
UPDATE floats SET f_value = f_value * 2 WHERE id = 1
SELECT * FROM floats


id             f_value
-----------    -------------------------------------
1                  0.66000000000000003
```

Exact Numeric Datatypes

To store numeric values with a fixed precision, you can use the `numeric` and `decimal` datatypes. Both datatypes are implemented the same way; `numeric` is a synonym for the `decimal` datatype.

When creating the column, you specify a precision and scale. Scale is the number of decimal digits that can be stored to the right of the decimal point.

In Listing 8.9, you use the decimal datatype instead of float (as in Listing 8.8).

LISTING 8.9   STORING EXACT NUMERICAL INFORMATION WITH THE decimal DATATYPE

```
CREATE TABLE exacts
(id int IDENTITY,
 e_value DECIMAL(4, 3))

INSERT exacts(e_value) VALUES(0.33)
SELECT * FROM exacts
id          e_value
..........  .......
.330

UPDATE exacts SET e_value = e_value * 2 WHERE id = 1
SELECT * FROM exacts

id          e_value
..........  .......
1              .660
```

The values are now represented with their exact values. If we enter a number that is too large, SQL Server returns an error message (8115). If we enter more decimal numbers than specified, SQL Server rounds the values to the specified scale. If rounding is unacceptable, you can SET NUMERIC_ROUNDABORT to ON:

```
SET NUMERIC_ROUNDABORT ON
INSERT exacts(e_value) VALUES(1./3.)

Server: Msg 8115, Level 16, State 2
Arithmetic overflow error converting numeric to data type numeric.
```

The storage requirements depend on the precision specified, as listed in Table 8.8.

TABLE 8.8   STORAGE REQUIREMENTS FOR decimal AND numeric

Precision	Storage Bytes
1–9	5
10–19	9
20–28	13
29–38	17

If you want to be able to use a precision higher than 28, you must start SQL Server with the /p switch.

8

LOGICAL DATABASE ARCHITECTURE

Money Datatypes

SQL Server provides two datatypes specifically for storing monetary data: money and smallmoney. Both are exact datatypes with a four-digit decimal precision. The difference is the range and storage requirements, as shown in Table 8.9.

TABLE 8.9   THE money AND smallmoney DATATYPES

	smallmoney	money
Storage size	4 bytes	8 bytes
Minimum value	–214,748.3648	–922,337,203,685,477.5808
Maximum value	+214,748.3647	922,337,203,685,477.5807

money and smallmoney can basically be considered synonyms for the decimal and numeric datatypes. The numeric and decimal datatypes were not available prior version 6.0, so money and smallmoney were useful for exact numeric representation.

The difference is the way that you specify a monetary value. You can (but don't have to) precede the value with a currency symbol:

```
CREATE TABLE money_values
(id int IDENTITY, m_value money)
INSERT money_values (m_value)
 VALUES ($123.45)
INSERT money_values (m_value)
 VALUES (£123123.45)
INSERT money_values (m_value)
 VALUES (123.45)
```

Note that SQL Server has no understanding about exchange rates and so on.

You cannot use a comma separator when you express monetary data to SQL Server. If you have a string with a comma separator, you can convert it using the CONVERT or CAST function:

```
INSERT money_values (m_value)
 VALUES (CAST('$444,123.45' AS MONEY) )
```

Datatype Synonyms

ANSI SQL-92 specifies different names for some datatypes. You can choose to use them because SQL Server has defined them as synonyms for the SQL Server datatypes. Table 8.10 lists the synonyms available in SQL Server.

TABLE 8.10 DATATYPES SYNONYMS

ANSI SQL-92 Synonym	*SQL Server Datatype*
character	char
char varying	varchar
character varying	varchar
national char	nchar
national character	nchar
national char varying	nvarchar
national character varying	nvarchar
national text	ntext
binary varying	varbinary
double precision	float
dec	decimal
integer	int

If you perform `sp_help` for the table or generate script in SQL Enterprise Manager, you will see the SQL Server names for the datatypes because the synonyms are translated into the corresponding SQL Server datatype when the table is created.

User-Defined Datatypes

You can create your own datatype through the User-Defined Datatypes (UDDTs) feature. They are not really new datatypes, such as for instance complex datatypes, structures, and so on. A UDDT is based on a system-supplied datatype, possibly with a precision and scale attribute.

To create and drop UDDTs, use `sp_addtype` and `sp_droptype`:

```
sp_addtype phone, 'char(13)'
sp_droptype phone
```

If the system datatype expression includes parentheses, you must surround it with quote signs. You can also create and manipulate UDDTs with SQL Enterprise Manager, as shown in Figure 8.2.

8

LOGICAL
DATABASE
ARCHITECTURE

FIGURE 8.2

Creating a user-defined datatype in SQL Enterprise Manager.

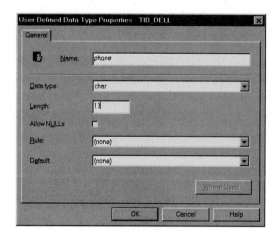

When you create a table, you can specify a UDDT instead of a base datatype, as shown in Listing 8.10.

LISTING 8.10 CREATING A TABLE WITH A USER-DEFINED DATATYPE

```
CREATE TABLE my_friends
(id int identity,
 name VARCHAR(20),
 phone phone)
INSERT my_friends (name, phone)
 VALUES('Pete K', '(408)496-7223')
```

You can use the datatype phone in all tables that have telephone number columns, which makes the database diagram easier to read. As you will find out later in this chapter, you can also bind default values and rules to UDDTs.

Views

A view is a logical way of looking at the physical data located in your tables. A view definition is a stored SELECT statement. Because a SELECT statement returns a resultset, you can work with a select statement as if it is a table. Therefore, when using a view, you use it just like a table. (This is thanks to the principle of *closure*; the output of one operation is the same kind as the input to that operation.) There are no limitations on querying through views, but there are some restrictions for modifying data.

> **NOTE**
>
> It is sometimes misunderstood that a view actually stores data. It does not.
>
> You can compare a view to a mathematical operator. The operator operates on an input set of values and returns a value. However, the function does not store data; it merely operates on stored or passed data.
>
> A view is only a window to the stored data.

Creating a view is as simple as creating a SELECT statement. In the following example, we create a view that returns au_lname and au_fname from the authors table for all authors living in California:

```
CREATE VIEW authors_names AS
SELECT au_lname, au_fname
 FROM authors
 WHERE state = 'CA'
```

The following query returns au_lname for all authors whose last names begin with the letter *M*. (Because we query against the view, we also have the restriction that the authors should live in California.)

```
SELECT * FROM authors_names
 WHERE au_lname LIKE 'M%'
```

To remove a view, use the DROP VIEW statement. This example drops the authors_names view:

```
DROP VIEW authors_names
```

> **NOTE**
>
> Be careful that you don't drop a view that other objects depend on. Other stored procedures and views might refer to the view. If you drop the view, the user who tries implicitly to use it through the other object will receive an error message. You can check for dependencies using SQL Enterprise Manager or sp_depends.

You can modify a view with the ALTER VIEW statement. This new feature in version 7.0 has an advantage over dropping and recreating the view because you don't have to worry about reassigning permissions to the view. The syntax for ALTER VIEW is the same as for CREATE VIEW.

You can also use SQL Enterprise Manager to create a view as shown in Figure 8.3.

FIGURE 8.3

Creating views in SQL Enterprise Manager.

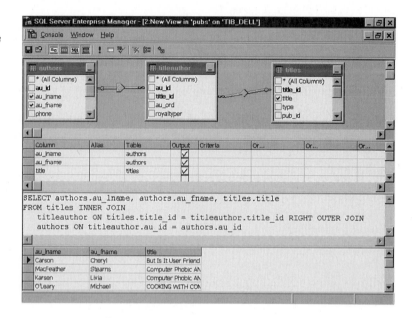

To add a table to the Create View window, just drag and drop a table onto the top pane on the window. You can then refine the view definition by specifying which columns to include, the join types between tables, the grouping, and so on.

Some situations when views can be valuable include

- Simplifying retrieval and modification of data.
- Enhancing security through views.
- Customizing the export format of data. Define a view with the desired export format and export from the view.

Views to Simplify Retrieval and Modification of Data

You can use views to simplify queries. A normalized data model can consist of many tables. If end users are allowed to query the data interactively, you probably want to simplify the data model, even if they are using some powerful analysis tool.

One common simplification is to perform a join in the view definition. Instead of the user performing the join each time a query is expressed, the user operates against the view.

Let's create a view that presents the author's last name and first name and the title that each author has co-written:

```
CREATE VIEW authors_titles AS
SELECT a.au_lname, a.au_fname, t.title
FROM titles t INNER JOIN
    titleauthor ta ON t.title_id = ta.title_id RIGHT OUTER JOIN
    authors a ON ta.au_id = a.au_id
```

A user wants to know the names of all authors who have been co-writing any books with the strings "Data" or "Computers" in the title:

```
SELECT * FROM authors_titles
 WHERE title LIKE '%data%' OR
       title LIKE '%computer%'
```

A view definition can of course be more complex, for instance, including

- More complex join operations
- Aggregate functions and grouping
- Operations on other views
- Unions

Views as a Security Mechanism

You can use views to restrict the amount of data that the user can operate on.

A vertical restriction means that the user is allowed to see some *columns*, but not all. In this example, the user should be able to see all columns in the titleauthor table except the royalty percentage column:

```
CREATE VIEW ta_limited AS
 SELECT au_id, title_id, au_ord
 FROM titleauthor
```

You could argue that we might as well deny the user select permission on the royal-typer column. The problem is that if the user performs a SELECT * FROM titleauthor without that permission, SQL Server will generate an error message. (Of course, the same error is returned if the user uses a tool that generates SELECT *.) If the user is presented with the view, the user doesn't even have to know that a royalty percentage column exists.

You can also use a view for horizontal restrictions, not presenting all *rows*. For instance, the following view presents all columns from the authors table for the authors who live in California:

```
CREATE VIEW authors_in_CA AS
SELECT *
 FROM authors
 WHERE state = 'CA'
```

Other examples of using views as security measures include

- Prohibiting users from correlating data in tables by excluding primary or foreign key columns.
- Presenting aggregations, but not detailed information. For instance, the user can see sales per day, but not each sales order.

The view should be owned (created) by the same user as the underlying objects. If there are different owners in the chain (a *broken ownership chain*), the user still needs access to the underlying object. Security and broken ownership chains are discussed in Chapter 10, "Security and User Administration."

Data Modifications and Views

Modifying data through views carries some restrictions.

A data modification statement (INSERT, UPDATE, or DELETE) cannot update more than one table. Therefore, you cannot insert or delete a row from the authors_titles view. You can update through the view as long as you do not change columns from more than one table.

You cannot update views with some derived values, which includes

- Aggregate functions and GROUP BY.
- DISTINCT, TOP, or UNION.
- Columns based on expressions. (Only columns based on real values are updatable.)

Views Created with WITH CHECK OPTION

A view returning a subset of rows that is not created with WITH CHECK OPTION can expose some strange behavior for data modification statements.

If we try to insert a row into the authors_in_CA view and specify the state as UT, the row will not be visible through the view, as shown in Listing 8.11.

LISTING 8.11 INSERTING AN OUT-OF-RANGE ROW INTO A VIEW CREATED WITHOUT WITH CHECK OPTION

```
INSERT authors_in_CA
(au_id, au_lname, au_fname, state, contract)
 VALUES('122-34-5567', 'Richard', 'Westman', 'UT', 1)
SELECT au_lname, au_fname, state
 FROM authors_in_CA
 WHERE au_id = '122-34-5567'

au_lname                              au_fname              state
-------------------------------- -------------------- -----

(0 row(s) affected)
```

This could, of course, be very confusing to the user. The row that you inserted is not there. (Well, it exists in the base table, but the view does not present it.) In Listing 8.12, you change the view definition to include WITH CHECK OPTION, and an error is returned if a row is inserted out of range.

LISTING 8.12 INSERTING AN OUT-OF-RANGE ROW INTO A VIEW CREATED WITH WITH CHECK OPTION

```
CREATE VIEW authors_in_CA AS
SELECT *
 FROM authors
 WHERE state = 'CA'
 WITH CHECK OPTION
GO
INSERT authors_in_CA
(au_id, au_lname, au_fname, state, contract)
 VALUES('122-34-5568', 'Richard', 'Westman', 'UT', 1)

Server: Msg 550, Level 16, State 1
The attempted insert or update failed because the target
view either specifies WITH CHECK OPTION or spans a view that
specifies WITH CHECK OPTION and one or more rows resulting
from the operation did not qualify under the CHECK OPTION
constraint.
Server: Msg 3621, Level 16, State 1
The statement has been aborted.
```

The same message is returned if you try to change the state to something other than CA with an UPDATE statement.

8

LOGICAL DATABASE ARCHITECTURE

Views Created WITH ENCRYPTION

The view definition (the SELECT statement) is saved in the syscomments table. The same applies for stored procedures, triggers, and so on. You can retrieve the source code by using sp_helptext or with the SQL Enterprise Manager:

```
EXEC sp_helptext authors_in_CA

Text
------------------------------
CREATE VIEW authors_in_CA AS
SELECT *
 FROM authors
 WHERE state = 'CA'
 WITH CHECK OPTION
```

Everyone has permissions to retrieve the source code. If you specify WITH ENCRYPTION in the view definitions, the source code in syscomments is encrypted (see Listing 8.13):

LISTING 8.13 ENCRYPTING THE SOURCE CODE FOR A STORED PROCEDURE DEFINITION

```
CREATE VIEW authors_in_CA
WITH ENCRYPTION AS
SELECT *
 FROM authors
 WHERE state = 'CA'
GO
EXEC sp_helptext authors_in_CA

The object comments have been encrypted.
```

> **CAUTION**
>
> Make sure that you save the source code to a file before creating an object WITH ENCRYPTION. The only programs that can decrypt the definition are SQL Server (if it has to re-create the object internally) and the SQL Server upgrade programs.
>
> As far as I know, Microsoft has never assisted a customer in decrypting the source code for objects created with WITH ENCRYPTION.
>
> Depending on your development environment, you might have a global compile switch that when turned on, includes WITH ENCRYPTION for your object creation statements.

Constraints

The value of the data in a database is (partly) determined by how correct the data is. Integrity rules can be maintained in the client applications, but this requires that the rules are applied in the first place, that they are consistently applied by programmers, and that users cannot change data through ad hoc front-end tools.

It is often better to let SQL Server maintain integrity rules. The features in SQL Server for maintaining integrity rules are

- Datatypes—By using suitable datatypes, SQL Server has a basic understanding of the semantics of the data. The datatype can also limit the number of values that you can insert into a column.
- Bound objects—Defaults and rules can be created and bound to columns or datatypes.
- Constraints, which are discussed in this section.
- Triggers—A trigger is the most powerful constraint mechanism.

Designing integrity rules is a lot of work when defining the data model. Each of the features has advantages and drawbacks, so I recommend that you understand each feature before diving into creating tables.

Constraints have one advantage over most of the other features: They are standardized in ANSI SQL-92. Tools that assist in building databases probably support constraints.

A constraint is declared with the table definition in the CREATE TABLE statement or after the table is created with ALTER TABLE:

```
CREATE TABLE customers
(customer_id INT IDENTITY PRIMARY KEY NOT NULL,
customer_name NVARCHAR(100) NOT NULL,
customer_comments NVARCHAR(1000) NULL)
```

If you do not name a constraint, SQL Server assigns a name automatically. Suppose you need to drop a constraint. Before you can use ALTER TABLE to drop the constraint, you need to find out the constraint name:

```
EXEC sp_helpconstraint customers
ALTER TABLE customers
 DROP CONSTRAINT PK__customers__7B5B524B
```

You can also name the constraint:

```
CREATE TABLE customers
(customer_id INT IDENTITY CONSTRAINT customers_pk PRIMARY KEY NOT NULL,
customer_name NVARCHAR(100) NOT NULL,
customer_comments NVARCHAR(1000) NULL)
```

Before the constraint name, you have to specify the keyword CONSTRAINT.

8

LOGICAL
DATABASE
ARCHITECTURE

> **TIP**
>
> Make sure that you name your constraints if you build an application that you need to maintain with scripts. An example of such an application is a commercially sold system.
>
> If at a later time (during an upgrade of your application, for instance) you need to modify the constraint, you must know the constraint name so that you can drop it (and possibly add a modified version).

Constraints can also be defined at the table level. Because we didn't specify the constraint with the column definition, we have to express which columns that the constraint applies to:

```
CREATE TABLE customers
(customer_id INT IDENTITY NOT NULL,
customer_name NVARCHAR(100) NOT NULL,
customer_comments NVARCHAR(1000) NULL
 CONSTRAINT customers_pk PRIMARY KEY(customer_id))
```

You can add a constraint to an existing table with the ALTER TABLE statement:

```
ALTER TABLE customers
 ADD CONSTRAINT customers_pk PRIMARY KEY(customer_id)
```

You can also manage constraints with SQL Enterprise Manager, as mentioned in Chapter 9, "The SQL Server Enterprise Manager," and as shown in Figure 8.4.

FIGURE 8.4

Use SQL Server's Enterprise Manager to manage constraints.

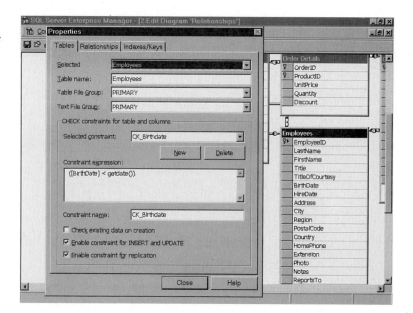

PRIMARY KEY and UNIQUE Constraints

When you design a table, you define a set of candidate keys. A candidate key is a column (or combination of columns) that uniquely identifies a row. Each table should have at least one candidate key. (Otherwise, there is no way of telling the rows apart in the table.)

A table can have several candidate keys. The American Embassy in Sweden, for instance, wants to store information about American citizens who are also Swedish citizens. You can identify the person by the American Social Security number or by the Swedish counterpart, personnummer. (For the sake of example, we ignore that these two concepts might not be suitable as candidate keys).

One of the candidate keys is (sometimes arbitrarily) made the primary key. Every table should have a primary key defined, and there can be only one primary key per table (but it can be composed of several columns). When you declare a primary key, SQL Server creates a unique index for the column. The column cannot allow NULL. If you add a primary key to a table, and the table has duplicates for the primary key columns, an error message is returned. If you don't want the index created to be a clustered index, you can use the keyword NONCLUSTERED:

```
CREATE TABLE customers
(customer_id INT IDENTITY CONSTRAINT customers_pk
 PRIMARY KEY NONCLUSTERED NOT NULL,
customer_name NVARCHAR(100) NOT NULL,
customer_comments NVARCHAR(1000) NULL)
```

> **TIP**
>
> If you have duplicate rows, there is no simple way to remove one of them. If you can tell them apart by some value in a column, you can use that value in the WHERE clause to differentiate the rows. If the rows are truly duplicates, you can execute SET ROWCOUNT 1 and then execute the DELETE statement. ROWCOUNT determines the maximum number of rows that will be affected by a statement. Remember to reset ROWCOUNT to 0 when you are done with the delete.

What about the other candidate keys (if we have any)? They are alternate keys. There is no constraint type called alternate, but there is a *unique* constraint. When you create a unique constraint, SQL Server guarantees that there can be no duplicates for the column. A unique constraint has the same attributes as the primary key with three differences:

- The column can allow NULL (but only one null value is allowed).
- The default index type is NONCLUSTERED.
- You can have more than one unique constraint per table.

Referential Integrity Constraint, FOREIGN KEY

Referential integrity (RI) is the property of all foreign keys in a referencing table having an associated primary key (or unique key) in referenced tables. For example, an order table contains a customer number, so the customer table should have a corresponding customer (see Listing 8.14):

LISTING 8.14 DEFINING THE RELATIONSHIP BETWEEN A CUSTOMER AND AN ORDER TABLE WITH A FOREIGN KEY CONSTRAINT

```
CREATE TABLE customers
(customer_id INT PRIMARY KEY NOT NULL,
customer_name NVARCHAR(25) NOT NULL,
customer_comments NVARCHAR(22) NULL)
CREATE TABLE orders
(order_id INT  PRIMARY KEY NOT NULL,
customer_id INT REFERENCES customers(customer_id),
order_date DATETIME )
GO

INSERT customers
 (customer_id, customer_name, customer_comments)
VALUES (1, 'Hardware Suppliers AB', 'Stephanie is contact.')
INSERT orders
 (order_id, customer_id, order_date)
VALUES(100, 2, '19980701')

Server: Msg 547, Level 16, State 1
INSERT statement conflicted with COLUMN FOREIGN KEY
constraint 'FK__orders__customer_id__1332DBDC'. The
conflict occurred in database 'Unleashed', table 'customers'
, column 'customer_id'.
Server: Msg 3621, Level 16, State 1
The statement has been aborted.
```

In this example, we tried to add an order with a customer number of 2, which does not exist in the customer table.

We define foreign keys without actually programming the code that performs the referential check; this is called *declarative referential integrity*.

The foreign key constraint implements restrictions on what you can do in a table. If we have any orders for a certain customer and want to delete that customer, SQL Server returns an error message. In some cases, we might want to automatically delete the referencing orders when we delete the customer, an operation called *cascading*. The section "Triggers," later in this chapter, includes some discussion on how to implement cascades.

CHECK Constraints

A CHECK constraint limits the number of values that you can store for a column. This is the domain from which the column can draw its values. You express a CHECK constraint as a boolean expression, which evaluates to either TRUE or FALSE.

The following CHECK constraints specify that a telephone number must follow a certain pattern and that the area code must be 415:

```
ALTER TABLE authors
ADD CONSTRAINT authors_chk_phone CHECK
 (phone LIKE '(415)[0-9][0-9][0-9]-[0-9][0-9][0-9][0-9]')
```

If we try to add this constraint, SQL Server generates an error message indicating there are rows in the table that do not conform to the constraint rule. By default, SQL Server validates existing rows against the constraint (for check constraints and foreign keys). If we want to keep the rows but still add the constraint, we can use WITH NOCHECK:

```
ALTER TABLE authors
 WITH NOCHECK
 ADD CONSTRAINT authors_chk_phone CHECK
 (phone LIKE '(415)[0-9][0-9][0-9]-[0-9][0-9][0-9][0-9]')
```

You can also disable a constraint (for CHECK constraints and foreign keys). For instance, we want to insert many rows into the orders table (which has a foreign key constraint). We know that the rows to be inserted do not violate the constraint and that the constraint checking will take a long time:

```
ALTER TABLE orders
 NOCHECK CONSTRAINT FK__orders__customer_number__1332DBDC
```

We can enable the constraint later with ALTER TABLE...CHECK CONSTRAINT.

You can create several CHECK constraints for a column. A check constraint cannot compare values against other tables. (For this, you can use triggers.) You can, however, compare values in other columns for the same row.

You can use functions in a check constraint as long as the function doesn't require any parameters. Examples of such functions are GETDATE() and CURRENT_USER().

8

LOGICAL
DATABASE
ARCHITECTURE

The following example might look a bit odd. We want to verify that modifications are made by a certain application. We create a CHECK constraint that uses the APP_NAME() function to check the application name. Note that we do not perform the check against a certain column; all we want is for the expression to evaluate to true:

```
CREATE TABLE my_friends
(id int identity,
 name VARCHAR(20),
 phone CHAR(15)
 CONSTRAINT app_check
   CHECK (APP_NAME() = 'MS SQL Query Analyzer'))
```

Guidelines on Constraints

Plan carefully before implementing constraints (or rules). There is great value in having business rules described in the database schema, and it would be unfortunate not to use such a good feature. You can save yourself some time by observing the following points before you start to develop your constraints:

- Constraint names must follow SQL Server object-naming conventions.
- Constraint names must be unique for the constraint creator (object owner).
- Rules (discussed later) and check constraints both enforce domain integrity.
- A table can have both rules and check constraints. The set of allowable values is the intersection of the rule and check constraints.
- Using rules and defaults (discussed later), and binding them to user-defined datatypes, you can centrally manage the data integrity requirements of many columns.

Rules

A rule is similar to a check constraint in functionality: It limits the domain of values that can be stored in a column. A rule is a bound object; you create the rule first and then bind it to a column in a table or to a user-defined datatype.

Rule Usage

Let's say that we want to implement the telephone number integrity rule (described previously), but with a rule instead of a check constraint.

First, we create the rule as an object in the database:

```
CREATE RULE phone_rule AS
 @phone LIKE '(415)[0-9][0-9][0-9]-[0-9][0-9][0-9][0-9]'
```

SQL Server will replace @phone with the value being inserted or updated. Because we might need to use AND or OR within your rule, we need a way to refer to the value. We might allow the string UNKNOWN to be stored as well:

```
CREATE RULE phone_rule AS
 @phone LIKE '(415)[0-9][0-9][0-9]-[0-9][0-9][0-9][0-9]'
 OR
 @phone = 'UNKNOWN'
```

We can now bind the rule to a column in a table or to a user-defined datatype:

```
-- Bind a rule to a column in a table
EXEC sp_bindrule phone_rule, 'authors.phone'

-- Bind a rule to a user defined datatype
EXEC sp_bindrule phone_rule, phone
```

If you add the futureonly parameter when you bind a rule to a user-defined datatype, existing tables that are using the datatype will not be affected.

Here are some other examples of rules:

```
--Discount must fall into a range
CREATE RULE discount_rule AS
 @discount BETWEEN 1 AND 50
GO
--A list of valid colors
CREATE RULE valid_colors AS
 @color IN ('Black', 'Red')
GO
--Date must be >= current date
CREATE RULE date_rule AS
 @date >= GETDATE()
GO
```

In the last rule, we used a function, which we can do as long as the function doesn't take any parameters.

You can unbind a rule with sp_unbindrule:

```
-- Unbind the phone rule from the phone UDDT
EXEC sp_unbindrule phone
```

Rule Limitations

I suggest that you think twice before you use rules. As you can see in the following list, rules are definitely being phased out in favor of constraints:

- You can have only one rule per user-defined datatype or column. If you bind a second, the first is automatically unbound.
- Rules cannot validate against other columns in the same row.

- Rules do not comply with the ANSI SQL-92 standard.
- SQL Server Books Online refers to rules as a "backward compatibility feature." This might seem like a minor detail, but if a similar problem appears with a rule and a check constraint, you could guess that Microsoft would prioritize to fix the check constraint bug first. There is also the risk that this feature might disappear from a future version of SQL Server.
- Development tools that generate data schema are more likely to support check constraints than rules.

There is one big advantage with rules: You can bind a rule to a user-defined datatype. That is, you can centralize rule handling for all columns that use that datatype.

Defaults

SQL Server supports two ways of generating default values for columns:

- Declarative defaults
- Bound defaults

Both types provide the same functionality; the difference is how you create and manage the default values. You can have only one default per column.

You cannot define a default for a column based on the timestamp datatype or a column that has the IDENTITY property.

Declarative Defaults

Declarative defaults belong to the *constraint* family. The default value is specified with the table definitions in CREATE TABLE or ALTER TABLE, and it is dropped when the table is dropped. The following example specifies UNKNOWN as default for phone number:

```
CREATE TABLE my_friends
(id int identity,
 name VARCHAR(20),
 phone phone CONSTRAINT def_phone DEFAULT 'UNKNOWN')
```

You can drop and add defaults with ALTER TABLE, just as you can with the other constraint types:

```
ALTER TABLE my_friends
DROP CONSTRAINT def_phone
GO
ALTER TABLE my_friends
ADD CONSTRAINT def_phone DEFAULT 'UNKNOWN' FOR phone
```

If you specify a default value in the Design Table dialog in SQL Enterprise Manager, a declarative default (in contrast to a bound default) is created.

Bound Defaults

A bound default is similar to a rule in the way that you create and manage the default.

You create the default as an object in the database:

```
CREATE DEFAULT def_phone AS 'UNKNOWN'
```

You can bind the default to a column in a table or to a user-defined datatype:

```
-- Bind a default to a column in a table
EXEC sp_bindefault 'def_phone', 'authors.phone'

-- Bind a default to a user defined datatype
EXEC sp_bindefault def_phone, phone
```

If you add the `futureonly` parameter when you bind a default to a user-defined datatype, existing tables using the datatype are not affected.

You unbind a default with `sp_unbindefault`.

Default Usage

The default you specify must be able to be evaluated to a constant at `INSERT` or `UPDATE`. You can use the following items as defaults:

- A constant
- A built-in function (if it doesn't take any arguments)
- A mathematical expression

In the preceding examples, we have already seen how a constant is used as a default.

Some of the built-in functions can be valuable as default values. In Listing 8.15, we create a table where all columns accept default values. The first is the NT Logon account, the second is the username (within the database), the third is the application name, and the fourth is the machine name.

LISTING 8.15 USING FUNCTIONS TO GENERATE DEFAULT VALUES

```
CREATE TABLE dflts
(nt_logon varchar(15) DEFAULT SUSER_SNAME(),
sql_user varchar(10) DEFAULT CURRENT_USER,
app varchar(22) DEFAULT APP_NAME(),
```

continues

8

LOGICAL
DATABASE
ARCHITECTURE

LISTING 8.15 CONTINUED

```
machine varchar(10) DEFAULT HOST_NAME())

INSERT dflts DEFAULT VALUES
SELECT * FROM dflts
nt_logon        sql_user    app                   machine
--------------- ----------- --------------------- ----------
TIB_DELL\Tibor  dbo         MS SQL Query Analyzer  TIB_DELL
```

Note that the column size should be large enough to accommodate the maximum length of the string the function returns. In the preceding example, the columns are smaller for formatting purposes.

If we script this table in SQL Enterprise Manager, we get the following script:

```
CREATE TABLE [dbo].[dflts] (
 [nt_logon] [varchar] (15) DEFAULT suser_sname(),
 [sql_user] [varchar] (10) DEFAULT user_name(),
 [app] [varchar] (22) DEFAULT app_name(),
 [machine] [varchar] (10) DEFAULT host_name()
) ON [PRIMARY]
```

(The keyword CONSTRAINT and the constraint name that SQL Enterprise Manager generates are removed for clarity.)

The function CURRENT_USER has been generated as USER_NAME(). CURRENT_USER is an example of an ANSI SQL-92 standardized niladic function. That's why it is not entered with parentheses after the function name. Niladic functions are scripted as their T-SQL counterparts. For more information on niladic functions and functions in general, refer to Chapter 21.

Quite often, there is a need to insert the current time or date when a row is inserted, such as when an invoice is created. The date could be generated by the client program or by SQL Server. By letting SQL Server generate the date, we get better consistency among the generated dates, and we are not depending on the client machines' internal clocks being synchronized.

Listing 8.16 displays some ways of generating time and date for defaults.

LISTING 8.16 GENERATING DEFAULT VALUES FOR DATETIME COLUMNS AND SETTING THE DATE AND TIME PARTS TO STANDARDIZED VALUES

```
CREATE TABLE dates
(dt datetime DEFAULT GETDATE(),
d datetime DEFAULT CONVERT(varchar(10), GETDATE(), 112),
t datetime DEFAULT CONVERT(varchar(15), GETDATE(), 114))
```

```
INSERT dates DEFAULT VALUES
SELECT * FROM dates
```

dt	d	t
1998-07-02 10:21:37.393	1998-07-02 00:00:00.000	1900-01-01 10:21:37.393

Because a datetime always contains both date and time, GETDATE() returns both parts. However, what if we are interested in only the date or the time, but not both? We certainly can use GETDATE() to generate both current date and current time. This makes it harder when querying the data, however, especially if you have to perform joins to correlate date values or time values. If the user wants to perform a join between two tables based on the same date value, the join condition must be expressed something like this:

```
FROM t_a JOIN t_b ON
 CONVERT(CHAR(10), t_a.dt_a, 112)
 = CONVERT(CHAR(10), t_b.dt_b, 112)
```

Not only is this harder to express, but also SQL Server will not be able to use any index on the datetime columns because we performed a function on the values.

Instead, we set the time in column d and date in column t to a standard value in the dates table. All inserted rows where the default is applied will get the same time or date.

When a Default Is Applied

There are four ways to get SQL Server to generate some default value when a row is inserted:

- Using a constraint default or a bound default
- Making the datatype datetime
- Specifying the IDENTITY property for the column
- Letting the column allow NULL

Columns based on the timestamp datatype and columns with the IDENTITY property cannot allow NULL. If there is a default for the column and an explicit NULL is passed with the insert, the NULL will be inserted (if allowed). If no value is passed and we don't have one of the first three conditions in the list, NULL will be inserted (if allowed).

There are three ways to express an INSERT statement to get a default applied. We will explore the three ways based on the following table:

```
CREATE TABLE dflt_insert
(id int IDENTITY NOT NULL,
 ts timestamp NOT NULL,
 phone char(13) NOT NULL DEFAULT 'UNKNOWN',
 comment VARCHAR(1000) NULL)
```

8

LOGICAL
DATABASE
ARCHITECTURE

If all columns have some default tied to them (as in the dflt_insert table), we can use the keywords DEFAULT VALUES to generate default values for the entire row:

```
INSERT dflt_insert DEFAULT VALUES
SELECT * FROM dflt_insert
```

```
id          ts                 phone         comment
----------- ------------------ ------------- -----------------
1           0x00000000000F4D95 UNKNOWN       NULL
```

We can also exclude the column for which we want a default generated in the column listing, as in the following example:

```
INSERT dflt_insert (phone, comment)
 VALUES('(408)496-7223', 'Phone no inserted')
SELECT * FROM dflt_insert
```

```
id         ts                 phone         comment
---------- ------------------ ------------- -----------------
1          0x00000000000F4D9B (408)496-7223 Phone no inserted
```

An identity will be generated for the id column and a timestamp generated for the ts column.

The third method is to specify the keyword DEFAULT in the value listing for the column:

```
INSERT dflt_insert (ts, phone, comment)
 VALUES(DEFAULT, DEFAULT, DEFAULT)
SELECT * FROM dflt_insert
id          ts                 phone         comment
----------- ------------------ ------------- -------
1           0x00000000000F4D9C UNKNOWN       NULL
```

> **NOTE**
>
> You cannot specify the DEFAULT keyword to generate an identity value. SQL Server will generate an error message stating that you tried to explicitly insert a value into an identity column. You must omit the column name from the column name listing.
>
> Although it seems a bit strange, this restriction has some advantages. You (the programmer) are not led into formulating constructs that explicitly try to insert values into identity columns. There is also less risk that you will construct INSERT statements that exclude the column name listing and refer to the columns by position (which conflicts to the relational model and may result in problems if the table is redefined).

Defaults on UPDATE

Assigning default values in UPDATE can be useful, not only for reassigning the default. If you want to keep track of who performed updates or when updates were performed, you can assign those columns to the default value. Listing 8.17 creates a table, inserts a row, and then updates the table and assigns default values to two columns.

LISTING 8.17   USING DEFAULT WITH UPDATE

```
CREATE TABLE dflt_update
(id int IDENTITY,
some_comment varchar(10),
upd_by varchar(15) DEFAULT SUSER_SNAME()
     CHECK (upd_by = SUSER_SNAME()),
upd_when datetime DEFAULT GETDATE(),
     CHECK (upd_when = GETDATE()))
INSERT dflt_update (some_comment)
 VALUES('Comment 1')
SELECT * FROM dflt_update

id      some_comment upd_by          upd_when
------- ------------ --------------- -----------------------
1       Comment 1    TIB_DELL\Tibor  1998-07-02 12:20:16.390

UPDATE dflt_update
 SET some_comment = 'Comment 2',
 upd_by = DEFAULT,
 upd_when = DEFAULT
 WHERE id = 1
SELECT * FROM dflt_update

id      some_comment upd_by          upd_when
------- ------------ --------------- -----------------------
1       Comment 2    TIB_DELL\Tibor  1998-07-02 12:21:46.940
```

8

LOGICAL
DATABASE
ARCHITECTURE

The UPDATE statement should explicitly set the upd_by and upd_when columns to DEFAULT; otherwise, SQL Server won't perform the check. If you need to keep track of these things regardless of how the UPDATE statement is constructed, you have to use a trigger.

Binding Precedence with Rules and Defaults

There are three ways to assign a default value, rule, or check to a column:

- Through a CHECK or DEFAULT constraint.
- By binding a RULE or DEFAULT object to the column.
- By creating the column on a user-defined datatype to which you have bound a RULE or DEFAULT object.

Using a combination of any of these ways can certainly be confusing.

The following restrictions apply for check constraints and rules:

- You can have only one rule bound to a column. If you bind a new rule to a column, the old rule is automatically unbound.
- You can have only one rule bound to a datatype. If you bind a new rule to a datatype, the old rule is automatically unbound.
- A rule bound to a column takes precedence over a rule bound to a datatype. If you want to reapply the rule bound to the datatype, first, you have to unbind the rule from the column. Then, you have to re-bind the rule to the datatype.
- You can have both a check constraint and a rule for a column. The rule is validated before the check constraint. If the verification for the rule fails, an error message is returned and the statement aborts.

The following restrictions apply for defaults:

- You can have only one type of default for a column at any given time.
- You cannot create a table with a default constraint if the column is based on a datatype to which a default object is bound.
- You cannot alter a table to add a default constraint if the column is based on a datatype to which a default object is bound or if a default object is bound to the column.
- If you have a table that uses a user-defined datatype and the table has a default constraint or default object bound to the column, binding a default to the datatype will not affect those columns.
- If you have a table with a datatype to which a default is bound, and then bind a default to a column, the binding to the column takes precedence.

Stored Procedures

A *stored procedure* is an executable database object stored in a database. It can be called from client applications, interactively, from other stored procedures, and from triggers. Parameters can be passed to and returned from the stored procedure. A stored procedure can also return a number of resultsets and a status code.

Advantages of Stored Procedures

Using stored procedures provides many advantages over executing large and complex SQL batches from client applications:

- Modular programming—Subroutines and functions are often used in ordinary 3GL and 4GL languages (such as C, C++, and Microsoft Visual Basic) to break up things into smaller, more manageable pieces of code. The same advantages are achieved when using stored procedures, with the difference that the stored procedure is stored in SQL Server and can be called by any client application.

- Restricted, function-based access to tables—Someone can have access to execute a stored procedure without having permissions to operate directly on the underlying tables.

- Reduced network traffic—Stored procedures can consist of many individual SQL statements but can be executed with a single statement. This allows you to reduce the number and size of calls from the client to the server.

- Faster execution—Stored procedures become memory resident after the first execution. The code doesn't have to be re-parsed and re-optimized on subsequent executions.

- Enforced consistency—If users modify data only through stored procedures, problems resulting from ad hoc modifications are eliminated.

- Reduced operator and programmer errors—There is less information to pass.

- Automated complex or sensitive transactions—If all modifications of certain tables take place in stored procedures, you can guarantee integrity on those tables.

Some of the disadvantages of using stored procedures follow (depending on environment):

- Less powerful programming language—There are more powerful and structured programming languages than T-SQL.

- Less integration with programming environment—Many of the larger software development projects use tools for version handling, debugging, re-use, and so on. Those tools might not support code stored within stored procedures.

8

LOGICAL
DATABASE
ARCHITECTURE

- Less portability—Although ANSI is working on a standard for writing procedural code and procedures in database management systems, few DBMS vendors support the standard. T-SQL is not based on that standard.
- Part of the code stored in SQL Server—In some situations, it might not be desirable to store some part of an application in a database management system.

The question is, "Should you use stored procedures?" The answer is (as it often is), "It depends."

If you are working in a two-tier environment, stored procedures are often advantageous. The trend is shifting to a three- (or more) tier environment. In this case, business logic is often handled in some middle tier (possibly ActiveX objects managed by Microsoft Transaction Server). If that is your environment, you might want to restrict the stored procedures to perform basic data-related tasks.

Performance Improvements in SQL Server 7.0

When dynamic SQL statements are executed, SQL Server performs a number of steps before the data can be returned to the client. Those steps include

1. Parsing the SQL statements.
2. Checking for permissions for each access to underlying objects.
3. Optimizing the SQL statements.
4. Executing the SQL statements.

The first time a stored procedure executes, all the steps are performed, and an execution plan is cached in memory. The optimization of SQL statements is based on the parameters passed, the index distribution statistics, and so on available at that execution. For subsequent executions, all SQL Server has to do is find the plan in cache and execute it.

The cached plans are lost when the server is shut down, so the four steps would be performed at the first execution of the procedure after startup.

Procedure Cache

In previous versions of SQL Server, memory was reserved for the procedure cache. The more that you set aside for the procedure cache, the less that was available for the data cache. Tuning the size of the procedure cache was a tedious task (partly because one procedure could exist as multiple plans in cache). Often, the procedure cache was left at the default value (30%), which in many configurations is unnecessarily high.

In version 7.0, the cache is unified. SQL Server uses the same cache area for data and index pages and for procedure plans.

Shared Query Plans

Procedure plans were not re-entrant in previous versions of SQL Server. If two users executed a procedure at the same time, two plans were used (or created) in cache memory. This led to suboptimal usage of the cache area, an environment that was harder to tune, and unpredictable execution times (because two plans could have different access paths).

There is never more than one plan per procedure in version 7.0. If the procedure is executed WITH RECOMPILE, a new plan is compiled to replace the old plan. In previous versions, new plans were created each time the procedure was executed WITH RECOMPILE, which could lead to many plans in cache for the same procedure.

SQL Server creates shared query plans (shareable between connections and application instances) for client applications that issue prepared statements. In earlier versions, SQL Server created a stored procedure in tempdb for each connection. Even applications that submit dynamic SQL statements can share plans (under certain circumstances).

The bottom line is that it is not as critical in version 7.0 for applications to use stored procedures to gain performance benefits. If the applications do, SQL Server will manage the cache memory in a better way.

8

LOGICAL
DATABASE
ARCHITECTURE

> **TIP**
>
> You can examine the procedure cache and plans with the DBCC MEMUSAGE and DBCC PROCCACHE commands.
>
> DBCC PROCCACHE returns the size of the procedure cache. (Remember that SQL Server grows and shrinks this size automatically.)
>
> DBCC MEMUSAGE displays the size of the object that occupies most space in the data cache and the procedure cache. If you are working on a server with a low load, you can for instance execute a dynamic SQL statement and see that SQL Server creates a plan for that statement.

Creating Stored Procedures

To create a stored procedure, you need to give the procedure a unique name and then write the sequence of SQL statements to be included in the procedure. It is good programming practice to always end a procedure with the RETURN statement. Listing 8.18 shows a simple stored procedure.

LISTING 8.18 A STORED PROCEDURE THAT RETURNS THE TITLE OF A BOOK AND THE NAMES OF THE AUTHORS WHO WROTE IT

```
CREATE PROCEDURE title_authors AS
SELECT a.au_lname, a.au_fname, t.title
FROM titles t INNER JOIN
 titleauthor ta ON t.title_id = ta.title_id RIGHT OUTER JOIN
 authors a ON ta.au_id = a.au_id
RETURN
```

To execute a stored procedure, simply invoke it by its name (the same way you probably have already executed system stored procedures, such as sp_help). If the procedure isn't the first statement in a batch, you have to precede the procedure name with the EXEC keyword. See Chapter 21 for more information on batches.

> **NOTE**
>
> The reason for the EXEC keyword rule is quite simple. SQL Server breaks down the string sent to it in a batch by searching for keywords. Stored procedure names aren't keywords. If SQL Server finds a procedure name among statements, chances are that SQL Server will return an error message. Sometimes the execution is successful, but SQL Server doesn't execute what you want:
>
> ```
> SELECT * FROM titles
> sp_help
> ```
>
> The procedure is not executed. The reason is that sp_help is considered a table alias in the SELECT statement.
>
> If you precede the procedure name with EXEC, you will get the expected behavior:
>
> ```
> SELECT * FROM titles
> EXEC sp_help
> ```
>
> Why don't you have to put EXEC in front of the procedure name if the procedure is the first statement in a batch? If SQL Server doesn't recognize the first string in a batch, it simply assumes that it is a name of a stored procedure. Execute the following string and notice the error message:
>
> ```
> Dsfdskgkghk
> Server: Msg 2812, Level 16, State 62
> Could not find stored procedure 'dsfdskgkghk'.
> ```
>
> Sometimes it helps to "think like the parser."

If you create a procedure with a name that already exists, you receive an error message that might not be expected. We try to create a procedure with the name `title_authors` (slightly modified):

```
CREATE PROCEDURE title_authors AS
SELECT a.au_lname, a.au_fname, t.title
FROM titles t INNER JOIN
 titleauthor ta ON t.title_id = ta.title_id RIGHT OUTER JOIN
 authors a ON ta.au_id = a.au_id
 WHERE a.state = 'CA'
RETURN
Server: Msg 2729, Level 16, State 1, Procedure title_authors,
 Line 7
Procedure 'title_authors' group number 1 already exists in
 the database. Choose another procedure name.
```

The reason for the error message is that the procedure can have an optional grouping number after the name. Add ; and an integer as in Listing 8.19.

LISTING 8.19 CREATING A STORED PROCEDURE WITH A GROUP NUMBER

```
CREATE PROCEDURE title_authors;2 AS
SELECT a.au_lname, a.au_fname, t.title
FROM titles t INNER JOIN
 titleauthor ta ON t.title_id = ta.title_id RIGHT OUTER JOIN
 authors a ON ta.au_id = a.au_id
 WHERE a.state = 'CA'
RETURN
GO
EXEC title_authors;2
```

8

LOGICAL
DATABASE
ARCHITECTURE

The first procedure will get an implicit group number (1). This is an odd feature. You can drop all procedures within a group by excluding the group number with the DROP PROCEDURE statement. (In fact, you cannot drop a single procedure within a group.) The grouping functionality can be used for version handling. For each new version of the procedure, you add to the grouping number. The old group number is available for clients that have not yet been modified to use the procedure correctly.

The stored procedure groups are based on the name; the stored procedures in the group all have the same name and are distinguished by their unique group number/ID.

You can modify a stored procedure with the ALTER PROCEDURE statement. This new feature in version 7.0 has an advantage over dropping and recreating the procedure in that you don't have to worry about reassigning permissions to the procedure. The syntax for ALTER PROCEDURE is the same as for CREATE PROCEDURE.

If you create a procedure with WITH ENCRYPTION, the source code in the syscomments table is encrypted. You cannot decrypt this data, so make sure that you store a copy of the source code for those procedures.

Delayed Name Resolution

The object names that a stored procedure refers to don't have to exist when the procedure is created. Earlier versions of SQL Server returned an error message if a procedure refers to an object that doesn't exist. Version 7.0 returns an error message at runtime if any object that a stored procedure refers to doesn't exist. In Listing 8.20, we mistype the name of a table in the stored procedure and try to execute it.

LISTING 8.20   DELAYED NAME RESOLUTION IN STORED PROCEDURES

```
CREATE PROCEDURE title_authors AS
SELECT a.au_lname, a.au_fname, t.title
FROM tttttitles t INNER JOIN
 titleauthor ta ON t.title_id = ta.title_id RIGHT OUTER JOIN
 authors a ON ta.au_id = a.au_id
 WHERE a.state = 'CA'
RETURN
GO
EXEC title_authors

Server: Msg 208, Level 16, State 1, Procedure title_authors,
 Line 2
Invalid object name 'tttttitles'.
```

If the object exists, the column names that the statements refer to must also exist.

One advantage of delayed (or deferred) name resolution is that it increases flexibility for the application developer because the order of creating stored procedures and the tables they reference do not need to be exact.

Executing with Input Parameters and Default Values

To perform more complex processing in stored procedures, we can pass parameters to the procedures. The parameters are used just like local variables within the procedure. For more information on how to use local variables, refer to Chapter 21.

Here's an example of a stored procedure that requires three parameters:

```
CREATE PROC myproc
 @parm1 int, @parm2 int, @parm3 int
```

```
AS
-- Processing goes here
RETURN
```

Parameter names in stored procedures are public, so I strongly recommend that you give your parameters meaningful names.

When you execute the procedure, you can pass the parameters by position or by name:

```
--Passing parameters by position
EXEC myproc 1, 2, 3
--Passing parameters by name
EXEC myproc @parm2 = 2, @parm2 = 1, @parm3 =3
--Passing parameters by position and name
EXEC myproc 1, @parm3 =3, @parm2 = 2
```

You cannot pass subsequent parameters by position after you name a parameter.

> **TIP**
>
> When embedding calls to stored procedures in client applications and script files, it is advisable to pass parameters by name. Reviewing the code and debugging it becomes a lot easier that way.

You can assign a default value to a parameter as in Listing 8.21.

LISTING 8.21 ASSIGNING A DEFAULT VALUE FOR A PARAMETER IN A STORED PROCEDURE

```
CREATE PROCEDURE title_authors @state char(2) = 'CA' AS
SELECT a.au_lname, a.au_fname, t.title
FROM titles t INNER JOIN
 titleauthor ta ON t.title_id = ta.title_id RIGHT OUTER JOIN
 authors a ON ta.au_id = a.au_id
 WHERE a.state = @state
RETURN
GO
EXEC title_authors
EXEC title_authors DEFAULT
EXEC title_authors @state = DEFAULT
EXEC title_authors 'UT'
```

8

LOGICAL
DATABASE
ARCHITECTURE

> **TIP**
>
> If you are involved in creating stored procedures that other people will use, you probably want to make the stored procedures as easy to use as possible.
>
> If you leave out a parameter that is required, SQL Server presents an error message. The MyProc procedure requires three parameters:
>
> ```
> EXEC myproc
> ```
>
> ```
> Server: Msg 201, Level 16, State 2, Procedure myproc, Line 0
> Procedure 'myproc' expects parameter '@parm1', which was not
>   supplied.
> ```
>
> Note that SQL Server only complains about the first missing parameter. The programmer passes the first parameter, only to find out that there are more parameters required. This is a good way to annoy a programmer (well, anyone).
>
> When you execute a command-line program, you probably expect that you can use /? to get a list of the parameters that the program expects. You can program the stored procedures the same way by assigning NULL (or some other special value) as a default value to the parameters and checking for that value inside the procedure. Listing 8.22 shows an outline of a stored procedure that presents the user with information about the parameters expected if the user doesn't pass any parameters.
>
> You can develop a standard for the way that the message is presented to the user, but what is important is that the information is passed somehow.

LISTING 8.22   PRESENTING INFORMATION TO THE USER ABOUT MISSING PARAMETERS FOR A STORED PROCEDURE

```
CREATE PROC MyProc2
 @parm1 int = NULL, @parm2 int = 32, @parm3 int = NULL
AS
IF @parm1 IS NULL OR
   @parm3 IS NULL
PRINT 'Usage:
 EXEC MyProc2
 @parm1 int,   (Required: Can be between 1 and 10)
 @parm2 = 32,  (Optional: Default value of 32)
 @parm3 int,   (Required: Any number within range)'
-- Processing goes here
RETURN
GO
EXEC MyProc2

Usage:
```

```
EXEC MyProc2
 @parm1 int,    (Required: Can be between 1 and 10)
 @parm2 = 32,   (Optional: Default value of 32)
 @parm3 int,    (Required: Any number within range)
```

Output Parameters

If a calling batch passes a variable as a parameter to a procedure, and that parameter is modified inside the procedure, the modifications will not be passed to the calling batch—unless you use the keyword OUTPUT when creating and calling the procedure.

If you want a procedure to be able to pass parameters out from the procedure, use the keyword OUT[PUT] when creating and calling the procedure. The following example accepts two parameters where one is used as an OUT parameter:

```
CREATE PROC ytd_sales
 @title varchar(80), @ytd_sales int OUTPUT AS
SELECT @ytd_sales = ytd_sales FROM titles WHERE title = @title
RETURN
```

The calling batch (or stored procedure) needs to declare a variable to store the returned value. The execute statement must include the keyword OUTPUT; otherwise, the modifications won't be reflected in the calling batch's variable:

```
DECLARE @sales_up_to_today  int
EXEC ytd_sales 'Life Without Fear', @sales_up_to_today OUTPUT
PRINT 'Sales this year until today''s date: ' +
      CONVERT(VARCHAR(10), @sales_up_to_today) + '.'
```

```
Sales this year until today's date: 111.
```

The print command simply returns output to the user. You can also pass the variable by name:

```
DECLARE @sales_up_to_today  int
EXEC ytd_sales 'Life Without Fear',
      @ytd_sales = @sales_up_to_today OUTPUT
PRINT 'Sales this year until today''s date: ' +
      CONVERT(VARCHAR(10), @sales_up_to_today) + '.'
```

OUTPUT parameters can also be passed to the client application (through ADO, ODBC, OLE DB, and so on).

Returning Procedure Status

Most programming languages have the ability to pass a status code to the caller of a function or a subroutine. A value of 0 generally indicates that the execution was successful. SQL Server is no exception.

8

LOGICAL
DATABASE
ARCHITECTURE

SQL Server will automatically generate an integer status value of 0 upon successful completion. If SQL Server detects an error, a status value between −1 and −99 is returned. You can use the RETURN statement to explicitly pass a status value less than −99 or greater than 0. The calling batch or procedure can set up a local variable to retrieve and check the return status.

In Listing 8.23, we want to return the year-to-date sales for a given title as a resultset. If the title does not exist, we do not want to return an empty resultset. Therefore, we perform a check inside the procedure and return the status value −101 if the title does not exist.

In the calling batch or stored procedure, we need to create a variable to hold the return value. The variable name is passed after the EXECUTE statement.

LISTING 8.23   RETURNING A STATUS CODE FROM A STORED PROCEDURE

```
--Create the procedure
CREATE PROC ytd_sales2 @title varchar(80) AS
IF NOT EXISTS (SELECT * FROM titles WHERE title = @title)
   RETURN -101
SELECT ytd_sales
 FROM titles
 WHERE title = @title
RETURN
GO

-- Execute the procedure
DECLARE @status int
EXEC @status = ytd_sales2 'Life without Fear'
IF @status = -101
 PRINT 'No title with that name found.'
```

RETURN values can also be passed to the client application (through ADO, ODBC, OLE DB, and so on).

SQL Server Status Codes

If a stored procedure terminates unexpectedly, SQL Server returns a status code. The values −1 to −99 are reserved by SQL Server, and −1 to −14 are currently in use. Table 8.11 lists the return codes currently in use by SQL Server and their meanings.

TABLE 8.11 SQL SERVER RETURN CODES

Status Code	Meaning
0	Successful execution
−1	Object missing
−2	Datatype error occurred
−3	Process chosen as a deadlock victim
−4	Permission error occurred
−5	Syntax error occurred
−6	Miscellaneous user error occurred
−7	Resource error, such as out of space
−8	Nonfatal internal problem encountered
−9	System limit reached
−10	Fatal internal inconsistency occurred
−11	Fatal internal inconsistency occurred
−12	Table or index corrupted
−13	Database is corrupt
−14	Hardware error

8

LOGICAL
DATABASE
ARCHITECTURE

Using Cursors in Stored Procedures

A cursor can be declared as local or global. A global cursor is available until deallocated or when the connection closes.

A local cursor goes out of scope when the stored procedure terminates. Procedures called from within the procedure (lower down in the call stack) can reference a higher-level cursor.

A cursor can pass a local cursor variable as an OUTPUT variable. Calling batches and procedures will be able to reference the cursor until the last referencing variable to the cursor goes out of scope. Chapter 21 contains more information about cursors and stored procedures in the section "Cursors."

Stored Procedures Guidelines and Limitations

A stored procedure cannot issue the USE statement, so the database context is limited to one database. You can qualify the object name with the database name if you need to reference an object in some other database.

System stored procedures are created in the master database (and the name begins with the prefix sp_), but they can be called from any database, without qualifying a database name. A system stored procedure is global in the sense that the system tables that it references are the current database system tables. This does not apply to user tables, however.

A stored procedure cannot create views, triggers, defaults, rules, or other stored procedures. You can, however, execute a string that creates the object:

```
CREATE PROC create_other_proc AS
   EXEC ('CREATE PROC au_lname AS
         SELECT au_lname from authors
         RETURN')
```

You can create tables in stored procedures. Generally, temporary tables are created in stored procedures. Temporary tables created in stored procedures are dropped at procedure termination. Global temporary tables, however, live until the creating connection terminates.

You cannot drop a table and re-create another table with the same name within the procedure unless you execute a string that creates the table.

Stored procedures can call other stored procedures up to a nesting level of 32. (The level was 16 in previous versions.)

If a stored procedure accepts parameters that are used as search arguments in the WHERE clause, you might consider creating the procedure WITH RECOMPILE, which means that an optimal execution plan is generated for each execution of the procedure. This advantage can be offset if the parsing and compilation time is relatively high, of course.

Remote Stored Procedures

You can execute a stored procedure residing on another server by using a four-part naming scheme:

```
EXEC server_name.db_name.owner_name.proc_name
```

This concept is (a bit misleadingly) called *remote stored procedures*. The name implies that the procedure called on the other server is some special type of stored procedure, but it is not. Any stored procedure can be called from another server.

A prerequisite to using *remote stored procedures* is that the remote server has been configured and login mapping has been done. The remote server is described in Chapter 15, "Remote and Linked Server Management."

The processing done by the remote stored procedure is by default not done in the local transaction context. If the local transaction rolls back, modifications done by the remote stored procedure are not undone. You can get the remote stored procedures to execute within the local transaction context, however:

```
BEGIN DISTRIBUTED TRANSACTION
EXEC purge_old_customers  --A local procedure
EXEC LONDON.customers.dbo.purge_old_customers
COMMIT TRANSACTION
```

Distributed transactions and the Microsoft Distributed Transaction Coordinator (DTC) service are discussed in Chapter 22, "Transaction Management and Distributed Transactions."

Debugging Stored Procedures with Microsoft Visual Basic and Visual Studio

Using a debugger is essential for all but the simplest programs. Stored procedures are no exception. With a debugger, you can set breakpoints, step through statements, and inspect the values of variables. Microsoft did not include a debugger in SQL Server, but you can refer to its tool suite for a T-SQL debugger.

If you don't find SQL Server Debugging in Control Panel, Add/Remove Programs, you have to add the software. Run the setup program, choose Server Applications and Tools, Launch BackOffice Installation Wizard, Install, Custom, and install SQL Server Debugging.

> **NOTE**
>
> You must have Visual Studio version 6.0 to debug stored procedures. The T-SQL debugger in Visual Basic 5.0 or Visual Studio 97 does not support SQL Server version 7.0.

The enterprise edition of Visual Studio (Visual InterDev, Visual J++, and Visual C++) includes a debugger for the Visual Studio developer environment. The solution you work with needs to include a database project.

Open a stored procedure, and then you can open the context menu (by right-clicking within your code) and set breakpoints. When you choose Debug from the context, a dialog asks for the parameters that the procedure expect. As you step through the code, you can inspect the values of variables in the Locals window.

The T-SQL debugger in Visual Basic is similar. Open your Visual Basic project, choose the Add-In Manager, and load the T-SQL debugger. Within the debugger, you define the connection attributes and choose which procedures you want to debug.

Triggers

A trigger is a special type of stored procedure that is executed automatically as part of a data modification statement. A trigger is created on a table and associated with one or more data modification actions (INSERT, UPDATE, or DELETE). When one of the actions for which the trigger is defined occurs, the trigger fires automatically. The trigger executes within the same transaction space as the data modification statement, so the trigger becomes a part of the data modification statement.

Triggers are the most powerful tool for maintaining database integrity because the trigger can perform whatever action is necessary to maintain data integrity. Triggers can do the following:

- Compare before and after versions of data
- Roll back invalid modifications
- Read from other tables (possibly in other databases)
- Modify other tables (possibly in other databases)
- Execute local and remote stored procedures

Benefits and Uses of Triggers

Declarative referential integrity (foreign key constraints) was introduced in version 6.0 of SQL Server. In previous releases, RI had to be performed by the client application through stored procedures or triggers. The vast majority of triggers written over the years perform referential integrity checks.

Because DRI is available now, triggers generally handle more complex integrity concepts, restrictions that cannot be handled through datatypes, constraints, defaults, or rules. Here are some examples of what triggers are useful for:

- Maintenance of duplicate and derived data—A denormalized database generally introduces data duplications (redundancy). Instead of exposing this redundancy to end users and programmers, you can keep the data in sync through triggers. If the derived data is allowed to be out of sync, you might want to consider handling refreshing through batch processing or some other method instead.

- Complex column constraints—If a column constraint depends on other rows within the same table or rows in other tables, a trigger is the best method for that column constraint.
- Cascading referential integrity—You can use triggers to implement cascading (or some other) actions for maintaining referential integrity.
- Complex defaults—You can use a trigger to generate default values based on data in other columns, rows, or tables.

You can use stored procedures for all of these tasks. The advantage of using triggers is that there is no way an application can bypass a trigger (except for bulk copy and TRUN-CATE TABLE). Even if a user uses an interactive tool, such as MS Query, the integrity rules cannot be bypassed once the trigger is debugged, tested, and implemented.

To achieve the same level of security when using stored procedures, you must be certain that access to your sensitive data occurs through your thoroughly tested stored procedures (and that the stored procedure does the integrity checking it is supposed to, of course).

Creating Triggers

You can create and manage triggers in SQL Enterprise Manager. Right-click the table for which you want to manage triggers and choose All Tasks, Manage Triggers from the pop-up menu (see Figure 8.5).

FIGURE 8.5

Managing triggers for the current table in SQL Enterprise Manager.

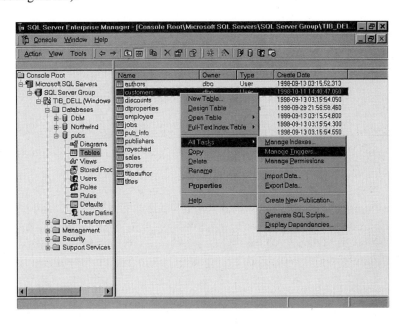

Figure 8.6 displays the Trigger Properties window.

FIGURE 8.6

The Trigger Properties window.

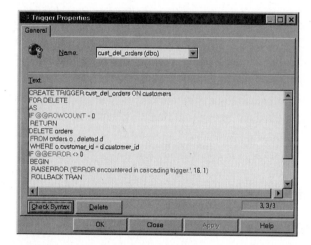

The best way to use the Trigger Properties window is to check for existing triggers for a table and to retrieve the source code for an existing trigger. The code can be transferred into SQL Query Analyzer through cut and paste for a more powerful editing tool.

Note that if you perform any changes in the Trigger Properties window and click OK, SQL Enterprise Manager executes an ALTER TRIGGER command. If you cut and paste the source code into SQL Query Analyzer, make sure that you change CREATE to ALTER. (Otherwise, you will receive an error message that the trigger already exists.)

The basic syntax for creating a trigger is

```
CREATE TRIGGER trigger_name
ON table_name
FOR { INSERT ¦ UPDATE ¦ DELETE }
AS
SQL statements
```

Here are a few things that are good to know about triggers:

- Triggers are objects, so they must have unique names within the database. (See Appendix C, "Defining System Administration and Naming Standards," for suggestions on naming standards.) If you try to add a trigger that already exists, an error message is returned. You can, however, ALTER an existing trigger (a new feature in version 7.0).

- A trigger is created on a table for an action or a set of actions. A trigger can respond to several actions (such as INSERT, UPDATE, or DELETE).

- You can have several triggers defined for the same action on a table (a new feature in version 7.0). If the database is in compatibility level 6.0 or 6.5, you have to specify WITH APPEND to be able to add a second trigger of the same type to a table. See Chapter 6, "Maintaining Backward Compatibility," for more information on database compatibility levels.

- A trigger cannot be placed on more than one table.

In Listing 8.24, we create a trigger that prints a message stating the number of rows updated by an UPDATE statement. We then execute a couple of UPDATE statements to see whether the trigger works.

LISTING 8.24 A SIMPLE TRIGGER

```
CREATE TRIGGER tr_au_upd ON authors
FOR UPDATE
AS
PRINT CONVERT(VARCHAR(5), @@ROWCOUNT) + " rows were updated."
GO
UPDATE authors
SET au_fname = au_fname
WHERE state = 'UT'
2 rows were updated.

UPDATE authors
SET au_fname = au_fname
WHERE state = 'CA'
15 rows were updated.
```

Even though we did not actually change the contents of the au_fname column, the trigger fired anyway (a simple example).

8

LOGICAL
DATABASE
ARCHITECTURE

> **NOTE**
>
> Triggers are meant to be a mechanism for guaranteeing the integrity of data. Although you can return resultsets and messages in triggers, it is not recommended. The programmers writing applications that perform modifications on your table are probably not prepared to get resultsets or messages when they submit data modification statements.
>
> The exception is returning an error with the RAISERROR command. If a trigger performs ROLLBACK TRAN, it should also execute RAISERROR to communicate the failure to the application.

You drop a trigger with the DROP TRIGGER statement. Triggers are automatically dropped when the table on which the trigger is created is dropped.

Executing Triggers on Column Updates

The UPDATE() function is available inside insert and update triggers. The function allows a trigger to determine whether a column was affected by the INSERT or UPDATE statement that fired the trigger. By testing whether a column was actually updated, you can avoid performing unnecessary work.

We might have a rule that you cannot change the city for an author (a silly rule, I agree, but it will show some points). Listing 8.25 creates a trigger for both INSERT and UPDATE.

LISTING 8.25 USING THE UPDATE() FUNCTION IN A TRIGGER

```
CREATE TRIGGER tr_au_ins_upd ON authors
FOR INSERT, UPDATE
AS
IF UPDATE(city)
 BEGIN
 RAISERROR ('You cannot change the city.', 15, 1)
 ROLLBACK TRAN
 END
GO
UPDATE authors
SET city = city
WHERE au_id = '172-32-1176'

1 rows were updated.
Server: Msg 50000, Level 15, State 1, Procedure
 tr_au_ins_upd, Line 5
You cannot change the city.
```

This is how you generally write triggers that verify the integrity of data. If the modification violates some integrity rule, an error message is returned to the client application and the modification is rolled back.

The UPDATE() function evaluates to true if you reference the column in the query. We did not actually change the value for city, but we referenced the column in the query.

We also got a message from the tr_au_upd trigger. We can have several triggers of the same kind in a table. The order in which they fire is arbitrary. Take care when using triggers; testing is imperative.

Let's try a couple of INSERTs on the authors table:

```
INSERT authors (au_id, au_lname, au_fname, city, contract)
VALUES('111-11-1111', 'White', 'Johnson','Menlo Park', 1)

Server: Msg 50000, Level 15, State 1
You cannot change the city.
```

The UPDATE() function evaluated to true because we referenced the column in the INSERT statement. Because the UPDATE() function is checked on INSERT as well, we cannot specify a value for the state when inserting a row.

In the following INSERT statement, we do not reference the city column, so the UPDATE() function evaluates to false, and the modification is not rolled back:

```
INSERT authors (au_id, au_lname, au_fname,  contract)
VALUES('111-11-2222', 'White', 'Johnson', 1)
```

We have a situation now where we can insert a NULL symbol in the city column, and we cannot change it. We had better clean up:

```
DROP TRIGGER tr_au_upd
GO
DROP TRIGGER tr_au_ins_upd
```

inserted and deleted Tables

In most situations, we need to know what changes were performed. You can find this information in the inserted and deleted tables. These tables are actually views of the rows in the transaction log that were modified by the statement. The tables have identical column structures and names as the tables that were modified. Consider the following statement:

```
UPDATE titles
  SET price = $15.05
  WHERE type LIKE '%cook%'
```

When the statement is executed, a copy of the rows to be modified is recorded in the log along with a copy of the rows after modification. These copies are available to the trigger in the deleted and inserted tables.

> **TIP**
>
> If you want to be able to see the contents of these tables, for testing purposes, create a copy of the table, and then create a trigger on that copy (see Listing 8.26).
>
> You can perform data modification statements and view contents in these tables without the modification actually taking place.

LISTING 8.26   VIEWING THE CONTENTS OF THE inserted AND deleted TABLES

```
SELECT *
 INTO titles_copy
 FROM titles
GO
CREATE TRIGGER tc_tr ON titles_copy
 FOR INSERT, UPDATE, DELETE
 AS
 PRINT 'Inserted:'
 SELECT title_id, type, price FROM inserted
 PRINT 'Deleted:'
 SELECT title_id, type, price  FROM deleted
 ROLLBACK TRANSACTION
```

The inserted and deleted tables are available within the trigger after INSERT, UPDATE, and DELETE. In Listing 8.27, we see the contents of inserted and deleted, as reported by the trigger when executing the preceding UPDATE statement:

LISTING 8.27   VIEWING THE CONTENTS OF THE inserted AND deleted TABLES WHEN UPDATING THE titles_copy TABLE

```
UPDATE titles_copy
 SET price = $15.05
 WHERE type LIKE '%cook%'

Inserted:
title_id type          price
-------- ------------  --------------------
MC2222   mod_cook      15.0500
MC3021   mod_cook      15.0500
TC3218   trad_cook     15.0500
TC4203   trad_cook     15.0500
TC7777   trad_cook     15.0500
```

```
Deleted:
title_id  type          price
--------  -----------   --------------------
MC2222    mod_cook      19.9900
MC3021    mod_cook       2.9900
TC3218    trad_cook     20.9500
TC4203    trad_cook     11.9500
TC7777    trad_cook     14.9900
```

When a trigger executes after more than one statement (INSERT, UPDATE, or DELETE), you can identify which statement initiated the trigger by examining the contents of the inserted and deleted tables, as shown in Table 8.12.

TABLE 8.12 DETERMINE THE ACTION THAT FIRED THE TRIGGER

Statement	*Contents of* inserted	*Contents of* deleted
INSERT	Rows added	Empty
UPDATE	New rows	Old rows
DELETE	Empty	Rows deleted

> **NOTE**
>
> Triggers do not fire on a row-by-row basis. One common mistake is to assume that only one row was modified. Triggers are set based. You must verify that the trigger works properly for multirow modifications.

8

LOGICAL
DATABASE
ARCHITECTURE

Trigger Restrictions

The following commands cannot be executed from a trigger:

- Create or drop objects (not even temporary tables). You can, however, execute SELECT...INTO (a new feature in version 7.0).
- Any ALTER statement.
- TRUNCATE TABLE.
- GRANT, REVOKE, or DENY.
- UPDATE STATISTICS.
- Any DROP command.
- Any RESTORE or LOAD command.
- RECONFIGURE.

WRITETEXT does not fire a trigger (regardless of whether it is logged or not).

TRUNCATE TABLE does not fire a trigger.

Nested Triggers

Triggers can be nested up to 32 levels. If a trigger changes a table on which there is another trigger, the second trigger is fired and can then fire a third trigger and so on.

If any trigger in the chain sets off an infinite loop, the nesting level is exceeded, the trigger is canceled, and the transaction is rolled back.

The following error message is returned if the nesting level is exceeded:

```
Server: Msg 217, Level 16, State 1, Procedure ttt2, Line 2
Maximum stored procedure nesting level exceeded (limit 32).
```

You can disable nested triggers by setting the nested triggers option of sp_configure to 0 (off):

```
EXEC sp_configure 'nested triggers', 0
RECONFIGURE
```

The default configuration allows nested triggers.

Recursive Triggers

The recursive triggers option is a new feature in version 7.0. If a trigger modifies the same table where the trigger was created, the trigger will not fire again unless recursive triggers is turned on. Recursive triggers is a database option, which by default is off.

The first command of the following example checks the setting of recursive triggers for the pubs database and the second sets recursive triggers to true:

```
EXEC sp_dboption pubs, 'recursive triggers'
EXEC sp_dboption pubs, 'recursive triggers', true
```

If you turn off nested triggers, recursive triggers is automatically disabled, regardless of how the database option is set. The maximum nesting level for recursive triggers is the same as for nested triggers, 32 levels.

Recursive triggers should be used with care. It is easy to create an endless loop, as shown in Listing 8.28.

LISTING 8.28 ERROR MESSAGE RETURNED FOR AN ENDLESS LOOP WITH RECURSIVE
TRIGGERS

```
EXEC sp_configure 'nested triggers', 1
RECONFIGURE
EXEC sp_dboption pubs, 'recursive triggers', true
CREATE TABLE rk_tr_test (id int IDENTITY)
GO
CREATE TRIGGER rk_tr ON rk_tr_test FOR INSERT
AS INSERT rk_tr_test DEFAULT VALUES
GO
INSERT rk_tr_test DEFAULT VALUES

Server: Msg 217, Level 16, State 1, Procedure rk_tr, Line 2
Maximum stored procedure nesting level exceeded (limit 32).
```

Enforcing Referential Integrity with Triggers

In Listing 8.29, we re-create and populate the customers and orders tables used earlier in
the chapter.

LISTING 8.29 RE-CREATING AND POPULATING THE customers AND orders TABLES

```
DROP TABLE orders
GO
DROP TABLE customers
GO

CREATE TABLE customers
(customer_id INT PRIMARY KEY NOT NULL,
customer_name NVARCHAR(25) NOT NULL,
customer_comments NVARCHAR(22) NULL)
CREATE TABLE orders
(order_id INT  PRIMARY KEY NOT NULL,
customer_id INT REFERENCES customers(customer_id),
order_date DATETIME )

INSERT customers (customer_id, customer_name, customer_comments)
VALUES(1, 'Hardware Suppliers AB','Stephanie is contact.')
INSERT customers (customer_id, customer_name, customer_comments)
VALUES(2, 'Software Suppliers AB','Elisabeth is contact.')
INSERT customers (customer_id, customer_name, customer_comments)
VALUES(3, 'Firmware Suppliers AB','Mike is contact.')

INSERT orders (order_id, customer_id, order_date)
VALUES(100, 1, GETDATE())
```

continues

8

LOGICAL
DATABASE
ARCHITECTURE

LISTING 8.29 CONTINUED

```
INSERT orders (order_id, customer_id, order_date)
VALUES(101, 1, GETDATE())
INSERT orders (order_id, customer_id, order_date)
VALUES(102, 1, GETDATE())

SELECT * FROM customers
SELECT * FROM orders
customer_id customer_name                customer_comments
----------- ------------------------     ----------------------
1           Hardware Suppliers AB         Stephanie is contact.
2           Software Suppliers AB         Elisabeth is contact.
3           Firmware Suppliers AB         Mike is contact.

order_id    customer_id order_date
----------- ----------- ----------------------------
100         1           1998-09-17 18:29:46.943
101         1           1998-09-17 18:29:46.973
102         1           1998-09-17 18:29:46.973
```

The foreign key constraint prohibits the following:

- Inserting rows into the orders table for customer numbers that don't exist in the customers table
- Updating the orders table, changing the customer number to values that don't exist in the customers table
- Deleting rows in the customers table, for which orders exist
- Updating the customers table, changing the customer number for which orders exist

To achieve the last two tasks, we might want a cascading action instead of a restriction (automatically cascade the DELETE or UPDATE statement executed on the customers table). You can do this with triggers.

Cascading Deletes

Cascading delete is not complex. Listing 8.30 shows a cascading delete trigger for the customers table.

LISTING 8.30 CASCADING DELETE FOR THE CUSTOMERS TABLE

```
CREATE TRIGGER cust_del_orders ON customers
FOR DELETE
AS
IF @@ROWCOUNT = 0
 RETURN
DELETE orders
 FROM orders o , deleted d
 WHERE o.customer_id = d.customer_id
IF @@ERROR <> 0
 BEGIN
  RAISERROR ('ERROR encountered in cascading trigger.', 16, 1)
  ROLLBACK TRAN
  RETURN
 END
```

This trigger has some error handling, so you can use it as a template for your cascading triggers.

The following DELETE statement deletes the row for customer number 1, so all three rows for that customer in the orders table should be deleted by the trigger:

```
DELETE customers WHERE customer_id = 1

Server: Msg 547, Level 16, State 1
DELETE statement conflicted with COLUMN REFERENCE constraint
 'FK__orders__customer_id__5D60DB10'. The conflict occurred
 in database 'Unleashed', table 'orders', column
 'customer_id'.
Server: Msg 3621, Level 16, State 1
The statement has been aborted.
```

This is not what we expected. The foreign key constraint restricted the DELETE statement, so the trigger never fired. Triggers in SQL Server are *after triggers*. The cascading action never took place.

We have four options:

- Remove the foreign key constraint from orders to customers.
- Disable the foreign key constraint from orders to customers.
- Keep the foreign key constraint and perform all cascading in stored procedures.
- Keep the foreign key constraint and perform all cascading in the application.

We are going to exploit the second option (see Listing 8.31).

8

LOGICAL
DATABASE
ARCHITECTURE

LISTING 8.31 DISABLING THE FOREIGN KEY CONSTRAINT TO THE CUSTOMER TABLE SO THAT CASCADING DELETE CAN OCCUR

```
ALTER TABLE orders
 NOCHECK CONSTRAINT FK__orders__customer_id__5D60DB10
GO
DELETE customers WHERE customer_id = 1
SELECT * FROM customers
SELECT * FROM orders
customer_id customer_name              customer_comments
----------- ------------------------- -----------------------
2           Software Suppliers AB      Elisabeth is contact.
3           Firmware Suppliers AB      Mike is contact.

order_id    customer_id order_date
----------- ----------- ---------------------------
```

The cascading took place because we disabled the foreign key constraint. The cascading updates option is more complex and not so common. We investigate that in the next section.

We have a potential integrity problem. If rows are inserted or updated in the orders table, there's no verification that the customer number exists in the customer table because we disabled the foreign key constraint. We can take care of that with an INSERT and UPDATE trigger on the orders table (see Listing 8.32).

LISTING 8.32 HANDLING A RESTRICTION WITH A TRIGGER ON THE ORDERS TABLE

```
DROP TRIGGER ord_ins_upd_cust
GO
CREATE TRIGGER ord_ins_upd_cust ON orders
FOR INSERT, UPDATE
AS
IF EXISTS (SELECT * FROM inserted
           WHERE customer_id NOT IN
           (SELECT customer_id FROM customers))
 BEGIN
  RAISERROR('No customer with such customer number', 16, 1)
  ROLLBACK TRAN
  RETURN
 END
```

Cascading Updates

The cascading update is tricky to achieve. Modifying a primary key, per definition, is really deleting a row and inserting a new row. That is the problem. We lose the connection between the "old" and the "new" row in the customer table, so how do we know what changes to cascade to which rows?

It's easier if we can restrict the changes to one row (see Listing 8.33) because we have only one row in the deleted and the inserted tables. We know the customer number before and after the modification.

LISTING 8.33   CASCADING UPDATE IN A TRIGGER

```
ALTER TRIGGER cust_upd_orders ON customers
FOR UPDATE
AS
DECLARE @rows_affected int, @c_id_before int, @c_id_after int
SELECT @rows_affected = @@ROWCOUNT
IF @rows_affected = 0
 RETURN -- No rows changed, exit trigger
IF UPDATE(customer_id)
BEGIN
 IF @rows_affected = 1
 BEGIN
   SELECT @c_id_before = customer_id FROM deleted
   SELECT @c_id_after = customer_id FROM inserted
   UPDATE orders
    SET customer_id = @c_id_after
    WHERE customer_id = @c_id_before
 END
ELSE
  BEGIN
     RAISERROR ('Cannot update more than 1 row.', 16, 1)
     ROLLBACK TRAN
     RETURN
  END
END
```

If several rows were updated, there is no way that we can know "which order belongs to which customer." You can easily modify the preceding trigger to handle if several rows change to the same value, but that is not allowed because of the primary key on the customer table. Modifying several rows and changing the primary key value is rare, and I doubt that you will encounter it.

> **NOTE**
>
> Cascading foreign key constraints is on the top of many customers' wish lists for SQL Server and will probably be implemented in a future release. I like simplicity and prefer sticking with constraints. That leaves handling cascading actions in stored procedures or in client applications.
>
> *continues*

8

LOGICAL DATABASE ARCHITECTURE

Stored procedures is often a good choice because they essentially give application developers a function-based interface to modifications. If the implementation details (table structure or rules) change, client applications can be isolated from the changes (as long as the interfaces to the stored procedures stay the same). The question on how to handle a cascade is a question of personal preference, however.

A note on cascading updates handled in a client application or stored procedure: This is a chicken-and-the-egg situation. You cannot change the referenced table first because other tables reference it. You cannot change the referencing table because there is no row in the referenced table with a corresponding value.

The solution is to insert a new row in the referenced table with the new primary key value, change the referencing rows, and then delete the old row in the referenced table.

System Databases

A system database is created to support the operation of SQL Server. When SQL Server is installed, the installation program creates four system databases (master, model, tempdb, and msdb). These databases cannot be deleted, even by a member of the sysdamin role. (Actually, msdb can be deleted, but it is definitely not recommended.)

NOTE

Previous versions of SQL Server did not separate data and transaction log for the model, tempdb, and master databases. In version 7.0, all databases have separate transaction logs, including the system databases.

master

The master database records all the system-level information for your SQL Server system. This includes login accounts, server-wide configuration settings, the existence of other databases, and so on. The master database is absolutely critical for your information, so you should always keep a recent backup of the master.

Most of the system stored procedures are also stored in the master database along with error messages.

msdb

The msdb database was introduced with version 6.0 of SQL Server. The main usage for msdb is to store information used by SQL Server Agent, such as job scheduling, operators, alerts, and so on.

Backup information is also stored in the msdb database. Therefore, msdb is important even if you do not use SQL Server Agent. The backup information in msdb assists with restoring a database.

model

The model database is a template database. Each time a database is created, the contents of model are copied into the new database. If you want certain objects, permissions, users, and so on to be automatically created each time you create a database, you can put them in the model database.

tempdb

The tempdb database holds all temporary tables and temporary stored procedures.

Temporary tables can be explicitly created by programmers. Those temporary tables are automatically deleted when the client connection is terminated.

SQL Server sometimes needs to create internal temporary tables (or work tables) for some operations. These operations include sorting, join operations, cursor handling, and so on. Those temporary tables are deleted as soon as the resultset is returned to the client application (or when the cursor is closed).

tempdb is re-created every time SQL Server is started, so there is no reason to back up the tempdb database.

Autogrow is set for tempdb by default. You probably want to increase the size anyway because autogrow "stalls" the system a bit when it happens. tempdb is reset to its default size each time SQL Server is started.

System Tables

SQL Server stores almost all configuration, security, and object information in its own *system tables*. Some system tables are actually views documented as tables.

Each database has a set of tables describing the database. These system tables are called the *database catalog*.

The master database has an additional set of tables describing the SQL Server installation. These tables are called the *system catalog*.

A number of tables hold replication information. These tables are stored in the master database, the distribution database, and the user database that uses replication.

The msdb database has a set of system tables in addition to the database catalog. These tables are used to store information used by SQL Server Agent and to hold information that Enterprise Manager uses to assist with restoring databases.

> **NOTE**
>
> Due to the architectural changes in version 7.0, the structure of some system tables has changed. Some system tables no longer exist. Where possible, Microsoft has provided views with the same structures and names as the old system tables.

System Catalog

Table 8.13 lists the tables and views in the system catalog. Table 8.14 lists undocumented system tables that are provided only for backward compatibility. Table 8.15 lists system tables that existed in earlier versions of SQL Server but not in 7.0.

TABLE 8.13 TABLES AND VIEWS IN THE SYSTEM CATALOG

Name	Type	Description
sysaltfiles	Table	Database file information for tempdb. Cannot be stored in tempdb.sysfiles because tempdb is rebuilt on each system startup.
syscharsets	Table	Installed character sets and sort orders.
sysconfigures	Table	System configurations values to be used at the next system startup.
syscurconfigs	Table	Current system configuration values. This is a virtual table, built from the configuration block each time it is queried.
sysdatabases	Table	Database name, owner, creation date, status, and other configuration values.
sysdevices	Table	Disk and tape backup files. Also used as a placeholder if DISK INIT is used to define a physical file, used later at execution of CREATE DATABASE (for backward compatibility).

Name	Type	Description
syslanguages	Table	Installed languages, added by `sp_addlanguage`.
syslogins	View	Information about each login ID, based on sysxlogins.
syslockinfo	Table	Current locks. This is a virtual table, built from the internal lock structures each time it is queried.
sysmessages	Table	System error or warning messages that can be returned by SQL Server.
sysoledbusers	View	User and password mapping for linked servers. Based on sysxlogins.
sysperfinfo	Table	Performance counters that can be displayed by Performance Monitor.
sysprocesses	Table	Process IDs, login information, and status information of each logged-in user. This is a virtual table, built from internal structures each time it is queried.
sysremotelogins	View	Users who are allowed to call remote stored procedures on the SQL Server. Based on sysxlogins.
sysservers	Table	Remote servers that SQL Server can access as an OLE DB data source.
sysxlogins	Table	Information about each login ID.

TABLE 8.14   TABLE PROVIDED FOR COMPATIBILITY WITH EARLIER VERSIONS OF SQL SERVER

Name	Description
syslocks	Current locks, replaced by syslockinfo.

TABLE 8.15   TABLE THAT IS NO LONGER PART OF THE SYSTEM CATALOG

Name	Description
sysusages	Data allocations and mapping of physical storage areas for databases. Replaced by sysfiles, which is part of the database catalog.

8

LOGICAL
DATABASE
ARCHITECTURE

Database Catalog

Table 8.16 lists the tables and views in the database catalog. Table 8.17 lists undocumented views that are provided only for backward compatibility. Table 8.18 lists system tables that existed in earlier versions of SQL Server but not in 7.0.

TABLE 8.16 TABLES AND VIEWS IN THE DATABASE CATALOG

Name	Type	Description
sysallocations	Table	Information about allocation units within the database.
syscolumns	Table	Names and characteristics for every column in every table and view and for each parameter in a stored procedure.
syscomments	Table	Contains the creation text of every stored procedure, trigger, view, check constraint, default constraint, rule, and default. This text can be read with sp_helptext.
sysconstraints	View	Mappings of constraints to the objects that own the constraints and type of constraint. Based on sysobjects.
sysdepends	Table	Relationships between dependent objects (views to tables, stored procedures to tables, and so on).
sysfilegroups	Table	Name and information about filegroups.
sysfiles	Table	Logical and physical name, size, and other information about database files.
sysfiles1	Table	Status information about database files.
sysforeignkeys	Table	Relationships for foreign keys in the database.
sysfulltextcatalogs	Table	One row for each full-text catalog.
sysindexes	Table	Index and space allocation information for every table and index.
sysindexkeys	Table	Information about index keys in the database.
sysmembers	Table	Members in database roles.
sysobjects	Table	Object definitions (tables, views, stored procedures, defaults, rules, default constraints and check constraints, and so on).
syspermissions	Table	Object and statement permission information.
sysprotects	Table	Object and statement permission information.
sysreferences	Table	Column mapping for foreign keys.
systypes	Table	System- and user-defined datatypes.
sysusers	Table	Information about the NT users, NT groups, SQL Server logins, or SQL Server roles that have access to the database.

TABLE 8.17 VIEWS PROVIDED FOR COMPATIBILITY WITH EARLIER VERSIONS OF SQL SERVER

Name	Description
sysalternates	User aliases, based on sysusers.
syssegments	Segment information. Returns three rows: `logsegment`, `system`, and `default`.

TABLE 8.18 TABLES THAT ARE NO LONGER PART OF THE SYSTEM CATALOG

Name	Description
syskeys	Documented keys, obsolete in version 6.0.
syslogs	The transaction log, no longer implemented as a system table.
sysprocedures	A binary representation of stored procedures, views, and other objects. This information is no longer kept in SQL Server. There is no longer a distinction between re-resolution and re-compilation.

Replication Catalog

A large number of system tables store replication configuration information. Some of these tables are stored in the master database, some in the distribution database, and some in the user database.

System Tables in msdb

The msdb database is used as a storage area for

- Configuration information used by SQL Server Agent—This includes information about jobs, jobsteps, alerts, operators, and so on.
- Backup history information—This is kept so that SQL Enterprise Manager can assist with restoring databases.

There were nine special system tables in the msdb database in version 6.5. These have been replaced by 21 tables in version 7.0.

Table 8.19 lists the tables used by SQL Server Agent.

8

LOGICAL
DATABASE
ARCHITECTURE

TABLE 8.19 TABLES IN MSDB USED BY SQL SERVER AGENT

Name	Description
sysalerts	Name, error number, and so on for all defined alerts.
syscategories	Name and so on for job, alert, and operator categories.
sysdownloadlist	Queue table for jobs to be downloaded to other servers.
sysjobhistory	History table for scheduled jobs.
sysjobs	Job information.
sysjobschedules	Scheduling information for jobs.
sysjobservers	Reference table for jobs and target servers.
sysjobsteps	Steps for each scheduled job.
sysnotifications	Information for how each operator should be notified (email, pager, Net send, or all) for each job.
sysoperators	Operator information (name, email address, and so on).
systargetservergroupmembers	Which target servers are included in each multiserver group.
systargetservergroups	Defined target server groups.
systargetservers	Enlisted target servers in the multiserver domain.
systaskids	Map tasks upgraded from earlier versions of SQL Server to jobs.

The tables in Table 8.20 are used to store information about backup and restore operations.

TABLE 8.20 TABLES IN MSDB USED TO STORE INFORMATION ABOUT BACKUP AND RESTORE OPERATIONS

Name	Description
backupfile	Filename, size, and so on for database backups.
backupmediafamily	Information about backup media families. (A media family is all the tapes used to store the backup of a database, for example.)
backupmediaset	Information about backup media sets. (For example, a media set is all the tape devices, including one or more media families, used as destination for a database backup.)
backupset	Information about backup sets.
restorefile	Restored database files.
restorefilegroup	Restored filegroups.
restorehistory	Information about performed restore operations.

Information about database maintenance plans is stored in tables in msdb, as described in Table 8.21. These tables are not documented, so the table structures and names might change in future versions and service packs.

TABLE 8.21 TABLES IN MSDB USED TO STORE INFORMATION ABOUT DATABASE MAINTENANCE PLANS

Name	Description
sysdbmaintplan_databases	One row for each database included in each plan.
sysdbmaintplan_history	History information for executed plans.
sysdbmaintplan_jobs	One row for each job included in each plan.
sysdbmaintplans	One row for each plan. Includes plan name, plan ID, creation date, and so on.

System Stored Procedures

A *system stored procedure* is a stored procedure with some special characteristics. These procedures, created when SQL Server is installed, are used to administer SQL Server. They shield the DBA from accessing the system tables directly. Some are used to present information from the system tables, whereas some modify system tables. Information about login IDs, for instance, can be viewed with the `sp_helplogins` procedure and modified with `sp_addlogin`, `sp_droplogin`, and so on.

8

LOGICAL
DATABASE
ARCHITECTURE

The earliest versions of SQL Server had no GUI-based administration tools, so a DBA had to have knowledge of these stored procedures. With version 4.2 of SQL Server, Microsoft shipped two graphical administration tools, and since version 6, we have SQL Enterprise Manager. Knowing the stored procedures is not an absolute must to administer SQL Server, but it is always good to know some of the basic system stored procedures. There are about 350 documented system stored procedures in version 7.0, so it would be a tough job to learn names and syntax for all of them. The total number of system stored procedures is about 600. Some of the undocumented stored procedures are called by other procedures, whereas other are called from SQL Enterprise Manager.

The following attributes characterize a system stored procedure:

- The stored procedure name begins with `sp_`.
- The procedure is stored in the master database.
- The procedure is owned by `dbo` (that is, created by `sa`).

These attributes make the procedure *global*. You can execute the procedure from any database without qualifying the database name. It executes in the current database context regarding system tables.

For instance, sp_helpuser shows information about usernames in the current database. If the procedure name did not begin with sp_ (for instance, helpuser), the database name in which the procedure exists would have to be qualified at execution:

```
USE pubs
EXEC master..helpuser
```

The procedure would list user information for the master database. The same thing occurs if you qualify a system stored procedure name with a database name:

```
USE pubs
EXEC master..sp_helpuser
```

The procedure is global only for the system tables. If a procedure refers to a user table, it will not be global even if it has the attributes listed.

In Listing 8.34, we create a global_example table in master and one in pubs. We also create a stored procedure that returns data from the global_example table. When we execute the sp_global_example procedure, we will see that it operates on the table in the master database, regardless of which database it is executed from because the global_example table is not a system table.

LISTING 8.34 SYSTEM STORED PROCEDURES, WHICH ARE GLOBAL ONLY FOR SYSTEM TABLES, NOT USER TABLES

```
USE master
GO
CREATE TABLE global_example (a_string VARCHAR(50))
INSERT global_example
 VALUES ('This is in the master database')
GO
CREATE PROC sp_global_example AS
 SELECT * FROM global_example

GO
USE pubs
CREATE TABLE global_example (a_string VARCHAR(50))
INSERT global_example
 VALUES ('This is in the pubs database')
GO
USE master
EXEC sp_global_example
a_string
- - - - - - - - - - - - - - - - - - - - - - - - - - - - - - - - - - - - - - - - - - - - - - - -
```

```
This is in the master database

USE pubs
EXEC sp_global_example
a_string
-----------------------------------------------
This is in the master database
```

If you write your own system stored procedures, remember to grant execute permissions (in the master database) to the procedure if anyone else but members of the sysadmins role should be able to use it. If the procedure modifies system tables, the `allow updates` configuration parameter must be set when the procedure is *created*.

CAUTION

Be careful if you write stored procedures that update system tables. It is easy to write a stored procedure that makes a database corrupt (or corrupts the whole server if any of the tables in the master database is modified). The same warning applies if you receive a stored procedure from anyone else.

Table 8.22 describes the eight categories of system stored procedures.

TABLE 8.22   SYSTEM STORED PROCEDURE CATEGORIES

Category	Description
System procedures	Used for general administration of SQL Server.
Security procedures	Used to manage login IDs, usernames, and so on.
Distributed queries procedures	Used to link remote servers and manage distributed queries.
Cursor procedures	Reports information about cursors.
Web Assistant procedures	Sets up and manages Web tasks (used by SQL Server Web Assistant).
Catalog procedures	Provides information about the system tables (used by ODBC).
SQL Server Agent procedures	Used by SQL Server Agent, provides access to the system tables in msdb. These are stored in msdb, so they are not global.
Replication procedures	Used to manage replication.

8

LOGICAL
DATABASE
ARCHITECTURE

Some of the most useful system stored procedures are listed in Table 8.23.

TABLE 8.23 SYSTEM STORED PROCEDURES

Procedure Name	Description
sp_who and sp_who2	Returns information about current connections to SQL Server.
sp_lock	Returns information about currently held locks.
sp_help [*object_name*]	Lists the objects in a database or returns information about an specified object.
sp_helpdb [*db_name*]	Returns a list of databases or information about a specified database.
sp_helptext [*object_name*]	Returns the CREATE statement for stored procedures, views, and so on.
sp_configure	Lists or changes configuration settings.

System Information Schema Views

ANSI SQL-92 defined a set of views that provides information about system data. These views are available in SQL Server 7.0. The advantage of using the views instead of querying the system tables directly is that the application is less dependent on the database management system or its particular version.

Both SQL-92 and SQL Server uses a three-part naming scheme for objects. Even though they use different names for each part, the names map quite nicely to each other (see Table 8.24).

TABLE 8.24 THREE-PART NAMING SCHEME FOR SQL SERVER AND SQL-92

SQL Server Name	SQL-92 Name
Database	Catalog
Owner	Schema
Object	Object

A user-defined datatype is called domain in the ANSI SQL-92 standard.

Warning About Querying System Tables Directly

Whenever possible, you should avoid embedding queries against the SQL Server system tables in your applications.

One of the areas that will involve the most work when porting an application to version 7.0 is handling queries to the system tables (if they exist). The engineers at Microsoft have done a good job of providing a high level of backward compatibility with earlier versions of SQL Server. Nevertheless, some of the information in the system tables does not correspond between the versions.

A better approach than querying the system tables is to use the information schema views or system functions to retrieve metadata information.

SQL Server ANSI-Compliant Views

The information schema views are owned by the user INFORMATION_SCHEMA. The user is created by the installation script that creates the views. Queries against these views must qualify the object name with INFORMATION_SCHEMA, as in the following example:

```
SELECT TABLE_NAME, TABLE_TYPE
  FROM INFORMATION_SCHEMA.TABLES
```

The information schema views display information applicable for the user who queries them (for instance, the tables that the user has permissions to use). Note that the names are in uppercase.

Table 8.25 lists the information schema views.

TABLE 8.25 INFORMATION SCHEMA VIEWS

Name	Description
CHECK_CONSTRAINTS	Information about check constraints.
COLUMN_DOMAIN_USAGE	Information about which column uses user-defined datatypes.
COLUMN_PRIVILEGES	Permissions at the column level.
COLUMNS	Information about columns in the database.
CONSTRAINT_COLUMN_USAGE	Table, column, and constraint name for each column that has a constraint defined.
CONSTRAINT_TABLE_USAGE	Table, column, and constraint name for each table that has a constraint defined.

continues

TABLE 8.25 CONTINUED

Name	Description
DOMAIN_CONSTRAINTS	Information about user-defined datatypes that has rules bound to it.
DOMAINS	One row for each user-defined datatype.
KEY_COLUMN_USAGE	Information about which columns are defined as PRIMARY KEY or UNIQUE.
REFERENTIAL_CONSTRAINTS	One row for each FOREIGN_KEY constraint.
SCHEMATA	Returns character set information for each database (always the same in SQL Server).
TABLE_CONSTRAINTS	Table constraints.
TABLE_PRIVILEGES	Permissions at the table level.
TABLES	One row for each table in the database for which the user has permissions.
VIEW_COLUMN_USAGE	Columns used in views.
VIEW_TABLE_USAGE	Tables used in views.
VIEWS	One row for each table in the database for which the user has permissions.

SQL-DMO and SQL-NS

SQL-DMO (Microsoft SQL Server Distributed Management Objects) is a COM-based (Component Object Model) programming interface. If you want to write a program that administers SQL Server, SQL-DMO is the API to choose.

To administer SQL Server at the command level, you use SQL statements, stored procedures, extended stored procedures, and so on. This process is abstracted and unified in SQL-DMO. You work with a set of objects, where each object might have properties, collections, and methods. For instance, a database object has a *collection* of tables, a *method* for checking the integrity of the database, and a *property* that specifies the amount of space available in the database.

SQL-DMO not only unifies the command syntax for you, but it also has some nice functionality built in. There are methods to script create statements for (all) objects in a database, transfer data between SQL Servers, and import data from a text file.

You can use SQL-DMO from any programming language that supports OLE Automation (for instance, Visual Basic, Microsoft Excel, Visual C++, and so on). SQL-DMO is relatively easy to use and effective. With a few lines of code, you can perform tasks that would require many lines of code using any of the other programming interfaces. You might want to consider SQL-DMO instead of stored procedures for scripts as well. A programming language such as Visual Basic has better features for error handling and so on than T-SQL.

Microsoft has given us access to the user interface elements in SQL Enterprise Manager in version 7.0: SQL-NS (SQL Namespace). If you want to display properties for a table or database, for example, you can use the dialog available in SQL-NS instead of creating your own dialog.

Considering that creating user interface elements is a time-consuming and tedious task, SQL-NS is quite helpful. Using SQL-NS provides better consistency across applications as well.

For more information about SQL-DMO, look in Appendix D, "Programming Tools and Interfaces."

ODS and Extended Stored Procedures

Open Data Services (ODS) is a set of libraries you can use to create an application that is accessed just like SQL Server. One common use of ODS concerns database gateways. A database gateway looks just like a SQL Server but translates incoming SQL statements and passes them to some other database management system. This feature was useful in the early 1990s because access to mainframe data, for example, was difficult from personal computers. If the mainframe can behave like SQL Server, we can use the programming libraries available or SQL Server. ODS has lost some of its importance as ODBC gained popularity.

There is still one useful application of the ODS library: *extended stored procedures*. You have probably come across stored procedures whose names begin with xp_. These are not built with T-SQL commands but map to a function stored in a DLL. To develop extended stored procedures, you use the ODS library.

You should be aware that an extended stored procedure executes within the same address space as SQL Server, so if it performs some illegal operations, it might bring down the whole server.

About 200 extended stored procedures are shipped with SQL Server. Most of them are undocumented. All extended stored procedures (or rather, references to) are stored in the master database. A folder in SQL Enterprise Manager under the master database lists the extended stored procedures.

If you plan to use an undocumented extended stored procedure, be careful. First, you have to find out what it does and what parameters it takes. You should also be aware that they are not supported by Microsoft. Moreover, there is no guarantee that the procedure is included in a later version of SQL Server or that it behaves in the same manner if it is included.

Table 8.26 lists the categories of extended stored procedures.

TABLE 8.26 EXTENDED STORED PROCEDURES CATEGORIES

Category	Description
General extended procedures	General functionality. Perhaps the most useful is `xp_cmdshell`, which executes external programs and returns the output from them as a resultset.
SQL Mail extended procedures	Used to perform email operations from within SQL Server.
SQL Server Profiler extended procedures	Used by SQL Server Profiler. These can also be used directly, for instance, to create a trace queue and start the trace from within a stored procedure.
OLE automation procedures	Allows SQL Server to create and use OLE automation objects.
API system stored procedures	Undocumented extended stored procedures used by the API libraries. The server cursor functionality, for instance, is implemented as a set of extended stored procedures.

One of the most used extended stored procedures is `xp_cmdshell`. `xp_cmdshell` can execute any operating system command or program (as long as it is a Win32 console program). The following example uses `xp_cmdshell` to list the files in a directory on the SQL Server computer's hard disk:

```
EXEC xp_cmdshell 'DIR c:\*.*'
```

`xp_cmdshell` returns a resultset of one `varchar(255)` column. A common use of `xp_cmdshell` is executing BCP and ISQL. This allows you to use T-SQL as a script language for importing and exporting data and so on.

Summary

Defining the logical database architecture is a big task. It includes choosing datatypes, implementing integrity features, and writing triggers. We have also looked at stored procedures, system tables, and system stored procedures. Understanding these concepts is crucial for a SQL Server DBA.

8

LOGICAL
DATABASE
ARCHITECTURE

SQL Server Administration Tasks and Tools

PART IV

IN THIS PART

The SQL Server Enterprise Manager

by Irfan A. Chaudhry

IN THIS CHAPTER

This chapter is geared toward two different audiences: those of you who are already familiar with SQL Server and those of you who are new to SQL Server. For users who are completely new to SQL Server, you have come in at the right time. With the release of version 7.0, Microsoft has made the lives of many DBAs even easier than before. With the new enhancements found in Enterprise Manager—such as the Microsoft Management Console (MMC), new and improved wizards, and the task pad—you will find yourself able to complete tasks quicker and easier without a big learning curve.

For users who are coming from version 6.x, you will find many enhancements in version 7.0 and the Enterprise Manager that you might wish that you had in the previous versions. Tools such as the Database Diagrammer and the Query Designer are just part of the new features. As in the past, Enterprise Manager allows users to accomplish tasks using a graphical user interface (GUI) that normally would require them to write SQL stored procedures. The ability to write stored procedures to accomplish tasks has not been taken away—far from it. Version 7.0 includes a new editor to help the user when writing stored procedures. However, this chapter concentrates on how to complete tasks under SQL Server using Enterprise Manager and its GUI.

Many basic tasks such as creating databases, tables, views, and triggers are covered in this chapter. In addition, many advanced topics such as publishing and subscribing are covered. I mainly discuss how to complete a task under Enterprise Manager, not so much the reasons behind the task. I have added cross-references to other chapters that go into more detail with the subject at hand, so when needed, you can reference these chapters.

Establishing Server Groups and Registering SQL Server in Enterprise Manager

You cannot register and manage servers running SQL Server 6.5 or older. You must upgrade these servers to SQL Server version 7.0 if you want to manage them through Enterprise Manger. To manage and configure SQL Server through Enterprise Manager, however, you must first register the server in Enterprise Manager.

Registering Servers with the Registration Wizard

To manage SQL Server through Enterprise Manager, you must register the server. Microsoft SQL Server 7.0 has several new wizards, including the Registration Wizard. Through the Registration Wizard, you can register multiple servers at one time and add the servers to an existing SQL Server group or a new server group.

In the following exercise, we will register a SQL Server and add it to a new server group:

1. Launch Enterprise Manager.
2. Select the Microsoft SQL Server icon and right-click; choose New SQL Server Registration.
3. Click Next at the welcome screen.
4. Type or select the server name and click Add, as shown in Figure 9.1. Click Next to continue.

FIGURE 9.1

The Register SQL Server Wizard makes it easy for you to register servers and add servers to a group.

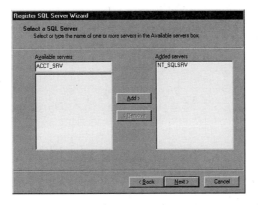

5. Select the authentication method; SQL Authentication is the default. Click Next to continue.
6. Type the SQL Server account information. You can request to be prompted to log in each time you connect. Click Next to continue.

TIP

In the case of large SQL Server shops, it's a good idea to have Enterprise Manager prompt the user each time to log on. Not only does this ensure the security of the SQL Server, but it also allows you to track who made what changes. On the other hand, in an environment where there is only a single DBA, it is not necessary to enforce a logon each time because that person is more than likely the only one allowed access to the SQL Server.

7. Select to create a new server group and type the name of the group.
8. Click Next and Finish. You will be prompted once the registration has completed successfully.

Server Groups

The purpose of forming server groups is to make it easier to manage a large number of SQL Servers as a few manageable groups. The server group is established according to some commonality shared between the servers, such as a specific task or location. A typical server group might consist of all the SQL Servers used in the Accounting department or might be broken down further to just the Finance department. Another example of a server group is all the SQL Servers located on the West Coast.

When creating server groups, you should remember that they are designed to help you manage your environment more efficiently. Place servers in groups that help you distinguish them—whether that be by location, specific task, or department.

To create a new server group, follow these steps:

1. Launch Enterprise Manager.
2. Select the Microsoft SQL Server icon and right-click; choose New SQL Server Group.
3. Type the name for the new group and click OK.

In enterprise environments where you need to subdivide the server groups into smaller groups, you have the option of creating subgroups. Examples of subgroups include Accounting, Engineering, and Finance.

Security

Microsoft SQL Server 7.0 uses two methods of authentication: Windows NT Authentication and SQL Server Authentication. When a user logs in using Windows NT Authentication, his network security attributes allow access to the SQL Server. SQL Server Authentication requires an individual login to be created at the SQL Server for each user. Along with creating SQL Server logins, administrators can create roles to help with the overall management of rights to the SQL Server.

Roles

Roles ease the management of assigning permissions to a database. You can assign roles to users in much the same way you add a Windows NT user to a group. SQL Enterprise Manager then allows you to assign object permissions to these roles, which saves the additional headache of assigning object permissions to each individual user.

Some of the predefined roles include

- Database creators
- Disk administrators
- System administrators

To view all the predefined roles, expand the security folder and select the Server Roles icon. The details pane displays all the roles along with descriptions of them. If the predefined roles do not fit the criteria you need, you can create a new role. To create a new SQL Server database role, complete the following:

1. Expand a server group and then expand the server.
2. Expand the database where the role will be created.
3. Right-click Roles and select New Database Role.
4. Enter a name for the role and either add users to the standard role or assign a password if it is an application role.

To add a user to a predefined role, perform the following steps:

1. Launch Enterprise Manager.
2. Expand the database where the role is defined.
3. Select the Roles icon.
4. From the details pane, select the predefined role and right-click. Choose Properties.
5. From the Database Role Properties window, click Add and select the user to be added to that role (see Figure 9.2).
6. Click OK to complete the task.

FIGURE 9.2

Assigning user Jsmith to the db_securityadmin role.

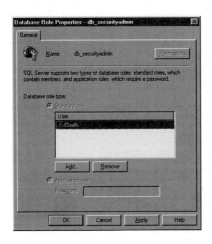

Logins

With SQL Server Authentication and Mixed Mode Authentication, you must create a login ID for a SQL Server user. In the following exercise, we will create a login ID using Enterprise Manager:

1. Launch Enterprise Manager.

2. Expand the SQL Server where the ID will be created.

3. Expand the Security folder and select the Logins icon.

4. Right-click the Logins icon and choose New Login.

5. Type the login ID and select SQL Server Authentication, as shown in Figure 9.3.

FIGURE 9.3

Creating a new user with the login ID TRoberts.

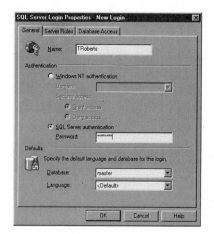

6. Type a password for the user and click OK.

7. You will be prompted to confirm the password. Click OK when done.

To set the user's server and database roles, select the user from the details pane and right-click. Select Properties so you can set the user's default database, server roles, database access, and database roles.

For more information on security, see Chapter 10, "Security and User Administration."

Creating Databases

Before creating a database through SQL Enterprise Manager, you must determine the following information:

- The name of the database
- The location of the database files
- Whether you want to permit automatic growth of the database
- How you want to restrict the maximum size of the database
- What options, such as access restrictions, you want to enable

In the following exercise, we will create a database using Enterprise Manager. The database will have the following parameters:

Name: MYDATABASE

Location: Default location

Automatic growth permitted in 20% increments

No restriction on the maximum file size

1. Launch Enterprise Manager.
2. Expand the server where the database will be created.
3. Select the Database folder and right-click to choose New Database.
4. Type the name of the database and change the database file Initial Size value to 30MB, as shown in Figure 9.4.

FIGURE 9.4

The Database Properties screen displaying the settings for the new database, MYDATABASE.

> **NOTE**
>
> The default value of the data and transaction log file size is the size of the model database. If you change the size of the model database, it will affect the default values of databases created in the future.

5. Change the file growth to increase automatically by 20%.
6. Click OK to complete the creation of the database.

> **TIP**
>
> You can generate SQL scripts for many of the objects such as databases, tables, and jobs through Enterprise Manager. For example, right-click the Northwind Database icon and select All Tasks, Generate SQL Scripts. You will be able to select whether you want to generate scripts for all the objects for that database or just the ones you select.

> **TIP**
>
> You can perform many of the tasks discussed in this chapter through the new wizards of Microsoft SQL Server 7.0. To gain access to these wizards, select the Run a Wizard button from the toolbar. You can also launch these tasks from the new task pad. Double-click the server, and the Getting Started task pad will appear in the details pane on the right side.

Creating Backup Devices

Backup devices are essential if you want to back up your databases. When creating a backup device, you can create a device that backs up the data either to a file or a tape drive. See Chapter 12, "SQL Server Backup, Restore, and Recovery," for more details on how to perform backups.

To create a backup device, follow these steps:

1. Launch Enterprise Manager.

2. Expand the server where the backup device will be created.

3. Double-click the Management folder and select Backup.

4. Right-click and select New Backup Device; type the name of the new backup device, as shown in Figure 9.5. If a tape drive is installed, you can select the tape drive name.

FIGURE 9.5

Backup device MYBACKUP being created.

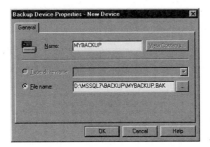

5. Click OK once the information is complete.

Server Activities

Enterprise Manager allows administrators to create and monitor day-to-day tasks such as backing up a database and viewing server alerts and SQL Server error log entries. Through Enterprise Manager, an administrator can also view information about processes, locks, and user activity. These jobs, alerts, operators, and notifications, as well as replication jobs, that you create through Enterprise Manager are all managed by the SQL Server Agent.

Monitoring the Server

Some of the SQL Server activities that you can monitor through Enterprise Manager include

- Currently running processes in SQL Server
- Blocked processes
- Locks
- User activity

To view current activity for the Microsoft SQL Server, follow these steps:

1. Launch Enterprise Manager.
2. Expand the server that will be monitored.
3. Double-click the Management folder.
4. Select the Current Activity icon.

From the details pane on the right side, you can select current Process Info, Locks/Process ID, or Locks/Object. For more information on performance monitoring, see Chapter 28, "Monitoring SQL Server Performance."

Scheduling Tasks

You can schedule tasks such as backing up a database, maintaining databases, and scheduling T-SQL commands through the SQL Server Agent.

The following exercise creates a scheduled task that dumps the transaction log for the Northwind database:

1. Launch Enterprise Manager.
2. Right-click the SQL Server.
3. Select New, Job.
4. Type Log Dump for the job name.
5. Change the Category to Database Maintenance and type a description for the job, as shown in Figure 9.6.

FIGURE 9.6

You can use Enterprise Manager to schedule routine jobs to make administration simpler.

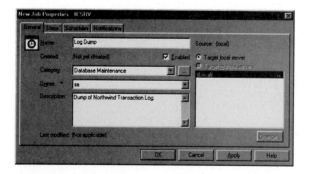

6. Select the Steps tab and click New.
7. Type a step name. (Each job must have a unique step name.)
8. Type the following T-SQL command:

```
Dump tran Northwind with no_log
```

9. Click the Advanced tab; change the On Success Action to Quit the job reporting success.

10. Click OK when done.

11. Click the Schedule tab and type a name for the schedule.

12. At this point, you can change the schedule from Recurring once a week, but keep the default time. Click OK to continue.

To manage the job, expand the Microsoft SQL Server and double-click the Management folder. Select the job from the details pane and right-click. From here, you can

- Start the job
- Stop the job
- Disable the job
- View the job's history
- Edit the job
- Delete the job
- Generate a SQL script for the job

Alerts

Enterprise Manager gives the administrator the ability to configure SQL Server to respond to alerts by executing predefined tasks and/or notifying the administrator via email or pager.

The following exercise creates an alert that writes an event to the SQL Server error log when the server reaches a predefined count for user connections:

1. Launch Enterprise Manager.

2. Select the server where the alert will be created.

3. Right-click the server and select New, Alert.

4. Type a name for the new alert.

5. To choose the type of alert, click the drop-down box to select SQL Server Performance Condition Alert, as shown in Figure 9.7.

6. Set the Object to SQLServer:General Statistics.

7. Set the Counter to User Connections.

8. Set Alert if Counter to Rises Above and type a value of 20.

9. Click the Response tab to set up the notification settings.

10. Click OK.

FIGURE 9.7

Creating a new alert.

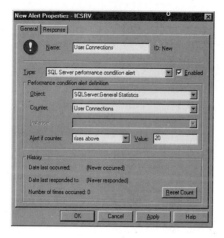

Error Logs

The SQL Server agent creates an error log that can log three types of errors. These errors include

- Information messages—These messages notify the administrator of general condition messages such as a notification that a particular task is complete. Information messages by default are not written to the error log because they can fill the log rapidly. To view information messages, select the dialog box in SQL Server Agent Properties.

- Warning messages—Warning messages are written to the error log because they warn about problems that can cause SQL Server to crash.

- Error messages—Error messages usually require the administrator to take some form of action. An error message could be generated, for example, if a SQL service such as the mail session fails to start.

You can view the error log:

1. Launch Enterprise Manager.
2. Select the server to be viewed.
3. Expand the server and select the Management folder.
4. Select the SQL Server Agent icon and from the menu bar, select Action, Display Error Log.

You can view error messages, warning messages, and information messages or all three types of messages at once.

For more information on the SQL Server Agent, see Chapter 11, "The SQL Server Agent."

Server Configuration

You can perform server configuration, such as reconfiguring memory settings, user connections, or setting locks, through Enterprise Manager. See Chapter 29, "Configuring, Tuning, and Optimizing SQL Server Options," for more information on configuring SQL Server.

Server Options

You can set several server options through Enterprise Manager. These options include processor allocation and determining maximum worker threads, memory settings, and user connections. Many of these options help the administrator to tune SQL Server for maximum performance and reliability.

Here's how you change or view these settings:

1. Launch Enterprise Manager.
2. Expand the SQL Server group.
3. Select SQL Server, right-click, and choose Properties.

From the SQL Server Properties screen, you can change or view these settings, including the startup parameters for SQL Server (see Figure 9.8). You can use the startup parameters to debug problems with the SQL Server.

FIGURE 9.8
The SQL Server Properties screen.

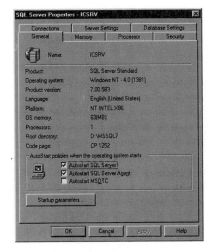

Security Options

You can set the security options for SQL Server from the SQL Server Properties window. The security options allow you to change the authentication mode for the server and the Startup Service account preferences.

> **NOTE**
>
> If you are running Enterprise Manager on a Windows 95 machine, you will not be able to change the Startup Service account settings; you must make these changes at the server.

Changing the Configuration

Rather than use cumbersome Transact-SQL commands to configure settings such as memory or user connections, you can use Enterprise Manager.

In the following exercise, we will set the SQL Server memory setting to dynamically use between 18MB and 63MB:

1. Launch Enterprise Manager.
2. Select the server to be configured.
3. From the menu bar, select Tools, SQL Server Configuration Properties.
4. Select the Memory tab.
5. Change the minimum setting for Dynamically Configure SQL Server Memory to 18MB (see Figure 9.9). Click OK.

FIGURE 9.9

Setting memory to dynamically use between 18MB and 63MB.

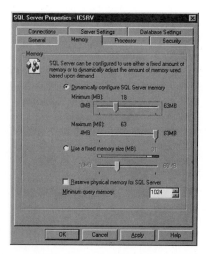

> **NOTE**
>
> The maximum amount of memory you can allocate to SQL Server is the total amount of RAM in your server. If the amount of load on the server fluctuates, set the memory to be dynamically configured; this way, additional memory will be there if needed.

System Tools

A number of systems tools available in Enterprise Manager assist the administrator with day-to-day activities. We will take a look at a number of them, including the new Query Tool.

Database Backup and Restore

The tools used to create and manage backup and restoration jobs appear in Enterprise Manager under the Tools menu. Using these tools, you can back up an entire database, its transaction log, its filegroups, and single or multiple files. The restoration tool allows you to restore an entire database and its transaction log, the transaction log only, the filegroups, or files only.

To back up a database using the new Backup Wizard, follow these steps:

1. Launch Enterprise Manager.
2. Expand the SQL Server where the database resides.
3. In the details pane, you see the Getting Started task pad. Select the Administer SQL Server icon.
4. Select the Back Up a Database icon.
5. Click Next at the welcome screen and choose the database to back up.
6. Click Next and type the name for the backup along with a description.
7. Select to back up the entire database and click Next to continue.
8. Select a device or file as the destination for the backup. Click Next to continue.
9. At the next window, you can set verification preferences along with schedule information.
10. Click Finish to create the backup task.

To restore a database using Enterprise Manager, follow these steps:

1. From Enterprise Manager, select the database to restore and right-click.
2. Select All Tasks, Restore Database.
3. You can choose to restore the database from a backup, filegroup, or device.
4. Select the Options tab to specify the transaction log settings.

By choosing a Point in Time Restore, you can specify a particular time and date from which to restore the database. This option is available only if you choose to restore a database. See Chapter 12 for more information on backing up and restoring a database.

> **NOTE**
>
> You can perform a backup while the database is in use. However, some actions cannot be taken during backups, such as creating indexes, shrinking the database, deleting database files, and nonlogged operations.

Database Object Transfer

Using the new DTS (Data Transformation Services), you can transfer database objects such as tables, views, stored procedures, indexes, rules, user roles, and logins between Microsoft SQL Servers. You can create a DTS job using one of the DTS wizards. To get access to the wizard, launch Run a Wizard by clicking the button on the toolbar. Expand Data Transformation Services and select one of the wizards. You can also gain access to DTS from the Data Transformation Services folder. Expand the SQL Server to view the DTS folder.

Query Tool ISQL/w

The new SQL Server Query Analyzer in SQL Server 7.0 has a new look and feel compared to the ISQL tool in older versions. Now, the main editor recognizes keywords, so when a user types a query statement, words such as select or from are displayed in a different color compared to the rest of the text.

Some of the tasks you can handle through the SQL Server Query Analyzer include creating and executing SQL Server scripts, querying SQL Server databases, performing index analysis, and returning query results in the form of a grid or text.

In the next exercise, we will execute a simple query to the master database.

Launch the SQL Server Query Analyzer from the menu bar:

1. From the menu bar, select Tools, SQL Server Query Analyzer.

2. Type the following:

   ```
   Select * from sysobjects
   ```

3. Press F5 to execute the query.

The screen will horizontally split and show the results in the bottom half of the screen, as shown in Figure 9.10.

FIGURE 9.10

A query executed against the master database.

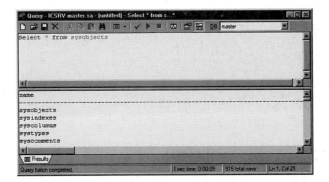

Working with the Visual Database Tools

The new visual database tools available in Microsoft SQL Server 7.0 will make an immediate impact on the lives of many administrators. Those administrators who rely on third-party tools to generate database designs or additional information about their existing servers will consider the new visual database tools a welcome addition.

Although these tools might not be as powerful as some third-party tools, they are certainly a step up from what was available in Microsoft SQL Server 6.x. With these new tools, an administrator can accomplish many tasks including graphically updating the database design, managing changes to the database, and building complex queries in a matter of minutes.

Using the Database Diagrammer

The Database Diagrammer allows you to view and modify database information. Viewable information includes columns within tables, indexes and constraints attached to tables, and relationships between tables. You can also use the tool to view different sce-

narios of the database structure without affecting the actual database. If you want, you can apply changes to the database after modifying the structure using the Database Diagrammer.

Creating Diagrams to Modify Database Structure

Using the Database Diagrammer, you can create tables, modify the existing table structure, and modify existing databases. In the following exercise, we will edit an existing table in the Northwind database and add a new table:

1. Launch Enterprise Manager.
2. Expand the SQL Server group and select the SQL Server.
3. Expand the server and expand the databases folder.
4. Expand the Northwind database.
5. Select the Diagrams icon and right-click; choose New Database Diagram.
6. The Create Database Diagram Wizard will launch. Click Next to continue.
7. Select the Employees table and select Add. Click Next to continue.
8. Select Finish to create the diagram.

Next, we will add a column to the table and then add a new table to the database:

1. From the toolbar, select the Show icon and choose to view the Column Properties for the table.
2. Add a new column to the table, as shown in Figure 9.11.

FIGURE 9.11

Editing the Employees table using the Database Diagrammer.

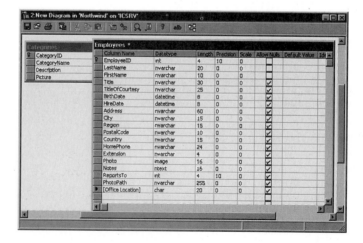

3. Right-click in the diagram window and select New Table.

4. Type MyTable for the table name and click OK.

5. Create new columns as desired and click the Save icon on the toolbar.

6. Type a name for the diagram and select Yes to save the changes to the database.

Expand the Northwind database and select the tables icon. In the details pane, you will find the newly created table. Double-click the Employees table to view the column you added.

Creating Diagrams to Document Database Structure

When dealing with extremely complicated databases, it is useful to have a structural diagram in front of you. However, the diagram is not helpful if no documentation describes aspects of the structure or if the diagram is congested and it is hard to decipher one table structure from the other.

Using the Database Diagram Wizard, we can diagram our database structure:

1. Launch Enterprise Manager.

2. Expand the server group and select SQL Server.

3. Expand the SQL Server and expand the Northwind database.

4. Select the Diagrams icon and right-click to choose New Database Diagram.

5. Click Next at the welcome screen.

6. Select the tables to be added to the diagram. Check Add Related Tables Automatically to have related tables diagrammed.

7. Click Next to continue.

8. Click Finish to complete the task.

You can zoom in or out by selecting the magnifying glass from the toolbar.

Annotating Database Diagrams

To create text annotation as part of the diagram, select New Text Annotation from the menu bar. In the text box, type the text required and click anywhere to get out of edit mode. Drag the text box by selecting the text and dragging it by the sides of the box. To increase or decrease the size of the box, select the text box and change the size by dragging on the squares on the corners and sides of the box.

9

**THE SQL SERVER
ENTERPRISE
MANAGER**

Defining Master Diagrams and Subdiagrams

Creating a master diagram along with subdiagrams allows you to view the database in more detail. First, you must create a master diagram; this diagram will contain all the tables that are part of the database. The subdiagram will contain the structure for a single table or multiple tables:

1. Create a master diagram.
2. Create a new database diagram.
3. From the Window menu, select Tile Horizontally.
4. From the master diagram, select the tables and copy them to the new subdiagram.

Using Database Diagrams to Manage Change Control

Using the Database Diagrammer, you can keep track of what changes are made to the database. You can roll back unwanted changes and apply specific changes to the database.

Source Code Control with Change Scripts

Change control scripts are saved to a text file named DbDgmiN.sql, where N represents the number for the change script. Each time you save the diagram, you have the option of creating a change script, which will allow you to keep track of changes, roll back from unwanted changes, or apply unsaved changes to the database.

To create a change script, complete the following:

1. Open any one of the tables in the Northwind database using the Database Diagrammer.
2. Edit the table by adding a new column.
3. Click the Save Change Script icon on the toolbar.
4. Click Yes to save the changes to the file.

You can view the script by opening the file in Notepad. The file is located in the MSSQL7/BIN directory. (MSSQL7 is located on the drive where SQL Server was installed.)

The change script will contain any error-handling code used to clean up temporary tables. In addition, it contains code to roll back transactions for unsuccessful changes.

Considerations in Multiuser Environments

If you are in an environment with more than one SQL Server administrator, using change control methods is imperative. By enforcing the use of change control scripts every time a database is changed, you can easily keep track of who made the changes, when they made those changes, and what those changes where.

Using the Query Designer

The Query Designer is a tool that administrators can use to build queries, change the database structure, and view the results of queries.

Diagram Pane

The diagram pane in Query Designer displays a graphical illustration of the current query. Additionally, the user can create table relationships by selecting columns from one table and creating the relationship with the other table.

Grid Pane

With the grid pane activated, a user can select the columns and tables needed to build the query via drop-down boxes.

SQL Pane

The SQL pane displays the T-SQL commands for the query being built. From here, you can also add your own T-SQL commands and run the query against the database.

Results Pane

The results pane displays the results of the query once it's executed.

Creating and Executing Queries

You can create and execute queries using the SQL pane, grid pane, and diagram pane. The following exercise outlines how you create and execute a query against the Employees table of the Northwind database.

1. Launch Enterprise Manager.
2. Expand the SQL Server group.
3. Expand the SQL Server.
4. Select the Northwind database and expand the tables object.
5. Select the Employees table from the details pane and right-click. Choose Open Table, Return All Rows.

6. The Query Designer will launch with the results pane visible. From the menu bar, select to show the grid pane and SQL pane.

7. Change the text in the SQL pane to the following (as shown in Figure 9.12):

```
Select * from Employees where employeeid > 2
```

FIGURE 9.12

Query built against the Employees table using the Query Designer.

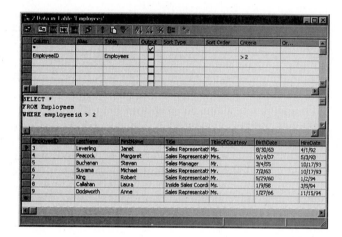

8. Click the exclamation icon on the menu bar to execute the query.

You will see the new results displayed in the results pane and the new query illustrated in the grid pane.

Parameter Queries

You can use parameter queries to help narrow down your resultset when building and executing a query. From the grid pane, you have the options of specifying parameters such as AND, >, and <.

Using Queries to Modify Data

You can build a query within the SQL pane and add T-SQL commands, which will let you modify the data or even database structure.

For further information on database design, see Chapter 23, "Database Design and Performance."

Database Management

A database contains objects such as tables, indexes, views, and stored procedures. In this section, we review the tools available in Enterprise Manager that you use to manage these objects.

Tables

When creating a table in Enterprise Manager, you must specify the table name, column names, and datatypes. Column names must be unique within each table, and each column must have a datatype.

In the next exercise, we will create a table in the Northwind database. Name the table HOME_ADDRESS and give the columns the following attributes:

Column Name	Datatype		Length
Employee_Name	Char	20	
Street_Address	Char	25	
City	Char	20	
Zip	Numeric	10	
Last_Updated	Date	8	

1. From Enterprise Manager, select the Northwind database.

2. Click to expand the database.

3. Select Tables and right-click New Table.

4. Type the name for the table.

5. Enter the column information.

6. Click the Save icon on the Table Design toolbar to save the table.

7. Close the window to exit.

> **NOTE**
>
> Unlike previous versions of Microsoft SQL Server, version 7.0 allows you to change column definitions without having to drop the table and recreate it.

9

THE SQL SERVER
ENTERPRISE
MANAGER

Double-click the Tables icon under the Northwind database. In the details pane, you will find the newly created table. Right-click the new table. Select Properties to view information regarding the table and its columns. Click Permissions to manage the permissions to the table. Exit the properties screen and right-click once more.

In addition to viewing the properties for the table, you can rename, copy, and delete the table. Selecting Open Table allows you to view the actual data in the table and selecting Design Table puts you back into design mode. From the All Tasks menu, you can manage indexes, triggers, permissions, and import and export data. Choosing Create New

Publication launches the Create Publication Wizard. Using this wizard, you can publish the data so it is available to other Microsoft SQL Servers. We will discuss this subject later in the chapter in the section "Installing Publishers."

You can generate SQL scripts and view dependencies for your table. It is a good idea to generate a SQL script once you have created the table and its objects. Creating a script allows you to easily recreate the table and all its objects as they were defined.

Indexes

The benefit to creating indexes comes mainly from performance. When you query or manipulate data, the process can be more efficient if you use indexes. To create an index, select the table where the index will be created and right-click. From the All Tasks menu, select Manage Indexes:

1. Select New and type a name for the index.
2. Select the columns to index (see Figure 9.13). You can change the column order with the Move Up or Move Down button.

FIGURE 9.13

Creating a new index on the Employees table of the Northwind database.

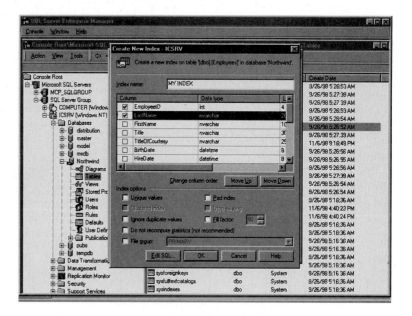

3. Click Edit SQL to change or view the SQL text for the index.
4. Click OK.

Triggers, Views, and Stored Procedures

Triggers enforce restrictions upon data entry, rejecting and rolling back changes that violate referential integrity and cascading changes throughout the database.

To create a trigger, select the table where the trigger will be created and right-click.

1. Select All Tasks.

2. Select Manage Triggers.

3. You can edit the SQL in the Text box to create the trigger. The following code creates a trigger that reminds the user to send out a report when changes are made to the Employees table:

```
CREATE TRIGGER reminder ON Employees
FOR INSERT, UPDATE, DELETE
AS
EXEC master..xp_sendmail 'Troberts',
'Send an updated report to HR with the changes you made'
```

4. Click the Check Syntax button to check the SQL and click OK to create the trigger.

   When you go back to manage the trigger, remember to select the name for the trigger from the drop-down box.

Views allow you to control the data users can see. A view not only consists of data retrieved from a single table but also can consist of data retrieved from multiple tables.

To create a view on the Northwind database, follow these steps:

1. Click the Northwind database to expand it.

2. Select the Views icon and right-click.

3. Select New View.

4. The Query Designer will launch. From the menu bar, select Add Table.

5. Select the Employees table and click Add.

6. Select the columns to be viewed.

7. Select Add Table from the menu bar.

8. Select the Customers table.

9. Select the columns to be viewed.

10. Click the Run icon to execute the view.

11. Click the Save icon to save the view.

Views can have permissions set; you can restrict which users can view the data retrieved. Expand the database and select the Views icon, select the newly created view, and right-click. From the Properties menu, you can check the T-SQL syntax and set the permissions. Permissions govern who can view data retrieved by the view and what type of data they can view.

Similar to the Open Table option, you can select Open View to view the actual data of the view. Selecting design view launches Query Designer so that you can edit the view using the SQL, grid, or diagram pane. From the All Tasks menu, you can select to manage permissions, generate SQL scripts, or display dependencies. In the following exercise, we will generate a SQL script for the view created in the previous exercise.

1. From the All Task menu, select Generate SQL Scripts.
2. Objects belonging to the Northwind database are displayed in the window. Scroll down until you find the view.
3. Click Add.
4. Click OK to generate the script.

For tasks you perform frequently or tasks that rely on the successful completion of previously executed commands, you can write a stored procedure to simplify the process:

1. Expand the database.
2. Select Stored Procedures and right-click.
3. Select New Stored Procedure. In the text box, type the T-SQL text.
4. Click Check Syntax to check the T-SQL text.
5. Click OK when done.

User-Defined Datatypes

User-defined datatypes are based on the system datatypes available in Microsoft SQL Server 7.0. User-defined datatypes are useful in keeping the data consistent within the database.

Follow these steps to define your own datatype:

1. Expand the database.
2. Select User Defined Data Types and right-click.
3. Select New User Defined Data Type and type the name for your datatype.
4. Select the datatype and type the length (see Figure 9.14).

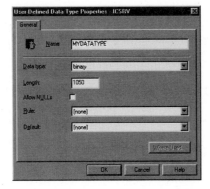

FIGURE 9.14

Creating a new user-defined datatype named MYDATATYPE.

5. If there are any predefined rules or defaults you would like to apply to the datatype, do so at this time and click OK to complete the task.

As with tables, views, and triggers, you can view additional information for the datatype by selecting the datatype and choosing Properties. From the Properties menu, selecting Where Used will list all the columns where the datatype is in use.

Object Permissions

In previous sections, we have reviewed the process for creating database objects. In this section, we will review the methodology for assigning permissions to these objects. You can set permissions by user or object.

Setting Permissions by User

By selecting a user from the Users object for a database, you can assign specific access to objects for that user. In the following exercise, we will assign a user access to the Customer and Suppliers by City view for the Northwind database:

1. Launch Enterprise Manager.
2. Expand the server.
3. Expand the Northwind database folder.
4. Select the Users object. In the details pane, select the user, right-click, and choose Properties.
5. Click the Permissions button.
6. You see listed all the database objects, such as tables, stored procedures, and views. Select the Customer and Suppliers by City view. Specify the type of access: SELECT, INSERT, or UPDATE.

Setting Permissions by Object

Setting permissions by object is useful if multiple users need access to an object. For more information on security, see Chapter 10.

To assign a user access to a stored procedure, follow these steps:

1. Launch Enterprise Manager.
2. Expand the SQL Server.
3. Expand the Northwind database.
4. Select Stored Procedures. From the details pane, select the Sales by Year stored procedure.
5. Right-click and select All Tasks, Manage Permissions.
6. Select the user and set the permissions.

Replication

Replicating data between Microsoft SQL Servers has become a need in more environments. Replication can involve sending and receiving data for the sake of redundancy or faster availability. Enterprise Manager has built-in wizards that can help manage the task of replication. For more information on replication, see Chapter 20, "Replication."

Installing Publishers

A publisher server has data that is published to another Microsoft SQL Server. This data could consist of master data, reports, or lists.

To install a publisher using Enterprise Manager, perform the following steps:

1. Launch Enterprise Manager.
2. Expand a server group and select SQL Server.
3. From the menu bar, select Tools, Replication, Create and Manage Publications.
4. Select the database to publish (see Figure 9.15).
5. The Create Publication Wizard will launch. Click Next to continue.
6. Click Next to specify the current server as the distributor server.
7. You will see the SQL Server Agent property settings. Click OK to continue.
8. Select the publication type and click Next.
9. Select Yes to allow Immediate-Updating Subscriptions and click Next.
10. Select the type of subscriber and click Next.

11. Select the articles to be published and click Next.

12. Specify the publication name and click Next.

13. Click Finish to complete the task.

FIGURE 9.15

Selecting the Northwind Database to be published by the SQL Server named ICSRV.

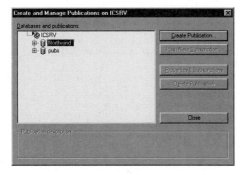

Setting Up Subscribers

Subscriber servers receive published data from either publisher or distributor servers. To install a subscriber server using Enterprise Manager, perform the following steps:

1. Launch Enterprise Manager.

2. Expand a server group and select SQL Server.

3. From the menu bar, select Tools, Replication, Pull Subscription to.

4. Click the button Pull New Subscription.

5. The Pull Subscription Wizard will launch. Click Next to continue.

6. Expand the distribution server and select the publication (see Figure 9.16). Click Next to continue.

FIGURE 9.16

Selecting the Northwind database for the subscription.

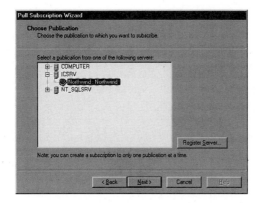

9

THE SQL SERVER ENTERPRISE MANAGER

7. Type the login information for the SQL Server Agent.

8. Select an existing database or create a new database where the subscription will be created.

9. Click Next to start the initialization process as scheduled.

10. Set the schedule for the distribution agent and click Next.

11. Click Next after verifying the service's startup status.

12. Click Finish to complete the task.

Getting Help

Microsoft SQL Enterprise Manager offers many online help features. The online help comes in the form of Books Online, online help for individual tasks, and new wizards. You can access the new wizards from the main menu bar.

The wizards belong to four categories: database, data transformation services, management, and replication. In the following exercise, we will launch one of the database wizards to create a new login.

1. From the toolbar, click Run a Wizard.

2. Expand the Database Wizard folder.

3. Double-click the Create Login Wizard.

4. Click Next at the welcome screen.

5. Select SQL Server authentication.

6. Type Wizard for the login ID and server for the password.

7. Select Database Creators for the security role and click Next.

8. Select Northwind for the database and click Next.

9. Click Finish to complete the wizard.

Summary

Microsoft SQL Enterprise Manager is a tool all administrators can find useful on an everyday basis. For this reason, it is important that any administrator understand the capabilities that Enterprise Manager has to offer. Microsoft SQL Server 7.0 introduces many new features and enhancements. An administrator who understands what the tool can do for her will spend less time learning how to do something and more time doing it.

Security and User Administration

by Greg Mable

CHAPTER 10

This chapter describes the security model on which SQL Server bases its security. You will learn how to administrate user accounts and apply permissions to database objects. This chapter also covers the use of database roles and how SQL Server is integrated with the Windows NT operating system.

An Overview of SQL Server Security

You can view SQL Server's security as operating at two different levels. The first level, authentication, is the layer that verifies that a given user who attempts to connect to SQL Server can be verified as having access to the system: The person is who he says he is, and the person has been granted access to the system. The second level, permissions, is applied at the object level. Once a user has been verified as the user and as having the access rights, the next level to check is whether the user has the appropriate permissions. One is the object level, and the other is the command level. To summarize, once the user has been verified and once the user's rights have been verified, the user can access the system or perform the function. Let's look at each of these layers more closely.

Authentication

Authentication is the process of validating a user's identity and access rights. SQL Server implements two different methods of authentication: Windows NT authentication and mixed security. Basically, the two different methods determine where the authentication takes place. Will the operating system perform the authentication, or will SQL Server do it? Because SQL Server runs on multiple platforms, including Windows 95/98, no single method works across all platforms.

Windows NT Authentication

In the early days of Windows NT and SQL Server, it was frustrating for users to remember the many passwords they had, and in those days, little, if anything, could be done about it. A typical user had a separate user ID and password for the network, SQL Server, email, and other application services. Now, the subsequent releases of SQL Server and Windows NT developed a method that integrates the accounts on the two systems. Integrated security, or as it is now known, Windows NT authentication, can synchronize the accounts between Windows NT and SQL Server. This mode of authentication introduces a term you may have encountered before: the concept of *trusted connections*. Trusted connections are network connections that operate over protocols which support authenticated connections between clients and servers. SQL Server supports the use of trusted connections, so you can manage SQL Server users from a single point of administration. No longer do you need to maintain a separate set of user IDs and passwords for SQL Server. You can simply use the trusted connection between SQL Server and Windows NT and maintain one set of user IDs and passwords in Windows NT. Once a user has been authenticated by the network, SQL Server will automatically authenticate the user using trusted connections. When the user accesses SQL Server, the user will not get a login dialog. Instead, the user, if given the appropriate permissions, will immediately receive access to SQL Server.

> **NOTE**
>
> Keep in mind, though, that the Windows NT authentication mode is available only on systems running SQL Server under Windows NT. It isn't available on systems running SQL Server under Windows 95 or 98.

Mixed Security

In addition to Windows NT authentication, SQL Server provides a mode of security known as mixed mode. In mixed mode, both Windows NT authentication and SQL Server authentication are used to validate user access. In particular, SQL Server authentication is used on SQL Server systems running under Windows 95/98 because these environments do not employ the Windows NT security database.

Permissions

Permissions in SQL Server are specified on two levels: The first is the object level, and the second is the statement level. Object-level permissions include the right to read, modify, and delete objects. For example, the ability to read, modify, and delete data in a table requires that the user have object-level permissions granted on the table before making changes. Object permissions comprise the ability to execute the select, insert, update, and delete statements on a table or view, as well as the ability to execute stored procedures.

Statement-level permissions are granted on the SQL statements that create database objects, such as the create table statement or the backup commands. These statements include the create table, database, view, rule, default, and stored procedure commands, as well as the backup database and log commands.

By separating the permissions into two levels, SQL Server makes it possible for an administrator to distinguish users who have the ability to create objects in the database from users who have the ability to read or modify objects in the database.

10

SECURITY AND USER ADMINISTRATION

SQL Server Security: Logins

SQL Server maintains a set of user login IDs that identify a user and give the user access to SQL Server. These may originate in a Windows NT security database or within SQL Server itself. These login IDs are also separate and distinct from user IDs, which allows a given login ID to have different user IDs associated with it. For example, the login ID Joseph could have Joe as his user ID in the Sales database and Joseph as his user ID in the Service database. The separation of a database user ID and the login ID permits a user to be known by one name in the system and by another name in the database. For example, a user's login ID might be somewhat cryptic or unfriendly, such as JosephMable3. You can define his user ID in the database as Joseph, which is a much friendlier name.

When SQL Server is installed, the system creates a special login called sa (system administrator). The sa login is a member of the sysadmin fixed server role and cannot be removed. In previous releases of SQL Server, the sa login was used as the primary means to administer the server.

> **TIP**
>
> I highly recommend that you create separate login IDs, assign them to the sysadmin role, and grant them to users who will perform administrative tasks rather than using sa. This allows you to remove users from the sysadmin role as needed and reserve the sa login for those occasions when it is absolutely necessary. I also recommend that you immediately assign a password to the sa login because one is not assigned by default.

SQL Server Security: Users

Every database created in SQL Server will contain a set of users who are allowed access to the database. The users of the database are specific to each database defined on SQL Server. The user John in the database Sales is distinct from the user John in the database Service. John might refer to the same person, but it might not. The identity of a user is specific to the database in which the user is defined.

SQL Server defines two special users that exist in every database defined on the system. The first user, dbo, is considered the owner of the database and by default is the owner of all objects in the database. The second user, guest, is a user that exists as a means to give a user access to the database without creating a user account especially for the person. Let's examine these two special users in more detail.

dbo

The dbo is a special user that exists in every database. The dbo is the database owner, and as such, this user cannot be deleted from the database. Any member of the sysadmin server role is automatically mapped to dbo in each database.

> **NOTE**
>
> When referencing objects created by the dbo, such as a table or stored procedure, you do not need to preface the object name with its owner. For example, in the database Pubs, because the authors table was created by the dbo, you do not need to prefix the table name with its owner name. You can simply refer to the authors table. However, for all other objects not created by the dbo, you will need to prefix the object name with its owner name. For example, if the user Joseph creates a table called Sales_Quotes, a user who makes a reference to the table must specify `Joseph.Sales_Quotes` in the SQL statement. Otherwise, SQL Server will attempt to reference the table dbo.Sales_Quotes.

guest

The guest user account permits a login without a user account to access a database. This will occur when a user with a login ID attempts to access a database and

- The login ID does not have a corresponding user ID in the database.
- The database contains a guest user account.

You can add and delete the guest user account from any database except the master and tempdb databases. By default, the guest user account is not added to any new database created in the system. However, you can change this default by adding the guest user to the model database. The model database is a template on which all newly created databases are built.

SQL Server Security: Roles

In the architecture of SQL Server security, database roles are similar to groups in previous versions of SQL Server. However, unlike group members, members of a database role can belong to more than one role. Prior versions of SQL Server limited users to membership in a single role or group. SQL Server 7.0 employs the concept of a role rather than a group to denote that members of a role perform some sort of function,

10

SECURITY AND
USER
ADMINISTRATION

either at the server level or at the database level. *Role* is a more descriptive term than *group*, and it captures the idea of a specific function given to a group of users, such as the backup operator role. SQL Server predefines a set of roles at the server level and at the database level. These roles are fixed, meaning that you cannot delete them. This provides consistency between SQL Server installations. You will always find a sysadmin or db_backupoperator role at any SQL Server installation.

The Public Role

By default, all users of a database are members of the public role. No users or other roles can be added or removed from this role because everyone is a member of this role by definition. The public role is useful as a means for you to configure the default permissions that apply in the database. For example, to make your database secure, you could revoke from all members of the public role all permissions to all objects in the database. Then, when a new user is added to the system, you will be assured that the user has only the object permissions that have been explicitly granted to the user.

Fixed Server Roles

Fixed server roles exist independently of any databases defined on the system. These built-in roles serve as a means for you to grant systemwide privileges to a user who requires them. With prior versions of SQL Server, you were unable to grant authority to a user if you wanted to allow him a certain level of privilege. Quite often, SQL Server functions in a corporate environment where various users serve different responsibilities. One person (group) is the Windows NT administrator. Another person (group) is the email administrator, and another person (group) is the database administrator. With previous versions of SQL Server, you had to be the Windows NT administrator to effectively administrate SQL Server. With the new version of SQL Server, the concept of systemwide server roles lets you assign a person or group to various administrative functions. You can assign a total of seven server roles. Even though you cannot create any new server roles, plenty of roles already exist on the server. Membership in these roles is cumulative; that is, permissions and rights inherited from different role membership are cumulative. Let's examine each of these server roles more closely and understand how you can use them to ease the administrative tasks for SQL Server.

sysadmin

The sysadmin role exists above all other roles and has the authority to perform any activity in SQL Server. It is the role assigned to the sa login created by default during installation. Windows NT users who are members of the BUILTIN\Administrators group are automatically made members of the sysadmin fixed server role.

serveradmin

The serveradmin role is used to grant a user the authority to make changes to SQL Server's configuration. This would include how much physical memory is dedicated to SQL Server and how much is dedicated to the operating system. This role would be useful to someone who is charged with maintaining the computer on which SQL Server runs. This person does not necessarily have to be a database administrator or understand how SQL Server works. This role would allow you to control who has the authority to make changes to the SQL Server's configuration. For example, you might develop an application that runs on SQL Server, and you install the application at a customer site. You want to ensure that SQL Server's configuration is not changed by anyone except those who have been given this responsibility. You can simply add the user to this server role and thus prevent unauthorized changes.

setupadmin

The setupadmin role is a role that you can assign a user (group) when you want to manage who has control over the setup of replication on the system and the extended stored procedures that are installed. This role would be useful in a situation in which the database administrator maintains the database and an application administrator maintains the development of the extended stored procedures, which systems are replicated, and how replication is implemented on the system. Often, the role that a database administrator plays focuses on the database and its objects. The setupadmin role exists to provide the ability for someone besides the database administrator to configure replication or manage the extended stored procedures defined on the system.

securityadmin

The securityadmin role is one that you might learn to appreciate immediately. The securityadmin role allows a user (group) the ability to manage SQL Server logins. This role would be appropriate in environments where database and network administration are managed by two different users or groups. This would allow network administrators to add SQL Server logins via Windows NT accounts and then allow SQL-Server–related tasks to be managed by some other person or group. Often, a database administrator in a corporate environment works in conjunction with a network administrator. In prior versions of SQL Server, the network administrator had to be given system administrator rights on SQL Server because there was no other way to manage SQL Server logins. A network administrator had to perform this function because it involved the Windows NT domain accounts. Thus, the network administrator would subsequently be given sa authority, which does not make for the most secure environment.

10

SECURITY AND USER ADMINISTRATION

processadmin

As another role that you might learn to appreciate, the processadmin role allows a user (group) to manage the processes running under SQL Server. This is particularly useful when you want to terminate a user process or query that has run astray. In previous versions of SQL Server, you had to be the system administrator to terminate a process running on SQL Server. With this version of SQL Server, you can designate someone (group) to manage processes running on SQL Server and grant her the ability to terminate a process, such as a user's ad hoc query that is overtaxing the server's resources. This provides you with the ability to delegate this responsibility to another user (group) without granting the person system administrator rights.

dbcreator

The dbcreator role gives a user (group) the ability to create and alter databases on SQL Server. This role would be useful in an environment where you want to delegate the responsibility of creating and maintaining databases to another person or group. For example, in a development environment, you could assign a user to the dbcreator role and allow the user to create and alter databases as needed without giving the user full administrative privileges on the system.

diskadmin

The diskadmin role gives a user (group) the ability to create disk files. Databases are defined in SQL Server as a set of operating system files. This diskadmin role can be used in conjunction with the dbcreator role to give a user or group the ability to create and maintain databases on SQL Server. This would be useful in a development environment where developers are creating and modifying a database or databases as the project progresses.

Fixed Database Roles

Unlike fixed server roles, fixed database roles are defined on a per-database level. Each database has the same set of predefined or fixed database roles. Unlike fixed server roles, with fixed database roles, you are free to create new database roles as you see the need to do so. Let's examine each of these fixed database roles in more detail and take a look at how you can use them in a typical SQL Server environment.

db_owner

The db_owner role is the role assigned to a user (group) that is the owner of the database. Like the system administrator and serveradmin role, the db_owner role can perform any activity in the database, including all the activities of other roles defined in the database, as well as configuration and maintenance tasks.

db_accessadmin

The db_accessadmin role gives a user (group) the ability to add or remove Windows NT groups, Windows NT users, and SQL Server users from the database. This role would be useful when you want to delegate the task of managing users in a database to another person. This would be especially relevant for remote sites or in environments where you are responsible for the setup and maintenance of an application that runs on SQL Server but would like to delegate the task of user administration to someone local to the site.

db_datareader

The db_datareader role permits the user (group) to select data from any user-defined table in the database. This role would be useful in an environment where user-defined tables are periodically created and you want to ensure that a given user will be able to read the data without any extra effort on your part. You can make the user a member of this group, and the user will be able to read the data in the tables as they are created.

db_datawriter

The db_datawriter role is similar to the db_datareader role except that members of this role have the ability to insert, update, or delete permissions on any user-defined table in the database. This role would be useful in a environment where you want to ensure that a given user will be able to add, modify, and delete data from any table in the database. This setup would be especially helpful in a development environment where tables are constantly defined, and you want to avoid the nuisance of having to grant permissions to users in the database to make changes to these tables. If they are members of the db_datawriter role, they will be able to make changes to any of the tables.

db_ddladmin

The db_ddladmin role allows its members to create, modify, and remove objects from the database. DDL is an abbreviation for data definition language, which is the nomenclature used to describe the SQL commands that create and modify database objects such as tables, indexes, and so on. This role would be useful in an environment where you want to centralize the DDL functions to a limited group of users.

db_securityadmin

The db_securityadmin role allows its members to create and maintain database roles and their members, as well as manage permissions in the database. This role would be useful in an environment where you want to delegate the responsibility of role administration and permissions to another user (group). For example, this role would be useful at a site where you install an application that runs on SQL Server and you want to delegate the administration of users and permissions to someone local to the site. With this role, the person or group can make the security-related changes for you while you still retain authority over other aspects of the database server.

db_backupoperator

Members of the db_backupoperator role can back up the database. Granting this role is useful in a production environment where you want to delegate the responsibility of backing up the database to a user (group) without having to grant the user any other rights in the database or server.

db_denydatareader

The db_denydatareader role is the inverse of the db_datareader role. Members of this group are denied the ability to select data from any user-defined table in the database. This would be useful when you want to ensure that a given user or group is unable to view any data in the database.

db_denydatawriter

The db_denydatawriter role is the inverse of the db_datawriter role. Members of this group are denied the ability to insert, update, and delete permission on any user-defined table in the database. This role would be useful when you want to ensure that a given user or group is unable to make changes to the database.

Configuring Windows NT Authentication

When SQL Server is first installed, it is configured to run in mixed mode. Mixed mode is the default authentication mode to provide backward compatibility with previous versions of SQL Server. Once SQL Server is installed, you can configure SQL Server's default security options using Enterprise Manager, as shown in Figure 10.1.

Let's examine each of these options as shown on the Security tab, which is found on the Properties page for a given SQL Server. Using Enterprise Manager, you highlight the server name in the left pane of the management console, right-click to select the Properties page for this SQL Server, and then select the Security tab from the resulting dialog window.

FIGURE 10.1

*Configuring SQL
Server security
options in
Enterprise
Manager.*

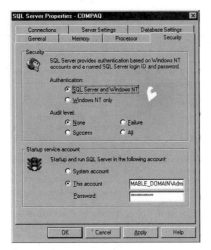

To enable Windows NT authentication only, simply select the corresponding check box.

> **CAUTION**
>
> When selecting the Windows NT Only option, be aware that many applications that were written to run under prior versions of SQL Server might rely on SQL Server authentication services and will fail to run.

In addition to specifying the authentication mode used by SQL Server, you can specify the level of auditing, if any, to perform when a user attempts to log in to the server. By default, auditing of login attempts is not enabled. You can specify audit login attempts that are successful, unsuccessful, or both.

The other option that appears on this property page is the option to designate the account under which SQL Server executes. By default, SQL Server will execute under the local system account.

> **NOTE**
>
> When SQL Server is configured to run under the local system account, you need to be aware that this account cannot access any resource outside of the local computer. This may or may not present a problem, depending on your particular environment.

10

SECURITY AND
USER
ADMINISTRATION

Managing SQL Server Logins

Using Enterprise Manager, you can easily add, modify, and delete SQL Server login IDs. To manage SQL Server logins, you highlight the server name shown in the left pane of the Enterprise Manager's management console and expand its entries. In the expanded list of objects, you will find a folder labeled Logins. You can simply right-click this folder and select New Login. You will then see the dialog window shown in Figure 10.2.

FIGURE 10.2

A SQL Server New Login Properties page: General settings.

In this configuration dialog window, you specify the login name for the user. Then you can specify, depending upon which authentication mode you select for this account, the Windows NT domain account and whether to grant or deny access to this user, or you can specify a password for SQL Server authentication. The last option on this window allows you to set the defaults for this login. When a user connects to SQL Server, you can automatically connect the user to a default database and language.

The second property page allows you to manage the login's membership in the fixed server roles, as shown in Figure 10.3.

You can simply select to which fixed server roles this login ID will be given membership. If you want to see what permissions apply to a given server role, you can select the Properties button to open a Server Role Properties dialog window. From this dialog window, you can select the Permissions property page. This page shows the permissions that are granted to the given fixed server role, as shown in Figure 10.4.

Figure 10.3

The Server Roles tab.

Figure 10.4

Permissions.

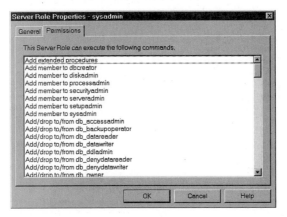

The last tab of the New Login properties pages is the Database Access property page, shown in Figure 10.5.

On this page, you can specify to which databases the login will be granted access. You also specify the user ID that will be used by the login when accessing the given database. By default, the user ID is given the same name as the login ID.

FIGURE 10.5

The Database Access tab.

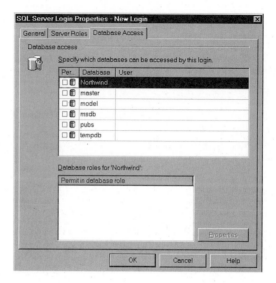

Running the Create Login Wizard

There is an alternative way to create a new login in SQL Server. You can run the Create Login Wizard. This wizard will walk you through the steps outlined in the previous section. You access this wizard from the Tools menu option. Select Tools, Wizards, and then expand the listing under the Database entry. Within this entry, you will find the Create Login Wizard. When you execute this wizard, it will open the first of a series of dialog windows.

The next dialog window, as shown in Figure 10.6, allows you to specify which authentication mode to use for this login ID.

FIGURE 10.6

The Create Login Wizard authentication mode.

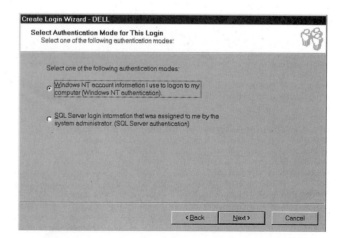

If you select the Windows NT authentication mode, you are presented with the access dialog in Figure 10.7.

FIGURE **10.7**

Windows NT
authentication.

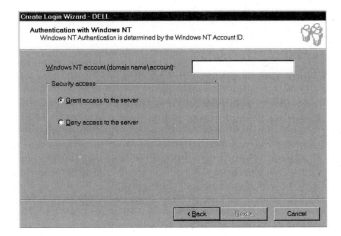

On this screen, you specify the Windows NT user account to use as the login ID and whether the specified login ID will be granted or denied access to SQL Server.

If you select SQL Server authentication mode, you are presented with a screen in which you simply enter the user's login ID and password. For SQL Server installations running on Windows 95/98 computers, this is the only option available.

The next dialog, shown in Figure 10.8, allows you to specify for which fixed server roles this login ID will be given membership.

FIGURE **10.8**

Server roles.

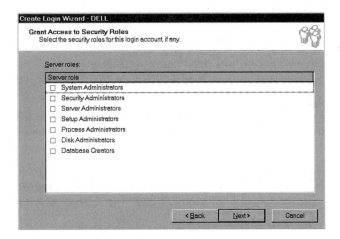

The next dialog, shown in Figure 10.9, allows you to specify for which databases this login ID will be given access. The wizard will create a user account with the same name as the login ID for each database that you select.

FIGURE 10.9

Database access.

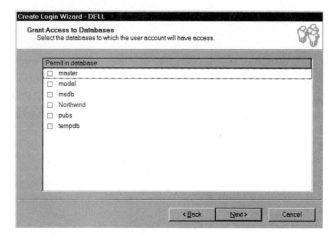

The last dialog window in the Create Login Wizard is a review screen that summarizes the selections you have made. You can easily navigate back to any of the previous screens to make any adjustments.

Managing SQL Server Users

You can use Enterprise Manager to administer SQL Server user accounts. From the left pane of the management console, highlight the server name and expand its objects, and under each database that has been defined on the server, you will find a folder labeled Database Users. Inside this folder, you will find all the users defined for the database. To edit an existing user, you can double-click the username. To add a new user, you can right-click one of the users and select New Database User. The dialog in Figure 10.10 will be displayed.

From this screen, you can specify the SQL Server login ID to be associated with the new database user, a database username, and any database roles to which you want the new user to belong.

For an existing user in the database, you can manage the permissions that apply to the user by first right-clicking the user's name in the Users folder and selecting Properties. This displays a window that lists the username and the database roles for which the user is a member. You can then click the Permissions button next to the username. This will display a dialog window similar to the one in Figure 10.11.

FIGURE 10.10

*SQL Server
Database User
Properties.*

FIGURE 10.11

*SQL Server
Database User
Permissions.*

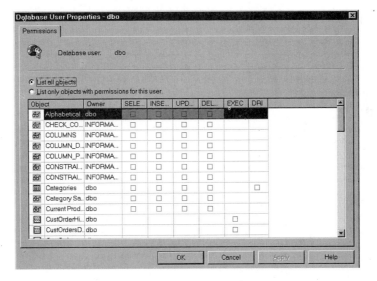

From this screen, you can apply various permissions to the user on any of the objects in the database. By default, this screen lists all objects in the database. It lists the name of the object and its owner, followed by a set of columns that designate the type of statement that can be performed on the object. These are select, insert, update, delete, execute, and DRI. DRI relates to ANSI compatibility for referential constraints. If checked, a reference to the table by another table will require the user to have select permission on the given table.

Those columns that contain check boxes are the columns that can be applied to the corresponding object. Marking the column using your mouse means that permission has been granted on the object for that statement. Those columns marked with an *X* are denied permission for that statement. Any check box left empty means that permission on the object has been revoked. You can filter the screen so that it will display only those objects to which the user has permissions applied.

Managing SQL Server Roles

Using SQL Server Enterprise Manager, you can administer SQL Server roles and their memberships. First, you highlight the server name in the left pane of the management console, and then, you expand its objects. In the list of objects, you will find under each database a folder labeled Database Roles. If you double-click this folder, it will display all the database roles for the given database. These roles include the fixed database roles and any user-defined database roles. To create a new database role, you can right-click the name of an existing role and then select Create New Database Role from the menu. This will display a dialog window similar to the one shown in Figure 10.12.

FIGURE 10.12

SQL Server Database Role Properties.

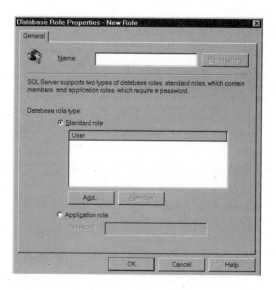

Using this screen, you can give the database role a name and then add existing members of the database (users and other database roles) to the database role. By default, the type of role created is a standard role. You can also specify that the role is an application. See the section later in this chapter "Granting Permissions Using Application Roles." For an existing database role, you can modify its role membership and permissions by double-clicking the role name displayed in the database role folder from Enterprise Manager. You then select the Permissions button located on the screen next to the database role name. It will display a dialog window similar to Figure 10.13.

FIGURE 10.13

SQL Server Database Role Permissions.

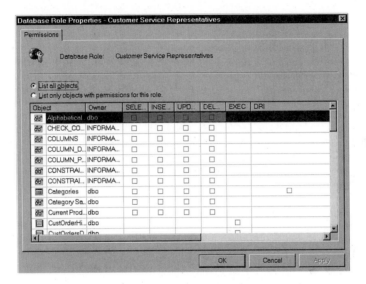

Using this screen, you can manage the permissions that the role has to any of the objects in the database. This screen is similar to the one used to manage database users. You can also filter objects on this screen to include only those objects that have permissions applied to this database role.

Managing SQL Server Permissions

As you have learned in the previous sections, you can manage SQL Server permissions using Enterprise Manager. In general, you can manage permissions on an object in SQL Server from Enterprise Manager. You simply highlight the object, right-click its name, and select its properties page. From the resulting dialog window, you can click a Permissions button to apply permissions on the object. For example, Figure 10.14 illustrates the permissions that can be applied to the stored procedure. Because it is a stored procedure, the only column that has a check box is the Execute column.

FIGURE 10.14

*SQL Server
Object
Permissions: a
stored procedure.*

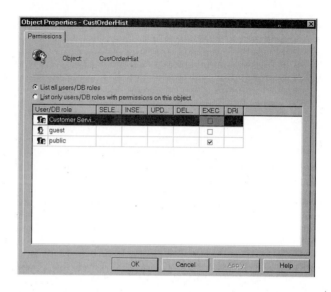

You can also use Enterprise Manager to manage permissions at the statement level. In
the left pane of the management console, you highlight the name of the database, right-
click its name, select Properties, and then select the Permissions property page. You will
see a screen similar to Figure 10.15.

FIGURE 10.15

*SQL Server state-
ment Permissions.*

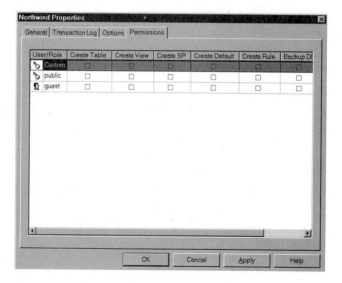

From this screen, you can manage which users and roles will have the ability to execute the statements. For this and all other permission screens, you mark the check box with a check mark to grant permission and mark the check box with an *X* to deny permission; a check box that is left unmarked is treated as a revoked permission. Revoking permission on an object or statement means that the user is denied permission. However, this does not guarantee that the user will not inherit the permission through membership in a database role that has been granted permission on the object or statement. For example, if the select permission on the table authors in the database pubs for the user Joseph is revoked, but Joseph is a member of a role called Writers that has been granted select permission, then Joseph will be able to select from the Authors table. If, however, Joseph had been *denied* rather than *revoked* the select permission, then Joseph would not be able to select from the authors table even though he inherits the right from membership in the Writers role.

> **NOTE**
>
> Denying permission always overrides any other permission on the object or statement. If a user is explicitly denied permission on an object or statement, or if the user inherits the denied permission, then the user will not be permitted any rights even if the user is explicitly granted permission. Deny permission always takes precedence.

SQL Server Permission Approaches

This section discusses the various approaches that you can take in applying permissions on SQL Server databases. Starting with the simplest model and working up, each approach is reviewed with the idea of ease of use while maintaining database integrity.

public

Because every user is automatically a member of the public role, you can simply apply permissions on database objects and statements with the public role. This is the simplest approach, but it is also the most restrictive. Everyone is given the same set of permissions, and no exceptions are made for any users.

public and guest

You can enhance the public permission approach described previously by applying permissions to the guest user. The guest user can be given a set of permissions that are different from the ones given to the public role. SQL Server then automatically uses the guest account whenever someone who does not have a database user ID accesses the database.

Granting Permissions to User-Defined Roles

You can manage permissions on database objects and statements through the creation of user-defined roles. By creating your own database roles and applying the permissions appropriate for that role, you can easily manage permissions for a large number of users. This is certainly preferable to granting permissions to each individual database user ID.

Granting Permissions Using Views

In addition to managing permissions with user-defined roles, you can also create database views and grant permissions on them to the appropriate roles. Using a view is one way of ensuring that users do not have access to data that is not appropriate for them. A view will hide the data and columns that you specify in your create view statement. You can then apply permissions to those roles that need to access the view. For a more in-depth discussion about views in SQL Server, see Chapter 8, "Logical Database Architecture."

Granting Permissions Using Stored Procedures

Another method to grant permissions on database objects and statements is to create stored procedures that contain the necessary SQL statements. Rather than grant permissions for database users to modify data directly using SQL statements, you can create stored procedures that make the modifications for them and then grant execute permission on the stored procedures to the appropriate database users. In this way, you can be assured that no user can make any changes to the database without your having explicitly granted the authority.

Granting Permissions Using Application Roles

Application roles are a new feature of SQL Server security. In the past, applications written to run on SQL Server would commonly implement their own form of security and would present the user with a logon dialog window. The application would receive the username and password and then check SQL Server for a corresponding username and password. Many of these applications would apply the same set of permissions for all the users of the application. It did not matter with which user ID you signed on. The application verified your user ID and then granted you access to run the application.

With application roles, you now have the ability to give the application its own database role. You can then apply permissions on objects and statements to the application role. When the application executes, instead of prompting the user for a user ID and password, it will pass SQL Server its application role name and password. SQL Server will then authenticate the application role before granting access to the database.

By definition, application roles contain no members. They are used by an application only and require a password. You can create them in the same way that you create other database roles, by indicating the type of database role—either a standard role or an application role in the dialog. (Refer to the previous section "Managing SQL Server Roles.")

Encryption

In addition to all the security mechanisms discussed so far, SQL Server also provides encryption services. For example, all passwords stored in the database are encrypted. No user, including the system administrator, can see a user's password. SQL Server can also encrypt all the data on the network communication link, provided the multiprotocol Net-Library is used. Finally, SQL Server can encrypt all stored procedure, view, and trigger definitions. This protects your investment in the code that you develop. You simply specify the `with encryption` option when creating them.

Summary

In this chapter, you learned how SQL Server implements its security mechanisms. At one level, SQL Server enforces security either by using authentication services provided by Windows NT or by using its own. The next level of security encompasses permissions on database objects and statements. These can be managed using database user IDs and roles. In the sections that followed, you learned about the various fixed server and database roles that SQL Server provides for your use. You then learned how to manage permissions and examined the various approaches that can be taken when applying them. Finally, you learned about the encryption services provided by SQL Server and how you can implement them in your database.

The SQL Server Agent

by Greg Mable

IN THIS CHAPTER

This chapter explores the SQL Server Agent, a built-in task scheduling service provided with SQL Server. One of the primary design goals of SQL Server 7.0 was to make it even easier than in previous releases to manage SQL Server. With this new release, Microsoft has improved the functionality of what was formerly known as the SQL Executive. In fact, the features have been enhanced so significantly that Microsoft decided that the service deserved a new name—the SQL Server Agent. This name more aptly describes what the service provides: an active, intelligent set of interfaces to manage SQL Server easily and efficiently.

This chapter is divided into the three main components of the SQL Server Agent: jobs, alerts, and operators. I describe each of these components in detail and provide an example to illustrate how to employ the components in a real-world scenario.

SQL Server Agent Overview

The SQL Server Agent is one of the major components for managing SQL Server. It features job scheduling, event alerts, and operator notification. Jobs can contain multiple steps and include dependencies such that you can program a job that fails to take appropriate action such as sending email. Jobs can also execute on multiple servers. (See Chapter 14, "Multiserver Administrative Support," for more information.) You can schedule jobs to run whenever the CPU utilization of the computer falls below a certain threshold level.

You can set up alerts to be triggered whenever a particular event in the Windows NT event log occurs. For example, if SQL Server were to run out of disk space, an event would be written to the Windows NT event log. You could set up this event to trigger an alert. From this alert, you can notify an operator that SQL Server has run out of disk space. Events can also be triggered on a performance threshold. For example, an alert can be generated should the SQL Server user connections counter exceed a certain value.

You can configure operators to receive email notifications and pager alerts using a third-party product. You can also configure a fail-safe operator to be used whenever the system cannot send notification to a designated operator.

Before discussing the features of the SQL Server Agent in more detail, let's review how you can set up its basic configuration options.

Startup Account

The SQL Server Agent is a Windows NT service. It appears in the list of services in the Services Control Panel applet. Because it is a NT-based service, you can configure the account under which the service runs. If you run the service under the local system account, any job you execute will be restricted to the resources available on the local system only. If you want to provide access to network resources to the SQL Server Agent, you should configure the service to run under a Windows NT domain account.

You can select which account the service will run under during the installation process or by using either the Services Control Panel applet or Enterprise Manager after the installation. From the console tree in Enterprise Manager, you can select the SQL Server Agent in the Management folder and edit its properties settings as shown in Figure 11.1.

FIGURE 11.1

SQL Server Agent Properties: Specify user account and mail profile.

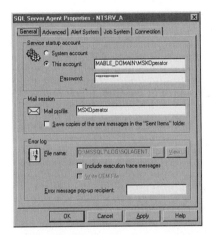

TIP

It is advisable to create a separate Windows NT domain account for the SQL Server Agent to run under, especially if you will be accessing network resources. By using a separate Windows NT domain account, you will be able to set up security and audit the resources accessed by the agent.

Under Windows 95/98, the SQL Server Agent account is not configurable because Windows 95/98 does not contain a local security database and is run as a separate application program.

Mail Profile

You can specify the default mail profile to be used by the SQL Server Agent, as shown earlier in Figure 11.1. This is the mail account that will be used when sending email messages to notify an operator about the status of a job. For example, you can configure a job to send an operator an email message whenever the job executes. As with the Windows NT domain account, it is advisable to create a separate mail profile for the SQL Server Agent. This way, you can determine the source of an email notification message as the SQL Server Agent.

User Connection

You can configure the SQL Server Agent service to connect to SQL Server using either one of the two authentication methods provided by SQL Server. You can configure the agent to connect to SQL Server using Windows NT integrated login, which means that the agent will run under the account specified in the startup service account. You can also use standard security and specify a particular SQL login account to use. Keep in mind that this account must be a member of the sysadmin role. For Windows 95/98 systems, you must specify a particular SQL Server account. As with the startup account, it is advisable to create an SQL Server account for this purpose.

Creating Jobs

The SQL Server Agent is a job scheduling service. In previous releases of SQL Server, jobs were referred to as tasks and each job could only contain a single function. Microsoft has enhanced the capabilities of the SQL Server Agent such that a task can now consist of multiple steps. Hence, it is no longer referred to as a task but as a job consisting of one or more steps. You can create a new job using Enterprise Manager. In the console tree, the SQL Server Agent object appears in the Management folder. Within the SQL Server Agent object are its three main components: jobs, alerts, and operators. You might want to create a job, especially if you are new to using the SQL Server Agent, by running the Create Job Wizard.

Running the Create Job Wizard

The simplest way to create a job in the SQL Server Agent is to run the Create Job Wizard from Enterprise Manager. The Create Job Wizard will walk you step-by-step through the process of creating a job consisting of a single step. Once the wizard has created the job, you can modify its properties and add more steps.

When you start the Create Job Wizard, you see the screen shown in Figure 11.2. You can specify the command type upon which the job will be based. You have three options: a Transact-SQL statement, an application or batch file, and an Active Script file written in either VBScript or JScript. When creating a job, you need to ensure that you are logged into SQL Server using an account that is a member of the sysadmin role.

FIGURE 11.2

Create Job Wizard: Specify the command type.

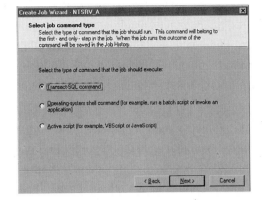

On the next screen (shown in Figure 11.3), you specify the text of the statement or operating system shell command. For Transact-SQL and Active Script commands, you can use the parse option to verify the syntax of your statement by clicking the Parse button. You can also specify a filename for the command rather than enter the text.

FIGURE 11.3

Specify the statement text.

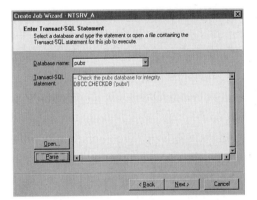

For jobs based on operating system shell commands, you can ensure that the job executes with the appropriate security. As shown in Figure 11.4, you can specify that the job must be executed by members of the sysadmin role by selecting the check box from the Properties page of the SQL Server Agent. If the user is not a member of sysadmin and attempts to start the job, the job will fail.

FIGURE 11.4

SQL Server Agent Properties: Enabling the security on shell and Active Script jobs.

The other options on the Job System tab of the SQL Server Agent's Properties page include the ability to limit the size of the job history log. You can specify the maximum number of rows that the log can contain and the maximum number of rows that a single job can contain. You can also clear the log. The Job Execution option enables you to set a limit on how long the SQL Server Agent will wait for a job to finish executing.

The next step in the Create Job Wizard is to specify the job's schedule, as shown in Figure 11.5.

FIGURE 11.5

Specify a schedule.

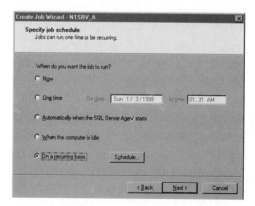

You have the options to run the job immediately, run the job once at the specified date and time, run the job on a recurring basis, run the job when the CPU is idle, or run the job when the SQL Server Agent starts. The last option might be useful in an environment in which you want to notify an operator that the agent has started. If you select the option to schedule a job on a recurring basis, you can then select the Schedule button to input the date, time, and frequency for the job.

As shown in Figure 11.6, you can specify the conditions that must occur for the SQL Server Agent to consider the CPU to be idle. You can access this dialog by selecting the Properties page for the SQL Server Agent and clicking the Advanced tab. For example, you can specify that the CPU must be below 10 percent and that it must remain this way for at least 10 minutes. The average CPU usage is one of the SQL Server Performance Monitor counters. Average CPU usage must remain below the percentage that you specify (across all CPUs on multiprocessor computers) in order for the job to begin executing.

FIGURE 11.6

SQL Server Agent Properties: Specify the CPU idle conditions.

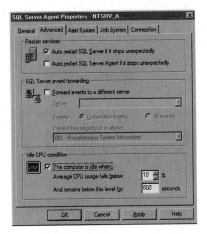

The next step in the Create Job Wizard is to specify the operator to be notified when the job is completed or has failed. As shown in Figure 11.7, you can notify an operator by using email or sending a network message. The latter will work only on a Windows NT Server or Workstation computer.

FIGURE 11.7

Create Job Wizard: Specify the operator notification.

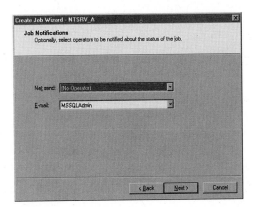

The last step in the Create Job Wizard, shown in Figure 11.8, is to give the job a name and review the prior options to see whether you want to make any changes. When you complete the wizard, the job is created and will appear in the details pane for the job object in Enterprise Manager.

FIGURE 11.8

Specify the job name.

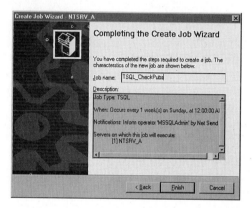

The Create Job Wizard is an excellent tool that you can use whenever you need to create a simple, one-step job on an ad hoc basis. When you need to create a job with more functionality, you will create the job by manually filling in the job's property pages as shown in Figure 11.9. Let's look at each of these options in more detail. As an example of a real-world scenario, I create a job that will check the integrity of a database and then perform a backup of the database if no errors are found.

FIGURE 11.9

A job property page in SQL Server Agent.

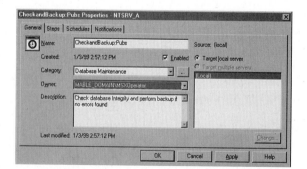

Defining Job Properties

You can define a job with many different properties. First, you need to give a job a name. This name must be unique to the server on which it is created. You can have a job with the same name on two different servers. Next, you need to determine whether the job will run on the local server or multiple servers. See Chapter 14 for more information on creating jobs that target multiple servers. Next, you can assign the job to a particular category or leave it assigned to the default category (unassigned). As shown in Figure 11.10, you can create your own category or choose one of the pre-existing categories. You access this dialog by selecting the Jobs icon from the Console pane in Enterprise Manager, selecting the All Tasks option, and then selecting Manage Job Categories. You also assign the job's owner so that only the job owner or someone in the sysadmin group can execute the job.

FIGURE 11.10

Choosing a job category.

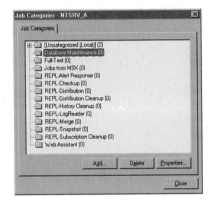

For this example, I have given the job the name CheckandBackupDatabase:Pubs and a description, enabled the job, assigned it to run on the local server, assigned MSXOperator as the owner, and placed it under the database maintenance category.

Defining Job Steps

A job can consist of one or more steps. Each of these steps can consist of Transact-SQL statements, an operating system shell command, Active Script statements, or a replication type. See Chapter 20, "Replication," for more information on replication jobs. You give each step a name and specify its command type, the commands for that step, and the database under which the commands will execute. A step can also contain some logic based on its success or failure. As shown in Figure 11.11, you can specify that if the step is successful, the job should continue—or the job should quit and report success (or failure, depending on your particular need). You can also specify that if the step should fail, the job should quit and report that it failed.

FIGURE 11.11

Advanced job steps.

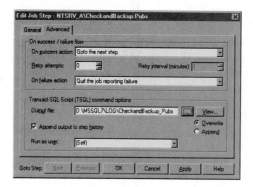

For jobs that are Transact-SQL or operating system shell types, you can also specify an output file to capture the results of the command that is run by each step. For Transact-SQL command types, you can specify the user in the database under which the step will run.

Defining Job Schedules

You can specify a particular schedule for a job to run. You can specify that the job run once at a specific date and time, run on a recurring basis, run whenever the SQL Server Agent starts, or run whenever the CPU is idle. You can also specify more than one schedule for a job. For example, you can configure a particular job to run on both a recurring basis and whenever the CPU is idle.

Defining Job Notifications

You can configure the job to notify an operator about its status once it has completed. You can either email an operator, page an operator if your system has the appropriate third-party software installed, or send a network message if the job is running on a Windows NT Server or Workstation. You can also specify that an event be written to the Windows NT event log when the job is completed. Maybe you want to specify that the job be automatically deleted when completed. This option would be useful in situations in which you have created a job that will run just once and you want to remove the job once it has finished.

Working with the SQL Server Agent Error Log

The SQL Server Agent maintains an error log for your use. Various informative, warning, and error messages are stored whenever the SQL Server Agent is running. You can use the error log as a means to debug your jobs as you begin to develop them and as a means to monitor or troubleshoot a job once the job has been placed into production. The error log is accessible from the SQL Server Agent object in the Enterprise Manager.

Viewing Job History

As with the SQL Server Agent error log, the SQL Server Agent maintains a job history log for each job that you create. You can use this job to monitor and troubleshoot your jobs. The job history is available by selecting the job history from the job details pane in Enterprise Manager.

System Tables

For the most part, you will rarely need to access the system tables that make up the SQL Server Agent. In case you need to modify an entry in one of the tables, you should be aware of which tables are used by the SQL Server Agent. These tables are stored in the msdb database. The sysjobs table contains the names and definitions of all jobs that have been created. The sysjobschedules table contains the schedules for these jobs, and sysjobsteps contains an entry for each of the steps for a given job. The sysjobhistory table stores the history of each job as it is executed.

> **CAUTION**
>
> All the information in these tables is available to you from Enterprise Manager. You should make any changes necessary from the Enterprise Manager. It is never advisable to directly edit system tables.

Configuring Alerts

You can configure an alert to be triggered whenever a particular error message is generated by SQL Server or when a particular Performance Monitor threshold has been reached. SQL Server error messages with severity levels 0 or 10 are informational only. Error messages with severity levels 11 through 16 can be corrected by the user. Severity levels 17 through 19 are generated by a resource or system errors. Severity levels 20 and higher are fatal errors. You can also create your own user-defined error messages using a range of error numbers from 50000 to 2147483647 from Enterprise Manager and trigger them using the Transact-SQL RAISERRROR command.

By default, the SQL Server Agent has preconfigured alerts for errors that occur with severity levels of 19 and higher. These alerts do not have any actions or notifications associated with them, so you can modify them to include any actions or notifications you want.

> **TIP**
>
> I suggest that you configure each of these alerts (errors with severity levels of 19 and higher) to send an email message to an operator who will be available to receive them in a timely manner. Errors with severity levels of 19 and higher must be corrected as soon as possible.

Running the Create Alert Wizard

The Create Alert Wizard from Enterprise Manager will guide you step-by-step through the process of creating an alert and its associated responses. You can access this wizard by selecting the Tools option from the menu, selecting the Wizards option, and then under the Management folder, selecting Create Alert Wizard.

The first step in the Create Alert Wizard is to specify the error message or text of the error message that must occur to trigger the alert, as shown in Figure 11.12.

FIGURE 11.12

Create Alert Wizard: Specify an error message.

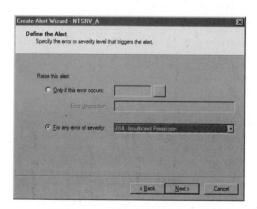

In the next step, you specify a database in which the error message must occur and the text that must appear in the error message. Both of these parameters are optional, as shown in Figure 11.13.

The next step of the Create Alert Wizard is to specify the responses to the alert when it is raised by its associated event. You can notify an operator via an email message, a pager, and a network message. You can also specify a job to execute in response to the alert, as shown in Figure 11.14.

FIGURE 11.13

Specify the optional parameters.

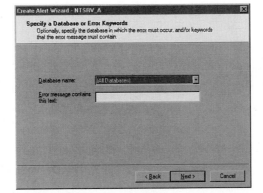

FIGURE 11.14

Specify the alert responses.

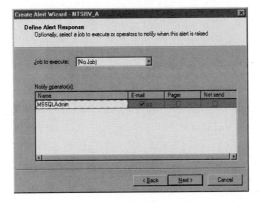

If you decide to send a notification message in response to an alert, you can also specify whether to include the error text in the notification message. You can also add your own message text, as shown in Figure 11.15.

FIGURE 11.15

Specify an optional notification message.

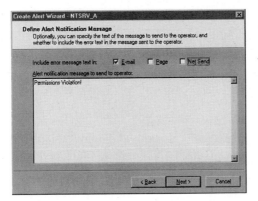

The last step of the Create Alert Wizard is to give the alert a name and confirm the selections that you have made. Once completed, the wizard creates an entry for the alerts object in the Management folder of Enterprise Manager.

Defining Alert Properties

When defining an alert using Enterprise Manager, you first give the alert a name. You then specify the type of alert—that is, whether the alert is raised by a SQL Server–generated error or by a SQL Server Performance Monitor counter.

> **TIP**
>
> You can define alerts that are raised in response to Performance Monitor counters. For example, you can set an alert whenever the SQL Server user connection counter exceeds a certain threshold. That way, you will automatically be notified when SQL Server is performing under a heavy load.

As shown in Figure 11.16, you can also specify that the error message contain the text that you specify. This is useful when defining your own messages or when configuring an alert to capture all messages that contain a specific phrase, such as `fatal error`.

FIGURE 11.16

Defining an alert's properties.

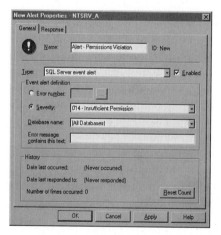

Defining Alert Responses

As shown in Figure 11.17, you can define an alert's responses to include sending a notification message to an operator or executing a job.

FIGURE 11.17

*Defining an
alert's responses.*

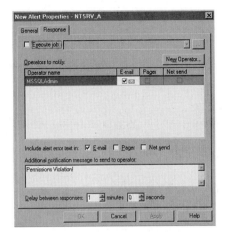

An alert's response can include sending an additional text message that you specify.

Configuring Operators

You can configure an operator as the recipient of notification messages sent in response
to an alert, as shown in Figure 11.18.

FIGURE 11.18

*Defining the
alert's operators.*

You can also specify what type of notification message to send (email, pager, or network
message). For the pager option, you can set up a schedule for when the operator will be
on duty and able to receive notification messages.

As an additional measure of assurance, you can define a fail-safe operator who will be notified when the alert is unable to notify any of the pager operators specified. See Figure 11.19 for the complete set of options available when using a third-party pager support program.

Figure 11.19

Defining a fail-safe operator.

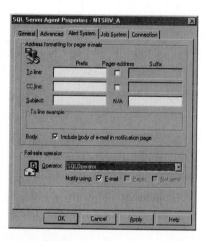

Tip

You can define a group of operators instead of a single operator to be the recipient of a notification message. You can do this by simply specifying a distribution list in the email notification address. That way, if any one of the operators is unavailable to receive messages, the other members of the group will be able to reply.

Summary

This chapter presents a comprehensive look at the new SQL Server Agent. Formerly called the SQL Server Executive, this service has been so significantly enhanced from its previous version that it deserved a new name: the SQL Server Agent. It consists of a comprehensive set of features that enable automated management of SQL Server. It provides a sophisticated scheduling component and will execute jobs based on response to system events, such as fatal errors. You can define operators as the recipient of alert notifications. Pager notification support has also been enhanced for use with third-party products. Tasks have also been enhanced and renamed as jobs. Jobs can consist of one or more steps, and these steps can also branch based on whether the step is successful. The SQL Server Agent is part of the overall design goal of SQL Server 7.0: reducing administration overhead and lowering the total cost of ownership.

CHAPTER 12

SQL Server Backup, Restore, and Recovery

by Sharon Bjeletich

IN THIS CHAPTER

Performing backups is a part of any database environment. A *backup* is a copy of a database (or portion of a database) stored on some type of media (tape, disk, and so forth). A *restore* is the process used to return a database to the state it was in at the time a backup was made.

It takes work to define an effective backup and recovery plan. This is especially true in very large database (VLDB) environments because the complexity of administrative activities is magnified. The timing of activities quickly becomes an issue. For large tables and databases, performing consistency checks (DBCC), updating index statistics, and creating indexes can take several minutes, hours, or days. When planning and scheduling automated backups, you must consider the impact these activities will have on the system, as well as the effect on other application activities.

The backup media you choose also can affect your plan. Backing up to tape devices means that you must manage the physical tapes. When a tape is full, any subsequent backups will fail, which will affect your entire backup and recovery process. When backing up to file system devices, you must consider issues such as directory structure and organization, file management, backup file location (local or network), and management of the backup files.

Why Back Up?

Backups are cumbersome. Why bother? Why do you have car insurance? Backups are the easiest and most foolproof way of ensuring that you can recover a database; they are a key element in any fault-tolerant environment. Without a backup, you could lose all your data, which would have to be recreated from the source. The lost data might not be reproducible.

Backups can guard against table or database corruption, media failure, or user error. They should be performed as frequently as needed for effective data administration. You can perform SQL Server backups while the target database is in use, although you must address concurrency issues. Generally, database backups (full) are performed during off-peak hours, whereas transaction log and differential database backups (incremental) can be scheduled during both peak and off-peak hours.

Roles and Responsibilities

In SQL Server, a backup is done with the Transact-SQL `backup` command; a restore is done with the `restore` command. The capability of executing the `backup` and `restore` commands defaults to the members of the database's db_owner and db_backupoperator roles.

> **NOTE**
>
> I for one am glad that Microsoft has changed the dump and load command names to backup and restore. Not only it is more intuitive, but also I have embarrassed myself once too often by reminding colleagues to be sure to "take a dump" before performing some operation. dump and load are still supported in this version of SQL Server 7.0, but only for backward compatibility, and all references to these commands should be replaced with the new syntax.

You should identify who is responsible for performing backups in your organization. If the designated individual (or individuals) does not access the database as a db_owner or db_backupoperator, grant the backup database and backup transaction statement permissions to the user account she will be using. Note that permission for the restore process (restore database and restore transaction statements) can't be granted; this is a sysadmin or db_owner role only.

Types of Backups

SQL Server 7.0 supports four main types of backups:

- Complete database backup
- Differential database backup
- Transaction log backup
- File and filegroup backups

A *complete database backup* copies the data as well as the transaction log in the backup set. This is similar to the behavior of a backup in SQL Server 6.5. The transaction log in SQL Server 7.0 is not implemented as a table in the database as it was in SQL Server 6.5, where the log was stored in a system table called syslogs. The transaction log is implemented in a series of log files and is optimized for that function.

A *differential database backup* is a copy of only the changes to the database since the last full database backup. Differential database backups are useful for supplementing full backups, especially in large environments, where it might not be possible to allow time for a full backup each evening. Differential backups still require the full backup to be restored before the differential can be restored, but only the last differential backup must be restored. Differential database backups are new to SQL Server in version 7.0 and are another example of how the product has been enhanced with support for large databases in mind. A differential database backup also includes the active portion of the transaction log.

A *transaction backup* is a copy of the committed transactions in the transaction log. The *transaction log* contains all current transactions since the last `backup log` command. This is similar to incremental backups of file systems, in which only the files that have changed are backed up. Backing up the transaction log also removes the backed-up transactions (clearing space in the transaction log), unless the `with no_truncate` option is specified. A transaction log is a serial record of all database transactions that can be replayed, if necessary, to return a database to a known state.

SQL Server 7.0 also allows backups of individual file or filegroups. This option is useful when there is not enough time for a full or differential database backup. A differential database backup can be thought of as a horizontal backup. A filegroup backup can be considered a vertical backup because a vertical slice of the database is taken. If files or filegroups are on separate hard drives and a hard drive is lost, only the missing file or filegroup need be restored. Using this type of backup requires that you back up transaction logs as well because obviously, a database could become inconsistent if only the file or filegroup were restored. You must also restore the transaction logs to ensure all data is consistent throughout all of the tables.

> **NOTE**
>
> Because transaction logs are required in conjunction with a file or filegroup restore, the server will not allow backups to files and filegroups on databases with `trunc. log on chkpt.` enabled.

You can restore files and filegroups inside of full database backup sets, so backing them up individually is not required to recover a specific file.

> **NOTE**
>
> In version 7.0, SQL Server no longer supports the ability to back up or restore a single table. If this functionality is important to your organization, you might want to consider a strategy to utilize the ability to restore files and filegroups, by grouping tables on specific files, as required.

> **CAUTION**
>
> The full-test index data used by the new full-text search functionality in SQL Server 7.0 does not ever get backed up. Enough information is backed up to recreate the indexes when a database is restored, but you should consider the amount of time required to rebuild these indexes when both planning and actually running a database restoration that includes a full-text search index. You will need to rebuild the indexes.

Backup Devices

A *backup device* is created for the exclusive use of the backup and restore commands. When backing up a database or transaction log, you must tell SQL Server where to create the backup. Creating a backup device enables you to associate a logical name with the physical backup media. The two most common types of media are tape devices and disk devices, as described in the following sections.

> **NOTE**
>
> In version 7.0, SQL Server no longer supports the ability to back up or restore to a diskette. You must back up to a hard disk and then copy the file to the floppy diskette.

Microsoft Tape Format

SQL Server now supports the Microsoft Tape Format (MTF) for backup devices. This lets you share SQL Server backups with NT Backup tapes. All backups, regardless of their type (tape or disk), use the Microsoft Tape Format. In version 7.0, SQL Server does not support MTF password protection.

Tape Devices

A *tape device* records backups to removable tapes. You can use tape drives alone or several in parallel for a single backup operation. Purchase as many drives as you can afford, based on the needs of your backup and recovery strategy. Tape devices are inherently more secure than disk devices because the media (tape) is removable and portable.

Tape devices are used by most production sites. Tape devices provide a removable source of backup media that can easily be moved offsite for additional security. Tape devices adapt to changing database size much more gracefully than do disk devices. Backing up a 50MB database to disk can be easily managed by your file system. As the database grows to 50GB, however, backing up to disk will probably prove impossible because most sites don't have that amount of free space in the file system. Additionally, to move the backup offsite, you must back up the files to tape.

Disk Devices

A *disk device* is just a file in a directory, usually stored in the file system of your database server. Backing up to a disk device is faster than backing up to a tape device. When you back up to a disk device, you can actually see the file grow if you check the file size at intervals during the backup. It is not recommended that you back up a database to the same physical drive as the database, for obvious reasons. If you lose the drive, you lose both the database and the backup.

> **NOTE**
>
> The line between tape and disk backups blurs as various removable media types (floptical and so on) gain both acceptance and increased capacity. Choose a strategy that fits your organizational requirements, whether it's tape, disk, floptical, or a combination.

Named Pipe Devices

Named pipe devices are included in SQL Server to support third-party backup and restore tools. You generally do not use named pipe devices with Transact-SQL.

Multiple Devices

You can perform backup and restore operations on multiple backup devices at once. These devices must all be of the same media type. Allowing multiple device backups and restores can significantly decrease the amount of time it takes to perform a backup or restore, depending on the number of devices. Again, Microsoft has added a critical feature in support of large databases with this ability. Using multiple devices in combination with the different types of backups supported allows for many different backup strategies.

To back up a database to multiple devices, create each device (ensuring that they are all of the same type), and use the following syntax:

```
backup database myDB to myDBDevice1, myDBDevice2, myDBDevice3
```

If you are using multiple tape devices to back up or restore a database, you cannot use the same media for another type of backup, such as an NT backup. Backup tape devices do not need to be the same type or capacity. SQL Server will prompt for reloading each tape device as needed. However, tape devices must be physically attached to the server.

Media Sets and Families

SQL Server uses the terms media sets and media families to describe the different components of a multiple media, multiple device backup. A media family is all of the media used by one device. For example, five tapes that might be used by one tape drive during a backup are called a media family. The first tape in the family is called the *initial* media, and all others are referred to as *continuation* media. All of the media families for all of the devices are referred to as the media set. If you have two tape drives, which require four tapes each to perform the backup, the media set refers to all four tapes. A media set can be given a description at backup time, using the `MEDIADESCRIPTION` parameter of the backup command.

Adding Backup Devices

Although the commands `dump` and `load` have been replaced with `backup` and `restore`, the system stored procedure `sp_addumpdevice` is still used to add a new backup device to a SQL Server. Here's the syntax:

```
sp_addumpdevice "tape", logical_name, physical_name
sp_addumpdevice "disk", logical_name, physical_name
```

> **TIP**
>
> As in SQL Server 6.5, you don't have to add backup devices with `sp_addumpdevice`; you can still provide the physical name as part of the `backup` syntax:
>
> ```
> backup database my_db to disk = "c:\mssql\backups\my_db.dmp"
> ```

> **NOTE**
>
> Execute permissions for adding backup devices defaults to members of the diskadmin server role.

Each backup device has both a logical and physical name. These names are discussed in the following sections.

Logical Name

A *logical name* is used to refer to a physical name in a friendly, easy-to-use (and remember) way. After executing the `backup` command, you can use the logical name for all backups and restores; a good practice is to choose the logical name based on the type of device being added. For tape devices, use a general name for the tape (`Tape1`, `Tape2`, and so forth). For disk devices, use a logical name indicating the database and backup type (`CustomerDB_backup` or `CustomerDB_tran`, for example).

Physical Name

The physical name is normally predefined for tape devices. Tape devices should be specified using the physical name defined by Windows NT. A common example of the physical name is `\\.\TAPE0`. The following example adds a tape device called `Tape1`:

```
sp_addumpdevice "tape", "Tape1", "\\.\tape0", 8000
```

For file devices, it's a good idea to organize a directory structure for all your databases. If you're using Enterprise Manager to create backup devices, SQL Server will put them in the `\mssql7\backup` directory. For convenience, you might want to use this same directory if you create a backup device using `sp_addumpdevice`. Each database in your server could be a subdirectory. The `CustomerDB` subdirectory would be `\mssql7\backup\CustomerDB`. The filename created is based on the backup type. Therefore, the two backup devices for the `CustomerDB` database would be created in the following manner:

```
sp_addumpdevice "disk", "CustomerDB_backup",
    "c:\mssql\backup\CustomerDB\CustomerDB_backup"
sp_addumpdevice "disk", "CustomerDB_tran",
    "c:\mssql\backup\CustomerDB\CustomerDB_tran"
```

By standardizing your structure, you can write scripts that accept a database name as a parameter. The entire `backup` command can be created dynamically. The location of the backup is also known, enabling you to move the file immediately to a different name to avoid having it overwritten.

Don't be stingy with the number of backup devices added. Using a different backup device for each database helps standardize your backup strategy, especially for disk devices.

> **NOTE**
>
> Backups to tape devices are not allowed under the Microsoft Windows 95/98 operating system.

SQL Server 7.0 Backup Functions

Backups in SQL Server 7.0 have received significant attention and optimization. The operations are much easier to perform, less intrusive to the system, and more flexible. Here are some new features:

- SQL Server has added differential database backups and restores. Restoring a differential backup, rather than a transaction log, avoids the time the server spends rolling forward the transactions, basically recreating all the activities that occurred during the transaction log time period. A differential database backup is more of a snapshot of the changes since the last backup, and only those changes are applied.

- You can perform backups and restores of files and filegroups. You must be sure to create a transaction log backup after the filegroup backup to ensure that database consistency is maintained. Although SQL Server will allow you to back up a filegroup without backing up the transaction log, when you restore the filegroup, an error message occurs indicating that the log must be backed up before continuing. Note that an index that affects multiple filegroups will require all of the filegroups to be backed up as a unit.

> **NOTE**
>
> You can now create a table and request that all of the text and image data be stored on a different filegroup. This can support a large database environment where textual and image data (which can be quite large) can be backed up and managed separately from the main data. However, as was noted earlier, if an index is created that spans filegroups, you must back up all the filegroups, so index planning must take this into consideration.

- Restoring databases is much simpler because the restore operation can create the database and the files, avoiding the bane of many a database administrator's existence: the inability to restore a database because the device setup and sizes do not match between the two servers.

- You can restart backup and restore operations if they involve multiple tape volumes.

- You can attach and detach files without a backup and restore. This is a great new feature, sort of "databases to go." Quite often, administrators need to move a database from one physical location to another (for instance, because a drive was out of space), and although it could be done in SQL Server 6.5, it was either time-consuming or fraught with danger.

Creating Backup Devices with SQL Enterprise Manager

You can also use SQL Server's Enterprise Manager to define tape devices via a GUI interface. In Enterprise Manager, expand the Management node of the desired server, right-click the Backup icon, and then click the New Backup Device menu item on the pop-up menu; the Backup Device Properties - New Device dialog box, which is shown in Figure 12.1, is displayed.

FIGURE 12.1

Defining new backup devices in the Backup Device Properties - New Device box in SQL Enterprise Manager.

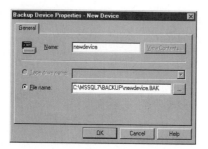

This dialog box enables you to define the logical and physical names, as well as assign the physical location of the device and indicate whether it's a disk or tape device. In the background, Enterprise Manager is simply running `sp_addumpdevice`, with the parameters containing the values you supply in this dialog box.

You can also create new backup devices in the Backup dialog box, accessed from the Tool menu option in Enterprise Manager, or by right-clicking a database name, selecting All Tasks from the pop-up menu item, and then selecting Backup Database from the pop-up menu.

Backup and Restore Commands

Now that I have defined the basics, you need to take a close look at the `backup` and `restore` commands. At this point, you should have SQL Server up and running and your backup devices identified. Look at the options for the `backup` and `restore` commands for both the entire database and the transaction log.

Backing Up the Database

Use `backup database` to make a full copy of your database. The simplified syntax for the `backup database` command follows:

```
backup database databasename to devicename
```

In SQL Server 7.0, however, the `backup` command needs to handle several other options, including differential database backups and file and filegroup backups. Following is the full syntax for the `backup database` command for backing up entire databases.

```
BACKUP DATABASE {database_name ¦ @database_name_var}
TO <backup_device> [,...n]
[WITH
[BLOCKSIZE = {blocksize ¦ @blocksize_variable}]
[[,] DESCRIPTION = {text ¦ @text_variable}]
[[,] DIFFERENTIAL]
[[,] EXPIREDATE = {date ¦ @date_var}
¦ RETAINDAYS = {days ¦ @days_var}]
[[,] FORMAT ¦ NOFORMAT]
[[,] {INIT ¦ NOINIT}]
[[,] MEDIADESCRIPTION = {text ¦ @text_variable}]
[[,] MEDIANAME = {media_name ¦ @media_name_variable}]
[[,] [NAME = {backup_set_name ¦ @backup_set_name_var}]
[[,] {NOSKIP ¦ SKIP}]
[[,] {NOUNLOAD ¦ UNLOAD}]
[[,] [RESTART]
[[,] STATS [= percentage]]]
```

Following is the full syntax for the `backup database` command for backing up files and filegroups:

```
BACKUP DATABASE {database_name ¦ @database_name_var}
<file_or_filegroup> [,...n]
TO <backup_device> [,...n]
[WITH
[BLOCKSIZE = {blocksize ¦ @blocksize_variable}]
[[,] DESCRIPTION = {text ¦ @text_variable}]
[[,] EXPIREDATE = {date ¦ @date_var}
¦ RETAINDAYS = {days ¦ @days_var}]
[[,] FORMAT ¦ NOFORMAT]
```

```
[[,] {INIT ¦ NOINIT}]
[[,] MEDIADESCRIPTION = {text ¦ @text_variable}]
[[,] MEDIANAME = {media_name ¦ @media_name_variable}]
[[,] [NAME = {backup_set_name ¦ @backup_set_name_var}]
[[,] {NOSKIP ¦ SKIP}]
[[,] {NOUNLOAD ¦ UNLOAD}]
[[,] [RESTART]
[[,] STATS [= percentage]]]
```

Remember that you must do a transaction log backup after a file or filegroup backup.

Table 12.1 presents detailed descriptions of each parameter of `backup database`.

TABLE 12.1   THE `backup database` PARAMETERS

Parameter	Description
database_name	The name of the database you're attempting to back up.
file_or_filegroup name	If you are backing up files or filegroups, enter the names, separated by commas. Filenames must be prefaced with `File =`; filegroup names must be prefaced with `Filegroup =`.
backup_device	The logical name of the backup device you defined with `sp_addumpdevice`. These can be multiple devices, separated by commas. You can create temporary backup devices by specifying `{disk ¦ tape ¦ pipe } = 'temp_backup_device'`. Be sure to specify the complete path and filename for a disk or tape temporary device. Multiple devices must all be of the same type.
blocksize = # of bytes	Backup will automatically determine the appropriate size for disk backups. You must use a blocksize of `2048` if you intend to copy the backup set to a CD for a later restore. The blocksize applies to a tape backup if the tape is being overwritten with the `format` parameter; otherwise, the appropriate blocksize is selected by the backup.
DESCRIPTION = *text*	A 255-character user-defined description for the backup set.
DIFFERENTIAL	This parameter is used to indicate that only a differential database backup should be performed.

Parameter	Description
expiredate = *date*	As an alternative to RETAINDAYS, you can specify the date when the backup media expires and can be overwritten.
retaindays = *#_of_days*	An option that you can use for any type of backup device. It doesn't allow the backup to be overwritten until the number of days specified has passed. This is an important option for any production backup strategy. If neither expiredate or retaindays is specified, the configuration value specified in sp_config will be used.
FORMAT ¦ NOFORMAT	Selecting the format option will overwrite the backup device and media header. It will invalidate any existing backup contents in the entire backup set. Obviously, you should use this with care. Specifying NOFORMAT indicates that the header should not be rewritten. The device is not rewritten as well unless INIT has also been specified. In SQL Server 6.5, SKIP and INIT together would overwrite a backup header. This is no longer always the case. Use FORMAT to ensure the media and the header are always overwritten.
INIT ¦ NOINIT	The INIT ¦ NOINIT option determines whether the backup will be appended to the device or reinitializes the entire device. Use INIT when backing up to a tape for the first time or when reusing an old device.
MEDIADESCRIPTION = *text*	A 255-character user-defined description of the media set. Use this to specify all of the parts of the media family included in the media set.
media_name = text	This option labels your media set, which then can be specified during a restore. For example, specify a value for *media_name* as a concatenation of your database name and the date (CustomerDB_Jan07). Then, if you have backups for January 7 on a single tape, you can easily restore the January 7 backup by specifying *media_name* as part of the restore. You must use a media name if a tape is to be used by both SQL Server and Windows NT backup programs. *media_name* replaces *volume* from previous versions of SQL Server. This parameter can be up to 128 characters in length.

continues

12

SQL SERVER BACKUP, RESTORE, AND RECOVERY

TABLE 12.1   CONTINUED

Parameter	Description
_name = text	A 128-character user-defined name for the backup set.
SKIP ¦ NOSKIP	This option indicates whether ANSI tape labels are read (NOSKIP) or ignored (SKIP). For example, when SKIP is specified and the ANSI label of a tape warns that it has expired or that you don't have permission to write to it, SQL Server ignores the warning. If the tape to which you're writing is new (and therefore has no ANSI label), SQL Server writes a new label on the first try. The SKIP option prevents unnecessary retries as SQL Server tries to find a label. Specifying NOSKIP tells SQL Server to read existing ANSI tape labels on the tape to which you're writing. The default is NOSKIP.
NOUNLOAD ¦ UNLOAD	Specifies whether a tape is automatically rewound and unloaded after the backup has completed. UNLOAD is the default.
RESTART	You use this new option to run the exact same backup command a subsequent time when a backup was interrupted. You can only use this for multiple tape backups.
stats = *percentage*	The percentage of pages backed up (or restored) in increments specified by the value. If *percentage* isn't specified, the statistics will be shown for each 10 percent of the operation.

Listing 12.1 shows an example of striped backups.

LISTING 12.1   EXAMPLE SYNTAX TO CREATE STRIPED BACKUPS

```
--   Back up the CustomerDB database across 4 backup devices (Tape1-4).
--   Name each media, initialize the tapes, do not rewind,
--   prevent other backups from overwriting this backup for 2 weeks,
--   and send the messages to the client terminal.
backup database CustomerDB to Tape1 medianame = "Volume1",
    Tape2 medianame = "Volume2",
    Tape3 medianame = "Volume3",
    Tape4 medianame = "Volume4"
    with init, nounload, retaindays=14
```

Listing 12.2 contains an example of multiple backups to a single tape.

LISTING 12.2 EXAMPLE SYNTAX TO PERFORM MULTIPLE BACKUPS TO A SINGLE TAPE

```
-- Back up the CustomerDB, ProductDB, and SecurityDB to Tape1
-- For the first backup, initialize the tape but do not rewind.
-- Back up the second database after the first.
-- After the third database is backed up, rewind the tape.
backup database CustomerDB to Tape1 medianame = "CustVol1"
    with init
backup database ProductDB to Tape1 medianame = "ProdVol1"
       /* nounload is the default */
backup database SecurityDB to Tape1 medianame = "SecVol1"
    with unload
```

NOTE

You can back up a database while the server is in use, but doing so can cause substantial performance degradation. Striping backups across even a small number of devices decreases the total amount of time required to execute the backup, decreasing the negative performance impact. You should benchmark user-response times with and without a backup process running to determine the impact on your system.

Backing Up Databases with SQL Enterprise Manager

Why, exactly, are we talking Transact-SQL syntax when Microsoft is shipping this nifty SQL Enterprise Manager utility? SQL Enterprise Manager, behind the scenes, is executing the syntax just described when you use it to back up databases.

There are a number of ways to access the backup tools in SQL Enterprise Manager. You can select the backup database option in the HTML page displayed on the right side of the SQL Enterprise Manager screen when the database name is selected on the left-hand side tree view. This HTML database description page will also indicate the last dates for full database, differential database, and transaction log backups. This screen is shown in Figure 12.2.

FIGURE 12.2

SQL Enterprise Manager displaying an HTML screen of database information, including backups.

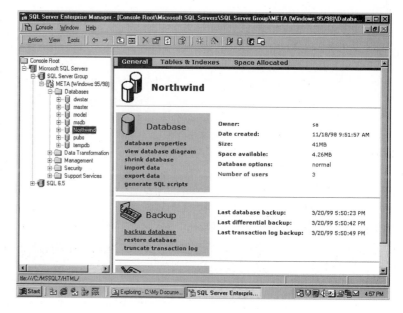

You can also choose Tools, Backup Database from the menu; SQL Enterprise Manager displays the Database Backup dialog box (see Figure 12.3). You can also access this dialog box by expanding the Management node in the Server Group, right-clicking the backup icon, and selecting Backup a Database. You will need to first select a database from the Server Group to use this option. From this dialog box, you can back up and restore databases, files and filegroups, and transaction logs. Enterprise Manager also enables you to create new backup devices, if they're needed.

FIGURE 12.3

SQL Enterprise Manager's graphical interface that hides many of the complexities of backup command syntax.

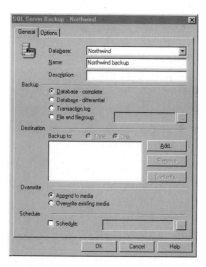

Selecting the database name from the combo box defines which database you're going to back up. The various syntax options discussed previously are represented as check boxes and other options.

You define striped backups by selecting backup devices from the list under the Destination label. Hold down the Ctrl key as you're selecting devices after the first one. SQL Enterprise Manager, when it builds the `backup database` statement it will eventually execute, will use the multiple devices selected to construct the multiple-device clause necessary for striped backup.

Whether used as native SQL syntax in a script, or used through SQL Enterprise Manager, the features of SQL Server backup are identical.

Backing Up Transaction Logs

Use `backup log` to make a copy of the transactions that have completed in your database since the last transaction log backup. Note that the older syntax used in previous versions of SQL Server of `dump transaction` is still supported in version 7.0. However, it is supported for backward compatibility only, and you should change all instances in your code to the new syntax as soon as possible. This is the simplified syntax for the `backup log` command:

```
backup log databasename to devicename
```

`backup log` works similarly to `backup database` and supports the same options. The only difference between the two is in the amount of work they do. This is the full syntax for the `backup log` command:

```
BACKUP LOG {database_name ¦ @database_name_var}{
[WITH
{ NO_LOG ¦ TRUNCATE_ONLY }]{
TO <backup_device> [,...n]
[WITH
[BLOCKSIZE = {blocksize ¦ @blocksize_variable}]
[[,] DESCRIPTION = {text ¦ @text_variable}]
[[,] EXPIREDATE = {date ¦ @date_var}
¦ RETAINDAYS = {days ¦ @days_var}]
[[,] FORMAT ¦ NOFORMAT]
[[,] {INIT ¦ NOINIT}]
[[,] MEDIADESCRIPTION = {text ¦ @text_variable}]
[[,] MEDIANAME = {media_name ¦ @media_name_variable}]
[[,] [NAME = {backup_set_name ¦ @backup_set_name_var}]
[[,] NO_TRUNCATE]
[[,] {NOSKIP ¦ SKIP}]
[[,] {NOUNLOAD ¦ UNLOAD}]
[[,] [RESTART]
[[,] STATS [= percentage]]]}
```

The special-purpose options are in the third line and the NO_TRUNCATE option. These options, NO_LOG, TRUNCATE_ONLY, and NO_TRUNCATE, are described in the following sections.

NO_LOG and TRUNCATE_ONLY

You use the NO_LOG and TRUNCATE_ONLY options to clear the transaction log without making a copy of it. In SQL Server 7.0, these commands are synonymous.

Both of these options throw away the log. When the command has been executed, you're exposed. If a disaster occurs before you can back up the database, you won't be able to recover any data that has been added since the last backup. The frequency of backing up transaction logs determines the scope of your exposure.

Database logs are now automatically created on a separate file if one is not specified during the creation. This alleviates the problem faced in previous versions of SQL Server, where it was not possible to back up transaction logs because the data and log were on the same database device. All databases, including master, msdb, and model, have a separate file created for the transaction logs. To see the current properties for the master, msdb, or model databases, in Enterprise Manager expand the Server Group, right-click the database name, and select Properties from the pop-up menu. The data files are shown in the first table called General, and the transaction log file is shown on the second tab—Transaction Log. Figure 12.4 shows the properties for a master database transaction log.

FIGURE 12.4

The Transaction Log properties for the Master database.

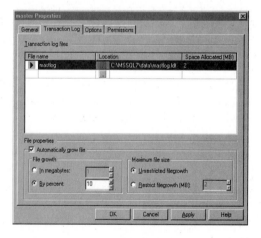

Even though the master database has a separate transaction log, SQL Server will not allow a backup of the log for the master database. You must use the backup database command. You can back up the model, msdb, and publication (if replication is enabled) transaction logs, if desired. However, you will need to change the default setting for these databases for the `trunc. log on chkpt.` option because it is enabled at the initial SQL Server setup. You perform full database backups for all of these system databases as for any user database, and you should include them in your regular backup strategy.

NO_TRUNCATE

The `NO_TRUNCATE` option is exactly the opposite of `TRUNCATE_ONLY` and `NO_LOG`. `NO_TRUNCATE` makes a copy of your transaction log but doesn't prune it. Use this option when you have a media failure of a data device being used by your database. The master database must be available. This option enables the server to back up the transaction log but doesn't try to touch the database in any way. (A checkpoint is executed in a normal backup transaction. If a database device is unavailable, the checkpoint process can't write the dirty pages. `NO_TRUNCATE` simply backs up the transaction log without checkpointing.)

> **CAUTION**
>
> The SQL Server documentation indicates that you can back up a transaction log with the `NO_TRUNCATE` option even though the database is damaged. Restoring the last database backup and all of the transaction logs, including this last log, would provide a recovery to the point of failure. However, this feature does not seem to actually work at this time if the primary data file is damaged. An error message is returned when a `backup log with no_truncate` command is attempted, indicating that the primary file is not available. Microsoft is working on fixing this problem. The best protection might be to mirror the primary data file.

Note that the ability to back up the transaction log is disabled after nonlogged operations such as nonlogged `writetext`, `select into` to a permanent table, and fast `bcp`. You must perform a complete database backup after any of these operations.

Transaction Log Backup with SQL Enterprise Manager

As with a database backup, SQL Enterprise Manager builds a `backup log` statement that reflects the backup options you select using the Backup/Restore Database dialog box. There's one important distinction. You can back up any database using `backup database`. Only those databases that do not have the `trunc. log on chkpt.` option enabled can have incremental backups done using `backup transaction`. As a result, SQL Enterprise Manager detects whether the database has the option enabled and automatically disables the Transaction Log option of the dialog box. The file and filegroup backup options are also disabled because this kind of backup requires a transaction log backup as well. In Figure 12.5, the master database is selected for backup, and therefore, the Transaction Log option is disabled.

FIGURE 12.5

The Transaction Log backup option disabled for the master database.

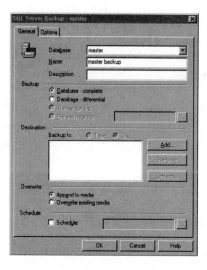

In SQL Server 7.0 Enterprise Manager, you can truncate the log right-clicking the database name, selecting All Tasks from the pop-up menu, and then selecting the Truncate Log option. The NO_TRUNCATE option appears on the Options tab of the Backup Database dialog box when a transaction backup is selected. The Remove inactive entries from transaction log option defaults to checked, but unchecking it is the equivalent of using the NO_TRUNCATE option for the backup log command.

Restoring the Database

SQL Server 7.0 uses the new restore syntax for restoring databases, logs, and files and filegroups. The older load syntax is still supported, but only for backward compatibility. The database that you restore can be the database used to create the backup, but this definitely isn't a requirement. The simplified syntax for the restore database command is as follows:

```
restore database databasename from devicename
```

You can use most of the options available to the backup command in restore. This is the full syntax to restore an entire database:

```
RESTORE DATABASE {database_name ¦ @database_name_var}
[FROM <backup_device> [,   n]]
[WITH
[DBO_ONLY]
[[,] FILE = file_number]
[[,] MEDIANAME = {media_name ¦ @media_name_variable}]
[[,] MOVE 'logical_file_name' TO 'operating_system_filename']
[,...n]
```

```
[[,] {NORECOVERY ¦ RECOVERY ¦ STANDBY = undo_filename}]
[[,] {NOUNLOAD ¦ UNLOAD}]
[[,] REPLACE]
[[,] RESTART]
[[,] STATS [= percentage]]]
```

The MEDIANAME, NOUNLOAD, UNLOAD, and STATS options are identical to those of the backup database command. The DBO_ONLY option sets the dbo use only option of sp_dboption to true, allowing only dbo_owner role members access to the database. The FILE option specifies the file number to be restored from a tape or disk device that contains multiple database backups. The default is 1.

The MOVE option lets you perform a restore to a different operating system filename and location. You can move multiple logical files to a new operating system file at the same time. You must use the NORECOVERY option if you're using subsequent restore statements. For example, if a full backup and then a differential backup are to be applied, then the first backup statement must include the NORECOVERY option. The final restore statement then can include the RECOVERY option (RECOVERY is the default, so you can omit it at this stage, if desired). This ensures that no recovery work occurs until all of the backups, both database and log, have been applied.

> **NOTE**
>
> A database remains in a load state after a restore with a NORECOVERY option. If you mistakenly set this option for a restore that was actually intended to be the final restore statement, run the restore database with recovery command and exclude the from clause. This forces the database to be recovered, and it can then be used.

The STANDBY option with an *undo_filename* allows the database to be in read-only mode between transaction log restores. In SQL Server 6.5, a database could be read between transaction log restores only when the no chkpt. on recovery option was set on the database. In SQL Server 7.0, the use of the STANDBY option with an undo file performs this function.

The REPLACE option deletes and recreates an existing database.

To determine what's contained in a multiple database device, use the command restore headeronly:

```
RESTORE   HEADERONLY
    FROM backup_device
```

You might consider using this command immediately after a database backup to verify that the restore process can read the backup. You can use it for tape or file devices.

To see a list of physical database filenames included in a backup set, use the command `restore filelistonly`:

```
RESTORE   FILELISTONLY
    FROM backup_device
```

The `restore labelonly` command will output media header information about the backup set, without restoring the database:

```
RESTORE   LABELONLY
    FROM backup_device
```

The `restore verifyonly` command will verify that a backup set is complete and valid and that all volumes are readable.

TIP

Because the `restore verifyonly` command returns a known message, an email or pager alert can be issued automatically by a system by running this command after a backup and validating that the `The backup set is valid` message is returned. The page or email can be sent to the database administrator, or the backup can be tried again.

NOTE

No one can use the database while `restore` is being executed, including the person executing the `restore` command.

Here are some restoring examples. The first shows a striped restore:

```
restore database accounting from Tape1, Tape2, Tape3, Tape4
```

The `restore database` command restores all used pages from the backup into the target database and runs a recovery of the transaction log to ensure consistency. Any unused pages are initialized by the restore process. This is the primary reason that a restore can take significantly longer than a backup. The time required to back up a database is proportional to the used pages in the database; the time required to restore a database is proportional to the overall number of pages in the database. Therefore, a 50GB database with 20MB of data might take only a few minutes to back up, but the restore could take several hours or days.

A restore is executed to restore a database normally after a corruption or user error occurs. SQL Server 7.0's restore command will create the actual database files and structures if they don't already exist. You must ensure that create database permissions exist for the restore user in this case.

12

SQL SERVER
BACKUP, RESTORE,
AND RECOVERY

> **NOTE**
>
> When databases are restored from one server to another, or detached and then reattached, and the users and logins might be different, the SUID can become null in the sysusers table and the users no longer appear in their roles. This problem existed in SQL Server 6.5, although in that version, names tended to become mismatched. It still needs to be addressed in version 7.0. There are two approaches. The sp_change_users_login system stored procedure works better in version 7.0 than it did in 6.5, but it is always good practice to have scripts to drop and re-create users as a backup.

Restoring Databases with SQL Enterprise Manager

You can open the Restore Database dialog box by right-clicking a database name in SQL Enterprise Manager and selecting All Tasks and then Restore Database from the pop-up menus. The resulting dialog box is shown in Figure 12.6. You can open the same dialog box also by selecting the Restore Database option from the SQL Server Enterprise Manager Tools menu or by clicking the restore database option in the HTML database description page shown when the database name is selected.

SQL Enterprise Manager supplies the same features and functions that are available in T-SQL for database restoration but presents them in a more usable format. In this dialog box, the three different icons included in the backup set indicate the backup type and their relationships. The first backup icon indicates a full backup, the second a differential backup that is associated with the full backup above it. The third icon indicates a transaction log backup, and the indentation indicates that it was backed up after the differential backup. As with the Backup tab, SQL Enterprise Manager automatically detects the database that you want to restore and determines whether you can apply a transaction log backup. If a transaction log backup is available, the Point In Time Restore option will be enabled. As with backing up databases, restoring databases requires a list of source backup devices and a destination database. Once you've supplied these, having made sure that the database isn't currently in use, SQL Enterprise Manager sends the appropriate `restore` command to SQL Server.

FIGURE 12.6

The SQL Server Enterprise Manager Restore Database dialog box.

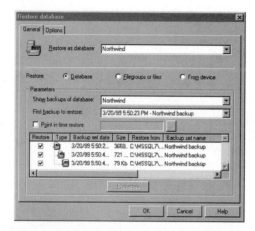

> **NOTE**
>
> If the database being restored includes full-text catalogs, the server must have Full-Text Search installed and the search engine started. Because the full-text indexes are not backed up, they will need to be repopulated with the sp_fulltext_catalog command. This system stored procedure is used to build catalogs for SQL Server 7.0 full-text search functionality.

Restoring After a Disaster

If the restore is a result of a disaster, you might want to first drop the database. In SQL Server 7.0, the `drop database` command should remove databases that are marked suspect. You can drop a database from the SQL Server Enterprise Manager by right-clicking the database name and selecting the Delete option from the pop-up menu. This operation will also delete the data and log operating system files. You can also use sp_dbremove:

`sp_dbremove database`

You can now restore the last full database backup and apply the last differential database backup, if created, or apply the transaction logs. Your database will be created as it was previous to the failure.

Restoring into a Different Database

Occasionally, you'll want to create an exact copy of a database in your system on the same server. This can be useful when you are supporting multiple, parallel development and test environments, and there is enough space to create a database for each development or test effort. This is a simple process in SQL Server 7.0. First, back up the existing database. Open the Restore Database dialog box, either from the Tools menu or by right-clicking a database name. In the Restore as database text box, enter the name of the new database. Select the database backup to be used from the Show backups of database text box. You can restore from a database backup, a filegroup backup, or a backup device. Once executed, the new database will be created and restored from the backup.

12

SQL SERVER
BACKUP, RESTORE,
AND RECOVERY

> **NOTE**
>
> You cannot back up and restore databases between SQL Server 7.0 and other versions of SQL Server. You will want to take this into account when upgrading your 6.5 servers to 7.0 because all your existing 6.5 backups will no longer be of value after you have upgraded, which leaves a window of vulnerability. You might want to actually use the bulk copy program (BCP) on all the data as well as take a secondary precaution at upgrade time. BCP is explained more in-depth in Chapter 16, "Using BCP to Import and Export Data."

To restore a database onto another server, you can use the same process described previously, but you must ensure that the two servers have the same code page and character set, sort order, and Unicode collation. If they do not, you need to use another data transfer method, such as BCP or Data Transformation Services. It is well worth establishing a known standard for these options in your organization to facilitate these cross-server backup and restore operations. Backups and restores between servers running on Intel processors and DEC Alphas are now supported.

Restoring a Differential Backup

If you're using differential backups, you must first restore the full database backup and then restore the last differential backup because each differential backup copies the changes to a database since the last full backup. SQL Enterprise Manager understands this and defaults to selecting both backups from the backup set when you open the Restore Database dialog box. Figure 12.7 shows an example of a differential database restore selection. You can see that the backup type icon indicates a differential backup under the full backup; selecting the differential backup check box also selects the full backup check box.

FIGURE 12.7

Selecting a differential database backup to be restored and activating the corresponding full database backup.

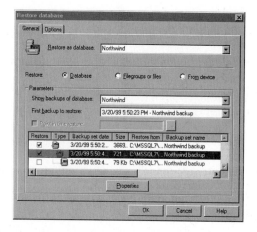

Restoring a Transaction Log

Use `restore log` to restore a transaction log backup. Transaction logs must be restored in the order in which they were backed up. If you attempt to restore a transaction log backup out of sequence, SQL Server will report an error. During a `restore database`, the data in the backup is copied over the database. After the `restore` is complete, the database contains all the data in the database at the time of the full database backup. Restoring a transaction log is different from restoring a database. After the log has been restored, a recovery takes place. SQL Server marches through the log, applying changes in the log that aren't reflected in the database. (Normally, all records in the log are new transactions.) The simplified syntax for the `restore log` command follows:

```
restore log <databasename> from <devicename>
```

You can use most of the options available to the `backup` command in the restore. This is the full syntax for the `restore log` command:

```
RESTORE LOG {database_name ¦ @database_name_var}
[FROM <backup_device> [,...n]]
[WITH
[DBO_ONLY]
[[,] FILE = file_number]
[[,] MEDIANAME = {media_name ¦ @media_name_variable}]
[[,] {NORECOVERY ¦ RECOVERY ¦ STANDBY = undo_filename}]
[[,] {NOUNLOAD ¦ UNLOAD}]
[[,] RESTART]
[[,] STATS [= percentage]]
[[,] STOPAT = {date_time ¦ @date_time_var}]]
```

Most of the options are explained in the `backup database` section. `FILE` is defined in the `restore database` section. `STOPAT` is discussed in the section "Restoring to a Point in Time" later in this chapter.

The restore of a transaction log backup usually requires significantly less time than a `restore database` because the size of the log is normally much smaller than the size of the database itself. No modifications should be made to the database between a `restore database` and a `restore transaction` (or between transaction log restores). Once any changes have been made to the database, no further transaction logs can be restored.

Restoring a File or Filegroup

SQL Server 7.0 allows you to restore a single file or filegroup, either from a file or filegroup backup or from a complete database backup. Here's the complete syntax for restoring files or filegroups:

```
RESTORE DATABASE {database_name ¦ @database_name_var}
<file_or_filegroup> [,...n]
[FROM <backup_device> [,...n]]
[WITH
[DBO_ONLY]
[[,] FILE = file_number]
[[,] MEDIANAME = {media_name ¦ @media_name_variable}]
[[,] NORECOVERY]
[[,] {NOUNLOAD ¦ UNLOAD}]
[[,] REPLACE]
[[,] RESTART]
[[,] STATS [= percentage]]]
```

All options are identical to those of the `restore database` command, except for the `NORECOVERY` and `MOVE` options. The `NORECOVERY` option in a filegroup restore keeps the database in a load state, which is useful if there are more restore commands to follow. The `MOVE` option is not available with filegroup restores. You must apply a transaction log restore after a filegroup restore to ensure that the database remains in a consistent state.

You can also restore files and filegroups using the Restore database dialog box. Figure 12.8 shows the `file or filegroup` option selected.

FIGURE 12.8

The Backup History list, showing only file backups and filegroup backups.

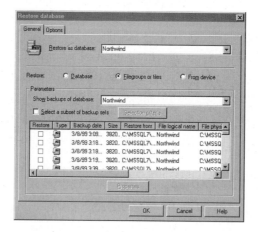

The backup icon for a file or filegroup backup includes a picture of a file folder.

Restoring to a Point in Time

SQL Server 7.0 allows you restore transaction logs to a specified point in time. You specify the desired date and time with the `STOPAT` option of the `restore transaction` command. If you refer to Figure 12.6, you can see the check box to indicate a point-in-time recovery, and the text boxes to allow you to enter the desired date and time. Point-in-time recovery is possible only while restoring transaction logs and isn't possible from a database or filegroup restore.

When restoring a sequence of transaction log backups, if you aren't sure which backup has the date and time needed, you can specify the same date and time for each of the restore operations; this way, you can be sure of stopping at the specified date and time.

Point-in-time recovery is possible because SQL Server writes an actual date/time timestamp in the transaction log. When doing point-in-time recovery, SQL Server checks the log for a timestamp greater than the specified time. Once one is encountered, that transaction and all subsequent transactions are rolled back. In this case, *subsequent* means records that occur in the log after the one that triggered a point-in-time recovery.

If the system time was incorrect when the log was written, for example, one hour ahead, the log will have timestamps that are one hour ahead. A log written to the transaction log at 4:30 will have a timestamp of 5:30 and will trigger point-in-time recovery if STOPAT was set to 5:30.

Backup and Restore History

SQL Server 7.0 has four new tables in the msdb database that record the history of backups and restores. In version 6.5, the tables were called sysbackuphistory, sysbackupdetail, sysrestorehistory, and sysrestoredetail. You must change all references to these names in any existing code to the new names in version 7.0, and the references are not one-to-one. In version 7.0, the history tables are backupfile, backupmediafamily, backupmediaset, backupset, restorefile, restorefilegroup, and restorehistory. SQL Enterprise Manager uses these tables when displaying the Restore dialog box; the tables allow you to see what backups are available for restoring. If you refer to Figure 12.6, you can see the Backup History list in the middle of the screen. As an administrator, you can also use these tables for generating your own reports of the history of your backups and restores.

Additional Backup Considerations

The pieces of the puzzle are starting to fall into place. You've defined the groundwork necessary to begin development of your backup and recovery approach. Now, you must consider several issues that can affect your plan.

Frequency of Backups

As mentioned previously, you should back up as frequently as necessary for effective database administration. This statement is intentionally vague because the frequency of backups varies based on your requirements. The deciding factor is the amount of time your business can afford for the database to be unavailable after a disaster. You now also have the ability to do a differential database backup.

The total time to restore a database is the sum of database restore time and transaction log restore time. The database restore happens only once during a recovery of a database, and the time can be predicted to some degree. The time to do the transaction log restores, however, is unpredictable. The time to restore transaction logs is based on the amount of activity since the database backup.

Consider the difference between a database backed up yearly versus a database backed up weekly, with transaction logs backed up every day between backups for both. The yearly backup scenario has 364 transaction log backups between database backups; the weekly backup scenario has 6 transaction log backups. If a disaster occurs on January 4, the time to recover in both cases is identical. Each scenario has a database restore (January 1 database backup) and three transaction log restores (January 2, 3, and 4 transaction log backups). Consider the worst-case scenario: A yearly backup approach could result in having to restore a full year's worth of activity one day at a time. The weekly backup approach would have a maximum of only a week's worth of activity to restore. Therefore, you should back up your database as often as possible. Ideally, database backups should occur with no activity on the system. Although this isn't a requirement, it assures you that the backup contains the state of your database before and after your backup was made. If this isn't possible, make your backups when activity is as light as possible.

You can execute backups during normal business hours, but they'll have an effect on the performance of your system. Database backups in SQL Server 7.0 are much less devastating to performance than those of earlier versions. This is due to code changes in the implementation of the database backup and increased speed of the process.

You can use differential backups for medium time-frame backups or when there is not enough time to perform a full backup. After any nonlogged operation, you should make a differential backup if the impact of a full database backup is too large because the transaction logs will no longer be usable for recovery.

Transaction log backups are often scheduled during normal business hours, but periods of low (or no) activity are obviously preferred. Backing up a transaction log takes significantly less time than backing up a database, and the time required is based on the amount of data in the log (which is based on modifications since the last backup transaction). A backup plan for a production system should include transaction log backups to provide up-to-the-minute recovery and differential database backups at low activity as well. Development environments normally don't back up transaction logs because this type of recovery isn't needed. Fairly frequent database backups usually suffice.

Capturing Statistics

Capture as many statistics as possible about the backup and restore processes. This information is invaluable in estimating durations and gives you real statistics about the performance of your system. These are important statistics to gather:

- Total database size (`sp_helpdb`).
- Total number of used pages (`sp_spaceused` and `dbcc sqlperf (logspace)`).
- Total execution time. (If you're using the command syntax in T-SQL, you can wrap the backup or restore command with `select getdate()`.)

For backups, the time to execute is fairly linear, based on used pages. For restores, the time to execute is based on total database size and used pages.

You need to understand and monitor database size and usage when planning backup regimens for databases that haven't leveled off in size. During the early stages of a system, data volume can be low. Data is added over time. This increase levels off when your purge and archive criteria kick in.

For example, you might create a 15GB database to support your production system. Initially, it might be restored with only 2GB of base information (used pages). If your application adds 5GB of data each year, and data is purged when it's two years old, the database size levels off at 12GB. Your statistics might show that the 2GB database can be backed up in one hour. If you have a four-hour backup window, you have to start investigating alternative approaches when your database reaches 8GB. By capturing statistics, you would be able to forecast this problem a full year in advance.

Transaction Logging

It's important to prevent the transaction log from running out of space. When the transaction log fills, no other logged operations can be executed until space is available in the log. This is disastrous in production systems. SQL Server 7.0 provides automatic log growth, but the log still cannot grow larger than the space available, and the growth rate needs to be optimized.

Ensure that a log is set to a reasonable size to start, to avoid the performance impact of the transaction log growth. It is also important to monitor and understand the optimal growth increment percentage, to prevent constant growth.

Although you can set the transaction log to grow and shrink automatically (allowing for an almost DBA-less development environment), many administrators find that on a production system, this is a function that they want to control manually, to ensure that growth and shrinking happen at the appropriate times. In this case, you must observe all of the previous problems with transaction logs filling up in version 6.5.

Even though you have the backup transaction activities scheduled, the system might experience peak activities (end of quarter, fiscal year end, and so forth) that cause the log to fill at a greatly accelerated rate. You must monitor the size of the log so that a full transaction log won't take you by surprise.

Monitoring Available Log Space

SQL Server offers the following two stored procedures to monitor space availability. You can use either to get a report on the syslogs table:

- sp_spaceused
- dbcc sqlperf (logspace)

sp_spaceused checks the reserved column to see how many pages are in use. Relate this to your overall log size to determine availability.

dbcc sqlperf (logspace) provides an accurate reporting of the number of data pages used. As with sp_spaceused, relate this value to overall log size to determine availability. It reports statistics regarding space used and space free in megabytes as well as a percentage of total space.

SQL Server can also use SQL Server's Performance Monitor to monitor log space. Performance Monitor's Alert subsystem can monitor total space used in megabytes, as well as a percentage of space used. This latter option is accurate only if the log is on its own device. Performance Monitor enables you to activate ISQL command-line scripts in response to particular events—most notably, setting a percentage threshold over which the log can't grow. Performance Monitor relies on a *polling interval* to determine how large the log is, and this polling action causes a performance hit.

SQL Server 7.0 includes a number of new Performance Monitor counters to help you manage and understand the growth of the log. The Databases object includes counters for log size (Log File(s) Size), the number of times a log growths (Log Growths), the number of times a log shrinks (Log Shrinks), and the percentage of log space used (Percent Log Used). Monitoring these counters along with the database size counter (Data File(s) Size) can help you understand the production server activity.

Developing Your Backup and Recovery Plan

Consider all your databases when developing the backup and recovery plan. System databases have different requirements from those of user databases.

Using a Standby Server

If the primary server is lost, you can bring a standby server online in a short amount of time. Because it is possible to use a standby server in a read-only mode between restore statements (by using the STANDBY with an undo file option described earlier), this server can also serve a function to the organization while it is waiting to save the day.

To use a standby server, you should restore each backup from the primary server to the standby server after the backup using the NORECOVERY option. This will ensure that the server is not recovered as it is waiting.

If the primary server databases become damaged, but the server itself is still running, immediately back up the log with the NO_TRUNCATE option, if possible. (At the time that this was written, this option did not work if the primary data file was unavailable, but Microsoft is working on the problem.) This normally will back up the entire log, even if the database is unavailable. You then apply this last log to the standby server, with the recovery option, to bring the server up to date to the primary server and to force the final recovery. If the last log is not available because the server itself has become unavailable, use the restore command without a FROM clause on the standby server to force the recovery.

System Databases

There are four system databases created as part of server installation: master, model, tempdb, and msdb (three for version 4.2*x*, which has no msdb). tempdb is temporary (it's actually rebuilt by SQL Server every time it's started); by definition, it should be considered exempt from backups. All other system databases should be backed up, however. If replication is installed, you might also have a distribution server to back up.

Threats

You should watch out for two things with system databases:

- Database or table corruption
- Damage to the master database filegroup

If corruption occurs, follow the steps to rebuild that individual database. If the master database filegroup is damaged, it must be rebuilt. This affects master, model, and tempdb.

The master Database

The master database isn't a high-activity database, and it tends to be fairly small. The following activities result in the insertion or modification of rows in various system tables:

- Creating, altering, or dropping databases
- Adding or dropping logins or users
- Adding or dropping backup devices
- Reconfiguring SQL Server
- Adding remote servers

Because the master database controls SQL Server, a database corruption or the loss of the master device can be devastating. SQL Server is unavailable until the master database is repaired. Not having a current backup of the master database can be fatal (or at least quite painful). To protect yourself, back up the master database whenever commands are executed that insert, update, or delete rows in the system tables. I cannot stress enough the importance of backing up this database. Recreating the master database from scratch can be extremely difficult, especially if you haven't saved the data from the system tables.

> **NOTE**
>
> Remember that only full database backups are allowed of the master database.

Detecting the Problem

If you lose the master device, the server goes down, alerting you to the problem. Alert messages appear in the errorlog file created by SQL Server, as well as in the Windows NT Event Log application. The normal method of detecting corruption in any database is using the suite of DBCC commands. If corruption occurs in the master database, the system likely will be affected instantaneously. Often, the server goes down and doesn't come up or major errors appear in errorlog.

> **TIP**
>
> If a DBCC detects corruption in master, log a call to Microsoft Product Support Services. Corruption in master or msdb might not be as serious on the surface, but it could be indicative of a problem with the underlying master device. If you're confident that you can solve the problem yourself, start executing the steps in the recovery process.

You must be proactive to avoid a painful recovery. First of all, avoid striping the master database backups, even if it's a standard for your user databases. Make sure that all of the master backup can fit on a single tape or in an operating-system file. (Based on the normal size of the master database, this shouldn't be a problem.) You must start SQL Server in single-user mode to start the recovery process. If the restore requires a volume change, you can't open another connection to tell the backup server that the new tape is in place.

Mitigating the Risk

You should regularly back up the master database, probably on the same schedule as your user databases. If you make a change and you don't want to wait for the backup scripts to run, execute it by hand. As always, you should have scripts saved for every activity that modifies master.

The SQL Server Setup utility has an option to rebuild the master device. (The check box says that you're rebuilding the master database, but what's really happening is that the master.dat file is overwritten with the original contents, so you get a whole new master device, including a whole new master database.) Rebuilding the master device, and allowing the setup process to complete, gives you a master device identical to when SQL Server was first installed. At this point, the master database has no knowledge of any user databases in your system. You have to execute one of the following:

- Restore your most recent backup of the master database (which is preferred).
- Transfer the data using Data Transformation Services or BCP.
- Re-create items from DDL scripts.

You should have all the resources to execute any of these approaches at any time. It's the only way to ensure that the master database (and SQL Server) will be available when you need it.

model and msdb

The model database is copied into any database created with `create database`. It houses those items you want to be available across all databases (rules, defaults, user-defined datatypes, and users). If you've made any modifications to model, save all DDL files and back up the database after changes are made.

The msdb database holds all the task-scheduling and error-processing instructions that SQL Executive uses for automated task and alert handling. You should back up this database any time you modify it so that you can restore your scheduled and error-based tasks as quickly as possible.

If you detect corruption in either of these databases, you must re-create the entire master database using the Setup utility described earlier.

User Databases

Your business requirements define whether a database should be backed up. Backups are normally a requirement for production systems. Your approach should define the following:

- *Who?* Identify the person or group responsible for backup and recovery.
- *Name?* Outline your naming standards for database names and backup devices.
- *Which databases?* Identify the databases in your system to be backed up.
- *Types of backups?* Indicate whether you'll back up only the database or whether you'll also back up the transaction log.
- *How?* Decide whether backups will use disk or file devices and whether the backup is a single process or striped.
- *Frequency?* Identify the schedule for backing up the database and the transaction logs.
- *Execution?* Determine whether backups will be initiated by hand or automated. If they will be automated, detail whether the backup is conducted by an off-the-shelf tool or custom program. Include all code (backup script and scheduler, if applicable) and make sure that it's commented extremely well.

For database recovery, detail the procedures involved in restoring each database. If you're using a tool, outline its use.

Considerations for Very Large Databases

When developing a backup and recovery plan for VLDB environments, you must consider several items. The challenge of a VLDB is its sheer size; everything is larger. Tables are measured in gigabytes, and databases are measured in tens or hundreds of gigabytes. The fact that several SQL Server VLDBs exist in industry today gives credence to the product's capability of handling vast amounts of data. VLDBs aren't easy to implement, however, for a variety of reasons. These are the top-10 VLDB issues:

- Impact of corruption
- Time for recovery
- Time of backups
- Time to perform initial restore of data
- Time to update statistics of indexes
- Time to perform database consistency checks

- Time to create indexes
- Impact of incremental batch data restoring routines
- Impact of online activity
- Backup media capacity and backup facilities

Based on these items, you need to make several database architecture choices:

- Physically implement a single logical database as several smaller physical databases
- Use multiple filegroups
- Segment tables horizontally and vertically
- Determine table or index placement
- Determine log size and placement
- Determine tempdb size and placement

Consider the issues in regard to your choices. The time required to perform database backups, restores, updates of statistics, and creation of indexes increases exponentially with size. Follow these steps:

1. First, consider the amount of time you're willing to be down while performing a recovery (the impact of corruption). If you need a database to be recovered within eight hours, determine the size of a database that can be recovered in that amount of time. Note that the restore process is much slower than the backup process. Assume that 4GB is the maximum database size that can be re-restored in the defined window.

2. Taking 4GB as a baseline, analyze table estimates for your database. If you have a 40GB logical database, you might need to implement 10 4GB databases. Are any tables greater than 4GB? How many tables can you fit in a database? Are any tables candidates for segmentation, based on this determination alone?

3. Develop your utopian administration schedule. For every day during a month, determine what periods of time can be dedicated to administrative activities. Weekends might be available, but this isn't always the case. If you determine that you have five hours per night to perform administrative activities, you then need to determine what activities must be completed and whether they can be distributed over your available administration time.

4. Determine the speed of the backup process. Take into consideration backup media

capacity, speed, and the number of databases to be backed up. Benchmark several scenarios. Create a database and restore it with about 2GB of data. Perform several database backups with a varying number of backup devices (striped backups). Run several backup processes (for different databases) simultaneously.

5. Determine periodic activity timings for each of your tables. This should be a matrix with table names down one axis and activities (such as DBCC, `update statistics`, and index creation) across the other axis. After you develop a baseline for these activities, you can easily group tables together to determine the total amount of administration time needed for a certain combination of tables.

6. Determine which activities must take place in a batch window. If you want to perform database consistency checks immediately prior to backing up a database, the time required to perform both activities can be determined from your timings. Assume that a backup takes three hours and a DBCC takes two hours. Although this total fits in your 5-hour window, it doesn't consider the fact that you have 10 of these to complete during the course of a week. Perform activities in parallel to determine concurrent processing times. Can you DBCC and back up two databases in a five-hour period?

7. Finalize your schedule and document accordingly.

8. Update your documents periodically based on actual experiences.

Summary

Developing a backup and recovery approach isn't a trivial process. You must consider internal and external forces and determine their impact. SQL Server 7.0 provides more options for a backup and recovery strategy and makes some of the work, such as automatic log growth, easier. In the end, you should document your approach so that it's clear how you plan to handle backup and recovery activities. Be sure to gather statistics on all activities, and use those statistics to predict future performance.

Although building a good backup and recovery plan seems like a tremendous amount of work, it's worth the effort in the long run. Your project plans must allocate time to create the plan, and the plan should be in place before you make your production database available.

Database Maintenance

by John J. Del Buono

IN THIS CHAPTER

Database maintenance is an integral part of sound SQL Server performance and stability. SQL Servers that have periodic maintenance generally have fewer problems for both the system administrator and database users. Placing more emphasis on the parameters of database maintenance helps the SQL Server perform to its optimal potential. Although this idea is important, maintenance should not be a troublesome or complicated task. It is imperative that you as the system administrator acquire the best tools to complete this task.

Microsoft SQL Server 7.0 has eased this burden for the system administrator by creating such tools as the Database Maintenance Plan and the Database Consistency Checker (DBCC). These two tools are basically integrated; the Database Maintenance Plan is actually a GUI interface of some of the DBCC statements. In the following pages, I discuss these tools in some detail and show their effect on SQL Server 7.0.

The Database Maintenance Plan Wizard

The Database Maintenance Plan helps you execute SQL Server's more frequently used built-in maintenance commands. These procedures let you run tasks immediately or schedule them for later or recurring times. The plan includes the following:

- Checking database integrity
- Updating database statistics
- Backing up the database

SQL Server 7.0 combines popular maintenance tasks in a user-friendly environment through the Database Maintenance Plan Wizard.

Start the wizard by selecting Tools, Database Maintenance Planner from the menu bar. You'll see the welcome screen shown in Figure 13.1. Click Next to proceed.

FIGURE 13.1

The Database Maintenance Plan Wizard.

Selecting Databases

Select the database or databases for maintenance. Figure 13.2 shows the choices:

- All Databases—As the selection suggests, you can schedule a maintenance plan for all the databases within the SQL Server.

- All System Databases—These databases are created by the SQL Server 7.0 setup to keep track of all databases, users, security, and other essential components within the server itself. These important databases should always have a periodic schedule for maintenance and backup.

- All User Databases—These databases are usually created by the administrators for data retrieval and storage. SQL Server 7.0 also creates two user databases (pubs and Northwind) during setup as samples for training purposes.

- These Databases—This selection lets you select individual databases within SQL Server 7.0.

FIGURE 13.2
Selecting the databases.

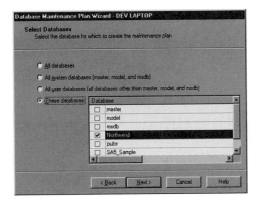

Updating Data Optimization Information

As information fills the data and index pages, updates to the database require more time to complete. If you reorganize these pages, the performance is greatly improved. The next section of the wizard lets you schedule data optimization procedures to "clean up" and reorganize the data. Figure 13.3 displays the options for this section.

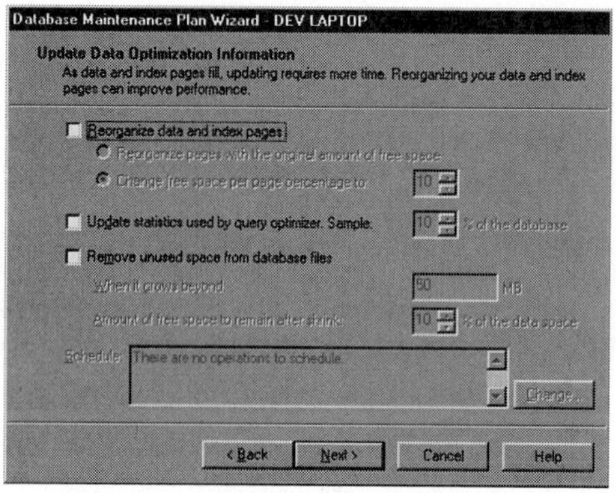

FIGURE 13.3

Updating data optimization information.

FIGURE 13.3

Updating data optimization information.

The following are the options that can be used for this section:

- Reorganize Data and Index Pages—When SQL Server is set up, a percentage of free space is set aside for each data page of an index within a table. This is known as the FILLFACTOR. The FILLFACTOR specifies the percentage that SQL Server will leave empty for each index page; this is referred to as the *leaf level* or *leaf page*. As an index page fills up, splits occur on the page to accommodate more data. The more splits that occur, the more time is used, which in turn impedes overall server performance. A properly set FILLFACTOR allows the SQL Server to perform optimally when the index page fills up.

  The user-specified FILLFACTOR values can be from 1 through 100. Lower numbers allow the SQL Server to create new indexes with leaf pages that are not completely full. This results in fewer splits and optimizes time. It is recommended that smaller numbers be used on tables that contain, or will contain, small amounts of data and UPDATE and INSERT statements that will be performed regularly. If, for example, 100 is the FILLFACTOR where the UPDATE and INSERT statements are used, the result will be a split for each INSERT and possibly for each UPDATE. When the default value of 0 is the FILLFACTOR, only the leaf page is filled, and space for at least one row is left for nonleaf pages.

> **NOTE**
>
> Note that the FILLFACTOR settings apply only when the index is created; the empty space percentage is not dynamically kept within the pages.

When this option is selected, the indexes on the tables are dropped and re-created with a new `FILLFACTOR` value as determined by the following:

> Reorganize Pages with the Original Amount of Free Space—When the indexes are dropped and re-created, the `FILLFACTOR` value is the same as the initial value before dropping.

> Change Free Space Per Page Percentage To—Indexes are dropped and re-created, and the `FILLFACTOR` is automatically calculated with the new value specified in the text box.

- Update Statistics Used by Query Optimizer—This option updates the distribution statistics used by Microsoft SQL Server to optimize navigation through tables. Every once in a while, SQL Server samples a percentage of the data in these tables for each index to check the integrity of the data.

  When you select this option, you can increase the percentage of the data being sampled.

- Remove Unused Space from Database Files—This option removes any unused space within the database and reduces the size of the data files. This option offers two choices:

  - When It Grows Beyond—Unused space will be recovered when the database has increased to the size specified in the text box.

  - Amount of Free Space to Remain After Shrink—When the database is reduced in size, possibly to increase disk space for other operating system tasks, this option will leave a percentage of the free space within the database. This percentage is based on the data within the database and not the database itself.

- Schedule—This option sets the frequency of this maintenance execution. Clicking Change changes the default schedule.

Checking Database Integrity

Unfortunately, no server is invulnerable. Electrical failures, voltage spikes, and unreliable software all contribute to server problems and can corrupt or damage a database. The Database Integrity Check can take some of the pain out of recovering from such problems.

This section of the wizard helps you detect problems with database integrity caused by software or hardware failures. Figure 13.4 displays the options for this section.

13

DATABASE MAINTENANCE

FIGURE 13.4

Running the data-base integrity check.

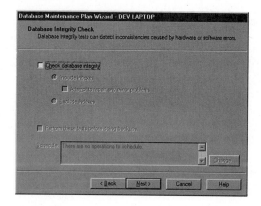

The following are the options that can be used for this section:

- Check Database Integrity—Click this to run the SQL-Transact statement DBCC CHECKDB (discussed later in this chapter). This selection reports any integrity issues that you can address. Additional options for this selection are

  - Include Indexes—Both the data pages and index pages are included in the scan.

  - Attempt to Repair Any Minor Problems—During the integrity operation, small problems are repaired automatically; I suggest that you select this option to avoid overlooking any repairs.

  - Exclude Indexes—Only data pages are scanned, reducing the time to complete the operation.

- Perform These Tests Before Doing Backups—When a backup is performed on the database, whether it is external or internal to SQL Server, this selection forces an integrity check of the data.

- Schedule—This option sets the frequency of this maintenance execution. Clicking Change changes the default schedule.

Specifying the Database Backup Plan

The next section of the Database Maintenance Plan Wizard deals with backups. Performing a periodic backup of the database reduces the risk of data loss. In addition to normal network backups—or with SQL 7.0 Desktop, standalone backups—this section allows you to schedule internal backups. For an internal backup, SQL Server 7.0 can place the backup copy in the SQL Server directory (which is not suggested), on another drive on the network, or on a tape device. Figure 13.5 shows the options for this section.

FIGURE 13.5

Specifying the database backup plan.

The following are the options that can be used for this section:

- Back Up the Database as Part of the Maintenance Plan—Schedule a database backup with the maintenance plan.
- Verify the Integrity of the Backup on Completion of the Backup—This option verifies that the backup completed normally and that all volumes have been mounted.
- Location to Store the Backup File—Here, you specify the location to store the backup copy. Clicking Tape places the file on a tape device attached to SQL Server. Clicking Disk places the file on a predefined drive location (described in the next section).
- Schedule—This option sets the frequency of this maintenance execution. Clicking Change changes the default schedule.

Specifying the Backup Disk Directory

The backup disk directory wizard page will appear only if you select Disk as the location to store the backup on the preceding page. This page lets you set the drive and directory in which the database backup file will be stored.

You can organize backup files in the following ways (see Figure 13.6):

- Use the Default Backup Directory—The backup file is placed in the default directory set by SQL Server, usually MSSQL\BACKUP.
- Use This Directory—The database file is placed in the directory you specify.
- Create a Subdirectory for Each Database—You can places the database file into a directory below the one you specify. If left unchecked, no directory is created.

13

DATABASE MAINTENANCE

- Remove Files Older Than—SQL Server will delete backed-up database files older than the date specified. If you select this option, I suggest that you have a reliable archival backup plan in place for the entire SQL Server.

- Backup File Extension—Specify the extension for the backup file.

FIGURE 13.6

Specifying the backup disk directory.

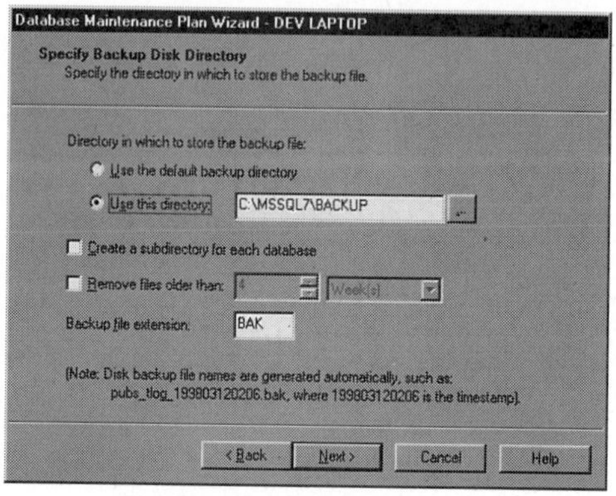

Specifying the Transaction Log Backup Plan

Transactions are performed continuously throughout the daily operation of SQL Server. These transactions include adds, updates, and deletes made by a number of users on a network or processes in a program. Each of these transactions is recorded in a log file, the transaction log. The purpose of this log is to keep an up-to-the-moment record of all transactions. SQL Server uses the transaction log as a reference point to the last transaction performed.

The transaction log is usually backed up on a daily basis. However, the more frequent the backup, the more up-to-date the retrieved information will be in the event of a SQL Server failure. You can restore the latest database file backup and then apply the latest transaction log backup to retrieve the most up-to-date information recorded in the database before the failure occurred.

The wizard page shown in Figure 13.7 is where you schedule the Transaction log backup:

- Back Up the Transaction Log as Part of the Maintenance Plan—You click this to schedule the transaction log backup.

- Verify the Integrity of the Backup on Completion of the Backup—This option ensures that the backup has been completed without problems or integrity issues.

- Location to Store the Backup File—Here, you specify the location to store the backup copy. Clicking Tape places the file on a tape device attached to SQL Server. Clicking Disk places the file on a predefined drive location (described in the next section).

- Schedule—This option sets the frequency of this maintenance execution. Clicking Change changes the default schedule.

FIGURE 13.7

Specifying the transaction log backup plan.

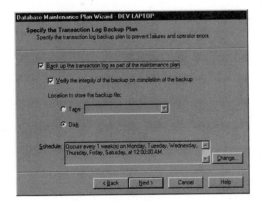

Specifying the Transaction Log Backup Disk Directory

The backup disk directory wizard page will appear only if you select Disk as the location to store the backup on the preceding page. This page lets you set the drive and directory for storing the transaction log file backup.

Administrators can organize transaction backups in the following ways (see Figure 13.8):

- Use the Default Backup Directory—The backup file is placed in the default directory set by SQL Server, usually MSSQL\BACKUP.

- Use This Directory—The transaction log file backup is placed in the directory you specify.

- Create a Subdirectory for Each Database—You can place the transaction log backup file into a directory below the one you specify. If left unchecked, no directory is created.

- Remove Files Older Than—SQL Server will delete the backed-up transaction log files older than the date specified. If you select this option, I suggest that you have a reliable archival backup plan in place for the entire SQL Server.

- Backup File Extension—Specify the extension for the backup file.

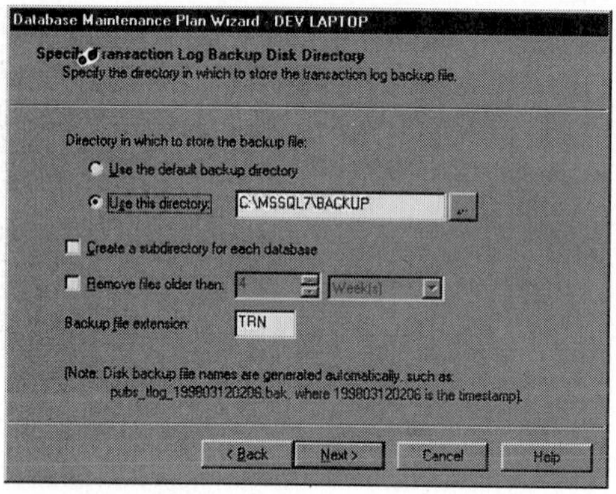

FIGURE 13.8

Specifying the transaction log backup disk directory.

Generating Reports

The Reports to Generate wizard page, shown in Figure 13.9, lets you specify the directory for any reports generated by the maintenance plan. The reports include detailed information about the procedures performed in the maintenance plan. The reports also include any errors encountered.

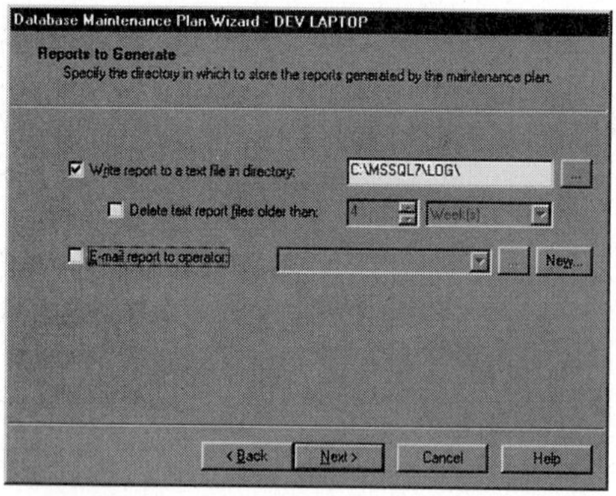

FIGURE 13.9

Generating reports.

The following are the options that can be used for this section:

- Write Report to a Text File in Directory—You can specify the directory for the report file. The default is a LOG directory below the SQL Server 7.0 directory.
- Delete Text Report Files Older Than—This option removes any reports older than the date specified.
- E-mail Report to Operator—This option specifies the operator who will receive the report via SQL mail. If the operator is not already set up to receive emails as alerts, you can click New to create a new operator.

Maintenance History

SQL Server can record a detailed history of the maintenance plan into a history table in the msdb database. This database can be on the same server as the maintenance plan or on another server.

Figure 13.10 illustrates the setup of this history table:

- Write History to the msdb.dbo.sysdbmaintplan_history Table on the Local Server—This options places the history in the msdb database on the server where the plan was created.
- Limit Rows in the Table To—You can specify the maximum rows to be used in the history table. If the number of rows exceeds this value, the earliest rows of history information will be deleted.
- Write History to the Server—Specify the name of the remote server and msdb database where the history table will be written.

FIGURE 13.10

*Keeping a mainte-
nance history.*

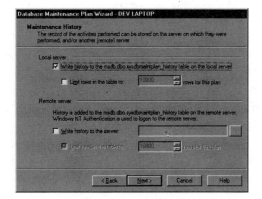

13

DATABASE
MAINTENANCE

Completing the Database Maintenance Plan Wizard

The final page in the wizard, shown in Figure 13.11, specifies a default plan name, which you can overwrite if you want, and a small description of the plan that was created. Clicking the Finish button saves and begins executing the plan according to its specifications.

FIGURE 13.11

Completing the Database Maintenance Plan Wizard.

The Database Consistency Checker

In situations that call for a higher level of maintenance, which the Database Maintenance Plan does not fully provide, SQL Server 7.0 can use the Database Consistency Checker, or DBCC. Run from the Query Analyzer, the DBCC has a full list of commands that perform complex database maintenance tasks. The DBCC performs the commands from the Database Maintenance Plan in addition to other commands that fine-tune or change the behavior of SQL Server 7.0. Figure 13.12 shows the syntax of a common DBCC statement, including the arguments used for this particular statement. This statement shows the database name to be checked without checking the indexes, and tells SQL Server to display any errors that are found.

FIGURE 13.12

The DBCC statement CHECKDB *in the Microsoft SQL Server Query Analyzer.*

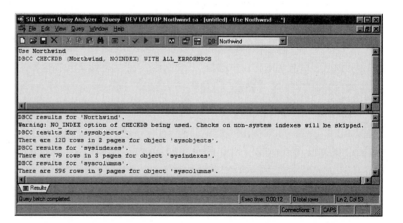

The following is a list of the more commonly used DBCC statements in SQL Server 7.0:

```
SHOWCONTIG
CHECKDB
CHECKFILEGROUP
CHECKCATALOG
DBREINDEX
OPENTRAN
SHRINKDATABASE
CHECKTABLE
UPDATEUSAGE
```

Detecting and Resolving Database Corruption

Programs that use databases can, from time to time, create data that is syntactically incorrect. Hardware "glitches" can cause SQL Server to receive information that is faulty or make it fail altogether. Both these situations can cause the database to become corrupt. The following DBCC statements can find and, in some cases, resolve these problems before they become too serious:

- DBCC SHOWCONTIG is used to determine heavy fragmentation of a database. Fragmentation occurs when data is inserted, updated, or deleted in a row of a table. These processes could lead to "holes" in the row, which tend to fill a data page. Tables with filled data pages can lead to longer running queries and updates. SHOWCONTIG removes these holes.

- DBCC CHECKDB checks for inconsistencies and integrity problems within the database. If the database is not too heavily damaged, CHECKDB will attempt to repair it.

  CHECKDB checks the following for each table in the database:

    - Correct linkage of index and data pages
    - Properly sorted indexes
    - Consistent pointers
    - Reasonable data on each page
    - Reasonable page offsets

- DBCC CHECKFILEGROUP checks for the page allocation and integrity of the tables within the database. This statement has the same functionality as the CHECKDB statement; the difference is that CHECKFILEGROUP checks tables and indexes multiple times on the different filegroups. No modifications can be performed on the tables or indexes while this statement is executing.

As with CHECKDB, CHECKFILEGROUP checks the following for each table in a file-group:

- Correct linkage of index and data pages
- Properly sorted indexes
- Consistent pointers
- Reasonable data on each page
- Reasonable page offsets.

- DBCC CHECKTABLE checks the linkages and sizes of pages for the specific table but does not check the allocation of the pages in the table.

  CHECKTABLE also checks for

  - Correct linkage of index and data pages
  - Properly sorted indexes
  - Consistent pointers
  - Reasonable data on each page
  - Reasonable page offsets

- DBCC CHECKCATALOG checks for the consistency between tables in a database. It verifies that every datatype in syscolumns will have a corresponding match in systypes and that views and tables in sysobjects will have at least one column in syscolumns. These system tables are used by the master database to keep track of all objects and processes within the SQL server.

- DBCC CHECKALLOC is the eventual replacement for the DBCC statement NEWALLOC. Although NEWALLOC is included in SQL Server 7.0 for backward compatibility, I suggest that you use CHECKALLOC.

  CHECKALLOC checks the allocation and use of all pages in the database. You do not need to use this statement if DBCC CHECKDB has already been executed because an allocation check is performed with CHECKDB. If allocation errors were the only errors reported, then you should perform CHECKALLOC with the repair option to save time.

- DBCC DBREINDEX rebuilds a single index for a table or all indexes for a table within the database. DBREINDEX accomplishes in a single statement what would take the equivalent of multiple DROP INDEX and CREATE INDEX statements.

  DBREINDEX allows indexes to be rebuilt dynamically. This would let you, in certain situations, rebuild indexes without knowing the structure and constraints of a table. These constraints are ignored when the bulk copy command is executed.

Trace Flags and Other Useful Commands

Trace flags are used to set certain characteristics or behaviors for SQL Server operation. You set these flags using the DBCC statements TRACEON and TRACEOFF. The following is a list of trace flags used in SQL Server 7.0:

106—Syntax errors display without the related line number for the error.

107—Use this to set numbers with floating decimal points.

206—This allows backward compatibility when the SETUSER statement is used.

237—REFERENCES permissions are disabled so you can create a foreign key on a table that is not owned by the original key owner.

244—Interim constraint violations checking is disabled.

260—Extended stored procedure dynamic link libraries (DLLs) versioning information is displayed.

325—This option prints performance-related details on nonclustered indexes to a sort when processing an ORDER BY clause.

326—Prints comparison information between estimated and actual sorts.

330—Enables complete information output to be displayed using the SET SHOW-PLAN option. This gives detailed information about joins.

506—You can enforce null values for comparisons between variables and parameters according to SQL-92 standards.

1204—This displays which type of locks are being used in the deadlock and the command being executed at that time.

1205—Use this to display detailed command information at the time of a deadlock.

1609—When executing sp_sqlexec in Open Data Services, this code allows the unpacking and checking of remote procedure call (RPC) information to be turned on.

2701—Use this to set the @@ERROR system function. Enabled sets @@ERROR to 50000 with a RAISERROR severity level at 10 or less. Disabled sets @@ERROR to 0 with the same RAISERROR conditions.

3205—Tape drive hardware compression is disabled.

3604—Allows the trace output to be sent to the client.

3605—Records trace output in the error log.

3640—DONE_IN_PROC messages are disabled in stored procedure output.

4022—Procedures automatically started are bypassed.

4030—Prints the receive buffer in ASCII and byte formats. This allows you to view any queries that are sent to the SQL Server.

13

DATABASE
MAINTENANCE

4031—Prints the send buffers in ASCII and byte formats (information sent back from the SQL Server).

4032—Use this to print the receive buffer output in ASCII format only. This usually replaces trace flag 4030 in order to increase the speed of the trace output.

7505—When calling dbcursorfetchex, this enables the handling of return codes for version 6.*x*. The cursor position is set on top of the end of the cursor result set.

8783—When enabling SET ROWCOUNT ON, this option allows the DELETE, INSERT, and UPDATE statements to recognize this setting.

The following is a list of available commands that might prove useful in the everyday life of the system administrator:

- DBCC TRACEON turns on the specified trace-flag number or numbers listed previously. These trace flags will remain on until the DBCC TRACEOFF statement has been executed for the corresponding numbers.

- DBCC TRACESTATUS returns the status of the trace flags. Two columns are returned in the resultset; the first represents the trace flag number, and the second is the status number. A status of 1 indicates the specified trace flag is turned on; a 0 represents off. To get a status of all flags on, include –1 as the first argument after the statement.

- DBCC SHRINKDATABASE is the SQL Server 7.0 replacement statement for DBCC SHRINKDB. This statement is used to reduce the size of data file and transaction log size allocation within a database. Reducing the size of these allocations frees space for other operating system usage. It should be noted that data files are reduced on a per-file basis; log files are reduced as if they were one continuous log.

- DBCC OPENTRAN informs the user of any older active transaction or distributed or nondistributed replication transactions on the database. Also, it displays any open transactions left in the transaction logs. This becomes useful when the log is truncated. Only a committed transaction of a log can be truncated. Using DBCC OPENTRAN, you can view the open transaction, inform the user to commit the transaction, or terminate the transaction yourself.

- DBCC UPDATEUSAGE displays a report of any inaccuracies within the master database sysindexes table and then attempts to correct the inaccuracies. These inaccuracies may be reported as incorrect space usage when the sp_spaceused system stored procedure is executed.

- UPDATEUSAGE is used to synchronize space-usage counters. This statement can take some time to run on large tables or databases; therefore, you should use it only when you believe that incorrect data has been returned by the sp_spaceused stored procedure.

Summary

Designing and implementing a good maintenance plan and tools will ensure that SQL Server 7.0 performs at its peak. Using tools such as the Database Maintenance Plan Wizard and Database Consistency Checker help you achieve this implementation goal.

Quite a few procedures, statements, and tools in SQL Server 7.0 customize the server to all users' specifications, but few are as important as the Database Maintenance Plan and the DBCC for the optimal performance of the server. If you use these tools, SQL Server 7.0 will run with fewer errors, the users will be more productive, and your life will be a little easier.

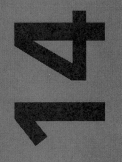

Multiserver Administrative Support

by Greg Mable

IN THIS CHAPTER

This chapter explores the multiserver administrative features of the SQL Server Agent, the built-in task-scheduling service provided with SQL Server. For more information on the SQL Server Agent, see Chapter 11, "The SQL Server Agent."

SQL Server 7.0 now includes features that make managing multiple SQL Server sites easier. To lower the total cost of ownership, Microsoft enhanced the features of the SQL Server Agent to let you create multiserver administrative jobs. This feature provides centralized control of job functions and event handling. You can designate one SQL Server to be the master SQL Server Agent and enlist other SQL Servers as target servers. The master SQL Server can distribute administrative jobs among the target SQL Servers. The target SQL Servers can then run the jobs designated for them and notify the master server of the results.

This enables you to administer a large number of remote SQL Server installations from a single, centralized location. And, using Enterprise Manager, this central SQL Server can serve as the console for monitoring the performance and activity of the remote SQL Servers.

Creating a Master SQL Server Agent

To create a master SQL Server Agent (MSX), you can run the Make Master Server Wizard. This wizard will guide you step-by-step through the process. To run the wizard, from Enterprise Manager highlight the SQL Server that you want to designate as the master SQL Server Agent and then select Make Master Server from the list of wizards. After you start the wizard, you see the screen shown in Figure 14.1.

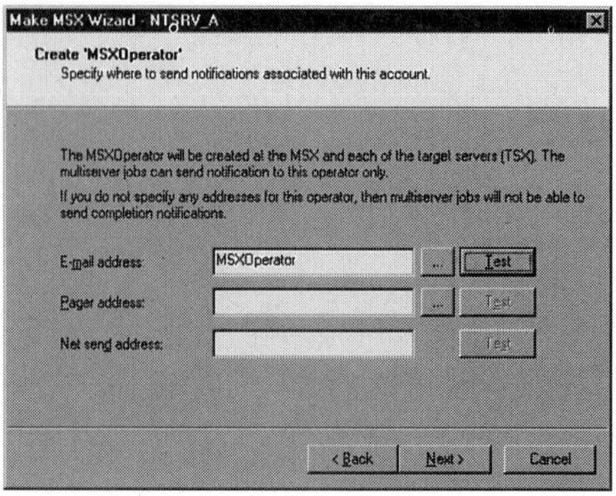

FIGURE 14.1

*Make Master SQL
Server Agent
Wizard: creating
the MSXOperator.*

The wizard will create the MSXOperator automatically. You need to specify which method you want the target servers to notify the master server about and then select an account to be used with the notification service.

> **TIP**
>
> To simplify your configuration, you can create an email and a Windows NT domain account with the same name as MSXOperator. That way, you can keep the association between the email account, NT domain account, and the SQL Server operator name consistent.

The next step in the wizard is to specify the target servers to enlist as shown in Figure 14.2. These will become the targets for any multiserver jobs created on the master.

FIGURE 14.2

Specifying target servers.

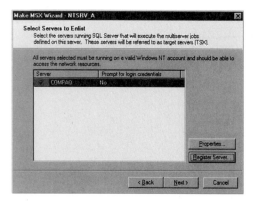

Those two steps are all that it takes to create a master SQL Server Agent. You might notice that the SQL Server Agent object in Enterprise Manager changes and has MSX appended to it. This visual clue indicates that this SQL Server is the master agent. You will also find that the jobs object has two entries beneath it: one for local jobs and one for multiserver jobs.

> **NOTE**
>
> You should note that the master server and all target servers must be running SQL Server 7.0. Multiserver administration is a new feature and is not backward compatible.

You can also create more than one master server, which might be useful in an environment where you must manage a large number of servers.

Enlisting Target Servers

You can enlist a target server (TSX) for a given master SQL Server Agent (MSX) using the Make Target Server Wizard. This wizard will walk you through the steps necessary to designate a server as the target server for a given MSX. A target server can be any SQL Server that you designate; however, the SQLServer and SQLServerAgent services must be running using an Windows NT domain account.

After you start the Make TSX Wizard, you see the screen shown in Figure 14.3.

FIGURE 14.3

Specifying the MSX and location of the target.

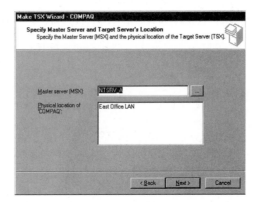

You specify the MSX server and provide a description of the location of the target server. The description is often useful when you want to know more about a target server than you can learn from its name.

Multiserver Jobs

To create a multiserver job, you can run the Job Wizard. The wizard will prompt you to specify the local server or any of the target servers. You can also create a new multiserver job using Enterprise Manager. You will be able to select any of the target servers to run the job. All the other options are the same as for local jobs. For more information on creating jobs, see Chapter 11.

Target servers periodically connect to the master server and download the list of jobs to perform. If a new job exists, the target server downloads the job. The target server then stores a copy of the job. Jobs created on the master server cannot be changed from the target server. When the job has run, the target server notifies the master server regarding the job's outcome. If the master server is unavailable when the target server attempts to notify it of the job's status, then the message is spooled until the master server is once again available.

As shown in Figure 14.4, you can monitor the status of the target server and the list of jobs for it to perform.

FIGURE 14.4

Managing a target server.

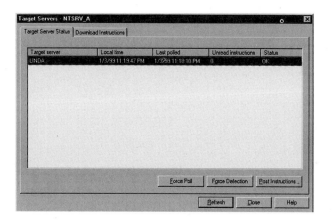

From this screen, you can force the target server to poll the master for any new jobs. You can also separate the target server from the master, which will allow the target server to be enlisted with another master server. You can explicitly specify which instructions should be downloaded to the target server. For example, you can specify that the target server synchronize its clock with the master server, specify the polling interval that the target server will use, or start a job on the target server. Periodically, you should synchronize the clocks on the target servers with the clock on the master server. You should also be aware whether your target servers are in the same time zone as the master server.

14

MULTISERVER ADMINISTRATIVE SUPPORT

> **TIP**
>
> If you have many target servers to manage, you should consider defining your master server on a nonproduction server. That way, a production SQL Server will not be affected by the job processing.

Event Forwarding

You can forward SQL Server event messages that meet or exceed a specific error severity level to a single SQL Server. This allows you to centralize event handling on one server. You can then define alerts and their associated operators only once. The server can also be the master SQL Server Agent.

CAUTION

If you forward events to a single SQL Server, network traffic as well as the processing load on the server can increase significantly. You should restrict the events to only those severity levels above a certain level, such as severity levels 19 through 25.

As shown in Figure 14.5, you can designate which server receives events from the Advanced properties page for the SQL Server Agent object. This option is only available on servers running Windows NT. You can select to forward either all events or only those events not handled by any local alerts that you might have defined.

FIGURE 14.5

Enabling event forwarding.

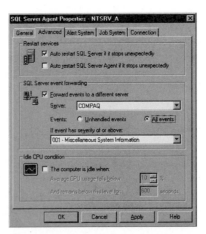

TIP

You should define local alerts for any events you want to be handled by the local server and avoid forwarding them. The alerts-forwarding server cannot distinguish between an event forwarded from Server A from the same event forwarded from Server B.

System Tables

When a target server polls the master server, it reads the sysdownloadlist table in the msdb database. The sysdownloadlist table contains all the operations assigned to a target server.

> **NOTE**
>
> Whenever you make changes to any multiserver job definition outside of Enterprise Manager, such as by using one of the stored procedures for modifying a job's definition, you must update the sysdownloadlist table so that the target servers will download the updated job definition. You can do this by running the following code:
>
> ```
> EXECUTE sp_post_msx_operation 'INSERT', 'JOB', <job_id>'
> ```

Summary

This chapter reviewed the multiserver administrative features provided with the SQL Server Agent. You can designate a master SQL Server Agent, where you can define a job to run on multiple servers and be notified regarding the job status. You can also designate an alerts-forwarding server, which would be the recipient of any events you forward from other SQL servers. The alert-forwarding server can then respond to these events as you deem appropriate. The multiserver administrative features ease the burden of maintaining a large number of servers and provide a means to centralize job maintenance and event handling.

Linked and Remote Server Management

by Matt Larson

IN THIS CHAPTER

CHAPTER 15

As your systems grow in size, complexity, or geographic distribution, you might find it necessary to enable your servers to communicate with each other directly. SQL Server does a terrific job of sharing data using linked servers. This chapter provides an overview of the new linked servers in SQL Server 7.0. It also briefly discusses remote servers, which are the predecessor to linked servers. Remote servers are only supported for backward compatibility.

Linked Servers Versus Remote Servers

Microsoft took a good, hard look at the current implementation of remote servers and decided to completely revamp it. Linked servers are the result. First, let's take a look at how remote servers worked and then compare them to linked servers.

Remote Servers

Remote servers are limited in functionality and relatively time-consuming to set up. The following list outlines the steps for setting up remote servers:

1. Define the local and remote servers on both servers.
2. Configure each server for remote access.
3. On the remote server, define the method for mapping logins and users to the server's own logins and users.
4. Set the remote option for password-checking.

It's easy to see how this was a frustrating process. You had to do work on both the local and remote servers. The data required on the remote server also severely limited what types of servers could be accessed. Login mappings were performed at the remote server instead of the local server. For example, the local user SandraLarson might be mapped to use the Guest user on the remote server. This works fine if the remote server is SQL Server, but how do you perform this task in another database that doesn't have user mappings? How do you tell an Oracle database to sign in the SandraLarson SQL Server user as Guest? These are just a few of the problems with remote servers.

Linked Servers

Unlike remote servers, linked servers have two simple setup steps:

1. Define the remote server on the local server.
2. Define the method for mapping remote logins on the local server.

Notice that all the configuration is performed on the local server. Using the preceding example, the mapping for the SandraLarson local user to the remote Guest user is stored in the local SQL Server database. In fact, you don't need to configure anything in the remote database. This setup allows SQL Server to use OLE DB.

OLE DB is an API that allows COM applications to work with databases as well as other data sources such as text files and spreadsheets. This lets SQL Server have access to a vast amount of different types of data.

Unlike remote servers, linked servers also allow distributed queries and transactions.

Distributed Queries

Distributed queries access data stored in OLE DB data sources. SQL Server treats these data sources as if they contained SQL Server tables. Due to this treatment, you can view or manipulate this data using the same basic syntax as other SQL Server SELECT, INSERT, UPDATE, or DELETE statements. The main difference is the table-naming convention. Distributed queries use this basic syntax when referring to the remote table:

```
linked_server_name.catalog.schema.object_name
```

The following query accesses data from a sales table in an Oracle database, a region table in a Microsoft Access database, and a customer table in a SQL Server database:

```
SELECT s.sales_amount
FROM access_server...region AS r,
oracle_server..sales_owner.sale AS s,
sql_server.customer_db.dbo.customer AS c
where r.region_id=s.region_id
and s.customer_id=c.customer_id
and r.region_name='Southwest'
and c.customer_name='ABC Steel'
```

Distributed Transactions

Distributed transactions are supported if the OLE DB provider has built in the functionality. This means it is possible to manipulate data from several different data sources in a single transaction. For example, suppose two banks decide to merge. The first bank (let's call it OraBank) stores all checking and savings accounts in an Oracle database. The second bank (let's call it SqlBank) stores all checking and savings accounts in a SQL Server 7.0 database. Let's also suppose a customer has a checking account with OraBank and a savings account with SqlBank. What would happen if a customer wants to transfer one hundred dollars from the checking account to the savings account? You can do it simply using the following code while maintaining transactional consistency. The transaction is either committed or rolled back on both databases:

```
BEGIN TRANSACTION
-- One hundred dollars is subtracted from the savings account.
UPDATE oracle_server..savings_owner.savings_table
 SET account_balance = account_balance - 100
WHERE account_number = 12345
-- One hundred dollars is added to the checking account.
UPDATE sql_server.checking_db.dbo.checking_table
 SET account_balance = account_balance + 100
WHERE account_number = 98765
COMMIT;
```

Adding, Dropping, and Configuring Linked Servers

The next few sections show you how to add, drop, and configure linked servers through system stored procedures.

sp_addlinkedserver

Before you can access an external data source through SQL Server, it must be registered inside the database as a linked server. You use the sp_addlinkedserver stored procedure for this purpose. Only users with the sysadmin or setupadmin fixed-server roles may run this procedure.

SQL Server delivers OLE DB providers for Oracle databases, Access databases, other SQL Server 6.5/7.0 databases, as well as databases that can be reached through ODBC. SQL Server also comes with OLE DB providers for Microsoft Excel spreadsheets and Indexing Service.

Some of the arguments for sp_addlinkedserver are only needed for certain OLE DB providers. It is fruitless to guess which arguments must be provided and the appropriate strings. Refer to the documentation for the OLE DB provider:

```
sp_addlinkedserver [@server =] 'server'
[, [@srvproduct =] 'product_name'][, [@provider =] 'provider_name']
[, [@datasrc =] 'data_source'] [, [@location =] 'location']
[, [@provstr =] 'provider_string'] [, [@catalog =] 'catalog']
```

The following list describes each element of the syntax:

server	The name of the linked server that will be added.
product_name	The product name of the OLE DB provider. If this argument is set to `'SQL Server'`, then only the `@server` argument is required. For all other OLE DB providers delivered with SQL Server, you can ignore this parameter.
provider_name	The unique programmatic identifier (PROGID). This value must match the PROGID in the Registry for the particular OLE DB provider. The following list shows the OLE DB providers delivered with SQL Server and corresponding values for this argument:

SQL Server	`SQLOLEDB`
Access/Jet/Excel Spreadsheets	`Microsoft.Jet.OLEDB.4.0`
ODBC	`MSDASQL`
Oracle	`MSDAORA`
File System (Indexing Service)	`MSIDXS`

data_source	A data source that points to the particular version of the OLE DB source. For example, for setting up an Access linked server, this argument holds the path to the file. For setting up a SQL Server linked server, this argument holds the machine name of the linked SQL Server. The following list shows the OLE DB providers delivered with SQL Server and corresponding values for this argument:

SQL Server	Network name of SQL Server.
Access/Jet/Excel Spreadsheets	Full pathname to the file.
ODBC	System DSN or ODBC connection string.
Oracle	SQL*Net alias.
File System (Indexing Service)	Indexing Service catalog name.

location	The location string possibly used by the OLE DB provider.
provider_string	The connection string possibly used by the OLE DB provider.
catalog	The catalog string possibly used by the OLE DB provider.

15

LINKED AND REMOTE SERVER MANAGEMENT

The following example adds an Oracle linked server called `'ORACLE_DATABASE'` that will connect to the database specified by the SQL*Net string `'my_sqlnet_connect_string'`:

```
EXEC sp_addlinkedserver @server='ORACLE_DATABASE',
@srvproduct='Oracle', @provider='MSDAORA',
@datasrc='my_sqlnet_connect_string'
```

The next example adds an Access linked server called `'ACCESS_DATABASE'` that will connect to the database `'Foodmart.mdb'` stored in the C:\temp directory:

```
EXEC sp_addlinkedserver @server='ACCESS_DATABASE',
@srvproduct='Access', @provider='Microsoft.Jet.OLEDB.4.0',
@datasrc='C:\temp\Foodmart.mdb'
```

This example adds a SQL Server linked server that resides on the `'SQL_SERVER_DATABASE'` machine:

```
EXEC sp_addlinkedserver @server='SQL_SERVER_DATABASE',
@srvproduct='SQL Server'
```

This example adds a Excel 5.0 spreadsheet as a linked server:

```
EXEC sp_addlinkedserver @server='EXCEL_SPREADSHEET',
@srvproduct='Excel', @provider='Microsoft.Jet.OLEDB.4.0',
@datasrc='C:\temp\MyExcelSpreadsheet.xls',
@catalog='Excel 5.0'
```

This example adds an ODBC data source as a linked server called `'ODBC_with_DATA_SOURCE'`. The ODBC connection string must be registered on the local server to use this linked server:

```
EXEC sp_addlinkedserver @server='ODBC_with_DATA_SOURCE',
@srvproduct='ODBC', @provider='MSDASQL',
@datasrc='My_ODBC_connection_string'
```

This example adds an ODBC datasource as a linked server called `'ODBC_with_PROVIDER_STRING'`. Unlike the previous example, an ODBC data source does not need to exist. The information normally stored as an ODBC datasource is stored in the `provstr` argument:

```
EXEC sp_addlinkedserver @server='ODBC_with_PROVIDER_STRING',
 @srvproduct='ODBC', @provider='MSDASQL',
 @provstr='DRIVER={SQL Server}; SERVER=MyServer; UID=sa;PWD=;'
```

sp_dropserver

You can unregister linked servers using `sp_dropserver`. Only members of the sysadmin and setupadmin fixed-server roles can execute this stored procedure:

```
sp_dropserver [@server =] 'server' [, [@droplogins =]
{'droplogins' ¦ NULL}]
```

The following list describes each element of the syntax:

> *server*   The linked server that will be unregistered.
>
> *droplogins*   Specifies that the logins associated with the server should be dropped. If this argument is not specified, then the server will only be dropped if logins do not exist for this linked server.

The following example unregisters an Oracle, Access, and SQL Server database:

```
EXEC sp_dropserver @server='ORACLE_DATABASE', @droplogins='droplogins'
EXEC sp_dropserver @server='ACCESS_DATABASE'
EXEC sp_dropserver @server='SQL_SERVER_DATABASE',
@droplogins='droplogins'
```

sp_serveroption

You can configure linked servers with `sp_serveroption`. Only users with the sysadmin or setupadmin fixed-server roles may run this procedure:

```
sp_serveroption [[@server =] 'server'] [,[@optname =] 'option_name']
[,[@optvalue =] 'option_value']
```

The following list describes each element of the syntax:

> *server*   The linked server that will be affected by this option.
>
> *option_name*   The name of the option to be configured. The valid option names follow:

> > `'collation compatible'`   If the `optvalue` is set to TRUE, SQL Server assumes the linked server has the same character set and collation sequence. Only set this option to true if you are sure the character sets and collation are identical.
> >
> > `'data access'`   If the `optvalue` is set to TRUE, distributed queries will be allowed if the OLE DB provider supports it. If the `optvalue` is set to FALSE, distributed queries will be disabled on this linked server.

15

`'dist'`	If the `optvalue` is set to TRUE, this specifies that the linked server is a distributor (used for replication).
`'dpub'`	If the `optvalue` is set to TRUE, this specifies that the linked server is a remote publisher to this distributor (used for replication).
`'pub'`	If the `optvalue` is set to TRUE, this specifies that the linked server is a publisher (used for replication).
`'sub'`	If the `optvalue` is set to TRUE, this specifies that the linked server is a subscriber (used for replication).
`'rpc'`	If the `optvalue` is set to TRUE, this allows remote procedure calls (RPC) from the linked server.
`'rpc out'`	If the `optvalue` is set to TRUE, this allows remote procedure calls (RPC) to the linked server.
`'system'`	For internal use only.
option_value	The value of this option. Valid values are TRUE (or ON) and FALSE (or OFF).

This example disables distributed queries to the ORACLE_DATABASE linked server:

```
EXEC sp_serveroption @server='ORACLE_DATABASE',
@optname='data access', @optvalue='FALSE'
```

This example enables remote procedure calls to the SQL_SERVER_DATABASE linked server:

```
EXEC sp_serveroption @server='SQL_SERVER_DATABASE',
@optname='rpc out', @optvalue='TRUE'
```

You can also run this stored procedure without certain parameters to query current settings. If no arguments are passed, the settable server options are displayed:

```
EXEC sp_serveroption
GO

Settable server options.
server_option
---------------------------------
collation compatible
data access
dist
dpub
pub
rpc
rpc out
sub
system

(9 row(s) affected)
```

If only the @server argument is provided, the options currently enabled for that server are displayed:

```
EXEC sp_serveroption @server='SQL_SERVER_DATABASE'
GO

The following options are set:
---------------------------------
rpc
rpc out
data access

(3 row(s) affected)
```

If the @server and @optname arguments are provided, the current setting for that option is displayed:

```
EXEC sp_serveroption @server='SQL_SERVER_DATABASE',@optname='rpc out'
GO

OptionName                         CurrentSetting
---------------------------------  --------------
rpc out                            ON

(1 row(s) affected)
```

Mapping Local Logins to Logins on Linked Servers

To gain access to a linked server, the user often must be validated by the linked server for security reasons.

sp_addlinkedsrvlogin

SQL Server provides the `sp_addlinkedsrvlogin` stored procedure to map local logins to logins on the linked servers. This stored procedure can be executed by members of the sysadmin and securityadmin fixed-server roles.

```
sp_addlinkedsrvlogin [@rmtsrvname =] 'rmtsrvname'
 [,[@useself =] 'useself'][,[@locallogin =] 'locallogin']
 [,[@rmtuser =] 'rmtuser'] [,[@rmtpassword =] 'rmtpassword']
```

The following list describes each element of the syntax:

rmtsrvname	The linked server that will use this login setting.
useself	The setting that determines whether a user or group of users will use their own usernames and passwords to log in to the linked server. There are two possible settings:

`'true'`	Local server logins use their own usernames and passwords to log in to the linked server. Consequently, the `rmtuser` and `rmtpassword` arguments are ignored. For example, the local MelanieHancock user with a password of LesMis would attempt to log in to the linked server with the MelanieHancock username and the LesMis password.
`'false'`	Local server logins will use the arguments specified in `rmtuser` and `rmtpassword` to log in to the linked server. For a linked server that does not require usernames and passwords (such as Microsoft Access), these arguments can be set to `NULL`.

locallogin	Specifies which local logins are affected by this mapping. You can designate either an individual login or all local logins. To specify that all logins be affected, pass a `NULL` to this argument.

rmtuser	The username that will be used to connect to the linked server if @useself is set to FALSE.
rmtpassword	The password that will be used to connect to the linked server if @useself is set to FALSE.

After you run sp_addlinkedserver, all local logins will automatically attempt to use their own usernames and passwords to log in to the new linked server. Essentially, SQL Server runs the following statement after sp_addlinkedserver:

```
EXEC sp_addlinkedsrvlogin @rmtsrvname='My_Linked_Server',
@useself='true', @locallogin=NULL
```

You can delete this default mapping with sp_droplinkedsrvlogin, which is described in the next section.

In NT authentication mode, SQL Server will submit the NT username and password to the linked server if the provider supports NT authentication, and security account delegation is available on both the client and server.

The first example will connect all users to the 'ORACLE_DATABASE' linked server using the 'guest' username and 'confio' password:

```
EXEC sp_addlinkedsrvlogin @rmtsrvname='ORACLE_DATABASE',
@useself='false', @rmtuser='guest', @rmtpassword='confio'
```

This example will connect all users to the 'SQL_SERVER_DATABASE' linked server using their own local usernames and passwords:

```
EXEC sp_addlinkedsrvlogin @rmtsrvname='SQL_SERVER_DATABASE',
@useself='true'
```

This example will log in the local 'RobinOrdes' user as the remote user 'ROrdes' with the 'new_orleans' password to the 'ORACLE_DATABASE' linked server:

```
EXEC sp_addlinkedsrvlogin @rmtsrvname='ORACLE_DATABASE',
@useself='false', @locallogin='RobinOrdes', @rmtuser='ROrdes',
@rmtpassword='new_orleans'
```

This example will log in the Windows NT user 'Domain1\DonLarson' as the remote user 'DLarson' with the 'five_sons' password:

```
EXEC sp_addlinkedsrvlogin @rmtsrvname='ORACLE_DATABASE',
@useself='false', @locallogin='Domain1\DonLarson',
@rmtuser='DLarson', @rmtpassword='five_sons'
```

This example will connect all users to the 'ACCESS_DATABASE' linked server without providing a username or password:

```
EXEC sp_addlinkedsrvlogin @rmtsrvname='ACCESS_DATABASE',
@useself='false', @rmtuser=NULL, @rmtpassword=NULL
```

15

**LINKED AND
REMOTE SERVER
MANAGEMENT**

sp_droplinkedsrvlogin

You can delete mappings for linked servers using sp_droplinkedsrvlogin. This stored procedure can be executed by members of the sysadmin and securityadmin fixed-server roles:

```
sp_droplinkedsrvlogin [@rmtsrvname =] 'rmtsrvname',
[@locallogin =] 'locallogin'
```

The following list describes each element of the syntax:

rmtsrvname	The linked server that will lose this login mapping.
locallogin	Specifies which local login will lose the mapping to the linked server. You can designate either an individual login or all local logins. To specify that all logins should be affected, pass a NULL to this argument.

This first example removes the login mapping for the 'RobinOrdes' user to the 'ORA-CLE_DATABASE' linked server:

```
EXEC sp_droplinkedsrvlogin @rmtsrvname='ORACLE_DATABASE',
 @locallogin='RobinOrdes'
```

This example removes the default login mapping for all users using the 'SQL_SERVER_DATABASE' linked server:

```
EXEC sp_droplinkedsrvlogin @rmtsrvname='SQL_SERVER_DATABASE',
@locallogin=NULL
```

sp_helplinkedsrvlogin

To determine the current linked server login settings, run the sp_helplinkedsrvlogin procedure:

```
sp_helplinkedsrvlogin [[@rmtsrvname =] 'rmtsrvname',]
[[@locallogin =] 'locallogin']
```

The following list describes each element of the syntax:

rmtsrvname	The linked server that will have its login settings displayed.
locallogin	Specifies which local login mappings will be displayed.

The first example shows the sp_helplinkedsrvlogin output if no arguments are provided. It displays one line for each linked server login mapping. The first column (Linked Server) shows which linked server owns this mapping. The second column (Local Login) shows which user is affected by this mapping. If set to NULL, this mapping applies to all users who do not have a specific mapping. The third column (Is Self Mapping) displays a 1 if the local username and password will be attempted on the remote server. If it displays a 0, the value in the last column (Remote Login) will be used to log in to the remote server. Note that the remote password is not listed for security reasons:

```
EXEC sp_helplinkedsrvlogin
GO
```

Linked Server	Local Login	Is Self Mapping	Remote Login
ACCESS_DATABASE	NULL	0	NULL
ACCESS_SERVER	NULL	1	NULL
EXCEL_SPREADSHEET	NULL	1	NULL
ODBC_with_DATA_SOURCE	NULL	1	NULL
ODBC_with_PROVIDER_STRING	NULL	1	NULL
ORACLE_DATABASE	NULL	0	guest
ORACLE_DATABASE	RobinOrdes	0	ROrdes

```
(7 row(s) affected)
```

The next example shows the sp_helplinkedsrvlogin output if only the rmtsrvname argument is provided. The output is identical to the preceding example except only the entries for the specified server are displayed:

```
EXEC sp_helplinkedsrvlogin @rmtsrvname='ORACLE_DATABASE'
GO
```

Linked Server	Local Login	Is Self Mapping	Remote Login
ORACLE_DATABASE	NULL	0	guest
ORACLE_DATABASE	RobinOrdes	0	ROrdes

```
(2 row(s) affected)
```

The final example shows the sp_helplinkedsrvlogin output if all arguments are provided. Again, the output is identical to the previous examples except that it is limited to the server and user specified:

```
EXEC sp_helplinkedsrvlogin @rmtsrvname='ORACLE_DATABASE',
 @locallogin='RobinOrdes'
GO
```

Linked Server	Local Login	Is Self Mapping	Remote Login
ORACLE_DATABASE	RobinOrdes	0	ROrdes

```
(1 row(s) affected)
```

15

LINKED AND REMOTE SERVER MANAGEMENT

Setting Up Linked Servers Through Enterprise Manager

Although you can set up linked servers and login mappings by directly executing these stored procedures, they can also be set up easily through Enterprise Manager.

To create a linked server, follow these steps:

1. Open Enterprise Manager.
2. Click the plus sign next to the local SQL Server.
3. Click the plus sign next to the Security folder.
4. Right-click Linked Servers and choose New Linked Server (see Figure 15.1).

FIGURE 15.1

Creating linked servers through Enterprise Manager.

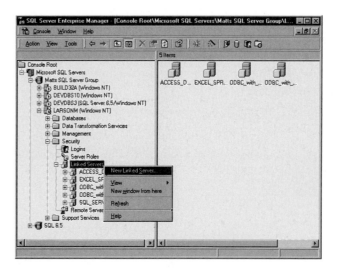

5. The General tab of the New Linked Server property box is displayed. The fields in the Server Type section are filled in the same way as the corresponding arguments for sp_addlinkedserver. The fields in the Server Options section at the bottom of this tab correspond to sp_serveroption arguments (see Figure 15.2).

6. The Security tab of the New Linked Server property box lets you map remote logins (see Figure 15.3). The code behind this dialog box actually runs the sp_addlinkedsrvlogin and sp_droplinkedsrvlogin stored procedures.

FIGURE 15.2

*The General tab
of the New
Linked Server
property box.*

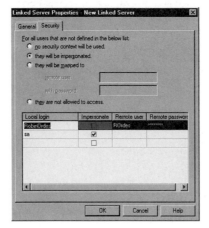

FIGURE 15.3

*The Security tab
of the New
Linked Server
property box.*

Summary

In this chapter, you have seen the difference between the new linked servers and remote servers. You also learned how distributed queries and transactions worked with linked servers. I also covered all the system stored procedures used to configure linked servers, including `sp_addlinkedserver`, `sp_dropserver`, `sp_serveroption`, `sp_addlinked-srvlogin`, `sp_droplinkedsrvlogin`, and `sp_helplinkedsrvlogin`. Finally, you learned to configure linked servers through Enterprise Manager.

15

**LINKED AND
REMOTE SERVER
MANAGEMENT**

Using BCP to Import and Export Data

by Simon Gallagher

In This Chapter

One of the most common tasks of data management is the transfer of information from one system to another. This information can be a file for, or from, a mainframe or a file to be used within Microsoft Excel.

With the arrival of SQL Server 7.0, you now have two options for transferring data to and from a flat file using a command interface: the Bulk-Copy Program (BCP) and the BULK INSERT command.

The Bulk-Copy Program is a data load and unload utility provided by Microsoft. It allows single-file-to-single-table data importation and exportation. Even with the introduction of the Microsoft Data Transformation Services (DTS), a huge number of existing data load scripts still make use of BCP. BCP also has the advantage over the DTS in that data loads can be made faster with large amounts of data. In these situations, BCP is still the mechanism of choice. For more information on the Data Transformation Services, see Chapter 35, "Data Transformation Services."

The version of BCP that comes with SQL Server 7.0 has additional enhancements that work with the query processor to speed up performance even more. Throughout this chapter we will see these new interactions.

The new addition to the SQL Server data transfer toolkit is the BULK INSERT statement. This command allows data loads into a table—but does so from a SQL statement rather than from the command line as does BCP.

Logged and Nonlogged Operations

There are two modes in which bulk-copy operations can occur: logged and nonlogged (also known as slow and fast BCP, respectively). The ideal situation is to operate in non-logged mode because this arrangement dramatically decreases the load time and the consumption of other system resources such as memory, processor use, and disk access. However, the default runs the load in logged mode, which causes the log to grow rapidly for large volumes of data.

To achieve a nonlogged operation, the target table must not be replicated (the replication log reader needs the log records to relay the changes made). The database holding the target table must also have its SELECT INTO/BULK COPY option set, and finally, the TABLOCK hint must be specified.

> **NOTE**
>
> Remember that setting the SELECT INTO/BULK COPY option disables the ability to back up the transaction log until a full database backup has been performed. Transaction log dumps are disabled because if the database had to be restored, the transaction log would not contain a record of the new data.

Although you can still perform fast loads against tables that have indexes, it is advisable to drop and re-create the indexes after the data transfer operation is complete. If there is existing data in the table, the operation will be logged; you achieve a nonlogged operation only if the table is initially empty. Generally, you get at least a 50% drop in transfer speed if the table has an index. The more indexes, the greater the performance degradation. This is due to the logging factor; more log records are being generated, and index pages are being loaded into the cache and modified. This can also cause the log to grow, possibly filling it (depending on your log file settings).

> **NOTE**
>
> Even the so-called nonlogged operation logs some things. In the case of indexes, index page changes and allocations are logged, but the main area of logging is of extent allocations every time the table is extended for additional storage space for the new rows.

Some third-party tool vendors, notably Platinum Technologies, have fast load and unload utilities that have proved faster than Microsoft's SQL Server 6.5 utilities. It will be interesting to see whether these tool vendors can provide still better performance than the newest version of BCP and the BULK INSERT command.

Parallel Loading

One of the advantages of data loads using SQL Server 7.0 over previous versions is that multiple clients can work in parallel to load the data from a file. To take advantage of this new feature, the following must be true:

- The bulk-copy operation must be nonlogged; all requirements specified in the discussion on nonlogged operations must be met.
- There must be no indexes on the target table.

The parallel loading feature is available only with the ODBC or SQLOLEDB-based APIs of version 7.0.

The procedure is straightforward. Once you have ascertained that the target table has no indexes (which may involve dropping primary or unique constraints) and is not being replicated, you must set the database option SELECT INTO/BULK COPY to true. The requirement to drop all indexes comes from the locking that has to occur to load the data. Although the table itself can have a shared lock, the index pages are an area of contention that prevents parallel access.

Now all that is required is to set up the clients (the clients can be different command windows on the server/client or on different client machines) to load the data into the table. You can make use of the -F and -L switches to specify the range of the data you want each client to load into the table if you are using the same data file. These switches remove the need to manually break up the file. Here is an example of the command switches involved for a parallel load with BCP:

```
bcp pubs..new_authors in newauthors.dat /T /Sraven /c /F1 /
➥L10000 /h"TABLOCK"
```

The TABLOCK hint provides better performance by removing contention from other users while the load takes place. If you do not use the hint, the load will take place using row level locks.

SQL Server 7.0 allows parallel loads without impacting performance by making each connection create extents in nonoverlapping ranges. The ranges are then linked into the table's page chain.

The Bulk-Copy Program

The Bulk-Copy Program is very customizable and comes with many switches. The switches are listed in Table 16.1. You should remember that these switches *are* case-sensitive.

TABLE 16.1   BCP SWITCHES

Switch	Description
-n	Native data format.
-c	Character data format.
-w	Unicode data format.
-N	Use Unicode for character data and native format for all others.

Switch	Description
-C	If you are loading extended characters, this switch allows you to specify the code page of the data in the data file.
-E	Use the identity values in the file rather than generating new ones.
-6	Use pre-7.0 datatypes; this option is required when loading native 6.*x* BCP files.
-b	The number of rows to include in each committed batch.
-m	The maximum errors to allow before stopping the transfer.
-e	The file to write error messages to.
-f	The format file used to customize the load or unload data in a specific style.
-F	The first row in the data file to start copying from when importing.
-L	The last row in the data file to end copying with when importing.
-t	The terminating character(s) for fields.
-r	The terminating character(s) for rows.
-i	A file for redirecting input into BCP.
-o	The file for receiving redirected output from BCP.
-a	The network packet size used to send to or receive from the server.
-q	Tells BCP to use quoted identifiers when dealing with table and column names.
-k	Overrides a column's default and enforces NULL values loaded into columns as part of the BCP operation.
-h	The 7.0 hint options.
-U	The user account to log in as; this account must have sufficient privileges to carry out either a read or write of the table.
-P	The password associated with the user account.
-S	The SQL Server's name.
-v	The version number of BCP to use.
-T	Makes a trusted connection to the SQL Server.

The following sections look at some of these switches, what they mean, and how and when they should be used. The remainder of the switches are obvious in their use. You can view the syntax for all the switches seen by executing the bcp /v command.

Batches

By default, BCP collects all the rows being inserted into the target table and commits them as one large transaction. This arrangement reduces the amount of work that the log must handle; however, it locks down the transaction log by keeping a large part of it active, which can make truncating or backing up the transaction log impossible or unproductive.

By using the BCP batch (-b) switch, you can control the number of rows in each batch or transaction. This switch controls the frequency of commits; although it can increase the activity in the log, it gives you the ability to trim the size of transaction log. You should tune the batch size in relation to the size of the data rows, transaction log size, and total number of rows to be loaded. The value you use for one load may not necessarily be the right value for a different table.

> **TIP**
>
> By making the batch size include just a few rows, you can more easily identify which ones are giving you problems. When you use the batch switch in conjunction with the -F and -L switches, you have an effective data file debugging tool.

Remember that specifying a value for the batch switch causes batches to commit on the server. If the third batch fails, the first and second batches *are* committed, and those rows are now part of the table. However, any rows copied up to the point of failure in the third batch are rolled back.

File Datatypes

BCP can handle data in one of three forms: character (ASCII), native, or Unicode. You have the choice of which character format is used, depending on the source or destination of the data file.

- The character format (-c) is the most commonly used of the three datatypes because it reads or writes using ASCII characters and carries out the appropriate datatype conversion for the SQL Server representations. The CHAR datatype is the default storage type; it makes use of tabs as field separators and the newline character as the row terminator.

- You use the native format (-n) when copying data between SQL Servers. This format allows BCP to read and write using the same datatypes used by SQL Server, leading to a performance gain. This format does, however, render the data file unreadable by any other means.

- The Unicode option (-w) makes use of Unicode characters rather than ASCII characters. The NCHAR datatype is the default storage type; it uses tabs as field separators and the newline character as the row terminator.

The Format File

By making use of a format file, you can customize the data file created by BCP or specify complex field layouts for data loads. There are two ways to create this format file: interactive BCP and the format switch.

Customizing a Format File Using Interactive BCP

If you do not specify one of the -n, -c, or -w datatype format switches, BCP prompts you for the following information for each column in the data set:

- File storage type
- Prefix length
- Field length
- Field terminator

BCP offers a default for each of these prompts which you can accept. If you accept all the defaults, you wind up with the same format file you would have by specifying the native format (with the -n switch). The prompts look like this:

```
Enter the file storage type of field au_id [char]:
Enter prefix length of field au_id [0]:
Enter length of field au_id [11]:
Enter field terminator [none]:
```

By pressing the Enter key at the prompt, you take the default. Alternatively, you can type your own value at the prompt.

Creating a Format File Using a Switch

By making use of the new version 7.0 format option, you can create a format file without actually transferring any data. Here is an example of creating a format file for the authors table in the pubs database:

```
bcp pubs..authors format junk /Sraven /T /fauthors.fmt /c
```

The format file created looks like this:

```
7.0
9
1    SQLCHAR    0    11    "\t"    1    au_id
2    SQLCHAR    0    40    "\t"    2    au_lname
3    SQLCHAR    0    20    "\t"    3    au_fname
4    SQLCHAR    0    12    "\t"    4    phone
5    SQLCHAR    0    40    "\t"    5    address
6    SQLCHAR    0    20    "\t"    6    city
7    SQLCHAR    0    2     "\t"    7    state
8    SQLCHAR    0    5     "\t"    8    zip
9    SQLCHAR    0    3     "\r\n"  9    contract
```

Table 16.2 provides a description of the lines and columns in the preceding format file example.

TABLE 16.2 THE CONTENTS OF THE FORMAT FILE

Line or Column	Description
1st line	Version of BCP
2nd line	Number of columns
3rd line 1st column	Data field position
2nd column	Datatype
3rd column	Prefix
4th column	Data file field length
5th column	Field or row terminator
6th column	Column position
7th column	Column name

You get different format files depending on your table and whether you chose character, native, or Unicode as your datatype. As you can see in the preceding example, only the last two columns in the format file relate to the actual table; the remaining columns specify properties of the data file.

File Storage Type

The storage type is the description of how the data is stored in the data file. Table 16.3 lists the definitions used during Interactive BCP and what appears in the format file. The storage type allows data to be copied as its base type (native format), as implicitly converted between types (`tinyint` to `smallint`), or as a string (in character or Unicode format).

Using BCP to Import and Export Data

CHAPTER 16

371

16

USING BCP TO
IMPORT AND
EXPORT DATA

TABLE 16.3 STORAGE DATATYPES

File Storage Type	Interactive Prompt	Host File Datatype
char	c[har]	SQLCHAR
varchar	c[har]	SQLCHAR
nchar	w	SQLNCHAR
nvarchar	w	SQLNCHAR
text	T[ext]	SQLCHAR
ntext	W	SQLNCHAR
binary	x	SQLBINARY
varbinary	x	SQLBINARY
image	I[mage]	SQLBINARY
datetime	d[ate]	SQLDATETIME
smalldatetime	D	SQLDATETIM4
decimal	n	SQLDECIMAL
numeric	n	SQLNUMERIC
float	f[loat]	SQLFLT8
real	r	SQLFLT4
int	i[nt]	SQLINT
smallint	s[mallint]	SQLSMALLINT
tinyint	t[inyint]	SQLTINYINT
money	m[oney]	SQLMONEY
smallmoney	M	SQLMONEY4
bit	b[it]	SQLBIT
uniqueidentifier	u	SQLUNIQUEID
timestamp	x	SQLBINARY

If the table makes use of user-defined datatypes, these customized datatypes appear in the format file as their base types.

If you are having problems loading certain fields into your table, you can try the following tricks:

- Try copying the data in as CHAR datatypes and forcing SQL Server to do the conversion for you.
- Duplicate the table and replace all the SQL Server datatypes with CHAR or VARCHAR of a length sufficient to hold the value. This trick allows you to further manipulate the data after it is loaded using Transact-SQL.

Prefix Length

For reasons of compactness in native data files, BCP precedes each field with a prefix length that indicates the length of the data stored. The space for storing this information is specified in characters and is called the *prefix length*.

Table 16.4 indicates the value to specify for prefix length for each of the datatypes.

TABLE 16.4 PREFIX LENGTH VALUES

Prefix Length	Use
0	Non-null data of type bit or numerics (int, real, and so on). Use this value when no prefix characters are wanted. This value causes the field to be padded with spaces to the size indicated for the field length.
1	Non-null data of type binary or varbinary, or null data with the exception of text, ntext, and image. Use this value for any data (except bit, binary, varbinary, text, ntext, and image) that you want stored using a character-based datatype.
2	When storing the datatypes binary or varbinary as character-based datatypes. Two bytes of char file storage and four bytes of nchar file storage are required for each byte of binary table data.
4	Use this value for the datatypes text, ntext, and image.

Prefix lengths are likely to exist only within data files created using BCP. It is unlikely that you will encounter a reason to change the defaults BCP has chosen for you.

Field Length

When using either the native or character data format, you must specify the maximum length of each field. When converting datatypes to strings, BCP suggests lengths large enough to store the entire range of values for each particular datatype. Table 16.5 lists the default values for each of the data formats.

TABLE 16.5 DEFAULT FIELD LENGTHS FOR DATA FORMATS

Datatype	*Length (/c)*	*Length (/n)*
bit	1	1
binary	Column length x 2	Column length
datetime	24	8
smalldatetime	24	4
float	30	8
real	30	4
int	12	4
smallint	7	2
tinyint	5	1
money	30	8
smallmoney	30	4
decimal	41	up to 17
numeric	41	up to 17
uniqueidentifier	37	16

You must specify a field length that is sufficiently long for the data being stored. BCP error messages regarding overflows indicate that the data value has been truncated in at least one of the fields. If the operation is a load, an overflow error usually results in BCP terminating. However, if you are dumping the data to a file, the data will be truncated without error messages.

The field length value is used *only* when the prefix length is 0 and you have specified no terminators. In essence, you are doing a fixed-length data copy. BCP uses the exact amount of space stated by the field length for each field; unused space within the field is padded out.

> **NOTE**
>
> Preexisting spaces in the data are not distinguished from added padding.

Field Terminator

If you are not making use of fixed-width fields or length prefixes, you must use a field terminator to indicate the character(s) that separate fields; for the last field in the data row, you must also indicate which character(s) end the line.

BCP recognizes the following indicators for special characters:

Terminator	Escape Code
Tab	\t
Backslash	\\
Null terminator	\0
Newline	\n
Carriage return	\r

You cannot use spaces as terminators, but you can use any other printable character. Choose field and row terminators that make sense for your data. Obviously, you should not make use of any character you are trying to load. You must combine the \r and \n characters to get your data into an ASCII data file with each row on its own line.

> **TIP**
>
> By specifying the -t and -r switches, you can override the defaults that appear for the prompts during Interactive BCP.

You can specify terminators for data copied in native format. You should be careful if you decide to go this route; the accepted approach is to use length prefixes.

The prefix length, field length, and terminator values interact. In the following examples, T indicates the terminator character(s), P indicates the prefix length, and S indicates space padding.

For data of type char, the data file has the following repeating pattern:

	Prefix Length=0	*Prefix Length=1,2,4*
No terminator	stringSstringS	PstringSPstringS
Terminator	stringSTstringST	PstringSTPstringST

For data of other types converted to char, the data file has the following repeating pattern:

	Prefix Length=0	*Prefix Length=1,2,4*
No terminator	stringSstringS	PstringPstring
Terminator	stringTstringT	PstringTPstringT

The next few sections examine how to load data into tables when there are differences in column number and layout.

Different Numbers of Columns in File and Table

If you have fewer fields in the data file than exist in the table, you have to "dummy up" an extra line in your format file.

Suppose that we want to load a data file that is missing the majority of the address information for each author. By making use of the format file we created in the section "The Format File," earlier in this chapter, we can still load the data file. Suppose that the data file looks like this:

```
100-10-1000 Gallagher Simon 317 638-7909 Indianapolis
100-10-1001 Herbert Simon 812 462-6700 St.Paul
```

To introduce a dummy value for the missing ones, we must make the following changes to the format file: make the prefix and data lengths 0 and set the field terminator to nothing ("").

The modified format file will look like this:

```
7.0
9
1       SQLCHAR         0       11      "\t"            1       au_id
2       SQLCHAR         0       40      "\t"            2       au_lname
3       SQLCHAR         0       20      "\t"            3       au_fname
4       SQLCHAR         0       12      "\t"            4       phone
5       SQLCHAR         0       0       ""              5       address
6       SQLCHAR         0       20      "\t"            6       city
7       SQLCHAR         0       0       ""              7       state
8       SQLCHAR         0       0       ""              8       zip
9       SQLCHAR         0       3       "\r\n"          9       contract
```

Now BCP can load the data file by making use of this new format file, with the address, state, and zip columns containing NULLs for the new rows.

For data files that have more fields than the table has columns, we change the format file to add additional lines of information. Suppose that the author data file contains a second address line and a country, as in this example:

```
100-10-1000 Gallagher Simon 317 638-7909 220 S.St Ste.220
➥Indianapolis IN 46225 US 1
100-10-1001 Herbert Simon 812 462-6700 6th St. Ste.123
➥St.Paul MN 76231 USA 0
```

Starting with the same format file as before, we modify it in two important areas: We change the second line to reflect the actual number of values, and we add new lines for each additional column in the file that is not in the table. Notice that the column position has a value of 0 to indicate the absence of a column in the table.

Thus the modified format file will look like this:

```
7.0
11
1     SQLCHAR     0     11     "\t"     1     au_id
2     SQLCHAR     0     40     "\t"     2     au_lname
3     SQLCHAR     0     20     "\t"     3     au_fname
4     SQLCHAR     0     12     "\t"     4     phone
5     SQLCHAR     0     40     "\t"     5     address
6     SQLCHAR     0     40     "\t"     0     address2
7     SQLCHAR     0     20     "\t"     6     city
8     SQLCHAR     0     2      "\t"     7     state
9     SQLCHAR     0     5      "\t"     8     zip
10    SQLCHAR     0     0      "\t"     0     country
11    SQLCHAR     0     3      "\r\n"   9     contract
```

These two examples show you the possibilities that the format file offers for customizing the loading and unloading of data.

Renumbering Columns

Using the techniques described in the preceding section, we can also handle data files that we want to place in a different order in the target tables. All that we have to do is change the column order number to reflect the desired sequence of the columns in the table.

For example, suppose the author data file came with the following layout:

```
<au_id><last name><first name><phone><zip><state><city><address>
➥<contract>
```

The SQL Server table itself has columns in a different order—specifically, the author's address information appears in the more familiar arrangement of address, city, state, and zip code. In order to load our data file into this table, we modify the format file to look like this:

```
7.0
9
1       SQLCHAR     0       11      "\t"            1       au_id
2       SQLCHAR     0       40      "\t"            2       au_lname
3       SQLCHAR     0       20      "\t"            3       au_fname
4       SQLCHAR     0       12      "\t"            4       phone
5       SQLCHAR     0       40      "\t"            8       address
6       SQLCHAR     0       20      "\t"            7       city
7       SQLCHAR     0       2       "\t"            6       state
8       SQLCHAR     0       5       "\t"            5       zip
9       SQLCHAR     0       3       "\r\n"          9       contract
```

The italics in the format file indicate the changes made. The principal thing to remember with the format file is that all but the last two columns deal with the data file. The last two columns specify the database table.

Using Views

The one big disadvantage of BCP is that it operates on a single table. Well, that is not strictly true—the ability to specify just a single table is actually a limitation of the syntax. Data can actually be unloaded from a view, which means that you can collect data from multiple tables (and with distributed queries even multiple servers).

You can also use BCP to back in through the view, but as is the case with normal Transact-SQL modifications, you can load into only one of the underlying tables at a time.

Loading Image Data

You can load binary large objects (BLOBs) into SQL Server tables. This operation requires a format file that specifies how much data is going in and into which column.

A format file used to load BLOBs would look like this:

```
7.0
1
1   SQLBINARY   0   12578          " "         1   column1
```

In this syntax, `column1` is the column name within the table to which you are loading the image.

You can then use the same format file to load a 12578-byte Word document into `column1` using this command:

```
bcp mydb..documents in analysis.doc -T -Smyserver -fmyfmt.fmt
```

You can also use the `BULK INSERT` statement to do the same operation on the Word document:

```
BULK INSERT mydb..documents FROM 'c:\analysis.doc'
WITH ( FORMATFILE = 'c:\myfmt.fmt' )
```

Supplying Hints to BCP

The new version of BCP comes with the ability to further control the speed of data loading by using hints. These hints are specified using the `-h` switch:

```
-h "hint [, hint]"
```

This option cannot be used when bulk copying data into versions of SQL Server before version 7.0 because BCP now works in conjunction with the query processor. The query processor optimizes data loads and unloads for OLE database rowsets that the latest versions of BCP and `BULK INSERT` can generate.

The `ROWS_PER_BATCH` Hint

The `ROWS_PER_BATCH` hint is used to tell SQL Server the total number of rows in the data file. This hint helps SQL Server to optimize the entire load operation. This hint and the `-b` switch heavily influence the logging operations that occur with the data inserts. If you specify both this hint and the `-b` switch, they must have the same values or you will get an error message.

When you use the `ROWS_PER_BATCH` hint, you copy the entire result set as a single transaction. SQL Server automatically optimizes the load operation using the batch size you specify. The value you specify does *not* have to be accurate, but you should be aware of what the practical limit is going to be based on the database's transaction log.

> **TIP**
>
> Do not be confused by the name of the hint. You are specifying the *total file size* and *not* the batch size (as is the case with the `-b` switch).

Using BCP to Import and Export Data

CHAPTER 16

379

16

USING BCP TO
IMPORT AND
EXPORT DATA

The CHECK_CONSTRAINTS Hint

The CHECK_CONSTRAINTS hint controls whether check constraints are executed as part of the BCP operation. By default, check constraints are not executed; this option allows you to turn the feature on. If you do not use this option, you should either be very sure of your data or should rerun the same logic as the check constraints you deferred after the data has entered the table.

> **TIP**
>
> A simple way to run the check constraints is to execute an UPDATE statement that sets one column to its current value. You may want to add a WHERE clause to restrict the operation to the new rows. Also be aware that the UPDATE trigger (not the INSERT trigger) is also fired.

The CHECK_CONSTRAINTS hint enables constraint checking on the target table only for the BCP operation. Any other data modifications occurring from other users still encounter the check constraints as normal.

The ORDER Hint

If the data you want to bulk load is already in the same sequence as the clustered index on the receiving table, you can use the ORDER hint. The syntax for this hint is shown here:

```
ORDER( {column [ASC | DESC] [,…n]})
```

There *must* be a clustered index on the same columns, in the same key sequence as you specify in the ORDER hint. Using a sorted data file helps SQL Server place the data into the table.

The KILOBYTES_PER_BATCH Hint

The KILOBYTES_PER_BATCH hint gives the size, in kilobytes, of the data in each batch. This is an estimate and is used internally by SQL Server to optimize the data load and logging areas of the BCP operation.

The TABLOCK Hint

The TABLOCK hint is used to place a table-level lock for the BCP load duration. This hint gives you increased performance at a loss to concurrency as described in "Parallel Loading" earlier in this chapter.

The BULK INSERT Command

The BULK INSERT statement is new with SQL Server version 7.0. BULK INSERT allows the bulk load of data into a database table. The main difference between this statement and BCP is that BULK INSERT is load- and SQL-based while BCP is bidirectional and command-line based.

The syntax for the BULK INSERT command is shown here:

```
BULK INSERT [['database_name'.]['owner'].]{'table_name' FROM data_file}
[WITH ( [ BATCHSIZE [ = batch_size]]  [[,] CHECK_CONSTRAINTS]
        [[,] CODEPAGE [ = ACP ¦ OEM ¦ RAW ¦ code_page]]
        [[,] DATAFILETYPE [ = {'char' ¦ 'native'¦ 'widechar' ¦
        ➥'widenative'}]]
        [[,] FIELDTERMINATOR [ = 'field_terminator']]
        [[,] FIRSTROW [ = first_row]] [[,] FORMATFILE [ =
        ➥'format_file_path']]
        [[,] KEEPIDENTITY] [[,] KEEPNULLS]  [[,] LASTROW [ = last_row]]
        [[,] MAXERRORS [ = max_errors]]
        [[,] ORDER ({column [ASC ¦ DESC]} [, …n])]
        [[,] ROWTERMINATOR [ = 'row_terminator']]  [[,] TABLOCK] )]
```

As you can see, the majority of the options for this command are the same as or similar to the switches for the BCP program.

The CODEPAGE option is used when you need to load extended characters (values greater than 127); this option allows you to specify one of the following values for char, varchar, and text datatypes:

ACP	Convert from the ANSI/Microsoft Windows code page (ISO 1252) to the SQL Server code page.
OEM	Convert from the system OEM code page to the SQL Server code page. This is the default.
RAW	No conversion, which makes this the fastest option.
<value>	Specific code page number (for example, 850 for the 4.2x default code page). For a list of the available code pages, look under the "Code Pages and Sort Orders" entry in the SQL Server Books Online.

The DATAFILETYPE option allows the specification of the data character set:

char	Data is in ASCII format.
native	Data is in SQL Server native format.
widechar	Data is in Unicode format.
widenative	Data is native, except for the char, varchar, and text columns, which are stored as Unicode.

The last option, widenative, is used when you need to transfer extended characters but want the performance offered by native data files.

To illustrate the various switches, the following sample statement loads customer data from the file c:\customer.dat, which is comma separated:

```
BULK INSERT mydb..customers
FROM 'c:\customer.dat'
WITH ( FIELDTERMINATOR = ',', ROWTERMINATOR = '\n' )
```

Improving Load Performance

To make some comparisons among the previous version of BCP, the new version, and the new hints, a series of tests were run. The basis of the test was a 40,000 (3MB) data row loaded into a duplicate of the authors table found in pubs. A new database was created with 20MB of data and 10MB of log, and a copy was made of the authors table from pubs using this command:

```
SELECT * INTO authors2 FROM pubs..authors WHERE 1=0
```

After each load, the table was truncated, and the transaction log was dumped. Each load was performed four times sequentially to end up with an average load speed. The results are shown in Table 16.6 and indicate the number of rows per second. All loads except where indicated are done in native mode and are noncumulative (this means that if one load was done with a CHECK constraint and another load was done with a clustered index, the second load was done without the CHECK constraint). Each of the servers was run with the installation defaults, and the database had only the SELECT INTO/BCP option set, except where indicated.

TABLE 16.6 ·DATA LOAD COMPARISONS (NUMBER OF ROWS PER SECOND)

Setup	6.5	7.0
SELECT INTO/BCP option off	3675	4338
Character mode	5410	4350
Native mode	5680	4655
Check constraint	5645	4195
CHECK_CONSTRAINT hint	N/A	4625
Clustered index on primary key	15	2385
ORDER hint with clustered index	N/A	2020
Nonclustered index on primary key	545	2360

continues

TABLE 16.6 CONTINUED

Setup	6.5	7.0
Batch size of 5,000	5650	4560
Batch size of 10,000	5775	4710
Batch size of 20,000	5626	4790
ROWS_PER_BATCH hint = 40,000	N/A	4630

The conclusion we can draw from this table is that the new version of BCP is, in fact, a little slower than the previous version in *some* areas, but greatly outperforms the older version in other areas. (Please note that these timings were taken from the beta 2 version of the product.)

Other conclusions we can draw from these values is that running without the CHECK_CON-STRAINT hint does speed up the data load (of course, we have to be sure of our data or perform the checks after the load), and that the choice of batch size is also an important influence on the overall speed.

We can therefore consider the following as rules for BCP operation:

- You can improve load performance by two or more times by dropping indexes from the target table.
- You can determine the tradeoffs between ignoring check constraints using the BCP hint, and allowing the check to take place as part of the operation. How sure of the data are you?
- Use native mode whenever possible; it is a bit faster than the other modes.
- If you have a recurring load, take the time to determine the best batch size for it. Otherwise, start with a batch size value on the order of a quarter to a half of the number of rows in the file, unless the number of rows is small (less than a few thousand).
- Consider the possibility of performing parallel data loads if you are loading large data files.
- Specify a large batch size for the ROWS_PER_BATCH hint. Ideally, the batch size should represent the total size of the file.
- Create ordered data files that match the clustered index.
- Lock the table to allow uninterrupted access by the bulk load.
- Perform nonlogged operations whenever possible.
- Turn the SELECT/INTO BCP database option on before performing a load. Remember to turn the option back off and back up the database after the load.

Microsoft recommends that you use the BULK INSERT statement instead of the BCP utility when you want to bulk copy data into SQL Server. The BULK INSERT statement is faster than BCP.

Working with Batch Files

The BCP utility is often used in command batch files with the isql or with the new favorite of SQL Server version 7.0: osql. To show the interaction between these two tools, let's look at a common process for loading data into production tables (see Figure 16.1).

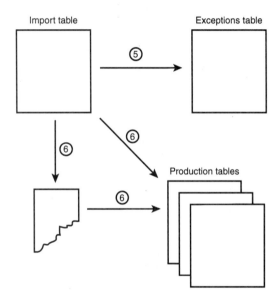

FIGURE 16.1
Loading data into production tables.

Here are the steps involved in loading data into production tables:

1. `osql -Q"create tables"`

   The first thing to remember is that, 99 times out of 100, you should bulk load data into a working table rather than directly into a production table. With this approach, you can be sure of the data quality, distribute the data among multiple production tables, and cause INSERT triggers to fire. Keeping these facts in mind, the osql -Q"create tables" statement creates a working import table and an exception table, which is described in step 5. Depending on how you do your cleanup, you may want to execute drop-table statements first.

2. `osql -Q"sp_dboption 'select into',true"`

   This optional statement puts the database into `SELECT INTO/BULK COPY` mode. This mode allows you to carry out a fast BCP but requires that the database be dumped at the end of the procedure.

3. `bcp data in`

   This statement bulk loads the data into the database, either using the `bcp` utility or with an `osql` executing a `BULK INSERT` command.

4. `osql -Q"create indexes"`

   When we created the import table, we did not specify any constraints that implicitly create indexes or any additional indexes. We ignored these options so that we could get the fastest possible bulk load. For the following steps, some indexes on the table can improve the speed at which we can carry out checks and joins. You should pick indexes appropriate for these operations.

5. `osql -Q"insert into exceptions"`

   To find out which, if any, rows in the import table are bad, we have to run a series of scripts that insert fields into the exception table. (We may choose to insert the entire data row, based on the checks, rules, and triggers in place for the production tables.) For example, if we want to consider data to be bad if the `state` field is not in a certain list, the SQL statement we execute might be as follows:

   ```
   INSERT INTO exceptions
   ( key1, key2, reason )
   SELECT author_id, title_id, 'Invalid state value.'
   FROM import_table
   WHERE state NOT IN ( 'IN', 'IL', 'ID' )
   ```

   This statement allows us to customize an error message detailing which check failed and store it in the exception table. We would follow each of these with a `DELETE` statement that acts on the `import_table`. This `DELETE` statement would use the same `WHERE` clause as the above `SELECT` so that we are working on only a smaller and smaller valid data set.

6. `osql -Q"insert...select"`

   The remaining data records in the import table are now ready to be moved into the production table(s). You have a choice depending on your requirements: You can either use `INSERT` statements with the `SELECT` statements, or use BCP to unload the data out of the import table and then back into the production table. Using `INSERT` statements allows you to positively verify that the data is good (the entire range of checks that normally occur are going to fire). Choose the `INSERT` method if you have set up any insert triggers to be fired; remember the BCP does not cause triggers to fire. The BCP unload and load method gives you the fastest performance; you can easily go against multiple tables with careful use of format files.

7. `osql -Q"sp_dboption 'select into',false"`

When you are finished with the transfer, remember to turn the
`SELECT INTO/BULK COPY` database option back off.

8. `osql -Q"backup database"`

Because we just carried out a bulk unlogged data transfer, we have to back up the
database. The backup captures our new data—and more importantly, re-enables
transaction log backups.

All that is left to do is to clean up and record what the operation achieved. You can use
BCP to unload the exceptions table to a file that you can then email to an operator using
another call to `osql`. Alternatively, you can execute an `osql` to query the table and send
the results to the operator. You can redirect the output of `osql` using the `-o` switch. The
various log files can also be collected for an operator to check over; place them in a specific directory or email them directly to the operator.

Once you have these commands set up, you can build them into a job that is executed by
the SQL Server agent. This approach allows you to build in dependencies between the
different tasks and provides all the other functionality supplied by the agent.

Summary

This chapter has shown you how to bulk load data into and out of SQL Server using the
BCP utility. The multitude of switches BCP offers can be bewildering, but this chapter
examines the switches and explains which ones offer tangible performance gains. With
the SQL Server version 7.0 of BCP, you can parallel load data into the same table; this
technique greatly reduces the time required to load very large data files.

Running the SQL Server Service Manager

by Greg Mable

IN THIS CHAPTER

A welcome enhancement to the set of SQL Server tools is the modification of the SQL Server Service Manager so that it executes as a task tray application. It now appears as a separate icon in the system tray. You can tell at a glance the status of a SQL Server service (MSSQLServer, SQLServerAgent, Microsoft Search, and DTC) without having to keep an application such as Enterprise Manager running on your desktop.

In this chapter, you will explore this utility and learn how to apply its benefits to fit your needs. This tool can quite easily simplify some of your day-to-day administrative tasks.

Using the Task Tray to Start and Stop SQL Server Services

When you start the SQL Server Service Manager application, the Service Manager icon appears in the system task tray, as shown in Figure 17.1.

FIGURE 17.1

The SQL Server Service Manager icon in the task tray.

The SQL Server Service Manager icon

You can right-click the icon to display a menu and open the application (see Figure 17.2).

FIGURE 17.2

The SQL Server Service Manager main screen.

The drop-down list boxes allow you to select a server and a SQL Server service on that server. Each of the services has its own icon and will be shown in green if it is running and red if stopped.

You have the option to set the polling interval. This is the interval used to determine how often the Service Manager checks whether the SQL Server services are running. You see a slight change in the icon shown in the task tray each time it polls. The default setting is 5 seconds.

> **TIP**
>
> You might want to increase the default polling interval from 5 seconds to a higher value, such as 60, especially if you are running multiple instances of the Service Manager in order to poll other SQL Server services and servers.

You also have the ability to turn off the service control verification. This is the confirmation message displayed whenever you select an option to stop or pause a service. By default, this option is checked.

> **CAUTION**
>
> Turning off this confirmation dialog will permit you to unintentionally stop a service by right-clicking the icon and inadvertently selecting the stop option. You should turn off this option only when you are not concerned about any of the services getting stopped unintentionally.

I offer a few brief words about pausing services. The pause command is only available for the MSSQLServer service on Windows NT, and it is not available for the SQLServerAgent, Microsoft Search, or the DTC. When you pause the MSSQLServer service, no new connections can be made to SQL Server. This function is useful when you want to shut down SQL server but want to let everyone currently on the system finish their work first.

When stopping the MSSQLServer service using the Service Manager, SQL Server will perform an orderly shutdown. The system does this by performing a checkpoint in each of the databases to ensure that the data cache has been written to the physical disk drive. In essence, it sends a service control message of SERVICE_CONTROL_STOP to SQL Server.

> **NOTE**
>
> If SQL Server was started from the command line, then the Service Manager will not be able to start, pause, or stop SQL Server. You must use Ctrl+C to shut down SQL Server.

An option in the Server Manager that is often overlooked is the About SQL Server Service Manager. If you right-click the Service Manager icon in the task tray and select the About option, you see the dialog box shown in Figure 17.3.

FIGURE 17.3

The About SQL Server Service Manager dialog box.

This option allows you to easily determine the version of SQL Server that is running. In addition, the dialog box includes a System Info button (if running under Windows NT). You can click this button to launch the Windows NT Diagnostics application.

Under Windows 95 and Windows 98, the System Info button does not appear.

> **TIP**
>
> This About option comes in handy when you need to quickly determine the versions of SQL Server and Windows NT running on a system. In particular, if you want to know whether a service pack has been applied to either the operating system or SQL Server, you can simply select the About option. It's quick and easy; you can walk anybody through this process.

Running Multiple Instances of the Service Manager

Multiple instances of the Service Manager are represented by multiple icons in the system task tray. Each time you start the Service Manager, another instance of the application appears in the task tray. Exiting the Service Manager only hides the application from the desktop; the application still runs and appears in the task tray. You must remember to right-click the icon in the task tray and select Exit in order to completely close the program.

Because you can run multiple instances of the Service Manager, you might want to set up your system to run an instance of the Service Manager for each service that you want to monitor. For example, in an environment where the MSSQLServer, SQLServerAgent, Microsoft Search, and the DTC are all used by a number of applications, you can place in the task tray an instance of the Service Manager for each service. This way, you can tell at a glance whether any of the services are unavailable.

You can extend this idea to more than one server. As an administrator responsible for the maintenance of several SQL Servers you can run an instance of the program for each SQL Server and have it focused on the MSSQLServer service. You can then tell immediately at a glance whether any of the SQL Servers are unavailable.

Summary

The SQL Server Service Manager is a small but handy tool that can ease your day-to-day administrative tasks. In previous versions, the utility was little used, only when a SQL Server service had to be restarted. The enhancement of the application as a task tray program enables you to use the program as a monitoring tool. It includes an often overlooked feature that allows you to perform some simple diagnostics. You might find yourself using the tool every day.

CHAPTER 18

SQL Server Command-Line Utilities

by Greg Mable

IN THIS CHAPTER

This chapter explores the various command-line utilities that ship with SQL Server. These utilities provide administrators with a set of tools for such tasks as automating routine maintenance procedures and verifying client connectivity to SQL Server. In this chapter, you will explore these command-line utilities. For each utility, this chapter provides the command syntax along with the most commonly used options. For the full syntax and options available for the utility, see the SQL Server Books Online help.

> **TIP**
>
> Because all these utilities run from a command line, you might find it easier to work with them by creating a folder of shortcuts. A shortcut could point to a set of .CMD files that execute the utility, calling it with the appropriate parameters. When you want to make changes, you can simply edit the .CMD files and then click the corresponding shortcut to execute them.

BCP

The SQL Server 7.0 version of the Bulk copy program (BCP) has been dramatically improved both in performance and functionality. It now uses the ODBC bulk copy API instead of DB-LIB to communicate with SQL Server and provides support for Unicode data. BCP uses the following syntax:

```
bcp {[[database_name.][owner].]{table_name¦ view_name} ¦ "query"}{
    in ¦ out ¦ queryout ¦ format} data_file
[-F first_row] [-L last_row] [
[-q]
[-E]
```

BCP also works in conjunction with the query optimizer so that importing and exporting data is more efficient than in earlier versions. For a more detailed look at BCP, see Chapter 16, "Using BCP to Import and Export Data."

Some of the commonly used options, other than the ones used to specify the database, such as user ID, password, and so on, are the -F and -L options. These options allow you to specify the first and last row of data (especially helpful in large batches). The -q option denotes that quoted identifiers are used. Quoted identifiers allow you to specify a table or field name that contains special characters such as spaces. The -E option allows you to import data into SQL Server fields that are defined with identity properties.

Data Transformation Services Utilities

There are two Data Transformation Services (DTS) command-line utilities included with SQL Server. The dtsrun utility allows you to edit the command used to execute a DTS package. DTS packages allow you to import, export, and transform data between Microsoft SQL Server and any OLE DB, ODBC, or text-file format. You can also use DTS to build a data warehouse from an online transaction processing (OLTP) system running on SQL Server or from import data from multiple heterogeneous sources.

The dtswiz utility allows you to start the Data Transformation Services Wizard using the options specified on the command line. You can use the Data Transformation Services Wizard to create DTS packages.

The DTS command-line utilities and the Data Transformation Services Wizard are discussed in more detail in Chapter 35, "Data Transformation Services."

ISQL/OSQL

How do you run a stored procedure from a batch file? For example, you want to run a batch process every night that copies some data into SQL Server and then executes a stored procedure to generate a report. How do you implement this?

You need a utility that allows you to run a SQL query from a command prompt. ISQL and, subsequently, OSQL were created to execute SQL queries and stored procedures from a command prompt. The ISQL utility uses DB-LIB to communicate with SQL Server, whereas OSQL uses ODBC.

Because ISQL is based on the DB-LIB interface, it does not support Unicode data. DB-Library has not been enhanced to support any of the new features in SQL Server 7.0 and is only maintained for backward compatibility. Microsoft recommends that you use OSQL instead of ISQL for any command-line procedures. You should consider migrating any utilities that you might have created with ISQL to use OSQL instead. Both utilities accept the same parameters and have the same syntax, so the migration should be a simple matter of search-and-replace. The syntax follows this example:

```
isql/osql -U login_id
```

In addition to using the utilities to run SQL queries, you can also use them by specifying the -L option. This option will list the names of the SQL servers currently on the network. You might want to use this option when you are troubleshooting a client's connection and you want to know which SQL servers the particular workstation can see.

18

SQL SERVER COMMAND-LINE UTILITIES

Makepipe and Readpipe

Makepipe and readpipe are a little known pair of utilities that are useful when you want to verify a client's connectivity to SQL Server through named pipes. The utilities work in conjunction with one another. To use these utilities, you first run makepipe from a command line on the server. Using the following syntax

```
Makepipe
Readpipe /Sserver_name
```

you can optionally pass it a pipe name, or it will create a default named pipe on the local SQL Server with a name of \\.\pipe\abc. Next, on the client computer, you run readpipe /Sserver_name. You can supply some optional parameters, but at minimum, readpipe needs the server name. If the named pipes interface is working properly between the client and the server, the client will display a message indicating that it sent data successfully to the server, and the server will echo the data sent from the client. You can press Ctrl+C to exit the utility on the server side. The -q option for the readpipe utility enables you to specify that it poll for incoming data. If not specified, the utility will wait for incoming data.

ODBCcmpt

ODBCcmpt allows you to enable or disable the 6.5 ODBC compatibility option, using the following syntax:

```
ODBCcmpt filename
```

This option permits the SQL Server ODBC driver (version 3.7) to be compatible with previous drivers. You might need to enable this option when running an application that SQL Server 7.0 should treat as a 6.5-level application. This allows backward compatibility for applications using either the ODBC 2.*x* or ODBC 3.*x* API.

ODBCPing

ODBCPing is a handy utility that allows you to test whether the ODBC and Microsoft SQL Server drivers are properly installed by connecting to SQL Server using the ODBC SQL Server driver. It uses this syntax:

```
ODBCPING { -Sserver_name ¦ -Ddata_source }
```

Unlike makepipe and readpipe, ODBCPing only runs on the client. You can use this utility whenever you need to verify that a client's ODBC connectivity is properly configured.

You can also incorporate the use of this utility as part of an installation procedure.

There are two ways you can run ODBCPing. You execute `ODBCPing -Sserver_name` to test a client's direct connectivity to SQL Server. You run `ODBCPing -Ddata_source` to use the specified data source to connect to SQL Server. In either case, if successful, ODBCPing displays the version of SQL Server and the version of the SQL Server ODBC driver.

Regrebld

Regrebld is a handy utility that you can use to back up and restore the SQL Server Registry entries. Initially, this utility is run automatically by the SQL Server setup program upon completion of an installation. It creates a set of files in the `\MSSQL7\Binn` directory with the .RBK extension. The syntax is

```
regrebld [-Backup ¦ -Restore ]
```

You can run this utility with `-Backup` to back up the Registry settings or use the `-Restore` option to restore the Registry settings and verify the state of SQL Server services. Be aware that if you run the utility without specifying an option, it will restore the Registry settings.

Replication Utilities

There are four utilities that you use to configure and execute the replication functionality of SQL Server. These utilities are covered in more detail in Chapter 20, "Replication":

- Replication Distribution Agent syntax:
  ```
  distrib -Publisher publisher
  -PublisherDB publisher_database
  -Subscriber subscriber
  ```
  The Replication Distribution Agent is a process that transfers jobs held in the distribution database to the various subscribers.

- Replication Log Reader Agent syntax:
  ```
  logread -Publisher publisher
  -PublisherDB publisher_database
  ```
  The Replication Log Reader Agent transfers transactions marked for replication on the publisher from the transaction log to the distribution database.

- Replication Merge Agent syntax
  ```
  replmerg
  -Publisher publisher
  ```

```
-PublisherDB publisher_database
-Publication publication
-Subscriber subscriber
-SubscriberDB subscriber_database
```

The Replication Merge Agent transfers the initial snapshots and any subsequent data changes in the publisher's database tables to the subscribers.

- Replication Snapshot Agent syntax

```
snapshot -PublisherDB publisher_database
-Publication publication_name
```

The Replication Snapshot Agent prepares the initial snapshots of tables in the publisher's database, stores the files on the distributor, and then maintains the status of its synchronization.

SQLDiag

The syntax is simply the following:

```
sqldiag
```

SQLDiag is a diagnostic tool that you can use to gather information regarding various SQL Server services. It is intended for use by Microsoft support engineers, but you might also find the information that it gathers useful in troubleshooting a problem. This tool collects the information into a text file, \Mssql7\log\Sqldiag.txt. The file contains all the SQL Server error logs, Registry data, file versions, configuration data, user and process information, and the output from the Microsoft diagnostic utility (Winmsd.exe).

SQLMaint

The syntax is simply the following:

```
sqlmaint
```

The SQLMaint utility is simple and convenient and is an alternative method to the Database Maintenance Wizard for setting up automated maintenance procedures for a given database.

The options for SQLMaint can be grouped as follows:

-CK is the prefix used with any option that performs a data integrity check, such as checking the integrity of the database tables and indexes. All of these options have the ability to bypass index checking, which speeds up the operation considerably.

-UpdSts and -RebldIdx are options that improve query performance. The first option updates the statistics used by the query optimizer and the second option rebuilds the indexes entirely.

-BkUp are options that back up either the database or the transaction log.

-DelBkUps determines how long the previous backups are saved.

-Rpt and -HtmlRpt are options that output the results of SQLMaint to a text file or an HTML file that can be published on a Web page.

SQLServr

The syntax is the following:

```
Sqlservr [-f] [-m]
```

The SQLServr application is the application that runs when SQL Server is started. You can use the SQLServr application to start SQL Server from a command prompt. You need to be aware, however, that if you start SQL Server from a command prompt, you cannot stop or pause it by using the Enterprise Manager, Service Manager, or the Services applet in the Control Panel.

Most commonly, you'll start SQL Server from the command prompt if you need to troubleshoot a configuration problem. The -f option starts SQL Server in minimal configuration mode. This allows you to recover from a change to a configuration setting that prevents SQL Server from starting. You use the -m option when you need to start SQL Server in single-user mode, such as when you need to rebuild one of the system databases, particularly the master database. (Hopefully, this will never happen to you.)

18

SQL SERVER COMMAND-LINE UTILITIES

VSwitch

The syntax is the following (see the Books Online Help for the full syntax of this utility):

```
vswitch -S {60 ¦ 65 ¦ 70}
```

You can use the VSwitch utility to switch between the currently active version of SQL Server (for systems that have SQL Server 7.0 installed alongside a previous version of SQL Server). You can call this utility from a batch file. Keep in mind, however, that it is recommended that only one version of SQL Server be installed on a computer. Each version uses a different set of Registry keys, so configuration changes made under one version will not be made under the other version. This utility is provided primarily as a means to assist in the upgrade process.

Summary

SQL Server provides a set of command-line utilities that allow you to execute SQL queries and stored procedures, perform diagnostics on client connectivity, and maintain the DTS packages and replication-based activities. In addition, the BCP utility allows you to import and export data easily from SQL Server.

Administering Very Large SQL Server Databases

by Matt Shepker

IN THIS CHAPTER

With data and data collection becoming more important in the business world, and hardware prices falling, a huge quantity of information is being stored worldwide. Many businesses are forming data warehouses to track business trends. These databases often grow into the hundreds of gigabytes, and sometimes even terabytes, in size.

These databases, often referred to as very large databases (VLDBs), provide new challenges for administrators. Due to the size of these databases, common maintenance tasks become difficult to perform because of the amount of time it can take to perform them.

Do I Have a VLDB?

While you are reading this, you are probably asking yourself whether you have a VLDB. Most definitions of VLDB are rather subjective. Is a database considered to be a VLDB when it reaches 1GB? 10GB? 100GB? 1TB? Granted, databases of these sizes are large, but they do not necessarily constitute VLDBs.

The actual definition of a VLDB is any database for which standard administrative procedures or design criteria fail to meet business needs due to the scale of the data. In other words, whenever you encounter a database that is so big that it makes you rethink your administrative procedures, you have a VLDB on your hands.

VLDB Maintenance Issues

When you are dealing with VLDBs, you must rethink how you are going to deal with everyday issues such as the following:

- Backing up and restoring databases
- Performing consistency checks on databases
- Updating index statistics
- Rebuilding indexes
- Purging and archiving historical data
- Partitioning data

Backing Up and Restoring Databases

Backing up databases is one of the most important things that an administrator can do. Backups can help you recover from disk failure as well as a multitude of other problems:

- Server hardware failure
- Software corruption
- Database corruption

- Natural disaster
- Vandalism
- User error

Because the size of the database is directly proportional to the amount of time that it takes to back up and restore the database, VLDBs can take an exceptionally long time to back up. In addition, it will actually take more time to restore the database than it will to back it up. SQL Server replaces the data in the database and then zeros out all the empty pages in the database.

SQL Server 7.0 added new functionality that helps with the amount of time it takes to perform database backups and restores. This new type of backup is known as file and filegroup backups. What this allows you to do is perform backups of individual database files at different times instead of backing up the full database all at once. For example, if you have two hours to perform backups and it takes four hours to complete a full backup, you can back up half of the files or filegroups now and then back up the rest later. This plan, combined with transaction log backups, provide a way of fully recovering your database. For more information on file and filegroup backups, see Chapter 12, "SQL Server Backup, Restore, and Recovery."

Performing Consistency Checks on Databases

Database consistency checks are used to check the internal structure of the database and verify the internal pointers and disk allocations. The database consistency checker, or DBCC, is the tool you use to do this. The problem with this tool is it can take a long time to run. A good formula for estimating the length of time that a DBCC will run is to figure 20 to 30 minutes for every gigabyte of data that you are checking. DBCCs are usually extremely CPU- and disk-intensive to run. SQL Server has to read into memory every data page that is being checked.

There are two ways to alleviate the time constraints of running DBCCs. The first option is to speed up the amount of time that a DBCC takes to run. The easiest way to do this is to increase the amount of memory available to the SQL Server. For example, increasing the amount of memory allocated to SQL Server from 128MB to 256MB will increase the speed by two times.

The other option is to offload the work of the DBCC onto another server. You can do this by restoring copies of the database onto another server and then running the DBCCs. When you perform your DBCCs in this fashion, you do not have to worry about impacting performance on your main server. However, you do have to determine what actions you are going to take if your DBCCs discover corruption in your database.

If you discover data corruption on your backup server, you have two options in dealing with it. First, you can stop all production on the primary server and attempt to fix the corruption on that server. When the database has been fixed, you can then perform a backup and transfer that copy over to the backup server. This option will usually result in little or no data loss.

The second option is to stop all data modification on the main server but allow users to query the data if they can. You then attempt to fix the problem that you found on the secondary server. When the database has been repaired, you back up the database on the secondary server and restore to the production server. This option will usually result in data loss from the time of the last database backup.

Updating Statistics

SQL Server creates and uses information known as index statistics to determine the correct way to access data in your tables. This information is used by the query optimizer to decide which index to use or whether a table scan is needed. The problem with these statistics is that SQL Server does not keep them updated. They are not kept up-to-date because SQL Server would have to spend more time during routine data processing to calculate these statistics, thus slowing down data modifications.

Updating statistics is an important thing for DBAs to perform because statistics can have a large impact on performance. Usually, this task is started by running the update sta-tistics command on a specific table—for example, update statistics authors. When the update statistics process is running on a table, it acquires a shared lock on the entire table. This allows users to query the data, but it does stop all data modification on the table.

With extremely large tables, this block can be a problem. One option to get around it is to update all the statistics on a table simultaneously. You do this by executing individual scripts that update different statistics on different indexes. For example, you can use one script that runs update statistics authors(index1) and another that runs update statistics authors(index2). This plan can greatly decrease the amount of time that the process takes.

You must determine whether you even need to update the statistics on the index. For example, for a table with a unique index that is queried for a single value, the index statistics are not even checked. If the only queries issued against this table are these types of queries, it is not extremely important for the statistics to be up-to-date. On the other hand, it is extremely important to have up-to-date statistics on indexes that are primarily used for range searches or when multiple values can match the query argument.

Rebuilding Indexes

With indexes on VLDBs, you also run into a problem with rebuilding the clustered indexes on your tables. This process is necessary to reapply the fill factor and to reclaim space from the table. When the clustered index on the table is rebuilt, the nonclustered indexes associated with that table are also rebuilt. When indexes are rebuilt, the statistics on the indexes are recreated as well. The command you use when rebuilding indexes is

```
DBCC DBREINDEX(tablename)
```

The biggest problem with rebuilding indexes is that SQL Server acquires an exclusive table lock on the table. This stops all queries and data modification on the table. Therefore, you must be careful when scheduling this process so there aren't any conflicts with user activity.

Purging and Archiving Data

A time will come for every VLDB that its size will approach the maximum size that hardware and software can handle. At this point, both the management team and the DBAs need to examine the business requirements and determine what can be done with the data. The process of purging or archiving data becomes extremely important in eliminating the problems discussed in this chapter.

There are really two different ways to take care of historical data in a database: purging and archiving. Purging simply means that you remove data from the database using a delete statement. Archiving data means that you are going to make a copy of the data in some way before you delete it, either through an insert and delete process or a backup and delete process.

When determining how you are going to deal with historical data, you need to ask yourself several questions:

- Is there a way to determine which data is no longer useful? For example, you might use a date stamp to determine which data is no longer valid or useful.
- Are there any legal ramifications or rulings that can be used to determine data retention? For example, if you are tracking shipments for a perishable product, laws frequently determine how long must you keep the data after the product was supposed to expire.
- Is it possible for the data requirements to change at some point? If you have an archival or storage process in place, it is important that you allow for changes in the archival requirements without major coding changes.
- Can the data that is being archived be recreated from some other source?

19

ADMINISTERING VERY LARGE DATABASES

Sometimes, data is simply summarization data that can be recreated through another source. The re-creation process might not be as easy, but it is often possible.

Whether you are creating a purge or archival system, you need to look into several factors before implementing a system. These factors all can impact the usability of the database:

- Locking
- Logging
- Referential integrity
- Transactional integrity

Locking Problems

When you are performing a lot of deletes on a table, you must examine the implications of how these deletes are going to affect other processes running on the same server. When you perform a delete on a single row, SQL Server automatically locks that row so no other user can access it. When that delete spans several rows on a single page, SQL Server will lock the entire page. When multiple pages are affected, SQL Server may determine that locking the entire table uses fewer resources. This means that all rows in the table are inaccessible to other processes.

You have several options in resolving locking problems:

- Timing—As they say, timing is everything. If you can, determine a maintenance window in which you can perform the archival or purge.
- Cursors—By using cursors, it is possible to select a group of rows that meet the criteria for deletion and then loop through the cursor and delete a single row at a time. Although this is an effective method, it is extremely slow.
- Row count—Another option is to use the set rowcount option to limit the number of rows that are affected at any point. This option forces SQL Server to stop processing after the number of rows affected reaches a certain level. You will want to ensure that you set this option to a low enough amount that you can ensure that SQL Server does not escalate the page locks to a table lock.
- Site specificity—If you can determine a value that makes data more site- or table-specific, you can limit the amount of data that is affected.

Logging Considerations

As with any other data modification process, data that is deleted from a database is logged in the transaction log. When you delete large amounts of data, the transaction log can get full very quickly. The problem is that although that actual data is gone from the database, the information is still in the transaction log until the log is dumped. When and if the transaction log becomes full, all data modifications in that database are stopped. Even if you have the `truncate log on checkpoint` option turned on, the transaction log can still become full. SQL Server can only truncate that portion of the transaction log that is not in use. If a large transaction, such as the batch delete of 50,000 rows, is still open, SQL Server cannot truncate that portion of the log. There are a few things that you can do to limit the chances that the transaction log is going to fill up:

- Limit the size of the delete statements that are committed in a single batch. This allows SQL Server to truncate the unused portion of the transaction log if needed.
- Correctly size the transaction log. This can be a difficult process if you are not accustomed to it. The rule of thumb is to make the transaction log one-fourth the size of the database.

Another problem that you can encounter with the transaction log is an I/O bottleneck. Deleting large amounts of data results in a large amount of disk I/O. Although data modifications are not always written to disk as soon as they are made, changes to the transaction log are. This can cause some contention if the data and the log reside on the same disk. It is always good practice to place the transaction log and the data on separate disk drives.

Referential Integrity

When purging or archiving data, you will frequently encounter scenarios in which related data is spread across several different tables. Because of this, you must be careful to take referential integrity into consideration when deleting data. Some of the different things you need to consider are the following:

- When deleting data in tables with declarative referential integrity (primary and foreign keys), you must delete the data in the related tables before you delete data from the main table.
- When deleting data in tables that have a cascading delete trigger, in which a delete in one table may affect many other tables, you must delete small amounts of data in the main table because it will affect many other tables. This could result in a great deal of log activity.

Transactional Integrity

The last issue you need to consider when purging or archiving data is that of transactional integrity. Every unit of work in SQL Server is known as a transaction. Every activity in a transaction must complete successfully, or all the activities are canceled. During the archival process, data is usually inserted into one table while it is deleted from another. If an error occurs during any portion of this process, all the process must be canceled. For example, if the insert into the table fails, you should not perform the delete from the other table. You enforce this integrity by placing the entire process into a transaction.

Partitioning Data

Another way to deal with large amounts of data is to partition it. With SQL Server 7.0, it is possible to separate different tables into different files within the same database. Data partitioning with VLDBs is slightly different in that the individual tables are placed in different databases or that large tables are broken up into several different databases. These different types of data partitioning are known as vertical and horizontal partitioning.

Vertical Partitioning

A vertical partitioning scheme uses an approach of placing tables from one database into different databases, as shown in Figure 19.1. This makes administration and development much easier because all the data from a single table is stored in one place.

FIGURE 19.1

Vertical partitioning places tables from one database into different databases.

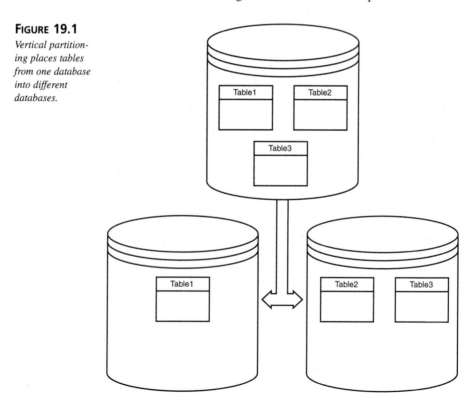

There are several advantages to vertically partitioning databases. One of the biggest advantages is that the separation of data can be hidden from the end user through the use of views. You can define these views in one main database that all the applications point to. The views then point to tables that are contained in other databases. An advantage to this approach is that you can change the actual location of the data without making any changes to the actual code of the application. Simply rewrite the views to point to the new storage location.

Another option in vertical partitioning is to break up tables and put different columns in different databases. This is an especially useful tool when you are dealing with large columns such as text and image data. It is often a good plan to put the smaller columns in one database and put the larger text and image columns in a different database.

Although using vertical partitioning and views might seem like a perfect solution, you need to be aware of several limitations before you jump into this solution. First and foremost, although views look like a single table, you must be aware of the limitations that you have when inserting, updating, and deleting data in a view.

When a view is spread across several tables and databases, you can only insert or update data from a single table in that view. If you must update or insert data into more than one table, you have to run different statements. SQL Server does not permit deletes from views that span multiple tables. You must run the deletes on each individual underlying table. Because of these limitations, developers can access the data without knowing where the tables exist, but they must know where the tables are when performing data modifications.

Another issue with vertical partitioning is that when you break up tables, you must determine a way to maintain the relational integrity of the database. You must also be careful to ensure that your backups are created so that all divided data is backed up as one unit. This way, if a database containing one portion of the data crashes, you can perform a restore on all of the divided table.

Horizontal Partitioning

The other option available for data partitioning is horizontal partitioning. Horizontal partitioning is the process of dividing a table into multiple portions and storing the different portions in different databases. The same columns are kept in each partition, and the table is split along a logical partition, such as a date, as shown in Figure 19.2. This can speed up database access by separating the current data from the historical data.

FIGURE 19.2
*Horizontal parti-
tioning is the
process of divid-
ing a table into
separate portions
based on a logi-
cal point.*

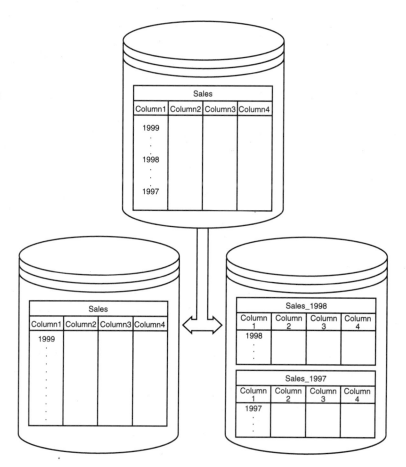

There are several reasons you might consider horizontally partitioning your tables. First, horizontal partitioning spreads the user activity across several database devices. This can help reduce I/O contention and locking and help speed up access. Another reason is that this can help you lock down portions of the data so only certain people see it.

The biggest issue with dealing with horizontally partitioned data is how you are going to access it. Through the union operator, you can combine the resultsets from several different queries into one resultset. You can hide the complexities of these queries from the end users by placing them within views. Unfortunately, because you cannot perform inserts, updates, and deletes in views, you are stuck with trying to determine how you will perform these complex updates.

There are basically two ways to horizontally partition the data in a database. The first option is to partition your data along logical boundaries. These boundaries can be geological, such as the location of a particular office, a date time field, such as the year, or another logical pattern, such as product information. The logical approach is good because it is easy to figure out where the data is. The downfall, however, is that it does not necessarily provide an even solution for dividing the data.

The other option for dividing data can provide an even way of distributing the data but makes figuring out where the data is stored difficult. This option is called hash partitioning. Hash partitioning is based on a hash key rather than a logical boundary. The hash key is usually generated using some random value. The major benefit to this is that you can evenly spread the data across several drives to distribute the disk I/O. When the data is spread across the drives in this fashion, it can be nearly impossible for you to determine the location of the data on those disks. This problem is evident when you encounter a failed disk partition or database. When your data is distributed logically, such as by order date, and the database that contains the data from 1996 crashes, you simply reload that data. If a database that contains hashed information crashes, it can be difficult to determine which rows were lost. You might need to reload data from several different sources, which can be time consuming.

Summary

With data becoming more important, VLDBs will become more prevalent in business. Without the proper planning and development, a VLDB can grow into a beast that will haunt you. With the release of SQL Server 7.0, VLDBs are easier to implement, but you will still have to plan creatively to get the job done.

19

ADMINISTERING VERY LARGE DATABASES

Replication

by Matt Shepker

In This Chapter

CHAPTER 20

With the business world becoming increasingly dependent on data, it has become important that data be in the correct place at the correct time. In the past, business data was created and distributed in papers and books, making distribution costly and time consuming. With the advent of the computer, data distribution became much easier. The first widely implemented computer systems were mainframes. With mainframes, data distribution was not necessary. All information created on the computer was available to all other portions of the computer. As client/server computing became more prevalent, it was not uncommon for businesses to store data on several computers at different geographic locations. Because of this, companies had to determine how all users who needed data had easy access to it in a timely manner. Solutions for this problem ranged anywhere from transferring backups from one location to another to using distributed transactions. To assist in the distribution of data, Microsoft added an extremely powerful tool to SQL Server. This tool, called replication, allows you to move data from one location to another.

What Is Replication?

Before setting up and using SQL Server replication, you should understand what replication is and how it works. Simply, replication is the process of copying data from one database to another. There are several different ways to set it up, and there are different ways to make it work in your business.

Setting up SQL Server replication provides several benefits. The first benefit that most people consider is that data can be delivered to different locations to eliminate network traffic and unnecessary load on a single server. For example, you can move all or some of the information from an online transaction processing database to a different server to allow for report generation. Another benefit is that you can move data off a single server onto several other servers to provide for high availability and decentralization of data. In this case, you could create a mirror of your main database on another server so that if the main server crashed, users could switch to the other server and continue to work with little downtime or data loss. This scenario could also allow different sites to operate independently from each other.

Replication Components

You must be familiar with several components of SQL Server replication before you can successfully understand and implement it.

The Publisher, Distributor, and Subscriber Metaphor

A SQL Server can play three separate roles in the replication process. These roles include the publication server, distribution server, and the subscription server.

The publication server contains the database or databases that are published. It makes data from the published databases available for subscription and sends updates to the distribution server.

The distribution server can either be the same server as the publication server or reside on a different server. This server contains the distribution database. This database, also called the store-and-forward database, holds changes that were forwarded from the publication database to the subscription servers. A single distribution server can support several publication servers.

The subscription server contains a copy of the database that is being distributed. Any changes made to the distributed database are sent and applied to the copy. In previous versions of SQL Server, any data sent to the subscription server was treated as read-only. There was no way to move replicated transactions from the subscriber back to the publisher. In SQL Server 7.0, subscribers can make updates, which are sent back to the publisher. It is important to note that an updating subscriber is not the same as a publisher.

Along with the server roles, two other terms fall into the publishing metaphor: *article* and *publication*. An article is simply a single table, or a subset of rows or columns out of a table, that is made available for replication. An article is always a part of a publication. A publication is a group of one or more articles that is the basic unit of replication. It is possible to have a single database that contains more than one publication. All articles in a publication are synchronized at the same time, thus maintaining referential integrity.

Filtering Articles

There are several different ways to create articles on SQL Server. The basic way to create an article is to publish all of the columns and rows that are contained in a table. Although this is the easiest way to create an article, your business needs might require that you send only certain columns or rows out of a table.

For example, your business might have a database that tracks product information for your company. This database resides at your main location and contains basic information about the products, such as product number, description, and prices, as well as proprietary information, such as formulation, that should not be released to the public. You have several branch locations that focus on selling the products. You can create an article for replication that contains a subset of the data in a table sent to the branch offices. This process, as shown in Figure 20.1, is known as vertical filtering.

20

REPLICATION

Figure 20.1

Vertical filtering is the process of creating a subset of columns from a table to be replicated to subscribers.

Publishing Server

au id	au lname	au fname	phone	city
172-32-1176	White	Johnson	408-796-7223	Menlo Park
213-46-8915	Green	Marjorie	415-986-7020	Oakland
238-95-7766	Carson	Cheryl	415-548-7723	Berkeley
267-41-2394	OLeary	Michael	408-286-2428	San Jose
274-00-9091	Straight	Dean	415-004-2919	Oakland
341-22-1782	Smith	Meander	913-843-0462	Lawrence
409-56-7008	Bennett	Abraham	415-658-9932	Berkeley
427-17-2019	Dull	Arn	415-006-7120	Palo Alto

Subscription Server

au lname	au fname	city
White	Johnson	Menlo Park
Green	Marjorie	Oakland
Carson	Cheryl	Berkeley
OLeary	Michael	San Jose
Straight	Dean	Oakland
Smith	Meander	Lawrence
Bennett	Abraham	Berkeley
Dull	Arn	Palo Alto

Another way to look at the differences between publishing all the data in a table and performing vertical filtering can be shown by running the following query in the SQL Query Analyzer:

```
use pubs
go
select * from authors
go
select au_lname, au_fname, phone from authors
go
```

In another example, you might have several branch locations that track information about users who call for technical support. You need to move all this information to one central location for reporting and then redistribute it back to the other sites. The problem with this plan is that it is possible for customers to speak to technicians at several different sites. When this data is rolled up and then redistributed, it is possible to overwrite data from one site with data from another. In this case, you would create an article that contains only a subset of rows from a particular database. This process, as shown in Figure 20.2, is known as horizontal filtering.

To see the actual dataset created when you perform horizontal filtering, run the following query in the SQL Query Analyzer:

```
use pubs
go
select * from authors
go
select * from authors where state = 'CA'
go
```

FIGURE 20.2

Horizontal filtering is the process of creating a subset of rows from a table to be replicated to subscribers.

au id	au lname	au fname	phone	city
172-32-1176	White	Johnson	408-796-7223	Menlo Park
213-46-8915	Green	Marjorie	415-986-7020	Oakland
238-95-7766	Carson	Cheryl	415-548-7723	Berkeley
267-41-2394	OLeary	Michael	408-286-2428	San Jose
274-00-9091	Straight	Dean	415-004-2919	Oakland
341-22-1782	Smith	Meander	913-843-0462	Lawrence
409-56-7008	Bennett	Abraham	415-658-9932	Berkeley
427-17-2019	Dull	Arn	415-006-7120	Palo Alto

Publishing Server

Subscription Server

au id	au lname	au fname	phone	city
238-95-7766	Carson	Cheryl	415-548-7723	Berkeley
267-41-2394	OLeary	Michael	408-286-2428	San Jose
274-00-9091	Straight	Dean	415-004-2919	Oakland
409-56-7008	Bennett	Abraham	415-658-9932	Berkeley
427-17-2019	Dull	Arn	415-006-7120	Palo Alto

It is possible for you to combine both horizontal and vertical filtering, as shown in Figure 20.3. This allows you to pare out unneeded columns and rows that aren't required for replication.

FIGURE 20.3

Combining horizontal and vertical filtering allows you to pare down the information in an article to only the important information.

au id	au lname	ua fname	phone	city
172-32-1176	White	Johnson	408-796-7223	Menlo Park
213-46-8915	Green	Marjorie	415-986-7020	Oakland
238-95-7766	Carson	Cheryl	415-548-7723	Berkeley
267-41-2394	OLeary	Michael	408-286-2428	San Jose
274-00-9091	Straight	Dean	415-004-2919	Oakland
341-22-1782	Smith	Meander	913-843-0462	Lawrence
409-56-7008	Bennett	Abraham	415-658-9932	Berkeley
427-17-2019	Dull	Arn	415-006-7120	Palo Alto

Publishing Server

Subscription Server

au lname	ua fname	city
Carson	Cheryl	Berkeley
OLeary	Michael	San Jose
Straight	Dean	Oakland
Bennett	Abraham	Berkeley
Dull	Arn	Palo Alto

You can visualize this dataset by running the following query in the SQL Query Analyzer:

```
use pubs
go
select * from authors
go
select au_lname, au_fname, phone from authors where state = 'CA'
go
```

Subscriptions

Before a subscription server can receive data from a publication server, it must subscribe to articles or publications. You can do this by performing either a push subscription or a pull subscription.

A pull subscription is set up and managed by the subscription server. In this case, the subscription server pulls the publication from the publication server. The biggest advantage is that pull subscriptions allow the system administrators of the subscription servers to choose what publications they will receive. Pull subscriptions can be created only on SQL Server 7.0 servers. With pull subscriptions, publishing and subscribing are separate acts and are not necessarily performed by the same user. Usually, pull subscriptions are best when the publication does not require high security.

A push subscription is created and managed by the publication server. In effect, the publication server is pushing the publication to the subscription server. The advantage of using push subscriptions is that all of the administration takes place in a central location. Publishing and subscribing can happen at the same time, and many subscribers can be set up at once.

Anonymous Subscriptions

In SQL Server 7.0, it is possible to add anonymous subscriptions. An anonymous subscription is a special type of pull subscription that is usually used when you are publishing databases to the Internet. Normally, information about all of the subscribers, including performance data, is stored on the distribution server. In the event that you have a large number of subscribers, or you do not want to track detailed information about the subscribers, you might want to allow anonymous subscriptions to a publication.

Anonymous subscriptions are always created by the subscriber. The subscriber is responsible for ensuring that the subscription is synchronized. An anonymous subscription is created using the same steps used to create a pull subscription.

The Distribution Database

The distribution database is a special type of database installed on the distribution server. This database is known as a store-and-forward database that holds all transactions waiting to be distributed to any subscribers. This database receives transactions sent from any published databases and holds them until they are sent to the subscribers.

Replication Agents

Along with the basic components, SQL Server also contains replication agents that are responsible for different actions during the replication process. Your replication scenario will contain at least two agents.

The Snapshot Agent

The snapshot agent is responsible for preparing the schema and initial data files of published tables and stored procedures, storing the snapshot on the distribution server and recording information about the synchronization status in the distribution database. Each publication will have its own snapshot agent that runs on the distribution server. The snapshot agent usually runs within the SQL Server Agent and can be administered using SQL Server Enterprise Manager.

The Log Reader Agent

The log reader agent is responsible for moving transactions marked for replication from the transaction log of the published database to the distribution database. Each database published using transactional replication has its own log reader agent that runs on the distribution server.

The Distribution Agent

The distribution agent moves transactions and snapshot jobs held in the distribution database out to the subscribers. Transactional and snapshot publications set for immediate synchronization when a new push subscription is created will have their own individual distribution agent that runs on the distribution server. Those not set up for immediate synchronization share a distribution agent that runs on the distribution server. Pull subscriptions to either snapshot or transactional publications have a distribution agent that runs on the subscriber. Merge publications do not have a distribution agent at all. Rather, they rely on the merge agent, discussed next. The distribution agent usually runs within the SQL Server Agent and can be administered using SQL Server Enterprise Manager.

The Merge Agent

When dealing with merge publications, the merge agent moves and reconciles incremental data changes that occurred after the initial snapshot was created. Each merge publication has a merge agent that connects to the publishing server and the subscribing server and updates both as changes are made. In a full merge scenario, the agent first uploads all changes from the subscriber where the generation is 0 or the generation is greater than the last generation sent to the publisher. The agent gathers the rows in which changes were made, and those rows without conflicts are applied to the publishing database.

A conflict is a row in which changes were made at both the publishing server and the subscriber. The conflicts are handled by the conflict resolver that is associated with the article in the publication definition. The agent then reverses the process by downloading

20

REPLICATION

any changes from the publisher to the subscriber. Push subscriptions have merge agents that run on the publishing server, whereas pull subscriptions have merge agents that run on the subscriber. Snapshot and transactional publications do not use merge agents.

Planning for SQL Server Replication

The process of sharing and moving data is often referred to as distributing data. When choosing a method to distribute data, you must consider several factors. These factors are heavily dependent on your business needs: the timing and latency of replication; the independence, or autonomy, of individual sites; and the ability to partition data to avoid conflicts.

Timing and Latency of Replicated Data

There are two models available to you in the distributed data process. In some applications, such as online transaction processing and inventory control systems, data must be synchronized at all times. This model, called immediate transactional consistency, was known as tight consistency in previous versions of SQL Server. In other applications, such as decision support systems and report generation engines, 100 percent data synchronization all of the time is not as important. This model, called latent transactional consistency, was known as loose consistency in previous versions of SQL Server.

SQL Server implements immediate transactional consistency data distribution in the form of two-phase commits. A two-phase commit, sometimes known as 2PC, ensures that transactions are committed on all servers or the transaction is rolled back on all servers. This will ensure that all data on all servers is 100 percent in sync at all times. One of the main drawbacks of immediate transactional consistency is that it requires a high-speed LAN to work. This type of solution is not feasible for large environments with many servers because occasional network outages can occur.

Latent transactional consistency is implemented in SQL Server via replication. Replication allows data to be updated on all servers, but the process is not a simultaneous one. The result is "real-enough time" data. This is known as real-enough time data or latent transactional consistency because there is a lag between the data updated on the main server and the replicated data. In this scenario, if you could stop all data modifications from occurring on all servers, then all of the servers would eventually have the same data. Unlike the two-phase consistency model, replication works over both LANs and WANs as well as slow or fast links.

Site Autonomy

When planning a distributed application, you must consider the effect of one site's operation on another. This is known as site autonomy. A site with complete autonomy can continue to function without being connected to any other site. A site with no autonomy cannot function at all without being connected to all other sites. For example, applications that utilize two-phase commits, or 2PC, rely on all other sites being able to immediately accept any changes that are sent to it. In the event that any one site is unavailable, then no transactions, on any server, can be committed. In contrast, sites using merge replication can be completely disconnected from all other sites and continue to work effectively, not guaranteeing data consistency. Luckily, some solutions combine both high data consistency and site autonomy.

Partitioning Data

When designing an application that will rely on replication, one way to avoid conflicts is to partition the data. In this case, you can set up safeguards in the application itself that will keep conflicts from occurring. It is always better to avoid conflicts before they happen than to try to fix them after they occur. Some replication methods do allow for detection and resolution of conflicts, which always result in one site's information being overwritten or rolled back. An example of data partitioning can be shown in a sales application in which phone operators take orders for products in several different locations. Each location is assigned its own unique set of order numbers. All of the locations can see all of the records, but a user can only update the records from her own site.

Methods of Data Distribution

After you have determined the amount of transactional latency and site autonomy, it is important to select the data distribution method that suits your business needs. Each different type of data distribution has a different amount of site autonomy and latency:

- Distributed transactions—Distributed transactions ensure that all sites have the exact same data at all times.
- Transactional replication with updating subscribers—Users can change data at the local location, and those changes are applied to the source database at the same time. The changes are then eventually replicated to other sites. This type of data distribution combines replication and distributed transactions. Because data is changed at both the local site and source database, conflicts do not occur.
- Transactional replication—With transactional replication, data is only changed at the source location and is sent out to the subscribers. Because data is only changed at a single location, conflicts cannot occur.

20

REPLICATION

- Snapshot replication with updating subscribers—This method is much like transactional replication with updating subscribers, when users can change data at the local location and those changes are applied to the source database at the same time. The entire changed publication is then replicated to all subscribers. This type of replication provides a higher autonomy than transactional replication.

- Snapshot replication—An entire copy of the publication is sent out to all subscribers. This includes both changed and unchanged data.

- Merge replication—All sites make changes to local data independently and then update the publisher. It is possible for conflicts to occur, but they are resolved.

SQL Server Replication Types

There are three major types of SQL Server replication: snapshot, transactional, and merge. Each replication type applies only to a single publication. It is possible to have multiple types of replication per database.

Snapshot Replication

As you can imagine, snapshot replication makes a picture of all the tables in a publication at a single moment in time and then moves the entire dataset to the subscribers. This type of replication requires little overhead on the server because snapshot replication does not track any data modifications, as the other forms of replication do. It is possible, however, for snapshot replication to require large amounts of network bandwidth, especially if the articles being replicated are very large. Snapshot replication is the easiest form of replication to set up and is used primarily with smaller datasets when subscribers do not have to perform updates. This can include price lists and phone lists where having the most critical data is not always critical.

Snapshot replication is performed by the snapshot agent and the distribution agent. The snapshot agent creates files that contain the schema of the publication and the data itself. The files are stored in the snapshot folder of the distribution server, and then the distribution jobs are recorded in the distribution database. The distribution agent moves the distribution jobs from the distribution database over to the target tables in the subscriber databases.

The Snapshot Agent Process

When the snapshot agent runs, it creates all schema and data files with the following steps:

1. The snapshot agent connects to the publisher and locks all the tables in a publication. The lock is required to ensure that no data modifications are made during the replication process.

2. The agent writes a copy of the schema of all published tables to the distributor. These files will be used to create the schema on the subscribing server; they have the .SCH file extension.

3. The agent creates a copy of the data in the publication and writes it to the distributor. If all the subscribers are SQL Servers, then the data will be written to the file using a SQL Server native format with a .BCP file extension. If you are replicating to databases other than SQL Server, the data will be stored in standard text files with the .TXT file extension. The .SCH file and the .TXT files are known as a synchronization set. Every table will have individual synchronization sets.

4. The agent adds rows to the distribution database, indicating the location of the synchronization set and the order in which they are to be created.

5. When all the synchronization sets have been created, the agent releases the locks on all of the tables.

The Distribution Agent Process

The distribution agent is responsible for moving the schema and data from the distributor to the subscribers, using the following steps:

1. The agent connects to the distributor from the server that it is currently running on. When using push subscriptions, the agent is located on the distributor. With pull subscriptions, the distribution agent is located on the subscriber.

2. The agent examines the distribution database to determine the location of the synchronization sets that were created by the snapshot agent.

3. The agent applies all of the schema and data to the subscription database.

Cleaning Up

When replication is installed on a SQL Server, three tasks are added to keep replication up and running for long periods of time. These tasks are agent cleanup, transaction cleanup, and history cleanup. In snapshot replication, after the snapshot has been delivered to all the subscribers, these tasks delete the associated .BCP and .SCH files from the distributor.

Immediate Updating Subscribers

Snapshot replication is basically designed as a one-way model for replication, meaning that data is modified on the publisher only and sent to the subscribers. SQL Server has built-in functionality that allows you to update data on the subscribers. This model,

20

REPLICATION

called immediate updating subscribers, implements two-phase commits to update the publishing server as soon as the changes are made on the subscribing server. The changes are then replicated to the other subscribers.

Transactional Replication

Transactional replication is the process of capturing transactions from the transaction log of the published database and applying them to the subscription databases. With SQL Server transactional replication, you can publish all or part of a table or one or more stored procedures as an article. All changes are stored in the distribution database and then sent and applied to the subscribed databases in the same order in which they were originally made.

In transactional replication, the publisher is where data changes are made. These changes are propagated to the other sites at nearly real time. Because changes are usually only made at the publishing server, data conflicts are avoided. Push subscribers usually receive updates from the publisher in a minute or less, depending on the speed and availability of the network. Subscribers can also be set up for pull subscriptions. This is useful for disconnected users who are not connected to the network at all times.

Transactional replication is performed by the snapshot agent, log reader agent, and distribution agent. The snapshot agent creates files that contain the schema of the publication and the data itself. The files are stored in the snapshot folder of the distribution server, and then, the distribution jobs are recorded in the distribution database. The log reader agent monitors the transaction log of all databases set up for replication and copies the transactions from the transaction log into the distribution database. The distribution agent moves the initial snapshot and transactions held in the distribution database to the subscribers.

The Snapshot Agent

The snapshot agent is the process that ensures that both databases start on an even playing field. This process is known as synchronization. The synchronization process is performed whenever there is a new subscriber to a publication. Synchronization only happens one time for each new subscriber and ensures that database schema and data are exact replicas on both servers. After the initial synchronization, all updates are made via replication.

When a new server subscribes to a publication, synchronization is performed. When synchronization begins, a copy of the table schema is copied to a file with a .SCH extension. This file contains all the information necessary to create the table and any indexes on the tables, if they are requested. Next, a copy is made of the data in the table to be synchronized and written to a file with a .BCP extension. The data file is a BCP, or bulk copy file. Both files are stored in the temporary working directory on the distribution server.

After the synchronization process has started and the data files have been created, any inserts, updates, and deletes are stored in the distribution database. These changes will not be replicated to the subscription database until the synchronization process is complete.

When the synchronization process starts, only new subscribers are affected. Any subscriber that has already been synchronized and has been receiving modifications is unaffected. The synchronization set is applied to all servers that are waiting for initial synchronization. After the schema and data have been recreated, all transactions that have been stored in the distribution server are sent to the subscriber.

When you set up a subscription, it is possible to manually load the initial snapshot onto the server. This is known as manual synchronization. For extremely large databases, it is frequently easier to dump the database to tape and then reload the database on the subscription server. If you load the snapshot this way, SQL Server will assume that the databases are already synchronized and will automatically begin sending data modifications.

The Log Reader Agent

After initial synchronization has taken place, the log reader agent begins to move transactions from the publication server to the distribution server. All actions that modify data in a database are logged to the transaction log in that database. Not only is this log used in the automatic recovery process, but also it is also used in the replication process. When an article is created for publication and the subscription is activated, all entries about that article are marked in the transaction log. For each publication in a database, a log reader agent reads the transaction log and looks for any marked transactions. When the log reader agent finds a change in the log, it reads the changes and converts them to SQL statements that correspond to the action that was taken in the article. The SQL statements are then stored in a table on the distribution server. The distribution server will read the changes and run them on the subscription server. The log reader agent is configured in the SQL agent in SQL Enterprise Manager.

Because replication is based on the transaction log, several changes are made in the way the transaction log works. During normal processing, any transaction that has either been successfully completed or rolled back is marked inactive. When you are performing replication, completed transactions are not marked inactive until the log reader process has read them and sent them to the distribution server. One of the major changes in the transaction log comes when you have the `truncate log on checkpoint` database option turned on. When the `truncate log on checkpoint` option is on, SQL Server truncates the transaction log every time a checkpoint is performed, which can be as often as every several seconds. The inactive portion of the log will not be truncated until the log reader process has read the transaction.

20

REPLICATION

NONLOGGED PROCESSES

For example, truncating a table and fast bulk-copying into a table are non-logged processes. In tables marked for publication, you will not be able to perform nonlogged operations unless you turn off replication on that table.

The Distribution Agent

Once the transactions have been moved into the distribution database, the distribution agent either pushes out the changes to the subscribers or pulls them from the distributor, depending on how the servers were set up. All actions that change data on the publishing server are applied to the subscribing servers in the same order they were made.

Cleaning Up

When replication is installed on a SQL Server, three tasks are added to keep replication up and running for long periods of time. These tasks are agent cleanup, transaction cleanup, and history cleanup. These tasks retain transaction information for a period of time, known as the retention period, after the replication has taken place and then deletes them from the distribution database.

Immediate Updating Subscribers

You can enable publications to support immediate updating subscribers in which a subscriber can modify replicated data. This process uses two-phase commits to send transactions to the publisher, so an application can be written as though it is updating just one site. In this setup, only the publisher needs to be available. After the change is made at the subscriber and sent to the publisher, it will eventually get sent to all other subscribers to the publication. Subscribers performing updates do not have full autonomy because the publisher must be available at the time of the data modification.

Replicating the Execution of Stored Procedures

Along with allowing you to replicate data in tables, SQL Server also allows you to replicate stored procedures. If you include stored procedures in an article, SQL Server will replicate the entire stored procedure from the publisher to the subscriber. When that stored procedure is used to modify data, instead of replicating the data changes caused by the stored procedures, SQL Server will instead replicate the execution of the stored procedure. This can be especially useful when you are dealing with data-maintenance stored procedures that affect a large amount of data. Instead of being replicated as a large amount of data modification language, it is instead replicated as a single EXEC statement.

There are two types of stored procedure articles you can create: articles for procedure execution and articles for serializable procedure execution. Procedure execution replicates the execution to all subscribers of an article. This occurs whether or not the individual statements successfully complete. Because changes made to the data can occur in multiple transactions, data at the subscribers is not guaranteed to be consistent with data at the publisher. In serializable procedure replication, the procedure execution is replicated only if the procedure is executed within a serializable transaction. If the stored procedure is executed from outside a serializable transaction, changes to data in published tables are replicated as a series of SQL statements. This guarantees that data at the subscribers is consistent with data at the publisher.

Merge Replication

Merge replication is a new feature in SQL Server 7.0. This technology tracks all changes to data in the replicated databases and then synchronizes changes so that all copies of the database have identical data. This type of replication will always involve conflict resolution. The publisher will not always win during the conflict. Instead, the winner is determined by whatever criteria you establish. All changes made on all servers are propagated back to the source database.

Merge replication is handled by the snapshot agent and the merge agent. The snapshot agent creates files that contain the schema of the publication and the data itself. The files are stored in the snapshot folder of the distribution server, and then, the distribution jobs are recorded in the distribution database. The merge agent takes the initial snapshot and applies it to all of the subscribers. It then reconciles all changes made on all the servers based on the rules that you configure.

Preparing for Merge Replication

When you set up a table for merge replication, SQL Server performs three different schema changes to your database. First, SQL Server must either identify or create a unique column for every row that is going to be replicated. This column is used to identify the different rows across all of the different copies of the table. If the table already contains a column with the ROWGUIDCOL property, SQL Server will automatically use that column for the row identifier. If not, SQL Server will add a column called rowguid to the table. SQL Server will also place an index on the rowguid column.

Next, SQL Server adds triggers to the table to track any changes that occur to the data in the table. The triggers track any changes and record them in the merge system tables. The triggers can track changes at either the row or the column level, depending on how you set it up. SQL Server 7.0 will support multiple triggers of the same type on a table, so merge triggers will not interfere with user-defined triggers on the table.

Last, SQL Server adds new system tables to the database that contains the replicated tables. The MSMerge_contents and MSMerge_tombstone tables track the updates, inserts, and deletes. These tables rely on the rowguid to track which rows have actually been changed.

The Snapshot Agent

The snapshot agent in merge replication operates in the same way it does in transactional replication.

The Merge Agent

The merge agent is responsible for moving changed data from the site where it was changed to all other sites in the replication scenario. When a row is updated, the triggers that were added by SQL Server fire off and update the new system tables, setting the generation column equal to 0 for the corresponding rowguid. When the merge agent runs, it collects the data from the rows where the generation column is 0 and then resets the generation values to values higher than the previous generation numbers. This allows the merge agent to look for data that has already been shared with other sites without having to look through all the data. The merge agent then sends the changed data to the other sites.

When the data reaches the other sites, the data is merged with existing data according to rules that have been defined by you. These rules are flexible and highly extensible. The merge agent evaluates existing and new data, and conflicts are resolved based on priorities or which data was changed first. Another available option is that you can create custom resolution strategies using the Component Object Model (COM) and custom stored procedures. After conflicts have been handled, synchronization occurs to ensure that all sites have the same data.

Conflict Resolution

The merge agent identifies conflicts using the MSMerge_contents table. In this table, a column called lineage is used to track the history of changes to a row. The agent updates the lineage value whenever a user makes changes to the data in a row. The entry into this column is a combination of a site identifier and the last version of the row created at the site. As the merge agent is merging all the changes that have occurred, it examines each site's information to see whether a conflict has occurred. If a conflict has occurred, the agent initiates conflict resolution based on the criteria mentioned earlier.

Cleaning Up

Cleanup in a merge replication environment involves two tasks that automatically purge data that is not longer needed. First, SQL Server adds a subscription cleanup at the publisher to delete the initial snapshots for each subscriber. The second task cleans up the history information on the distributor.

Replication Scenarios

You can choose from several scenarios when setting up replication. There are specific things that you can do with each scenario:

- Central publisher
- Central publisher with a remote distributor
- Publishing subscriber
- Central subscriber
- Multiple publishers or multiple subscribers

Central Publisher

The central publisher replication scenario, as shown in Figure 20.4, is the most common scenario. In this scenario, one server performs the function of both publisher and distributor. The publisher/distributor services any number of subscribers.

FIGURE 20.4
The central publisher scenario is the simplest and most frequently used scenario.

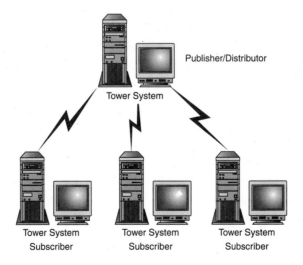

Publisher/Distributor

Tower System

Tower System
Subscriber

Tower System
Subscriber

Tower System
Subscriber

20

REPLICATION

The central publisher scenario can be used in the following situations:

- Creating a copy of a database for ad hoc queries and report generation
- Sending out a copy of a master price list to remote locations
- Maintaining a local copy of an online transaction processing database during communications outages

Central Publisher with Remote Distributor

The central publisher with remote distributor scenario, as shown in Figure 20.5, is similar to the central publisher subscriber and would be used in the same situations. The major difference in the two is that a second server is brought in to perform the role of distributor. This is useful when you need to free the publishing server from having to perform the distribution task. A single distributor server can distribute changes for several publishers. The publisher and distributor must be connected to each other via a reliable, high-speed data link.

FIGURE 20.5

The central publisher with remote distributor is used when the task of replication must be removed from the publishing server.

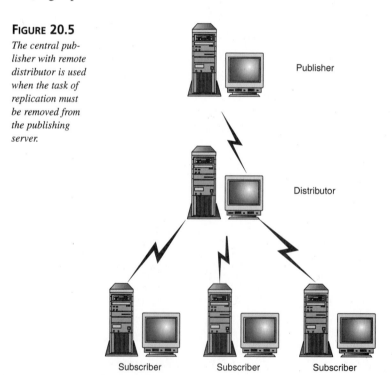

Publisher

Distributor

Subscriber   Subscriber   Subscriber

Publishing Subscriber

In the publishing subscriber scenario, as shown in Figure 20.6, the distribution server acts as both a subscriber to the original database and a publisher of the local copy. This scenario is best used when there is a slow or expensive network link between the primary server and the rest of the subscribers. For example, ABC Corp's main office is in San Diego and has several branch offices in Japan. Instead of replicating changes to all the branch offices in Japan, ABC Corp chooses to send all the updates to a server in Tokyo. The server in Tokyo then replicates the updates to all other subscriber servers in Japan. The major benefit to using this scenario is a reduction in network traffic and a reduction in communication costs.

FIGURE 20.6

The publishing subscriber scenario is appropriate when you must replicate across a slow and expensive WAN link.

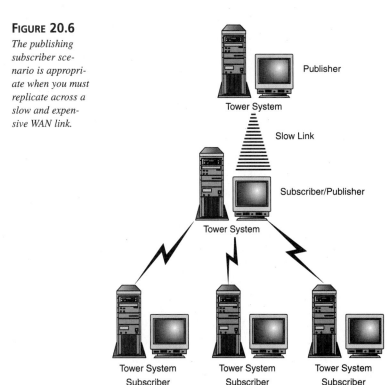

Central Subscriber

In the central subscriber scenario, as shown in Figure 20.7, several publishers replicate data to a single, central subscriber. You would use this scenario when you need to provide a central location that has all the data from the remote locations. When you implement this scenario, you need to take several precautions to make sure that all the data remains synchronized and is not overwritten.

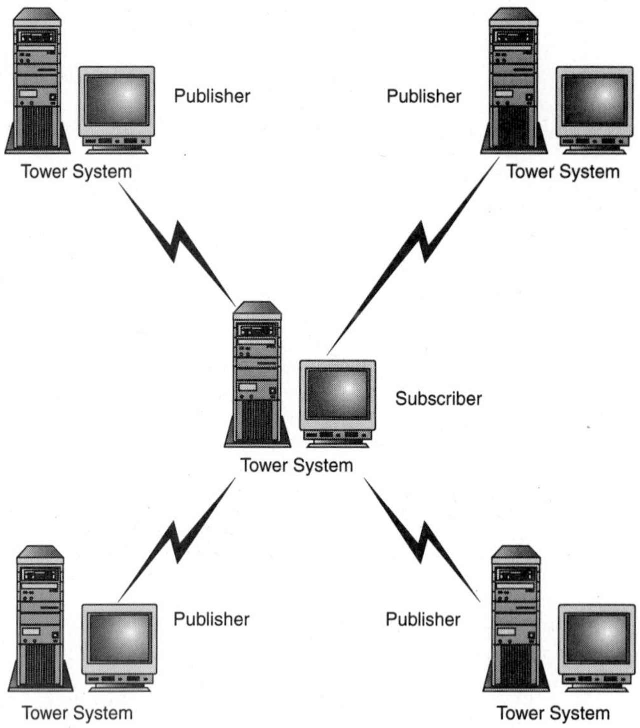

Figure 20.7

When using the central subscriber scenario, several publishers send data to a single, central subscriber.

Before implementing this scenario, you need to perform the following tasks:

1. Create a column that contains a unique identifier for the data that will be replicated from each site. You will then use this identifier to partition the rows.

2. Add the column that contains the unique identifier to the primary key.

3. Perform a manual synchronization of the table.

Multiple Publishers or Multiple Subscribers

In the multiple publishers or multiple subscribers scenario, as shown in Figure 20.8, a single, horizontally partitioned table is maintained on every server participating in the scenario. Each server publishes a particular set of rows that pertain to it and subscribe to the rows that all the other servers are publishing. You must be careful when implementing this scenario to ensure that all sites remain synchronized. The most frequently used applications of this system are regional order processing systems and reservation tracking systems. When setting up this system, you should make sure that only local users can update local data. This check can be implemented through the use of stored procedures, restrictive views, or a check constraint.

FIGURE 20.8
In the multiple publishers of a single table, a single, horizontally partitioned table is maintained by every server in the scenario.

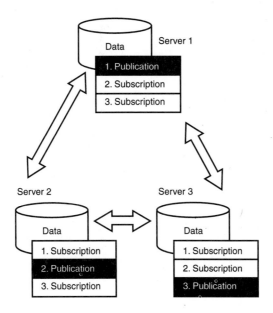

Setting Up Replication

Luckily, SQL Server 7.0 replication is much easier to configure than SQL Server 6.5 replication was. Microsoft has added a number of wizards to assist you in setting it up. Before I get too far into looking at the different wizards, first understand the order and steps that you have to go through to set up replication:

1. Create or enable a distributor.
2. Create a publication and define articles within the publication.
3. Define subscribers and subscribe to a publication.

Enabling Publishing

Before setting up a publisher, you should designate a distribution server to be used by that server. As you have seen, you can either configure the local server as the distribution server or choose a remote server. You can create a distributor in one of two ways. First, you can configure the server as a distributor and publisher at the same time, or configure the server as a dedicated distributor. You can do this using the Configure Publishing and Subscribers Wizard. You must be a member of the sysadmin server role to use this wizard. Use the following steps to configure a server as a distributor:

20

REPLICATION

1. Connect to the server you are setting up as a distributor within SQL Enterprise Manager. From the Tools menu, choose Replication and then select Configure Publishing and Subscribers. This will open the Configure Publishing and Distribution Wizard.

2. At the introduction screen, select the Next button.

3. From the Choose Distributor screen, you are prompted to either set up the local server as the distribution server or select a remote distributor (see Figure 20.9). For this example, I assume that you are configuring a new distributor on the local server. If you have already created a distributor, choose that server for use with the publisher you are creating. After you click the Next button, SQL Server will verify the account context that it is currently running in. If SQL Server is running under the LocalSystem account, you will not be able to perform multisite replication. This is because the LocalSystem account does not have access to network resources.

FIGURE 20.9

You must either select or install a distributor for this publisher to use.

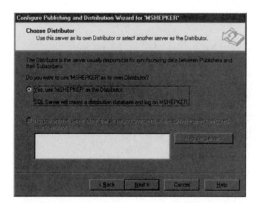

4. From the Use Default Configuration Screen, you can either choose to use the default settings or select to specify your own options. Specify your own options in this example.

5. The next screen allows you to choose the name of the distribution database and the location of the files.

6. The Enable Publishers dialog allows you to configure which publishers are allowed to use the distributor that you are currently setting up (see Figure 20.10). If you click the button with the ellipsis (...) after the publisher's name, a screen allows you to choose specific options about that publisher. From this screen, you can also choose which accounts the distribution agents will use to log in to the publisher.

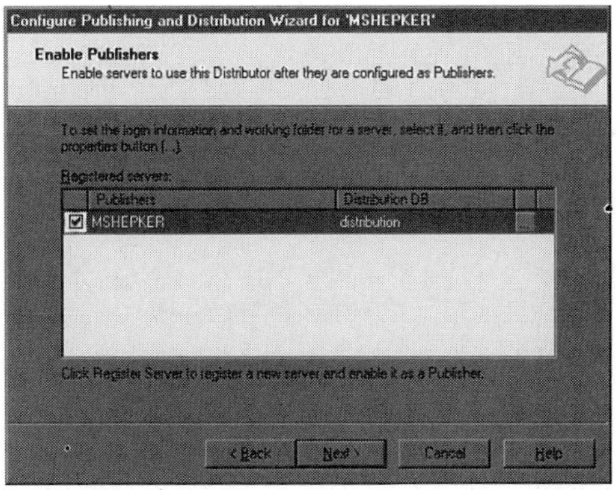

FIGURE 20.10

The Enable Publishers dialog.

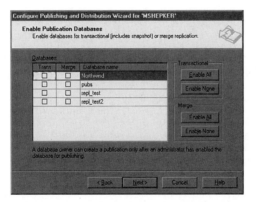

7. From the Enable Publication Databases screen, you can select any user database shown in the window for either transactional or merge replication (see Figure 20.11). If you are setting up this server to act as a distribution server only, do not select any of these databases.

FIGURE 20.11

The Enable Publication Databases dialog.

8. From the next screen, the Enable Subscribers dialog, you can select which servers are allowed to connect to this server. If you click the button with the ellipsis (...) after the subscriber's name, you can set up specific options about that subscriber. On the General tab, you can specify the account that will be used to connect to the subscriber. From the Schedules tab, you can select the times both the distribution and merge agent will run. By default, these are both set to run continuously.

9. The next screen provides you with a summary of what steps the server is going to perform to set up the distributor and publisher (see Figure 20.12).

20

REPLICATION

FIGURE 20.12

The summary screen outlines all the steps that SQL Server is going to take in setting up replication.

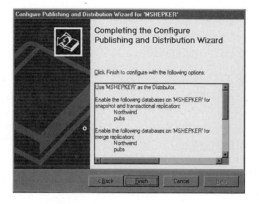

Creating a Publication

Now that the distribution database has been created and publishing has been enabled on the server, the next step you need to take is to create and configure a publication for subscribers to connect to. You can use the Create and Manage Publications Wizard to do this. You must be a member of the sysadmin server role to use this wizard. The following steps will walk you through setting up a new publication:

1. Connect to the server that you are setting up as a distributor within SQL Enterprise Manager. From the Tools menu, choose Replication and then select Create and Manage Publications. This will open the Create and Manage Publications Wizard.

2. At the Create and Manage Publications screen, you are prompted to select the database on which you are going to set up a publication (see Figure 20.13). These were the databases you selected while you were setting up replication. Choose the database and click the Create Publication button.

FIGURE 20.13

The Create and Manage Publications dialog.

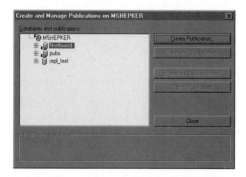

3. The next screen is an introduction screen that outlines what steps you will take while setting up the publication. Click Next.

4. The Choose Publications dialog enables you to choose which type of replication you will be using for this publication. The types presented to you are based on what you selected in the Configure Publishing and Subscribers Wizard.

5. If you choose either snapshot or transactional replication, the next screen allows you to configure whether you are going to allow immediate updating subscribers. Otherwise, you will skip to the next step.

6. The Specify Server Types screen allows you to choose what type of subscription server will be connecting to this server. If servers other than SQL Server will be connecting to this server, make sure you select that option.

7. From the Specify Articles screen, you are prompted to create articles in your publication (see Figure 20.14). You must include at least one article in your publication. After you select an article, a button with an ellipsis (...) appears after the article name. If you push this button, you are able to select options for your article. For snapshot and transactional replication, you can determine how the snapshot portion of the replication will occur. If you have selected merge replication, you will be able to select the conflict resolver that you are going to use. You can either select the default SQL Server resolver or create your own stored procedure or COM objects. For more information on creating a custom conflict resolver, search for "using a custom resolver" in SQL Server Books Online.

FIGURE 20.14

The Specify Articles screen allows you to choose which tables you are going to publish.

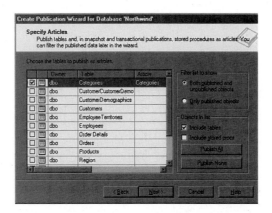

8. The next screen allows you to configure the name of your publication and provide a description of it.

9. On the next screen, you are asked whether you want to define data filters, enable anonymous subscriptions, or customize other properties. If you select that you do not want to, the next screen will allow you to finish the publication.

20

REPLICATION

10. If you select that you do want to further customize your publication, on the next screen you are asked whether you want to filter data. If you select no, you will skip the next two steps.

11. If you select that you want to filter the data, the next screen, Filter Table Columns, presents a list of all the articles in your publication and the columns contained in them (see Figure 20.15). You can select columns that you want to publish instead of the entire table.

FIGURE 20.15

The Filter Table Columns dialog enables you to choose individual columns to publish.

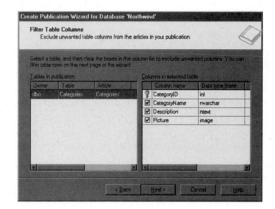

12. From the next screen, you are prompted to filter individual rows for each article. If you push the button with the ellipsis (...), you are asked for the criteria for the row filters. For example, if you want to publish data out of a table that comes only from a single store, you would place that criteria in the box.

13. On the next screen, you are asked whether you want to allow anonymous subscribers. If you select that you do want to create anonymous subscribers, SQL Server will allow any server to connect to and receive data from your publication. SQL Server also does not track all the performance data that it normally does when you are not using anonymous subscribers.

14. The Set Snapshot Agent Schedule screen allows you to choose the frequency with which snapshots occur. Remember that creating the snapshots can be an intensive process and should be configured to happen during off hours.

15. The last screen is a summary screen that outlines what steps and options you have selected. Once you select the Finish button, SQL Server will create the publication for you.

Creating Subscriptions

Now that you have installed and configured replication and set up the publications, the next step is to create subscriptions. Remember that there are two different types of subscriptions that you can create: push and pull. Push subscriptions are easier to create because all of the subscription process is performed and administered from one machine. Pull subscriptions allow remote sites to subscribe to any publication that they want, but you must be confident that the administrators at the other sites have properly configured the subscriptions at their sites. The following steps will walk you through creating a push subscription. The next section will assist you in creating a pull subscription.

1. Connect to the publishing server within SQL Enterprise Manager. From the Tools menu, choose Replication and then select Create and Manage Publications. This will open the Create and Manage Publications Wizard.

2. The Create and Manage Publication Wizard will open and allow you to select the publication that you will push out to the other sites. Select the publication and click the Push New Subscription button. This will open the Push Subscription Wizard.

3. After the introductory screen, you are prompted to choose which servers you will publish to.

4. From the Choose Destination Database screen, you are prompted to choose which database you will publish to (see Figure 20.16). If you click the Browse Database button, you can see a list of all the databases on the destination server. If you want to create a new database on the destination server, click the Create New button.

FIGURE 20.16

The Choose Destination Database screen.

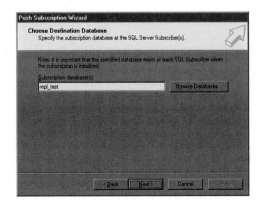

5. The next screen allows you to configure how the distribution agent will run. If you want to provide the lowest latency, select the Run Continuously option. Otherwise, configure the distribution agent to run at specific times during the day. By default, the distribution agent runs once an hour every day.

6. After you have configured when the distribution agent will run, you are prompted to configure the initialization of the database schema. This task is performed by the snapshot agent. The wizard will check the contents of the destination database and might force you to initialize if the table schema is not already there.

7. The next part of the process, the Start Required Services dialog, checks whether the required services are running on the destination server (see Figure 20.17). These include the MSSQLServer service and the SQLServerAgent service. If these are not running, you need to start them before going any further.

FIGURE 20.17

The Start Required Services dialog displays the required services and whether they are running.

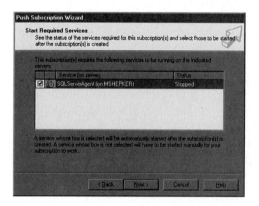

8. The last screen is a summary screen that outlines the options you selected and the steps SQL Server will perform to create the subscription. Once you click the Finish button, SQL Server will create the subscription.

The other option is to create pull subscriptions from the subscribing servers:

1. Connect to the publishing server within SQL Enterprise Manager. From the Tools menu, choose Replication and then select Pull Subscriptions to *server name*. This will open a window called Pull Subscription to *server name*. Click the Pull New Subscription button.

2. The Pull Subscription Wizard will open. An introductory screen details the actions you need to take to create a pull subscription.

3. The next screen of the Pull Subscription Wizard allows you to select a publication from any server that you currently have registered on the server (see Figure 20.18).

If you need to connect to another server, select the Register Server button. Once you select the server name, you get a list of all the publications on that server. Select the publication that you want to pull, and click the Next button.

FIGURE 20.18

You must select the publication that you want to pull from the server.

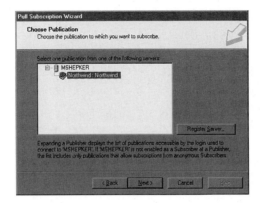

4. In the next screen, you are prompted to enter the login that the synchronization agent will use to connect to the publisher and the distributor. Enter the correct information and select the next button.

5. From the next screen, you are prompted to choose which database you will publish to. If you click the Browse Database button, you can see a list of all the databases on the destination server. If you want to create a new database on the destination server, click the Create New button.

6. From the next screen, you are prompted to configure the initialization of the database schema. This task is performed by the snapshot agent. The wizard will check the contents of the destination database and might force you to initialize if the table schema is not already there.

7. The Set Distribution Agent Schedule screen enables you to configure how the distribution agent will run (see Figure 20.19). If you want to provide the lowest latency, select the Continuously option. Otherwise, you can configure the distribution agent to run at specific times during the day. A new option using pull subscription enables you to synchronize the subscription on demand. By default, the distribution agent runs once an hour every day.

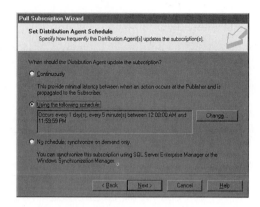

FIGURE 20.19

The Set Distribution Agent Schedule dialog.

8. The next part of the process checks whether the required services are running on the destination server. These include the MSSQLServer service and the SQLServerAgent service. If they are not running, you need to start them before going any further.

9. The last screen is a summary screen that outlines the options you selected and the steps SQL Server will perform to create the subscription. Once you click the Finish button, SQL Server will create the subscription.

Now that replication is set up, the only thing left to do is wait. If you have properly configured replication, it will only be a matter of time before you begin to see replication actions beginning to occur.

Monitoring Replication

Once replication is up and running, it is important for you to monitor the replication and see how things are running. There are several ways to do this, including SQL statements, SQL Enterprise Monitor, and Windows NT Performance Monitor.

SQL Statements

The easiest way to monitor replication is to look at the actual data that is being replicated. To do this, simply run a select statement against the table where data is being replicated. Is the most current data available in the database? If you make a change to the data in the published table, do the changes show up in the replicated tables? If not, you might need to investigate how replication was configured on the server.

SQL Enterprise Manager

SQL Enterprise Manager provides a great deal of information about the status of replication. You select the Replication Monitor within SQL Enterprise Manager. In the Replication Monitor, you can use folders to find information about replication. These folders track information about publishers, agents, and any alerts that are triggered by replications:

- Publishers—This folder contains information about publishers on the machine. By selecting any publisher on the machine, you can view information about any computers that have subscribed to the publication. This will tell you the current status and the last action taken by the subscriber.

- Agents—The agents folder contains information about the different agents on the machine. By choosing any agent's folder, you can see the current status of that agent. If you select an agent and double-click it, it will display the history of that agent.

- Replication Alerts—The replication alerts folder allows you to configure alerts to fire in response to events that occur during replication. These can activate when errors occur or in response to success messages.

The Performance Monitor

If you are running SQL Server on a Windows NT computer, you can use Windows NT Performance Monitor to monitor the health of your replication scenario. Installing SQL Server adds several new objects and counters to Performance Monitor:

- SQLServer:Replication Agents—This object contains counters used to monitor the status of all replication agents, including the total number running.

- SQLServer:Replication Dist.—This object contains counters used to monitor the status of the distribution agents, including the latency and the number of transactions transferred per second.

- SQLServer:Replication Logreader—This object contains counters used to monitor the status of the log reader agent, including the latency and the number of transactions transferred per second.

- SQLServer:Replication Merge—This object contains counters used to monitor the status of the merge agents, including the number of transactions and the number of conflicts per second.

- SQLServer:Replication Snapshot—This object contains counters used to monitor the status of the snapshot agents, including the number of transactions per second.

20

REPLICATION

Replication in Heterogeneous Environments

SQL Server 7.0 allows for transactional and snapshot replication of data into and out of environments other than SQL Server. The easiest way to set up this replication is to use ODBC and create a push subscription to the subscriber. SQL Server can publish to the following database types:

- Microsoft Access
- Oracle
- Sybase
- IBM DB2/AS400
- IBM DB2/MVS

SQL Server can replicate data to any other type of database, providing that the ODBC driver supports the following:

- The driver must be ODBC Level-1 compliant.
- The driver must be 32-bit, thread-safe, and designed for the processor architecture on which the distribution process runs.
- The driver must support transactions.
- The driver and underlying database must support Data Definition Language (DDL).
- The underlying database cannot be read-only.

Replicating to Internet Subscribers

Another advance in SQL Server 7.0 is the ability to replicate data to Internet subscribers. The first requirement for this feature is that your publication must allow pull and anonymous subscriptions. You must take three steps to configure an Internet subscription:

1. Configure the publisher or distributor to listen on TCP/IP.
2. Configure a publication to use FTP.
3. Create a subscription to use FTP.

Configuring a Publisher or Distributor to Listen on TCP/IP

Before you can set up replication to Internet subscribers, you must configure SQL Server to communicate on TCP/IP or the multiprotocol network library. You can configure this area using the SQL Server Network Utility. You must also have Internet Information

Server set up on the distribution server because Internet replication relies on the FTP service to transfer the snapshots from the distribution server to the subscribers. You have to set up the FTP home directory to the snapshot folder and configure the FTP home directory as an FTP site.

Configuring a Publication to Use FTP

After you have configured the server to use FTP, the next step is to set up the publication to allow for Internet replication. You can do this using SQL Enterprise Manager. Once it is configured, the distribution or merge agents will use FTP to download the snapshot files to the subscriber server. Once the snapshot files are copied to the subscriber, the agent applies the files to the tables at the subscriber. The following steps walk you through setting up an existing database to use the Internet:

1. Connect to the publishing server in SQL Enterprise Manager. From the Tools menu, choose Create and Modify Publications. This will open the Create and Manage Publication dialog.

2. From the dialog box, choose the publication that you want to edit and click the Properties & Subscriptions button. This will open the publication's properties box.

3. From the Subscription Options tab, put a check in the Allow Subscriptions to Be Downloaded Using FTP.

Configuring a Subscription to Use FTP

Once the publication has been configured to use FTP, you must create a pull or anonymous subscription to the database. These subscriptions are created the same way that you would create any other subscription. The difference is that you need to configure the FTP options. The following steps walk you through setting up Internet-enabled subscriptions:

1. Connect to the publishing server in SQL Enterprise Manager. From the Tools menu, choose Pull Subscriptions. This will open the Pull Subscriptions dialog.

2. From the dialog box, choose the publication that you want to edit and click the Properties button. This will open the publication's properties box.

3. From the Pull Subscriptions Properties screen, choose the Snapshot Delivery tab. Put a check in the Use the File Transfer Protocol When Downloading Snapshot Files from the Distributor. Enter the options in the FTP parameters section.

Summary

Replication is a powerful feature of SQL Server that can be used in many business situations. Companies can use it for anything from roll-up reporting to relieving the main server from ad hoc queries and reporting. Replication is the best solution for moving data from server to server in a quick and efficient manner.

Transact-SQL

Using Transact-SQL in SQL Server 7.0

by Tibor Karaszi

IN THIS CHAPTER

The focus for this chapter is the elements of the Transact-SQL (T-SQL) language. I discuss most of the language constructs in T-SQL. The chapter is not intended as a learning tool for the general SQL language. There are several such books on the market, from beginning to advanced level; some describe the standard ANSI SQL syntax and some specialize in T-SQL. Look for the *Sams Teach Yourself* line of books on SQL and Transact-SQL, *SQL Unleashed*, and *Microsoft SQL Server Programming Unleashed* from Sams Publishing for more specific information on each of these.

New in SQL Server 7.0

Transact-SQL is an evolving language. As with any new release of SQL Server, version 7.0 includes enhancements to the Transact-SQL dialect. What follows is an outline of some of the major enhancements.

Unicode Support

The character set chosen at installation time cannot be changed later without transferring data and rebuilding the installation. Because storage usage for each character is one byte, the maximum number of characters that can be represented is 256. Some of these characters are special characters, so the actual number of available characters is lower. Unicode uses a two-byte storage area for each character, which means that 65,536 characters can be represented. Unicode is supported through three new datatypes: `nchar`, `nvarchar`, and `ntext`. Note, however, that twice as much storage area is needed for Unicode data than for the old `char`, `varchar`, and `text` data. Refer to Chapter 8, "Logical Database Architecture," for more information on datatypes.

ALTER TABLE, ALTER PROCEDURE, ALTER TRIGGER, and ALTER VIEW

It is now possible to change the definition of an object without having to drop and re-create the object. When re-creating an object, you must re-grant or re-revoke permissions.

`ALTER TABLE` was restricted in earlier versions of SQL Server. Except for adding and dropping constraints, adding a column was all that you could do. This new column had to allow `NULL`.

Developers wrote scripts to create an intermediate table with the desired table structure, copying over data and renaming the tables. Some tools, such as Visual Database Tools in Visual InterDev, could perform these operations behind the scenes.

With version 7.0, you can drop columns from a table, alter data, and add a column with `NOT NULL` if a default value or identity attribute is defined for that column.

You can also modify a view, trigger, and stored procedure definition with the ALTER VIEW, ALTER PROCEDURE, and ALTER TRIGGER statements.

T-SQL and ANSI/ISO SQL-92

T-SQL has evolved significantly over the years, and so have the ANSI standards for the SQL language. ANSI SQL-92 is a significantly larger standard than its predecessors. There are three levels defined in ANSI SQL-92: entry, intermediate, and full.

SQL Server supports the entry level of ANSI SQL-92. Naturally, you will find a number of special statements and features in SQL Server that are not defined by the ANSI standard. Examples of such features are

- Operating-system–dependent statements, such as defining physical database storage.
- Legacy syntax and commands—Even if the current version supports the ANSI way of expressing a command, backward compatibility is a major issue.
- Extensions to the ANSI standards—All vendors strive at implementing competitive features. Microsoft is no exception.

Version 7.0 is a superset of the entry level of the ANSI SQL-92 standard. Although this level was achieved in version 6.5, Microsoft continues to add support for the ANSI standard. This includes adding new language constructs as well as encouraging developers to express statements as the ANSI standard defines.

Cursor Enhancements

We now have the same expressive power when working with SQL cursors as we have with API cursors. Microsoft has introduced an alternative syntax to declaring a cursor in T-SQL. You can explicitly define whether the cursor should be STATIC, INSENSITIVE, or DYNAMIC.

If we do not declare the cursor as read-only, we can also define the level of concurrency with our cursor definition. We can define a cursor for READ_ONLY, SCROLL_LOCKS, or OPTIMISTIC concurrency.

In version 6.x, all cursors had global scope; a cursor ran out of scope when the connection was terminated. We now have the ability to define local cursors, whose scope is within the creating batch.

We can also return a cursor variable from a stored procedure and process the cursor from the calling batch or stored procedure. This can improve re-use because we can define a generic cursor and call it from several stored procedures or batches.

Creating Database Objects

A database consists of a number of elements, or objects. Information about a particular object appears in a system table. Table 21.1 lists the various object types and where information about the objects is stored.

TABLE 21.1   OBJECTS AND SYSTEM TABLES IN SQL SERVER

Object Type	System Table
Table, view, stored procedure, trigger, default, rule	sysobjects
Constraints	sysconstraints, sysreferences
Index	sysindexes
Datatypes	systypes

To be able to create a database objects, the user must have CREATE permissions. The creator of an object becomes the object owner (sometimes referred to as DBOO, database object owner). The database owner (DBO) can create an object with another username as owner. The object will be created in the current database unless another database is specified. In the following example, the customers table will be owned by the creator and created in the current database:

```
CREATE TABLE customers
```

In the next example, the customers table will be created in the pubs database if the login ID that executes the statement has a username in pubs:

```
CREATE TABLE pubs..customer
```

The following command, which can be executed by DBO, creates a table that will be owned by the username steve. The table will be created in the current database:

```
CREATE TABLE steve.customer
```

Tables

The table is the only type of information carrier in a relational database. The table has a structure containing a set of rows and a set of columns…well, perhaps not a proper set. Columns can be addressed not only by name but also by position when performing an INSERT. Rows can contain duplicates. There has been a debate for a rather lengthy time regarding these subjects, and we will not dive further into that debate here.

Using Transact-SQL in SQL Server 7.0
CHAPTER 21

453

21

USING TRANSACT-
SQL IN SQL
SERVER 7.0

> **NOTE**
>
> The relational model uses different terminology for tables, columns, and rows. A table is called a *relation*; a column is an *attribute* and a row is a *tuple*. Note, however, that the current ANSI SQL standard does not use this terminology, nor is it widely used.

Each column (or rather, the data to be stored in the column) is based on a datatype, which limits the possible values that can be stored in the column and also defines behavior when adding, subtracting, and so on. The column can have further restrictions as well.

Restrictions can be defined at the table level, for instance, such that a combination of two columns must be unique within the table.

You can create a table using the CREATE TABLE statement. You can also use Enterprise Manager, which has a more powerful interface in version 7.0. Enterprise Manager is covered in Chapter 9, "The SQL Server Enterprise Manager." Note that Enterprise Manager acts as a graphical front end which, in turn, generates the CREATE TABLE command.

This is the basic syntax for the CREATE TABLE command:

```
CREATE TABLE table_name
(column_name datatype {identity NOT NULL ¦ NULL}
[, ...])
```

The following example creates a customers table with three columns: the customer's ID, the customer's name, and a comment.

```
CREATE TABLE customers
(customer_id INT IDENTITY NOT NULL,
customer_name VARCHAR(100) NOT NULL,
customer_comments VARCHAR(5000) NULL)
```

SQL Server Object Names

All objects in SQL Server are named. Examples of objects are tables, views, and stored procedures. Names for objects must be unique within the database, but remember that the object owner is a part of the name. The table steve.customer is not the same as john.customer.

> **TIP**
>
> It is recommended that DBO own all objects in most cases. This simplifies administration and makes it easier for programmers and end users to refer to an object. Handling permissions on stored procedures and views is also easier if the same user owns all the objects.

Whether object names are case sensitive depends on the case sensitivity chosen at SQL Server installation time. Case sensitivity applies to object names as well as character data stored in tables.

> **NOTE**
>
> To determine case sensitivity for a SQL Server installation, execute the stored procedure sp_helpsort.

> **TIP**
>
> Choose case sensitivity carefully when you install SQL Server for product development. Ideally, an application should not depend on the case sensitivity of SQL Server. If an application is to be sold commercially, you might find the customers a bit annoyed if they find out that they cannot use their existing SQL Server because your application demands another case-sensitivity option.
>
> Case sensitive is the recommended collation sequence for development SQL Servers. Watch out for name clashes, however. You can name one table Customer_Details and another customer_details. These are different names in a case-sensitive SQL Server, but a name clash would also occur in a case-insensitive SQL Server. This applies to variable names as well.
>
> Case insensitive is a less-restrictive option. For an object named Customer_Details, a SELECT statement that refers to it as customer_details works in a case-insensitive SQL Server. However, a case-sensitive SQL Server would return an error message saying that the object does not exist.

Object names (or *identifiers*) can be up to 128 characters in length, including letters, symbols (_, @, or #), and numbers. The first character must be an alphabetic character (a–z or A–Z). Variables and temporary tables have special naming schemes. Note that an object name cannot include spaces. By using quoted identifiers, you can use characters that would otherwise be illegal in object names. If possible, do not use quoted identifiers. You might find some great utility that does not support quoted identifiers. An example is SQLMAINT.EXE in SQL Server 6.5.

Column Properties

A column can have several properties. Some properties restrict what can be stored in the column, whereas others provide functionality (such as a counter). The NULL or NOT NULL keywords define whether a column can contain the null symbol:

```
NULL ¦ NOT NULL
```

You cannot define NULL for a column that is to be used as the primary key or the identity column. It is generally recommended to keep the columns allowing NULL to a minimum because it is difficult to deal with missing information. IDENTITY defines a counter:

```
IDENTITY(seed, increment)
```

A new value is generated for each row inserted into the table.

The IDENTITY property can only be defined for the integer type of columns. This includes INT, SMALLINT, TINYINT, DECIMAL, and NUMERIC, provided that the last two have a scale of 0.

ROWGUIDCOL defines the column as a row global unique identifier. It can only be defined for columns of the datatype UNIQUEIDENTIFIER. The purpose of this property is to generate unique values across tables and across SQL Servers. To generate the unique value, you use the function NEWID(), which returns a value that is useful only for the UNIQUEIDENTIFIER datatype.

Available column constraints are primary key, unique, foreign key, check, and default. A constraint does exactly what the name implies: constrain the possible values that can be used within the column. The constraint feature is used to achieve as consistent data as possible within the database. For more information on constraints, refer to Chapter 8.

Example

We want to create an orders table with the following columns:

- Order number—A globally unique ID. This column is defined as a primary key. For each value inserted, a new value is issued through a default constraint.

- A customer number that is a foreign key to the customer table.

- Order date, which can be automatically inserted through a default constraint. Note that the default constraint removes the time part of the value returned from GETDATE().

LISTING 21.1 THE CREATE TABLE STATEMENT FOR THE ORDERS TABLE

```
CREATE TABLE orders
(order_id UNIQUEIDENTIFIER DEFAULT NEWID() PRIMARY KEY
➥ NOT NULL,
customer_id INT REFERENCES customers(customer_id)
➥NOT NULL,
order_date DATETIME DEFAULT CONVERT(CHAR(8), GETDATE(), 112))
➥NOT NULL
```

Identity Columns

The identity functionality is not designed to produce continuous values in all situations. If a row is deleted, that value will not be reused. If an insert is rolled back, the value will not be reused.

An explicit value cannot be inserted for the identity column unless you SET IDENTITY_INSERT *table_name* ON. Only the table owner can explicitly insert the identity value.

To reset the value to the current highest (or lowest) value, run DBCC CHECKIDENT(*table_name*).

A primary key (or unique key) constraint should always be defined for a column if the column is a key. The identity feature is not designed for uniqueness per se. Duplicates can occur if you use IDENTITY_INSERT or if SQL Server loses track of its internal counter for the identity value and starts over again at the seed value. This behavior happened quite often in versions 6.0 and 6.5, especially if SQL Server was unexpectedly shut down.

Renaming Objects

You can rename an object using the sp_rename system stored procedure. The syntax for renaming an object is

```
sp_rename {'object_name'} [, 'new_name'] [, 'object_type']
```

object_type can be COLUMN, DATABASE, INDEX, OBJECT, or USERDATATYPE.

Using Transact-SQL in SQL Server 7.0

CHAPTER 21

457

21

USING TRANSACT-
SQL IN SQL
SERVER 7.0

> **CAUTION**
>
> Make sure that you revise the objects that depend on the renamed object (views, stored procedures, and so on). SQL Server will give you a warning that changing an object name may break scripts and stored procedures, which is absolutely true.
>
> I strongly encourage you to check which objects depend on the renamed object, edit the dependant's source code, and re-create them. The system stored procedure sp_depends will give you a report about which objects depend on another object.

Adding Columns to a Table

Sometimes, you must add a column to a table, generally because you find out that there are more attributes that you want to store for the entity described by the table. You can add a column with the ALTER TABLE command.

A column added to a table with earlier versions of SQL Server had to allow NULL. This was a bit annoying because we generally try to avoid NULL if possible.

What do we insert in the current rows for the new column? With version 7.0, you can define a default value or define the added column with the identity attribute.

Let's say that we want to add a column to the customer table. As a customer service measure, you give an estimated shipping date for each order. Estimated shipping dates for existing orders will be set to 1900-01-01 to clearly mark the rows that were inserted before this column was added:

```
ALTER TABLE orders ADD estimated_shipping_date DATETIME
➥ NOT NULL DEFAULT '19000101'
```

The default value could later be removed or changed to something more meaningful.

Temporary Tables

A temporary table exists for the duration of the connection that created it. When you use a hash sign (#) as the first letter in the table name, SQL Server makes the table a temporary table. A temporary table can be explicitly created with the CREATE TABLE statement or implicitly with SELECT INTO.

The temporary table is available only for the connection that created the table. All temporary tables are created in the tempdb database, but do not worry about name clashes.

SQL Server will append a unique identifier on the table name so that even if another connection creates a temporary table with the same name, they will be named differently in
the tempdb database.

Why create temporary tables? It might be easier to solve a complex query by breaking it
into steps. You might want to store some values so that you can do further calculations
on them.

> **NOTE**
>
> The default size of the tempdb database is too small for almost all production
> installations. It is impossible to recommend a "right" size for tempdb offhand,
> but a good rule of thumb is to make it either as big as your biggest table in the
> system or half the size of your biggest database.
>
> The tempdb database is also used to store the internal worktables that SQL
> Server creates for some operations, such as sorting and group by.
>
> Other operations that might require storage area in tempdb are batch process-
> ing, data transfer, backup, and some of the DBCC commands.

Global and Permanent Temporary Tables

You create a global temporary table by preceding its name with two hash signs. A global
temporary table can be useful when an application uses several connections and you
want the temporary table to be available for all connections. If a stored procedure creates
a local temporary table, it is removed when the procedure terminates. The procedure is
considered a connection in this aspect. However, a global temporary table is available
after the procedure executes.

You can also create a permanent temporary table. When you explicitly create the table in
the tempdb database, it remains available after the connection that created it terminates.
It disappears when SQL Server restarts because tempdb is re-created at startup.

> **TIP**
>
> It is always a good idea to drop the temporary table when it is not needed any-
> more. This will free up space in tempdb, which might become critical if your
> connections live for a long time.

SELECT, INSERT, UPDATE, and DELETE

Four basic SQL statements allow us to retrieve and modify data in our tables. SELECT retrieves data from one or more tables, INSERT inserts rows into one table, UPDATE modifies rows in one table, and DELETE remove rows from one table.

> **NOTE**
>
> If you are already familiar with these statements, you might want to skim this section.

You could easily fill a book with examples and explanations of these statements. This section covers the major parts of syntax and shows some simple examples.

The SELECT Statement

The SELECT statement has the following basic syntax:

```
SELECT column1[, column2, ...]
 FROM table1[, table2, ...]
 [WHERE search_conditions]
 [GROUP BY expression]
 [HAVING search_condition]
 [ORDER BY order_expression [ASC ¦ DESC]]
```

We want to return all the Utah authors' first and last names from the authors table. We also want to rename the column heading in our result.

```
SELECT au_lname AS 'First', au_fname AS 'Last'
 FROM authors
 WHERE STATE = 'UT'
```

By default, SQL Server returns all the rows that meet our search conditions. If you specify SELECT DISTINCT, the duplicates are removed.

The columns that we base our search condition on do not have to be returned in the resultset. You can filter rows in several ways with the WHERE clause. The following expressions are available for the WHERE clause:

Operators: =, <> (not equals), <, >, >=, and >=.

BETWEEN *expression1* AND *expression2*. Between is inclusive.

IN(*element1*, *element2*, ...). Returns all rows whose values are equal to the elements specified in the list.

LIKE *string_expression*. Used for pattern matching. Table 21.2 lists the available wildcard characters.

TABLE 21.2 WILDCARDS AND LIKE

Wildcard	Meaning
%	Any number of characters
_	Any single character
[]	Any character listed in the bracket

Logical OR and AND are used to connect multiple search arguments.

The ORDER BY clause sorts the resultset by the specified column or columns. Ascending sorting is the default, but you can use ORDER BY column_name DESC to specify descending ordering. You should always specify ORDER BY if you expect a certain order for your data. Rows in a table compose a set, and a set is not ordered.

Listing 21.2 shows an example that uses some of the clauses.

LISTING 21.2 USING WHERE AND ORDER BY

```
SELECT au_lname, au_fname, state
 FROM authors
 WHERE state IN('CA', 'KS')
   AND au_lname LIKE 'S%'
ORDER BY au_lname
```

You can use the TOP keyword to restrict the number of rows returned. In Listing 21.3, we want to retrieve the title and price for the five most expensive books.

LISTING 21.3 USING TOP TO RESTRICT THE NUMBER OF ROWS RETURNED

```
SELECT TOP 5 price, title
FROM titles
ORDER BY price DESC
price                   title
--------------------    ------------------------------------
22.9500                 But Is It User Friendly?
21.5900                 Computer Phobic AND Non-Phobic Indi...
20.9500                 Onions, Leeks, and Garlic: Cooking ...
20.0000                 Secrets of Silicon Valley
19.9900                 The Busy Executive's Database Guide
```

Using Transact-SQL in SQL Server 7.0

CHAPTER 21

461

21

USING TRANSACT-
SQL IN SQL
SERVER 7.0

You can add WITH TIES, which might produce more than the requested number of rows. Several books have the price $19.99. In Listing 21.4, we add WITH TIES so that all those books are returned.

LISTING 21.4 USING TOP WITH TIES

```
SELECT TOP 5 WITH TIES price, title
FROM titles
ORDER BY price DESC
price                  title
--------------------   -------------------------------------
22.9500                But Is It User Friendly?
21.5900                Computer Phobic AND Non-Phobic Indi...
20.9500                Onions, Leeks, and Garlic: Cooking ...
20.0000                Secrets of Silicon Valley
19.9900                The Busy Executive's Database Guide
19.9900                Straight Talk About Computers
19.9900                Silicon Valley Gastronomic Treats
19.9900                Prolonged Data Deprivation: Four Ca...
```

If you don't use ORDER BY with TOP, the number of rows returned is chosen arbitrarily, based on the execution plan chosen by the optimizer. You can also specify TOP *n* PER-CENT to restrict the number of rows based on a percentage value instead of an absolute value.

> **NOTE**
>
> The TOP keyword is new to version 7.0. To get the same functionality, SET ROW-COUNT *n* was often used in previous versions. TOP is used by the optimizer, so it will often result in better performance than ROWCOUNT.

We can store the resultset in a table instead of retrieving it by using SELECT column(s) INTO *table_name*. The table specified will be created with the same structure as the resultset. A temporary table is created in tempdb if you precede the table name with one or two hash signs. If you want to create a permanent table with SELECT...INTO, you must set the database option select into/bulkcopy to TRUE.

When you use the UNION keyword, a logical union between two or more resultsets is returned. This query returns the city and state of each author and publisher as a single resultset:

```
SELECT city, state FROM authors
UNION ALL
SELECT city, state FROM publishers
```

By default, SQL Server removes all the duplicates. You can add the keyword ALL if you do not want the duplicates to be removed.

GROUP BY and HAVING

GROUP BY and HAVING are used with aggregate functions (which are described in the section "SQL Server Functions," later in this chapter). GROUP BY allows us to calculate aggregates for groups within our tables. The following example calculates the average price for each book category in the titles table:

```
SELECT type, AVG(price)
FROM titles
GROUP BY type

business       13.7300
mod_cook       11.4900
popular_comp   21.4750
psychology     13.5040
trad_cook      15.9633
UNDECIDED      NULL
```

If a WHERE clause is used, it is applied before the grouping takes place. The following query calculates the average price per book category for books published by the publisher with the ID 1389:

```
SELECT type, AVG(price)
FROM titles
WHERE pub_id = 1389
GROUP BY type

business       17.3100
popular_comp   21.4750
```

HAVING lets us restrict the number of aggregations returned. The clause is applied after the grouping is applied. We want to return the average price for book categories, but only the categories with an average that is higher than $14:

```
SELECT type, AVG(price)
FROM titles
GROUP BY type
HAVING AVG(price) > $14

popular_comp   21.4750
trad_cook      15.9633
```

CUBE, ROLLUP, and the GROUPING Function

CUBE, ROLLUP, and GROUPING are used in conjunction with GROUP BY.

Using Transact-SQL in SQL Server 7.0

CHAPTER 21

463

21

USING TRANSACT-
SQL IN SQL
SERVER 7.0

When you use CUBE, you will get extra rows in the resultset. The extra rows are super aggregates. If we add CUBE to the query that returns the average price for book categories, we get an extra row with the average price of all books, as shown in Listing 21.5.

LISTING 21.5   USING CUBE TO CALCULATE SUPER AGGREGATES

```
SELECT type, AVG(price) AS average
FROM titles
GROUP BY type
WITH CUBE

type          average
------------- --------------------
business      13.7300
mod_cook      11.4900
popular_comp  21.4750
psychology    13.5040
trad_cook     15.9633
UNDECIDED     NULL
NULL          14.7662
```

The book type is returned as NULL for the extra row. In Listing 21.6, we use the GROUPING function to present the extra row in a more explicit manner.

LISTING 21.6   USING THE GROUPING FUNCTION

```
SELECT type, AVG(price) AS average, GROUPING(type) AS super
FROM titles
GROUP BY type
WITH CUBE

type          average              super
------------- -------------------- -----
business      13.7300              0
mod_cook      11.4900              0
popular_comp  21.4750              0
psychology    13.5040              0
trad_cook     15.9633              0
UNDECIDED     NULL                 0
NULL          14.7662              1
```

The value 1 is returned for each super aggregate presented for the grouped column specified.

CUBE is more useful if we group over several columns. In Listing 21.7, we want to return the average price grouped by book type and publisher.

LISTING 21.7   GROUPING OVER SEVERAL COLUMNS

```
SELECT type, pub_id, AVG(price) AS average
FROM titles
GROUP BY type, pub_id

type          pub_id average
-----------   ------ --------------------
business      0736   2.9900
psychology    0736   11.4825
mod_cook      0877   11.4900
psychology    0877   21.5900
trad_cook     0877   15.9633
UNDECIDED     0877   NULL
business      1389   17.3100
popular_comp  1389   21.4750
```

In Listing 21.8, we add WITH CUBE, which gives us the total average, the average for each
book type, and the average for each publisher.

LISTING 21.8   GROUPING OVER SEVERAL COLUMNS WITH CUBE

```
SELECT type, pub_id, AVG(price) AS average
FROM titles
GROUP BY type, pub_id
WITH CUBE

type          pub_id average
-----------   ------ --------------------
business      0736   2.9900
business      1389   17.3100
business      NULL   13.7300
mod_cook      0877   11.4900
mod_cook      NULL   11.4900
popular_comp  1389   21.4750
popular_comp  NULL   21.4750
psychology    0736   11.4825
psychology    0877   21.5900
psychology    NULL   13.5040
trad_cook     0877   15.9633
trad_cook     NULL   15.9633
UNDECIDED     0877   NULL
UNDECIDED     NULL   NULL
NULL          NULL   14.7662
NULL          0736   9.7840
NULL          0877   15.4100
NULL          1389   18.9760
```

Using Transact-SQL in SQL Server 7.0

CHAPTER 21

465

21

USING TRANSACT-
SQL IN SQL
SERVER 7.0

ROLLUP is similar to CUBE, but it produces a subset of the super aggregates. It is sensitive to the position of the column in the GROUP BY clause; it moves from right to left and produces super aggregates along the way. In Listing 21.9, super aggregates are calculated for publishers and for all titles, but not for book types.

LISTING 21.9 USING THE ROLLUP CLAUSE

```
SELECT type, pub_id, AVG(price) AS average
FROM titles
GROUP BY type, pub_id
WITH ROLLUP
type          pub_id average
------------- ------ --------------------
business      0736   2.9900
business      1389   17.3100
business      NULL   13.7300
mod_cook      0877   11.4900
mod_cook      NULL   11.4900
popular_comp  1389   21.4750
popular_comp  NULL   21.4750
psychology    0736   11.4825
psychology    0877   21.5900
psychology    NULL   13.5040
trad_cook     0877   15.9633
trad_cook     NULL   15.9633
UNDECIDED     0877   NULL
UNDECIDED     NULL   NULL
NULL          NULL   14.7662
```

Joining Tables

You can also correlate two tables, performing a join. Generally, we connect the tables using a common column, which is most often a column for which a foreign key and primary key relationship has been specified.

There are two ways that you can specify a join. First, you can specify the join condition in the WHERE clause. This is an older way of specifying a join, but it is still supported. Those of you who have been using SQL for a while are probably more familiar with this method.

You can also specify the join condition in the FROM clause. This method complies with the ANSI-92 standard.

> **NOTE**
>
> The ANSI-92 join syntax (or ANSI JOIN for short) was introduced in version 6.5 and is now the preferred way of expressing joins.
>
> One advantage with the ANSI JOIN syntax is that the actual join operation performed is easier to read because it is explicitly stated in the FROM clause. You can also assume that Microsoft is more eager to fix problems regarding ANSI joins than those of the older T-SQL join syntax.

The following example shows both ways of expressing a join. Both statements return the same resultset:

```
SELECT title, qty
 FROM titles t, sales s
 WHERE t.title_id = s.title_id

SELECT title, qty
 FROM titles t INNER JOIN sales s ON t.title_id = s.title_id
```

We also introduced a table alias in the example. We aliased the title table to the name t and sales to s. Aliasing is useful when you have to refer to a table in several places in the query; you don't have to type the whole table name each time.

The different types of joins are INNER, OUTER, and CROSS. An INNER join is based on equality between the column values. The OUTER join returns all the rows from a controlling table (specified with LEFT OUTER or RIGHT OUTER), even if there is no match from the other table. Columns returned from that other table will have the NULL symbol for the returned rows. A CROSS join returns all possible combinations of rows, also called a *cartesian product*.

With the ANSI syntax, you specify the join type explicitly in the FROM clause, but the join type in the older join syntax is specified in the WHERE clause.

Subqueries

You can use a subquery in place of an expression. Depending on the context, restrictions exist on the subquery. The query might be allowed to return only one column and even one row.

If the subquery returns only one row and one column, it can be used in place of any expression. This example returns all books published by Binnet & Hardley:

```
SELECT title FROM titles
 WHERE pub_id =
```

Using Transact-SQL in SQL Server 7.0

CHAPTER 21

467

21

USING TRANSACT-
SQL IN SQL
SERVER 7.0

```
(SELECT pub_id FROM publishers
  WHERE pub_name = "Binnet & Hardley")
```

An error message is returned if the subquery would have returned several rows.

A subquery must always appear in parentheses.

> **NOTE**
>
> You will often find that you can achieve the same result with a subquery or a
> join. A join is often more efficient that a subquery (with the exception of when
> you want to remove duplicates, where a subquery with EXISTS is more effi-
> cient).

You can use a subquery that returns one column and several rows with the IN predicate.
The following example returns all publishers of business books:

```
SELECT pub_name FROM publishers
 WHERE pub_id IN
 (SELECT pub_id FROM titles
  WHERE type = 'business')
```

You can use a subquery that returns several rows and several columns (in fact, all
columns) with the EXISTS keyword. The following example returns the same resultset as
the preceding example:

```
SELECT pub_name FROM publishers p
 WHERE EXISTS
   (SELECT * FROM titles t
    WHERE p.pub_id = t.pub_id
    AND type = 'business')
```

We return all columns from the subquery. We do not have a column relationship
between the queries; our relationship is between the tables. The subquery is a
correlated subquery. The inner query refers to the outer in the WHERE clause
(WHERE p.pub_id = t.pub_id). SQL Server executes the inner query for each row in
the outer query, testing for a match on pub_id.

Adding Rows with INSERT

You use the INSERT statement to add rows to a table. The following example adds one
row to the authors table:

```
INSERT authors (au_id, au_lname, au_fname, phone, contract)
VALUES('123-65-7635', 'Johnson', 'Lisa', '408 342 7845', 1)
```

The number of values in the VALUES list must match the number in the column list. You can omit the column list, but I strongly recommend that you keep it. That INSERT statement depends on the column ordering and would break if the table were re-created with another column ordering.

You can also omit columns from the table, but the column you want to delete must allow NULL, have a default value, be the timestamp datatype, or have the identity property defined for it.

To insert more than one row, you must use INSERT with a subquery. The following query inserts all authors from California into a table called authors_archive:

```
INSERT authors_archive
 (au_id, au_lname, au_fname, phone, city, state, zip)
SELECT au_id, au_lname, au_fname, phone, city, state, zip
FROM authors
 WHERE state = 'CA'
```

A useful feature is that you can execute any statement as the subquery as long as it returns a resultset that is compatible with the table. Listing 21.10 creates a table to hold information from DBCC SQLPERF(logspace) and inserts the resultset returned by that command into the table.

LISTING 21.10 USING INSERT WITH A SUBQUERY THAT IS NOT AN ORDINARY SELECT STATEMENT

```
CREATE TABLE log_space
(cap_date DATETIME DEFAULT GETDATE(),
 db sysname,
 log_size FLOAT,
 space_used FLOAT,
 status BIT)

INSERT log_space(db, log_size, space_used, status)
EXEC ('DBCC SQLPERF(logspace)')
```

Modifying Rows with UPDATE

The update statement is straightforward. You specify the table to be updated, the columns, the new values, and the rows to be updated. The following statement changes the royalty to 15% and price to $25 for title 1032:

```
UPDATE titles
 SET royalty = 15, price = $25
 WHERE title_id = 'BU1032'
```

If you omit the WHERE clause, all rows are updated.

Removing Rows with DELETE

To remove rows from a table, use the DELETE statement. To remove the title BU1032:

```
DELETE titles WHERE title_id = 'BU1032'
```

If you omit the WHERE clause, all rows are removed.

If you really want to remove all rows, it is much more efficient to use the TRUNCATE TABLE statement, which does not log each deleted row to the transaction log.

SQL Server Functions

With version 7.0, Microsoft has added more than 30 functions to an already large number of functions. Some of the functions are shortcuts to get information that could be retrieved in other ways. For instance, there is a function to get an object ID (OBJECT_ID()) if you know the object's name, but looking it up in the sysobjects table could also work.

Other functions such as some of the mathematical functions are more essential. (Okay, it could be argued that you can calculate the square root, for instance, in T-SQL, but it is not efficient.)

Most functions have the structure

```
FUNCTION_NAME(parameter1, parameter2, ...)
```

The parameters might be an expression (such as a column name), a constant, or a special code (such as a formatting code).

A function returns a value. The datatype for the value depends on what function you are using. Let's take a look at the available functions grouped by category.

String Functions

The string functions let you perform concatenation, parsing manipulation, and so on with strings.

> **TIP**
>
> Excessive use of string functions against a column might indicate that the column should be split into several columns. For example, if you find yourself frequently parsing out first name and last name from a name column, perhaps you should split the name into two columns.

Table 21.3 lists the available string functions. They can be used against any string expression.

TABLE 21.3 STRING FUNCTIONS

Function Name	Returns	New in 7.0
ASCII(char)	The ASCII code for the leftmost character in char.	
CHAR(int)	A character for int (an ASCII code).	
CHARINDEX(char_pattern, char, [int_start])	Starting location of char_pattern within char, optionally starting search at int_start.	
DIFFERENCE(char1, char2)	The difference between the two character expressions. Used for a phonetic match.	
LEFT(char, int)	int characters from left of char.	
LEN(char)	Number of characters in char, excluding trailing blanks.	Yes
LOWER(char)	char in lowercase.	
LTRIM(char)	char without leading spaces.	
NCHAR(int)	The character for a given Unicode value.	Yes
PATINDEX(char_pattern, char)	Starting position of char_pattern in char or 0 if the pattern is not found.	
REPLACE(char1, char2, char3)	Replaces all occurrences of char2 with char3 in char1.	Yes
QUOTENAME(char, [char_quote])	char is a valid quoted identifier. Adds the characters [and] (this default can be changed to ' or ", specified as char_quote) at beginning and end of char. Returns a Unicode string.	Yes
REPLICATE(char, int)	Repeats char int times.	
REVERSE(char)	Reverses char.	
RIGHT(char, int)	int characters from right of char.	
RTRIM(char)	char without trailing spaces.	
SOUNDEX(char)	A four-character string, used for comparison of a phonetic match.	
SPACE(int)	A string of int spaces.	

Function Name	Returns	New in 7.0
STR(*float*, [*length*, [*decimal*]])	*float* as a character string, with length of *length* and *decimal* numbers of decimals. Default *length* is 10 and default number of decimals is 0.	
STUFF(*char1*, *start*, *length*, *char2*)	Replaces *length* of characters from *char1* with *char2*, starting at *start*.	
SUBSTRING(*char*, *start*, *length*)	Returns *length* number of characters from *char*, from *start* position.	
UNICODE(*char*)	Returns the Unicode code for the leftmost character in *char*.	Yes
UPPER(*char*)	Returns *char* in uppercase.	

You can use the operator + to concatenate strings.

The following example uses SUBSTRING and string concatenation to present each author's first letter of the first name and then the last name:

```
SELECT SUBSTRING(au_fname,1,1) + '. ' + au_lname FROM authors
```

Mathematical Functions

The mathematical functions in Table 21.4 perform calculations based on the input values and return a numeric value. There are no new mathematical functions introduced in version 7.0.

TABLE 21.4 MATHEMATICAL FUNCTIONS

Function Name	Returns
ABS(*numeric*)	The absolute (positive) value of *numeric*.
ACOS(*float*)	The arc cosine for *float*.
ASIN(*float*)	The arc sine for *float*.
ATAN(*float*)	The arc tangent for *float*.
ATAN2(*float1*, *float2*)	Returns the arc tangent whose tangent is between *float1* and *float2*.
CEILING(*numeric*)	The smallest integer value that is higher than or equal to *numeric*.

continues

TABLE 21.4 CONTINUED

Function Name	Returns
COS(*float*)	The trigonometric cosine of *float*.
COT(*float*)	The trigonometric cotangent of *float*.
DEGREES(*numeric*)	The number of degrees for a given angle, *numeric*, given in radians.
EXP(*float*)	The exponential value of *float*.
FLOOR(*numeric*)	The largest integer value that is lower than or equal to *numeric*.
LOG(*float*)	The natural logarithm of *float*.
LOG10(float)	The base-10 logarithm of *float*.
PI()	The constant pi.
POWER(*numeric1*, *numeric2*)	The value of *numeric1* to the specified power, given in *numeric2*.
RADIANS(*numeric*)	Radians of *numeric*, given in degrees.
RAND([*seed*])	A random value between 0 and 1. *seed* can be specified as the starting value.
ROUND(*numeric*, *length*,*func*)	Rounds the specified *numeric* to specified *length*. If *func* is specified and not 0, *numeric* is truncated to *length*.
SIGN(*numeric*)	1 if *numeric* is positive, 0 if *numeric* is 0, and −1 if *numeric* is negative.
SIN(*float*)	The trigonometric sine of *float*.
SQUARE(*float*)	The square of *float*.
SQRT(*float*)	The square root of *float*.
TAN(*float*)	The trigonometric tangent of *float*.

The operators +, −, *, /, and % (modulo) are also available for numeric expressions.

Date Functions

The date functions perform operations such as formatting and subtracting. The expression given is a datetime datatype.

Some of the functions take a *datepart* as argument. The datepart specifies what part of our datetime datatype we want to operate on. Table 21.5 provides the codes for the datepart.

Using Transact-SQL in SQL Server 7.0

CHAPTER 21

473

21

USING TRANSACT-
SQL IN SQL
SERVER 7.0

TABLE 21.5 AVAILABLE CODES FOR DATEPART

Datepart	Abbreviation	Possible Values
Year	yy	1753–9999
Quarter	qq	1–4
Month	mm	1–12
Day of year	dy	1–366
Day	dd	1–31
Week	wk	1–53
Weekday	dw	1–7
Hour	hh	0–23
Minute	mi	0–59
Second	ss	0–59
Millisecond	ms	0–999

The date- and time-related functions are listed in Table 21.6.

TABLE 21.6 DATE- AND TIME-RELATED FUNCTIONS

Function Name	Returns	New in 7.0
DATEADD(*datepart*, *int*, *date*)	Adds *int dateparts* to date.	
DATEDIFF(*datepart*, *date1*, *date2*)	The number of dateparts between *date1* and *date2*.	
DATENAME(*datepart*, *date*)	A character string with the datepart name of *date*.	
DATEPART(*datepart*, *date*)	The *datepart* of *date*.	
GETDATE()	The current date and time.	
DAY(*date*)	The day-of-month part integer.	Yes
MONTH(*date*)	The month as an integer.	Yes
YEAR(*date*)	The year as an integer.	Yes

You can use the operators + and – directly on datetime expressions in version 7.0. The implied datepart is days. In this example, we use the + operator to add one day to the current date:

```
SELECT GETDATE(), GETDATE() + 1

1998-03-28 16:08:33    1998-03-29 16:08:33
```

System Functions

The system functions, listed in Table 21.7, are useful for retrieving information such as column names, table names, and so on. Basically, many of the functions are shortcuts for querying the system tables.

> **TIP**
>
> It is better to use the system functions than to directly query the system tables. If the system tables change in forthcoming releases of SQL Server (as they did with version 7.0), your applications and scripts will still work if you use the system functions. You can also use a new set of views in SQL Server 7.0 for retrieving system-table–related information. The views are independent of the system tables, and all have the object owner INFORMATION_SCHEMA.

TABLE 21.7   SYSTEM FUNCTIONS

Function Name	Returns	New in 7.0
APP_NAME()	The name of the application that executes the function.	
CASE *expression*	Evaluates a list of conditions and returns one of multiple possible expressions. See the section "Cursors" for an example of using the CASE function.	
CAST(*expression* AS *datatype*)	The CAST function is a synonym for the CONVERT function and converts *expression* to *datatype*.	Yes
COALESCE(*expr1*, [*expr2*,,,])	The first non-null expression.	
COL_LENGTH(*table*, *column*)	The length of *column* in *table*.	
COL_NAME(*table_id*, *column_id*)	The name of *column_id* in *table_id*.	
COLUMNPROPERTY(*id*, *column*, *property*)	Information about a *column* in a table, given the *id*. Returns information for a parameter, given in *column*, for a stored procedure. The *property* parameter defines the type of information to be returned.	Yes

Function Name	Returns	New in 7.0
CONVERT(*datatype[(length)]*, *expression*, *style*)	Converts *expression* to *datatype*. For conversion of datetime or float expressions, *style* defines the formatting.	
CURSOR_STATUS(*local*, *cursor_name* ¦ *global*, *cursor_name* ¦ *variable*, *cursor_name*)	A code to the caller of a stored procedure that indicates whether the procedure has returned a cursor and whether the resultset contains any rows.	Yes
DATABASEPROPERTY (*database_name*, *property*)	Information defined in *property* for *database_name*.	Yes
DATALENGTH(*expression*)	The storage area of *expression*, including trailing blanks for character information.	
DB_ID([*db_name*])	The database ID of *db_name* or the current database.	
DB_NAME([*db_id*])	The database name of *db_id* or the name of the current database.	
GETANSINULL([*db_name*])	The default nullability of *db_name* for the current database.	
GETCHECKSUM(*col_name*)	A checksum value for the values in *col_name*.	Yes
HOST_ID()	The process ID of the client application's process.	
HOST_NAME()	The client's workstation name.	
IDENT_INCR(*table*)	The identity increment for the identity column in *table*.	
IDENT_SEED(*table*)	The identity seed for the identity column in *table*.	
INDEX_COL(*table*, *index_id*, *key_id*)	The column name for the specified *table*, *index_id*, and *key_id*.	
IS_MEMBER(*group* ¦ *role*]	1 if the user is a member of specified NT *group* or SQL Server *role*; otherwise, 0.	Yes

continues

TABLE 21.7   CONTIUNED

Function Name	Returns	New in 7.0
IS_SRVROLEMEMBER (*role* [, *login*])	1 if the user's login ID is a member of the specified server *role*; otherwise, 0. An explicit *login* name can be specified.	Yes
ISDATE(*char*)	1 if *char* is in a valid datetime format; otherwise, 0.	
FILE_ID(*filename*)	The ID for *filename*.	Yes
FILE_NAME(*file_id*)	The filename for *file_id*.	Yes
FILEGROUP_ID(*filegroupname*)	The ID for *filegroupname*.	Yes
FILEGROUP_NAME(*filegroup_id*)	The filegroup *filegroup_id*.	Yes
ISNULL(*expression*, *value*)	*value* if *expression* is NULL.	
ISNUMERIC(*char*)	1 if *char* can be converted to a numeric value; otherwise, 0.	
NEWID()	A generated global unique identifier.	Yes
NULLIF(*expr1*, *expr2*)	Null if *expr1* equals *expr2*.	
OBJECT_ID(*object_name*)	The ID for *object_name*.	
OBJECTPROPERTY(*object_id*, *property*)	Information for *object_id*. *property* defines the type of information to be returned.	Yes
PARSENAME(*object_name*, *object_part*)	*object_part* of *object_name*.	Yes
PERMISSIONS(*object_id*[, *column*])	A bitmap indicating permissions on *object_id* and optionally *column*.	Yes
STATS_DATE(*table_id*, *index_id*)	Date when the distribution page was updated for *index_id* on *table_id*.	
SUSER_ID(*login_name*)	The loginid of the specified *login_name*. Included for backward compatibility; use SUSER_SID instead.	
SUSER_NAME([*login_id*])	The login name of *login_id*. Included for backward compatibility; use SUSER_NAME instead.	

Function Name	*Returns*	*New in 7.0*
SUSER_SID([*login*])	Security identification number (SID) for *login*.	Yes
SUSER_SNAME([*login_id*])	The login name of *login_id*.	Yes
TRIGGER_NESTLEVEL ([*tr_object_id*])	Nesting level of specified or current trigger.	Yes
TYPEPROPERTY(*datatype*, *property*)	Information defined in *property* for *datatype*.	Yes
USER_ID([*username*])	The user ID for *username*.	
USER_NAME([*user_id*])	The username for *user_id*.	

The following example returns the title ID and price for all books. If the price is not set (NULL), we return a price of 0:

```
SELECT title_id, ISNULL(price, 0) FROM titles
```

Let us expand the example. We want to display the string 'Not Priced' for those who have NULL. We have to convert the price to a character value before replacing NULL with our text string:

```
SELECT title_id, ISNULL(CONVERT(CHAR(10),price), 'Not Priced')
➥FROM titles
```

Niladic Functions

The niladic group of functions, listed in Table 21.8, is basically a set of system functions. The reason for grouping them separately is that they are used without parentheses after the function name. They are defined in the ANSI SQL-92 standard.

You often find niladic functions used as defaults in CREATE TABLE and ALTER TABLE.

> **NOTE**
>
> Niladic functions are basically aliases to SQL Server system functions. If you use them for default values in tables and run sp_help for the table, edit the table, or script the table in Enterprise Manager, you will notice that they get translated to the corresponding system function.

TABLE 21.8   NILADIC FUNCTIONS

Function Name	Returns	Corresponding System Function
CURRENT_TIMESTAMP	Current date and time	GETDATE()
CURRENT_USER	The user's username	USER_NAME()
SESSION_USER	The user's username	USER_NAME()
SYSTEM_USER	The user's login name	SUSER_NAME()
USER	The user's username	USER_NAME()

In Listing 21.11, we create a table with three columns with defaults for the current date-time, the user's login name, and the username. The INSERT statement inserts default values for all columns, and the SELECT statements retrieve the row inserted.

LISTING 21.11   USING NILADIC FUNCTIONS WITH THE INSERT STATEMENT

```
CREATE TABLE my_defaults
(the_datetime DATETIME DEFAULT CURRENT_TIMESTAMP,
users_login CHAR(20) DEFAULT SYSTEM_USER,
users_name CHAR(20) DEFAULT CURRENT_USER,)

INSERT my_defaults DEFAULT VALUES

SELECT * FROM my_defaults

1998-03-29 19:09:52.377      sa                      dbo
```

Aggregate Functions

The aggregate functions differ from those in the other groups. Aggregate functions perform an aggregation for a column over a set of rows.

Table 21.9 lists the aggregate functions available in SQL Server.

TABLE 21.9   AGGREGATE FUNCTIONS

Function Name	Returns	New in 7.0
AVG([ALL ¦ DISTINCT] *expression*)	The average of all values given in *expression*.	
COUNT([ALL ¦ DISTINCT] *expression* ¦ *)	The number of non-NULL values in *expression*. NULLS are counted if * is specified.	
MAX([ALL ¦ DISTINCT] *expression*)	The maximum value in *expression*.	

Function Name	Returns	New in 7.0
VARP(*expression*)	The statistical variance for the population for all values in the given *expression*.	Yes
STDEVP(*expression*)	The statistical standard deviation for the population for all values in the given *expression*.	Yes
MIN([ALL ¦ DISTINCT] *expression*)	The minimum value in *expression*.	
SUM([ALL ¦ DISTINCT] *expression*)	The sum of all values in *expression*.	
VAR(*expression*)	The statistical variance of all values in the given *expression*.	Yes
STDEV(*expression*)	The statistical standard deviation of all values in the given *expression*.	Yes

If you add the keyword DISTINCT, only distinct values will be aggregated. The default is ALL. You should note that NULL values are not included in the aggregates, except for COUNT(*), which counts the number of rows returned from the relational expression.

Say that we want to count the number of rows, prices, and distinct prices in the title table:

```
SELECT COUNT(*) AS Total, COUNT(price) AS Prices,
➥ COUNT(DISTINCT price) AS "Distinct prices"
 FROM titles
```

```
Total      Prices     Distinct prices
18         16         11
```

Apparently, two books are not priced yet, or we do not know the price (NULL), and we have a total of five duplicate prices.

Now, we want to perform some real aggregation over the prices:

```
SELECT MAX(price) AS 'Max', MIN(price) AS 'Min', AVG(price) AS 'Average'
 FROM titles
```

```
Max                Min                Average
22.9500            2.9900             14.7662
```

Note that even though NULL usually counts low, the minimum price is 2.99 because NULL is excluded from the aggregate.

Aggregate functions are often used in conjunction with GROUP BY. The following example retrieves the average price for each book category:

```
SELECT type, AVG(price) AS Average
 FROM titles
 GROUP BY type
```

```
type          Average
business      13.7300
mod_cook      11.4900
popular_comp  21.4750
psychology    13.5040
trad_cook     15.9633
UNDECIDED     NULL
```

Programming Constructs

The languages that interface to database management systems are sometimes divided into three categories:

- DML, Data Manipulation Language—This includes the ability to read and manipulate the data. Examples are SELECT, INSERT, DELETE, and UPDATE.

- DDL, Data Definition Language—Creating and altering the storage structures; an example is CREATE TABLE.

- DCL, Data Control Language—Defining permissions for data access; examples are GRANT, REVOKE, and DENY.

T-SQL includes other statements that can be useful, for instance, in tying together the DML statements in a stored procedure, such as IF, ELSE, and WHILE.

The IF Statement

The IF statement takes one argument: *boolean_expression*, which is an expression that can evaluate to TRUE or FALSE. The code to be conditionally executed is a statement block:

```
IF boolean_expression
    statement_block
ELSE
    statement_block
```

Using Transact-SQL in SQL Server 7.0

CHAPTER 21

481

21

USING TRANSACT-
SQL IN SQL
SERVER 7.0

You define a statement block with the statements BEGIN and END. In Listing 21.12, a script checks for the existence of a table, prints a message if the table exists, and, if it does, drops the table.

LISTING 21.12 USING THE IF STATEMENT TO PERFORM CONDITIONAL PROCESSING

```
IF OBJECTPROPERTY(OBJECT_ID('orders'), 'istable') = 1
BEGIN
 PRINT "Dropping orders Table"
 DROP TABLE orders
END
ELSE
 PRINT "Table orders does not exist"
```

WHILE, BREAK, and CONTINUE

The WHILE statement allows you to loop while an expression evaluates to true. The syntax for WHILE is

```
WHILE boolean_expression
statement_block
BREAK
statement_block
CONTINUE
```

BREAK exits the WHILE loop, and CONTINUE stops unconditionally and evaluates the *boolean_expression* again.

RETURN

RETURN is used to stop execution of the batch and thus the stored procedure and trigger. When used in a stored procedure, RETURN can take an integer as an argument. The value 0 indicates successful execution. The values -1 to -99 are reserved by Microsoft (currently, -1 to -14 are in use), so you should use values outside that range.

GOTO

GOTO (yes, there is a GOTO statement in T-SQL) branches to a defined label. GOTO can be useful for error handling in stored procedures, for example. In Listing 21.13, a fragment of a stored procedure checks for errors after each statement and exits the procedure with a return code if an error occurs.

LISTING 21.13   GOTO AND RETURN

```
BEGIN TRAN
INSERT orders(customer_number) VALUES(1)
 IF @@ERROR <> 0 GOTO err_handle
RETURN 0
...
err_handle:
RAISERROR ('An error occurred in the stored procedure.
➡ The transaction has been rolled back', 12, 1)
ROLLBACK TRANSACTION
RETURN -101
```

WAITFOR

You can use WAITFOR to halt execution for a specified delay (WAITFOR DELAY) or until a specified time (WAITFOR TIME). In the following example, we want to generate a deadlock. (For instance, we might have defined an alert for the deadlock error that we want to test.) We must be able to start execution of both batches more or less simultaneously for the deadlock to occur, so we introduce a wait for 10 seconds.

Execute the two code blocks in Listing 21.14 from two separate windows (connections) in the Query Analyzer.

LISTING 21.14   USING WAITFOR TO INTRODUCE A DELAY OF 10 SECONDS

```
--Execute from one connection
BEGIN TRAN
UPDATE authors SET au_lname = au_lname
WAITFOR DELAY '00:00:10'
UPDATE titles SET title = title
ROLLBACK TRAN
--Execute from another connection
BEGIN TRAN
UPDATE titles SET title = title
UPDATE authors SET au_lname = au_lname
ROLLBACK TRAN
```

EXECUTE

The EXEC (or EXECUTE) command is used as a keyword for executing stored procedures. Introduced in version 6.0, EXEC also gives us the ability to execute strings and variables containing strings. This can be very useful.

We want to perform UPDATE STATISTICS for all tables in the database. The UPDATE STA-TISTICS command does not accept a variable as its parameter, so we build the command in a variable and execute the contents of the variable:

```
DECLARE @tbl_name NVARCHAR(128)
SELECT @tbl_name = 'authors'
EXEC('UPDATE STATISTICS ' + @tbl_name)
```

This is powerful in conjunction with cursors, which we examine later in the chapter in the section "Cursors."

Another example is if we want to write a stored procedure that will SELECT rows from a table name passed to it as an argument.

The following syntax will produce an error message:

```
SELECT * FROM @tbl_name
```

SQL Server does not accept variables for table names, column names, and so on:

```
CREATE PROC general_select @tbl_name NVARCHAR(128) AS
 EXEC('SELECT * FROM ' + @tbl_name)
GO
EXEC general_select authors
```

> ### TIP
>
> If the string you want to execute is longer than 8,000 characters (or 4,000 if you use Unicode), you can concatenate the contents of two or more variables in the EXECUTE command:
>
> ```
>     EXEC(@var1 + var2)
> ```
>
> This is a more useful trick if you are running version 6.x because the maximum length of a CHAR or VARCHAR is 255 characters.

Batches

A batch is simply a set of commands sent to SQL Server for execution. Do not confuse the batch term as used here with traditional batch processing, where mass modifications are performed, often at low-activity periods.

Basically, SQL Server receives a string (containing T-SQL commands) from the client application. SQL Server parses this string as a unit, searching for keywords. If a syntax error is found, none of the statements in the batch is executed, and an error message is returned to the client application.

In the Query Analyzer, ISQL, and OSQL, the string GO is used to separate batches. When the tool finds the string GO, it takes all text up to the preceding GO and submits it to SQL Server for execution.

Some restrictions for batches concern what commands can be combined with other commands within a batch. Some examples follow:

- You cannot combine any command within a batch. Most CREATE commands must be executed in a single batch. The exceptions are CREATE TABLE, CREATE INDEX, and CREATE DATABASE.

- When calling a stored procedure, you must precede the procedure name with EXECUTE if it's not the first string in a batch. If SQL Server doesn't recognize the first string in a batch, it simply assumes that the string is a call to a stored procedure.

A related concept is the script. A script is a text file containing one or more batches. Scripts are often used with the Query Analyzer, ISQL, and OSQL. You do not have to specify GO after the last command in a script file; the tools will automatically generate an end-of-batch signal.

Listing 21.15 creates a table and then a view. Note that the CREATE commands are separated by GO.

LISTING 21.15   CREATING A TABLE AND A VIEW THAT ONLY DISPLAY RECENT ORDERS

```
CREATE TABLE orders
(order_number UNIQUEIDENTIFIER DEFAULT NEWID()
➥ PRIMARY KEY NOT NULL,
customer_number INT REFERENCES customers(customer_number),
order_date DATETIME DEFAULT CONVERT(CHAR(8), GETDATE(), 112))
GO
CREATE VIEW recent_orders AS
SELECT order_number, customer_number, order_date
 FROM orders
 WHERE order_date > GETDATE() - 14
```

Comments

Anyone who's ever had to review or change some code recognizes the importance of comments. Even if it seems obvious when you're writing it what the code does, the meaning will most certainly not be that obvious at a later time.

When SQL Server finds a comment, it does not execute anything until the end of the comment. The Query Analyzer's syntax coloring indicates commented text with a green color by default. SQL Server supports two types of comment markers:

```
/* Comments */
```

Using Transact-SQL in SQL Server 7.0

CHAPTER 21

485

21

USING TRANSACT-
SQL IN SQL
SERVER 7.0

These comment markers are useful for commenting several lines. None of the text between the comment markers is parsed, compiled, or executed. For shorter comments, you can use

```
-- Comments
```

SQL Server will not execute the text following the markers until the end-of-line. The -- comment markers are defined in ANSI SQL-92.

Both types of comments can be nested within a /*...*/ comment block. You cannot specify the end-of-batch (GO) separator within a /*...*/ comment block.

Here is an example of a batch with an opening comment block that describes what the batch performs and a comment line later in the code that can be altered for debugging purposes:

```
/* Retrieves all orders that have been submitted the last day.
The SELECT COUNT is only for debugging purposes */
SELECT order_number, customer_number, order_date
 FROM orders
 WHERE order_date > GETDATE() -1
--SELECT 'Number of orders returned':, @@ROWCOUNT
```

Local Variables

Local variables allow you to store values temporarily. The variable is always declared as a certain datatype with the DECLARE statement. The datatype can either be system supplied or user defined. The variable's name always begins with the @ sign.

The variable is assigned a value with the SELECT statement or (new in version 7.0) the SET statement.

Listing 21.16 prints the number of distinct book types in the titles table. First, we declare a local variable, then, we assign it a value, and finally, we print the contents of the variable.

LISTING 21.16   ASSIGNING A VALUE TO A LOCAL VARIABLE AND PRINTING ITS CONTENTS

```
DECLARE @user_msg VARCHAR(255)
SELECT @user_msg = 'There are ' + CONVERT(VARCHAR(3),
➥(SELECT COUNT(DISTINCT type) FROM titles))
➥ + ' book types in the titles table.'
PRINT @user_msg

There are 6 book types in the titles table.
```

> **NOTE**
>
> The life span of a local variable is a batch. After the batch has processed, the variable ceases to exist.
>
> If you want to store a value to live between batches in T-SQL, you must create a (temporary) table to store the value in.

Local variables are often used in stored procedures.

Functions Called Global Variables in Earlier Releases

A set of functions was called *global variables* in earlier releases of SQL Server. The name *global* was confusing because it implied that the scope of the variable is longer than a local variable. Global variables were often mistaken for variables that a user can declare and that live across batches, which is not the case. You can name a variable starting with two at signs (@@), but it will still behave as a local variable.

These functions (now categorized as connection-specific, monitoring-related, and general functions) contain information that is maintained by SQL Server. They exist so that an application can check things such as the error code for the last executed command.

The functions are useful because some of them contain information that cannot be found elsewhere or would be hard to obtain with other means.

For connection-specific functions, outlined in Table 21.10, SQL Server maintains separate values for each connection.

TABLE 21.10 CONNECTION-SPECIFIC FUNCTIONS

Function Name	Description
@@CURSOR_ROWS	Number of rows populated in the last opened cursor.
@@DATEFIRST	Indicates the first day of the week (7 is Sunday, 1 is Monday, and so on).
@@ERROR	The error number generated by the last executed command. This is valuable for error checking in stored procedures, batches, and triggers.
@@FETCH_STATUS	Indicates whether a fetch operation from a cursor was successful.

Using Transact-SQL in SQL Server 7.0

CHAPTER 21

487

21

USING TRANSACT-
SQL IN SQL
SERVER 7.0

Function Name	Description
@@IDENTITY	The identity value generated by the last insert statement. The @@IDENTITY value is not affected by other connections' inserts.
@@LOCK_TIMEOUT	The locking timeout value in milliseconds.
@@LANGID	The connection's language ID in use.
@@LANGUAGE	The connection's language in use; a character string.
@@NESTLEVEL	The nesting level for stored procedures and triggers.
@@PROCID	The ID of the currently executing stored procedure.
@@ROWCOUNT	The number of rows affected (modified or read) by the last command.
@@SPID	The connection ID.
@@TEXTSIZE	The maximum number of bytes returned by a SELECT statement when reading text and image data. Note that this can be further limited by the client application.
@@TRANCOUNT	The transaction nesting level.
@@ERROR	Useful for error handling in stored procedures and triggers. In Listing 21.17, we check @@ERROR after each statement and branch into an error-handling routine if an error occurs.

LISTING 21.17   USING THE @@ERROR FUNCTION TO CHECK FOR ERRORS

```
BEGIN TRAN
INSERT orders(customer_number) VALUES(1)
 IF @@ERROR <> 0 GOTO err_handle
RETURN 0
...
err_handle:
RAISERROR ('An error occurred in the stored procedure.
➥ The transaction has been rolled back', 12, 1)
ROLLBACK TRANSACTION
RETURN -101
```

In Listing 21.18, we need to find out the identity value generated by our last insert, so we use the @@IDENTITY function. Note that we need to save the value returned from @@IDENTITY into a local variable if we need it after the next INSERT statement. All INSERT statements update @@IDENTITY, even those that insert into a table without an identity column. We do not have to worry about other connections' inserts because `@@IDENTITY` is maintained per connection.

LISTING 21.18   USING THE `@@IDENTITY` FUNCTION TO GET THE LAST GENERATED IDENTITY VALUE

```
CREATE TABLE customers
(customer_id INT IDENTITY PRIMARY KEY NOT NULL,
customer_name NVARCHAR(100) NOT NULL,
customer_comments NVARCHAR(1000) NULL)
Go

CREATE TABLE orders
(order_number UNIQUEIDENTIFIER DEFAULT NEWID() PRIMARY KEY
➥ NOT NULL,
customer_number INT REFERENCES customers(customer_id),
order_date DATETIME DEFAULT CONVERT(CHAR(8), GETDATE(), 112))
GO

DECLARE @cust_id INT
INSERT customers (customer_name, customer_comments)
VALUES ("Hardware Suppliers AB", "Stephanie is contact.")
SELECT @cust_id = @@IDENTITY
INSERT orders (customer_number)
VALUES (@cust_id)
```

The monitoring-related functions are listed in Table 21.11 for completeness. Typically, `DBCC SQLPERF` and SQL Performance Monitor give similar information in a more useful fashion.

TABLE 21.11   MONITORING-RELATED FUNCTIONS

Function Name	*Description*
`@@CONNECTIONS`	The number of login attempts since the last restart of SQL Server.
`@@CPU_BUSY`	The number of time ticks (currently 1/100 second) that the machine's CPU has been performing SQL Server work since the last restart of SQL Server.
`@@IDLE`	The number of time ticks (currently 1/100 second) that the machine's SQL Server has been idle since the last restart of SQL Server.
`@@IO_BUSY`	The number of time ticks (currently 1/100 second) that SQL Server has been performing I/O operations since the last restart of SQL Server.

Using Transact-SQL in SQL Server 7.0

CHAPTER 21

489

21

USING TRANSACT-
SQL IN SQL
SERVER 7.0

Function Name	Description
@@PACK_RECEIVED	The number of packets received by SQL Server since the last restart of SQL Server.
@@PACK_SENT	The number of packets sent by SQL Server since the last restart of SQL Server.
@@PACKET_ERRORS	The number of times that an error occurred while sending a packet since the last restart of SQL Server.
@@TOTAL_ERRORS	The number of times that an error occurred while reading or writing since the last restart of SQL Server.
@@TOTAL_READ	The total number of physical reads since the last restart of SQL Server.
@@TOTAL_WRITE	The total number of physical writes since the last restart of SQL Server.

Outlined in Table 21.12, the general functions are useful for administration purposes. The most useful one is @@VERSION, which returns the version number, including the service pack level.

TABLE 21.12 GENERAL FUNCTIONS

Function Name	Description
@@DBTS	The current timestamp for the database.
@@MAX_CONNECTIONS	The maximum number of user connections that the installation can support. @@MAX_CONNECTIONS does not reflect the currently configured value of user connections.
@@MAX_PRECISION	The maximum precision value for decimal and numeric datatypes.
@@MICROSOFTVERSION	A Microsoft internal version number. This should not be used for version checking and handling. Use @@VERSION instead.
@@SERVERNAME	The name of the SQL Server. This should match the machine name; if it doesn't, you might want to drop the old (wrong name) with sp_dropserver and add the new (correct name) with sp_addserver.
@@SERVICENAME	The name of the service that executes SQL Server. This should be MSSQLServer if the service name is not changed.
@@TIMETICKS	The number of microseconds per time tick.
@@VERSION	The SQL Server version number.

Listing 21.19 shows how you can use @@VERSION to check the version number of the SQL Server.

LISTING 21.19   USING THE @@VERSION FUNCTION TO DETERMINE THE VERSION OF SQL SERVER

```
SELECT @@VERSION

SELECT
 SUBSTRING(@@VERSION, (CHARINDEX('Server  ', @@VERSION) + 8),
➡ 1) AS Major,
 SUBSTRING(@@VERSION, (CHARINDEX('Server  ', @@VERSION) + 10),
➡ 2) As Minor,
 SUBSTRING(@@VERSION, (CHARINDEX('Server  ', @@VERSION) + 20),
➡ 3) AS 'Service Pack'


Microsoft SQL Server  7.00 - 7.00.390 (Intel X86)
    Dec 13 1997 03:16:48
    Copyright (c) 1988-1997 Microsoft Corporation

Major Minor Service Pack
7    00    390
```

RAISERROR

The RAISERROR command originates from the Db-Library programming API. A Db-Library application registers two callback functions. SQL Server executes a callback function when it sends a message or an error message to the client.

The *message handler* is called when messages are sent from SQL Server to the clients, such as messages generated from the PRINT command.

The *error handler* is called from SQL Server when an error occurs. You can generate an error message with the RAISERROR command.

An ODBC application cannot register callback functions, so a program can check for these messages and errors with function calls. The same applies for OLE-DB applications, which can retrieve message and error information through the SQLOLEDB interfaces.

Managing SQL Server Errors

Most error messages are stored in the sysmessages table in the master database. An error message consists of the error number, a severity level, and a description. Table 21.13 describes the columns in the sysmessages table.

Using Transact-SQL in SQL Server 7.0

CHAPTER 21

491

21

USING TRANSACT-
SQL IN SQL
SERVER 7.0

TABLE 21.13 COLUMNS IN THE SYSMESSAGES TABLE

Column Name	Description
Error	The error number. Every error message has a unique error number.
Severity	The severity level. A higher severity level (generally) indicates a more severe problem. SQL Server will terminate the connection and perform a rollback (if a transaction was started) for severity levels over 19.
Description	The message string with placeholders.

Some error messages are stored in the sysservermessages table in the msdb database. Some of these are informational messages. One example of these messages is the message written to NT's Event Log for each backup that SQL Server performs. The messages in sysservermessages table have the severity levels 110, 120, and 130.

When a message is written to the Event Log or sent to a client application, it also includes state. The state is an internal value that can further describe the error. If you report a problem to Microsoft, the technician might ask for the state.

Microsoft has done a rough grouping of the severity levels. It is not as consistent as you might wish because the messages have evolved over a long time from two different companies (Sybase and Microsoft). Take the descriptions in Table 21.14 with a grain of salt.

TABLE 21.14 DESCRIPTIONS OF SEVERITY LEVELS

Severity Level	Description
0–10	Informational messages
11	Object not found
12	Not used
13	Transactional syntax errors
14	Insufficient permissions
15	Syntax errors in SQL
16	Miscellaneous
17	Insufficient resources
18	Internal errors, non-fatal
19	Resource problems, fatal
20–25	Fatal errors

continues

TABLE 21.14   CONTINUED

Severity Level	Description
110	Server information
120	Server warnings
130	Server errors

You can also add your own error messages, which can be useful for centralizing error reporting from your application. Chapter 11, "The SQL Server Agent," describes how to add messages in Enterprise Manager. You can also manage messages with the stored procedures sp_addmessage, sp_dropmessage, and sp_altermessage. The error number must be greater than 50,000. For more information on these commands, refer to Chapter 11.

The RAISERROR and PRINT Commands

You can generate a message with the RAISERROR command. This is a good way to communicate to a client application that an error has occurred from triggers and stored procedures. The RAISERROR command has the following syntax:

```
RAISERROR([err_no]¦[err_string], severity, state,
➡ [argument1[, ...]] options
```

If you supply an error string, the error number will be 50,000. If you supply an error number, that error number has to be defined in the sysmessages table. Arguments are used to insert data (table name and so on) into the message string. If you want to use arguments, you have to define the error message with placeholders for the arguments.

User-defined error messages must have an error number that is greater than 50,000. The maximum value for an error number is 2,147,483,647.

The available options are

LOG—The message is sent to NT's Event Log.

NOWAIT—The message is sent directly to the client. This is useful for long-running operations so that the application can display a status indicator, for instance.

SETERROR—The function @@ERROR returns 50,000, even if the severity is lower than 11.

Listing 21.20 adds a user-defined message and calls it from T-SQL code.

Using Transact-SQL in SQL Server 7.0

CHAPTER 21

493

21

USING TRANSACT-
SQL IN SQL
SERVER 7.0

LISTING 21.20 ADDING AN ERROR MESSAGE TO SQL SERVER AND GENERATING THE ERROR

```
sp_addmessage 50001, 16, 'The row(s) from table %s could not
➡ be deleted. There are rows in table %s that refer to this row.
➡ Delete those rows first.'
RAISERROR (50001, 16, 1, 'Titles', 'Titleauthor')
Server: Msg 50001, Level 16, State 42000
The row(s) from table Titles could not be deleted. There are
➡ rows in table Titleauthor that refer to this row.
➡ Delete those rows first.
```

One situation where you might find the *state* parameter useful is when you execute a script using ISQL or OSQL. If you execute the RAISERROR with a state of 127, the processing of the script file terminates. Suppose we have a simple batch file that executes

```
ISQL /Usa /P /iMyBatch.SQL /n
```

And the script file (MyBatch.SQL) contains the code in Listing 21.21.

LISTING 21.21 USING STATE 127 TO TERMINATE A BATCH PROCESSED WITH ISQL OR OSQL

```
-- Exit if users connected to database.
IF (SELECT COUNT(*) FROM master..sysprocesses
    WHERE dbid = DB_ID('pubs')) > 0
RAISERROR ('Cannot proceed with batch, users connected
➡ to database.', 16, 127)
GO
-- If not, continue with whatever you want to do
SELECT au_fname, au_lname FROM pubs..authors
```

If the IF statement evaluates to true, the RAISERROR statement will terminate the processing of the script file. This is not the same result as you get from issuing a RETURN statement. The return statement would have terminated the batch but executed the following batches.

The PRINT command returns a string to the client application's message handler. This should not be considered as an error. PRINT is commonly used for batch processing where you want to print information to the log about the processing. The PRINT command takes one argument, a string expression, which can be a string constant, local variable, or function. In version 7.0, string expressions can be concatenated in the PRINT command. The following example uses that feature to display the name of the current month:

```
PRINT 'The current month is ' + DATENAME(mm, GETDATE()) + '.'
The current month is April.
```

SET Options

You can use the SET command to alter the connection's behavior. Options set with the SET command stay active until the connection terminates. Most SET commands take ON or OFF as arguments, whereas some take a specific value. Many of the SET statements do not take effect until the next batch. In the tables that follow, the default behavior is displayed in a bold typeface.

The tuning-related SET parameters are generally used when analyzing and optimizing queries. They can give you information about how a query is executed by SQL Server and also, to some extent, control how a query is executed. The default options are noted by asterisks (*) in Table 21.15.

TABLE 21.15 TUNING-RELATED SET PARAMETERS

Parameter	Arguments	Description
FORCEPLAN	ON¦OFF *	Makes SQL Server process a JOIN in the same order as specified in the FROM clause.
NOEXEC	ON¦OFF *	SQL Server will optimize the query but not execute it. Used in conjunction with SHOWPLAN in earlier releases of SQL Server.
PARSEONLY	ON¦OFF *	SQL Server will parse the query but not optimize or execute it.
SHOWPLAN_ALL	ON¦OFF *	Displays the query plan that SQL Server uses to execute the query and does not execute the query. This is intended for programs that parse the out put, such as the Query Analyzer. For textual output, use SHOWPLAN_TEXT instead.
SHOWPLAN_TEXT	ON¦OFF *	Displays the query plan that SQL Server uses to execute the query and does not execute the query.
STATISTICS_IO	ON¦OFF *	Displays information regarding I/O activity for each query.
STATISTICS_TIME	ON¦OFF *	Displays information regarding execution time for each query.

In Listing 21.22, we turn on SHOWPLAN_TEXT so that the execution plan is returned to the client.

Using Transact-SQL in SQL Server 7.0

CHAPTER 21

495

21

USING TRANSACT-
SQL IN SQL
SERVER 7.0

LISTING 21.22 USING SHOWPLAN_TEXT

```
SET SHOWPLAN_TEXT ON
GO
SELECT title, au_fname, au_lname
 FROM titles t
   JOIN titleauthor ta ON t.title_id = ta.title_id
   JOIN authors a ON ta.au_id = a.au_id

StmtText
SELECT title, au_fname, au_lname
 FROM titles t
   JOIN titleauthor ta ON t.title_id = ta.title_id
   JOIN authors a ON ta.au_id = a.au_id

StmtText
¦--Nested Loops(Inner Join)
      ¦--Nested Loops(Inner Join)
      ¦     ¦--Index Scan(pubs..authors.aunmind)
      ¦     ¦--Index Seek(pubs..titleauthor.UPKCL_taind,
➡ titleauthor.au_id=authors.au_id)
      ¦--Index Seek(pubs..titles.UPKCL_titleidind,
➡ titles.title_id=titleauthor.title_id)
```

With the transaction-handling–related SET parameters, you can override SQL Server's default transaction-handling semantics. By default, one transaction (connection) cannot read or modify another transaction's modified data, but a transaction can both read and modify data that another transaction has read. In Table 21.16, the default options are noted by asterisks (*).

TABLE 21.16 TRANSACTION-HANDLING–RELATED SET PARAMETERS

Parameter	Arguments	Description
CURSOR_CLOSE_ON_COMMIT	ON¦OFF *	Controls whether cursors should be closed on commit.
IMPLICIT_TRANSACTIONS	ON¦OFF *	An implicit BEGIN TRANSACTION is triggered for most DML statements when turned on.
REMOTE_PROC_TRANSACTIONS	ON¦OFF *	A distributed transaction is started when a remote procedure is executed from a local transaction when turned on.

continues

TABLE 21.16 CONTINUED

Parameter	Arguments	Description
TRANSACTION_ISOLATION _LEVEL	READ_ COMMITTED * ¦READ_ UNCOMMITTED¦ REPEATABLE_ READ¦ SERIALIZABLE	Specifies the degree of isolation between concurrent transactions.
XACT_ABORT	ON¦OFF *	When this option is turned on, SQL Server will roll back the current transaction if a runtime error occurs.

In Listing 21.23, we turn on IMPLICIT_TRANSACTIONS, issue two DELETE statements, print the nesting level, and perform a ROLLBACK.

LISTING 21.23 SETTING IMPLICIT_TRANSACTIONS TO GET AN IMPLICIT BEGIN TRANSACTION

```
SET IMPLICIT_TRANSACTIONS ON
GO
DELETE FROM titles WHERE title_id = 'BU1032'
DELETE FROM titleauthor WHERE title_id = 'BU1032'
SELECT 'Transaction nesting level is: ' +
➡ CAST(@@TRANCOUNT AS VARCHAR(5))
ROLLBACK TRAN
Server: Msg 547, Level 16, State 23000
DELETE statement conflicted with COLUMN REFERENCE constraint
➡ 'FK__sales__title_id__1CF15040'. The conflict occurred in
➡ database 'pubs', table 'titleauthor', column 'title_id'
Transaction nesting level is: 1
```

With the formatting-related SET parameters, you can specify, for instance, the order in which day, month, and year parts are specified when entering data. In Table 21.17, the default options are noted by asterisks (*).The default specified applies for the U.S. English language.

TABLE 21.17 SET PARAMETERS, WHICH CONTROL DATA FORMATTING

Parameter	Arguments	Description
DATEFIRST	number	Specifies which day is the last weekday. The default is 7 (Saturday).

Parameter	Arguments	Description
DATEFORMAT	*mdy*	Specifies how SQL Server will interpret the date, month, and year parts when inserting datetime data in numeric format.
FMTONLY	ON¦OFF *	SQL Server will only return metadata to the client when turned on.
IDENTITY_INSERT	*tblname* ON¦OFF *	Allows you to enter an explicit value for an identity column when turned on.
LANGUAGE	*language_name*	Controls in which language error messages should be returned. The language must be available on the server. It also controls the language used when returning the weekday and month with the DATENAME function.
NOCOUNT	ON¦OFF *	Controls whether the number of rows affected by the last command should be returned to the client application. Even if turned off, the count is still available in the @@ROWCOUNT global variable.
OFFSETS	ON¦OFF *	Controls whether the offset for certain T-SQL keywords should be returned to DB-Library applications.
PROCID	ON¦OFF *	Controls whether the ID of a stored procedure should be returned to the calling DB-Library application.
ROWCOUNT	*number*	Causes SQL Server to stop processing the query after the specified number of rows are processed. Note that this also applies to data modification statements. In version 7.0, use the TOP keyword if you want to control how many rows to return from a SELECT statement.
TEXTSIZE	*number*	Controls how many bytes a SELECT statement returns from text and ntext columns. Note that ntext uses two bytes per character.

In Listing 21.24, we want to return the weekday and month that a book is published in the Swedish language. First, the language is added with the call to sp_addlanguage. The call to sp_addlanguage appears in the script file instlang.sql.

LISTING 21.24 USING sp_addlanguage TO ADD A LANGUAGE TO SQL SERVER

```
exec sp_addlanguage 'Svenska','Swedish',
'januari,februari,mars,april,maj,juni,juli,augusti,september
➥,oktober,november,december',
'jan,feb,mar,apr,maj,jun,jul,aug,sep,okt,nov,dec',
```

continues

LISTING 21.24   CONTINUED

```
'mandag,tisdag,onsdag,torsdag,fredag,lördag,söndag',
ymd,1
SET LANGUAGE swedish
GO
SELECT '"' + RTRIM(title) + '"' is published on a '
➥ + DATENAME(dw, pubdate) + ' in ' + DATENAME(mm, pubdate) + '.'
 FROM titles
WHERE title_id = 'PC1035'
"But Is It User Friendly?" is published on a söndag in juni.
```

Listing 21.25 sets the date format for specifying datetime data. Note that the SELECT statement shows the three available options to specify datetime data. SET DATEFORMAT applies only to the numeric format.

LISTING 21.25   USING SET DATEFORMAT TO SPECIFY DEFAULT DATEPART INTERPRETATION FOR THE NUMERIC DATE FORMAT

```
SET DATEFORMAT ymd
GO
SELECT CONVERT(smalldatetime, '1999.12.31') as 'Numeric',
 CONVERT(smalldatetime, '19991231') as 'Unseparated',
 CONVERT(smalldatetime, 'Dec 1999 31') as 'Alphabetic'

Numeric              Unseparated          Alphabetic
1999-12-31 00:00:00  1999-12-31 00:00:00  1999-12-31 00:00:00
```

The ANSI-related and miscellaneous SET parameters control behavior for comparison to NULL, division with 0, and so on. In Table 21.18, the default options are noted by asterisks (*).

TABLE 21.18   ANSI AND MISCELLANEOUS SET PARAMETERS

Parameter	Arguments	Description
ARITHABORT	ON¦OFF *	Terminates a query if overflow or divide-by-zero occurs when turned on. Note that rows can be returned before the abort occurs.
ARITHIGNORE	ON¦OFF *	Returns NULL if overflow or divide-by-zero errors occur when turned on. No warning message is sent to the client. Default behavior is that NULL and a warning message are returned.
NUMERIC_ROUNDABORT	ON¦OFF *	Controls level of reporting when loss of precision occurs.

Using Transact-SQL in SQL Server 7.0

CHAPTER 21

499

21

USING TRANSACT-
SQL IN SQL
SERVER 7.0

Parameter	Arguments	Description
ANSI_NULL_DFLT_OFF	ON¦OFF *	Set this to on if you do not want a column to allow NULL when you create a table and do not specify NULL or NOT NULL.
ANSI_NULL_DFLT_ON	ON¦OFF *	Set this to on if you want a column to allow NULL when you create a table and do not specify NULL or NOT NULL.
ANSI_NULLS	ON¦OFF *	Controls how comparison to NULL should be handled. By default, NULL = NULL equals TRUE. SETANSI_NULLS to ON to change the evaluation to false.
ANSI_PADDING	ON¦OFF *	Specify whether char, varchar, and varbinary columns should be padded with blanks and zeroes. Behavior is specified at the CREATE time of the table.
ANSI_WARNINGS	ON¦OFF *	Generates a warning if an aggregate function is applied over rows that contain NULL and if INSERT or UPDATE specifies data with a length that exceeds the column definitions for character, Unicode, or binary data. A division by 0 or overflow will result in the rollback of the statement if this option is set.
ANSI_DEFAULTS	ON¦OFF *	If set to ON, the following set parameters will be activated: ANSI_NULLS, ANSI_NULL_DFLT_ON, ANSI_PADDING, ANSI_WARNINGS, CURSOR_CLOSE_ON_COMMIT, IMPLICIT_TRANSACTIONS, and QUOTED_IDENTIFIER.
DEADLOCK_PRIORITY	NORMAL *¦LOW	If LOW, this connection will be the preferred victim if a deadlock occurs. If your application handles deadlock gracefully, set this to LOW to increase the chance that an application that does not handle deadlock can continue processing in the event of a deadlock situation.
DISABLE_DEF_ CNST_CHK	ON¦OFF *	Set to on if you want SQL Server to halt execution immediately if a statement is performed that violates a constraint. By default, SQL Server will continue processing and recheck at end of statement.

continues

TABLE 21.18 CONTINUED

Parameter	Arguments	Description
FIPS_FLAGGER	OFF * ¦ ENTRY ¦ INTERMEDIATE ¦ FULL	Specifies whether SQL Server will generate a warning if a statement does not comply with the specified level of the FIPS 127-2 standard.
QUOTED_IDENTIFIER	ON ¦ OFF *	Will not check for keyword violation with strings surrounded with double quotes.

In Listing 21.26, we explore the differences when checking for the NULL symbol, depending on how ANSI_NULLS is set. The preferred way of checking for the NULL symbol is to use IS NULL and IS NOT NULL, which is consistent regardless of how ANSI_NULLS is set.

LISTING 21.26 CHECKING FOR NULL

```
SET ANSI_NULLS OFF
GO
SELECT title_id, price FROM titles WHERE price = NULL
SELECT title_id, price FROM titles WHERE price IS NULL

title_id price
MC3026    NULL
PC9999    NULL
title_id price
MC3026    NULL
PC9999    NULL

--Note that both statements return two rows.
SET ANSI_NULLS ON
GO
SELECT title_id, price FROM titles WHERE price = NULL
SELECT title_id, price FROM titles WHERE price IS NULL

title_id price
title_id price
MC3026    NULL
PC9999    NULL
--Note that the first statement returns zero rows.
```

You can specify many of the SET parameters in the ODBC client configuration (the ODBC DSN). This feature introduced some problems. For instance, you could write a stored procedure so that the parameter was assigned NULL as default and a check for a value was done inside the procedure. This check is sometimes written as IF @parameter = NULL (which evaluates to false when ANSI_NULLS is ON).

Cursors

In contrast to most programming languages, SQL is a set-based language. This leads to an impedance mismatch between languages. You need some way of interfacing between two languages. Most programming interfaces to SQL Server are based on function calls: You specify a query to execute through one function call and execute the query through another function call, and so on. What do you do with the result?

For a data modification statement, you probably only check for the return code and give the user some feedback. For a SELECT statement, you probably want to read through the rows returned and display them or perform further processing for the rows (unless you know in advance you will retrieve only one row).

We build some kind of loop to go through our resultset and perform some processing for each row. If we only want to display the rows, we can simply fetch them as they arrive to the client, reading from our input buffer. What if we need to perform further processing for each row, such as performing some calculations and update the current row? You can do this through a cursor.

A cursor is a placeholder in a resultset from a query. We cannot navigate in a table because a table (or rather, the contents in a table) is a set, but we can navigate through the result from a query.

Let's say that we have a leads table, and we want to predict the value of sales for the forthcoming three months. The leads table appears in Listing 21.27.

LISTING 21.27 THE LEADS TABLE

```
CREATE TABLE leads
(l_id INT IDENTITY,
customer INT,
est_sale FLOAT,
close_date SMALLDATETIME DEFAULT DATEADD(dd, 30, GETDATE()),
prob FLOAT DEFAULT 20,
sales_person CHAR(8),
category VARCHAR(30))

SELECT * FROM leads

l_id customer est_sales close_date prob sales_person category
---- -------- --------- ---------- ---- ------------ --------
1    1        600       Apr 15 199 30   Steve        books
2    1        200       Apr 25 199 55   John         paper
3    5        400       May  1 199 40   Kelly        books
4    3        900       May 12 199 25   Lisa         misc
```

continues

LISTING 21.27   CONTINUED

5	7	200	Jun	1	199	15	John	misc
6	6	700	May	10	199	50	Bob	paper
7	5	450	Apr	10	199	10	Richard	books
8	13	600	May	15	199	80	John	misc
9	5	1200	Apr	10	199	50	Ann	books
10	16	200	Jun	15	199	50	Andy	books
11	7	800	May	20	199	40	Bob	misc
12	9	600	Apr	20	199	30	Lisa	paper
13	3	900	Apr	15	199	60	John	paper
14	16	300	May	25	199	25	Kelly	misc
15	11	700	Jun	20	199	45	Lisa	books

We want to make a projection by multiplying the estimated sale with the probability of a sale occurring, and then summarize the projections:

```
SELECT SUM(est_sale * probability/100) FROM leads
```

What if we want to be more precise? Based on experience

- Some salespeople are too optimistic, whereas others are conservative. Lisa's probability is usually 20% low and Steve's is usually 30% high.

- In June, we always offer an additional 20% discount.

- The books' projections are usually low, so we want to increase it by 15%.

- Customer 2 has a tendency to ask for a bid but seldom buys. We want to lower the probability to 50% for Customer 2.

Some Approaches

We certainly could retrieve all the rows to the client computer and perform all the aggregations in the client application. This would make a poor use of SQL Server's power. We would have to write a lot of code and retrieve many records to the client computer. You can imagine what amount of network bandwidth that would take if the table has tens of millions of rows.

We decide to use a cursor. We loop through each row, save relevant column information in variables, and perform our calculations.

> **NOTE**
>
> You might think that we should use a set-based operation instead of a cursor. I agree, so hold on. I discuss that later in the chapter.

Cursor Example and Some Syntax

In Listing 21.28, you find the code for performing the projection. Take a look at it; I explain it in detail later.

LISTING 21.28 CALCULATING SALES PROJECTIONS USING A CURSOR

```
DECLARE lead_cur CURSOR FOR
SELECT customer, est_sale, close_date, prob, sales_person,
       category
 FROM leads
FOR READ ONLY

DECLARE
 @sum_sales FLOAT,
 @customer INT,
 @est_sale FLOAT,
 @close_date SMALLDATETIME,
 @prob FLOAT,
 @sales_person CHAR(8),
 @category VARCHAR(30)

SELECT @sum_sales = 0
OPEN lead_cur

FETCH lead_cur INTO
 @customer, @est_sale, @close_date, @prob, @sales_person,
 @category

WHILE @@FETCH_STATUS = 0
 BEGIN
  IF @sales_person = 'Lisa'  -- Lisa usually projects low
     SELECT @prob = @prob * 1.2
  IF @sales_person = 'Steve' -- Steve usually projects high
     SELECT @prob = @prob * 0.7
  IF @customer = 2 -- Customer 2 has a low buying rate
     SELECT @prob = @prob * 0.5
  IF DATEPART (mm, @close_date ) = 6 -- Discount June sales
SELECT @prob = @prob * 0.8
  IF @category = 'Books' -- Increase book projections
     SELECT @est_sale = @est_sale * 1.15

  SELECT @sum_sales = @sum_sales + @est_sale * @prob / 100
  FETCH lead_cur INTO
   @customer, @est_sale, @close_date, @prob, @sales_person,
   @category
 END

CLOSE lead_cur
SELECT @sum_sales AS "Estimated Sales"
DEALLOCATE lead_cur
```

Declaring Cursors

A cursor is declared for a SELECT statement. The ANSI defines the following syntax to declare a cursor:

```
DECLARE cursor_name [INSENSITIVE] [SCROLL] CURSOR
FOR select_statement
[FOR {READ ONLY ¦ UPDATE [OF column_list]}]
```

Version 7.0 introduced an alternative way of declaring a cursor to give the cursor the same capabilities as the API-based cursor. I discuss API cursors later in the chapter.

> **NOTE**
>
> The cursor types actually use the same code in SQL Server, so it is natural that we have the ability to use the same features at the SQL level that we have at the API level.

The syntax for Transact-SQL cursors is

```
DECLARE cursor_name CURSOR
[LOCAL ¦ GLOBAL]
[FORWARD_ONLY ¦ SCROLL]
[STATIC ¦ KEYSET ¦ DYNAMIC]
[READ_ONLY ¦ SCROLL_LOCKS ¦ OPTIMISTIC]
FOR select_statement
[FOR {READ ONLY ¦ UPDATE [OF column_list]}]
```

You cannot use COMPUTE, COMPUTE BY, FOR BROWSE, and INTO in *select_statement*.

Let's use our example to discuss the DECLARE statement:

```
DECLARE lead_cur CURSOR FOR
SELECT customer, est_sale, close_date, probability,
➥ sales_person, product_category
 FROM leads
FOR READ ONLY
```

Our cursor declares a SELECT statement that reads from a single table. We do not want to update any data based on cursor position, so we declare the cursor as READ ONLY.

As for all queries, it is a good idea to limit the number of rows that the cursor will process through a WHERE clause. If SQL Server can use an index to find the rows, it's even better.

The cursor name must follow the general rules for identifiers.

Local and Global Cursors

A new feature in version 7.0 is that you can specify whether the cursor should be local or global.

If you used cursors with version 6.*x*, you used global cursors. The cursor is implicitly deallocated at termination of the connection.

A local cursor's scope is a batch (which implies a stored procedure or trigger). The cursor is implicitly deallocated when the batch terminates unless a reference to it is passed to a calling stored procedure, batch, and so on. Then, it will go out of scope when the last variable referring to it goes out of scope.

In Listing 21.29, we write a general stored procedure that returns the names of all tables in a database. Then, we can use that procedure for performing certain maintenance routines against our tables, such as running UPDATE STATISTICS, rebuilding indexes, and so on.

LISTING 21.29 CREATING A STORED PROCEDURE THAT RETURNS A CURSOR THAT CAN BE USED TO OPERATE AGAINST EACH TABLE IN A DATABASE

```
CREATE PROC cur_tbl_names @tbl_cur CURSOR VARYING OUTPUT AS
SET @tbl_cur = CURSOR LOCAL FORWARD_ONLY FOR
 SELECT TABLE_NAME FROM INFORMATION_SCHEMA.TABLES
  WHERE TABLE_TYPE = 'BASE TABLE'
OPEN @tbl_cur
```

First, you can see that the parameter @tbl_cur is defined as CURSOR VARYING OUTPUT. This is needed if we want to return a reference to the cursor from the procedure.

The select statement returns all the table names in the database. It might look a bit strange to those who have worked with SQL Server's earlier versions. INFORMATION_SCHEMA.TABLES is one of the system-table–independent views that are used for looking at catalog information. These views are defined in the ANSI standard, so I encourage you to use them when possible.

Listing 21.30 contains the code that calls our procedure.

LISTING 21.30 CALLING THE PROCEDURE IN LISTING 21.29

```
DECLARE @tbls CURSOR
DECLARE @table_name sysname
EXEC cur_tbl_names @tbl_cur = @tbls OUTPUT
FETCH NEXT FROM @tbls INTO @table_name
WHILE @@FETCH_STATUS = 0
```

continues

LISTING 21.30 CONTINUED

```
BEGIN
  EXEC('DBCC DBREINDEX( ' + @table_name + ')')
  FETCH NEXT FROM @tbls INTO @table_name
END
```

We get a reference to the cursor and execute our stored procedure, and then we have a standard loop for that cursor. Now, we can write several batches (or stored procedures) that use the same cursor, and if we want to exclude any tables, we modify the code only once: in the stored procedure.

You might wonder what sysname is. It is a built-in datatype, used for identifiers.

Declaring Variables

How do we process values from the cursor?

We could simply display each row to the user as a one-row resultset, but that does not make much sense. It would be much simpler to issue an ordinary SELECT statement and display the rows to the user as we read the rows from the input buffer.

What we really want to do is store the values for some of the columns into local variables and perform some processing based on those values.

Note that I have chosen the same variable names as those returned from the SELECT statement. This makes it easier to remember the variable names when processing the cursor, and it makes it easier to maintain the code:

```
DECLARE
  @sum_sales FLOAT,
  @customer INT,
  @est_sale FLOAT,
  @close_date SMALLDATETIME,
  @probability FLOAT,
  @sales_person CHAR(8),
  @product_category VARCHAR(30)
```

We also need to initialize the summary variable:

```
SELECT @sum_sales = 0
```

Opening Cursors

When you open a cursor, the SELECT statement is executed and the cursor becomes populated. At that point in time, the cursor will be positioned above the first row:

```
OPEN lead_cur
```

You can check how many rows the resultset contains with the global variable @@CURSOR_ROWS. If the value is –1, the cursor is being populated asynchronously.

If you close a cursor and open it again, the SELECT statement is re-executed. Bear this in mind, so you don't re-execute your select statement if you don't have to.

Fetching Rows

Now, it is time to start reading rows from your cursor, which you do with the FETCH command:

```
FETCH lead_cur INTO
 @customer, @est_sale, @close_date, @probability,
 @sales_person, @product_category
```

The default for FETCH is to get the next row from the cursor. We will look at scrolling capabilities later in the chapter. If you specify too many or too few variables after INTO, you will get a runtime error. You also get a runtime error if you specify a variable type for which SQL Server cannot perform an implicit datatype conversion.

The Main Loop

The main loop is where the real processing occurs. The loop looks like this:

```
WHILE @@FETCH_STATUS = 0
 BEGIN
  IF @sales_person = 'Lisa'  -- Lisa usually projects low
     SELECT @probability = @probability * 1.2
  IF @sales_person = 'Steve' -- Steve usually projects high
     SELECT @probability = @probability * 0.7
  IF @customer = 2 -- Customer 2 has a low buying rate
     SELECT @probability = @probability * 0.5
  IF DATEPART (mm, @close_date ) = 6 -- Discount June sales by 20%
     SELECT @probability = @probability * 0.8
  IF @product_category = 'Books' -- Increase book projections
     SELECT @est_sale = @est_sale * 1.15

  SELECT @sum_sales = @sum_sales + @est_sale * @probability / 100
  FETCH lead_cur INTO
   @customer, @est_sale, @close_date, @probability, @sales_person,
@product_category
END
```

We loop while @@FETCH_STATUS = 0. A value of –1 means that we have navigated outside the cursor. A value of –2 means that the row that we are trying to fetch has been deleted; all columns will contain the NULL symbol.

Closing the Cursor

We want to close the cursor as soon as we don't need it anymore. Open cursors hold locks on the underlying tables or use valuable resources.

You can re-open the cursor, which means that the statement is executed again and the cursor is re-populated:

```
CLOSE lead_cur
SELECT @sum_sales AS "Estimated Sales"
```

Deallocating Cursors

When we are finished with the cursor definition, we deallocate it. You cannot declare a cursor with the same name until you have deallocated the previous cursor:

```
DEALLOCATE lead_cur
```

It is a good idea to deallocate a cursor when you do not need it anymore. The query plan is released from memory at that time, and it makes the structure of your code clearer.

Updating with Cursors

How can you update a cursor when the cursor is a resultset, not the data itself? What you do is update based on the cursor position. The modification can be either an UPDATE or a DELETE.

Declaring a Cursor FOR UPDATE

To update based on the cursor position, the cursor must be declared FOR UPDATE:

```
[FOR {READ ONLY ¦ UPDATE [OF column_list]}]
```

If you do not specify a *column_list*, all columns are updateable.

If your select statement is a join, you can update several tables through the same cursor. This probably does not have that much meaning for ANSI cursors, but it is possible.

Listing 21.31 shows an example of an updateable cursor.

LISTING 21.31 AN UPDATEABLE CURSOR

```
DECLARE upd_cur CURSOR FOR
SELECT title, au_lname, au_fname
 FROM titles t
 JOIN titleauthor ta ON t.title_id = ta.title_id
 JOIN authors a ON ta.au_id = a.au_id
 WHERE state = 'CA'
```

Using Transact-SQL in SQL Server 7.0

CHAPTER 21

509

21

USING TRANSACT-
SQL IN SQL
SERVER 7.0

```
ORDER BY title
FOR UPDATE
```

Obviously, columns with computed values and aggregates cannot be updated.

Scrolling Capabilities

If you declare the cursor with the SCROLL keyword, you can navigate as you want within the resultset. An example of the leads cursor declared with scroll capabilities looks like

```
DECLARE lead_cur SCROLL CURSOR FOR
SELECT customer, est_sale, close_date, probability,
 sales_person, product_category
 FROM leads
FOR READ ONLY
```

For a scrollable cursor, you can use the FETCH statement to navigate in a more flexible way:

```
FETCH [NEXT ¦ PRIOR ¦ FIRST ¦ LAST ¦ ABSOLUTE n ¦ RELATIVE n]
```

If you omit the navigational argument, NEXT is performed. You do not need a scrollable cursor in order to FETCH NEXT.

Scrollable cursors are most useful as API cursors, where a user, for instance, can move up and down a listbox and choose some entry based on a cursor value.

INSENSITIVE Cursors

A cursor declared as insensitive will not be affected by updates done through the tables that it is based on. SQL Server will simply make a copy of the cursor data and store it in the tempdb database.

An insensitive cursor is useful if you want to take a snapshot of the data and you do not want to be disturbed by changes to the underlying data while you process the cursor data.

An insensitive cursor is not updateable.

Cursors and Concurrency

We must be careful when using cursors so we do not block other users' access to the data. If the executing code is not in the scope of a transaction, SQL Server will only apply shared locks for the duration of the fetch request. SQL Server will automatically implement optimistic concurrency. If we try to update a row through the cursor, and some other user updated it, SQL Server will issue an error message to the client application.

> **CAUTION**
>
> If a cursor is used inside a transaction, shared locks are held on all rows that are fetched until the end of the transaction. This can lead to poor concurrency.

If you use the T-SQL extension to `DECLARE CURSOR`, you can control the cursor concurrency behavior:

```
[READ_ONLY ¦ SCROLL_LOCKS ¦ OPTIMISTIC]
```

- If we use `READ_ONLY`, we cannot update through the cursor, and shared locks are only held during each fetch operation.
- When using `SCROLL_LOCKS`, SQL Server acquires scroll locks as we read data into the cursor. Subsequent updates based on the cursor are guaranteed to succeed.
- With `OPTIMISTIC`, we get optimistic concurrency as described in the preceding text.

API Cursors

So far, we have looked at how we can use cursors through T-SQL. The most common use of cursors, however, is through the application programming interface (API). Each API has calls or methods for defining cursor capabilities.

In fact, you can say that all results from SQL Server are returned through a cursor. The simplest case is that the client retrieves rows one at a time, scrolling forward (reading from the input buffer) through the resultset. This is called a default resultset.

If we need more advanced scrolling capabilities, part of the resultset must be cached somewhere, so we can use, say, a key when searching for the previous row. This caching can occur at the client or at the server.

Client cursors are implemented at the client side. ODBC or OLE-DB caches the necessary information. There are no cursor calls sent to SQL Server. Client cursors are useful if

- We have a slow network connection to the SQL Server.
- There aren't too many rows in the resultset or we will navigate through a major part of the resultset.
- We will allow the user to interact rapidly through the cached resultset.

Using Transact-SQL in SQL Server 7.0

CHAPTER 21

511

21

USING TRANSACT-
SQL IN SQL
SERVER 7.0

A Web-based application is a good example of where client cursors can be valuable. For example, a SQL statement is sent to SQL Server to retrieve a number of customer names. This resultset is buffered at the client side. When the user chooses a customer, another SQL statement is executed, and customer details are presented in the Web browser.

API server cursors are implemented through the API cursor support in SQL Server. SQL Server has a number of sp_cursor extended stored procedures used by ODBC and OLE-DB, which implements API server cursors.

By default, server-side cursors are used in the programming APIs, but the programmer can choose to use client cursors instead.

We can also choose how many rows are to be returned with each fetch operation sent to SQL Server (*fat* cursors). This is not possible with Transact-SQL cursors; it would not make any sense because all processing is done at the server.

> **CAUTION**
>
> The cursor model chosen can have a severe impact at performance. See the next section, "Avoiding Cursors," for some examples.

Avoiding Cursors

I have encountered numerous situations where performance was slow due to the improper use of cursors. You should always aim at letting SQL Server perform what it's good at: set-based operations. It makes little sense to have an advanced RDBMS and only use it for one-row-at-a-time retrievals.

Our cursor example can be performed with one SELECT statement, as shown in Listing 21.32.

LISTING 21.32 THE LEADS CURSOR EXAMPLE PERFORMED WITH ONE SELECT STATEMENT INSTEAD

```
SELECT "Sum of Sales" = SUM(
  est_sale * prob / 100
  *
  CASE category WHEN 'Books' THEN 1.15 ELSE 1 END
  *
  CASE DATEPART (mm, close_date ) WHEN 6 THEN 0.8 ELSE 1 END
  *
  CASE sales_person WHEN 'Lisa' THEN 1.2 WHEN 'Steve' THEN 0.7
➡ ELSE 1 END
  *
  CASE WHEN customer = 2 THEN 0.5 ELSE 1 END)
```

The advantage with this approach is a significant performance improvement. The possible disadvantage is that you obviously need to know SQL.

As another example, imagine that we want to increase the discount for all customers who have bought a certain amount.

We could retrieve all rows and check the amounts bought, and if a customer's amount is over the target, we can update that customer's discount. This would require that we retrieve all rows, with one network roundtrip for each customer and one UPDATE statement for each row that we want to update.

Thinking set-based, we could simply issue an UPDATE statement that raises the discount for all customers who meet the requirements (in the WHERE clause). SQL Server can use an index to find the rows, and all processing is done at the server. This update statement would be easier to construct than the procedural processing.

The performance implications are obvious. Okay, it is a simple example, but the same reasoning applies for more advanced operations.

 On the companion CD-ROM, you will find a Visual Basic application (leads.zip) that demonstrates the differences. I performed some timing, and Table 21.19 presents the results.

Let us take a look at some details first. My server is a Pentium II, 333MHz with 128MB RAM. I used the leads table with 50,000 rows. I performed several tests:

- SQL-based cursors through RDO and ADO.
- A SELECT statement, using CASE through RDO and ADO.
- All calculations at the client side, fetching all rows. I used both the default resultset and fetching a number of rows at a time (executing an sp_cursor procedure at the server for each fetch). I fetched 100 rows at a time with RDO and 1 row at a time with ADO.

The client I used is a Pentium 120MHz with 72MB RAM. The machines were connected through an isolated 10MB Ethernet. Table 21.19 displays execution time in seconds when running the Visual Basic program both at the server and at the client.

TABLE 21.19 PERFORMANCE COMPARISON BETWEEN DIFFERENT USES OF CURSORS

Cursor	API	Server	Client
SQL	RDO	8.8	8.5
SQL	ADO	8.8	8.6
None	RDO	2.0	2.0

Cursor	API	Server	Client
None	ADO	1.9	1.9
Default resultset	RDO	20	106
Server cursor	RDO	23	101
Default resultset	ADO	20	116
Server cursor	ADO	650	983

There is quite a difference between 2 seconds and 983 seconds of execution time.

> **NOTE**
>
> Note the difference between ADO and RDO using a server cursor. Without any further investigation, we can safely assume that this is due to the difference in the number of rows retrieved with each fetch. SQL Server executes an sp_cursor procedure for each fetch. I used a block size of 100 for RDO and 1 for ADO.

The numbers speak for themselves.

Summary

SQL is a powerful data-access and data-modification language. In SQL Server, the language has been extended with operations such as controlling execution flow. To interface with procedural programming languages, we can use cursors, but it is almost always a good idea to use set-based operations as much as possible.

Transaction Management and Distributed Transactions

by Simon Gallagher

In This Chapter

This chapter discusses the very important area within database coding we call *transaction management*. Whether the Transact-SQL is executed directly on the server or through a custom application you are developing, the transactions you construct and issue can have a huge impact on the performance of SQL Server and the consistency of your databases.

New in SQL Server 7.0

New keywords to SQL Server 7.0 are the SQL-92 keywords COMMIT WORK and ROLLBACK WORK. These are similar but *not* identical to the SQL Server commands COMMIT TRAN and ROLLBACK TRAN.

Transaction Processing

A *transaction* is often called a *Logical Unit of Work* (LUW), which means that it is a way of collecting and associating a number of actions into a serial all-or-nothing action. Consider a bank transaction in which you move $1,000 from your checking to your savings account. This transaction is, in fact, *two* actions: a decrement of your checking account and an increment to your savings account. Consider the impact on your finances if the bank's server went down after completing the first stage and never got to the second! By collecting the two operations together, as a transaction, they either both succeed or both fail.

A transaction is a logical unit of work that has four special characteristics known as ACID properties:

- Atomicity—Associated modifications are an all-or-nothing proposition; they either all are done or none is done.

- Consistency—After a transaction finishes, all data is in the state it should be, all internal structures are correct, and everything accurately reflects the transaction that has occurred.

- Isolation—One transaction cannot interfere with the processes of another transaction.

- Durability—After the transaction has finished, all changes made are permanent.

The responsibility for these characteristics of a transaction is split between us (as developers) and SQL Server. The developer is responsible for ensuring that the modifications are correctly collected together and that the data is going to be left in a consistent state that corresponds with the actions being taken. SQL Server ensures that the transaction is isolated and durable and undertakes the atomicity requested and ensures the consistency of the final data structures. The durability of the transaction is handled by the transaction log of each database. As we will see in this chapter, we have some control over how SQL Server handles some of these properties. For example, we can modify a transaction isolation by enlisting bound connections.

Transactions and Locking

SQL Server issues and holds onto locks for the duration of a transaction to ensure the isolation and consistency of the modifications. As work progresses within a transaction, *update locks* become *exclusive locks*, which are then held until the completion of the transaction. *Shared locks*, or read locks, are held for as long as the statement needs them; usually, a shared lock is released as soon as that resource (row, page, table) has been finished with. The length of time a lock is held can be modified by the use of keywords such as HOLDLOCK in a query. At this point, even shared locks are held onto until the completion of the transaction.

22

TRANSACTION MANAGEMENT

What this means for database application developers is that you should try to hold onto as few locks or as small a lock as possible for as short a time as possible. The simple rule when working with transactions is "Keep them short and keep them sweet!" In other words, do what you need to do in the most concise manner in the shortest possible time.

To modify the manner in which a transaction and its locks can be handled by a SELECT statement, you can issue the SET TRANSACTION ISOLATION LEVEL statement. This statement allows the query to choose how much it is protected against other transactions modifying the data being used. The SET TRANSACTION ISOLATION LEVEL statement has the following mutually exclusive options:

- READ COMMITTED—This default behavior causes the transaction to hold shared locks on the data for as long as it is reading. However, these locks are not held past the page that is being read; the transaction can encounter *non-repeatable reads* or *phantom data* because other transactions are not blocked from modifying the data after we have read it.

- READ UNCOMMITTED—With this level of isolation, one transaction can read the dirty pages of other transactions. This is, therefore, the least restrictive isolation level, but one that allows the reading of dirty and uncommitted data. This option has the same effect as issuing NOLOCK within your SELECT statements, but only has to be set once for your connection.

- REPEATABLE READ—As data is read, locks are placed and held for the pages. These locks prevent other transactions from modifying the data you have read, so that you can carry out multiple passes across the same information. This isolation level is obviously more restrictive and can block other transactions. However, it does not prevent the addition of new rows or *phantom rows* because only *existing* data is locked.

- SERIALIZABLE—This is the most restrictive isolation level because it places an entire range lock on the data. This prevents *any* modifications to the tables being read from until the end of the transaction.

> **CAUTION**
>
> Pre-SQL Server 7.0 REPEATABLE READ and SERIALIZABLE statements were completely interchangeable. You received both functionalities together. With SQL Server 7.0, this is no longer true; if you want serializable behavior, you have to modify your scripts that make use of REPEATABLE READ appropriately.

For more information on locks, locking behavior, and performance, see Chapter 30, "Locking and Performance."

How SQL Server Keeps Track of Transactions

SQL Server makes extensive use of a database's transaction log to record the modifications occurring within user's transactions. The primary responsibility of logging is to ensure transaction durability—whether this is ensuring that the changes make it to the physical database files, or ensuring that any unfinished transactions are rolled back should there be an error or a server failure.

So, what is logged? Obviously, the start and end of a transaction are logged, but also the before and after images of data being modified, page allocations and deallocations, and changes to indexes. SQL Server keeps track of a number of pieces of information, all with the aim of ensuring the ACID properties of the transaction.

For SQL Server to keep straight what is currently happening within a connection, it uses a global session variable called @@trancount.

As a transaction is started, this variable is incremented; as a transaction completes, this variable is decremented. In the following sections, we will see how this variable is affected by different commands.

There are three ways to carry out transaction processing with Microsoft SQL Server:

- AutoCommit—Every Transact-SQL statement is its own transaction and commits when it finishes. This is the default mode in which SQL Server operates.
- Explicit—This approach provides programmatic control of the transaction using the BEGIN TRAN and COMMIT/ROLLBACK TRAN/WORK commands.
- Implicit—SQL Server is placed into a mode of operation in which issuing certain SQL commands starts a transaction. The developer finishes the transaction by using the COMMIT/ROLLBACK TRAN/WORK commands.

Each of these methods is discussed in the following sections.

AutoCommit Transactions

AutoCommit transactions are the default mode of behavior for SQL Server. Each Transact-SQL command issued commits or undoes its work at the end of its execution. Each SQL statement is considered to be its own transaction, with begin and end control points implied.

```
[implied begin transaction]
UPDATE account
SET balance = balance + 1000
WHERE account_no = "123456789"
[implied commit or rollback transaction]
```

If there is an error within the execution of the statement, the action is undone (rolled back); if there were no errors, the action is completed and the changes are saved.

Later in this chapter, we will see how AutoCommit works if the statement being executed causes a trigger or multiple triggers to fire, as well as when it is the execution of a stored procedure.

Transactions and Batches

The failure of a batch can appear to generate the same behavior as that of a transaction. It is, however, quite different—the difference coming from the sequence of actions with which the commands are executed. Before a batch is executed, it is first compiled. If a compilation error occurs anywhere in the batch, the whole batch is considered suspect, is not compiled, and is not executed. Execution then continues with the next batch. Consider the following example:

```
1:  CREATE TABLE testable ( column1 INT PRIMARY KEY, column2 INT )
2:  go
3:  INSERT INTO testable ( column1, column2 ) VALUES ( 1, 1 )
4:  INSRET INTO testable ( column1, column2 ) VALUES ( 2, 2 )
```

```
 5:  go
 6:  INSERT INTO testable ( column1, column2 ) VALUES ( 1, 3 )
 7:  INSERT INTO testable ( column1, column2 ) VALUES ( 3, 4 )
 8:  INSERT INTO testable ( column1, column2 ) VALUES ( 3, 5 )
 9:  INSERT INTO testable ( column1, column2 ) VALUES ( 4, 6 )
10:  go
11:  SELECT * FROM testable
12:  go
```

When you run this, you will get two errors: a syntax error caused by the misspelling of
INSERT in line 4, and a constraint violation caused by the attempt to add a second 3 value
in line 8. Even though the very first INSERT statement is valid, it is in the same batch as
the line with the syntax error. Therefore, it is never executed, leaving the second batch to
finish without a primary key constraint violation for the value 1. The first insert of a
value 3 succeeds, but the second generates an error with a primary key constraint violation. The second batch, however, *is* executed with the following results:

column1	column2
1	3
3	4
4	6

A new feature in SQL Server 7.0 is *delayed name resolution*. This is the moving of the
verification of an object's name from the time of compilation to the time of execution.
Consider the following code:

```
1:  CREATE TABLE testable ( column1 INT PRIMARY KEY, column2 INT )
2:  go
3:  INSERT INTO testable ( column1, column2 ) VALUES ( 1, 3 )
4:  INSERT INTO testble ( column1, column2 ) VALUES ( 2, 4 )
5:  INSERT INTO testable ( column1, column2 ) VALUES ( 3, 5 )
6:  INSERT INTO testable ( column1, column2 ) VALUES ( 4, 6 )
7:  go
8:  SELECT * FROM testable
9:  go
```

You might expect the entire batch to fail because of the error on the fourth line, right?
Actually, because of delayed name resolution, the first line of the batch will still be executed and committed. The remainder of the batch is not executed.

> **NOTE**
>
> Delayed name resolution results in a change in behavior from previous versions
> of SQL Server (which would not execute the entire batch). Running the preced-
> ing code under SQL Server 6.5 gives you an empty table.

The delayed name resolution feature makes it much easier to create stored procedures that operate on objects that do not exist at the time of creation, but are there at runtime. For example, populating a temporary table with results for the stored procedure to operate on used to require the creation of the temporary table before the procedure would create. This is no longer a burdensome requirement.

User-Defined Transactions

To have complete control of a transaction, you need to code user-defined transactions. Any user can make use of the transaction control statements; no special privileges are required.

To start a transaction, you use the command `BEGIN TRAN`, which optionally takes a name. This name is *completely* meaningless in all versions of Microsoft SQL Server.

```
BEGIN TRAN[SACTION] [transaction_name]
```

A transaction can then be completed successfully with either `COMMIT TRAN` or `COMMIT [WORK]`, or can be undone using either `ROLLBACK TRAN` or `ROLLBACK [WORK]`.

> **TIP**
>
> `COMMIT [WORK]` and `ROLLBACK [WORK]` are very similar to the pre-7.0 `COMMIT TRAN` and `ROLLBACK TRAN` commands, except that they do not operate against transaction names. The advantage of the SQL Server 7.0 syntax `COMMIT [WORK]` and `ROLLBACK [WORK]` is that they use SQL-92–compatible syntax.

The `COMMIT` statement marks the successful conclusion of the transaction. This statement can be coded as `COMMIT`, `COMMIT WORK`, or `COMMIT TRAN`, it makes no difference—other than the first two versions are SQL-92 standard.

The `ROLLBACK` statement unconditionally undoes all work done within the transaction. This statement can also be coded as `ROLLBACK`, `ROLLBACK WORK`, or `ROLLBACK TRAN`. The only difference is when you use savepoints, which require the use of `ROLLBACK TRAN` to a named transaction point.

Certain commands *cannot* be specified within a user-defined transaction. In most cases, because of their long-running nature, you would not want them to be user specified. Here are the commands you cannot specify in a user-defined transaction:

ALTER DATABASE	CREATE DATABASE	DROP DATABASE
BACKUP DATABASE	RESTORE DATABASE	RECONFIGURE
BACKUP LOG	RESTORE LOG	UPDATE STATISTICS

Savepoints

A *savepoint* is a point within the transaction you want to mark—with an eye to possibly undoing a portion of (but not the entire) transaction. You must use the SQL Server-specific transaction management commands that were available before version 7.0 and are the only commands that allow you to name a point within the transaction and then recover back to it. The following code illustrates the differences between these two types of syntax:

SQL-92 Syntax	*SQL Server-Specific Syntax*
BEGIN TRAN mywork	BEGIN TRAN mywork
UPDATE table1...	UPDATE table1...
SAVE TRAN savepoint1	SAVE TRAN savepoint1
INSERT INTO table2...	INSERT INTO table2...
DELETE table3...	DELETE table3...
IF @@error = -1	IF @@error = -1
ROLLBACK WORK	ROLLBACK TRAN savepoint1
COMMIT WORK	COMMIT TRAN

Note the difference between the SQL-92 syntax on the left and the SQL Server-specific syntax on the right. The SQL-92 syntax will do what you told it to, not what you might have intended: When you reach the ROLLBACK WORK command, the *entire* transaction is undone, rather than undoing only to the point marked by the savepoint.

When SQL Server encounters a SAVE TRAN statement, it marks that fact within the transaction log for recovery purposes. As we will see in a later section, savepoints are very different from nested transactions. They behave differently and produce different outcomes.

Implicit Transactions

Implicit transactions for a connection are enabled by issuing the IMPLICIT_TRANSACTIONS statement. The syntax is as follows:

```
SET IMPLICIT_TRANSACTIONS {ON ¦ OFF}
```

When turned on, transactions are implicitly started, if not already in progress, whenever any of the following commands are executed:

ALTER TABLE	CREATE	DELETE
DROP	FETCH	GRANT
INSERT	OPEN	REVOKE
SELECT	TRUNCATE TABLE	UPDATE

Note that neither the `ALTER VIEW` nor `ALTER PROCEDURE` statement starts an implicit transaction.

Implicit transactions must be explicitly completed by issuing a `COMMIT` or `ROLLBACK`, and a new transaction is started again on the execution of any of the preceding commands. If you plan on using implicit transactions, the main thing to be aware of is that locks are held until you explicitly commit the transaction. This can cause problems with concurrency and the ability of the system to back up the transaction log.

In "Transactions and Triggers," later in this chapter, you will see how implicit transactions affect the `@@trancount` variable.

Nested Transactions

The `@@trancount` connection variable allows SQL Server to monitor what type of commands are happening within the transaction. For example, what would SQL Server do when encountering the following transaction (which produces an error)?

```
BEGIN TRAN
   DELETE FROM authors
   WHERE au_id = "100-000-000"
```

The `@@trancount` indicates a value of 1 (transaction open and in progress). This value indicates to SQL Server that it should not clean up and undo the deletion action. The deletion occurs only when a `COMMIT` or `ROLLBACK` is explicitly executed.

Although there is nothing to prevent you from coding a `BEGIN TRAN` within another `BEGIN TRAN`, there is no benefit from doing so, but such cases might occur. In fact, if you nest transactions in this manner, you must execute a `COMMIT` for each `BEGIN TRAN`. This is because SQL Server modifies the `@@trancount` with each transaction statement and considers the transaction finished only when the count returns to `0`. Table 22.1 shows the effects that transaction statements have on `@@trancount`.

TABLE 22.1   TRANSACTION STATEMENTS EFFECTS ON `@@trancount`

Statement	*Effect on* `@@trancount`
`BEGIN TRAN`	+1
`COMMIT`	-1
`ROLLBACK`	Sets to 0
`SAVE TRAN` *savepoint*	No effect
`ROLLBACK TRAN` *savepoint*	No effect

The following points address some issues brought up by the information in the table:

- The ROLLBACK pays no attention to what the nesting level currently is, causing the entire transaction to be undone and the nesting level to be reset to 0.

- Because the BEGIN TRAN statement increments @@trancount, each BEGIN TRAN statement must be paired with a COMMIT for the transaction to successfully complete.

We will use some sample code to show the values of @@trancount as the transaction progresses. In this first example, we have a simple explicit transaction with a nested BEGIN TRAN.

SQL Statements	@@trancount *Value*
SELECT "Starting....."	0
BEGIN TRAN	1
DELETE FROM table1	1
BEGIN TRAN	2
INSERT INTO table2	2
COMMIT	1
UPDATE table3	1
COMMIT	0

In this next example, we have turned IMPLICIT TRANSACTIONS ON to see what effect this has the value of @@trancount.

SQL Statements	@@trancount *Value*
SET IMPLICIT_TRANSACTIONS ON	0
go	0
INSERT INTO table1	1
UPDATE table2	1
COMMIT	0
go	
BEGIN TRAN	1
DELETE FROM table1	1
COMMIT	0
go	
DROP TABLE table1	1
COMMIT	0

As you can see in this second example, if a transaction is already started and a statement occurs that would have caused a transaction to start, SQL Server "knows" that a transaction is already in progress thanks to the @@trancount variable and does not nest down a level, which would then have required a second COMMIT to actually finish the transaction!

Transactions and Triggers

A *trigger* is the last point within a transaction at which a determination of failure can be made. So the *only* transaction statement you should *ever* code within a trigger is a ROLLBACK statement. The trigger will already be operating within the context of a transaction whether it is an explicit BEGIN TRAN or is implied by the statement executing.

To show the relationship between a trigger and the transaction, we will use the following trigger code:

```
use pubs
go
CREATE TRIGGER tD_employee ON employee
FOR DELETE
AS
    DECLARE @msg VARCHAR(255)

    SELECT @msg = 'Trancount in trigger = ' + CONVERT(VARCHAR(2),
    ➥@@trancount)

    PRINT @msg

    ROLLBACK TRAN
go
```

The purpose of the trigger is to simply show the state of the @@trancount within the trigger as the deletion is taking place.

If we now execute code for an implied and an explicit transaction, we can see the values of @@trancount and the behavior of the batch. First, here's the implied transaction:

```
DECLARE @msg VARCHAR(255)
SELECT @msg = 'Trancount before delete = ' + CONVERT(VARCHAR(2),
@@trancount)
PRINT @msg
DELETE FROM employee WHERE emp_id = 'PMA42628M'
SELECT "Trancount after delete = " + CONVERT( VARCHAR(2), @@trancount)
go
```

The results of this are as follows:

```
Trancount before delete = 0
Trancount in trigger = 1
```

As you will notice in this and the next example, the batch is finished by the trigger rolling back the transaction. The SELECT statement is *not* executed. Because no transaction starts until the DELETE statement executes, the first value of @@trancount indicates this with a value of 0. Within the trigger, the transaction count has a value of 1; we are now inside the implied transaction caused by the DELETE. The ROLLBACK within the trigger resets this value to 0—as would the successful completion of a trigger.

Now let's see what happens within an explicit transaction:

```
BEGIN TRAN
    DECLARE @msg VARCHAR(255)
    SELECT @msg = 'Trancount before delete = ' +
    ➡CONVERT(VARCHAR(2), @@trancount)
    PRINT @msg
    DELETE FROM employee WHERE emp_id = 'PMA42628M'
    SELECT @msg = "Trancount after delete = " +
    ➡CONVERT( VARCHAR(2), @@trancount)
    PRINT @msg
ROLLBACK TRAN
SELECT @msg = "Trancount after tran = " +
➡CONVERT( VARCHAR(2), @@trancount)
PRINT @msg
go
```

This code gives the following results:

```
Trancount before delete = 1
Trancount in trigger = 2
```

Again, the batch and transaction are finished by the trigger rolling back; the following SELECT, PRINT, and ROLLBACK statements are not executed. The BEGIN TRAN causes the transaction count to increase by 1, and then the DELETE increments it again. This value remains for the duration of that statement and the trigger it causes to fire.

If we remove the ROLLBACK TRAN statement from the trigger and execute the previous code, we will get these results:

```
Trancount before delete = 1
Trancount in trigger = 2
Trancount after delete = 1
Trancount after tran = 0
```

It is important to understand that, by themselves, data modification statements (insert, delete, and update operations) do not affect the @@trancount variable. Instead, the execution of triggers caused by the modification statement is what will affect @@trancount.

Transactions and Stored Procedures

Stored procedures are an excellent place to contain all the statements for a transaction. The client calls the stored procedure, which then runs locally on the server (no network traffic to slow things down). The procedure starts the transaction, carries out the data modifications, completes the transaction, and returns the status or data to the client! Stored procedures have the added benefit that if you need to fix, fine tune, or expand the duties of the transaction, you can do it all at one time in one central location.

This might seem to be the ideal situation, but it does require you to think about how transactions work and to code for them appropriately. Consider what happens when one stored procedure calls another, and they both do their own transaction management. Obviously, they now need to work in concert. If the called stored procedure has to stop the transaction, how can it do this correctly?

To explain the issues involved, we will use the following stored procedure. The procedure takes a single integer argument, which it then attempts to place in a table (testable). All data entry attempts—whether successful or not—are logged to a second table (auditlog). The code for the stored procedure is as follows:

```
CREATE PROCEDURE trantest @arg INT
AS
BEGIN TRAN
    IF EXISTS( SELECT * FROM testable WHERE col1 = @arg )
    BEGIN
        RAISERROR ('Value %d already exists!', 16, -1, @arg)
        ROLLBACK TRANSACTION
    END
    ELSE
    BEGIN
        INSERT INTO testable (col1) VALUES (@arg)
        COMMIT TRAN
    END

INSERT INTO auditlog (who, valuentered) VALUES (USER_NAME(), @arg)
```

Now let's see what happens if we call this stored procedure in the following way and check the values of the two tables:

```
EXEC trantest 1
EXEC trantest 2
SELECT * FROM testable
SELECT valuentered FROM auditlog
go
```

The execution of this code gives the following results:

```
col1
- - - - - - - - - - -
1
2


valuentered
- - - - - - - - - - -
1
2
```

These would be the results we would expect. We can further test the operation of the stored procedure by running the same code a second time. `Testable` would still only have two rows, but the `auditlog` will now contain four rows: additional rows for the values 1 and 2 will have been added during the second execution of the script. This happens because the stored procedure issues a rollback after the error is raised.

Now what happens when we execute the calls from within a transaction?

```
BEGIN TRAN
EXEC trantest 3
EXEC trantest 1
EXEC trantest 4
COMMIT TRAN
SELECT * FROM testable
SELECT valuentered FROM auditlog
go
```

The execution of this code gives the following results:

```
Server: Msg 50000, Level 16, State 42000
Value 1 already exists!
Server: Msg 266, Level 16, State 25000, Procedure trantest, Line 14
Transaction count after EXECUTE indicates that a COMMIT or
                              ROLLBACK TRAN is missing.
Previous count = 1, Current count = 0.
Server: Msg 3902, Level 16, State 25000
The commit transaction request has no corresponding BEGIN TRANSACTION.
col1
- - - - - - - - - - -
1
2
4


valuentered
- - - - - - - - - - -
1
2
1
4
```

Hmmm, looks like a number of problems are occurring now! For starters, we get back a message telling us that the transaction nesting level got messed up. More seriously, the results show that the value 4 made it into the table anyway, and that the audit table picked up the 1 and the 4 but lost the fact that we tried to insert a value of 3. What happened?

Let's take this one step at a time. First, we start the transaction and execute trantest with the value 3. The stored procedure starts its own transaction, adds the value to testable, commits that, and then adds a row to the auditlog. Next, we execute the procedure with the value 1; this value already exists within the table, so the procedure raises an error and rolls back the transaction. Remember that a ROLLBACK undoes work to the outer most BEGIN TRAN—that means the start of the batch. So what gets rolled back? The whole of the call to trantest for the value 3; the insert into testable and auditlog. The auditlog entry for this value of 1 *is* saved because it is a standalone statement now. We now receive the error regarding the change in the transaction nesting level because a transaction should leave the state of a governing transaction in the same way it was entered. Next, we call trantest with the value 4, an operation that completes successfully. Finally, we try to commit the transaction; because none is currently in operation, we receive the last error regarding a mismatch between BEGIN TRAN and COMMIT TRAN.

So what is the correct way to code this and other stored procedures? The crux of the problem is identifying within the stored procedure that it is being called from within a transaction. We do this by checking the current value of @@trancount and determining what needs to be done:

```
DECLARE @trancount INT
/* Capture the value of the transaction nesting level at the start */
SELECT @trancount = @@trancount
IF (@trancount = 0)
   BEGIN TRAN mytran
ELSE
   SAVE TRAN mytran
 .
 .
 .
/* This is how we would trap an error. We rollback either to our
   own BEGIN TRAN or we rollback to the savepoint. We return an
   error code to the caller to indicate an internal failure.
   How the caller handles the transaction is up to the caller.*/
IF (@@error <> 0)
BEGIN
   ROLLBACK TRAN mytran
   RETURN —1969
END
 .
 .
```

```
/* Once we reach the end of the code, we need to pair the BEGIN TRAN
    if we issued it with a COMMIT TRAN. If we executed the SAVE TRAN
    instead, we have nothing else to do...end of game! */
IF (@trancount = 0)
    COMMIT TRAN

RETURN 0
```

Notice that we capture the state of the transaction nesting at the very start of the code, in case calls are made to other procedures that also affect the value of @@trancount. If a transaction is not already in progress, we start one. If a transaction is in progress, we just make a savepoint we can get back to. On an error, the ROLLBACK will return the @@trancount to the value it had when the procedure was first called.

These same concepts should be applied to the code that calls the stored procedures. You should check the return value of the stored procedure and determine whether the whole batch should be failed, or whether that one call is of little importance to the overall outcome.

Coding Effective Transactions

Transactions have a detrimental affect on concurrency of access to data. SQL Server can hold a number of resources while the transaction is open; modified rows have exclusive locks, and other locks may also be held. To reduce locking contention over resources, transactions should be kept as short and effective as possible. During development, you may not even notice that there is a problem; it may become noticeable only after the system load is increased. Following are some guidelines to consider when coding transactions:

- Do not return result sets within a transaction. Doing so prolongs the transaction unnecessarily. Perform all data retrieval and analysis outside the transaction.
- The principal crime with transaction coding is to prompt the user for a response. I have seen even the best programmers miss this one in magazine listings. On the failure of a transaction, you must roll back before putting up a message box telling the user that a problem occurred.
- Keep the start and end of a transaction together in the same batch—alternatively, use a stored procedure for the operation.
- Keep the transaction short. Start the transaction at the point you need to do the modifications. Do any preliminary work beforehand.
- Make careful use of different locking schemes and transaction isolation levels.

- Carry out optimistic locking rather than using actual resource locks. Optimistic locking makes use of the WHERE clause to update the data rather than holding onto a page or table lock. Chapter 21, "Using Transact-SQL in SQL Server 7.0," and Chapter 30, "Locking and Performance," both cover optimistic locking.

- Collect multiple transactions into one transaction, if appropriate. This may seem to go against some of the other suggestions, but it reduces the amount of work SQL Server has to do to start and finish transactions.

Long-Running Transactions

As we have already seen, transaction information is recorded in each database's transaction log. However, this can be a cause of consternation to the system administrator attempting to back up the transaction log. Only the inactive portion of the log can be truncated during this operation. The inactive portion is defined by the oldest still-active transaction.

To find the oldest active transaction in a database, you can use the DBCC OPENTRAN command:

```
DBCC OPENTRAN [('DatabaseName' ¦ DatabaseId)]
[WITH TABLERESULTS [, NO_INFOMSGS]]
```

The TABLERESULTS option allows you to load the results into a table defined as follows:

```
CREATE TABLE #opentran_results
( result_label VARCHAR(30), result_value VARCHAR(46))
```

Now you can identify which transactions are potential problems based on their longevity. If you capture the process information at the same time using sp_who, you can identify who or what application is causing the longest running transaction(s). Using this information, you can have a quiet word with the offender if the query is *ad-hoc* or with the application developers if it is a custom application. The best-behaved transaction is a concise transaction.

Bound Connections

As already mentioned in this chapter, transactions are important for maintaining data consistency across data modification statements, rows, tables, and—as you will see in the "Distributed Transactions" section—even servers. Transactions do, however, interfere with concurrent access by users to the objects being modified because of the exclusive locks being held until the end of the transaction. If you have excessively long data modification transactions that interfere with other users' query capabilities, you can use tricks like the NOLOCK query hint. If, however, you need to hold onto exclusive locks and have some sort of cooperative processing occurring, bound connections may be an alternative to consider. Here are some other scenarios in which bound connections can be useful:

- Multithreading batch operations—If operations against a table or tables are long running and can be logically broken down into distinct independent operations, these can be carried out through multiple connections running in parallel.

- Multiconnected applications—An application may present multiple views or windows of information. Modifications can be carried out through one connection; to allow continued and updated browsing of the information, additional connections can be bound together to see the data without being blocked.

These examples illustrate the two types of bound connections: local and distributed. *Local bound connections* are connections within one server that are bound into a single transaction space. *Distributed bound connections* make use of the Microsoft Distributed Transaction Coordinator (described in the section "The Distributed Transaction Coordinator (MS DTC)") to the same transaction space that is shared across connections from more than one server.

Using bind tokens, multiple connections can be bound to share a single transaction lock space. This lasts until the completion of the transaction—either by COMMIT or ROLLBACK.

There is one important downside to bound connections: sequential processing. Only one connection out of all the connections bound together can actually be doing any work. This means that during a result set retrieval, the entire result set must be retrieved or the command canceled before any other work can be done by a participating connection. Any attempt to work while such is going on results in an error that should be trapped so that you can resubmit the work after some time interval.

How to Bind Connections

Binding connections together is actually very simple and requires the acquisition of a token that identifies the transaction space with which you want to join.

A bind token is acquired using the stored procedure sp_getbindtoken. This stored procedure creates a bound connection context and returns the unique identifier for this through an output argument:

```
sp_getbindtoken TokenVariable OUTPUT [, @for_xp_flag]
```

The *TokenVariable* is a variable defined as a varchar(255) and is used to receive the bind token from the stored procedure. If you pass the @for_xp_flag argument a 1, the stored procedure will create a bind token that can be used by extended stored procedures to call back into SQL Server.

> **NOTE**
>
> Only the owner of a connection can gain the bind token for it.

After you have the bind token, you have to pass it to the intended co-client, who then uses a different stored procedure, sp_bindsession, to participate in your transaction context:

```
sp_bindsession [TokenVariable | NULL]
```

The *TokenVariable* is the value created in the previous step. The NULL value is used to unbind a connection from another. You can also unbind a connection by executing sp_bindsession without any arguments.

> **CAUTION**
>
> In this author's experience, attempting to unbind from a connection causes all the involved connections to hang. I recommend that once a connection is bound to another, you should wait until the completion of the transaction.

To illustrate the use of these procedures together, consider the following code:

```
DECLARE @token VARCHAR(255)
EXECUTE sp_getbindtoken @token OUTPUT
```

This results in the following value for @token:

```
NQ9---5----.Q>Z4YC:T>1F:N-1-288TH
```

Each call to sp_getbindtoken results in a different value. Depending on who the intended recipient is, you somehow communicate this value to him, which he then uses in the call:

```
EXEC sp_bindsession 'NQ9---5----.Q>Z4YC:T>1F:N-1-288TH'
```

22

TRANSACTION
MANAGEMENT

> **CAUTION**
>
> Be careful if you have the option REMOTE_PROC_TRANSACTIONS turned on for the transaction and you execute a remote stored procedure; the bind token is changed to a distributed token distributed identification number. This new token is what must be sent to connections that want to join; it is *not* the token you might have obtained before the remote procedure call.

Binding Multiple Applications

If you bind connections across applications, you have to find a way of communicating the bind token so that it can be used with sp_bindsession. SQL Server does not provide a simple solution to this problem; you can consider mechanisms like these:

- Using an IPC such as Remote Procedure Calls (RPC), Dynamic Data Exchange (DDE), or Net-DDE.
- Using a file on a server.
- Coordinate through a SQL Server table. You might also make a stored procedure manage the assignment of the token to the requesting applications.
- If the applications are local, you might be able to pass the token through global memory, or directly with a function call.

Distributed Transactions

With the increasing interest and implementation of distributed systems, there is a need to access and modify distributed data. Consider a system in which customer information is stored and maintained within one server, and product information is kept on another. When a customer purchases an item, we have to start a transaction that records the order on the server with the customer information and that also decrements the stock level on the product server. This transaction must be one logical transaction, yet it is physically spread across two servers. We need a way to ensure that the distributed transaction operates in the same way a local transaction does, and that it adheres to the same ACID properties of a transaction.

Any approach we choose is going to be based around what is known as the *two-phase commit protocol*.

Two-Phase Commit Protocol

Distributed transactions require some extra thought and control to implement. The service providing the two-phase commit functionality is based around one SQL Server which is known as the *commit server*. This server is in charge of maintaining the current state of the transaction and is used by the servers to determine the overall success or failure of the transaction.

The transaction goes through the following steps:

1. The transaction is started and identifies itself to the commit server.
2. Data modification statements are issued against the servers involved.
3. The commit server collects information about each server and enlists them into the transaction.
4. The transaction indicates that it wants to finish the transaction by issuing a PREPARE TRANSACTION statement.
5. Phase One: During the first phase of the commit, all servers communicate to the commit server that they are ready to commit.
6. Phase Two: A COMMIT TRANSACTION is issued to all servers after a consensus on preparedness is reached.

If an error occurs between the two phases, all servers communicate with the commit server to see whether the transaction is being committed or canceled. Here is a list of some of the errors that can occur between Phase One and Phase Two:

- One of the enlisted servers goes down—The request to COMMIT on that server fails because the server cannot be reached, but the request to carry out the commit may have succeeded. The downed server uses *probe* to identify what action it should take.
- Commit server becomes unavailable—The transaction must be rolled back. The application executes a ROLLBACK TRANSACTION to each enlisted server.
- An enlisted server and commit server are lost—The application executes a ROLLBACK TRANSACTION against all still-active servers. The enlisted server that went down communicates with the commit server, which is not aware that the transaction completed, and informs the enlisted server to roll back.

If one of the enlisted SQL Servers is unable to communicate with the commit server, the database involved is marked as suspect. When the commit server is "visible" again, the affected server should be restarted so that the database and the in-doubt transaction can be recovered.

22

TRANSACTION
MANAGEMENT

The commit server is contacted only once when such failures occur; the commit server returns the state of the transaction as it was last updated by the controlling application.

Thankfully, the really hard work has been done for us by Microsoft, which implemented the two-phase commit service for us. All we have to do is understand how to interact with it to achieve the desired results. We can do this by making use of the two-phase commit functions available in either the DB-Library dynamic link library or the Microsoft DTC service.

The Distributed Transaction Coordinator (MS DTC)

The Microsoft Distributed Transaction Coordinator (DTC) service is installed along with the SQL Server and SQL Agent. Within your network, you can be running any number of Microsoft DTC services, one on each SQL Server if you want. From the Control Panel of the client, you can control which Microsoft DTC server is used. By making use of multiple DTC servers, you can spread the work load.

The MS DTC is the commit server for distributed transactions and makes use of a log file to record the outcome of all transactions that have made use of its service.

THE IMPORTANCE OF MSDTC.LOG!

You should never modify or delete the MSDTC.LOG file. If you delete this file, nothing is going to work.

Setup

During the setup of the service (which is done as part of the server installation), the DTC DLLs and executables are copied to the \BINN subdirectory under the SQL root. The DTC log file is installed in the \DATA directory under the SQL root.

CAUTION

Before you apply any service packs or upgrades, make sure that all in-doubt transactions are resolved. Microsoft reserves the right to change the format of the DTC log file between versions.

Once you have started the DTC service, you can try a simple test to verify that everything is working as it should.

Open the DTC Services Statistics window and watch the Current/Active counter as you bring up a query window and execute BEGIN DISTRIBUTED TRAN. When you see the counter increment, issue a ROLLBACK; the counter should return to 0.

How To

Thankfully, we need not concern ourselves with the underlying protocols and functions being called to make a distributed transaction happen. As developers, we just change the way we code very subtly by using BEGIN DISTRIBUTED TRAN instead of the more usual BEGIN TRAN.

On the execution of BEGIN DISTRIBUTED TRAN, the transaction is enlisted with the MS DTC. This action makes us the transaction originator and controller of the COMMIT or ROLLBACK request to the DTC, which then manages the completion of the transaction across the servers involved.

SQL Servers are enlisted into our transaction in one of the following ways:

- A remote stored procedure call is made against a server.
- We provide a bind token to our distributed transaction.
- A distributed query is executed.

In previous versions of SQL Server, remote stored procedures like this one were the only way to carry out distributed transactions:

```
USE pubs
GO
BEGIN DISTRIBUTED TRANSACTION

UPDATE sales
SET qty = qty + 10000
WHERE au_id = 'GAL-06-1269'

EXECUTE remotesrv.pubs..update_sales_qty 'GAL-06-1269', 10000

COMMIT TRAN
GO
```

22

TRANSACTION MANAGEMENT

> **NOTE**
>
> To have your remote stored procedures always execute within the context of a distributed transaction, you can use SET REMOTE_PROC_TRANSACTIONS ON, which is set at the connection level, or you can configure it at the server level using sp_configure 'remote proc trans', '1'.

When the target OLE DB data source of a distributed query supports ItransactionLocal, the transaction is *automatically* elevated to a distributed transaction. If, however, the data source does not support ItransactionLocal, only queries can be carried out; the data source is considered read-only. See Chapter 26, "Advanced Query Processing," for more information about distributed queries.

> **NOTE**
>
> After you have set up linked servers, you can undertake distributed transactions without being restricted to executing just remote stored procedures.

Troubleshooting

Obviously, because we have made our transaction more complicated and have involved more components (servers, the network, and so on), things are going to go wrong—later rather than sooner, we hope.

The simplest way to determine whether your server can communicate with a commit server is to open a query window and execute BEGIN DISTRIBUTED TRANSACTION. If the service cannot be found, you will get a service is unavailable error.

If a commit server is proving to be unreliable for certain clients, perhaps because of transitory network problems, you may want to install the DTC Client utility on those clients and install the DTC service on a closer server. The DTC Client allows you to specify a specific DTC service and network protocol to be used by distributed transactions.

The Microsoft DTC Admin Console provides you with a comprehensive set of statistics and information on the DTC service running on the server. This tool gives you access to five areas:

- General—Version information, coordinator name, and the ability to start and stop the DTC service.

- Transactions—The currently active transactions and their state. From this window, you can also resolve a transaction by forcing a commit, abort, or forget.

- Trace—This area has log information from the DTC service. The amount of tracing is set on the Advanced tab.

- Statistics—This area shows the current number of active and in-doubt transactions, together with historical information on the total number committed, aborted, and so on.

- Advanced—From this tab, you can control the trace amount, the display refresh rate, and the size and location of the DTC log file.

The DTC Admin Console is your principal tool in debugging distributedtransactions.

Summary

A transaction is a Logical Unit of Work (LUW) and a unit of recovery. The successful control of transactions is of the utmost importance to the correct modification of related information. In this chapter, we learned how to control transactions, examined different management schemes, and determined how to correctly code transactions within triggers and stored procedures. We have discussed methods of optimizing transactions and how to carry out distributed transactions using the Microsoft DTC service.

22

TRANSACTION
MANAGEMENT

Performance and Tuning

Part VI

IN THIS PART

Database Design and Performance

by Vipul Minocha

CHAPTER 23

Various factors contribute to the optimal performance of an application. Some of these factors include logical design (rules of normalization), physical design (denormalization, indexes, and so on), choice of hardware (SMP servers), network bandwidth (LAN versus WAN), client and server configuration (memory, CPU, and so on), data access techniques (ODBC, ADO, and so on), and application architecture (two-tier versus n-tier). This chapter will help you understand some of the key application design issues that will ensure that you have a reliable and high-performance application.

Logical Database Design Issues

A good database design is fundamental to the success of any application. Database design primarily consists of two parts: logical design and physical design. Logical database design requires following certain sets of rules called rules of normalization. As a result of normalization, you create a data model that's usually, but not necessarily, translated into a physical data model. A logical database design does not depend on the relational database you intend to use. On the other hand, a physical data model makes extensive use of the features of the underlying database engine to yield optimal performance for the application.

Normalization Conditions

Any database designer must address two fundamental issues:

- Storing data on the disk that is most efficient in disk space usage—resulting in low cost
- Fetching and saving data with the fastest response time—resulting in high performance

Ideally, you want to implement a system with low cost and high performance. Unfortunately, one goal is usually achieved at the expense of the other. Normalization is a technique of spreading data across many tables so that relevant information is kept together based on certain guidelines. Normalization results in controlled redundancy of data and therefore provides good balance between disk space usage and performance.

Normalization Forms

There are six rules of normalization. Here, I discuss the first three because most database designers follow only the first three rules.

The first rule of normalization requires removing repeating data values and specifies that no two rows can be identical in a database. This means that each entity must have a primary key (one or more columns of the table), which uniquely identifies a row in the table.

An entity is in the second normal form if it conforms to the first normal form and all nonkey attributes of the table are fully dependent on the entire primary key. If the primary key consists of multiple columns, then nonkey columns should depend on the entire key and not just on the subset of the key.

An entity is in the third normal form if it already conforms to the first two normal forms and none of nonkey attributes are dependent on any other nonkey attributes. All such attributes should be removed from the table. For example, suppose there are three columns in the emp table (with a primary key empid): salary, bonus, and total_salary, where total_salary = salary + bonus. Existence of the total_salary column in the table violates the third normal form because a nonkey attribute (total_salary) is dependent on two other nonkey attributes (salary and bonus). Therefore, to conform to the third rule of normalization, you must remove the total_salary column from the emp table.

Benefits of Normalization

The following are the major advantages of normalization:

- Because information is logically kept together, normalization provides a better overall understanding of the system.

- Because of controlled redundancy of data, normalization can result in substantial cost savings in terms of disk space usage.

- Because tables are smaller with normalization, index creation and data sorts are much faster.

- SQL Server allows only one clustered index per table. A clustered index usually provides the fastest search capability. Using normalization rules, you typically have multiple smaller tables; therefore, you can create more clustered indexes, resulting in better performance.

- With less redundant data, it is easier to maintain referential integrity for the system.

- Normalization also results in narrower tables. Because you can store more rows per page, more rows can be read and cached for each I/O performed on the table. This results in better I/O performance.

Drawbacks of Normalization

The main goal of normalization is to reduce redundancy in the system. As a result of normalization, data is stored in multiple tables. To retrieve or modify information, you usually have to establish joins across multiple tables. Joins are expensive from an I/O standpoint. Multitable joins can have an adverse impact on the performance of the system. In the following sections, I discuss some of the denormalization techniques that you can use to improve the performance of the system.

Denormalizing the Database

After a database has been normalized to the third form, database designers intentionally backtrack from normalization to improve the performance of the system. This technique of rolling back from normalization is called denormalization. Denormalization allows you to keep redundant data in the system, thereby reducing the number of joins to retrieve data.

> **NOTE**
>
> Denormalization is recommended where the data does not change very much, such as data warehouses, or data marts. If the data changes often, the redundancies become a problem in the system from a data integrity standpoint.

Denormalization Guidelines

When should you decide to denormalize a database? Consider the following points first:

- Be sure you have a good overall understanding of the logical design of the system. This knowledge helps in determining how other parts of the application are going to be affected when you change one part of the system.
- Don't make an attempt to denormalize the entire database at once. Instead, focus on the specific areas and queries that are accessed more frequently and are suffering from performance problems.
- Understand the types of transactions and the volume of data associated with specific areas of the application having performance problems. You can resolve many such issues by tuning the queries without denormalizing the tables.
- Determine whether you need virtual (contrived) columns. Virtual columns can be computed from other columns of the table.
- Understand data integrity issues. With more redundant data in the system, maintaining data integrity is more difficult and data modifications may be slower.
- Understand storage techniques for the data. Using RAID and SQL Server filegroups can also help improve performance without denormalizing the database tables.
- Determine the frequency at which data might change. If the data is changing too often, the cost of maintaining referential integrity might outweigh the benefits provided by redundant data.

> **TIP**
>
> If you are experiencing severe performance problems, denormalization should not be the first step you take to rectify the problem. Identify specific issues causing performance problems. Usually, you'll discover factors such as poorly written queries or poorly configured hardware or SQL Server. You should try to fix such issues before taking steps to denormalize database tables.

Essential Denormalization Techniques

You can employ various methods to denormalize a database table and achieve desired performance goals. Some of the useful techniques used for denormalization are

- Keeping redundant data
- Using virtual columns
- Performing horizontal data partitioning
- Performing vertical data partitioning

Redundant Data

Joins are inherently expensive in a relational database from an I/O standpoint. Sometimes to avoid common joins, it helps to add redundancy to the table by keeping exact copies of the data in multiple tables. The following example demonstrates this point. The example shows a three-table join to get authors' names and the titles of the books written by each author:

```
select a.au_lname, a.au_fname, c.title
from authors a, titleauthor b, titles c
where a.au_id = b.au_id
and b.title_id = c.title_id
order by 1,2
```

You can improve join performance in this example by adding a title column to the titleauthor table. This will eliminate the join from the title table. The new query will look as follows:

```
select a.au_lname, a.au_fname, b.title
from authors a, titleauthor b
where a.au_id = b.au_id
order by 1,2
```

As you can see, the column title is now redundantly stored in two places—the title table and the titleauthor table. It is obvious here that with more redundant data in the system, maintaining referential integrity is more difficult. For example, if the title of the book changes in the title table, to preserve referential integrity, you must also change the title column value in titleauthor to reflect the correct value. You can use SQL Server triggers to maintain referential integrity.

> **TIP**
>
> It is usually a good idea to add redundancy for columns that are static in nature. If redundant data is dynamic in nature, data modification statements are slower in order to preserve data integrity. For the same reason, it is also important to store a redundant column with the same attributes (the datatype, length, rules, defaults, and so on) as the original column.

Virtual Columns

A number of queries calculate aggregate values derived from one or more columns of a table. Such computations can sometimes be CPU intensive and can have an adverse impact on performance if they are performed frequently. One of the techniques to handle such situations is to create an additional column that stores the computed value. Such columns are called virtual columns or contrived columns. In the earlier versions of the SQL Server, virtual columns physically existed in the table and their values were maintained through triggers or stored procedures. SQL Server 7.0 natively supports virtual columns. You can specify such columns during create table or alter table commands. The following example demonstrates the use of virtual columns:

```
Create table emp ( empid int, salary money, bonus money,
total_salary as ( salary+bonus ))
go
Insert emp (empid, salary, bonus) values 100, $150000.00, $15000
Go
Select * from emp
Go
empid        salary         bonus                  total_salary
----------   -------------  ---------------------  ----------------
100          150000.0000    15000.0000             165000.0000
```

Virtual columns are not physically stored in SQL Server tables. SQL Server internally maintains a column iscomputed in the system table syscolumns to determine whether a column is computed. The value of the virtual column is calculated at the time the query is run. Virtual columns supported by SQL Server cannot participate in joins to get values. For complex calculations that depend on columns in various tables, create a column (an actual column instead of a virtual column) in the table and use stored procedures or triggers to maintain its value.

Horizontal Data Partitioning

As tables grow larger (in terms of the number of rows) in a database, data access time also tends to increase. Queries that access tables with a large number of rows tend to get slower because of the large amount of data being scanned. Even when you have proper indexes on such tables, access time might still be unacceptable because of the time taken by the optimizer to navigate through the B-tree itself to locate the correct pointers to the data pages. The solution is splitting the table into multiple tables such that each resultant table has the same table structure as the original one but stores a different set of data. Figure 23.1 shows a billing table with 9 million records. You can split this table into 12 monthly tables (each with an identical table structure) to store billing records for each month.

FIGURE 23.1

Horizontal partitioning of data.

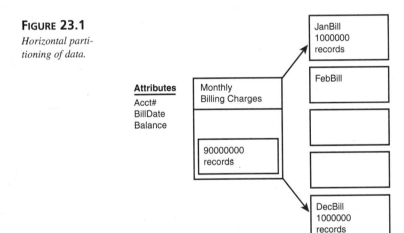

You should carefully weigh the options when performing horizontal splitting. Queries become more complex. Also, queries that are self-referencing do not benefit much from horizontal partitioning. For example, the business logic might dictate that each time you add a new billing record to the billing table, you need to check any outstanding account balance for any previous billing dates. In such cases, before you do an insert in the current monthly billing table, you must check the data for all the other months to find any outstanding balance.

> **TIP**
>
> Horizontal splitting of data is useful where a subset of data might see more activity than the rest of the data. For example, in a healthcare provider setting, 98 percent of the patients are inpatients and only 2 percent are outpatients. In spite of the small percentage involved, the system for outpatient records sees a lot of activity. In this scenario, it makes sense to split the patient table into two tables, one for the inpatients and one for the outpatients.

Vertical Data Partitioning

As you know, a database in SQL Server consists of a multiple of 8KB pages and a row cannot span across multiple pages. Therefore, the total number of rows on a page depends on the width of a table. This means the wider the table, the fewer the number of rows per page. More I/Os are needed to fetch the same number of rows from a table that is wider than the other table. You can achieve significant performance gains by reducing the number of I/Os on the table. Vertical splitting is a method of reducing the width of a table by splitting the columns of a table into multiple tables. Usually, all frequently used columns are kept in one table and others are kept in the other table. This way, more records can be accommodated per page, fewer I/Os are generated, and more data can be cached into SQL Server memory. Figure 23.2 illustrates a vertically partitioned table. The frequently accessed columns of the authors table are stored in the author_primary table, whereas less frequently used table are stored in author_secondary table.

FIGURE 23.2

Vertical partitioning of data.

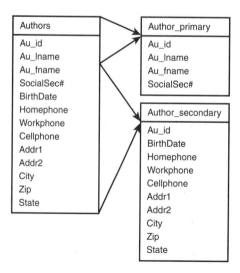

> **TIP**
>
> Make the decision to split data very carefully, especially when the system is already in production. Changing the data structure might have a system-wide impact on a large number of queries that reference the old definition of the object. In such cases, to minimize risks, SQL Server views can be effective in providing vertical partitioning of data. You can also modify data from the underlying tables through views.

Indexes and Performance

I/O is typically the slowest part of most applications. The challenge for the database designer is to build a physical data model that provides efficient data access. Creating indexes on database tables allows SQL Server to access data with a reduced number of I/Os. Defining useful indexes during the logical and physical data modeling step is crucial. The SQL Server optimizer relies heavily on index key distribution and density. The optimizer in SQL Server can use multiple indexes in a query (through index intersection) to reduce the number of I/Os to retrieve information. In the absence of indexes, the optimizer will choose to perform a table scan, which can be costly from an I/O standpoint.

Although indexes provide a means for faster access to data, they slow down data modification statements. Therefore, it is important to choose indexes carefully for a good balance between data search and data modification performance. The application environment usually governs the choice of indexes. For example, if the application is mainly OLTP with transactions requiring fast response time, creating too many indexes might have an adverse impact on performance. On the other hand, the application might be a decision support system (DSS) with few transactions doing data modifications. In that case, it makes sense to create a number of indexes on the columns that are frequently used in the queries.

23

DATABASE DESIGN AND PERFORMANCE

> **NOTE**
>
> For very large database applications where OLTP and DSS requirements conflict and compete with one another, creating an OLTP database and a separate DSS database is useful. One main challenge is to keep the data and structure in sync between the OLTP and DSS databases. You can use SQL Server replication to synchronize the databases. SQL Server replication in the past has been unstable and somewhat difficult to manage and troubleshoot. SQL Server 7.0 promises to bring more stability in replication implementation. Still, replication is a complex task, so be careful before you take this path.

The following sections explain how to evaluate useful indexes and understand index density and key distribution.

Evaluating Index Usefulness

SQL Server provides indexes for faster access to data and to enforce the uniqueness of the data in the database tables. Creating the appropriate indexes for a database is one of the most important aspects of database design. Because you can't have an unlimited number of indexes on a table, choose indexes on columns that have high selectivity. The selectivity of an index can be defined as follows:

> Selectivity ratio = [100 * (Total number of rows uniquely identified by the key)] / (Total number of rows in the table)]

If the selectivity ratio is low—that is, a large number of rows can be uniquely identified by the key—then the index is highly selective and useful to the optimizer. Based on the selectivity of data, the SQL Server optimizer decides whether to use any indexes in a query. The higher the selectivity, the faster SQL Server can get to a specific row.

As an example, let's say you are evaluating useful indexes on the authors table. Assume that most of the queries access the table either by the author's last name or by state. Because a large number of concurrent users modify data in this table, you are allowed to choose only one index—author's last name or state. Which one would you choose? Let's perform some analysis to see which one is a more useful index. First, let's determine the selectivity based on the author's last name:

```
select au_lname, Total = count(*)
from authors
group by au_lname
au_lname                              Total
------------------------              -----
Bennet                                1
Blotchet-Halls                        1
Carson                                1
DeFrance                              1
McBadden                              1
O'Leary                               1
Panteley                              1
Ringer                                2
Smith                                 1
Straight                              1
Stringer                              1
White                                 1
Yokomoto                              1
```

As you can see, all the authors except Ringer can be uniquely identified by the key.

Selectivity ratio is low for all the key values in this table. Therefore, a key on the au_lname column is highly selective and is a good candidate for an index.

Now, consider the selectivity based on the state column:

```
select state, Total = count(*)
from authors
group by state

state Total
--- ------.
CA    750
IN    100
KS    250
MD    1
MI    10
OR    51
TN    12
UT    29
```

Let's determine the selectivity ratio for the state of CA:

Selectivity ratio = (100 * 750) / 1203 = 62%

As you can see, the selectivity on the state column is poor, especially for the state of California, and therefore, state is not a good candidate for an indexed column. If the selectivity ratio for a key is less than 15 percent (the optimizer cannot discard 85 percent of the rows based on the key value), then the optimizer will choose a table scan. In such cases, performing a table scan is more efficient than scanning through the B-tree to locate data.

How do you determine the selectivity of all your indexes in your environment? You don't need to write queries as described previously. SQL Server internally stores the selectivity information of each index on a distribution page. You cannot access the distribution page directly, but you can use a few DBCC commands to determine the selectivity of a key.

The Distribution Page

As mentioned earlier, the selectivity of a key is an important factor that determines whether an index will be used in a query. SQL Server stores the selectivity and the distribution values of the key in pages pointed to by STATBLOB column on the sysindexes system table. Based on the values stored in this table, the query optimizer decides which index to use. To see statistical information about the distribution page, use the DBCC SHOW_STATISTICS command, which returns the selectivity and density of indexed column on a table. The syntax for this command is

```
DBCC SHOW_STATISTICS (tablename, target)
```

tablename is the name of the table and *target* is the name of the index you want to get statistics on.

The following command displays distribution information about the aunmind nonclustered index on the au_lname and au_fname columns of the authors table.

```
dbcc show_statistics (authors, aunmind )
go
Statistics for INDEX 'aunmind'.
Updated              Rows   Rows Sampled Steps Density    Average key
                                                          length
------------------  ----  ------------ ---- -----------  ----------.
Dec 13 1997 7:30AM  23     23           23   3.9697543E-2  34.956524

(1 row(s) affected)

All density              Columns
------------------------  ------------------------
4.7258981E-2             au_lname
4.3478262E-2             au_lname, au_fname

(2 row(s) affected)

Steps
------------------------------
Bennet
Blotchet-Halls
Carson
DeFrance
del Castillo
Dull
Green
Greene
Gringlesby
Hunter
Karsen
Locksley
MacFeather
McBadden
O'Leary
Panteley
Ringer
Ringer
Smith
Straight
Stringer
White
Yokomoto

(23 row(s) affected)
```

You can see from the example that this index is very low density (high selectivity); therefore, this index will be useful if the optimizer chooses to use it. Now, the questions you might ask are "How does a distribution page get created, and how is it maintained?" A distribution page is added when you first create the index on a table or when you run the UPDATE STATISTICS command. In the earlier versions of SQL Server, distribution information did not get updated automatically. If you inserted a large number of rows after creating an index, the distribution statistics reflected by the distribution page varied widely from the actual key distribution. As a result, the optimizer in versions 6.5 and earlier sometimes chose an access plan that was inefficient. As part of regular maintenance, DBAs had to create a schedule for the UPDATE STATISTICS command in order to keep the distribution values accurate. With version 7.0, distribution page statistics are automatically updated by SQL Server. SQL Server constantly monitors the data sample and updates the statistics through an internal process. It is possible to turn off this behavior by using the sp_autostats system stored procedure. This stored procedure allows you to change the automatic update statistics for a specific index or all the indexes of a table. The following command turns off the automatic update of statistics for an index named aunmind on the authors table:

```
Exec sp_autostats "authors", "OFF", "aunmind "
Go
Automatic statistics maintenance turned OFF for 1 indices.
```

When you run sp_autostats and simply supply the table name, it displays the current setting for the table. Following are the settings for the authors table:

```
Exec sp_autostats "authors"
Go
Index Name              AUTOSTATS    Last Updated
— — — — — — — — — — —.   — — — —.    — — — — — — — — — — —.
authors.UPKCL_auidind    ON          1997-12-13 07:30:59.540
authors.aunmind          OFF         1997-12-13 07:30:59.540
authors.authors_Index_1  ON          1998-03-28 22:03:31.733

(3 row(s) affected)
```

You can still manually update distribution statistics by using the update statistics T-SQL command. In SQL Server 7.0, this command was enhanced to support more features. The new syntax of this command is

```
UPDATE STATISTICS {table} [index ¦ (index_or_column [, ...n])
  [WITH [FULLSCAN],SAMPLE number {PERCENT ¦ ROWS}]
    ][[,] NORECOMPUTE][[,] [INDEX ¦ COLUMNS ¦ ALL]
```

The option FULLSCAN forces SQL Server to perform a full scan of the data in the table or index. This is the default behavior of the command. When you use the SAMPLE option, you can specify a specific number of rows or percentage of rows to sample to build or update the distribution statistics. As stated before, SQL Server 7.0 automatically updates the key distribution statistics. By using the NORECOMPUTE option with UPDATE STATISTICS, you can tell SQL Server not to perform an automatic update of the statistics. After issuing a TRUNCATE TABLE command, or when the automatic update statistics option is turned off, you should run this command. To determine the last time statistics were updated, run the following command:

```
DBCC STATS_DATE(tableid, indexid)
```

> **TIP**
>
> You can get the *tableid* from sysobjects by using the following query:
> ```
> Select id from sysobjects where name = 'tablename' and type = "U"
> ```
> You can get the *indexid* from sysindexes by using the following query:
> ```
> Select indid, name from sysindexes
> Where id = object_id('tablename') and indid > 0
> ```

> **NOTE**
>
> What actually happens when you execute sp_autostats or use the NORECOMPUTE option in the UPDATE STATISTICS command to turn off auto update statistics for a specific index or a table? SQL Server internally sets a bit in the status column of the sysindexes table to inform the internal SQL Server process not to update the key distribution statistics for the indexes that are turned off using these commands. To turn on auto-update, either run UPDATE STATISTICS without the NORECOMPUTE option or pass the ON parameter to the sp_autostats system stored procedure.

Index Densities

You know by now that SQL Server keeps key distribution statistics on the distribution page for each of the indexes on the table. Before I jump into the details of index density, look at an example. Assume that the composite index nc2 is indexed on state and zip of the authors table. The following is the output of the DBCC SHOW_STATISTICS command for this index:

```
dbcc show_statistics("authors", nc2 )
go
Statistics for INDEX 'nc2'.
```

```
Updated              Rows   Rows Sampled Steps  Density    Average key
                                                           length
_____  __._____  ___ _____  _____.
Apr  5 1998  8:44AM 23    23                23    1.1342155E- 2 24.869562

(1 row(s) affected)

All density             Columns
_____  _____
0.4442344               state
6.6162571E-2            state, zip

(2 row(s) affected)

Steps
__.
CA
CA
CA
 .
 .
 .
IN
OR
TN
UT
UT
```

Look at the output and notice the results under the heading Steps. This heading displays distribution steps *only* for the first part of the composite key (au_state). The optimizer uses these distribution step statistics when you have a simple case of equality joins in your where clause (such as select * from authors where state = "MD"). However, not all such queries are this simple. Some queries might specify multiple columns as SARGs (search arguments) in the where clause (such as select * from authors where state = "CA" and ZIP = "90210") or participate in joins with other tables. For such queries, SQL Server stores the density of each column in the key. For composite keys, SQL Server stores the density for the first column of the composite key, first and second column, first, second, and third column, and so on. This is shown in the example under the All density and Columns output of the DBCC command.

Index density essentially represents the inverse of all unique key values of the key. The density of each key is calculated by the following formula:

Key density = 1.00 / (Count of key values in the table)

Therefore, the density for the column state is calculated as follows:

Select Density = 1.00/ (select count(distinct state) from authors)

```
Go
Density
— — — — — — — —
.1250000000000
```

The density for the column's state and zip follows:

```
Select Density = 1.00/ (select count(distinct state+zip) from authors)
Go
Density
— — — — — — — —
.0555555555555
```

Let's assume there were 1 million rows in this table, only state was specified in the where clause of the query, and the statistics are up to date; the optimizer will have a selectivity for 125,000 (1,000,000 * 0.125000) number of rows. If state and zip both were specified in the where clause of the query, the optimizer will have a selectivity for 55,555.55 (1,000,000 * .0555555555555) number of rows. If you only specified the zip code in the where clause of the query, because there is no index on the table with zip code as the first column of the key, there are no values stored for the zip code alone on the distribution page. Therefore, the index density will be 1, and the optimizer estimates hitting 1,000,000 (1,000,000 * .1.0). SQL Server uses these statistical values to determine the selectivity of an index. The higher the density of a key, the lower the selectivity—and that determines whether the optimizer will choose an index when it creates the query plan. If the selectivity is poor (usually less than 15-20%), then in spite of the index, the optimizer will choose to do a table scan because it is more cost effective.

> **TIP**
>
> Watch out for such indexes in your databases. Such indexes are in fact detrimental to the performance of the system. They not only are useless for data retrieval, but they also slow down your data modification statements. Identify such indexes and drop them.

Index Design Guidelines

SQL Server indexes are mostly transparent to users with a few exceptions where users can pass optimizer hints. Based on the key distribution values, the SQL Server cost-based optimizer chooses the index that is least expensive from an I/O standpoint. Query optimization is covered in detail in Chapter 25, "Optimization." Following are some of the main guidelines that will help you build useful indexes in your environment.

Clustered Index Indications

Because the data is physically sorted on the clustered key, searching a clustered index is almost always faster than searching a nonclustered one. Because you are allowed to create only one clustered index per table, choose this index judiciously. The following guidelines will help you decide when to choose a clustered index:

- Columns in that index have a few unique values.

  Because the data is physically sorted, all the duplicate values are kept together. Any query that tries to fetch records against such keys will find all the values with a minimum number of I/Os.

- Columns that are often specified in the order by clause.

  Because the data is already sorted, SQL Server does not have to re-sort the data.

- Columns that are often searched for a range of values.

  Because the bottom of the leaf page in a clustered index is actually a data page, pointers in a clustered index point to a page on which data resides. SQL Server can use this index to locate the starting and ending page for the specified range, resulting in a faster scan of the range.

- Columns that are most frequently used in the join clause.

- Queries that may return large resultsets with adjacent key values.

> **NOTE**
>
> The SQL Server optimizer invariably chooses a clustered index over a nonclustered index. Therefore, if you want to create only one index on a table, create a clustered index.

Nonclustered Index Indications

SQL Server 7.0 allows you to create a maximum of 250 (compared with 249 in SQL Server 6.5) nonclustered indexes on a table. Always keep in mind that as you add more indexes to the system, database modification statements get slower. The following guidelines will help you choose the right nonclustered index in your environment:

- Columns that have a large number of unique values or queries that return small resultsets.

  Because the bottom of the leaf page in a nonclustered index is actually a pointer to the row ID of the data page, SQL Server can use a nonclustered index quite efficiently to get to individual records.

23

DATABASE DESIGN AND PERFORMANCE

- Queries that use indexed columns in the where and the order by clauses.

  If a nonclustered index is selected by the optimizer, the order of the key values in the B-tree will be the same as the columns specified in the order by clause. In such cases, SQL Server can eliminate creating an internal temporary work table for a data sort. The following query is an example where SQL Server avoids the extra step of creating a work table for a sort:

  ```
  select * from authors where state like "c%"
  order by state
  ```

Index Covering

Index covering is a situation where all the columns in the SELECT and WHERE clauses of the query are also part of the nonclustered index. This results in faster retrieval of data because all the information can come directly from the index page, and SQL Server avoids trips to the data pages. The following example has a nonclustered index on the au_lname and au_fname columns of the authors table:

```
Select au_lname, au_fname
From authors
Where au_lname like "M%"
Go
```

Many other queries that use an aggregate clause (such as min, max, avg, and so on) or check for existence of a criteria also benefit from index covering. The following query is an example of index covering using aggregates:

```
select count(au_lname) from authors where au_lname like "m%"
```

Composite Indexes Versus Multiple Indexes

As your key gets wider, the selectivity of the key becomes higher as well. It may appear as if creating wide indexes should result in better performance. This is generally not true. The reason is that the wider the key, the fewer rows SQL Server stores on the index pages, resulting in a higher number of levels of B-tree. To get to specific rows, SQL Server must perform more I/Os. To get better performance from queries, instead of creating a few wide indexes, create multiple narrower indexes. The advantage here is that with smaller keys, the query optimizer can quickly scan through multiple indexes to create the most efficient access plan. Also, with more indexes, the optimizer can choose from various alternatives. If you are deciding on a wide key, check the distribution of each member of the composite key individually. If the selectivity on the individual columns is very high, you might want to break up the index into multiple indexes. If the selectivity of individual columns is low but is high for combined columns, it makes sense to have wider keys on a table. To get to the right combination, populate your table with real-world data, experiment with creating multiple indexes, and check the distribution of each column. Based on the distribution steps and index density, you can make a decision that works best for your environment.

SQL Server Index Maintenance

SQL Server indexes are self-maintained, which means that any time a data modification (such as update, delete, or insert) takes place on a table, the index B-tree is automatically balanced to reflect correct pointers. This does not solve the problem of fragmentation in the data and index pages. Fragmentation on an index page can happen for the following reasons:

- As more records are added to a table, space is used on the data page and on the index page. As a result, the page eventually becomes completely full. If another insert takes place on that page, because there is no more room for the new row, SQL Server splits the page into two. Each new page becomes 50 percent full. Figure 23.3 illustrates page splitting due to inserts.

FIGURE 23.3

Page splitting due to inserts.

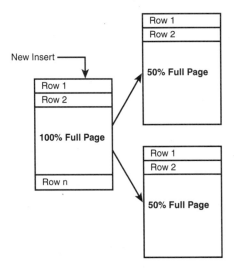

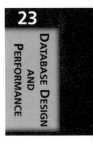

- Frequent update statements can cause fragmentation in the database at the data and index page level. Figure 23.4 depicts an update scenario, where as a result of an update statement, most of the rows move to a different page (a deferred update). The page that used to be 80 percent full becomes only 10 percent full. Because SQL Server indexes are self-maintained, the index page will be balanced automatically, but this page will have a lot of unused space. A number of such updates occurring on a system can lead to heavy fragmentation.

FIGURE 23.4

Fragmentation due to updates.

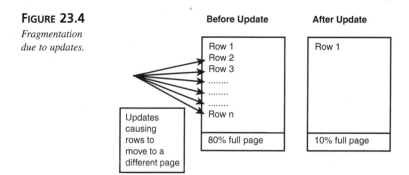

• Figure 23.5 shows a scenario where fragmentation can take place because of delete statements. As you can see from the figure, a delete statement causes a page to become only 10 percent full. This page will remain allocated to the extent even if it has only a single row.

FIGURE 23.5

Fragmentation due to deletes.

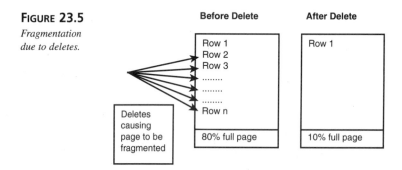

Usually in a system, all these factors contribute to the fragmentation of data in the data pages and the index pages. In an environment with a lot of data modification, you might see a lot of fragmentation on the data and index pages over a period of time. Data fragmentation adversely impacts performance because the data is spread across more pages than necessary. More I/Os will be required to retrieve the data. SQL Server provides a DBCC command to monitor the level of fragmentation in the database. The syntax for this command is

```
DBCC showcontig(tableid[,indexid])
```

This command is covered in more detail in Chapter 28, "Monitoring SQL Server Performance." Once you have determined that data is fragmented, SQL Server allows you to reorganize the data on index and data pages so that each page is filled to an optimal level. SQL Server provides the Fill Factor option, which allows you to specify the fullness at the data and index page levels. Fill factor is described in the next section.

Setting the Fill Factor

The Fill Factor option allows you to define the percentage of free space on a data page or an index page when you create an index or a table. The value can be from 1 to 100. Setting the value to 80 would mean that each page will be 80 percent full at the time you create the index. It is important to note that as more data gets modified on a table, the fill factor is not maintained at the level specified during the `create index` command. Over a period of time, you will find that each page has a different percentage of fullness. You can also specify the fill factor value at the server level by using the following command:

```
Exec sp_configure 'fill factor', Percentage_Value
```

You can override this value by specifying a value during the `create index` statement:

```
CREATE [UNIQUE] [CLUSTERED ¦ NONCLUSTERED]
    INDEX index_name ON table (column [, ...n])
[WITH
        [PAD_INDEX]
        [[,] FILLFACTOR = fillfactor]
        [[,] IGNORE_DUP_KEY]
        [[,] SORTED_DATA_REORG]
        [[,] {IGNORE_DUP_ROW ¦ ALLOW_DUP_ROW}]
        [[,] DROP_EXISTING]
        [[,] STATISTICS_NORECOMPUTE
]
[ON filegroup]
```

If you specify only `fillfactor`, only data pages are affected by this command. To specify the level of fullness, use the `PAD_INDEX` option together with `fillfactor`. This option allows you to specify how much space to leave open on each node of the index. You don't need to specify a value with `PAD_INDEX`; it uses the same percentage value that is specified with `fillfactor` option.

TIP

If you don't specify a value for `fillfactor`, the default value is zero. This does not mean that all the pages are completely empty. A `fillfactor` value of 0 is actually treated like a value of 100, except that data pages for a clustered index and leaf pages for a nonclustered index are created completely full. However, a space for two rows is left open at each internal node of the index.

When you use `PAD_INDEX`, the value specified by `fillfactor` cannot be such that the number of rows on each index node falls below two. If you do specify such a value, SQL Server will internally override it.

Reapplying the Fill Factor

As data gets modified in a table, the value of `fillfactor` is not maintained at the level specified during the `create index` statement. As a result, each page can reach a different level of fullness. Over a period of time, this can lead to heavy fragmentation in the database and may start to impact performance. The DBA must reapply the fill factor to improve performance of the system. SQL Server provides the `DBCC DBREINDEX` option to reapply the fill factor without having to drop and create the index. The syntax is

```
DBCC DBREINDEX (['database.owner.table_name' [, index_name
[, fillfactor ]]])
[WITH NO_INFOMSGS]
```

For example, if you want to apply a fill factor of 80 for an index UPKCL_auidind on the authors table, run the following command:

```
DBCC DBREINDEX("authors", "UPKCL_auidind", 80)
```

Updates and Performance

SQL Server supports two types of update mechanisms: deferred update and update in place.

Deferred Update

Deferred mode when the original rows are deleted and new rows can be inserted on different pages from those of the original rows. This mode of update can logically be treated as a `DELETE` followed by an `INSERT` statement. Although SQL Server does split such an update into actual `DELETE` and `INSERT` operations, it does keep the deleted and inserted records in the transaction log file. Therefore, this mode of update can be expensive. Usually, not many operations result in deferred updates. A deferred update occurs on a table when the column being updated is a part of a clustered index. Assume that there is a clustered index on the empid column of the *emp* table. If you run the following command, SQL Server will use a deferred update:

```
Update emp - increment employee id of each employee by 1000
Set empid = empid + 1000
```

Deferred updates can be costly because SQL Server has to store more rows in the transaction log file. Because an indexed column is modified, a lot of movement of data can take place at the data and index pages. To avoid deferred updates, choose your indexes wisely so that they are not frequently modified as part of your update statements.

Update in Place

Internally, SQL Server implements an `update` statement by performing a `delete` and then an `insert` statement. This means that the row is physically deleted from the page and potentially inserted on a different page. However, this is an exception to the rule called *update in place*. An update in place involves no physical movement of the rows being updated; that is, there is no `delete` followed by an `insert`. Instead, the row is updated in its current place. Update in place is efficient because there is no movement at the data page level as well as at the index page level. In the earlier versions of SQL Server, you had to meet a number of conditions to perform an update in place. These restrictions included that the table being modified cannot

- Participate in replication
- Have a trigger
- Participate in a join during an update

All such restrictions have been removed in SQL Server 7.0, and the only condition in which update in place will not take place is when a column being updated is also a part of the clustered index.

Database Filegroups and Performance

Earlier in this chapter, I discussed horizontal and vertical partitioning of the data to improve performance. To improve performance further, you can spread horizontally or vertically partitioned tables across multiple stripe sets. Earlier versions of SQL Server provided segments as a means to place data and indexes to partition the data. Segments were difficult to manage, and no one used them. SQL Server 7.0 does not support segments. Instead, the concept of filegroups was added to SQL Server. Filegroups are discussed at length in Chapter 7, "Physical Database Architecture." In this section, I discuss how portioning the data can be combined with filegroups to further improve the performance of the system.

The basic idea behind partitioning is to split a large table (with a large number of rows or columns) into multiple tables. As a result of partitioning, if all the resultant tables are kept on the same stripe set, you will not gain much performance from an I/O standpoint. If you create multiple filegroups across different stripe sets, you can create tables and indexes on these filegroups to spread I/Os across such tables.

> **NOTE**
>
> Because the data page and the leaf level of a clustered index are the same, if you create a clustered index on a filegroup, the entire table moves from the existing filegroup to the new filegroup.

The following example demonstrates the use of filegroups when you create a table or an index:

```
Create table JanBill ( billdate datetime, acct# int,
bill_amt money ) on filegroup1

Create table FebBill (billdate datetime, acct# int,
bill_amt money ) on filegroup2

Create index nc1janbill on JanBill (billdate datetime,
acct# int ) on filegroup3
```

The filegroups must exist before you use them in the `create table` or `create index` statements. You can create filegroups using the `create database` or `alter database` T-SQL commands. Performance gains are not going to be significant if you are not using underlying disk striping provided by the operating system or the hardware. To maximize gains from data partitioning on various filegroups, create your filegroups on the stripe sets using RAID.

RAID Technology

RAID (Redundant Array of Inexpensive Disks) is used to configure a disk subsystem in a way to provide optimal performance and fault tolerance for an application. The basic idea behind using RAID is that you spread data across multiple disk drives so that I/Os are spread across multiple drives. RAID has special significance for database-related applications, where you want to spread random I/Os (DMLs) and sequential I/Os (for the transaction log) across different disk subsystems to minimize head movement and maximize I/O performance.

There are six (0-5) levels of RAID implementation, based on the level of fault tolerance provided by each level. With different RAID levels, you can achieve higher performance at the cost of data reliability and vice versa. You can implement RAID at the hardware level or under Windows NT. Windows NT supports levels 0, 1, and 5. In most cases, people use hardware-based RAID implementation because it is more efficient and does not consume any extra processor cycles. RAID 0, 1, and 5 are the most common RAID implementations for SQL Server.

RAID Level 0

RAID level 0 is most commonly known as disk striping, where data is written across multiple partitions on multiple drives. Stripe sets are not stored with parity; therefore, in case of a media failure, there is no fault tolerance provided by RAID 0. RAID 0, however, provides the best I/O performance among all other RAID levels because I/O is spread across multiple devices. Figure 23.6 depicts a RAID 0 disk array configuration.

FIGURE 23.6
RAID Level 0.

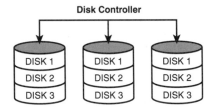

RAID Level 1

RAID Level 1 is most commonly known as disk mirroring. Every write to the primary disk is written to the mirror set. Therefore, data written to the primary disk is the same copy as the mirrored set. RAID 1 devices provide excellent fault tolerance because in a media failure, either on the primary disk or the mirrored disk, the system can still continue to run. Also, read performance is much better with RAID 1 because data can be read from the device, which is closer to the head, minimizing head movement. Figure 23.7 shows a RAID 1 configuration.

23

DATABASE DESIGN AND PERFORMANCE

FIGURE 23.7
RAID Level 1.

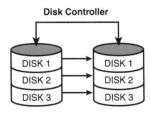

> **TIP**
>
> There is a trend of implementing RAID 0+1, which is a combination of disk striping and mirroring. Although it has the same cost issues as RAID 1, it does provide a good balance between fault tolerance and read/write performance.

RAID Level 5

RAID 5 is most commonly known as striping with parity. In this configuration, data is striped across multiple disks in large blocks. At the same time, parity is written across all the disks. Parity information across disks keeps information about data redundancy. Information is always stored in such a way that data parity information is written to the different disk. Therefore, in the event of a disk failure, the system can still continue to run without any downtime. RAID 5 provides excellent read performance, but the cost of implementation is high. Figure 23.8 shows a RAID 5 configuration. You can see that RAID 5 is similar to RAID 0; the only difference is that RAID 5 provides better fault tolerance. RAID 5 provides excellent read performance combined with robust fault tolerance. However, writes are slower with RAID 5.

FIGURE 23.8
RAID Level 5.

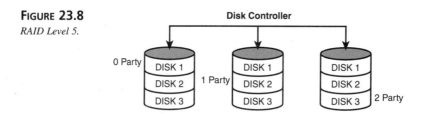

RAID Levels Commonly Used with SQL Server

RAID 0 provides the best overall performance of all the RAID levels but provides no fault tolerance. This configuration may be desired in environments where data availability is secondary to performance requirements. You might want to use RAID 0 for testing or development environments.

RAID 1 and RAID 5 are the most commonly used configurations for production environments. RAID 5 provides excellent fault tolerance and is more cost effective than RAID 1. Although RAID 1 implementation is somewhat more expensive, it provides better fault tolerance and I/O performance compared to RAID 5. Because RAID 1 is a mirrored implementation, the system will continue to run, even when two disks fail (provided both the disks are not the mirrored sets). In RAID 5 configuration, if two drives fail at the same time, some data will be lost. If you lose a disk in RAID 1 configuration, the only impact you will see is a little degradation in the read performance on the data that was stored on the failed mirror set. In a RAID 5 configuration, every I/O operation against the failed drive will perform against all the drives in the volume.

Different RAID levels provide a balance between cost and performance. The decision about which RAID level to pick for your particular environment also depends upon the nature of application you are planning to deploy. In an OLTP environment, I/Os are usually small but quite frequent. Also, OLTP environments have random I/Os (data modification statements) combined with sequential I/Os (writes to a transaction log file). Using SQL Server filegroups with data striping can provide excellent performance for random I/Os. Activity on the log file is always a write operation and is also sequential. Therefore, the performance of the write operations may be critical. If the log files are constantly backed up, you might want to put transaction log files on a RAID 0 configuration to improve write performance. A DSS environment usually has few writes, and a majority of the operations on the database are read only in nature. For OLTP environments, my recommendation is the RAID 1 configuration, which provides the optimal price and performance combination. RAID 5 is usually the choice in data-warehousing applications. You should experiment with these configurations, and based on the I/O requirements in your own environment, you should determine your own optimal RAID configuration.

Summary

A good database design is the foundation of any application. Normalization techniques allow you to create logical relationships between entities in the database with controlled redundancies. To improve the performance of the system, denormalization techniques can be useful. The biggest performance gains, however, come from designing proper indexes on the tables. It involves understanding selectivity, density, and the distribution of the key values. You can gain further performance gains by using SQL Server filegroups and RAID levels.

23

DATABASE DESIGN
AND
PERFORMANCE

Query Analysis

by Sharon Bjeletich

In This Chapter

What's New in SQL Server 7.0

The SQL Server query processor and storage engine were both completely rewritten for SQL Server 7.0, and the familiar ISQL/w was transformed into the SQL Server Query Analyzer tool. This tool still functions much in the same way as the previous version of ISQL, but is a more powerful and productive tool for understanding the new engine and analyzing queries.

The largest change is the addition of the graphical execution plan. This tool visually displays queries categorized by the subtask by the optimizer. Although the Query Analyzer (QA) output is a bit confusing at first, it provides enough support in the ToolTips it displays and in Books Online that you can understand the graphics.

Another feature added to the QA is a better text editor, which includes color-coding for Transact-SQL syntax, more configuration options, and the Index Tuning Wizard. The QA also uses ODBC rather than DB-Lib to access the server.

> **NOTE**
>
> One of the advantages of naming this tool Query Analyzer is that its optimal usage is clearer to users. Too many developers in the past used the SQL Server 6.5 Enterprise Manager or ISQL/w to develop back-end code. They never actually ran showplan to evaluate and optimize the queries and never saved the code in a file that can become part of the application source code and kept under configuration control. The removal of a query window from the SQL Server 7.0 Enterprise Manager discourages that bad habit, and the Query Analyzer encourages just what it says: query analysis.

There are a number of types of query processor optimization:

- Syntactic—Queries are optimized according to the statement syntax. Joins are processed in the order written and have the same execution plan every time. The user must an excellent knowledge of the database and its structures.

- Semantic—This is still a theoretical technique based on the assumption that the optimizer understands the schema and relies heavily on constraints. There are a number of new initiatives in this area, both in query processing and in modeling methodologies.

- Heuristic (also called *rules-based*)—This is a rules-based method for reordering the individual query operations. It focuses on relational algebraic rules. Queries are represented as trees, and sets of algebraic rules are performed in a specific order.

For example, selects can be broken apart first, then associative rules are applied, then commutative rules are applied, and so on.

- Cost-based (also called *systematic*)—This approach is based on the optimizer's knowledge of the data and underlying structures, not the user's, and I/O tends to be a dominant factor.

As it was in the previous version, the SQL Server optimizer is still cost-based.

A number of new features in the SQL Server 7.0 query processor affect query analysis and optimization. (Note that query optimization is covered in Chapter 25, "Optimization.") They include

- Execution plan management
- The addition of merge joins and hash joins
- The ability to use multiple indexes in a query
- Parallel processing
- Larger page size (8KB)
- The clustered index value as row identifier in nonclustered indexes
- The Query Governor
- The Index Tuning Wizard

SQL Server 7.0 manages execution plans in a new way, which may affect how queries are written and how the procedure cache setting is managed. Execution plans are now stored for both stored procedures and statement batches. In previous versions, an execution plan for a stored procedure was saved in the procedure cache for each user. In SQL Server 7.0, there is only one plan saved, which is read-only and reentrant. Individual user execution data is stored separately for each user execution.

When any statement batch is executed, the procedure cache is searched to determine if an existing plan can be used. These plans will be marked for recompilation if there are any changes to the underlying structures, when an index is dropped on the underlying structure, if there are a large number of inserts and deletes, and whenever statistics are rebuilt.

The addition of merge and hash joins brings more sophistication to the product, and Microsoft has indicated that these new technologies were introduced to support decision support systems, very large databases, heterogeneous queries, and large complex queries. SQL Server 6.5 had only one way to perform a join—nested iteration. The addition of the merge and hash joins provides some powerful choices for the optimizer, and understanding these approaches will be helpful. These joins are explained in more detail in the section "Logical and Physical Operators," later in the chapter.

24

QUERY ANALYSIS

> **CAUTION**
>
> SQL Server 7.0 requires that all object references be fully qualified for the engine to match an existing plan with a statement. This is a discipline that is required by some organizations, but it can reduce flexibility when a database name is required, as you must change the code to use it against another database. There is also overhead associated with the engine trying to analyze and match every statement with an existing query plan. Although Microsoft indicates that the algorithm used is efficient, some short-running queries (such as those used in transaction-intensive environments where subsecond response is a requirement) can show a performance hit. This new feature does support dynamic SQL and data warehousing applications. Users will need to spend some time analyzing and understanding the impact of this new feature on their environment.

Allowing the use of multiple indexes on a query makes multiple, small indexes more effective because you can use them together to form the equivalent of a covering index. The optimizer can also perform index intersection and index union. For example, in a query that has two search arguments—both on different columns in one table—and an index on each of the two columns used in the search argument, the analyzer can return the subset of rows that form the intersection of the two resultsets. Figure 24.1 shows an example of a graphical execution plan using multiple indexes on one table. Note the two inputs at the far right side, both from the Orders table but with two different indexes. One index is supporting the ShippedDate criteria, and the other is supporting the EmployeeID criteria.

Note that all examples use the Northwind database that is installed with SQL Server 7.0. The Orders and Order Details tables were enlarged by adding more rows to provide more obvious results in the execution plans.

The SQL Server query processor has the ability to break down queries into multiple steps, and on SMP (symmetric multiprocessor, meaning more than one processor is installed) machines, you can run some of these steps in parallel. How much parallelism occurs depends on a number of things, including the number of processors and the SQL Server edition (the desktop edition supports two processors, the standard edition supports four processors, and the enterprise edition supports eight processors), how many concurrent users are on the system, the load on the CPU, how much memory is installed in the system, and the type of query being processed. Parallelism lets you either optimize multiple queries at one time or break a single query into subtasks.

FIGURE 24.1

Using multiple indexes.

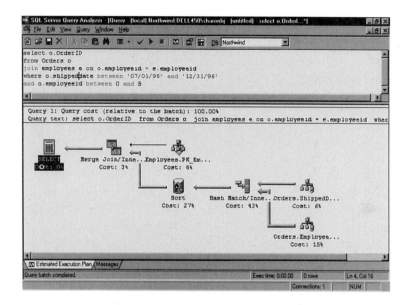

Because the SQL Server 7.0 storage engine and the query processor (now referred to as the relational engine) were rewritten, some changes impact query analysis. Two such changes include the change in page size from 2KB to 8KB and the storage of the clustered index key value as the row identifier for nonclustered indexes. The larger page size means fewer page splits and larger amounts of data read in per I/O request. The change in how indexes are created and the ability of the optimizer to use multiple indexes in queries also change optimization strategies. Probably one of the largest efforts database administrators will make in the transition from SQL Server 6.5 to SQL Server 7.0 is in understanding their indexing strategies. Some strategies may change as users begin to fully understand the impact on their systems. However, some of the issues that needed to be addressed in SQL Server 6.5 still exist in SQL Server 7.0. Hot spots (index or data pages that are commonly in locking contention by multiple users) can still occur with clustered indexes on primary keys, and you still need to find a balance between the indexes needed to support data insertion and those needed to support data selection.

You can use the Query Governor to limit a query according to execution cost, as opposed to number of rows returned. In SQL Server 6.5, you could limit an individual query by setting the rowcount parameter, and many shops imposed these limits on applications that supported ad-hoc queries. This was not effective against runaway queries and may have unnecessarily restricted a valid query. The Query Governor limit in SQL Server 7.0 can be set both serverwide and per connection, and it stops queries that it estimates will run longer in seconds than the current setting.

> **NOTE**
>
> Locking is much more configurable in SQL Server 7.0. The new system stored procedure `sp_indexoption` allows page and/or row-level locking to be disallowed for a specific table or index. If there is a table that is often in contention, a *hot spot*, it may be beneficial to disallow page locks. Disallowing both page and row-level locks will force a table lock, so the option should be used by experienced users after analysis.

The Index Tuning Wizard will suggest an optimal indexing strategy for tables, based on the actual usage. Because the major critical factor for query optimization, after table design and query design, is indexing and join selection, the Index Tuning Wizard is a powerful and welcome tool. The wizard requires a workload, either a query or a trace captured in SQL Profiler, and the recommendations are more accurate the larger the workload, up to the 32,767 tunable queries allowed. Also note that queries with quoted identifiers are not considered.

The Query Analyzer will also indicate tables that are missing statistics by using red in the graphical execution plan. The statistics can be updated immediately in the Analyzer window. SQL Server is better able to manage statistics itself, so you have less need to run the Update Statistics statement. However, updating statistics is still a critical factor in query optimization, and many database administrators may find that they will continue to regularly schedule this maintenance.

> **NOTE**
>
> Constraint processing has now been integrated into the query optimizer, which better supports distributed data solutions. For example, an organization may horizontally partition tables by region or office for local insert and retrieval optimization. You can then run union queries to report on data transparently across the multiple tables to support management reporting. If there is a check constraint on the partitioning column, and that column is used in the search argument, the optimizer knows to include only the table with a matching check constraint.

Queries that utilize the in subquery statements are more optimized in SQL Server 7.0 than in previous versions. Insert, update, and delete changes can now be sorted in index order and applied in a single pass over each index.

One of the best new features of the Analyzer is the ability to evaluate execution plans for queries within a batch against each other. Although individual execution plans may be difficult to evaluate in themselves, seeing a query evaluated against another query trying to return the same result can be educational. One of the best ways to understand the new Analyzer is to write queries in as many different ways as possible in a single batch that are meant to return the same results. The Analyzer will clearly indicate their performance in relation to each other. Figures 24.2 and 24.3 show the execution plan for two queries meant to return the distinct names of suppliers with products that have been sold (using the Northwind database). (The execution plan has been split into two figures to show both plans.) It is clear that the new Query Processor provides many advantages for SQL Server users and administrators.

FIGURE 24.2

The top section of a multiple query execution plan showing the query cost relative to the batch (3.54%).

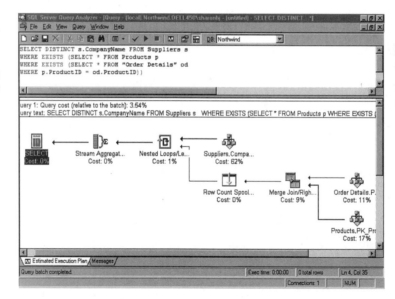

24

QUERY ANALYSIS

FIGURE 24.3

The bottom section of a multiple query execution plan showing the query cost relative to the batch (96.46%).

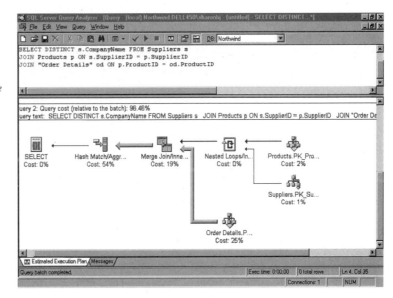

Query Analyzer Graphical Execution Plan

The Query Analyzer produces a graphical execution plan that provides analysis information in a more intuitive manner. I outline in detail the different operators that you can display graphically, and I assume that you understand how to use the Query Analyzer tool and its configuration.

The QA displays icons to represent a logical and or physical operator, and the movement occurs from right to left and top to bottom, eventually ending with the statement type of the query. This might be a SELECT, INSERT, UPDATE, TABCREATE, and so on. The arrows in between the icons indicate the movement of rows between operators. To understand the query, start with the farthest icon on the right, and read each ToolTip as you move left and down through the tree. Each column on the query tree is called a node, and icons displayed under each other participate in the same parental operation.

> **NOTE**
>
> The displayed width of each of the arrowhead lines in the graphical execution plan can indicate the estimated number of rows and their row size being moved through the query. The smaller the width of the arrow, the smaller the estimated row count or row size. Moving the cursor over the line also displays a ToolTip indicating the estimated row count and row size.

Figure 24.4 shows a sample Query Analyzer graphical execution plan window.

FIGURE 24.4

Query Analyzer graphical execution plan.

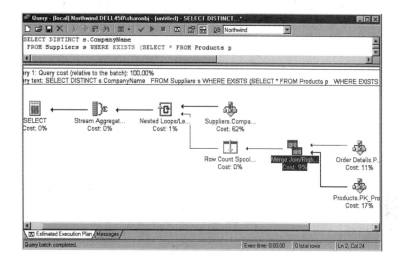

Analyzer ToolTips

When a graphical execution plan is presented in the Query Analyzer, you can get more information about the step in the execution plan by moving the mouse cursor over the icon. The ToolTip that is displayed will detail more information about the logical and physical operator being used, (including a helpful brief explanation of the operator), warning information, such as missing statistics, and the estimated row count, row size, I/O cost, and CPU cost, as well as the total subtree cost. You may also see an Argument section that outlines the predicate and any parameters used by the argument.

The ToolTip provides a large amount of information, and it might be difficult at first to determine the critical factors in analyzing the performance of the query displayed, but there are a few items to quickly check that will help start that analysis of the performance.

Figure 24.5 displays a sample ToolTip for one of the operators in the same execution plan as Figure 24.4.

In this example, the ToolTip displays the information for the Merge Join physical operator icon, which is hidden behind the ToolTip in Figure 24.5. This query also has a nested loop operator, which appears to the left of the ToolTip. Both of these physical operators require two inputs, which are shown as stacked icons to the right. The different thickness in the lines moving between the operators indicates the relative amount of data being moved.

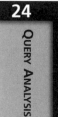

FIGURE 24.5

*A ToolTip
example.*

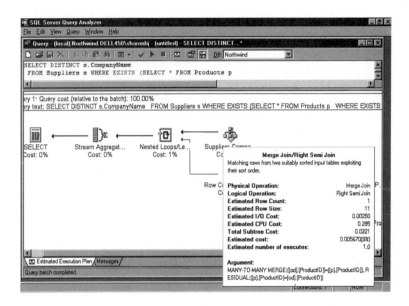

In this ToolTip, the physical operation is a merge join (described further later in this chapter in the section "Logical and Physical Operators"). Although the physical operation of a merge join can implement different logical operations, in this case, the logical operation is a right semi-join. A right semi-join means that the operation returns each row from the second input (in this display, the bottom) where there is a matching row in the first input (in this display, the top).

The Estimated Row Count returned from this operation is 1, and the line width indicates a small flow. The Estimated Row Size is 11. The Estimated I/O Cost and Estimated CPU Cost provide critical information about the performance of this query. These numbers should be as low as possible.

The Estimated Subtree Cost will display cumulated costs for this node and any previous nodes. This number increases as you move to the left. With the last icon, the ToolTip displays the total Estimated Subtree Cost for the entire query, as well as the Estimated Row Count. This number should also be as small as possible. The Estimated Cost and Estimated Number of Executes also provide helpful information about this particular part of the query operation. Because merge joins make only one pass through input data, the Estimated Number of Executes should be 1 for both of the inputs to this parent node. Because nested loops are iterative (described in more detail later in this chapter), generally one of the inputs will have an Estimated Number of Executes that is more than 1. You can see this for this query by selecting the ToolTips for the two inputs to the nested loops operation.

The Argument section outlines the predicates and parameters that are used by the query. In this case, the operation is performing a Many-to-Many Merge on the `ProductID` key. The `RESIDUAL` keyword indicates any other predicates for the query. Because this is a many-to-many merge, the residual displays the keys again in the opposite order.

Putting all of the information together provides the keys to understanding each operation and its potential cost. Adding similar queries to the batch and having the optimizer analyze them against each other will also help users better understand performance impact.

Logical and Physical Operators

The graphical execution plan displays execution information in a different way than was used in SQL Server 6.5. To fully understand the plan, you should recognize each of the icons displayed. The following sections cover most of the more common logical and physical operators displayed in the QA.

Assert

Assert acts as a road block, allowing a result stream to continue. The argument displayed in the Assert ToolTip will spell out each check being performed. This might include the constraints on columns or tables included in the query or an expression that is the result of a previous join created to check referential integrity.

For example, an insert into the Order Details table in the Northwind database needs to validate the existence of the inserted ProductID in the Products table, the existence of the inserted OrderID in the Orders table, the value of the inserted Discount against the check constraint on that column, and the value of the inserted Quantity against the check constraint on that column. If the result of the Assert returns a null, the stream continues through the query. Figure 24.6 shows the execution plan and ToolTip of an Assert that appears in a query to update a column with a check constraint. The argument indicates that the check constraint rejects any value less than zero.

Bookmark Lookup

The Bookmark Lookup icon in the execution plan indicates that the query processor needed to look up the row in the table or clustered index. One example of when this can happen is when the nonclustered index being used for the operation needs to make the pointer jump because of a column in the statement that is not included in the nonclustered index. Adding the column to create a covering index, if appropriate, should eliminate the bookmark lookup. This situation is an example of when the columns in the `select` clause of the statement can influence the execution plan. The `WITH PREFETCH` clause indicates that the query optimizer will use asynchronous prefetch (read-ahead) on this lookup. Figure 24.7 shows an example of a query that does not require a bookmark and the same query with an additional column in the select clause that is not part of the clustered index and requires a bookmark to that data.

FIGURE **24.6**

Assert example.

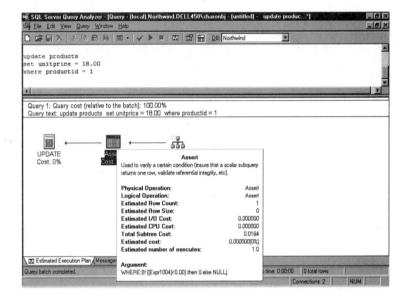

FIGURE **24.7**

Bookmark example.

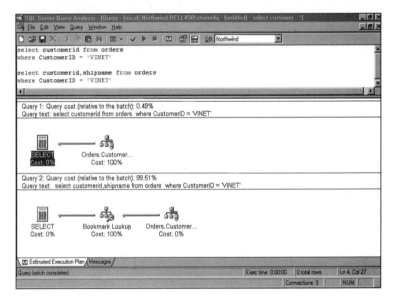

Clustered Index or Index: Delete, Insert, and Update

The Clustered Index or Index physical operators Delete, Insert, and Update indicate that a delete, insert, or update is being made to a clustered index or a nonclustered index.

> **NOTE**
>
> In SQL Server 6.5, if a clustered index page was split, the physical row identifier (used as pointers in the nonclustered index) changed, requiring the nonclustered indexes to be rebuilt. Because SQL Server 7.0 now uses the clustering key itself, these indexes are not rebuilt on a page split. However, changing the data in a column used as a clustering key does have an impact that it did not in SQL Server 6.5 because the nonclustered indexes need to reflect the new key value. For example, using the Order Details table in the Northwind database, the query execution plans for an update to the Products column (which is part of the clustered index) shows a cost that is much larger than an update of the Quantity column (which is not part of the clustered index).

Clustered Index or Index: Scan and Seek

The seek is a logical and physical operator that indicates the optimizer is using either the clustered index or a nonclustered index to find rows. An index scan (also a logical and physical operator) indicates the optimizer is scanning a subset of the table rows using the index. A clustered index scan might occur even when there is a nonclustered index on the search argument. For instance, if a select statement requests all the columns in the table based on a column value that had a nonclustered index, it might be more efficient to scan the clustered index to retrieve all column data. Requesting only one or two columns returned in the resultset might cause the optimizer to change its strategy and use a nonclustered index seek.

Figure 24.8 shows a Clustered Index Seek ToolTip. The ToolTip indicates that the seek is being performed against the PK_Suppliers index on the Suppliers table in the Northwind database. The Argument section indicates that the seek is looking for the value in the parameter, and the optimizer has determined that the results need to be output in clustered index order, as indicated by the ORDERED keyword at the end of the Argument.

FIGURE 24.8

Clustered Index Seek ToolTip example.

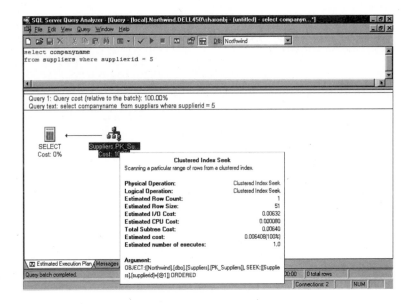

Collapse and Split

A Split physical and logical operator indicates that the query optimizer has decided to break the rows input from the previous update optimization step into a separate delete and insert operation. The Estimated Row Count in the Split icon ToolTips will normally be double the input row count, reflecting this two-step operation. If possible, the optimizer may then choose later in the plan to collapse those rows, grouping by a key value. Figure 24.9 shows an example of an update to a column not in a clustered or nonclustered index where no split is occurring and an update to a column participating in the clustered index.

Compute Scalar

The optimizer uses the Computer Scalar operator to output a computed scalar value.

Concatenation

The Concatenation operator indicates that the resultsets from two output sources are being concatenated. You often see this when a UNION ALL is being used. You can force a concatenation union strategy by using the OPTION clause in the query and specifying a CONCAT UNION. Query optimization is covered in Chapter 25.

FIGURE 24.9

Split example.

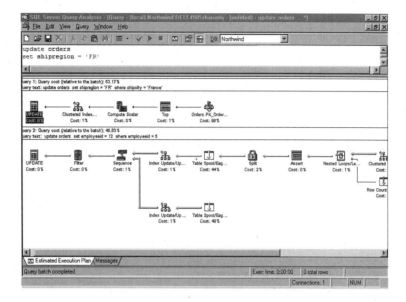

> **NOTE**
>
> Optimizer hints are not always executed. In the example using the UNION ALL statement, the optimizer will probably ignore a HASH UNION hint. Because a UNION ALL means to return all rows whether they are duplicates or not, there is no need to hash these values (which might be required to determine uniqueness), so the concatenation will probably still occur.

Figure 24.10 shows the execution plan for a union query using a Concatenation operator.

Deleted Scan and Inserted Scan

The Deleted Scan and Inserted Scan icons in the execution plan indicate that a trigger is being fired and that within that trigger, the optimizer needs to scan either the deleted or inserted tables.

Filter

The Filter icon indicates that the input rows are being filtered according to the argument indicated in the ToolTip. This seems to occur mostly for intermediate operations that the optimizer needs to perform.

FIGURE **24.10**

Example of union query execution plan using concatenation.

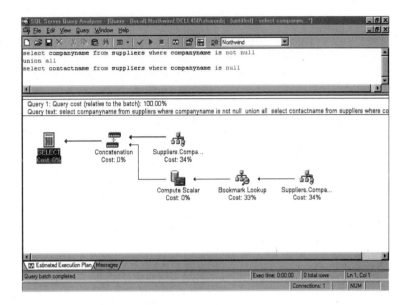

Hash Match, Hash Match Root, and Hash Match Team

Hash joins are new to SQL Server 7.0, and are covered more in depth in Chapter 25, but to understand these three physical operators, you must understand the concept of hash joins to some degree.

In a hash join, the keys that are common between the two tables are hashed using the same hash function into a hash bucket. This bucket will usually start out in memory and then move to disk as needed. The type of hashing that occurs depends on the amount of memory required. Hashing is commonly used for inner and outer joins, intersections, unions, and differences. It is often used by the optimizer for intermediate processing.

Pseudo-code for a simple hash join might look like this:

```
for each row in the smaller table
read the row
    hash the key value
insert the hashed key into the hash bucket
next row
for each row in the larger table
    read the row
    hash the key value
    if key value is already in the hash bucket
        output key and both row identifiers
next row
```

If the two inputs are too large to fit into memory, you may use a modified method, called the grace hash join. This method partitions the smaller input table (also referred to as the build input) into *n* buckets. The number of buckets is selected so that each can fit into memory. The larger table (also referred to as the probe input) is then also partitioned into the same number of buckets. Each bucket from each input can then be read into memory and the matches made. A hybrid join is a join method that uses elements of both a simple in-memory hash and a grace hash.

A hash aggregation uses the same basic method for aggregates (for the sum operator, for example). At the point where the probe input row is checked to determine whether it already exists in the hash bucket, the aggregate is computed if it does.

> **NOTE**
>
> A hash aggregation does not produce ordered results. The Group By clause may cause the optimizer to use a hash method, and you cannot assume the result is in order. The ANSI standard requires the use of the Order By clause with a Group By, and you should get into the habit of using it right away. The method that SQL Server 6.*x* used happened to cause the resultset to be ordered, so a large number of aggregation queries were written without Order By clauses. You should analyze this area of your queries before upgrading an existing database to SQL Server 7.0.

You can use a group optimizer hint with the OPTION clause to hint an ordered group by, which will not use a hash aggregation and will return the result rows in order. However, allowing the optimizer to use the hash aggregation method and including an explicit Order By clause is much faster than using the Order Group optimizer hint, which results in a stream aggregation. The query execution plans for both approaches are shown in Figure 24.11.

A hash join requires at least one equality clause in the predicate, which includes the clauses used to relate a primary key to a foreign key. Usually, the optimizer will select a hash join when the input tables are unsorted or are different in size, there are no appropriate indexes, or a result ordering is not required.

The addition of hash joins to SQL Server 7.0 further supports large databases, complex queries, and distributed tables.

24

QUERY ANALYSIS

FIGURE 24.11

Graphical execution plans for a group by using hash aggregation and a `Group By` using stream aggregation.

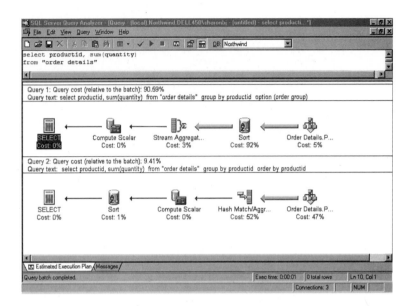

A hash match uses the hash join strategy described previously and may also include any other criteria required to be considered a match. This other criteria are indicated in the RESIDUAL clause shown in the Hash Match ToolTip.

A hash match team is a group of operators sharing a common hash function and strategy. The hash match root is the operator that coordinates the hash match team and is responsible for outputting the results to the next step in the process.

Index, Row Count Spool, and Table Spool

An Index, Row Count Spool, or Table Spool icon indicates that the rows are being stored in a temporary spooling table in the tempdb database. This is similar to the worktable that was created in SQL Server 6.5. Generally, this spool will be created to support a nested iteration operation because the optimizer may need to use the rows over again. Often, you see a spool icon under a Nested Loops icon in the execution plan. A Table Spool ToolTip will not show any predicate because no index is used. An Index Spool ToolTip will show a SEEK predicate. A temporary worktable is created for an index spool, and then, a temporary index is created on that table. These temporary worktables are local to the connection and live only as long as the query. Figure 24.12 shows an example of a row count spool.

FIGURE 24.12

Example of a query execution plan using a row count spool.

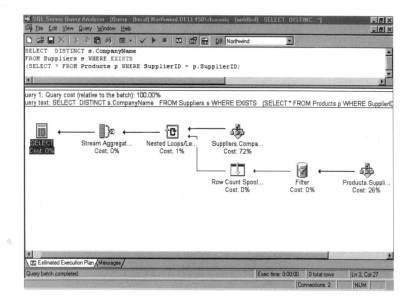

Eager or Lazy Spool

The optimizer will select to use either an Eager or Lazy method of filling the spool, depending on the query. The Eager method means the spool table is built all at once upon the first request. The Lazy method builds the spool table as a row is requested.

Log Row Scan

The Log Row Scan icon indicates the transaction log is being scanned.

Merge Join

The merge join is a new strategy for SQL Server in version 7.0. Merge joins require that both the inputs be sorted on the common columns, defined by the predicate. This allows one pass through each input table, matching the merge columns defined in the WHERE clause as it steps through each input. It looks similar to a simple nested loop but occurs in only one pass.

Pseudo-code for a simple merge join might look like this:

```
while there are still rows in the left table and the right table,
    get a left table row and a right table row
    if keys are equal,
        output rows a
```

24

QUERY ANALYSIS

```
        loop on inner row
   if keys are not equal,
        discard row with lower value
get another left table row and  right table row
```

Merge joins are fast but require the input to be sorted. The introduction of this strategy can be especially optimal in decision support systems and data warehousing where there are very large amounts of data that is already sorted or indexed.

Figure 24.13 shows an example of an execution plan using a merge join. Note that this query moves large amounts of rows through the query, which can be expensive. It also uses a nested loops join and a hash aggregation.

FIGURE 24.13

*Example of a
merge join.*

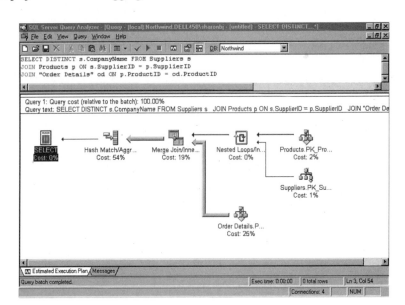

Nested Loops

Nested loop joins are also known as nested iteration, which is familiar to SQL Server 6.5 users. This is the join strategy used fairly exclusively in SQL Server 6.5. Basically, in a nested iteration, every row in the outer table is compared to every row within the inner table. This is why you will often see a Spool icon of some flavor providing input to a Nested Loop icon. This allows the inner table rows to be reused—or "rewound." When every row in each table is compared, it is called a "naive nested loops join." If an index is used, it is referred to as an "index nested loops join."

Pseudo-code for a nested loops join might look like this:

```
for each row in the outer table
    read the row
    for each row in the inner table
        read the row
        if the row matches the outer row
            output row
    next inner table row
next outer table row
```

You can see the number of comparisons for this method to be the calculation of the number of outer rows times the number of inner rows, which can become expensive. Generally, a nested loops join is considered to be most effective when both input tables are quite small.

Figure 24.14 shows the execution plan for a query that uses an index scan on the outer input table (shown as the top icon in the plan) and an index seek on the inner table (shown on the bottom in the plan) for each outer table row. Stream aggregation is then used to perform the `Distinct` function.

FIGURE 24.14

Example of a nested loops join.

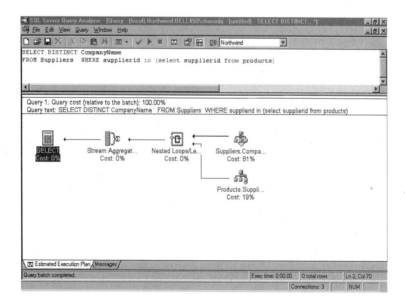

24

QUERY ANALYSIS

Remote Delete, Remote Insert, Remote Query, Remote Scan, and Remote Update

These various operators—Remote Delete, Remote Insert, Remote Query, Remote Scan, and Remote Update—simply indicate that the operation is being performed against a remote server.

Sequence

The Sequence operator executes each operation in its child node, moving from top to bottom in sequence, and returns only the end result from the bottom operator. You see this most often in the updates of multiple objects.

Sort

The Sort operator indicates that the input is being sorted. The sort order will be displayed in the ToolTip Argument section.

Stream Aggregation

You will most often see the Stream Aggregation operation when aggregating a single input, such as a `distinct` clause, or a `sum`, `count`, `max`, `min`, or `avg` operator. Figure 24.15 shows a sample execution plan with a Stream Aggregation operator.

FIGURE 24.15

Example of stream aggregation.

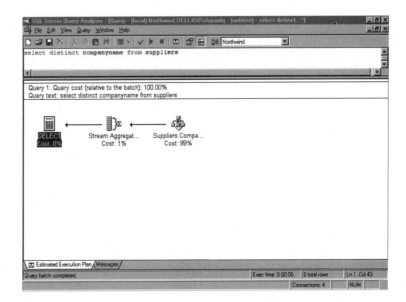

Table Delete, Table Insert, Table Scan, and Table Update

You see the Table Delete, Table Insert, Table Scan, and Table Update operators when the indicated operation is being performed against that table as a whole. This does not always mean there is a problem, although as in SQL Server 6.5, a table scan can be an indicator that you need some indexes to support the query. A table scan can still occur on small tables. A `select into` statement would produce a Table Insert operator. A table update might also be an indicator that you need a better indexing strategy.

Top

The Top operator indicates a limit set on the number of results to be returned. Top differs from `set rowcount` in that `top` limits a resultset after an ordering, whereas `set rowcount` limits before the ordering if there is an `order by` clause.

Analyzing Stored Procedures

A welcome addition to the SQL Server 7.0 Query Analyzer is the ability to analyze stored procedures. Analyzing stored procedures in batches, supplying different, widely disparate parameters can provide excellent feedback on how a stored procedure may actually perform at different times and under different circumstances.

Because the stored procedure never executes when it is being analyzed, any objects created within the procedure do not actually get created, and references to these objects later in the procedure will fail. Because it is considered good practice to create all tables, both temporary or not, with a `create` statement, and then insert into these tables, you can copy and save the `create` statements with the stored procedure file to be used for analysis.

Because stored procedures can become complex with multiple SQL statements, seeing the graphical execution plan in the Query Analyzer window can be difficult. As with development in SQL Server 6.5, the best approach might be to create stored procedures as SQL statement batches first, analyzing and optimizing each statement as you go, and only converting the batch into a stored procedure once the Analyzer is showing an optimized execution plan for all of the statements.

SHOWPLAN_ALL and SHOWPLAN_TEXT

SQL Server 7.0 no longer supports the `set showplan on` statement as used in SQL Server 6.5, but it provides two variants of `showplan` output: `set showplan_text` and `set showplan_all`. Both of these statements stop the query from executing (which was not the case in SQL Server 6.5).

You can turn on this option for a user session by typing the following command in a Query Analyzer window:

```
set showplan_all on
go
```

Setting this option will then cause the query to not execute and the textual showplan to display. The set command must be the only statement in the batch. To turn off the textual showplan, enter the following command:

```
set showplan_all off
go
```

The same syntax will work for the showplan_text statement. You can also turn the showplan_text output by selecting the Show Query Plan check box in the Current Connections property box, accessed from the Query menu in the Query Analyzer.

set showplan_all outputs much the same data as the graphical execution plan, in textual format. Figure 24.16 shows a query with its graphical execution.

FIGURE 24.16

Sample graphical execution plan.

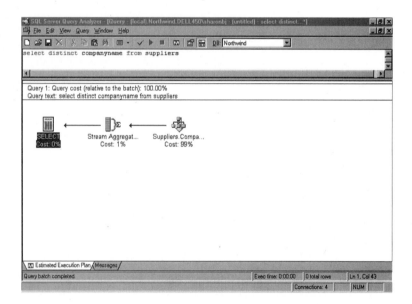

The same query run with set showplan_all will produce the following output, broken down by column:

```
StmtText:
|—Clustered Index Seek(OBJECT:([Northwind].[dbo].[Suppliers].
➥[PK_Suppliers]),
SEEK:([Suppliers].[supplierid]=[@1]) ORDERED)
```

This is the same information shown in the graphical execution plan ToolTip under the main heading and the Argument section. The optimizer is performing a clustered index seek using the index named PK_Suppliers on the Suppliers table. The seek is for a sup-plierid, and the ORDERED clause indicates that the results must be returned in the clustered index order.

Following is the second statement in the batch:

```
StmtId:
2
```

The first statement, not displayed, is the query statement itself. Following is the ID for the node of this subtask of the query:

```
NodeID:
3
```

A node ID should be unique within a showplan_all output. Following is the ID for the parent of this subtask node:

```
Parent:
1
```

In this case, it is the query itself that is the parent. In a query that might have a merge join or a nested loops operator that would take input from two other operators, the input operator's parent would be the node ID for the merge join or nested loops operator.

The physical operation is a clustered index seek:

```
PhysicalOp:
Clustered Index Seek
```

The logical operation is a clustered index seek:

```
LogicalOp:
Clustered Index Seek
```

In the case of join operations, such as a merge join or nested loops, the physical operator would be the join operation, but the logical operator would be the type of join performed (left join, inner join, and so on). A showplan_all output may show more information about a join than the graphical execution plan. For instance, a merge join may indicate a MANY-TO-MANY MERGE or a simple MERGE.

Following are the predicates and parameters, which make up the argument for the operation:

```
Argument:
OBJECT:([Northwind].[dbo].[Suppliers].[PK_Suppliers]),
SEEK:([Suppliers].[supplierid]=[@1]) ORDERED
```

24

QUERY ANALYSIS

This will usually be prefaced with the argument type, which might include HASH (indicating a hash join or aggregate), OBJECT (indicating a scan or seek against an object, usually a table), or a MERGE (indicating a merge join). Nested loops usually show a NULL in this column.

The following column lists the values introduced by this operator:

```
DefinedValues:
[Suppliers].[companyname]
```

Following is the estimated number of output rows:

```
EstimateRows:
1.0
```

This is the estimated I/O cost for this node:

```
EstimateIO:
6.3284999E-3
```

This is the estimated CPU cost for this node:

```
EstimateCPU:
7.9600002E-5
```

Following is the estimated average row size for this node:

```
AvgRowSize:
51
```

This is the estimated cumulative cost for this node and its children:

```
TotalSubtreeCost:
0.0064081
```

This is the list of columns output by this node:

```
OutputList:
[Suppliers].[companyname]
```

This is a list of warnings issued by the analyzer:

```
Warnings:
NULL
```

These may include NO STATS, which indicates that the statistics need to be updated, or NO JOIN PREDICATE.

The following section will indicate either the type of query (SELECT, INSERT, and so on) or PLAN_ROW, which indicates a row that is part of the execution plan:

```
Type:
PLAN_ROW
```

This is a boolean indicator for parallel query plans:

```
Parallel:
0
```

This is the estimated number of executions of this operation:

```
EstimateExecutions:
1.0
```

The `set showplan_text` statement returns only the query statement and the `StmtText` results, as explained in the previous section. The `set showplan_text` option is meant to be output data that is readable by MS-DOS applications, such as ISQL or OSQL (the ODBC-based DOS tool).

Statistics

SQL Server 7.0 still supports both the `set statistics io` option and the `set statistic time` option, which will display the actual logical and physical page reads incurred by a query. These two `set` options return actual execution statistics, as opposed to the estimates returned by the Query Analyzer and the two `showplan` options discussed earlier. These two tools are invaluable for determining actual query impact. The `set statistics profile` option has been added as well. The SQL Profiler is a more sophisticated tool that you can use to actually trace all server activity or subsets of server activity. You can replay these traces to better understand and optimize a server. The SQL Profiler is covered in depth in Chapter 27, "Using the SQL Server Profiler."

statistics io

You set the `statistics io` option for individual user sessions, and you can turn it on in a Query Analyzer window by typing

```
set statistics io on
```

You can also set this option for the user session by selecting the Show Stats IO check box in the Current Connections property box, accessed from the Query menu in the Query Analyzer.

The `statistics io` option displays the scan count (number of iterations), the logical reads (from cached data), the physical reads (from physical storage), and read-ahead reads.

The following is an example of a query and the `statistics io` that was output:

```
SELECT DISTINCT s.CompanyName
FROM Suppliers s
```

```
JOIN Products p ON s.SupplierID = p.SupplierID
JOIN "Order Details" od ON p.ProductID = od.ProductID
Table 'Order Details'. Scan count 1, logical reads 310,
physical reads 0, read-ahead reads 0.
Table 'Suppliers'. Scan count 77, logical reads 183,
physical reads 0, read-ahead reads 0.
Table 'Products'. Scan count 1, logical reads 2,
physical reads 0, read-ahead reads 0.
```

This indicates that the first table, Order Details, was scanned once, with all reads coming from cache. The second table, Suppliers, was scanned 77 times, with all reads coming from cache, and the third table, Products, was scanned once, with all reads coming from cache. Note that a physical read requires a logical read, so there will never be more physical reads than logical reads.

Although it is positive that there were no physical reads in this case, there are a large amount of scans and logical reads, which might be lower with a better-optimized query. Writing the same query in a different manner, as shown in the following code, produces a lower scan and logical read count. The query and its statistics output follow:

```
SELECT DISTINCT s.CompanyNameFROM Suppliers s
WHERE EXISTS
(SELECT * FROM Products p
JOIN "Order Details" od
ON p.ProductID = od.ProductID
WHERE SupplierID = p.SupplierID)
Table 'Products'. Scan count 1, logical reads 2,
physical reads 0, read-ahead reads 0.
Table 'Order Details'. Scan count 1, logical reads 2,
physical reads 0, read-ahead reads 0.
Table 'Suppliers'. Scan count 1, logical reads 1,
physical reads 0, read-ahead reads 0.
```

The information displayed by the `statistics io` option is very different from the information displayed by the Query Analyzer graphical execution plan and does not estimate the number of physical or logical reads, but you can compare the scan counts to determine how the Analyzer is performing.

The graphical execution plan for the first query estimates one clustered index scan of the Products table, 77 clustered index seeks for the Suppliers table, and one index scan of the Order Details table. This matches the actual scan counts output by the `statistics io` option.

The graphical execution plan for the second query estimates one clustered index seek for the Products table, one index scan for the Order Details table, and one index scan for Suppliers. This also matches the actual scan counts reported by the `statistic io` option.

You can use the `statistics io` option to evaluate the effectiveness of the size of the data cache, and to evaluate over time how long a table will stay in cache.

statistics time

You set the `statistics time` option for individual user sessions. In a Query Analyzer window, type

```
set statistics time on
```

You can also set this option for the user session by selecting the Show Stats Time check box in the Current Connections property box, accessed from the Query menu in the Query Analyzer.

The `statistics time` option displays the total CPU and elapsed time it takes to actually execute a query. The `statistics time` output for the first query described in the preceding section returns the following:

```
SELECT DISTINCT s.CompanyName
FROM Suppliers s
JOIN Products p
ON s.SupplierID = p.SupplierID
JOIN "Order Details" od
ON p.ProductID = od.ProductID
SQL Server parse and compile time:
   CPU time = 0 ms, elapsed time = 30 ms.

SQL Server Execution Times:
   CPU time = 1352 ms,  elapsed time = 535746 ms.
```

The `statistics time` output for the second query described earlier returns the following:

```
SELECT DISTINCT s.CompanyName
FROM Suppliers s
WHERE EXISTS
(SELECT * FROM Products p
JOIN "Order Details" od
ON p.ProductID = od.ProductID
WHERE SupplierID = p.SupplierID)
SQL Server parse and compile time:
   CPU time = 0 ms, elapsed time = 22 ms.

SQL Server Execution Times:
   CPU time = 0 ms,  elapsed time = 288 ms.
```

You again see that the second query is faster than the first. The `statistics time` option provides a powerful tool for benchmarking and comparing performance.

24

QUERY ANALYSIS

statistics profile

The set statistics profile option returns the same textual information that is displayed with the set showplan_all statement, with the addition of two columns displaying actual execution information. The Rows column displays the actual number of rows returned in the execution step, and the Executions column shows the actual number of executions for the step. The Rows column can be compared to the EstimatedRows column, and the Execution column can be compared to the EstimatedExecution column to determine the efficacy of the execution plan.

You set the statistics profile option for individual user sessions. In a Query Analyzer window, type

```
set statistics profile on
```

Other Analysis Tools

With the enhancement of the analysis tools provided by SQL Server 7.0, you will find much less need to use trace flags, whereas trace flags were commonly used in SQL Server 6.5 to see full analysis information. You can also perform more in-depth analysis of performance implications by using the SQL Server Profiler tool provided with SQL Server 7.0. This tool is covered in Chapter 27 and provides a powerful optimization and impact-analysis mechanism.

Summary

The new SQL Server 7.0 Query Analyzer can provide critical information about how your queries will perform, and it is also an excellent tool for better understanding how queries are processed in SQL Server 7.0. Such an understanding can only help ensure that users' queries become more optimized through experience with the tool. The statistics io and statistics time options can also provide excellent feedback on how queries actually perform.

Optimization

by Kevin Viers

In This Chapter

CHAPTER 25

By its nature, SQL is not a procedural language. In other words, when you issue an SQL statement, you are telling the database what results you want and not how you want the database to get those results. A SELECT statement is simply a set of instructions that you issue to the database defining the results that you want. The database must figure out how it is going to get those results for you. The process of determining the most efficient way of processing these requests is known as optimization.

> **NOTE**
>
> To understand the concepts presented in this chapter, you should have a good understanding of how SQL Server uses implements indexes and how they affect performance. Refer to Chapter 23, "Database Design and Performance," for more information about indexes.

What Is a Query Optimizer?

For any given SQL statement, there are many ways to access the source tables to build the desired resultset. The query optimizer analyzes all the possible ways that the resultset can be built and chooses the most appropriate method. This method is called the query execution plan. SQL Server uses a cost-based optimizer. The optimizer assigns a cost to every possible execution plan in terms of CPU resource usage and disk I/O. The optimizer then chooses the execution plan with the least associated cost.

Of course, the process of query optimization is extremely complicated and is based on sophisticated costing models and data-access algorithms. This chapter is intended to help you better understand some of the concepts related to how the query optimizer chooses an execution strategy and how the query optimizer has been enhanced to improve query processing performance.

Optimizer Basics

When SQL Server processes a query, it performs the following basic steps:

1. The query is parsed to break it into keywords, expressions, operators, and identifiers.
2. The query is analyzed to determine search arguments and join clauses. A search argument is defined as a WHERE clause comparing a column to a constant. The join clause is a WHERE clause comparing a column from one table to a column in another table.

3. Indexes are selected based on search arguments and join clauses (if any exist). Indexes are evaluated based on their distribution statistics and are assigned a cost.

4. The join order is evaluated to determine the most appropriate order in which to access tables. Additionally, the optimizer evaluates the most appropriate join algorithm to match the data.

5. Execution costs are evaluated and a query execution plan is created that represents the most efficient solution.

6. The relational engine executes the query execution plan.

To understand how the optimizer works, it is helpful to walk through a simple example. Let's consider processing the following single SELECT statement:

```
SELECT *
From Orders o, Customers c
Where o.CustomerId = c.CustomerId
And o.CustomerId = '12345'
```

Figure 25.1 shows a graphical showplan that illustrates how the optimizer will choose to execute this query. You can refer to Chapter 24, "Query Analysis," for a more detailed discussion of the graphical showplan feature of SQL Server 7.0.

FIGURE 25.1

Graphical show-plan illustration.

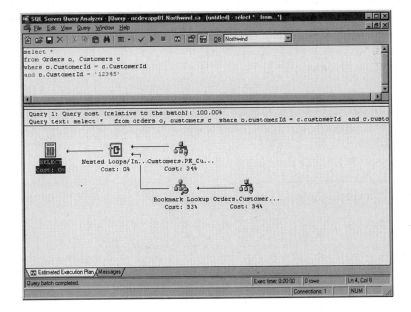

In the example, the optimizer knows that the query has a search argument defined where the CustomerId is equal to '12345'. The first thing the optimizer will do is to look for an index on the CustomerId column. If there is an index, it can scan this index to return only those rows that match the search argument. In this case, the optimizer finds an index on the CustomerId column in the Orders table.

The next step is to join the Orders table with the Customer table based on the CustomerId column. Again, the optimizer will look for any indexes that will help speed the search. The optimizer has already determined which rows it needs from the Orders table, but it needs to determine how to access the Customers table. The optimizer finds an index on the CustomerId column in the Customers table.

At this point, the optimizer has determined that it can use the two indexes to join the tables. The optimizer determines the appropriate join strategy to match the rows from each index. The final step will be to return the desired information to the user. These steps collectively will be compiled into an execution plan, which will be handed off to the query processor for execution.

Of course, this is not the only possible way that SQL Server could have executed this query. The optimizer made many decisions to come up with this execution plan, and each decision was based on the relative cost in CPU resource usage and disk I/O of each alternative.

Improvements for SQL Server 7.0

The query optimizer has been almost completely redesigned for SQL Server 7.0. Microsoft made many improvements to the query processing architecture. Some of the more notable improvements follow:

- Autoupdate statistics—SQL Server 7.0 will automatically update and maintain distribution statistics. Previous versions required a DBA to manually update statistics.
- Additional join strategies—SQL Server 7.0 supports merge and hash joins. These new join strategies greatly improve query processing performance.
- Multiple index support—SQL Server 7.0 can utilize multiple indexes per table. Previous versions of SQL Server could only utilize one index per table when processing a query.
- Improved query-tuning tools—SQL Server 7.0 includes a graphical showplan to illustrate the execution plan chosen by the optimizer, a Query Profiler to analyze poor performing queries, and an Index Tuning Wizard to automatically recommend indexes to help improve performance.

Each of the items mentioned here are significant changes to the architecture of the SQL Server query optimizer and add significantly to query processing performance. The remainder of the chapter focuses on each in more detail.

Statistics

As I mentioned previously, one of the primary jobs of the query optimizer is to evaluate all the available indexes for a given query and make decisions about how to best use those indexes, if at all. How does the optimizer know how to make these decisions? The answer is statistics.

SQL Server maintains statistics about the distribution of data values within columns. These statistics can be maintained for both indexed and nonindexed columns. The basic statistical information concerns the distribution of data within a column. In its simplest form, the statistics keep track of the uniqueness of data within a column. The optimizer can use this information to assign a cost to using a particular index or column to resolve a query.

Automatic Statistics Updating

As you can imagine, keeping accurate statistics is extremely important for the query optimizer to make the most efficient decisions. To ensure that statistics remain accurate as the underlying data changes, SQL Server utilizes automated statistics updating. In previous versions of SQL Server, the DBA was responsible for manually updating statistics at periodic intervals. Statistics could become stale if not updated appropriately. When the statistics become out of date, the query optimizer might make incorrect decisions about how to best process a query.

In SQL Server 7.0, the statistics are automatically updated by managing update counts on tables. Whenever SQL Server determines that an appropriate number of updates have occurred on a table, it will automatically update the statistics for the columns of that table. Typically, SQL Server will automatically update statistics when the update count exceeds 10 percent of the cardinality of the table. If a table has 10,000 rows, the statistics will be automatically updated when 1,000 index values have changed due to update.

Data Sampling

You might wonder what impact the automated updating of statistics will have on performance. Actually, the overhead is quite minimal because SQL Server uses page sampling to gather statistics.

When the statistics are updated automatically, SQL Server takes a random sampling of data pages and assumes that those data pages are a good statistical representation of the entire table. It then updates the statistics based on this sampling. Of course, it is possible that the sample is not an accurate statistical reflection of the entire table, and SQL Server can create inaccurate statistics. If you suspect this is the case, you can force SQL Server to do a full scan by manually updating the statistics.

Manually Controlling Statistics

Although it is nice that SQL Server will automatically maintain statistics for you, there will certainly be times when you want to manually force a statistics update. Likewise, you might not want automatic statistics updating on a certain column or index.

To manually update the statistics on an index or column, use the UPDATE STATISTICS command with the following syntax:

```
UPDATE STATISTICS {table}
[index ¦ (statistics_name[,...n])]
[WITH [[FULLSCAN]
¦ SAMPLE number {PERCENT ¦ ROWS}]]
[[,] [ALL ¦ COLUMNS ¦ INDEX]
[[,] NORECOMPUTE]]
```

You can use the FULLSCAN clause to force SQL Server to scan the entire table when gathering statistics. The SAMPLE clause will allow you to specify either a percentage or a number of rows to scan while gathering statistics.

If you do not want SQL Server to automatically update statistics, you can set the auto create statistics and auto update statistics database options to false by using the sp_dboption system stored procedure.

> **CAUTION**
>
> I would not recommended turning off automatic statistics updating. If you do this, you will have to manually update statistics to prevent them from becoming out of date. The query optimizer relies heavily on these statistics when making decisions about the most efficient execution plan.

Query Optimization Algorithms

The job of the query optimizer is amazingly complex. There are literally thousands of things the optimizer must consider when determining the optimal execution plan. The statistics are simply one of tools that the optimizer can use to help in the decision making process.

In addition to examining the statistics to determine the appropriate use of indexes, the optimizer must consider the order in which to access tables, the appropriate join algorithms to use, the appropriate sorting algorithms, and many other details that are too many to list here.

I attempt to cover some of the most common query processing algorithms that the optimizer uses to determine an appropriate execution plan. In addition, I highlight some of the improvements that have been made in the query processor to improve performance in SQL Server 7.0.

> **NOTE**
>
> Throughout this section, I use the graphical showplan to illustrate some of the principles discussed. If you have not already done so, read Chapter 24 for a more detailed discussion of the graphical showplan.

Join Processing Strategies

If you are familiar with SQL, then you are very familiar with joins as they are used in creating SQL statements. As far as the SQL Server query processor is concerned, a join occurs any time it has to compare two inputs to determine an output. The join can occur between one table and another table, between an index and a table, or between an index and another index.

The SQL Server query processor uses three types of join strategies when it must compare two inputs: nested loops join; merge join; and hash join. The optimizer must consider each one of these algorithms to determine the most appropriate algorithm for a given situation. Keep in mind that a single query might require the processor to perform several joins.

Nested Loops Join

The nested loops join algorithm is by far the simplest of the three supported algorithms. In fact, this is the only join algorithm that was supported in SQL Server 6.5.

The nested loops join uses one input as the "outer" loop and the other input as the "inner" loop. As you might expect, SQL Server processes the outer input one row at a time. For each row in the outer input, the inner input is searched for matching rows. Figure 25.2 illustrates a query that uses a nested loops join.

FIGURE 25.2

A nested loops join.

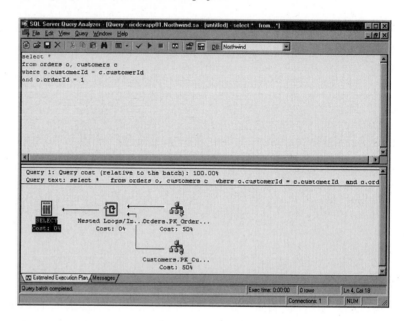

Note that in the graphical showplan, the outer loop is represented as the top input table and the inner loop is represented as the bottom input table. In most instances, the optimizer will choose the input table with the least number of rows to be the outer loop.

The nested loops join is effective on transactions that only affect a small number of rows. As the number of rows in the outer loop increases, the effectiveness of the nested loops join strategy diminishes. This is because of the increased disk I/O required as the loops get larger.

Merge Join

The merge join algorithm is new to SQL Server 7.0. This algorithm is much more effective than the nested loops join when dealing with large data volume. The merge join works by retrieving one row from each input and comparing them. Figure 25.3 illustrates a query that will use a merge join.

FIGURE 25.3

A merge join.

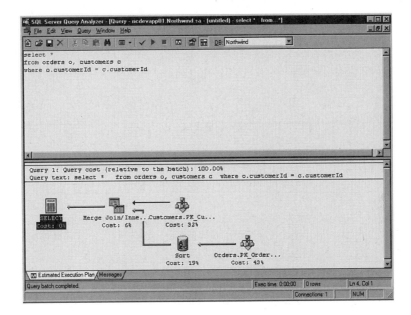

The merge join requires that both inputs be sorted on the merge columns. The merge join does not work if both inputs are not sorted. Usually, the optimizer will choose a merge join strategy when the data volume is large and both columns are contained in an existing pre-sorted index, such as a primary key. If either of the inputs is not already sorted, the optimizer has to perform an explicit sort before the join. This might cause the merge join to be too expensive.

Hash Join

The final, and most complicated, join algorithm is the hash join. Like the merge join, the hash join is new to SQL Server 7.0. The hash join is an effective join strategy for dealing with large data volumes where the inputs might not be sorted. Figure 25.4 illustrates a query that uses a hash join.

The basic hash join algorithm involves separating the two inputs into a "build" input and a "probe" input. The optimizer will assign the smaller input as the build input. The hash join scans the build input and creates a hash table either in memory or on the data files. Each row from the build input is inserted into the hash table based on a hash key value, which is computed. The probe input is then scanned one row at a time. A hash key value is computed for each row in the probe, and the hash table is scanned for matches. The hash join is an effective join strategy when dealing with large data volumes and unsorted data inputs.

25

OPTIMIZATION

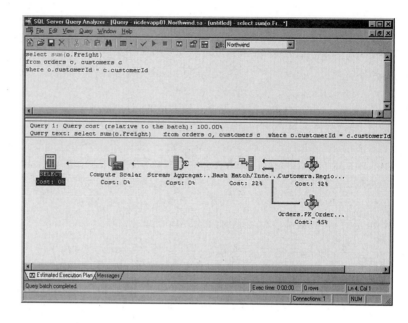

Each of the three supported join algorithms could be used for any join operation. The query optimizer examines all of the possible alternatives, assigns costs to each, and chooses the least expensive join algorithm for a given situation. The addition of the merge and hash joins has greatly improved the query processing performance of SQL Server in the data warehousing and very large database environment. In previous versions that only supported nested loops join strategies, SQL Server was not as effective at handling large data requests.

Multiple Index Support

In addition to the merge and hash join algorithms, SQL Server 7.0 has added support for multiple indexes. Of course, you have always been able to create multiple indexes on a table. Until SQL Server 7.0, however, the query processor could only exploit one index per table per query. That restriction has been eliminated, and the optimizer can now exploit multiple indexes in a couple of interesting ways.

Index Intersection

Index intersection is a mechanism that allows SQL Server to use multiple indexes on a table when you have multiple restrictions in a query. Consider the following example:

```
SELECT count(*)
FROM Orders
WHERE OrderDate between '1/1/1999' and '3/31/1999'
AND ShippedDate between '1/1/1999' and '3/31/1999'
```

The Orders table contains two nonclustered indexes, one on the OrderDate column and one on the ShippedDate column. The optimizer will search each index to find the rows that meet the restrictions. The two resultsets will then be intersected, and all rows that satisfy all restrictions will be returned. This is a much more efficient means of satisfying this query than was previously available.

Index Joins

Another way of using multiple indexes on a single table is to join two or more indexes to create a covering index. In case you don't remember, a covering index is an index that contains all of the columns required for a given query. Consider the following example:

```
SELECT OrderDate, ShippedDate, count(*)
FROM Orders
GROUP BY OrderDate, ShippedDate
```

Again, the Orders table contains indexes on both the OrderDate and ShippedDate columns. In this instance, the optimizer will join the two indexes using a merge join to return the appropriate resultset. By joining the two indexes, SQL Server created the same effect as having one covering index on the table.

Data Warehousing and Large Database Strategies

In a data warehousing environment, your data is more than likely contained in a star or snowflake schema. These schemas are characterized by having a few fact tables with many rows that contain your detailed transactional data. You also then have several smaller dimension tables that are related to the fact table via foreign keys. The dimension tables often have few rows.

SQL Server has introduced several optimizer enhancements to improve query performance in a star or snowflake schema environment.

Cartesian Product of Dimension Tables

One way in which the SQL Server query optimizer has been enhanced is to support performing a cross join on dimension tables (creating a Cartesian product) before joining to the fact table. This means that the fact table has to participate in fewer joins, which will reduce the overall cost of the operation. This might sound strange, but it makes sense.

Consider the following example:

```
SELECT count(*)
FROM fact f, dimension1 d1, dimension2 d2
WHERE f.key1 = d1.key1
AND f.key2 = d2.key2
```

In this example, the fact table is being joined with both the dimension1 and dimension2 tables. We will assume that the fact table contains 1,000,000 rows and that each dimension table contains 10 rows. The SQL Server optimizer will actually cross join dimension1 and dimension2 first. This will create a Cartesian product of 100 rows. This resultset is then joined with the fact table to produce the final result. As a result, the fact table only has to be scanned once. I am sure you can see the logic behind this.

Semijoin Reduction

Another optimizer enhancement is a concept known as semijoin reduction. In this scenario, the optimizer will use index intersection on multiple indexes from the fact table. The fact table contains many foreign keys. If you have indexes on each of the foreign keys, SQL Server will use those indexes effectively when processing a query.

The optimizer will actually join each dimension table with an appropriate index of the fact table. Next, the optimizer intersects the results of those joins. Finally, the optimizer fetches rows from the fact table. By doing this, the optimizer avoids performing any full row fetch of the fact table until it is absolutely necessary.

Predicate Transitivity

We all learned about the transitive property in junior high school algebra. The transitive property simply states that if A=B and B=C then A=C. As it turns out, this property holds true in the world of SQL as well.

SQL Server 7.0 supports a concept known as predicate transitivity. Predicate transitivity enables SQL Server to infer a join equality from two given equalities. Consider the following example:

```
SELECT *
FROM table1 t1, table2 t2, table3 t3
WHERE t1.column1 = t2.column1
AND t2.column1 = t3.column1
```

You might expect that the query processor would require the following execution plan:

1. Join table1 with table2 to produce a resultset of matching rows.

2. Join table2 with table3 to produce a resultset of matching rows.

3. Join the outputs of the first two joins to retrieve the final query resultset.

In all, this type of execution plan would require three joins. In SQL Server 6.5, this is exactly the type of execution plan that might have been recommended to produce the query results. SQL Server 7.0, however, uses predicate transitivity to arrive at the following execution plan:

1. Join table1 with table3 to produce a resultset of matching rows. Remember, SQL Server infers this join based on the transitive property.

2. Join the output of the first join with table2 to retrieve the final query resultset.

As you can see, using the principle of predicate transitivity, SQL Server is able to optimize this query using only two joins. This results in a much cheaper execution plan.

Creative Group-By Usage

The SQL Server query optimizer has also implemented some creative usage of grouping to enhance performance in some queries. As you might recall, the correct ANSI SQL sequence for executing a query is as follows:

1. Execute the necessary joins as defined in the FROM and WHERE clauses.

2. Reduce the resulting data by applying the GROUP BY clause.

3. Apply any predicates in the HAVING clause.

In some instances, it is more effective to perform the grouping operation before the join. This has the effect of reducing the join input size and therefore lowering the overall cost of the operation. Of course, this is not always the case, but the point is that the query optimizer will consider this possibility.

Query-Tuning Tips

By now, you should have a better understanding of the how the SQL Server query optimizer works to evaluate the most cost-effective execution plan for a given query and some of the architectural improvements that have been made in the product. Although the improved optimizer and the autoupdating statistics certainly reduce the burden of the DBA when it comes to query tuning, you are not completely off the hook.

There are still things that every good DBA must do to ensure that database applications are running at peak performance. This section outlines a basic recipe for query tuning and using some of the new SQL Server 7.0 tools to most effectively tune query performance.

Query-Tuning Cookbook

The following is an effective approach to tuning any of your database applications. It requires you, as the DBA, to understand the database that you are tuning and the application that is accessing that database. The basic steps are as follows:

1. Declare all constraints that you know to be true for a database. These constraints should include primary keys, foreign keys, Declaritive Referential Integrity (DRI), NULL value, and checks.

25

OPTIMIZATION

2. Create indexes on all foreign keys and any other columns you suspect will be heavily used search columns. This should be a best guess. Do not over index at this point.

3. Start the query profiler. You should set the profiler to look for slow-running queries and to show all warnings.

4. Run your application for a period of time. Make sure that the application is run long enough to collect a good sampling of the queries that are likely to be executed during normal operation.

5. Stop the query profiler and create any statistics that are flagged by the query profiler.

6. Run the Index Tuning Wizard against the profiled queries. The Index Tuning Wizard will highlight additional indexes that might be of value.

7. Continue to profile and tune. You should run the profiler and Index Tuning Wizard at periodic intervals to ensure that the application is still appropriately tuned.

The steps listed here will require you to use the new SQL Server query profiler and Index Tuning Wizard tools. The following sections highlight how to use those tools to tune your application.

SQL Server Profiler

The SQL Server Profiler is a tool that you can use to identify slow-running queries and other performance bottlenecks. (Refer to Chapter 27, "Using the SQL Server Profiler," for a detailed discussion of how to use this tool.) For the purposes of this discussion, all you need to understand is how to use the profiler to capture a workload. A workload is simply a set of queries that are compiled into one trace file. This workload can then be used as the source for the Index Tuning Wizard.

Follow the instructions in Chapter 27 for capturing a trace. You need to make sure that you capture your trace output to a file. This file will be the workload input for running the Index Tuning Wizard.

Index Tuning Wizard

The Index Tuning Wizard is a utility provided by SQL Server that will analyze a set of queries and make recommendations about indexes that could be applied to improve performance. The Index Tuning Wizard does a great job of quickly analyzing a database and recommending a basic set of indexing options. Of course, it is not perfect, and it can make mistakes by not recommending an index that it should or by recommending a less than optimal index.

As a DBA, I recommend using the Index Tuning Wizard as a starting point for any indexing strategy. You should not rely completely on this tool because there will certainly be some instances in which you know an index should be applied and it is not recommended by the Index Tuning Wizard.

As part of the "Query-Tuning Cookbook," you should have collected a workload or trace file using the SQL Server query profiler. You can then use the Index Tuning Wizard to analyze the workload and make recommendations for query processing performance enhancement.

To use the Index Tuning Wizard, follow these steps:

1. Within the SQL Server Query Profiler, select the Tools menu. From the Tools menu, select the Index Tuning Wizard menu option. You will see the Index Tuning Wizard dialog box (see Figure 25.5). Click Next to continue. The Select Server and Database dialog box will appear, as shown in Figure 25.6.

FIGURE 25.5

The Index Tuning Wizard dialog box.

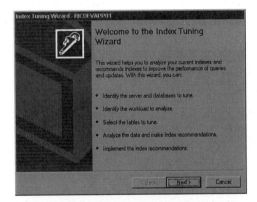

FIGURE 25.6

The Select Server and Database dialog box.

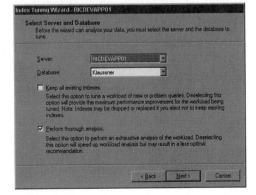

25

OPTIMIZATION

2. In the Select Server and Database dialog box, enter the name of the SQL Server and the database you want to tune. The Index Tuning Wizard will consider only one database at a time. Choose the appropriate optimization type. Following are the available options:

- Keep All Existing Indexes—If you check this option, the Index Tuning Wizard will only consider adding new indexes. If you do not check this option, the Index Tuning Wizard will consider dropping and re-creating indexes. This method will offer the best chance for performance improvement but is also the most risky.

- Perform Thorough Analysis—This option is used to specify how thoroughly you want the Index Tuning Wizard to analyze your database. This is a classic trade-off between performance and thoroughness. I recommend keeping this checked, especially on the first pass.

Click Next to continue. The Identify Workload dialog box will appear as shown in Figure 25.7.

FIGURE 25.7

The Identify Workload dialog box.

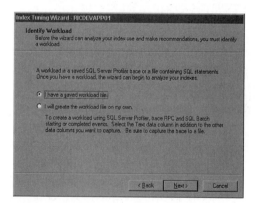

3. On the Identify Workload dialog box, choose whether you have an existing workload file or you are going to create a new workload file. In our example, we have already created a workload file using the Query Profiler. Click Next to continue. The Specify Workload dialog box will appear as shown in Figure 25.8.

4. On the Specify Workload dialog box, select the My workload file and enter the location of the trace file you created using the Query Profiler. Click Next to continue. The Select Tables to Tune dialog will appear as shown in Figure 25.9.

FIGURE 25.8

The Specify Workload dialog box.

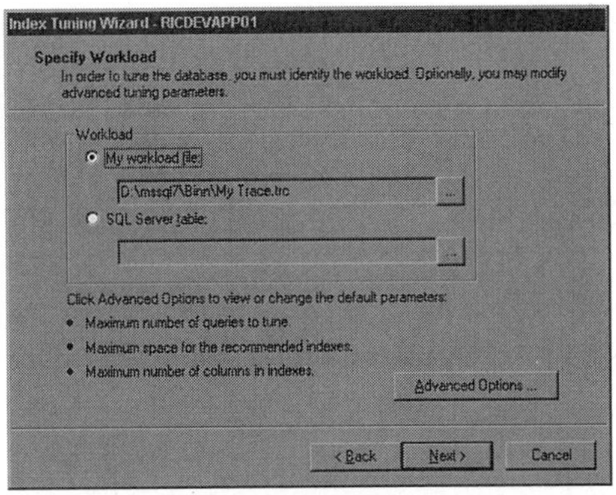

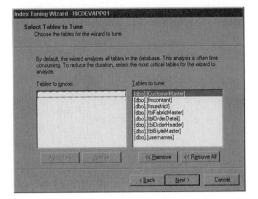

FIGURE 25.9

The Select Tables to Tune dialog box.

5. On the Select Tables to Tune dialog box, you can choose to exempt certain tables from index analysis consideration. For example, if you are only concerned about one or two specific tables, you can tell the Index Tuning to ignore all other tables. Click Next to continue. The Index Recommendations dialog box will appear as shown in Figure 25.10.

6. The Index Recommendations dialog box will show you all of the indexes that have been recommended to potentially improve query performance. This dialog box will show indexes that it recommends even if they already exist. Remember, if you chose not to keep existing indexes, these indexes will be dropped and re-created. Click Next to continue. The Schedule Index Update Job dialog box will appear, as shown in Figure 25.11.

25

OPTIMIZATION

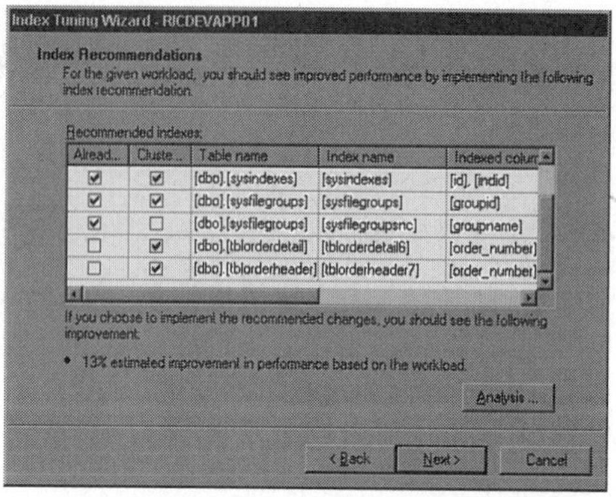

FIGURE 25.10

The Index Recommendations dialog box.

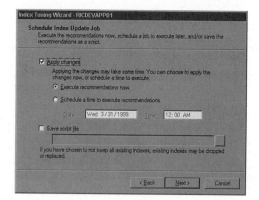

FIGURE 25.11

The Schedule Index Update Job dialog box.

7. The Schedule Index Update Job dialog box allows you to make several choices about when and how to implement the index changes. You can choose to implement the changes immediately, schedule an execution, or create a script file that you can run manually at any later time. Click Next to continue. The Completing the Index Tuning Wizard dialog box appears, as shown in Figure 25.12.

8. Click Finish on the Completing the Index Tuning Wizard dialog box to implement the index changes.

TIP

As mentioned in the "Query-Tuning Cookbook" section, it is a good idea to perform this procedure periodically on your databases. It is possible that your users could begin accessing data in ways that you haven't analyzed before. This is especially true in data warehousing and ad-hoc querying environments. By continually sampling workload information, you can ensure that you are applying appropriate indexes based on usage patterns.

FIGURE 25.12
*The Completing
the Index Tuning
Wizard dialog box.*

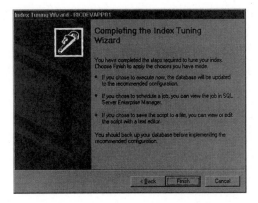

Query Governor

Another interesting tool available in SQL Server 7.0 is the query governor. Because SQL Server uses a cost-based optimizer, the cost of executing a given query is always estimated before the query is actually executed. The query governor allows you to set a cost threshold to prevent certain long-running queries from being executed. This is not so much a tuning tool as it is a disaster-prevention tool.

If you have an application with an English Query front end, you have no way of controlling what the user is going to request from the database. The query governor will allow you to prevent a run-away query from executing and avoid eating up valuable CPU time processing a bad query.

To set the query governor, open Enterprise Manager. Right-click the server and choose Properties from the menu. Next, select the Server Settings tab. In the Server Behavior group box, check the Use Query Governor option and specify a cost threshold. The cost threshold is given in cost units as used by the query optimizer (see Figure 25.13).

Things to Beware Of

No matter how much you tune your queries, there are still some things the query optimizer can miss. You should be on the look-out for certain things that can cause you problems when attempting to optimize a query.

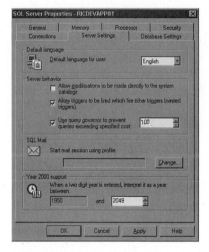

FIGURE 25.13

The SQL Server Properties dialog box.

Using Non-Search Arguments

As mentioned previously, the query optimizer uses search arguments to help it narrow down a specific resultset to evaluate. The search argument is in the form of a WHERE clause that equates a column to a constant, as seen in this example:

```
SELECT column1
FROM table1
WHERE column1 = 123
```

The query optimizer can use the search argument to examine an index, arrive at a result-set, and avoid doing a full table scan. The following example is not a valid search argument:

```
SELECT column1
FROM table1
WHERE column1 / 10 = 123
```

In this example, the query optimizer does not know the search value until runtime. As a result, the optimizer must perform a table scan to find the correct values. In general, always make sure that the column is on the left side of the predicate equation and the search conditions are on the right side of the equation.

Datatype Mismatches

Another common problem is datatype mismatches. If you attempt to join tables on columns of different datatypes, the query optimizer might not be able to effectively use indexes to compute the join. This will result in a table scan because the SQL Server will have to convert all values first before it can process the query. Avoid this situation by maintaining good datatype consistency across your database.

Triggers

If you are using triggers on INSERT, UPDATE, or DELETE, it is possible that your triggers can cause problems. You might think that the query is performing poorly when actually, it is the trigger that needs to be tuned. Additionally, you might have triggers that fire other triggers. If you suspect you are having problems with the triggers, drop the trigger to see if the performance improves. If it does, you might need to tune the trigger itself.

Summary

The SQL Server query optimizer has been greatly improved for version 7.0. The addition of the merge and hash join algorithms to the query processor make SQL Server a truly robust and scalable database. These enhancements, along with the addition of multiple index support and automated statistics updating, will make your life as a DBA much simpler when it comes to query performance tuning. SQL Server provides you with several tools that you can use to create a basic and effective indexing strategy with little more than few clicks of the mouse.

622

Advanced Query Processing

by Ted V. Daley

IN THIS CHAPTER

Today's database reporting environment provides unique and challenging demands. The need for quicker execution times and seamless access to heterogeneous data stores has prompted development of two important new features: parallel queries and distributed queries.

A popular feature of Microsoft Windows NT and its BackOffice products is scalability. The same program that runs on desktop computer systems also runs on multiple processor superservers. SQL Server 7.0 takes maximum advantage of multiprocessor configurations with parallel execution of a single query. Allowing the query to run on multiple processors has significant advantages, especially when the query requires several processor cycles or examines a large number of rows. SQL Server 7.0 breaks the processing of a query into several subtasks. Each subtask can run on a different CPU at the same time, generating resultsets more quickly and more efficiently than executing the different parts serially. During query execution, SQL Server automatically determines which queries will benefit from parallelism and generates a parallel execution plan.

Businesses are increasingly discovering the need to construct reports that use a variety of data stores. SQL Server 7.0 uses linked servers to go beyond simple data access and create distributed queries that access data from Access, DB2, Oracle, Sybase, and any other data provider with an OLE DB driver—the emerging standard for data access. Distributed queries access data that can be stored in multiple data sources on either the same computer or different computers. SQL Server 7.0 also supports referencing these heterogeneous OLE DB data sources in Transact-SQL statements—giving you the ability to generate queries, data modifications, commands, and transactions against multiple data sources and return a single resultset.

Parallel Queries

Microsoft SQL Server version 7.0 introduces significant changes in the way execution plans are created. The query processor includes parallel query processing, a new execution strategy that can improve the performance of complex queries on computers with more than one processor.

SQL Server inserts exchange operators into each parallel query to build and manage the query execution plan. The exchange operator is responsible for providing process management, data redistribution, and flow control. It is possible that a parallel query execution plan can use more than one thread, whereas a serial execution plan, used by a nonparallel query, uses only a single thread for its execution. Prior to query execution time, SQL Server determines whether the current system state and configuration allow for parallel query execution. If parallel query execution is justified, SQL Server determines the optimal number of threads, called the degree of parallelism, and distributes the query workload execution across those threads. The parallel query uses the same number of threads until completion. SQL Server reexamines the optimal degree of parallelism each time a query execution plan is retrieved from the procedure cache. Individual instances of the same query could be assigned a different degree of parallelism.

SQL Server calculates the degree of parallelism for each instance of a parallel query execution using the following criteria:

- **How many processors does the computer running SQL Server have?**

  If your computer has two or more processors, it can use parallel queries.

- **What is the number of concurrent active users?**

  The degree of parallelism is inversely related to CPU usage. SQL Server assigns a lower degree of parallelism if the CPUs are already busy.

- **Is sufficient memory available for parallel query execution?**

  Queries, like any process, require resources to execute, particularly memory. Obviously, a parallel query will demand more memory than a serial query. More importantly, as the degree of parallelism increases, so does the amount of memory required. Realizing this, SQL Server carefully considers this in a query execution plan. SQL Server could either adjust the degree of parallelism or use a serial plan to complete the query.

- **What is the type of query being executed?**

  Queries that use several CPU cycles justify using a parallel execution plan. Some examples are joins of large tables, substantial aggregations, and sorting large resultsets. SQL Server determines whether to use a parallel or serial plan by checking the value of the cost threshold for parallelism.

- **Is there a sufficient amount of rows processed in the given stream?**

  If the optimizer determines that the number of rows in a stream is too low, it does not execute a parallel plan. This prevents scenarios where the costs exceed the benefits of executing a parallel plan.

Two server configuration options—the maximum degree of parallelism and cost threshold for parallelism—affect the consideration for a parallel query. Although it is not recommended, you can change the default settings for each.

The maximum degree of parallelism option limits the number of threads to use in a parallel plan execution. The range of possible values is 0 to 32. This value is automatically configured to 0, which uses the actual number of CPUs. If you desire to suppress parallel processing, set the value to 1.

You can affect the query optimizer's choice to use a parallel execution plan by changing the values for the maximum degree of parallelism and the cost threshold for parallelism server configuration options using either the `sp_configure` system stored procedure or the Enterprise Manager program. It is strongly recommended that you do not change this value on SMP computers. For single processor machines, these values are ignored.

To set the maximum degree of parallelism option, you can use the following:

- The `sp_configure` system stored procedure

```
USE master
sp_configure 'show advanced options', 1
GO
RECONFIGURE
GO
sp_configure 'max degree of parallelism', 1
GO
RECONFIGURE
GO
```

- The Enterprise Manager

    1. Right-click a server; then click Properties.

    2. Click the Processor tab. The Processor settings dialog box appears (see Figure 26.1).

FIGURE 26.1

*SQL Server
Properties—the
Processor settings
tab.*

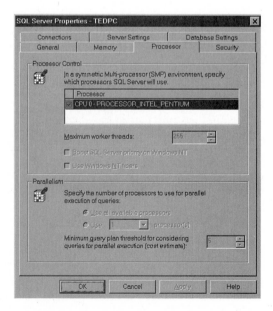

3. Under Parallelism, select the number of processors to execute queries in parallel.

The cost threshold for parallelism option establishes a ceiling value the query optimizer uses to consider parallel query execution plans. If the calculated value to execute a serial plan is greater than the value set for the cost threshold for parallelism, a parallel plan is generated. This value is defined by the estimated time in seconds to execute the serial plan. The range of values for this setting is 0 to 32767. The default value is 5. If the maximum degree of parallelism is set to 1 or the computer has a single processor, the cost threshold for parallelism value is ignored.

You can configure this option using either the sp_configure system stored procedure or the Enterprise Manager:

- The sp_configure system stored procedure

```
USE master
sp_configure 'show advanced options', 1
GO
RECONFIGURE
GO
sp_configure 'cost threshold for parallelism', 15
GO
RECONFIGURE
GO
```

- The Enterprise Manager

  1. Expand a server group.

  2. Right-click a server; then click Properties.

  3. Click the Processor tab.

  4. In the Parallelism box, enter a value from 0 through 32,627.

Microsoft SQL Server provides two useful tools for monitoring the degree of parallelism for queries. One choice is the SQL Server Profiler and event classes. *Event classes* refer to an activity generated within SQL Server—for example, the execution and completion of a remote procedure call (RPC), a batch, Transact-SQL statement, or a successful or failed connection to SQL Server. SQL Server Profiler groups event classes into event categories (collections) that describe the type of event class. For example, all Transact-SQL classes are grouped within the T-SQL event category. Table 26.1 outlines the necessary event classes and data columns to capture when defining your trace.

TABLE 26.1 SQL OPERATORS EVENT CATEGORIES

Event Class	Data Column	Description
Delete	Event Sub Class	Degree of parallelism or number of CPUs used to perform the DELETE.
Insert	Event Sub Class	Degree of parallelism or number of CPUs used to perform the INSERT.
Select	Event Sub Class	Degree of parallelism or number of CPUs used to perform the SELECT.
Update	Event Sub Class	Degree of parallelism or number of CPUs used to perform the UPDATE.

Table 26.2 provides explanations of the possible values for the Event Sub Class data column.

TABLE 26.2 SQL OPERATORS FOR THE EVENT SUB CLASS DATA COLUMN

Event Sub Class Value	Description
0	The computer has only a single processor, or the estimated cost of a query is less than the cost threshold for parallelism value.
1	A parallel query was considered. However, either the calculated cost was less than the cost threshold for parallelism value or not enough resources are available for a parallel query execution plan.
>1	A parallel execution was chosen with the shown degree of parallelism.

The other choice is to view the parallel execution plan using the SQL Server Query Analyzer. Two formats are available for viewing the execution plan: graphical and tabular. The graphical execution plan uses icons to represent the execution of specific statements and queries in SQL Server. The tabular representation is produced by the SET SHOWPLAN_ALL or SET SHOWPLAN_TEXT statements. The showplan output for every parallel query will have at least one of these three logical operators:

- Distribute Streams receives a single input stream of records and distributes multiple output streams. The contents and form of the record are unchanged. All records enter through the same single input stream and appear in one of the output streams, preserving the relative order.

- Gather Streams assembles multiple input streams of records and yields a single output stream. The relative order of the records, contents, and form are maintained.

- Repartition Streams accepts multiple input streams and produces multiple streams of records. The record contents and format are unchanged.

Distributed Queries

Using distributed queries, you can access data from multiple heterogeneous data sources on the same or different computers. Connectivity to the data sources is possible using OLE DB, the Microsoft specification of an application programming interface (API) for universal data access.

Because OLE DB providers expose their data in tabular objects called rowsets, they can be referenced in Transact-SQL statements as if they were a SQL Server table.

A typical scenario where distributed queries are helpful might be with an automobile parts manufacturer that has four regional warehouses across the country. All warehouses manage their own resources. When the quantity for a part falls below the reorder point, the inventory control manager at the warehouse places an order with the supplier. Each warehouse stores its inventory data in different formats: Oracle, SQL Server 7.0, and Microsoft Access. You can create a central report showing the entire company's parts inventory using a single distributed query.

Setting Up a Distributed Environment

You must first create a linked server before you can work with data from a remote SQL Server or another OLE DB data source. A linked server consists of an OLE DB data source that is registered on the local SQL Server. It is used as a reference by the local server to resolve the location of remote data and objects. Linked servers allow you to send Transact-SQL statements directly to a remote data source. These actions can also be treated as distributed transactions. It is possible to reach distributed data stored in multiple SQL servers and heterogeneous data that is stored in both relational and nonrelational sources. If you want to define a source other than a SQL Server 7.0 as a linked server, an OLE DB provider must exist. This information regarding linked servers is stored in the sysoledbusers system table.

Linking to a Remote Data Source

To execute Transact-SQL statements on a remote SQL Server or OLE DB data source, you must create a link to the server or data source. You can do so using either the Enterprise Manager or the `sp_addlinkedserver` system stored procedure:

```
sp_addlinkedserver 'server', 'product_name', 'provider_name',
 'data_source', 'location', 'provider_string'
```

This step defines a remote data source on the local computer and includes the OLE DB provider. The parameters for the `sp_addlinkedserver` system stored procedure follow:

Parameter	Description
server	Name of the linked server to create
product_name	The product name of the OLE DB data source
provider_name	Friendly name for the OLE DB provider corresponding to this data source
data_source	Name of the data source used by the OLE DB provider
location	Location of the data source used by the OLE DB provider
provider_string	OLE DB provider-specific connection string that identifies a data source

Connecting to a Remote SQL Server

You do not need to specify the *provider_name*, *data_source*, *location*, and *provider_string* when you are connecting to a SQL Server 7.0 source. Here's how you add the SalesServer, a SQL Server 7.0 server to the list of linked servers on the local SQL Server system:

```
EXEC sp_addlinkedserver
@server = 'SalesServer'
@product_name = 'SQL Server'
```

Connecting to an OLE DB Data Source

Table 26.3 lists some common OLE DB provider names. For a more complete listing of OLE DB provider names, refer to SQL Server Books Online.

TABLE 26.3   COMMON OLE DB PROVIDER NAMES

Product	Provider Name
Microsoft SQL Server 7.0	N'SQLOLEDB'
Microsoft OLE DB provider for Access (Jet)	'Microsoft.Jet.OLEDB.4.0'
Microsoft OLE DB provider for Oracle	'MSDAORA' (*data_source* refers to the SQL*Net alias name for the Oracle database.)
OLE DB Provider for ODBC	'MSDASQL'—*provider_name* 'LocalServer'—*data_source* (using the *data_source* parameter)
OLE DB Provider for ODBC	'MSDASQL'—*provider_name*'DRIVER={SQL Server}'—*provider_string* (using *provider_string* parameters) SERVER—*servername* UID=login;PWD=password;

26

This example shows how you add the Oracle server OracleMarketing to the linked servers list:

```
EXEC sp_addlinkedserver
@server = 'OracleMarketing'
@product_name = 'Oracle'
@provider_name = 'MSDORA'
@data_source = 'OracleDB'
```

Establishing Linked Server Security

When users execute a distributed query, the local SQL Server logs into the remote SQL Server on behalf of the user. Therefore, it might be necessary to establish security between the local and remote data sources. However, if the user's login ID and password exist on both the local and remote SQL servers, the local SQL Server can use the account information of the user to log into the remote SQL Server. This case often exists when SQL servers participate in a Windows NT domain environment.

To map login IDs and passwords between local and remote SQL Servers, use the `sp_addlinkedsrvlogin` system stored procedure. Keep in mind that this system stored procedure does not create user accounts. It merely maps a login account created on the local server to an account created on the remote server.

The syntax for the `sp_addlinkedsrvlogin` system stored procedure is

```
sp_addlinkedsrvlogin 'rmtsrvname', 'useself', 'locallogin', 'rmtuser',
 'rmtpassword'
```

The parameters are described as follows:

Parameter	Description
`rmtsrvname`	Name of the linked server
`useself`	Determines whether the user's own account information is used or `rmtuser` and `rmtpassword` arguments are used
`locallogin`	Uses account information from an already created local login ID
`rmtuser`	The username on the remote server to be used if the `useself` parameter is set to `FALSE`
`rmtpassword`	Password associated with the `rmtuser`

In the next example, a user who logs onto the local SQL Server using `SalesMngr` can access data on the remote server `SalesServer` SQL Server. The local account information will be mapped to the remote account `rmtSalesMngr`:

```
EXEC sp_addlinkedsrvlogin 'SalesServer', 'false', 'SalesMngr',
 'rmtSalesMngr', 'salespass'
```

Getting Information About Linked Servers

You can use both SQL Server Enterprise Manager and the system stored procedures to gather information about linked servers. Some of these stored procedures follow:

- `sp_linkedservers` returns a list of linked servers that are defined on the local server.
- `sp_catalogs` displays a list of catalogs and descriptions for a specified linked server.
- `sp_indexes` shows index information for a specified remote table.
- `sp_primarykeys` returns the primary key columns for the specified table.
- `sp_foreignkeys` lists the foreign keys that are defined for the remote table.
- `sp_tables_ex` displays table information from the linked server.
- `sp_columns_ex` returns column information for all columns or a specified column for a remote table.

Querying a Linked Server

When you write a distributed query, you must use the four-part name to refer to linked objects:

`linked_server_name.catalog_name.schema_name.object_name`

The elements of this name have the following descriptions:

`linked_server_name`	The unique networkwide name of the linked server
`catalog_name`	Name of the database
`schema_name`	The name of the object owner
`object_name`	The name of the table

If you want to include the employees table that is owned by the database owner in the sales database on the SalesServer linked SQL Server, use the following four-part name:

`SalesServer.sales.dbo.employees`

You can use the following Transact-SQL statements:

- `SELECT` statement with a `WHERE` clause or a `JOIN` clause
- `INSERT`, `UPDATE`, and `DELETE` statements

You cannot use the following:

- `CREATE`, `ALTER`, or `DROP` statements

- Inserting an ORDER BY clause in a SELECT statement if a large object column from a linked table is in the select list of the SELECT statement

- READTEXT, WRITETEXT, and UPDATETEXT statements

The next example joins the employees table in the salesremote database on a linked server to the orders table on the local SQL Server:

```
USE sales
SELECT empname, order_detail
FROM orders o JOIN SalesServer.salesremote.dbo.employees e
ON o.empid = e.empid
```

Executing a Stored Procedure on a Linked Server

It is possible to execute a stored procedure on a linked server. The server hosting the client connection will accept the client's request and send it to the linked server. The EXECUTE statement must contain the name of the linked server as part of its syntax:

```
EXECUTE servername.dbname.owner.procedure_name
```

This example executes sp_helpsrvrole, which shows a list of available fixed server roles on the Sales remote server:

```
EXEC sales.master.dbo.sp_helpsrvrole
```

Modifying Distributed Data

To ensure the integrity of data modifications on a linked server, you must perform a distributed transaction by using the BEGIN DISTRIBUTED TRANSACTION statement.

The next example shows how to add the SQL Server login name Sam to two different servers. The transaction will either commit or roll back on both of the servers:

```
BEGIN DISTRIBUTED TRANSACTION
EXEC sp_addlogin Sam
EXEC remoteserver.master.dbo.sp_addlogin Sam
COMMIT TRAN
```

Keep in mind the following considerations regarding distributed transactions:

- BEGIN DISTRIBUTED TRANSACTION statements cannot be nested.
- ROLLBACK TRANSACTION statements roll back the entire distributed transaction.
- Savepoints are not supported.

Summary

This chapter gives you an introduction to working with distributed data. It begins by showing you how to set up a linked server environment and then how to configure linked servers and establish security between the two servers. It also gives examples of how to execute an ad hoc query, use stored procedures, and modify data on a linked server.

Using the SQL Server Profiler

by Tibor Karaszi

IN THIS CHAPTER

In this chapter, you will take a look at a useful tool: the SQL Server Profiler, which can answer many questions for you—questions that were hard to answer in previous versions of SQL Server:

- Which queries are table-scanning my invoice history table?
- Am I experiencing many deadlocks, and, if so, why?
- What SQL queries is each application submitting?
- Which were the 10 worst-performing queries last week?
- If I implement this alternate indexing scheme, how will it affect my batch operations?

SQL Server Profiler records activity made against SQL Server. You can direct SQL Server Profiler to record output to a window, a file, or a table. You specify what events to trace, what information to include in the trace, how you want it grouped, and what filters you want to apply.

SQL Server Profiler Architecture

SQL Server version 6.5 included SQL Trace, which you could use to trace SQL calls submitted to SQL Server. It was a popular tool, for instance, with developers who could see the SQL calls submitted from their programs. SQL Trace was basically an ODS (Open Data Services) sniffer that limited the event types it could trace.

Even though you will find similarities between SQL Server Profiler and SQL Trace, SQL Server Profiler is a completely new design. Because SQL Server was modularized in version 7, each component can now submit information to SQL Server: an *event-driven* model. The architecture of the SQL Server Profiler is shown in Figure 27.1.

The figure illustrates the following four steps in the process:

1. Event producers, such as the Query Processor, Lock Manager, ODS, and so on, submit events to SQL Server Profiler.
2. The filters define what information to submit to SQL Server Profiler. A producer will not produce events if the event is not included in the filter.
3. All events are queued by SQL Server Profiler.
4. SQL Server Profiler writes the events to each defined consumer, such as a flat file, a table, the Profiler window, and so on.

FIGURE 27.1
SQL Server Profiler's architecture.

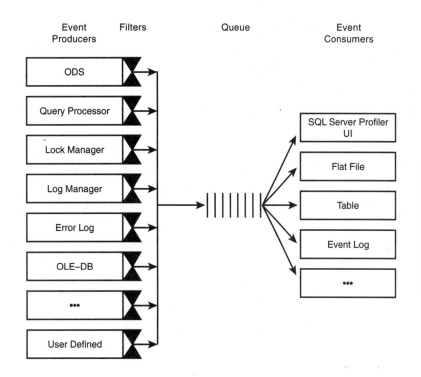

Creating Traces

Because SQL Server Profiler can trace numerous events, it is easy to "get lost" when reading the trace. Determine roughly the information you need and how you want the information grouped. For example, if you want to see what SQL statements each user is submitting through her applications, you could trace incoming SQL statements and group them by user and by application.

When you have decided what type of information you want from the trace, start SQL Server Profiler and choose File, New Trace, which displays the Trace Properties dialog. The information for each trace (or queue) is stored in the Registry on the SQL Server.

With the Create Trace Wizard, you can choose from a number of predetermined trace settings, define some properties, name the trace, and choose a destination. If you want to add events, change grouping, and so on, you can modify the trace definition that the wizard creates for you.

The following predefined traces are available in the Create Trace Wizard:

- Find the worst performing queries.
- Identify scans of large tables.
- Identify the cause of a deadlock.
- Profile the performance of a stored procedure.
- Trace SQL activity by application.
- Trace SQL activity by user.

General Properties

You can start the SQL Server Profiler from the SQL Server Program group in the Start menu or from the Tools menu in Enterprise Manager.

General properties for the trace are defined in the General tab in the Trace Properties window, as shown in Figure 27.2.

FIGURE 27.2

General properties.

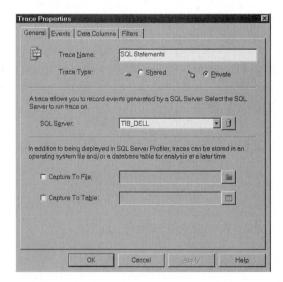

There are two types of trace definitions: private and shared. A private trace definition can only be used by the NT account that created it. A shared trace definition is available for all accounts on the machine. The trace information is stored in the Registry, either under HKEY_CURRENT_USER or HKEY_LOCAL_MACHINE. To administer traces (creating, starting stopping, and so on), you must have system administrator (sa) privileges in SQL Server.

> **NOTE**
>
> You can grant other SQL Server logins the sa right to administer traces, although it's not recommended. First, make sure that the login has a username in the master database. Then, grant execute rights for the user to the appropriate xp_trace... extended stored procedures.
>
> Note that this move can produce a potential security risk if you allow the user to trace all incoming SQL statements. Performance can also suffer if many traces are running against SQL Server simultaneously.

Also on the General tab, you can specify the server where the trace is to run. Choose <New Server> in the drop-down list to register a new server. If you click the command button to the right of the server name, you see the Source Server dialog, shown in Figure 27.3.

FIGURE 27.3

The Source Server dialog.

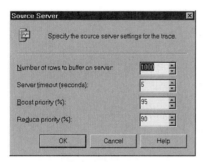

The attributes in the Source Server dialog are listed in Table 27.1.

TABLE 27.1 ATTRIBUTES FOR A TRACE QUEUE

Text Box	Description
Number of Rows to Buffer on Server	Number of events that can be held in the queue that SQL Server creates for buffering events from the producers. Valid range is 1–20,000.
Server Timeout (Seconds)	If the queue becomes full, producers stop submitting events temporarily and buffer the events. The producers start submitting events as soon as at least one event is removed from the queue. If the timeout period occurs before any events are removed from the queue, however, an autopause occurs until the number of items in the queue drops to the Reduce Priority level. No events are generated during the autopause. Valid range is 1–10.

continues

TABLE 27.1   CONTINUED

Text Box	Descriptionon
Boost Priority (%)	Number of items in the queue, in percent, before the consumer's thread priority is increased. Valid range is 1–100.
Reduce Priority (%)	When the number of items in the queue drops to this level, the consumer's thread priority is decreased to its normal level. Valid range is 0–99 and must be less than the Boost Priority.

You should generally leave the default values unless you have problems with frequent autopauses. After you make your selections for the source server, finish the general properties with the capture selections.

Check Capture To File if you want to save to trace to a file. You will be prompted for a filename. You can use the file later to replay the trace or import the trace to other tools, such as the Index Tuning Wizard.

You can also save the trace to a table if you check Capture To Table. You will be prompted for a SQL Server name, a database name, and a table name.

Events

In the Events tab, you specify what events you want to catch in the trace.

> **TIP**
>
> If you capture too many events in one trace, the trace becomes difficult to review. Instead, you can create several traces, one for each type of information that you want to examine.
>
> You can choose not to view events after the trace was taken, but you have to stop and save the trace (to a table or a file) and re-open it first.

Expand an event group to list the available events within the group. Add or remove a single event by double-clicking the event or selecting the event and clicking the Add/Remove button. You can also add or remove all events within a group by marking the event group. Figure 27.4 shows the events available by default. Even more events are available if you enter the trace options dialog (Tools, Options) and select Events, All Event Classes. The extra events available are not that useful, though.

FIGURE 27.4

Event properties.

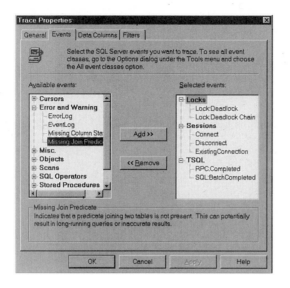

The available event groups and events are listed in Table 27.2.

TABLE 27.2   EVENT GROUPS AND EVENTS

Event Group	Event	Logs
Cursors	CursorClose	A cursor has been closed. (The cursor events are triggered only for API cursors.)
	CursorExecute	A prepared cursor has been executed.
	CursorOpen	A cursor has been opened.
	CursorPrepare	A cursor has been prepared.
	CursorUnprepare	A cursor has been unprepared.
Error and Warning	Errorlog	Messages written to the SQL Server error log.
	EventLog	Messages written to the Windows NT Application event log.
	Missing Column Statistics	Distribution statistics for a column would have been useful but have not been collected.
	Missing Join Predicate	A join predicate was missing for the query. This is often unintentional and results in lengthy execution time for the query.

continues

27

USING THE SQL
SERVER PROFILER

TABLE 27.2 CONTINUED

Event Group	Event	Logs
Locks	`Lock:Deadlock`	Processes rolled back due to a dead-lock.
	`Lock:Deadlock Chain`	One row for each deadlock participant.
Misc.	`Exec Prepared SQL`	A previously prepared SQL statement has been executed.
	`Execution Plan`	The actual plan chosen for the query.
	`CursorOpen`	Each time a cursor is opened.
	`LoginFailed`	When a login attempt fails.
	`Prepare SQL`	A prepare was executed through an ODBC, OLE DB, or DB-Library application.
	`ServiceControl`	When SQL Server is started, paused, continued, or stopped.
	`Unprepare SQL`	A previously prepared SQL statement has been unprepared.
Objects	`Object:Closed`	Opening of database objects, such as for SELECT and INSERT statements.
	`Object:Created`	Creation of database objects, such as for CREATE TABLE and CREATE INDEX statements.
	`Object:Deleted`	Deletion of database objects, such as for DROP TABLE and DROP INDEX statements.
	`Object:Opened`	Closing of database objects, such as after SELECT and INSERT statements.
Scans	`Scan:Started`	Scanning of tables and indexes.
SQL Operators	`Delete`	Occurrence of DELETE statements. Note that the actual statement text is not included in these events.
	Insert	Occurrence of INSERT statements.
	Select	Occurrence of SELECT statements.
	Update	Occurrence of UPDATE statements.
Stored Procedures	`SP:Completed`	Completion of execution of a stored procedure. The SQL statements are included in the event's text portion.

Event Group	Event	Logs
	SP:Starting	Start execution of a stored procedure. The SQL statements are included in the event's text portion.
	SP:StmtCompleted	Start execution of a SQL statement within a stored procedure. The SQL statement is included in the event's text portion.
	SP:StmtStarting	Completion of execution of a SQL statement within a stored procedure. The SQL statement is included in the event's text portion.
Transactions	DTCTransaction	Distributed transaction statements.
	SQLTransaction	SQL Server transaction statements.
TSQL	RPC:Starting	Start execution of a stored procedure executed via ODBC using the CALL escape clause.
	SQL:BatchStarting	Start of a SQL batch. Includes SQL statements.
	SQL:StmtCompleted	Completion of a SQL statement. Includes the SQL statement.
	SQL:StmtStarting	Start of a SQL statement. Includes the SQL statement.

NOTE

If you are going to use SQL Server Profiler, I recommend that you spend a couple of hours going through the events. Start a trace with a few events at a time and execute some relevant statements. You will soon realize the strength of SQL Server Profiler.

Data Columns

In the Data Columns tab, you specify what information to store for your events and how they will be grouped within the trace. Storing too much data can make the trace file or table grow too large and can affect performance as well.

You should only include columns that make sense to the events being traced. Figure 27.5 displays the Data Columns tab.

FIGURE 27.5

Defining what information to be captured in the trace.

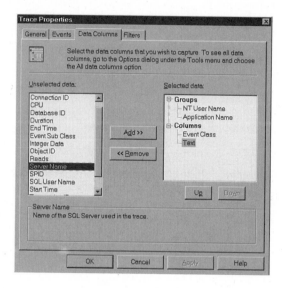

The Event Class column is the event name (event class) captured. If you capture more than one event, you probably want to include this column. If you want to capture the actual text, for instance, the SQL command, include the Text column. The type of information stored in this column depends on the event class.

To differentiate between activities generated from different applications, include the Application Name column; to differentiate between different users, include the NT User Name column or SQL User Name column.

The CPU, Reads, and Writes columns are useful if you want to find out how many resources the event requires. The Duration column specifies the elapse time in milliseconds. To trace activities against a specific object, include the Object Name column.

> **TIP**
>
> The easiest way to learn about each column is to create a trace that includes all the events and all the columns and generate some activities against SQL Server while the trace is running. Do not run such a trace on a heavily used production server because it would greatly affect the server's performance.

When you analyze the data, you probably want to perform some grouping with the columns. You can group all the columns you include in the trace. If you group over several columns, you should note that the column ordering makes a difference.

To specify grouping, mark the column you want to group over and choose the Up and Down button until you move the column to the desired location.

Suppose you want to find out which application performs the most table scans and then group that information by each user of the application. In that case, you group by Application Name, NT User Name. You might also want the reverse grouping to see which user is performing the most tables scans and what application the user is running—so then you group over NT User Name, Application Name.

> **TIP**
>
> If you save the trace to a file or a table, you can open it later and specify whatever grouping you want. This flexibility gives you almost endless possibilities for analyzing the trace data.

Filters

You can restrict what to trace based on certain event criteria. If the event does not pass the restriction, the event is not produced. Depending on what criteria you define the restriction for, the parameters can be of one of three types:

- Include Only and/or Exclude—Specify whether you want to include or exclude a certain value. For instance, by default, there is a restriction for the application name to exclude SQL Server Profiler. You can define several inclusion or exclusions by separating them with semicolons. For instance, to exclude SQL Server Profiler and Query Analyzer, specify the following exclusion string:

  `SQL Server Profiler%;%Query Analyzer%`

- Minimum and/or Maximum—You can define a minimum or maximum value for Duration, for example.

- Value—Define a value that the event must match—for instance, a certain object ID.

To define a filter, simply select the event criteria and enter the desired parameters. If you want to remove the filter, delete the text. Figure 27.6 shows the Filters tab.

27

USING THE SQL
SERVER PROFILER

FIGURE 27.6

Producing manageable results with filters.

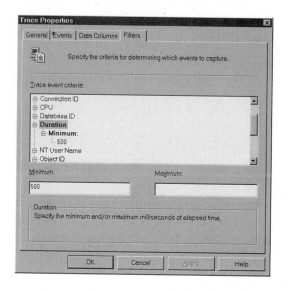

Table 27.3 lists the available event criteria and their respective parameter type.

TABLE 27.3 EVENT CRITERIA

Event Criteria	Include Only and/or Exclude	Minimum and /or Maximum	Value	Description
Application Name	Yes	No	No	Name of the application that generated the event.
Connection ID	No	No	Yes	The SQL Server generated connection ID.
CPU	No	Yes	No	CPU time in milliseconds.
Database ID	No	No	Yes	The DBID as stored in sysdatabases.
Duration	No	Yes	No	Execution time for the statement or stored procedure in milliseconds.

Event Criteria	Include Only and/or Exclude	Minimum and /or Maximum	Value	Description
NT User Name	Yes	No	No	Name of NT account.
Object ID	No	No	Yes	The object ID as stored in sysobjects.
Reads	No	Yes	No	Number of logical reads.
Server Name	Yes	No	No	Name of the SQL Server.
SPID	No	No	Yes	The system process ID.
SQL User Name	Yes	No	No	The login ID as defined in sysxlogins.
Text	Yes	No	No	The text submitted. You can use the _ and % wildcards.
Writes	No	Yes	No	Number of physical writes.

27
USING THE SQL
SERVER PROFILER

Replaying Trace Data

To replay a trace, you must have a trace saved to a file or a table. You can define a trace to be saved when you create or modify the trace queue. You can also save a trace as long as it is open in SQL Server Profiler. To save a trace, choose File, Save As and indicate whether you want to save it to a file or a table.

When you replay a trace, you first specify which server it should run on. You can, for instance, save a trace on the production server and replay it on a test server, elaborating the use of different indexes.

You can also set the degree of synchronization, which specifies whether you want all commands to run in the same sequence or run regardless of other commands. If you have a trace file with many updates, you might want to run with synchronization so that you do not encounter problems with dependencies between the modifications.

The Read Rate specifies whether you want to replay the trace over the same time period as when you captured it or as fast as possible. If you modified the indexing scheme or some other parameters, you might want to run it as fast as possible to see what level of improvement you achieved.

In a similar manner as with a programming tool, you can set breakpoints, step through statements, or position the cursor at a statement and run to the cursor.

Saving and Exporting Traces

You can save a trace to a file and to a table. The number of columns in the trace table depends on how many data columns you defined in the trace. Saving to a table is useful if you want to perform analysis on the trace with some other tool, such as Microsoft Access. A trace file is a binary file, so only applications with support for reading SQL Server Profiler trace files can read it.

You can also save a trace to a script file. The file will contain all the SQL statements in the trace. The character set can be either ANSI or Unicode.

You can export a trace definition to a file to be used on another machine. The trace definition file is in Unicode (text) format. Basically, this feature reads the definition from the Registry and saves it to a text file—and vice versa when you import a trace definition file.

Exporting Data to Showplan

Exporting trace data to showplan is easy. In SQL Server Profiler, select the rows you want to analyze and choose Edit, Copy from the menu. Then, you can paste into Query Analyzer. All nonexecutable information will have a comment at the beginning of the row. In Query Analyzer, you can re-execute the statements or choose to display the query execution plan.

The trace can be a running, stopped, or saved trace.

Exporting Data to the Index Tuning Wizard

SQL Server Profiler is an excellent tool if you want to capture a workload, tune the indexing scheme, and re-run the trace.

You can certainly plan and create the indexes manually, but you can get some help from the Index Tuning Wizard. The Index Tuning Wizard uses a trace saved to a table or a file.

Because the Index Tuning Wizard analyzes SQL statements, make sure that the trace includes one or more of the following events:

> SP:StmtCompleted
>
> SP:StmtStarting
>
> SQL:BatchCompleted
>
> SQL:BatchStarting
>
> SQL:StmtCompleted
>
> SQL:StmtStarting

One of each class (one SP: and one SQL:) is sufficient to capture dynamic SQL statements and statements embedded in stored procedures.

You should also make sure that the trace includes the Text data column.

The Index Tuning Wizard analyzes the trace and gives you recommendations along with an estimated improvement in execution time. You can choose to create indexes now or at a later time or save the CREATE INDEX commands to a script file.

SQL Server Extended Stored Procedures

Much of the SQL Server Profiler functionality is available through a set of extended stored procedures, whose names all begin with xp_trace. Through the procedures, you can start a trace at a given time, include trace functionality within an application, and so on.

Use xp_trace_addnewqueue to create a trace queue along with the queue size and the data columns to be included in the trace output. You define the events to trace with xp_trace_seteventclassrequired. Filters are defined with the xp_trace_set...filters procedures, one for each filter. If you want a queue to be started each time SQL Server is started, execute xp_trace_setqueueautostart. This is useful for auditing the activity against a SQL Server. You can autostart several queues.

The statements in Listing 27.1 create a queue with a set of data columns, set the event classes and filters, specify that the trace is to be saved to a file, and start the trace.

LISTING 27.1   TRACING WITH EXTENDED STORED PROCEDURES

```
USE master
DECLARE @q_handle int, @column_value int
-- Set the Data columns according to bit-mask as
--   documented in Books Online.
-- We want to store Text, Duration and Event_class.
SET @column_value = 1¦4096¦1048576

-- Add the Queue.
EXEC xp_trace_addnewqueue 1000, 5, 95, 90, @column_value,
➥ @q_handle OUTPUT

-- Set application filter to exclude the Profiler application.
EXEC xp_trace_setappfilter @q_handle, NULL,
➥ 'SQL Server Profiler%'

-- Include event RPC:Completed.
EXEC xp_trace_seteventclassrequired @q_handle, 10, 1
-- Include event SQL:BatchCompleted.
EXEC xp_trace_seteventclassrequired @q_handle, 12, 1

-- Saves the trace data to the file SQL_Text.SQL.
-- Other destination types are available.
EXEC xp_trace_setqueuedestination @q_handle, 2, 1, NULL
➥ 'd:\SQL_Text.trc'
--Start the consumer that actually writes to a file.
EXEC xp_trace_startconsumer @q_handle

-- Save the queue for future use, not required.
EXEC xp_trace_savequeuedefinition @q_handle, 'SQL_Text', 1
```

Summary

SQL Server Profiler has been enhanced considerably since SQL Trace in version 6.5. It is an excellent tool for tracing, profiling, and analyzing activities against SQL Server. You can start several traces and define the events to trace, the data to store, and the filters for each trace. A trace can be stored to a table or a file. You can use the trace later for analyzing and alter grouping when analyzing the trace. You can also use a trace with the graphical showplan and the Index Tuning Wizard.

Monitoring SQL Server Performance

by Simon Gallagher

IN THIS CHAPTER

The optimal configuration and setup of SQL Server is a primary responsibility of a system administrator. In this chapter, we will examine some of the methods available for looking at how SQL Server is handling user requests and its interaction with the Windows NT operating system and hardware.

Windows NT Performance Monitor

Performance Monitor is a graphical tool supplied as part of the installation of any Windows NT Server or Workstation that lets you monitor various performance indicators. There are hundreds of counters related to certain objects. These counters can be monitored on the local machine or over the network and can be set up to monitor any object and counter on multiple systems at once from one session.

You can set up the Performance Monitor to run other applications in the event of reaching certain thresholds. One such application is the SQL Alerter (SQLALRTR.EXE), which you can use to write errors or messages to the Windows NT Application event log, which the SQL Agent can then react to.

Performance Views

You can switch the Performance Monitor between any of four views:

- Chart—This is the default view that shows the selected counters as colored lines with the y-axis representing the value and the x-axis representing time.
- Alert—In this view, you can set thresholds for counters, and the Performance Monitor will maintain a visual log of when they are reached.
- Log—This option allows you to capture counter values with times to a file. This gives you a set of values that you can load back into the Performance Monitor model at a later time. That way, you can monitor the system after hours and capture statistical data.
- Report—In this mode, you see the current values for counters collected under their parent object.

You choose the view according to what area of the server you want to monitor, how you will examine the values, and when you will undertake the monitoring. The following list suggests when one type of view is more appropriate than another:

For This Purpose	Use This
You want instant and obvious indications for actions you are performing.	Chart
You are monitoring counters that are not impacted by drawing processes.	Chart
You need to kick off applications when thresholds are past.	Alert
You want to capture the maximum value reached for a set of counters.	Report
You want to capture values for counters over a period of time for replay or comparison.	Log
You want minimal impact on the server, and you do not need to check network counters.	Remote Monitoring

28

MONITORING SQL
SERVER
PERFORMANCE

Obviously, you need to be aware of what counters you will examine, whether you should monitor from another machine, and how the counter values are to be tracked.

Monitoring Values

If you open the Performance Monitor using the shortcut in the SQL Server program group, you will see a default set of counters. If you open the monitor from the Windows NT Administrative Tools group, you will have an empty workspace. Either way, you will want to customize the view you have.

To remove a counter, simply highlight the line in the bottom area of the window and press the Delete key. You can add a counter by selecting the command from the Edit menu or by clicking the large plus sign toolbar button. The Add dialog (see Figure 28.1) allows you to select a computer (for remote monitoring), an object, an associated counter, and an instance of the counter if applicable.

You can customize the look of the line in the chart view by specifying color, width, and style.

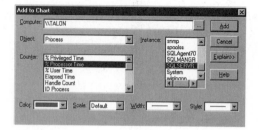

The following steps illustrate how you add the SQL Server processor time for monitoring:

1. Select the Add to Chart option from the Edit menu.
2. Choose Process from the drop-down list of objects.
3. Select the % Processor Time Counter from the list below the object.
4. Scroll the Instance list until you find SQLSERVR and select it.
5. Choose a color, line width, and style.

By clicking the Explain button, you can get a simple explanation of the counter. You can change the scale of a counter's value as well. In this case, you don't need to change the scale because it is a percentage, and the chart y-axis is numbered to 100.

You follow the same process whether you're adding the counter to chart view or report view. In the next section, we will learn about some of the counters and when you want to monitor them.

Windows NT Performance Counters

You need to be able to tell how Windows NT is reacting to the presence of SQL Server running within it: how SQL Server is using memory, the processors, and other important system resources. A large number of objects and counters relate to Windows NT and the services it is running. In the next few sections, we will look at which objects and counters provide useful information in investigating certain areas of the system.

> **TIP**
>
> Some of the network counters are only available if you add the Network Monitor Agent to Windows NT. You can add this software component through the Network applet in Control Panel.

Monitoring the Processors

The main processor of your server is doing the majority of all the hard work, executing the operating system code and all applications. This is a logical point to start looking at the performance of your system.

Two counters directly relate to the load on the CPU, yet they only give some of the picture of the work being done. These counters are System: % Total Processor Time and System: Processor Queue Length. Along with these counters you should examine a third: Process: % Processor Time.

You should display Process: % Processor Time for each process instance running on the server. By displaying all of this information together, you get a fuller picture of how much work the CPU is doing and how much of a queue develops waiting for processor time. A set of values show you which processes are contributing to the overall load.

> **TIP**
>
> A good way to show these counters is as a histogram. You can change the graph to display as a bar chart under the Options menu.

Once you identify which processes are causing a burden on the CPU, check whether they can be either turned off or moved to a different server. If they cannot, then you might want to consider upgrading the processor.

No one should use the SQL Server box as a workstation because using the processor for client applications can cause SQL Server to starve for processor time. The ideal Windows NT setup for SQL Server is on a standalone member server to the Windows NT domain. Do not install SQL Server onto a Primary Domain Controller (PDC) or Backup Domain Controller (BDC) because they run additional services that consume memory, CPU, and network resources.

Before you upgrade to the latest processor just because the % Processor Time counter is constantly high, you might want to check the load placed on the CPU by your other adapters. By checking System: % Interrupt Time and System: Interrupts/sec, you can tell whether the CPU is interrupted more than normal by adapters such as disk controllers.

The % Interrupt Time should be as close to zero as possible; any processing requirements should be handled by controller cards. The optimum value of Interrupts/Sec varies with the CPU used; DEC Alpha processors generate a nonmaskable interrupt every 10ms, whereas Intel processors interrupt every 15ms. The lowest absolute values are 100 interrupts per second and 67 interrupts per second, respectively.

By upgrading inefficient controllers to bus-mastering controllers, you can take some of the load from the CPU and put it back on the adapter. You will also want to keep the controller patched with the latest drivers from the hardware vendor.

Monitoring Memory

Memory, like the processor, is divided into segments for each process running on the server. If there is too much demand for memory, the operating system (Windows NT or 95/98) has to use virtual memory to supplement the physical memory. Virtual memory is storage allocated on the hard disk; it is named PAGEFILE.SYS under Windows NT and WIN386.SWP under Windows 95/98. At the points where any operating system leaves the electronic world (memory modules) and interacts with the mechanical world (disk drives), things slow down. You therefore need to eliminate this process, known as swapping or page faulting. To observe the level of the page faulting, you can look at the Memory: Page Faults/sec counter.

Another memory counter is an indicator for *thrashing*, which occurs when a large number of requests for memory cannot be satisfied directly from physical memory. The counter you observe is Memory: Pages/sec.

Because the memory used by SQL Server 7.0 is dynamically grown and shrunk, you might want to track the exact usage using either Process: Working Set: SQLServr or SQLServer: Memory Manager: Total Server Memory (Kb). These counters indicate the current size of the memory used by the SQL Server process. If you see a performance degradation because SQL Server must continually grow and shrink its memory, you should either remove some of the other services or processes running or use the configuration option Use a Fixed Memory Size on the Memory tab to fix the total amount of memory. Be aware that you have now made a static choice, and dynamic changes such as additional user connections might increase the need for memory, and you will have to revisit your fixed configuration value for the memory.

You can use the Memory: Available Bytes counter to identify extra memory that can be given to SQL Server. If this value indicates additional memory in excess of 4MB, you can assign it for use by SQL Server. Windows NT uses 4MB as a magic number to start trimming the working sets of processes, which is obviously an expensive task that should be avoided. To this end, you should remove any unnecessary services, process, and protocols to free memory for use by SQL Server and the operating system.

Monitoring Disk Usage

It is important to monitor the interaction of the operating system and the processes running under it with the hard disk. The goal of any system administrator is to reduce the time spent by the mechanical area of the computer: the hard drive. Any time the process requires a switch from electronic to mechanical, the operation takes a performance hit. This is why Windows NT and SQL Server use memory caches.

By monitoring the portion of the system cache used for the server services (synchronous) and that related to the SQL Server (asynchronous), you can see how much disk access is related to SQL Server. Not all asynchronous disk activity is SQL Server, but on a dedicated box, it should be. You can watch a number of different synchronous and asynchronous counters, depending on the type of activity you want to monitor.

Slow disk I/O causes a reduction in the transaction throughput. To identify which disks are receiving all the attention, you can monitor the Physical Disk: % Disk Time counter for each physical disk drive. This counter will show you the percentage of time that the disk is active; a continuously high value could indicate an under-performing disk subsystem.

Before you can get information from this counter, or any of the other disk-related counters, you must first turn on the performance counters using `diskperf`. From a command prompt, you need to execute `diskperf -y` and then reboot the computer.

> **CAUTION**
>
> Remember to turn off the disk-performance counters when you are finished by executing `diskperf -n`. Running your system with these counters on will impact your performance.

You can also monitor the queue that builds up for particular physical drives by watching Physical Disk: Avg. Disk Queue Length. If this counter is consistently greater than zero, then you need to examine the hard drive and the controller characteristics to see if they can be improved upon. If one physical drive has a high value in relation to the values for the other drives, look at how you redistribute your database and system files to spread out the I/O.

> **TIP**
>
> If you are running disk striping, you need to turn on the disk counters using `diskperf -ye`.

Of course, this monitoring will only show half the picture if drives are partitioned into multiple logical drives. To see the work on each logical drive, you need to examine different counters; in fact, you can monitor read and write activity separately with Logical Disk: Disk Write Bytes/sec and Logical Disk: Disk Read Bytes/sec.

You can see not only the actual work on each drive but also the queue length for each drive. This allows more detailed investigation of which files or directories are getting the most attention on the disk.

Monitoring the Network Card

One area of possible congestion is the network card; it does not matter how fast the server's work is if it has to queue up to go out through a small pipe.

Unfortunately, additional activity on the server consumes some of the bandwidth through the network card. You can identify the activity by comparing the counters for reading and writing through the network card for the Server object and for SQL Server. For monitoring reads, the counter is Server: Bytes Received/sec.

> **NOTE**
>
> Under previous versions of SQL Server, a counter called SQLServer:Network Reads/sec indicated SQL Server's contribution. With SQL Server 7.0, you need to use the `DBCC PERFMON` command to find the same information.

If the SQL Server counter is lower than the server's counter, then other activity is occurring. The same applies to the write counter, Server: Bytes Transmitted/sec.

> **NOTE**
>
> Under previous versions of SQL Server, a counter called SQLServer:Network Writes/sec indicated SQL Server's contribution. With SQL Server 7.0, you need to use the DBCC PERFMON command to find the same information.

You will also want to check the counter showing how many requests are queuing up, waiting to make use of the network card. You can check this by using DBCC PERFMON command.

> **NOTE**
>
> Under previous versions of SQL Server, a counter called SQLServer:Network Command Queue Length indicated SQL Server's contribution.

If this counter is constantly greater than zero, then the network card could be a bottleneck; check the bus width of the card. Obviously, a 32-bit PCI card is faster than an 8-bit ISA one. Also, check that you have the latest drivers from the hardware vendor.

You will want to consider these values together with the actual number of user connections made to the SQL Server by examining the SQLServer:General Statistics:User Connections counter.

SQL Server Performance Counters

Once SQL Server is installed, the Windows NT Performance Monitor gains a number of SQL-Server–specific statistical objects (see Table 28.1), each with a number of associated counters.

TABLE 28.1 SQL SERVER PERFORMANCE MONITOR OBJECTS

Performance Monitor Object	Description
SQLServer:Access Methods	Information on searches and allocations of database objects.
SQLServer:Backup Device	Information on throughput of backup devices.
SQLServer:Buffer Manager	Memory buffers used by SQL Server.

continues

TABLE 28.1 CONTINUED

Performance Monitor Object	Description
SQLServer:Cache Manager	Information on any cacheable objects such as stored procedures, triggers, and query plans.
SQLServer:Databases	Database-specific information, such as the log space usage or active transactions within the database.
SQLServer:General Statistics	Server-wide activity.
SQLServer:Latches	Information regarding latches on internal resources.
SQLServer:Locks	Individual lock information, such as lock timeouts and number of deadlocks.
SQLServer:Memory Manager	SQL Server's memory usage, including counters such as the connection and lock memory use.
SQLServer:Replication Agents	Provides information about the SQL Server Replication agents that are currently running.
SQLServer:Replication Dist.	Tracks commands and transactions read from the distribution database and delivered to the subscriber databases by the distribution agent.
SQLServer:Replication Logreader	Tracks commands and transactions read from the published databases and delivered to the distribution database by the logreader agent.
SQLServer:Replication Merge	Information about merge replication.
SQLServer:Replication Snapshot	Information about snapshot replication.
SQLServer:SQL Statistics	Query statistics, such as the number of batches of SQL received by SQL Server.
SQLServer:User Settable	Customizable counters return anything you might want to monitor.

In the following sections, we will examine some of these objects and counters.

SQLServer:Cache Manager Object

For finding information about the operation of SQL Server's caches, the SQLServer:Cache Manager object holds a number of useful counters that measure such things as procedure and trigger cache operations.

These cache counters allow you to watch how each of the caches are used and the upper limits of their use. These useful counters help indicate whether additional physical memory would benefit SQL Server:

Cache Pages—The number of pages used by the cache

Cache Object Counts—The number of objects using the cache pages

Cache Use Counts/sec—Object usage

Cache Hit Ratio—Difference between cache hits and lookup

You can display each of these counters for specific cache instances, ranging from ad hoc SQL plans to procedure plans and trigger plans.

A few related cache counters provide more of an overview on the cache operations: SQLServer:Memory Manager:SQL Cache Memory and SQLServer:Memory Manager:Optimizer Memory.

The SQLServer:Buffer Manager object also contains a counter that pertains to the operation of the Read Ahead manager: Readahead Pages/sec. The information returned by this counter will indicate how much work is done populating the page cache due to sequential scans of data. This may indicate the need to optimize certain queries, add more physical memory, or even consider pinning a table into the cache.

In the following sections, we will discuss these and some of the other objects and counters.

Monitoring SQL Server's Disk Activity

In the section "Monitoring Disk Usage" earlier in this chapter, you saw how to monitor disk activity. In this section, you examine what SQL Server's contribution is to all of this activity. Disk activity can be categorized into reads and writes.

SQL Server carries out writes to the disk for the following processes:

- Logging records
- Dirty cache pages at the end of a transaction
- Freeing space in the page cache

Logging is a constant occurrence in any database that allows modifications, and SQL Server attempts to optimize this process by batching a number of writes together. To watch how much work is done on behalf of the database logs, we would examine the SQLServer:Databases:Log Bytes Per Flush and SQLServer:Databases:Log Flushes/sec counters. The first tells us the quantity of the work, and the second the frequency.

The third kind of write occurs to make space within the page cache. This is carried out by the Lazy Writer process, which we can track with the counter SQLServer:Buffer Manager:Lazy Writes.

It is easy to monitor the amount of reading SQL Server is doing using the counter SQLServer:Buffer Manager:Page Reads.

There is unfortunately no way to see work done on a database-by-database basis. All read and write counter values are combined server-level values.

You will also want to check how many operations are queuing up for servicing by the disks by using the DBCC PERFMON command.

> **NOTE**
>
> Under previous versions of SQL Server, a counter called SQLServer:I/O Outstanding Reads indicated the values we are interested in.

If this is constantly greater than zero, your disk subsystem is a potential bottleneck. Check the interrupts per second to see whether the controller and not the disk is at fault.

Locks

One of the necessary areas of performance degradation is locking. However, you need to ensure that the correct types of locks are issued and that the worst kind of lock, a blocking lock, is kept to a minimum. A blocking lock, as its name implies, prevents other users from continuing their own work. An easy way to identify the level of blocking locks is to use the counter SQLServer:Memory Manager:Lock Blocks. If this counter indicates a value greater than zero on a frequent basis, you need to examine the queries being executed or even revisit the database design.

Users

Even though you cannot always relate performance problems to the number of users connected, it is a good idea to occasionally monitor how this number fluctuates.

The current level is shown with SQLServer:General Statistics:User Connections and is most useful when monitored in conjunction with other objects and counters. It is easy to say that the disk subsystem is a bottleneck, but how many users is SQL Server supporting at the time?

Procedure Cache

Another area of memory usage by SQL Server is the procedure cache, and corresponding to the procedure cache is a large number of counters that provide insight on its utilization.

To understand the information provided by the counters, you need knowledge of how the cache operates (see Figure 28.2).

FIGURE 28.2

Procedure cache architecture.

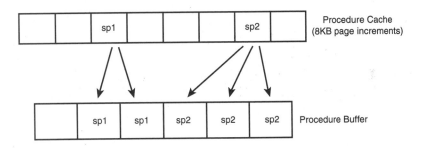

The procedure cache maintains pointers to the procedure buffer, which is where the executable from the stored procedures is actually kept. You can monitor the amount of memory used by the procedure buffers and cache separately.

For the procedure buffers, you can track how many are currently in use with SQLServer:Cache Manager:Object Counts:Procedure Plans. SQL Server also maintains a separate set of counters for the parts of the cache that are active as opposed to only in use. You can also track the total size of the procedure cache using the SQLServer:Cache Manager:Cache Pages:Procedure Plans counter, which is in 8KB pages. This counter value will fluctuate with the execution of each new stored procedure and other server activity.

Transaction Logs

The log counters provide less useful information in version 7.0 than they did before because the logs are now allowed to grow and shrink automatically. However, it is useful to know the upper limits of a database log size for capacity-planning reasons.

The log counters, which are available on a database-by-database basis under the SQLServer:Database Manager object, include the following information:

Counter	Description
Log Bytes Per Flush	Amount of log information contained in each flush.
Log File Size(KB)	The size of the log file.
Log Flush Wait/sec	The number of commits waiting to flush.
Log Growths	The number of times the log file grows.
Log Shrinks	The number of times the log file shrinks.
Percent Log Used	The current transaction log size.
Repl. Pending Xacts	The number of transactions being held for pick up by the replication process.

You can also use these counters to fire off warning messages to the administrator as a database's log reaches a certain level. This kind of functionality is better constructed using the Task Manager and a stored procedure that can check the values and alert the administrator without the overhead of keeping the Performance Monitor constantly open.

User-Defined Counters

You can extend the range of information that the Performance Monitor displays by creating up to 10 of your own counters. These user-defined counters appear under the SQLServer:User Settable:Query object, which contains as instances the 10 counters starting with User Counter 1. You define your own counters by calling stored procedures with the names sp_user_counter1 through sp_user_counter10, which are found in the master database.

These counters work very differently than they did under previous versions and require you to call the stored procedures in order to update the information they return to the Performance Monitor. To make any real use of these stored procedures, you now need to call them within a loop or as part of a job that is scheduled on some recurring basis.

Using these counters allows you to monitor any information you want, whether it is system, database, or even object specific. The only restriction is that the stored procedure can only take a single integer value argument.

The following sample procedure sets the average connection time for all user connections. Processes that have a kernel ID (kpid) of zero are system ones: checkpoint, Lazy Writer, and so on:

```
DECLARE @value INT

SELECT @value = AVG( DATEDIFF( mi, login_time, GETDATE()))
FROM sysprocesses
WHERE kpid > 0

EXEC sp_user_counter1 @value
```

You could further extend this information by creating additional user procedures for returning the minimum and maximum times connected, as well as database usage. Your only limitation is that you can monitor only 10 pieces of information at one time.

> **TIP**
>
> Create script files that contain a set of counter stored procedures that you can use to create and re-create as you want to monitor them.

SNMP Support

An aid for monitoring the status and performance of SQL Server is the Simple Network Management Protocol (SNMP). This service is widely used across the industry for enterprisewide management, using its cross-platform capabilities, monitoring, and event-processing features.

Ideally, you will have SNMP support installed for Windows NT before you install SQL Server. The SQL Setup program will then copy the files MSSQL.MIB and SQLSNMP.DLL. If SNMP is not installed before you install SQL Server, you can turn this feature on once you have installed the service. The SNMP files for SQL Server will already have been copied into the MSSQL7\BINN directory, and all you need do is open the Server Network utility and select the Enable SNMP check box at the bottom of the dialog.

SNMP's architecture can be broken into two main pieces: the SNMP network management machine and the SNMP agent (the system being monitored, which in our case is SQL Server). The SNMP agent responds to requests from the management machine for information, but can also trap and notify when certain critical events occur (see

FIGURE 28.3

SNMP monitoring and trap operation.

1. Management request and response
2. SNMP trap issued by agent on event occurence

Figure 28.3).

Under Windows NT, the data being accessed by SNMP is held in the Registry, and the agent service makes this information available in a form readable by SNMP monitors. The events that elicit SNMP traps are not defined in an ad hoc way by users, but rather through a Management Information Base (MIB). The MIB is a data file that has all the

28

MONITORING SQL SERVER PERFORMANCE

details about the objects available to be managed via SNMP. Different services provide different MIBs; for example, Internet Information Server (IIS) has an INETSRV.MIB file that is implemented using the IIS.DLL file.

Security for SNMP is implemented using a shared password (the community name) so that only systems with the correct name can manage associated agents. To further increase the security of your SNMP installation, you can configure an SNMP packet filter so that control packets are accepted only from certain host systems.

When the SNMP service is started on the SQL Server machine, the SQLSNMP.DLL file is loaded. This process contains a trap mechanism for raising SQL Server alerts and is what coordinates SQL Server with the Windows NT-based SNMP service.

On the Windows NT Server Resource Kit CD-ROM, you will find a number of SNMP utilities, one of which will allow you to carry out simple management tasks (`snmputil`). Using other utilities, you can compile new MIBs to allow monitoring of other performance counters.

`snmputil` gives you a good means for testing your installation, but you will need a full management tool for use in your production environment, such as HP OpenView, Unicenter TNG, SunNet Manager, Advent, or Intraspection. Each of these provides a different variety of graphical tools, add-ons, and foundation objects for developing tools in Visual Basic, Java, and many other development languages.

Using DBCC to Examine Performance

The DBCC command may have been targeted by Microsoft for extinction, but it can still provide useful information on the current state of SQL Server. The next several sections detail the available options. A lot of the same commands are used and presented in a more friendly format by the SQL tools; however, we can capture information from these DBCC commands into tables for historical statistics.

MEMUSAGE

The DBCC MEMUSAGE command has changed from previous versions. A lot of the information that it used to return is now dynamically grown and shrunk. With that in mind, Microsoft modified MEMUSAGE to take either or both of two arguments to return specific useful information:

```
DBCC MEMUSAGE( ['BUFFER'][,]['PROCEDURE'] )
```

The BUFFER option shows the amount of page cache memory in use by the 20 largest objects. The PROCEDURE option shows the amount of procedure cache used by the 12 largest compiled objects (stored procedures, triggers, views, rules, and defaults). The amount of memory shown by either of these options is in 8KB pages.

The procedure cache usage is shown for the following:

- Trees—Precompiled versions of the object
- Compiled plans—Compiled versions of the object
- Execution plans—Executable versions of the object

This information can aid you in deciding which tables might be worth pinning into memory and which stored procedures might be worth revisiting for optimal execution.

SQLPERF

The DBCC SQLPERF command has been drastically altered from previous versions and now only reports transaction-log space usage for all databases. The syntax is

```
DBCC SQLPERF( LOGSPACE )
```

The results of this command are tabular and can be captured into a database table to maintain historical statistics on log usage on the server. The information returned is

Data	*Description*
Database Name	Name of the database
Log Size (MB)	Current size of the log file
Log Space Used (%)	Percentage of the log file currently used
Status	Status of the log file (always contains 0)

This information can actually be captured into a table and then used for historical monitoring of log usage and growth:

```
CREATE TABLE #logspace
( dbname sysname,
  logsize real,
  logused real,
  status tinyint
)

INSERT INTO #logspace EXEC('DBCC SQLPERF(LOGSPACE)')
```

PERFMON

Another DBCC command useful for finding performance information on SQL Server is DBCC PERFMON. This command returns information about the I/O work that SQL Server has been performing, the page cache state and operation, and network statistics.

As with the DBCC SQLPERF command, the results of the execution can be redirected into a table:

```
CREATE TABLE #perfmon
( statistic varchar(32),
  value real
)
```

SHOWCONTIG

The DBCC SHOWCONTIG command has been discussed in other chapters and is only mentioned here for completeness. The DBCC SHOWCONTIG command illustrates the internal state of extents and pages and is helpful in determining how SQL Server is likely to perform when reading data from a table.

PROCCACHE

The DBCC PROCCACHE command returns the following information on the procedure cache:

Data	Description
num proc buffs	Number of possible cache slots in the cache
num proc buffs used	Number of cache slots in use by procedures
num proc buffs active	Number of cache slots that have currently executing procedures
proc cache size	Total size of the procedure cache
proc cache used	Amount of the procedure cache holding stored procedures
proc cache active	Amount of the procedure cache holding stored procedures that are currently executing

Even though SQL Server 7.0 grows and shrinks the procedure cache size as required, you will still want to monitor how much of the memory allocated to SQL Server is in use by the procedure cache. This need makes the DBCC command very useful. You can capture the information into a table for historical monitoring of the system.

INPUTBUFFER and OUTPUTBUFFER

You use the DBCC INPUTBUFFER/OUTPUTBUFFER command to examine the statements sent by a client to the SQL Server. The syntax for these commands is

```
DBCC INPUTBUFFER(spid)
DBCC OUTPUTBUFFER(spid)
```

INPUTBUFFER shows the last statement sent from the specified client, and OUTPUTBUFFER shows the results sent back from the SQL Server.

SQL tools use these commands to display current activity, and you can also use them to examine the commands sent by certain processes that are affecting system performance.

SQL Enterprise Manager

Within the SQL Enterprise Manager (SQL-EM), you have access to the Current Activity window. This a three-tabbed interface allows you to view the current locks held and the current user connections in two different formats. The window provides easy-to-decipher information with a high level of detail.

Activity

The Server Activity window shows you the number of connections for each login. For each of these lines, you can see the database in use, the last command executed, and the hostname of the computer the connection is made from.

The Detail Activity window, as its name implies, provides much more information about a user connection than the Server Activity window. It displays lock information, disk and CPU utilization, and blocking process IDs.

These activity windows also allow you to execute the following actions by clicking the appropriate button on the side of the window:

- Send Message allows you to do a NET SEND to a selected connection.
- More Info provides detailed information on a connection, such as disk and CPU usage and the last SQL command issued.
- Kill Process will execute the kill command on the selected connection.

Locking

The Locking window provides information on all of the current locks, including the type of lock, who is holding it, and the object being locked. This view allows you to quickly and easily see who is holding a large quantity of locks and also identify which process is blocking others on what resources.

Summary

This chapter introduces you to the Windows NT Performance Monitor and the different data views that are available. You have seen the relevant counters to monitor for specific areas of system operation and what the expected values or range of values should be. We also examined various forms of the DBCC command, which gives you direct access to some of the performance statistics.

Configuring, Tuning, and Optimizing SQL Server Options

by Vipul Minocha

IN THIS CHAPTER

For a system to perform well, you should optimize various components of the system to yield high performance. These components include client hardware configuration, server hardware setup, network configuration, database design techniques, and so on. In this chapter, I examine another important aspect of SQL Server: tuning. By setting the values of numerous SQL Server configuration parameters, you can configure SQL Server to provide excellent performance and throughput.

Configuration Variables

SQL Server provides a number of configuration parameters that the system administrator can set to maximize the performance of a system. You can set these parameters either by using the sp_configure system stored procedure or by using SQL Server Enterprise Manager. The syntax of the command is

```
Exec sp_configure  [parameter_name [, parameter_value ]]
```

parameter_name is the name of the configuration parameter you want to set, and parameter_value is the value for the parameter. Both these parameters are optional. Parameters set by sp_configure take effect at the server level. By default, all SQL Server users have permission to run this stored procedure, but only an sa can set the value of a parameter. If you execute this procedure without specifying any parameters, sp_configure returns the current configuration values of SQL Server. The following example displays the output of the sp_configure procedure executed without any parameters:

```
Exec sp_configure
```

name	minimum	maximum	config_value	run_value
affinity mask	0	2147483647	0	0
allow updates	0	1	0	0
cost threshold for parallelism	0	32767	5	5
cursor threshold	-1	2147483647	-1	-1
database size	2	10000	2	2
default comparison style	0	2147483647	1	1
default language	0	9999	0	0
default locale id	0	2147483647	1033	1033
default sortorder id	0	255	52	52
fill factor	0	100	0	0
language in cache	3	100	3	3
locks	5000	2147483647	0	0
max additional query mem.	0	2147483647	1024	1024
max async IO	1	255	32	32
max degree of parallelism	0	32	0	0

```
max query wait            0        2147483647  2147483647  2147483647
max text repl size        0        2147483647  65536       65536
max worker threads        10       1024        255         255
media retention           0        365         0           0
memory                    0        3072        0           0
nested triggers           0        1           1           1
network packet size       512      32767       4096        4096
open objects              100      2147483647  500         500
priority boost            0        1           0           0
procedure cache           1        99          30          30
recovery interval         1        32767       5           5
remote access             0        1           1           1
remote login timeout      0        2147483647  30          30
remote proc trans         0        1           0           0
remote query timeout      0        2147483647  0           0
resource timeout          5        2147483647  10          10
set working set size      0        1           0           0
show advanced options     0        1           1           1
sort pages                32       511         64          64
spin counter              1        2147483647  10000       0
time slice                50       1000        100         100
user connections          5        32767       30          30
user options              0        4095        0           0

(38 row(s) affected)
```

If you specify only the parameter name, SQL Server returns the current configuration value for that particular parameter.

At the SQL Server installation, the setup program makes certain assumptions for configuration parameters and uses default values for all SQL Server configuration parameters. However, for a number of parameters, such as memory, read-ahead parameters, cost threshold of parallelism, and so on, the values chosen by the setup program might not be appropriate for a given environment. Based on the nature of the application, a DBA should tune these parameters appropriately.

Dynamically Adjusted and Advanced Variables

There are two types of configuration parameters:

- Dynamic parameters—Dynamic parameters take effect immediately after you change their value and execute the `reconfigure` command.

- Static parameters—Static parameters require SQL Server to be restarted after the new values are set, and they take effect upon next startup of SQL Server.

29

CONFIGURING,
TUNING, AND
OPTIMIZING SQL

Here is a brief explanation of the output of the `sp_configure` command. As you can see, the output consists of five columns:

- Name—Name of the configurable option.
- Minimum—This is the minimum legal value allowed for this parameter. Passing an illegal value causes SQL Server to return an error.
- Maximum—This is the maximum legal value allowed for this parameter. Passing an illegal value causes SQL Server to return an error.
- Config_value—This column reflects the values that are going to take effect the next time SQL Server is started. If you change any static parameters, the new values are listed under this column.
- Run_value—This column reflects the values that are currently being used by SQL Server. If you change any dynamic parameters, the new values are listed in this column. At the time of SQL Server startup, the `config_value` for all the parameters is copied into `run_value`. Immediately after restart, both columns (`run_value` and `config_value`) should display the same values corresponding to each parameter.

SQL Server internally maintains two tables: syscurconfigs and sysconfigures. The syscurconfigs table contains the current configuration values of SQL Server parameters. These values are shown under the run_value column. The sysconfigures table stores the new values of the parameters that were changed since the last SQL Server startup. These values are shown in the config_value column. Dynamic parameters are written to both of these tables. Static parameters are written only to the sysconfigures table. At SQL Server restart, all the values are copied from the sysconfigures table to the syscurconfigs table.

Setting a value too high for a parameter might cause SQL Server to crash during startup. For example, if you set the value of the memory option to a value that is higher than the physical memory on the machine, SQL Server will not start. In this case, you start SQL Server with the `-f` option. This causes SQL Server to start with the default parameter values (the same values used by the setup program when you installed SQL Server). Once SQL Server is running, change the incorrect value to the right one and restart SQL Server without the `-f` option.

SQL Server parameters are further divided into two categories:

- Basic options
- Advanced options

When SQL Server is installed for the first time, `sp_configure` will show only the basic options. To see advanced options as well, run the following command: ·

```
Exec sp_configure 'show advanced option' , 1
Go
```

```
Reconfigure with override
Go
```

Advanced options are meant to be used by highly experienced SQL Server users who are familiar with the internal operations of SQL Server.

Setting Configuration Options with SQL Enterprise Manager

You can set SQL Server parameters by using SQL Server Enterprise Manager (SEM). To set a specific parameter value, do the following:

1. Start Microsoft Management Console (MMC).

2. Right-click the server.

3. Click Properties.

4. Choose the appropriate tab for specific parameters.

This process is depicted in Figure 29.1.

FIGURE 29.1

Setting parameter values using Enterprise Manager.

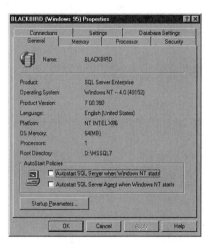

Some of the configuration options available in SQL Server 6.5 are obsolete in the new version of SQL Server. There have also been some additions to the list of variables that you can configure. The following parameters are obsolete in SQL Server 7.0:

backup buffer size	backup threads
free buffers	hash buckets
LE threshold maximum	LE threshold minimum

LE threshold percent	logwrite sleep
max lazywrite IO	open databases
procedure cache	RA cache hit limit
RA cache miss limit	RA delay
RA pre-fetches	RA slots per thread
RA worker threads	recovery flags
remote conn timeout	SMP concurrency
sort pages	

The new variables available in SQL Server 7.0 follow:

cost threshold for parallelism

default comparison style

default locale id

max degree of parallelism

max additional query mem

max additional query wait

time slice

remote sites

The following sections explain the significance of all the SQL Server parameters and their impact on SQL Server performance.

Affinity Mask

Type—Advanced, static

Default value—0

Setup configuration using SEM—Click the Processor tab; then, in the Processor Control box, choose one or more processors to define the affinity mask for the server.

SQL Server supports Symmetric Multiprocessing (SMP). SMP support means that a thread is not tied to a particular processor on the machine. This allows SQL Server to run multiple threads simultaneously, resulting in a high level of load balancing. However, when a server is experiencing a heavy load because of other applications running on the same server, it might be desirable to bind thread affinity to a processor.

The affinity mask is a bitmapped field. Starting from the least significant digit, each bit that's set to 1 represents the processor on which SQL Server will spawn its threads. An example is follows; decimal values are shown in parentheses:

Bit Mask	Processors Used
00000001 (1)	1
00000011 (3)	1, 3
00000100 (4)	4
00000110 (5)	2, 5
00000111 (7)	1, 3, 7

> **TIP**
>
> I don't recommend changing this option for a machine with up to four processors. If you have more than four processors on the machine and applications other than SQL Server are major consumers of a processor's cycle, you might want to use this option to make sure that SQL Server gets the processing cycles it needs.

Allow Update

Type—Basic, dynamic

Default value—0

Setup configuration using SEM—Click the Settings tab; then, from the Server Behavior box, choose Allow Modifications to Be Made Directly to the System Catalogs.

By default, SQL Server does not allow ad hoc updates to internal system tables. When you set the allow update value to 1, any user with proper permissions can update system tables. Because system tables are critical to the functioning of SQL Server, someone can create havoc by improperly modifying these tables.

Why modify system tables? Here are a couple scenarios:

- In many database applications, business logic is written in stored procedures and triggers. To protect your intellectual property, you might not want anyone to see and modify this logic. One way to accomplish this goal is to delete entries from the syscomments table for the objects you want to protect.

- My database is currently running off a Jaz drive connected to my machine, and sometimes, my Jaz drive is disconnected. In such cases during startup, SQL Server fails to initialize the database file and marks the database corrupt by setting the status bit in sysdatabases table to 256. To bring the database back to life, I connect my Jaz drive, change the status bit to the original value, and restart the machine, and then, SQL Server recognizes the drive and starts the database normally.

> **CAUTION**
>
> The allow update option should only be used by highly experienced users of SQL Server. For example, if you create a stored procedure that modifies system tables when the allow update option is turned on, the procedure will continue to be able to modify the system table even if you turn allow update to off again. Therefore, be very careful when you set this parameter value to 1. Turn it off as soon as you are done with the task of modifying system tables.

Cost Threshold for Parallelism

Type—Advanced, dynamic

Default value—5

Setup configuration using SEM—Click the Processor tab; then, in the Parallelism box, choose a value (between 0 and 32,627) for this parameter.

SQL Server now supports parallel query execution. Before any query is executed, SQL Server's cost-based optimizer estimates the cost of execution for a serial plan, a plan that uses a single thread. The option to set the cost threshold for parallelism allows you to specify a threshold in seconds, where if the cost of serial execution plan (in seconds) is greater than the value specified by this parameter, SQL Server will consider a parallel query execution plan. It is important to remember that a query will not become a candidate for parallel query execution simply based on this fact. Because parallel query execution is supported only on an SMP server, this value is ignored for non-SMP hardware. For an application that uses a lot of complex queries, set this value to a lower number so that you can take advantage of the parallel query execution capabilities of SQL Server.

Cursor Threshold

Type—Advanced, dynamic

Default value—-1

Setup configuration using SEM—N/A

This option allows you to specify when SQL Server should generate a cursor resultset asynchronously. If the optimizer estimates that the number of rows returned by the cursor is greater than the value specified by this parameter, it will generate the resultset asynchronously. The optimizer makes this decision based on the distribution statistics for each table participating in the join in the cursor. To determine the optimal value for this parameter, make sure that statistics are up to date (by running update statistics) for the tables used in the cursors. By default, SQL Server generates a cursor resultset synchronously. If you are using a fair amount of cursors that return a large number of resultsets, setting this value to a higher value will result in better performance. Setting this value to 0 will force SQL Server to always generate a cursor resultset asynchronously.

Database Size

Type—Basic, static

Default value—6

Setup configuration using SEM—Click the Database Settings tab; then, in the Initial Database Size (MB) box, choose a value (between 2 and 10,000) for this parameter.

This option allows you to specify the default database size for each new database. When you create a new database, SQL Server will create the database of the size supplied during the `create database` command. If you don't supply the size information, SQL Server uses the larger of the size of the model database and the value defined by the parameter value. If all the databases are bigger than the size of the model database, change this value to the desired value.

Default Comparison Style

Type—Advanced, read-only

Default value—N/A

Setup configuration using SEM—N/A

This is a read-only parameter. This parameter displays the sort option for a given locale ID on the machine. This value is set during the SQL Server installation based on the choices you make for the sort order.

Default Language

Type—Basic

Default value—0

Setup configuration using SEM—Click the Settings tab; then, in the Default Language box, choose the language SQL Server should use for displaying messages.

This option specifies the language ID currently in use by SQL Server. The default value is 0, which specifies the U.S. English system. As you add languages on the server, SQL Server assigns a new ID for each language. You can then use these IDs to specify the default language of your choice. You can add languages using SQL Server setup program. Adding a language allows SQL Server to display error messages and date/time values in the format that is appropriate for that language.

Default Locale ID

Type—Advanced, read-only

Default value—N/A

Setup configuration using SEM—N/A

This is a read-only option that specifies the locale ID for the Unicode character set installed on your machine. To change this parameter value, you have to reinstall SQL Server by using the setup program or buildmaster utility.

Default Sortorder ID

Type—Advanced, read-only

Default value—N/A

Setup configuration using SEM—N/A

This is a read-only option that specifies the default sort order installed on your machine. To change this parameter value, you have to reinstall SQL Server by using the setup program or buildmaster utility.

Fill Factor

Type—Basic, static

Default value—0

Setup configuration using SEM—Click the Database Settings tab; then, in the Settings box, choose Fixed and use the slider control to select the value.

The fill factor option allows you to define the percentage of free space on a data page or an index page when you create an index or a table. The value can range from 1 to 100. Setting the value to 80 would mean each page would be 80 percent full at the time of the create index. SQL Server also allows you to specify the value of fill factor at the server level by providing a fill factor parameter. The significance and performance implications of fill factor were discussed in Chapter 23, "Database Design and Performance."

Language in Cache

Type—Basic, static

Default value—3

Setup configuration using SEM—N/A

SQL Server can support multiple languages for handling system error messages and warnings. This option specifies the maximum number of languages that SQL Server can keep simultaneously in memory.

Locks

Type—Advanced, static

Default value—0

Setup configuration using SEM—N/A

In earlier versions of SQL Server, the DBA had to specify the number of locks available to SQL Server. If this parameter was set to a low value, a query requiring a large number of locks would fail at runtime. Setting it too high would result in wasting memory that otherwise could be used to cache data. SQL Server 7.0 can handle locks dynamically if this parameter is set to the default value (0). SQL Server initially allocates 2 percent of memory available to SQL Server, and as lock resource structures are consumed, the lock manager allocates more lock resources to the pool to a maximum of 40 percent of the memory available on SQL Server. Unless you are certain of the overall lock consumption of your application, there is hardly a reason to change this value.

Max Additional Query Mem

Type—Advanced, dynamic

Default value—1024

Setup configuration using SEM—Click the Memory tab; then, in the Memory box, choose a value (between 512 and 2,147,483) for this parameter.

Each query that executes on SQL Server needs a minimum amount of memory that's required for it to run (based on the plan size). SQL Server, by default, provides this much memory for each query. A number of queries that perform hash joins and sorts can run faster if more memory was assigned for each such query. SQL Server now provides the max additional query mem parameter, which allows you to specify how much additional memory to provide to each query on top of the minimum amount needed by the query. This is quite a useful feature if you have a large amount of memory available on your server.

Max Async IO

Type—Advanced, static

Default value—32

Setup configuration using SEM—N/A

This parameter defines the number of asynchronous threads that can be issued for highly disk-intensive I/Os such as checkpoints, bulk copy, and so on. Usually, there is no reason to change the default value. If you are using multiple controllers attached to multiple drives or hardware-based RAID for disk striping, however, you might want to increase this value to a higher number.

29

CONFIGURING,
TUNING, AND
OPTIMIZING SQL

Max Degree of Parallelism

Type—Advanced, dynamic

Default value—0

Setup configuration using SEM—Click the Processor tab; then, in the Parallelism box, choose the number of processors for parallelism from the drop-down listbox.

This parameter specifies the number of threads to be used for parallel query execution. On a non-SMP server, this value is always ignored. For an SMP server, a default value of 0 signifies that all the CPUs will be used for parallel query execution. If you set this value to 1, all query plans will be serialized. If the affinity mask parameter is set on, parallel query execution will take place only on the CPUs for which the affinity mask bit is turned on.

Max Query Wait

Type—Advanced, dynamic

Default value—2147483647

Setup configuration using SEM—N/A

Queries that are memory intensive (involving huge sorts) might take a long time to execute based on the available memory during execution. SQL Server internally calculates the timeout interval for such queries. Usually, this is quite a large number. You can override this value by specifying a value (in seconds) using the max query wait parameter of SQL Server. If you set this value too low, then when your system is under a heavy load and a highly concurrent environment, you risk more frequent query timeouts.

Max Text Repl Size

Type—Basic, dynamic

Default value—65536

Setup configuration using SEM—N/A

This parameter specifies the maximum size of the text and image datatypes for columns participating in replication during single insert, update, writetext, and updatetext statements.

Max Worker Threads

Type—Basic, dynamic

Default value—255

Setup configuration using SEM—Click the Processor tab; in the Processor Control box, choose a value (between 10 and 1,024) for this parameter.

SQL Server uses native operating system threads. This parameter specifies the maximum number of threads available for SQL Server processes. One or more threads are used for supporting each network protocol (such as TCP/IP, named pipes, and so on). SQL Server is configured to listen. Threads are also consumed by the `checkpoint` and `lazywriter` processes. A pool of threads is used to handle user connections. When the number of connections is lower than the max worker thread parameter value, a thread is created for each connection. When there are more connections on the server than the value defined by the max worker thread parameter, SQL Server provides thread pooling for efficient resource utilization. More threads can create overhead on the system processors. Therefore, lowering this value might sometimes improve the performance of the system. For a system with a few hundred user connections, a reasonable value for this parameter is around 125. You might want to experiment with various values to determine the appropriate value for this parameter.

Media Retention

Type—Advanced, static

Default value—0

Setup configuration using SEM—Click the Database Settings tab; then, in the Default Backup Media Retention (days) box, choose a value (between 0 and 365) for this parameter.

This parameter allows you to specify a time in days to protect the database and transaction log dumps to be overwritten by another such command. If you try to back up a database or a transaction log within the specified length of time, SQL Server will give you a warning, which the operator can override. The default value of 0 means that no warning will be issued by SQL Server. You can override the value specified by this parameter during `BACKUP DATABASE` or `BACKUP LOG` commands by specifying the `RETAINDAYS` option.

Memory

Type—Advanced, static

Default value—0

Setup configuration using SEM—Click the Memory tab; in the Memory box, choose Use a Fixed Memory Size (MB) for the fixed-memory option or choose Dynamically Configure SQL Server Memory for dynamic allocation of memory.

This parameter specifies the amount of memory (in terms of MB) available to SQL Server. SQL Server uses this memory for user connections, locks, internal data structures, and caching the data. The default value of 0 means that SQL Server will perform dynamic allocation of memory from the operating system based on available physical

29

memory on the machine. The SQL Server `lazywriter` process is responsible for making sure that there is enough memory available to SQL Server for the optimal number of buffers and Windows NT so that there is no excess paging at the operating-system level. The `lazywriter` process frequently checks physical memory available on the machine. If the memory available is greater than 5MB, then `lazywriter` assigns excess memory to the SQL Server buffer cache.

If SQL Server is the only application running on the machine, you might want to perform static memory allocation. Be careful when you allocate fixed memory to SQL Server. If you allocate more memory to SQL Server than there is on the machine, SQL Server will fail to start. Use the `-f` option during startup to bring up SQL Server with the default configuration. Change the value to the correct value, and restart SQL Server.

Nested Triggers

Type—Basic, dynamic

Default value—1

Setup configuration using SEM—Click the Settings tab; then, in the Server Behavior box, select Allow Triggers to Be Fired Which Fire Other Triggers (Nested Triggers) to set the value for this parameter.

As the name suggests, this parameter specifies whether a trigger event on a table will fire another trigger and so on. The nesting level of triggers is 16. If you reach this limit, SQL Server will give an error and roll back the transaction. The default value of 1 means that a trigger on a table can cause another trigger to fire.

> **NOTE**
>
> In the earlier versions of SQL Server, a trigger could not be fired recursively. (A trigger could not invoke itself if it modified the data in the table on which it was created.) The workaround was to execute a stored procedure from the trigger, which would modify the data, causing the trigger to fire again. This workaround is not necessary any more. You can turn on recursion for triggers by specifying the `recursive triggers` option in the `sp_dboption` stored procedure. For example, to turn recursive triggers on for the database pubs, issue the following statement:
>
> ```
> Exec sp_dboption 'pubs', 'recursive triggers' , TRUE
> ```

Network Packet Size

Type—Basic, dynamic

Default value—`4096`

Setup configuration using SEM—N/A

This parameter specifies the default network packet size for SQL Server. Setting this value to a higher number (which should be divisible by 512) can improve the performance of applications that involve a large amount of data transfer from the server. You should check your network configuration and set an appropriate value for this parameter.

> **TIP**
>
> You can also specify the network packet size from the client when you connect to SQL Server (using the `-a` option for `isql` and `bcp`). Setting the network packet size from a client can be useful when the default network packet size is adequate for general application needs, but a larger packet size might be needed for some specific operations (such as bulk copy).

Priority Boost

Type—Advanced, static

Default value—`0`

Setup configuration using SEM—Click the Processor tab; then, in the Processor Control box, choose Boost SQL Server Priority on Windows NT.

This parameter is used to specify the process priority of SQL Server process on the Windows NT operating system. The default value of `0` means that SQL Server should run on the same priority level as other applications on the machine. Do not set this option value to `1`, even if SQL Server is the only major application running on the machine. This can cause all sorts of problems, including a tremendous slowdown on the machine.

> **NOTE**
>
> Don't set the value of this parameter to `1`, except in the case of a dedicated SQL Server with SMP hardware.

29

CONFIGURING,
TUNING, AND
OPTIMIZING SQL

Recovery Interval

Type—Basic, dynamic

Default value—5

Setup configuration using SEM—Click the Database Settings tab; then, in the Recovery box, choose a value (between 1 and 32,767) for this parameter.

This parameter is used to specify the maximum time (in minutes) that SQL Server would require to recover a database during startup. During startup, SQL Server rolls forward all the changes that were committed during a SQL Server crash and rolls back the changes that were not committed. Based on the value specified by this parameter, SQL Server determines when to issue a checkpoint in every database of SQL Server so that in the event of a SQL Server crash, it can recover the databases in a time specified by this parameter. If the value of the recovery interval parameter is low, SQL Server will issue checkpoints more frequently. This is to allow a recovery to be faster, but frequent checkpoints can slow down the performance. On the other hand, setting this value too high will create a longer recovery time for databases in the event of a crash.

Remote Access

Type—Basic, dynamic

Default value—1

Setup configuration using SEM—Click the Connections tab; then, in the Remote Server Connections box, choose Allow Other SQL Servers to Connect Remotely to This SQL Server via RPC.

This parameter controls whether remote logins are allowed on the SQL Server. The default value of 1 allows remote access to SQL Server. To turn off remote access, set this parameter to 0.

Remote Login Timeout

Type—Advanced, dynamic

Default value—0

Setup configuration using SEM—N/A

This parameter sets the timeout interval (in seconds) for remote connections. If for some reason, a remote server does not respond to a login request, the login request will "error out" after a timeframe specified by this parameter. The default value of 0 signifies an indefinite wait.

Remote Proc Trans

Type—Basic, static

Default value—0

Setup configuration using SEM—Click the Connections tab; then, in the Remote Server Connections box, choose Enforce Distributed Transactions (MTS).

This parameter allows remote procedures taking part in multiserver transactions to use MS-DTC so that transaction integrity is maintained across servers. The default value of 0 means the remote procedure calls will not use MS-DTC: Data modification at the remote server will not be a part of transactions at the local server. If you set this parameter to 1, then SQL Server uses MS-DTC to preserve transaction integrity across servers.

Remote Query Timeout

Type—Advanced, dynamic

Default value—0

Setup configuration using SEM—Click the Connections tab; then, in the Query Timeout (sec) box, choose a value (between 0 and 2,147,483,647) to configure this parameter.

This option specifies the amount of time in seconds that SQL Server should wait for the query execution at a remote server. The default value of 0 means that SQL Server will wait indefinitely for a query to finish its executions.

Resource Timeout

Type—Advanced, dynamic

Default value—10

Setup configuration using SEM—N/A

This parameter controls the I/O timeout interval. This option specifies the number of seconds SQL Server should wait for a resource before it times out. The default value for this parameter is 10. In environments with high transaction volume and slower disk subsystem, you might see `logwrite` and `bufwait` timeout messages in the error log of SQL Server. In such cases, you might want to increase the value of this parameter.

Set Working Set Size

Type—Advanced, static

Default value—0

Setup configuration using SEM—Click the Memory tab; then, in the Memory box, choose Reserve Physical Memory for SQL Server.

29

CONFIGURING,
TUNING, AND
OPTIMIZING SQL

When this parameter is set, on startup SQL Server will request from the operating system an amount of memory defined by the memory configurable option. This option has no effect when the memory option is set to 0; SQL Server is configured for dynamic memory allocation.

Show Advanced Options

Type—Advanced, dynamic

Default value—0

Setup configuration using SEM—N/A

By default, you will not see the advanced configuration parameters of SQL Server. By setting this parameter to 1, you will be able to see all the SQL Server parameters that can be set by the sp_configure command.

Spin Counter

Type—Advanced, dynamic

Default value—10 for a single processor; 10000 for a multiprocessor server

Setup configuration using SEM—N/A

This parameter specifies the number of attempts SQL Server will make to acquire a resource (such as locks, index page, data page, and so on). Set this parameter to a higher value if you see errors related to resource timeouts.

Time Slice

Type—Advanced, static

Default value—100

Setup configuration using SEM—N/A

This parameter specifies the number of milliseconds a process is to wait for execution before it yields. SQL Server does not oversee the time a process takes for execution; it simply schedules the process. It is the responsibility of the process itself to yield after the time specified by the parameter. If the process does not yield, the SQL Server kernel assumes the process to be a runaway and kills it.

User Connections

Type—Basic, static

Default value—30

Setup configuration using SEM—Click the Connections tab; then, in the Maximum Concurrent User Connections box, choose a value (between 5 and 32,767) for this parameter.

This parameter specifies the number of concurrent users allowed on SQL Server. The memory allocation for user connections is static. Each connection takes up 40KB of memory space. If you configure SQL Server for 100 connections, SQL Server will pre-allocate 4MB (40KB * 100) for user connections. Therefore, setting this value too high might impact performance because the extra memory could have been used to cache data.

User Options

Type—Basic, static

Default value—0

Setup configuration using SEM—Click the Connections tab; then, in the Default Connection Options box, check one or more options to configure this parameter.

This option allows you to specify certain defaults for all the parameters allowed with the SET T-SQL command. Individual users can override these values by using the SET command. This parameter is a bit-mask field, and each bit represents a user option. Table 29.1 outlines the values that you can set with this parameter.

TABLE 29.1 SPECIFYING USER OPTIONS

Bit Mask Value	Description
1	DISABLE_DEF_CNST_CHK controls interim/deferred constraint checking.
2	IMPLICIT_TRANSACTIONS controls whether a transaction is started implicitly when a statement is executed.
4	CURSOR_CLOSE_ON_COMMIT controls the behavior of cursors once a commit has been performed.
8	ANSI_WARNINGS controls truncation and null in aggregate warnings.
16	ANSI_PADDING controls padding of fixed-length variables.
32	ANSI_NULLS controls null handling when using equality operators.
64	ARITHABORT terminates a query when an overflow or divide-by-zero error occurs during query execution.
128	ARITHIGNORE returns NULL when an overflow or divide-by-zero error occurs during a query.
256	QUOTED_IDENTIFIER differentiates between single and double quotation marks when evaluating an expression.
512	NOCOUNT turns off the message returned at the end of each statement that states how many rows were affected by the statement.

29

CONFIGURING, TUNING, AND OPTIMIZING SQL

continues

TABLE 29.1   CONTINUED

Bit Mask Value	Description
1024	ANSI_NULL_DFLT_ON alters the session's behavior to use ANSI compatibility for nullability. New columns defined without explicit nullability are defined to allow NULLs.
2048	ANSI_NULL_DFLT_OFF alters the session's behavior to not use ANSI compatibility for nullability. New columns defined without explicit nullability are defined not to allow NULLs.

For a given user connection, you can use the @@options global variable to see the values that have been set.

Summary

SQL Server 7.0 is a step toward a self-administrating database management system. Many of the parameters available with SQL Server 6.5 are obsolete now. Moreover, the existing parameters require little tuning from the DBA. These self-administering features might provide a big help to a large segment of administrators. However, there are situations in which a DBA would want more control over administration to fine-tune the database. Therefore, the removal of some of the key parameters might not be appreciated by everybody. However, there are still quite a few parameters that the administrator can configure to fine-tune the performance of the system.

CHAPTER 30

Locking and Performance

by Vipul Minocha

IN THIS CHAPTER

In this chapter, you will examine various locking and transaction management features in SQL Server. You will look at the lock types and their impact on performance. You will also review locking hints provided by SQL Server to change default locking behavior.

Need for Locking

Any relational database must support the following properties for transaction management:

- Atomicity—Atomicity defines the unit of work; that is, either all commands within a transaction succeed, or if one or more commands fail, then all the individual commands abort as well. Atomicity in SQL Server is provided by the use of transactions (`begin transaction`, `commit transaction`, `rollback transaction`, and so on).

- Consistency—Consistency ensures that at the end of the transaction, the result of the query is valid and correct. Consistency validates whether there is any kind of corruption either at the internal level (such as an index page pointing to the wrong data page) or at the data level (as a result of an incomplete or failed transaction.)

- Isolation—Isolation ensures that individual transactions don't interfere with one another. This means that a given transaction does not read or modify the state (uncommitted data) of another transaction. SQL Server locking features provide isolation for individual transactions. Locking in a concurrent environment provides isolation in the following cases:

  - Multiple transactions try to modify the same row.

  - Uncommitted data by one transaction is read by other transactions, also known as *dirty* reads.

  - Data read with same SELECT clause during various stages of the transaction results in different values of the same set of data, also known as *nonrepeatable* reads.

  - Data read with same SELECT clause during various stages of the transaction results in different sets of data, also known as inconsistent or *phantom* reads.

- Durability—Durability ensures that once a transaction has been committed, it will withstand hardware and software failures. The transaction logging feature of SQL Server provides durability for transactions.

Locking provides isolation for the transactions. Locking has a significant impact on the integrity of the transaction and performance of the system. For a system that's performing well, transactions are short and non-interfering. In this chapter, I explore the locking features of SQL Server that provide complete isolation to transactions. I also focus on some locking features that allow a transaction to read dirty and nonrepeatable reads for performance reasons.

Lock Resources

Locking in SQL Server is automatic and is provided by an internal lock manager process. The lock manager is responsible for deciding the lock type (shared, update, and so on) and the granularity of locks (row, page, and table). Locking occurs at the data-page level as well as the index-page level. Based on the type of transaction, the SQL Server lock manager chooses different types of lock resources. For example, a `create index` statement will lock the entire table, whereas an `update` statement might lock only a specific row. The lock manager can choose to lock the following resources:

- Table—The entire table inclusive of data and indexes. Used for table-level locking.
- Extent—Consists of eight contiguous pages (8KB), representing 64KB of data or index pages. Used for locking the extent.
- Page—Consists of 8KB of data or index information. Used for locking the page.
- RID—Represents a row identifier within a page. Used for row-level locking.
- Key-range—SQL Server must provide isolation for each transaction. Not only must each transaction be provided isolation, but it should also not be affected by the inconsistent state of any other transaction. Figure 30.1 depicts a scenario where Transaction A is modifying rows with the key values 1, 3, and 5. Before Transaction A can commit its changes, Transaction B adds two rows on the same page with the key values 2 and 4 and commits it. Assuming there is row-level locking enabled for the table, Transaction A and Transaction B both can run in isolation with no threat to data integrity. However, what happens if Transaction A reads data from the page at Stage 1 and reads data again at Stage 4? The data read at Stage 1 is going to be different than that at Stage 4, therefore violating the transaction rule of isolation called *serialization*. SQL Server provides data serialization with key-range locking. Key-range locking locks the entire key range in the query (the key values 1 through 5 in Figure 30.1) by locking the index pages. Therefore, when Transaction B starts, it will be blocked from inserting the new rows until Transaction A commits or rolls back the transaction.

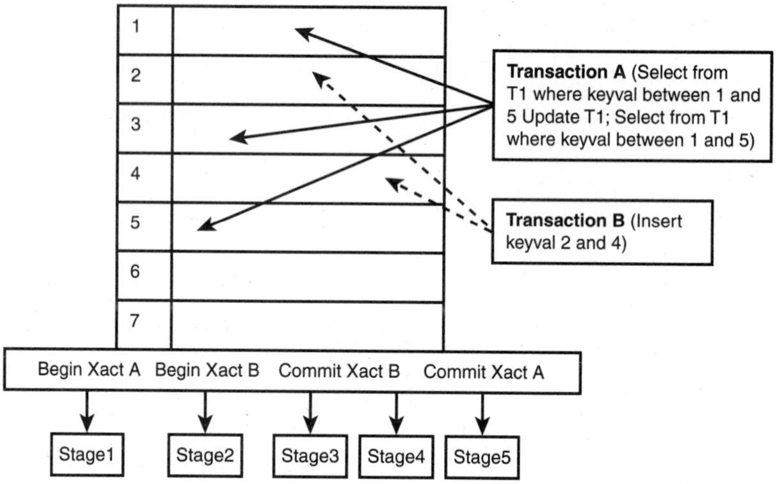

FIGURE 30.1

Key-range locking.

SQL Server Lock Types

Locking is handled automatically by SQL Server. The lock manager chooses the type of locks based on the type of transaction (such as select, insert, delete, and so on). The various types of locks used by lock manager follow:

- Shared
- Update
- Exclusive
- Intent
- Schema

In the previous versions of SQL Server, locking was implemented by locking the entire page on which the data resided. The most granular locking for SELECT, DELETE, and UPDATE statements was at the page level. Therefore, if a transaction modified a single row on a page, other transactions trying to access other records on the same page were blocked until the lock was released. Locking at the page level had significant impact on performance, especially in OLTP environments. SQL Server 7.0 brings a significant shift in the locking strategy. The lock manager was improved to provide full implementation of row-level locking. SQL Server automatically adjusts the granularity of locking based on the nature of the transaction.

Shared Locks

SQL Server uses shared locks for all read-only operations such as SELECT statements. Multiple shared locks can be held at any given time for a number of transactions because these transactions don't interfere with one another. Any transaction that is attempting to modify data on a page (or a row) on which a shared lock is placed will be blocked until all the shared locks are released.

> **NOTE**
>
> It is a common misconception that within a transaction, shared locks are held for the duration of the transaction. Shared lock resources (row, page, table, and so on) are released as soon as the read operation is complete. SQL Server provides HOLDLOCK clause as a part of the SELECT statement if you want to continue holding the shared lock for the duration of the transaction. I explain holdlock later in this chapter. Another way to hold shared locks for the duration of the transaction is to set the isolation to repeatable reads or higher.

Update Locks

Update locks are used for data modification statements. The idea behind an update lock is to provide isolation for a transaction. Before I explain the usefulness of this type of lock, it is important to understand data modifications in relation to locking resources. When a transaction tries to update a row, it must first read the row to ensure that it is modifying the appropriate record. Therefore, the transaction will put a shared lock on the resource. To modify the row now, it must get an exclusive lock on the resource so that no other transaction can modify the same record. The SQL Server lock manager escalates from the lock type shared to the lock type exclusive on the resource. As a result, this transaction can modify the row, and locks are released after the commit (or rollback). In theory, all data modifications can be done by escalating the lock type directly from shared mode to exclusive mode. The problem is that it can lead to dead locks in an environment where multiple transactions are trying to modify data on the same resource. Figure 30.2 explains how deadlocks can occur if lock escalation takes place from shared to exclusive.

FIGURE 30.2

Deadlock scenario with shared and exclusive locks.

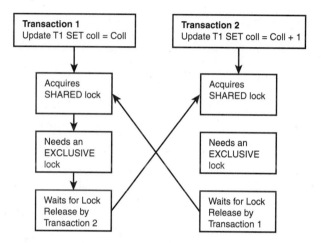

Update locks in SQL Server are provided to prevent this kind of deadlock scenario. Update locks essentially represent progression from a shared lock to an exclusive lock. No data modification can take place by a transaction holding the update lock. An update lock must escalate to an exclusive lock for any data modification to take place on a resource. Update locks prevent deadlocks by allowing only one transaction at any time to put an update lock on a resource. When a transaction acquires an update lock, it waits until all previously held shared locks are released, and at that time, the update lock is escalated to an exclusive lock.

Exclusive Locks

As explained earlier, an exclusive lock is granted to a transaction when it is ready for data modification. An exclusive lock on a resource makes sure that no other transaction can interfere with the data locked by the transaction holding the exclusive lock. SQL Server releases the lock at the end of the transaction.

Intent Locks

The intent lock is a mechanism used by the transactions to declare their intent of acquiring a shared, update, or exclusive lock. An intent lock on a table merely represents the desire to obtain a lock on a resource with a table. It does not put any locks on the table. For example, a shared intent lock on a table by a transaction signifies that no other transaction can acquire an update lock on the resource requested by this transaction.

> **NOTE**
>
> Intent locks improve performance because they make SQL Server examine locks on the table level, rather than the potential multiple locks on the page or row level within the table.

Schema Locks

SQL Server uses schema locks to maintain structural integrity of SQL Server tables. Unlike other types of locks that provide isolation for the data, schema locks provide isolation for the schema of database objects such as tables, views, indexes, and so on within a transaction. The lock manager uses two types of schema locks:

- Schema stability—When a transaction is referencing either an index or data page, SQL Server places a schema stability lock on the object. This ensures that no other transaction can drop the index, stored procedures, or table while other transactions are still referencing it.

- Schema modification—If a transaction needs to modify the structure of an object (alter the table, recompile a stored procedure, and so on), the lock manager places a schema modification lock on the object. For the duration of this lock, no other transaction can reference the object.

Lock Types and Syslockinfo

I have stated before that the different types of locks placed on SQL Server objects are automatically managed by the lock manager. SQL Server keeps all this information in its internal lock structures. However, it provides a view of these structures through a table called syslockinfo. This table is used by the `sp_lock` stored procedure to provide a snapshot of SQL Server locks.

The following query displays the columns of this table:

```
select name from master..syscolumns
where id = object_id("master..syslockinfo")
go
name
- -- -- -- -- -- -- -- -- -- -- -- -- -- -- -- -- -- -- -- -- -- -- -
rsc_text
rsc_bin
rsc_valblk
rsc_dbid
rsc_indid
```

```
rsc_objid
rsc_type
rsc_flag
req_mode
req_status
req_refcnt
req_cryrefcnt
req_lifetime
req_SPID
req_ecid
req_ownertype
```

(16 row(s) affected)

Some of the significant columns are described in the following:

- RSC_DBID—This column describes the database associated with the object on which the lock is held.

- RSC_INDID—This column describes the index ID of the object on which the lock is held. This value is NULL if there are no locks on the index pages (or the rows of the index pages).

- RSC_OBJID—This is the ID of the object on which the lock is placed.

- RSC_TYPE—This column signifies the type of resource being locked by a transaction. The possible values for this column are outlined in Table 30.1.

TABLE 30.1 RESOURCE TYPE

Column Value	Description
1	No resources used
2	Database
3	File
4	Index
5	Table
6	Page
7	Key
8	Extent
9	Row ID

- REQ_MODE—This column describes the lock that is being requested by the transaction. The status of the request is kept in another column called REQ_STATUS. Possible values for this column are shown in Table 30.2.

TABLE 30.2 LOCK REQUEST MODE

Value	Lock Type	Description
0	N/A	No access provided to the requestor
1	Schema	Schema stability lock
2	Schema	Schema modification lock
3	Intent	Intent for shared lock
4	Intent	Intent for shared lock without key-range
5	Intent	Intent for shared lock with key-range
6	Intent	Intent for an exclusive lock
7	Intent	Intent for a shared lock with intent for an exclusive lock (an update statement)
8	Shared	Acquisition of a shared lock on the resource
9	Update	Acquisition of an update lock on the resource
10	Intent/Key-Range	Intent for row-level locking on an index page with key-range
11	Intent/Key-Range	Intent for insert exclusive row-level locking on an index page with key-range
12	Intent/Key-Range	Intent for update exclusive row-level locking on an index page
13	Intent/Key-Range	Intent for delete exclusive row-level locking on an index page
14	Exclusive	Exclusive lock granted on the resource.
15	Bulk	Used for bulk copy operations.

- REQ_STATUS—This column provides the status of a request lock. It can have the values indicated in Table 30.3.

TABLE 30.3 LOCK STATUS

Value	Description
1	Request for lock approved (granted)
2	Request in the process of converting to approved (converting)
3	Waiting to be approved (waiting)

30

LOCKING AND PERFORMANCE

SQL Server Lock Granularity

Lock granularity is defined as the minimum number of locks needed on resources to provide complete isolation and serialization for a transaction. In the previous versions of SQL Server, lock granularity was page level. Locking was implemented by locking the entire page (data or index) even if a query modified only a single row. Microsoft tried to remedy this problem by introducing row-level locking during inserts in version 6.5 of SQL Server, but other DML statements such as DELETE and UPDATE continued to use page-level locking.

SQL Server 7.0 represents a significant shift in the locking strategy. The lock manager was improved to provide complete row-level locking for all kinds of transactions. Locking is dynamic in SQL Server. This means that based on a number of factors, such as key distribution, number of rows, density, search arguments (SARGs), and so on, the lock manager automatically adjusts the lock granularity—from row to page to table level. Locking granularity has a direct impact on the concurrency (and hence performance) of the system. For example, in OLTP environments, row-level locking provides significant advantage over page- or table-level locks on a resource. However, this might not be true in applications such as data warehousing. In such cases, row-level locking might not be the best choice because tables usually contain an extremely large number of records, and the overhead of maintaining row-level locks might be high on the lock manager. Therefore, the benefits of page-level or table-level locking might outweigh the concurrency benefits provided by row-level locking. Fortunately, the query optimizer makes lock granularity decisions internally, and the programmer does not have to worry about such issues. SQL Server 7.0 does provide a number of T-SQL extensions that give you better control over query behavior from a locking standpoint. These optimizer overrides are discussed later in this chapter.

Lock Compatibility

If a resource already has a lock, then locks placed by other transactions on the same resource are governed by the state lock compatibility matrix within SQL Server. For example, if a transaction has acquired a shared lock, the possible lock state transitions for other transactions are intent shared and update. Figure 30.3 shows the lock compatibility diagram for the SQL Server lock manager. The check mark indicates compatibility, and *X* indicates incompatibility between lock modes.

FIGURE 30.3

Lock compatibility diagram.

Requested Lock Mode→ Existing Lock Mode↓	Intent Shared	Shared	Update	Intent Exclusive	Shared Intent Exclusive	Exclusive	Schema Stability	Schema Modification
Intent Shared	√	√	√	√	√	X	√	X
Shared	√	√	√	X	X	X	√	X
Update	√	√	X	X	X	X	√	X
Intent Exclusive	√	X	X	√	X	X	√	X
Shared Intent Exclusive	√	X	X	X	X	X	√	X
Exclusive	X	X	X	X	X	X	√	X
Schema Stability	√	√	√	√	√	√	√	X
Schema Modification	X	X	X	X	X	X	X	X

Optimistic Locking

With most applications, clients fetch the data to browse, make modifications to it, and then post it to SQL Server. Most client software with a user interface falls into this category. The data is read and presented to the user, the user makes some changes or enters some new data, and the changes are put back into the database. These human-speed operations are very slow in comparison to machine-speed operations, and the time lag between the fetch and post may be significant. Although you are able to lock resources for the entire duration of the transaction, the concurrency is adversely affected. Optimistic locking is a technique used in such situations where reading and modifying data processes are widely separated in time. Optimistic locking helps a client avoid overwriting another client's changes to a row without holding any locks on the database.

Optimistic Locking Using the Timestamp Datatype

SQL Server has a special datatype called timestamp. A timestamp is an eight-byte binary datatype. SQL Server automatically generates the value for a timestamp whenever a row containing a column of this type is stored, either by an INSERT or an UPDATE statement. Other than a guarantee that the value is unique and monotonically increasing, the value is not meaningful; you cannot look at the individual bytes and make any sense out of them. Despite the name of the datatype, the value has no relation to the time. It is, in fact, simply a counter that gets changed monotonically (and automatically by SQL Server) during each insert and update. The purpose of the timestamp datatype is to serve as a version number in optimistic locking schemes.

The following two conditions must be met in order to provide optimistic locking:

- The table must have a primary key so that each row can be uniquely identified.
- The table must have a column with the timestamp datatype. The following is an example of how to create a table with a timestamp column:

```
create table mytable ( col1 int, timestamp)
go
```

30

LOCKING AND
PERFORMANCE

The client reads the row with the current value of the timestamp column but does not maintain any locks in the database server. At some later time, when the client wants to update the row, it must ensure that no other client has changed the same row in the intervening time. (Because there are no locks, it is the client's responsibility to make sure that the other client's changes are preserved.) The client prepares the T-SQL UPDATE statement in a special way, using a timestamp column as a versioning marker:

```
UPDATE theTable
SET theChangedColumns = theirNewValues
WHERE primaryKeyColumns = theirOldValues AND timestamp = itsOldValue
```

Because the WHERE clause includes a primary key, the UPDATE applies to exactly one row or to no rows; it cannot apply to more than one row because the primary key is unique. The second part of the WHERE clause is what provides the "locking." If some other client has updated the row, the timestamp will no longer have its old value (remember that the server changes the timestamp value automatically with each update), and the WHERE clause will fail to pick out any rows. The client uses this signal, a zero-row UPDATE, as an indication of lock failure. It can then choose to re-read the data or do whatever recovery it deems appropriate.

> **NOTE**
>
> Using a timestamp column is a popular strategy among database designers and application architects. However, there are performance-related inefficiencies associated with optimistic locking using the timestamp column. This section will highlight these inefficiencies and propose a scheme that's simpler and superior in terms of performance.

Optimistic Locking Using an INT Datatype

In the preceding example, you actually do not need a timestamp datatype to do optimistic locking. An INT column (let's call it RevisionColumn) dedicated to the same purpose will work just fine. The only difference is that because the server does not alter the value of the column, the client must do so. The T-SQL UPDATE statement looks like this:

```
UPDATE theTable
SET theChangedColumns = theirNewValues, RevisionColumn = itsOldValue + 1
WHERE primaryKeyColumns = theirOldValues AND RevisionColumn = itsOldValue
```

Notice the only change to the SQL statement is the explicit change to the value of the designated optimistic-locking revision column in the SET clause.

Optimistic Locking—Server-Side Versioning Versus Client-Side Versioning

The timestamp and int datatype techniques are pretty much the same. However, there are a few differences:

- The int uses only four bytes, in comparison to the eight-byte timestamp, so it is more efficient in terms of storage space.

- When an int is used, the client must remember to put the version update into the SET clause, in addition to remembering to put the version check into the WHERE clause.

- After an UPDATE statement, the timestamp value at the client is not the same as that of the server. Therefore, another read must be performed from the server to synchronize the timestamp values of the client and the server. This is true for inserts as well; whenever the server generates primary key or versioning data on behalf of the client, the client must read the generated data as a part of the same transaction in which the data is generated. Otherwise, the client will not have the correct values to use in the WHERE clause for a subsequent UPDATE it might want to make. However, if versioning is performed by the client, the client already has an up-to-date picture of the row's data (including the version number) following the UPDATE and need not follow the update with a query for the new timestamp value. The difference is not between the two UPDATE statements documented previously but occurs in the state in which the client remains "after" the UPDATE is done. The following example demonstrates this point:

```
- - optimistic locking using a timestamp

UPDATE theTable
SET theChangedColumns = theirNewValues
WHERE primaryKeyColumns = theirOldValues
AND timestamp = itsOldValue

/* Read the data in the same transaction to
   synchronize the timestamp values
   at the client and the server. */

SELECT timestamp FROM theTable
WHERE primaryKeyColumns = theirNewValues
Versus
- - optimistic locking using an int
UPDATE theTable
SET theChangedColumns = theirNewValues,
revisionColumn = itsOldValue + 1
WHERE primaryKeyColumns = theirOldValues
AND revisionColumn = itsOldValue
```

As you can see from the two segments of SQL, optimistic locking with an int keeps the client in an identical state with respect to knowledge of the data on the server without an additional read from the database. The second method is clearly simpler, provides better performance, and from a purist standpoint, meets better standards compliance because it does not rely on a special SQL Server datatype not supported by other DBMSs.

Index Locking

Similar to locks on the data pages, SQL Server manages locks on index pages internally. Compared to data pages, index pages have more contention. Contention at the B-tree root page is the highest because the root is the starting point of the search. Contention usually decreases as you move down the various levels of the B-tree. SQL Server provides a system stored procedure called sp_indexoption that allows expert users to control locking behavior at the index level. The syntax of this stored procedure is

```
Exec sp_indexoption {[@IndexNamePattern = ] 'index_name'}[,
[@OptionName = ] 'option_name'] [,
[@OptionValue = ]'value']
```

The following variables apply:

- *index_name* is the name of the table or a specific index name on the table.
- *option_name* can have the following two values:

  AllowRowLocks—When set to false, this will prevent any row-level locking on the index pages. Only page- and table-level locks will be applied.

  AllowPageLocks—When set to false, this will prevent page-level locks. Only row- or table-level locks will be applied.

- *value* can be true or false for the option_name parameter.

SQL Server usually makes good choices for the index locks, but based on the distribution of data and nature of the application, you might want to force this option on a selective basis. The following example turns off row-level locking for index pages on an index named aumind for the authors table:

```
Exec sp_indexoption "authors.aunmind", "AllowRowLocks", false
Go
All 1 matched objects now have their 'allowrowlocks' setting as
 'false'. Updates were required for 1 objects.
```

Using Transaction Isolation Levels in SQL Server

Isolation levels determine the proportion to which inconsistent data of one transaction is protected by other transactions. In theory, each transaction must be fully isolated from other transactions, but in practice, for practical and performance reasons, this might not always be true. In a concurrent environment in the absence of locking and isolation, the following four scenarios can happen:

- Lost update—In this scenario, no isolation is provided to a transaction from other transactions. Multiple transactions can read the same copy of data and modify it. The last transaction to modify the dataset prevails, and the changes by all other transactions are lost.

- Dirty reads—In this scenario, one transaction can read data that is being modified by other transactions. Data read by the first transaction is inconsistent because the other transaction may choose to roll back the changes.

- Nonrepeatable reads—This is somewhat similar to zero isolation. In this scenario, a transaction reads the data twice, but before the second read occurs, some other transaction modifies the data; therefore, the values read by the first read will be different from those of the second read. Because the reads are nonrepeatable each time, it is called nonrepeatable reads.

- Phantom reads—Refer to Figure 30.1, which depicts a scenario where Transaction A is modifying rows with the key values 1, 3, and 5. Before Transaction A can commit its changes, Transaction B adds two rows on the same page with the key values 2 and 4 and commits it before Transaction A. Assuming that Transaction A and Transaction B both can run independently without blocking each other, data read by Transaction A at Stage 1 is going to be different from that at Stage 4. This phenomenon is called phantom reads because in the second pass, you are getting records you did not expect to retrieve.

Ideally, a DBMS must provide isolation levels to prevent all of these scenarios. Sometimes because of practical and performance reasons, databases do relax some of the rules. ANSI has defined four transaction isolation levels, each providing a different degree of isolation to cover the previous scenarios. ANSI SQL-92 defines the following four standards for transaction isolation:

30

LOCKING AND PERFORMANCE

- Read uncommitted (Level 0)
- Read committed (Level 1)
- Repeatable read (Level 2)
- Serializable (Level 3)

SQL Server does support all these levels. In your application, you can set these isolation levels by using the SET TRANSACTION ISOLATION LEVEL T-SQL command.

Read Uncommitted

If you set the read uncommitted mode, there is no isolation provided to any transaction. For a transaction running with this isolation level, the transaction is not immune to dirty reads, nonrepeatable reads, or phantom reads.

To set read uncommitted mode for a transaction, run the following statements from the client:

- T-SQL—SET TRANSACTION ISOLATION LEVEL READ UNCOMMITTED.
- ODBC—Use the function call SQLSetConnectAttr with Attribute set to SQL_ATTR_TXN_ISOLATION and ValuePtr set to SQL_TXN_READ_UNCOMMITTED.
- OLE DB—Use the function call ITransactionLocal::StartTransaction with the isoLevel set to ISOLATIONLEVEL_READUNCOMMITTED.
- ADO—Set the IsolationLevel property of the Connection object to adXactReadUncommitted.

Read Committed

The read committed mode is the default behavior for SQL Server. In this mode, there is no implicit begin transaction by SQL Server; therefore, as soon as a DML statement is complete, changes are applied to the underlying table immediately. During the execution of a DML statement, SQL Server places an update lock on the resource undergoing modification; no other transaction can acquire a shared or an update lock, preventing any dirty reads. In this mode, a transaction is not immune to lost updates, nonrepeatable reads, or phantom reads.

To set read committed mode for a transaction, run the following statements from the client:

- T-SQL—SET TRANSACTION ISOLATION LEVEL READ COMMITTED.
- ODBC—Use the function call SQLSetConnectAttr with Attribute set to SQL_ATTR_TXN_ISOLATION and ValuePtr set to SQL_TXN_READ_COMMITTED.

- OLE DB—Use the function call `ITransactionLocal::StartTransaction` with `isoLevel` set to `ISOLATIONLEVEL_READCOMMITTED`.

- ADO—Set the `IsolationLevel` property of the `Connection` object to `adXactReadcommitted`.

Repeatable Read

In repeatable read mode, SQL Server implicitly starts a transaction. Because of that, SQL Server will not commit a DML statement until there is an explicit `COMMIT` or `ROLLBACK` of the transaction from the application. This mode allows a transaction to put shared and exclusive locks on the resources undergoing modification. Transactions using repeatable mode don't suffer from lost update, dirty read, or nonrepeatable read problems. However, such transactions can still have phantom read problems.

To set repeatable read mode for a transaction, run the following statements from the client:

- T-SQL—`SET  TRANSACTION ISOLATION LEVEL REPEATABLE READ`.

- ODBC—Use the function call `SQLSetConnectAttr` with `Attribute` set to `SQL_ATTR_TXN_ISOLATION` and `ValuePtr` set to `SQL_TXN_REPEATABLEREAD`.

- OLE DB—Use the function call `ITransactionLocal::StartTransaction` with `isoLevel` set to `ISOLATIONLEVEL_ REPEATABLEREAD`.

- ADO—Set the `IsolationLevel` property of the `Connection` object to `adXact REPEATABLEREAD`.

Serializable

Serializable is the strictest mode that guarantees complete isolation for a transaction. In this mode, SQL Server implicitly starts a transaction and uses key-range locking on the index pages. Any transaction using this mode places shared locks, exclusive locks, and key-range locks to prevent interference from any other transaction. Transactions using serializable mode don't suffer from lost update, dirty read, nonrepeatable read, or phantom read problems. However, because a relatively large number of resources may be locked to provide complete isolation, applications using this mode may reveal some concurrency issues.

To set the serializable mode for a transaction, run the following statements from the client:

- T-SQL—`SET TRANSACTION ISOLATION LEVEL SERIALIZABLE`.

- ODBC—Use the function call `SQLSetConnectAttr` with `Attribute` set to `SQL_ATTR_TXN_ISOLATION` and `ValuePtr` set to `SQL_TXN_SERIALIZABLE`.

30

LOCKING AND PERFORMANCE

- OLE DB—Use the function call `ITransactionLocal::StartTransaction` with `isoLevel` set to `ISOLATIONLEVEL_SERIALIZABLE`.

- ADO—Set the `IsolationLevel` property of the `Connection` object to `adXact SERIALIZABLE`.

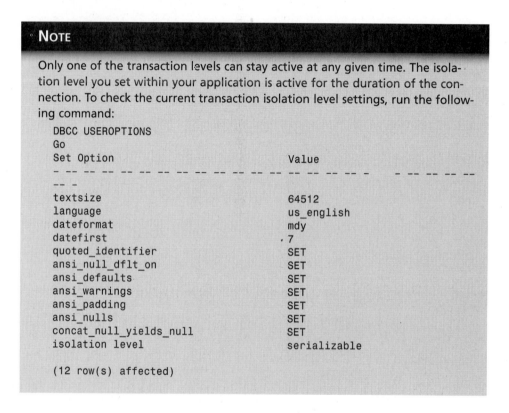

> **NOTE**
>
> Only one of the transaction levels can stay active at any given time. The isolation level you set within your application is active for the duration of the connection. To check the current transaction isolation level settings, run the following command:
>
> ```
> DBCC USEROPTIONS
> Go
> Set Option                       Value
> - -- -- -- -- -- -- -- -- -- -- -- -- -- -- -- -- -   - -- -- -- --
> -- -
> textsize                         64512
> language                         us_english
> dateformat                       mdy
> datefirst                        .7
> quoted_identifier                SET
> ansi_null_dflt_on                SET
> ansi_defaults                    SET
> ansi_warnings                    SET
> ansi_padding                     SET
> ansi_nulls                       SET
> concat_null_yields_null          SET
> isolation level                  serializable
>
> (12 row(s) affected)
> ```

Serialization and Key-Range Locking

As mentioned in the previous section, SQL Server provides serialization (isolation level 3) through the `SET TRANSACTION ISOLATION SERIALIZABLE` command. One of the isolations provided by this command is the prevention against phantom reads. Prevention against phantom reads means that the recordset obtained by a query within a transaction must return the same resultset when it is run multiple times within the same transaction. That is, while a transaction is active, no new rows should be inserted by any other transaction that will cause these rows to appear in the original transaction if the recordset is fetched multiple times in the transaction. SQL Server 7.0 provides this capability though key-range locking, which is described in the following sections.

As described earlier, key-range locking within SQL Server provides isolation for a transaction from an inconsistent state of any other transaction. This means that a transaction should return the same recordset each time. In this section, I describe how key-range locking works with various lock modes. Key-range locking covers the following scenarios:

- Range search—In this scenario, SQL Server places locks on the index pages for the range of data covered in the WHERE clause of the query. Because the index range is locked, no other transaction will be able to insert any new rows that fall within the range. In Figure 30.4, Transaction B tries to insert a row with a key value (stor_id = 7200) that falls within the range being used by Transaction A (stor_id between 6000 and 7500). To provide key-range isolation, SQL Server places intent-shared (IS) locks on the index pages for the key values between 6,000 and 7,500 and shared locks (S) for the data pages. Other processes can read the values within this key range but will not be able to insert any new rows. The shared lock on the data page protects the rows from being updated by any other transaction.

FIGURE 30.4

Key-range locking with range search.

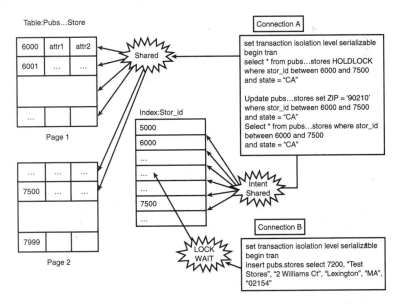

- Searching or deleting nonexistent rows—In this scenario, if a transaction is trying to delete or fetch a row that does not exist in the database, it still should not find any rows at a later stage in the same transaction and same query. For example, in

30

Figure 30.5, Transaction A is trying to fetch a nonexistent row with the key value 7200, and another concurrent transaction (Transaction B) is trying to insert a record with the same key value (stor_id = 7200).

SQL Server in this mode will prevent Transaction B from inserting a new row by placing a intent-shared (IS) lock on the index page for the rows in the range between MAX(stor_id) < 7200 (key value 7100 in Figure 30.5) and MIN(stor_id) > 7200 (key value 7300 in Figure 30.5).

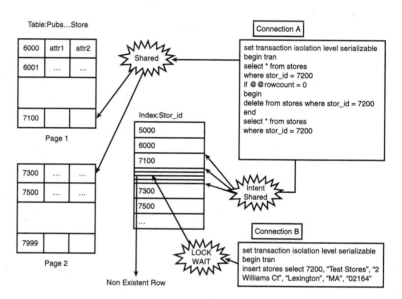

FIGURE 30.5

Key-range locking with a nonexistent dataset.

Following is the sample output of the sp_lock command for these two transactions:

```
Exec sp_lock
Go
spid  dbid  ObjId       IndId  Type  Resource          Mode    Status
- --  -- - - -- -- - - -- -- -- -- -. - -- -- - - -- - - -- -- -- -- -- --
-- - - -- -- -- - - -- -- -
7     5     0           0      DB                      S       GRANT
7     5     405576483   1      PAG   1:109             IS      GRANT
7     5     405576483   0      TAB                     IS      GRANT
7     5     405576483   1      KEY   (0e0e37383936)    IS-S    GRANT
8     1     0           0      DB                      S       GRANT
8     5     0           0      DB                      S       GRANT
8     5     405576483   1      PAG   1:109             IX      GRANT
8     5     405576483   0      TAB                     IX      GRANT
8     5     405576483   1      KEY   (0e0e37383936)    IIn-Nul WAIT
```

- Insert operations—In this scenario, SQL Server places a intent-insert lock on the index page only for the key that's being inserted. Other key-range values are still open for other transactions to access or modify the data. Figure 30.6 depicts this scenario.

FIGURE 30.6

Key-range locking in insert operations.

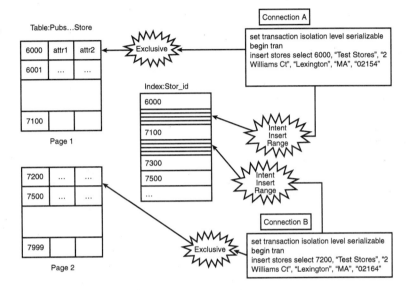

• Delete operations—In this scenario, SQL Server places an exclusive lock on the index page only for the key that's being deleted. Other key-range values are still open for other transactions to access or modify the data. Figure 30.7 depicts this scenario.

FIGURE 30.7

Key-range locking in delete operations.

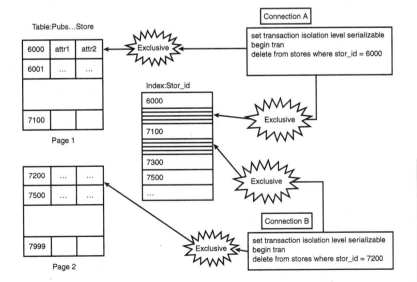

Table Hints for Locking

As mentioned in the previous section, you can set an isolation level for your connection using the SET TRANSACTION ISOLATION LEVEL command. This command creates a global isolation level for your session, which is useful if you want to provide a consistent isolation level for your application. However, sometimes you want to create different isolation levels for different queries in the system or different isolation levels within a single query for tables participating in joins. SQL Server allows you to do that by supporting table hints in the SELECT, DELETE, UPDATE, and INSERT clauses of the query. This allows you to override the isolation level set at the connection level.

In this chapter, I have mentioned that locking is dynamic in SQL Server; based on certain factors (such as SARGs, key distribution, data volume, and so on), the query optimizer chooses the granularity of the lock (row, page, or table level) on a resource. Although it is generally a good idea to leave such decisions to the cost-based optimizer, you might encounter certain situations where you want to force a lock granularity on the optimizer. SQL Server provides certain table hints that you can use in the query to force lock granularity for various tables participating in a join. In the following section, I discuss various locking hints that can be passed to an optimizer to manage isolation levels and the lock granularity of a query.

Transaction Isolation Level Hints

You can use seven hints within a query to override the default transaction isolation level:

- HOLDLOCK—Within a transaction, a shared lock is released as soon as the T-SQL statement holding the shared lock is complete. To maintain a shared lock for the duration of the entire transaction, use the HOLDLOCK clause in the statement. The following example demonstrates the usage of the HOLDLOCK statement within a transaction:

```
declare @seqno int
begin transaction
- - get a UNIQUE sequence number from sequence table
SELECT @seqno = isnull(seq#,0) + 1
from sequence WITH HOLDLOCK

    - - in the absence of HOLDLOCK, shared lock will be released
    - - and if some other concurrent transaction ran the same
    - - command, both of them will get the same sequence number

UPDATE sequence
set    seq# = @seqno

    - - now go do something else with this unique sequence number
```

- NOLOCK—You can use this option to specify that no shared lock be placed on the resource and requests for update or exclusive locks be denied. This option will allow dirty reads for other transactions. The NOLOCK option is a useful feature in reporting environments where approximate values are good enough.

- READCOMMITTED—This is same as specifying the read committed mode when you use the SET TRANSACTION ISOLATION LEVEL command.

- READPAST—This hint applies only to the SELECT statement. By specifying this option, you can skip over the rows that are locked by other transactions. In the absence of the READPAST option, the SELECT statement will wait (or time out if lock timeout values are set) until the locks are released on the rows by other transactions. For a statement with the READPAST clause, all blocking transactions should be in the transaction-isolation read committed mode, and all the locks held by them should be row-level locks. Given these restrictions, in an OLTP multiuser concurrent environment, it is practically impossible to implement this option.

- READUNCOMMITTED—This is the same as specifying the read uncommitted mode when using the SET TRANSACTION ISOLATION LEVEL command, and it is the same as NOLOCK table hint.

- REPEATABLEREAD—This is same as specifying repeatable read mode with the SET TRANSACTION ISOLATION LEVEL command.

- SERIALIZABLE—This is same as specifying serializable with the SET TRANSACTION ISOLATION LEVEL command.

NOTE

In previous versions, *tables hints* were called *optimizer hints*. The syntax and behavior of some of these hints have changed from previous versions. In SQL Server 7.0, all the hints in the FROM clause must be preceded by the WITH clause with the hints listed in parentheses. The only exception is the HOLDLOCK hint, which can still be specified without the WITH clause.

In SQL Server 6.5, the REPEATABLE READ transaction isolation level option behaved identical to SERIALIZABLE option; it protected transactions against phantom reads. In SQL Server 7.0, the REPEATABLE READ option provides level 3 isolation. (It does not, and rightfully so, protect against phantom reads.) Use the SERIALIZABLE option if you want to provide level 4 isolation for transactions in your system.

30

LOCKING AND PERFORMANCE

Lock Granularity Hints

You can use five optimizer hints to override lock granularity:

- ROWLOCK—You can force the lock manager to place a row-level lock if it is considering a page-level or a table-level lock.

- PAGLOCK—You can force a page-level lock on a resource if the optimizer is considering a table-level lock.

- TABLOCK—You can use this option to hold a table-level lock if the optimizer is considering a row-level or a page-level lock.

- TABLOCKX—This option allows you to specify an exclusive lock on a table. No shared or update locks are granted to other transactions as long as this option is in effect. If you are planning maintenance on a SQL Server table and you don't want interference from any other transaction, this is one of the ways to bring a table into a single user mode.

- UPDLOCK—This option is similar to HOLDLOCK except that although HOLDLOCK places a shared lock, UPDLOCK places an update lock on the resource for the duration of the transaction.

Examining Current Lock Activity

To monitor the performance of the system, it is necessary to keep track of locking activity at SQL Server. There are three possible ways to do so:

- Using the sp_lock stored procedure
- Viewing locking activity with SQL Enterprise Manager
- Viewing the current quantity of locks with Performance Monitor

Using the sp_lock Stored Procedure

The stored procedure sp_lock provides a snapshot of locks being held on resources by various transactions. The syntax of this command follows:

```
Exec sp_lock [SPID1] [,SPID2]
```

Following is the sample output of this command:

```
Exec sp_lock
Go
SPID   dbid   ObjId        IndId  Type Resource          Mode    Status
- -- -- - - -- -- - - -- -- -- -- -- - - -- -- - - - -- - - -- -- -- -- -- --
-- - - -- -- -- - - -- -- -
1      1      0            0      DB                     S       GRANT
```

6	1	0	0	DB		S	GRANT
7	5	0	0	DB		S	GRANT
7	5	117575457	1	PAG	1:122	IX	GRANT
7	5	117575457	1	PAG	1:96	IX	GRANT
7	5	117575457	2	KEY	(f59632855aa0)	X	GRANT
7	5	117575457	2	KEY	(d59632855aa8)	X	GRANT
7	5	117575457	0	TAB		IX	GRANT
7	5	117575457	1	KEY	(02c094e89f8a)	X	GRANT
8	5	0	0	DB		S	GRANT
8	5	117575457	1	PAG	1:96	IU	GRANT
8	5	117575457	0	TAB		IX	GRANT
8	5	117575457	1	KEY	(02fd89ed9d9e)	U	GRANT
8	5	117575457	1	KEY	(02c094e89f8a)	U	WAIT
8	5	117575457	1	KEY	(0dff8ce59982)	U	GRANT
8	5	117575457	1	KEY	(0afe9ce59186)	U	GRANT
8	5	117575457	1	KEY	(0fc693fd9b86)	U	GRANT
8	5	117575457	1	KEY	(3dfab8f09596)	U	GRANT
9	1	0	0	DB		S	GRANT
9	2	0	0	DB		S	GRANT
9	5	0	0	DB		S	GRANT
9	1	117575457	0	TAB		IS	GRANT

```
(22 row(s) affected)
```

The columns provide the following information:

- The SPID is the process ID for a transaction. It is retrieved from the sysprocesses table in the master database.
- The dbid is the ID of the database on which locks are held. This information comes from the sysdatabases table in the master database.
- The ObjId is the ID of the resource on which locks are held. This information comes from the sysobjects table from the databases on which the locks are placed.
- The IndId is the ID for the table index on which locks are held.
- The Type is the type of lock being held on the resource. This information comes from the syslockinfo memory structure in the master database. Possible values for this column are shown in Table 30.4.

TABLE 30.4   POSSIBLE VALUES FOR THE Type FIELD

Value	Description
1	Unused
2	Database
3	File
4	Index

continues

TABLE 30.4 POSSIBLE VALUES FOR THE Type FIELD

Value	Description
5	Table
6	Page
7	Key
8	Extent
9	RowID

- The Resource is the internal name of the resource on which locks are placed. This information comes from the syslockinfo table in the master database. Information displayed by this column is directly governed by the type of lock held on the resource. Table 30.5 displays the resource format based on the value of the lock type.

TABLE 30.5 RESOURCE TYPE

Lock Type	Resource Format
Table	ObjectId
Page	FileNumber:PageNumber
RowID	FileNumber:PageNumber:RowID
KeyRange	ObjectID:IndexID

- The Mode is the type of lock requested by the transaction. All the lock types were discussed at the beginning of this chapter.

- The Status is the status of request. The possible values follow:
  GRANT
  WAIT
  CNVRT

Viewing Locking Activity with SQL Enterprise Manager

You can see that the output of sp_lock is somewhat unfriendly because it displays the IDs of the database and objects. For a more user-friendly output, use the object_name(id) and db_name(dbid) functions to convert IDs into more meaningful information. You can also use the SQL Server Enterprise Manager to display the locking information. To see the output from the Enterprise Manager, right-click the server, choose Tools, click Current Activity, and click the Object Locks tab to display locking information on SQL Server. You can click the More Info button to see the SQL text of the command for a specific process ID. Figure 30.8 displays a sample snapshot for the object locks held on SQL Server.

FIGURE 30.8

Viewing locks using SQL Enterprise Manager.

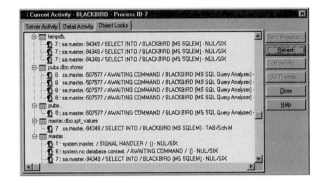

Viewing the Current Quantity of Locks with Performance Monitor

You can also get SQL Server lock information using the Performance Monitor. The stored procedure `sp_lock` and the Enterprise Manager provide a snapshot of locks on the server. If you want to monitor locking activity on a continuous basis, use the Performance Monitor. Two objects are significant in the context of locking:

- SQLServer:Lock Manager
- SQLServer:Locks

SQLServer:Lock Manager

The SQLServer:Lock Manager object allows you to monitor locking activity at the server. You can measure the following counters using this object:

- Lock Blocks—This counter represents the number of locked resources on SQL Server.

- Lock Blocks Allocated—This counter represents the number of locks allocated at any given time. Because the number of locks is dynamic in SQL Server 7.0, this value can change periodically.

- Lock Owner Blocks—This counter represents the total number of locks on each thread. For example, if a query is chosen for parallel execution on multiple threads (say five) and each thread puts a lock on some resource, assuming there is no other lock activity on the server, the value of this counter will be 5.

- Lock Owner Blocks Allocated—This counter represents the number of locks allocated for lock owner blocks. This value can change dynamically as threads acquire or release locks on resources.

- Table Lock Escalations—This counter represents the number of times locks were escalated on a table (such as from shared intent to shared to update to exclusive).

SQLServer:Locks

You can use the SQLServer:Locks object in detecting bottlenecks in the system. Various counters allow you to measure parameters based on the feedback provided by Performance Monitor counters so you can take corrective actions to improve concurrency and the overall performance of the system. The counters belonging to the SQLServer:Locks object follow:

- Average Wait Time—This counter represents the average wait time for each lock request. This value is represented in milliseconds. A high value is an indication of low concurrency of the system.

- Lock Requests—This counter represents the total number of new locks and lock conversion requests. A high value for this counter is not necessarily a cause for alarm; it may simply indicate a system with a very high number of concurrent users.

- Lock Timeouts—This counter represents the total number of timeouts that occurred for lock request on a resource. By default, a blocked process will wait indefinitely unless the application specifies a maximum timeout limit using the SET LOCK_TIMEOUT command. If you see a high value for this counter, make sure that the timeout limit is not set to a low value in your application.

- Lock Wait Time—This counter represents the cumulative wait for each lock request. It is given in milliseconds.

- Lock Wait—This counter represents the total number of lock requests that had to wait before a lock request on a resource was granted. A high value indicates a poorly implemented system where a large number of transactions block one another.

- Number of Deadlocks—This number represents the total number of deadlocks taking place in the system. I discuss deadlocks and how to avoid them in the next section.

Deadlocks and Minimizing Locking Contention

A deadlock is a scenario in which two connections are waiting for a locked resource. SQL Server automatically detects a deadlock situation with a method called circular chain lock detection. An internal SQL Server process continues to monitor for deadlocks. In the first pass, this process detects all the processes that are waiting on some resource. In the second pass, this process tries to detect lock situations that can lead to a deadlock situation and kills the process that has caused a circular chain of locks. A typical dead-lock scenario is depicted in Figure 30.9. The two concurrent processes (SPIDs 10 and 20) have acquired a shared lock on the sequence table. Both SPIDs try to escalate the lock level to UPDATE, but for SPID 10 to acquire an update lock, SPID 20 must release its shared lock from the table. Similarly, for SPID 20 to acquire an update lock, SPID 10 must release its shared lock from the table. This is a classic case of deadlock. The SQL Server internal process detects this and determines that SPID 10 is responsible for causing the loop lock and kills it. SPID 20 then acquires the update lock and proceeds normally.

FIGURE 30.9

Deadlock due to HOLDLOCK*s.*

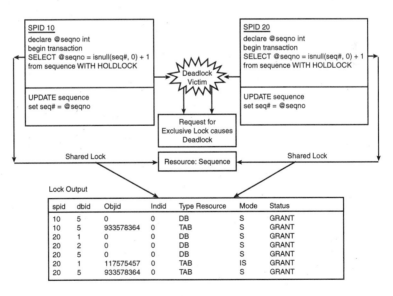

spid	dbid	Objid	Indid	Type	Resource	Mode	Status
10	5	0	0	DB		S	GRANT
10	5	933578364	0	TAB		S	GRANT
20	1	0	0	DB		S	GRANT
20	2	0	0	DB		S	GRANT
20	5	0	0	DB		S	GRANT
20	1	117575457	0	TAB		IS	GRANT
20	5	933578364	0	TAB		S	GRANT

It is a misconception to assume that deadlocks happen at the data page level. In fact, many deadlocks occur at the index page level. Figure 30.10 depicts a scenario where deadlock takes place due to contention at the index page level.

30

LOCKING AND PERFORMANCE

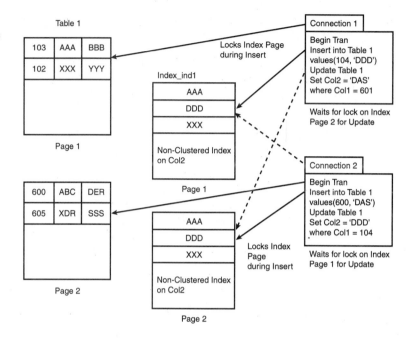

FIGURE 30.10
Deadlocks due to locks on index pages.

Avoiding Deadlocks

You can do a variety of things to minimize, if not completely eliminate, the number of deadlocks in the application. The following is a list of general guidelines you might want to follow when designing your application:

- Keep transactions short. Fetch small amounts of data so that fewer locks are placed on resources.

- Use the optimistic locking method described earlier in this chapter.

- Use SET DEADLOCKPRIORITY LOW or SET DEADLOCKPRIORITY NORMAL. Setting a low deadlock priority will cause the current transaction to be the victim in case a deadlock situation occurs involving the current process. You might want to set a low priority for DSS queries and a high priority for OLTP queries.

- Be consistent about the order in which you access the data from tables.

- Minimize the use of HOLDLOCK. For example, the query in Figure 30.9 (earlier in the chapter) can be rewritten as follows:

```
declare @seqno int
begin transaction
UPDATE sequence set @seqno = isnull(seq#,0) + 1
from sequence
select @seqno
```

This way, a query directly acquires the update lock mode, and the chance for a deadlock is eliminated.

- SQL Server 7.0 fully supports row-level locking. Finer lock granularity results in better concurrency and fewer deadlocks. Use table hints to obtain finer lock granularity on resources.

- Avoid user interaction within a transaction. This will increase the duration of the transaction if it has to wait for user input and will cause the locks to be held on the underlying tables for a longer duration.

- Choose the transaction isolation level judiciously. You might be able to reduce deadlocks by choosing lower isolation levels.

Handling and Examining Deadlocks

SQL Server returns an error number 1205 to the client when it kills a process as a result of deadlock. Because deadlock is not a logical error, but merely a resource contention issue, the client can resubmit the same transaction. To handle deadlocks on the client, trap for message 1205 in your application. If you want to resubmit the batch, make sure that you put in a delay of a few milliseconds in the code.

You can use a number of trace flags to monitor a deadlock situation. Always remember that trace flags are useful for debugging and tuning performance. You should turn them off once you have diagnosed and fixed the problems. Some of useful lock-related trace flags follow:

- Trace flag 1200—T1200 prints all of the lock request/release information when it occurs, whether a deadlock is involved or not. This is expensive in terms of performance, but it can be useful for analysis. The following code displays the output of this trace flag:

```
DBCC TRACEON (3604) - display dbcc messages on the client
DBCC TRACEON (1200)
go
declare @seqno int
begin transaction
UPDATE sequence set @seqno = isnull(seq#,0) + 1
from sequence
select @seqno
go
Process 7 acquiring IX lock on TAB: 5:933578364 [] result: OK
Process 7 acquiring IX lock on TAB: 5:933578364 [] result: OK
Process 7 acquiring IU lock on PAG: 5:1:160 result: OK
Process 7 acquiring U lock on RID: 5:1:160:0 result: OK
Process 7 releasing lock on PAG: 5:1:160
Process 7 releasing lock on RID: 5:1:160:0
Process 7 releasing lock reference on TAB: 5:933578364 []
```

- Trace flag 1204—T1204 prints useful information once a deadlock is detected. The output consists of the SPIDs and T-SQL causing the deadlock to occur. It also displays the lock resources requested by the victim. The following is a sample output of this trace flag:

```
DBCC TRACEON(3605) - send the output to errorlog
DBCC TRACEON(1204)
go
*** Deadlock Detected ***
 ==> Process 7 chosen as deadlock victim
 == Deadlock Detected at: 98/07/19 14:08:14.22
 == Session participant information:
 SPID: 7 ECID: 0 Statement Type: UPDATE
 Input Buf: U P D A T E   s e q u e n c e    s e t
➥ s e q #  =  2
 SPID: 8 ECID: 0 Statement Type: UPDATE
 Input Buf: U P D A T E   s e q u e n c e    s e t
➥ s e q #  =  2
 == Deadlock Lock participant information:
 == Lock: TAB: 5:933578364 []
 Database: pubs
 Table: sequence
  - Held by: SPID 7 ECID 0 Mode "S"
  - Requested by: SPID 8 ECID 0 Mode "IX"
 == Lock: TAB: 5:933578364 []
 Database: pubs
 Table: sequence
  - Held by: SPID 8 ECID 0 Mode "S"
  - Requested by: SPID 7 ECID 0 Mode "IX"
```

- Trace flag 1205—T1205 provides an insight into how the SQL Server internal process for monitoring deadlock works. The output shows the scan of resource lock requests for the processes causing deadlock to occur:

```
DBCC TRACEON(3605) - send the output to errorlog
DBCC TRACEON(1204)
go
**** Starting deadlock search: SPID 7 ****
- -- Searching deadlock
TAB: 5:933578364 []              CleanCnt:2 Mode: S Flags: 0x0
 Grant List::
   Mode: S       Flg:0x0 Ref:2 Life:02000000 SPID:8 ECID:0
   Mode: S       Flg:0x0 Ref:2 Life:02000000 SPID:7 ECID:0
 Convert List:
   Mode: IX      Flg:0x2 Ref:1 Life:02000000 SPID:7 ECID:0
   Mode: IX      Flg:0x2 Ref:1 Life:02000000 SPID:8 ECID:0
- -- Searching deadlock
TAB: 5:933578364 []              CleanCnt:3 Mode: S Flags: 0x0
```

```
Grant List::
   Mode: S          Flg:0x0 Ref:2 Life:02000000 SPID:8 ECID:0
   Mode: S          Flg:0x0 Ref:2 Life:02000000 SPID:7 ECID:0
Convert List:
   Mode: IX         Flg:0x2 Ref:1 Life:02000000 SPID:7 ECID:0
   Mode: IX         Flg:0x2 Ref:1 Life:02000000 SPID:8 ECID:0

**** Starting deadlock search: SPID 8 ****
- -- Searching deadlock
TAB: 5:933578364 []                 CleanCnt:2 Mode: S Flags: 0x0
 Grant List::
   Mode: S          Flg:0x0 Ref:2 Life:02000000 SPID:8 ECID:0
   Mode: S          Flg:0x0 Ref:2 Life:02000000 SPID:7 ECID:0
Convert List:
   Mode: IX         Flg:0x2 Ref:1 Life:02000000 SPID:7 ECID:0
   Mode: IX         Flg:0x2 Ref:1 Life:02000000 SPID:8 ECID:0
```

Summary

Locking is critical for providing transaction isolation. With SQL Server 7.0, Microsoft has shifted its locking strategy significantly. The lock manager has been improved in various ways, especially through the full implementation of row-level locking. SQL Server now truly supports all transaction isolation levels, including serialization. A number of enhancements give the developer better control over lock granularity.

30

LOCKING AND PERFORMANCE

BackOffice
Integration

PART
VII

IN THIS PART

SQL Mail

by John Del Buono and Sharon Bjeletich

IN THIS CHAPTER

One of the unique features of the SQL Server 7.0 is its ability to integrate with the existing server architecture of an established network. It supplies the functionality to send and receive messages and send query results to mail recipients via the mail provider. SQL Mail and the SQL Server Agent are the tools that orchestrate this integration.

To send this mail, you must first start SQL Mail from the SQL Server Enterprise Manager, which in turn establishes a connection with either Microsoft Exchange, Windows NT Mail, or a Post Office Protocol 3 (POP3) server. Once that is completed, you can start the SQL Server Agent, which lets you set up jobs, operators, and alerts. Alerts can be triggered on specific events and then notify the intended recipient by sending an email message or paging through the SQL Mail system.

Setting Up Your Mail Provider

Before you can use SQL Mail, a mail provider must be in place on the same server as SQL Server 7.0. There are three providers:

- Microsoft Exchange Server
- Microsoft Windows NT Mail
- Post Office Protocol 3 Server

You must also create and test a client profile for these providers prior to establishing connections using SQL Mail. Refer to your mail administrator to request a client profile for SQL Mail.

Microsoft Exchange Server

The Exchange server provides connectivity for the mail client on a centralized network hub. This connectivity is commonly used on larger Windows NT networks.

Microsoft Windows NT Mail

Where NT has been installed and a centralized mail network hub has not been implemented, using Windows NT Mail is the best way to establish connectivity for the mail client. To implement Windows NT Mail, you must create a workgroup postoffice and share folders for each SQL Mail recipient created in that workgroup.

Post Office Protocol 3 Server

A POP3 server allows you to connect to an external source with a mail server if your network doesn't provide one or you are restricted from using Windows NT Mail. To use POP3, you must configure the client mail profile to use Simple Mail Transfer Protocol (SMTP) and provide POP3 addresses.

Using SQL Mail

SQL Mail is the vehicle by which special stored procedures can interact with MAPI systems. For these procedures to run correctly, you must start the SQL Mail service and configure a mail profile. To start SQL Mail, using the SQL Server Enterprise Manager (see Figure 31.1), right-click SQL Mail under the Support Services folder of your SQL Server. Choose Start from the menu. You can automatically start SQL Mail by clicking the box Autostart SQL Mail when SQL Server starts under SQL Mail Properties.

FIGURE 31.1

Starting SQL Mail in SQL Server Enterprise Manager.

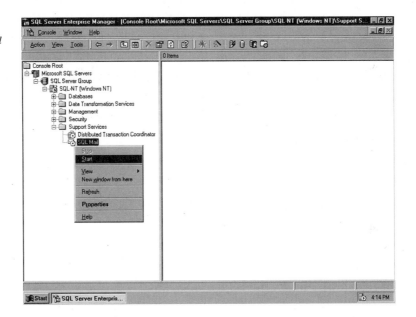

The mail profiles must be from the user domain account that was activated when you logged on to Windows NT. The profile that SQL Mail uses must be created in the same domain account where SQL Server was started.

To configure a mail profile, right-click your SQL Server in the SQL Server Enterprise Manager and select Properties.

You can select the mail profile from the SQL Mail section of the Server Settings tab (see Figure 31.2). As stated earlier, you must set up the mail profiles on the mail provider side prior to configuring the profile for SQL Mail. Once you're finished with the configuration, email requests can be processed automatically using the stored procedures, or by jobs and scheduled tasks through the SQL Server Agent, which is discussed later in the chapter.

FIGURE 31.2

*Setting the SQL
Mail profile under
the Server
Settings tab.*

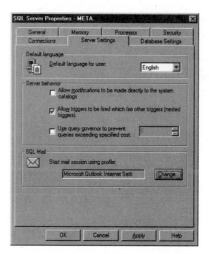

Using SQL Server Agent Mail

Another way to allow email messaging and alerts is to use SQL Server Agent. SQL Server Agent lets you set up scheduled tasks or jobs to notify users or operators via email when certain events are triggered or send messages that describe a job's status. It is used in conjunction with SQL Mail. You must configure both SQL Server Agent and SQL Mail for the same domain and profiles; otherwise, a request initialized from the Agent to a SQL Mail recipient fails.

You can configure SQL Server Agent to send email notifications in the following ways:

- When an alert is triggered
- As a scheduled task

You can configure alerts to send email messages about specific events when you select Alerts under the SQL Server Agent folder. (The SQL Server Agent is located in the Management folder of the SQL Server.) When setting up a new alert, you have the opportunity to select a type of response for this alert under the Response tab (see Figure 31.3). When this alert is triggered, a message is sent to the designated operator, with any additional instructions.

FIGURE 31.3

The Response tab for the newly configured alert.

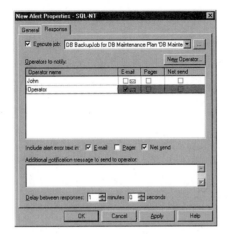

Jobs and scheduled tasks, also located under the SQL Server Agent, can include email notifications as well. Figure 31.4 shows an example; right-click a predefined Job, select Properties, and then select the Notifications tab. Here, if the job DB Backup Job for DB Maintenance Plan 'DB Maintenance Plan2' fails, the operator Sam will be notified via email. Sam is a previously defined operator with a valid email address.

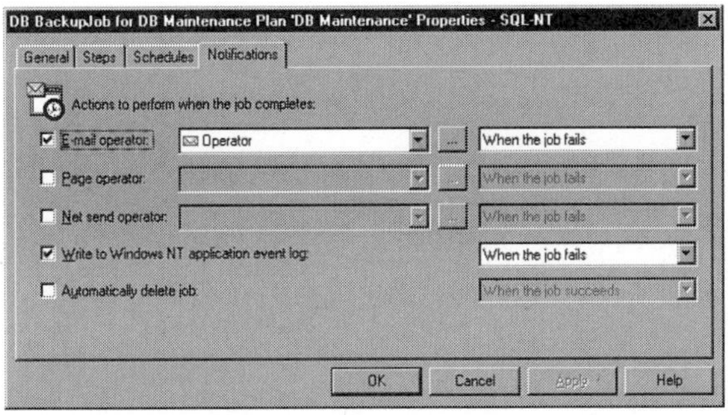

FIGURE 31.4

Notifications tab under a predefined job property.

SQL Mail Stored Procedures and Extended Stored Procedures

SQL Server 7.0 provides built-in stored procedures and extended stored procedures that perform many system services, including the SQL Mail service. These stored procedures are used by SQL Server to process email messages received in a predefined SQL Mail account mailbox or to send email messages generated by the mail stored procedure to recipients on the network.

The following sections describe the stored procedures (with their corresponding syntax) that can be run individually or executed within the instructions of another stored procedure on a specific event or job. Extended stored procedures are external commands created in a programming language that extend the capabilities of the SQL Server. These procedures are run through the SQL Server Query Analyzer as normal stored procedures and are usually designated with the xp_ prefix. An example of the xp_startmail extended stored procedure is shown in Figure 31.5.

FIGURE 31.5

The xp_startmail *extended stored procedure within SQL Server Query Analyzer.*

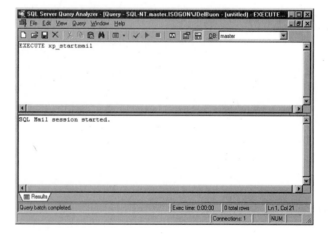

xp_startmail

You use the xp_startmail procedure to start a mail client session. For any of the mail stored procedures to work, this procedure must be initiated. The syntax for xp_startmail follows:

```
xp_startmail [@user = 'username'], [@password = 'password']
```

'*username*' is optional; when it's specified, the SQL Server attempts to log on to a MAPI provider such as NT mail using this name.

'*password*' is optional; when specified, it's used as the password for the '*username*'.

'*username*' and '*password*' are both sysnames with no defaults. If these arguments are not provided, SQL Server will substitute the names specified in the SQL Server Properties dialog box.

> **NOTE**
>
> sysname is a user-defined datatype. It is used for table columns, variables, and stored procedure parameters that store object names.

xp_sendmail

Once a mail session has been started, you can invoke the xp_sendmail procedure. It lets the system send messages and query resultsets to specified mail recipients. On SQL Server, only one user at a time can send a message. The other users sending mail messages are queued until the first user's message is sent. In the following syntax, the @*variablename*s are needed when not all options are used; otherwise, you can just enter the value for each of the options in the order listed, separated by commas. The syntax for xp_sendmail is as follows:

```
xp_sendmail @recipients = 'recipients [;...n]'
,[@message = 'message']
,[@query = 'query']
,[@attachments = attachments]
,[@copy_recipients = 'copy_recipients [;...n]]'
,[@blind_copy_recipients = 'blind_copy_recipients [;...n]]'
,[@subject = 'subject']
,[@type = type]
,[@attach_results = 'attach_value']
,[@no_output = 'output_value']
,[@no_header = 'header_value']
,[@width = width]
,[@separator = separator]
,[@echo_error = 'echo_value']
,[@set_user = user]
,[@dbuse = database]
```

The following paragraphs describe each element of the syntax:

`@recipients = 'recipients [;...n]'`

This is the list of recipients separated by semicolons.

`[@message = 'message']`

You can specify a message of up to 8,000 bytes in size.

`[@query = 'query']`

You can provide any T-SQL query, up to 8,000 bytes. The resultset of the query will be sent in the mail. Note that bound connections are used here so there is no blocking with the client that issued the `xp_sendmail` command.

`[@attachments = attachments]`

This is the filename for an attachment.

`[@copy_recipients = 'copy_recipients [;...n]]'`

This is the list of "copy to" recipients, separated by semicolons. This is what would appear in the Cc: box of a mail message dialog box.

`[@blind_copy_recipients = 'blind_copy_recipients [;...n]]'`

This is a list of recipients, separated by semicolons, that are to receive a blind copy. This list would appear in the Bcc: section of a mail message dialog box.

`[@subject = 'subject']`

Here, you provide a subject line for the message.

`[@type = type]`

This is the input message type, and the default is null. This is a fairly esoteric setting that for most uses is left null. For more information, investigate SQL Mail in the Windows NT Resource Kit.

`[@attach_results = 'attach_value']`

The default setting for this is False, which will cause a query resultset to be appended to the message. A True value will cause the query result to be sent as an attachment.

`[@no_output = 'output_value']`

If set to True, this option will send the mail but not output anything to the client session. The default is False.

`[@no_header = 'header_value']`

If set to `True`, this option does not send the column header information with the query resultset; it sends only the rows. The default is `False`.

`[@width = width]`

This parameter is the same as the `/w` parameter in the ISQL utility. It indicates the output width for a query resultset. The default is 80 characters. Use a larger width to send a wide resultset without line breaks inside the output lines.

`[@separator = separator]`

Here, you specify a configurable column separator for the resultset. Tabs are the default separator, but using a comma here with the attach_results option will product a comma-delimited file.

`[@echo_error = 'echo_value']`

Setting this option to `True` will cause server messages and errors to be appended to the message rather than written to the error log. Setting this option to `True` causes the `xp_sendmail` stored procedure to always return a success status (`0`).

`[@set_user = user]`

This is the security context for the query. This allows a query to be run under a different security context from the session initiating the `xp_sendmail` command. The default is `guest`.

`[@dbuse = database]`

This is the database name from which the query should be run.

xp_readmail

The `xp_readmail` procedure reads a mail message from the SQL Server inbox. The syntax follows:

```
xp_readmail [@msg_id = 'message_number']
,[ @type = 'type' [OUTPUT]]
,[@peek = 'peek']
,[@suppress_attach = 'suppress_attach']
,[@originator = 'sender' OUTPUT]
,[@subject = 'subject' OUTPUT]
,[@message = 'message' OUTPUT]
,[@recipients = 'recipients [;...n]' OUTPUT]
,[@cc_list = 'copy_recipients [;...n]' OUTPUT]
,[@bcc_list = 'blind_copy_recipients [;...n]' OUTPUT]
,[@date_received = 'date' OUTPUT]
,[@unread = 'unread_value' OUTPUT]
,[@attachments = 'attachments [;...n]' OUTPUT]
```

```
,[@skip_bytes = bytes_to_skip OUTPUT]
,[@msg_length = length_in_bytes OUTPUT]
,[@originator_address = 'sender_address' OUTPUT]
```

The following paragraphs describe each element of the syntax:

```
[@msg_id = 'message_number']
```

This is a varchar(255) string indicating the message number to be read.

```
[ @type = 'type' [OUTPUT]]
```

This is a message type; the default is null. This is a fairly esoteric setting that for most uses is left null. For more information, investigate SQL Mail in the Windows NT Resource Kit.

When the OUTPUT clause is used, an output parameter is specified for one or more of the xp_readmail parameters, and the result is returned to this parameter.

```
[@peek = 'peek']
```

This parameter causes the message status to change to read when set to False, the default. A True value causes the message status to remain unread.

```
[@suppress_attach = 'suppress_attach']
```

If this parameter is set to True, messages with attachments that create temporary files are suppressed.

```
[@originator = 'sender' OUTPUT]
```

This is the mail address of the message sender.

```
[@subject = 'subject' OUTPUT]
```

This is the message subject line.

```
[@message = 'message' OUTPUT]
```

This is the actual text of the message, a varchar(8000) parameter.

```
[@recipients = 'recipients [;...n]' OUTPUT]
```

This is a list of recipients separated by semicolons.

```
[@cc_list = 'copy_recipients [;...n]' OUTPUT]
```

This is a list of copied recipients separated by semicolons.

```
[@bcc_list = 'blind_copy_recipients [;...n]' OUTPUT]
```

This is a list of blind-copied recipients separated by semicolons.

`[@date_received = 'date' OUTPUT]`

This is the date of the mail message.

`[@unread = 'unread_value' OUTPUT]`

If this parameter is set to `True`, the message was previously unread.

`[@attachments = 'attachments [;...n]' OUTPUT]`

This is a semicolon-separated list of the temporary paths of the attachments.

`[@skip_bytes = bytes_to_skip OUTPUT]`

This parameter indicates the number of bytes to skip before reading the next 255 bytes of a message.

`[@msg_length = length_in_bytes OUTPUT]`

This is the total length in bytes of the message. Using this parameter with the `bytes_to_skip` output parameter in a stored procedure allows a message to be read in chunks of 255 bytes.

`[@originator_address = 'sender_address' OUTPUT]`

This is the resolved mail address of the sender.

xp_findnextmsg

The `xp_findnextmsg` procedure is used with `sp_processmail` to process mail in the Microsoft SQL Server inbox by accepting a message ID for input. It returns the message ID for output. The syntax follows:

```
xp_findnextmsg [@msg_id = 'message_number' [OUTPUT]]
,[@type = type]
,[@unread_only = 'unread_value']
```

The following paragraphs describe the elements of the syntax:

`[@msg_id = 'message_number' [OUTPUT]]`

This is the number of the message, stored as a string. When the OUTPUT clause is used, the message number is placed in this parameter. Otherwise, it is returned as a resultset.

`[@type = type]`

This is the MAPI mail type. The default is null.

`[@unread_only = 'unread_value']`

When this is set to `True`, only unread messages are processed by the stored procedure. The default is `False`.

xp_deletemail

The `xp_deletemail` procedure deletes the specified message from the SQL Server inbox. The syntax is

```
xp_deletemail {'message_number'}
```

`'message_number'` is the number, stored as varchar(255), of the message that is to be deleted.

sp_processmail

The `sp_processmail` procedure invokes the extended stored procedures `xp_findnextmsg`, `xp_readmail`, and `xp_deletemail` to process incoming mail messages. It uses `xp_sendmail` to return the resultset to the message sender. The syntax is

```
sp_processmail [@subject = 'subject']
,[@filetype = 'filetype']
,[@separator = 'separator']
,[@set_user = 'user']
,[@dbuse = 'dbname']
```

The following paragraphs describe the different elements of the syntax:

```
[@subject =] 'subject'
```

If you enter a subject line in this parameter, only messages with that subject line are processed. The default is null to process all messages.

```
[@filetype = 'filetype']
```

This is the varchar(3) file extension that will be used when sending the resultset. The default is txt.

```
[@separator = 'separator']
```

This is the column separator to be used between each column in the resultset. This is a varchar(3) parameter with a default of a tab character.

```
[@set_user = 'user']
```

This is the security context under which the query will be run.

```
[@dbuse = 'dbname']
```

This is the name of the database where the query should be run.

xp_stopmail

You use the `xp_stopmail` procedure to stop the mail client session. The syntax is simple:

```
xp_stopmail
```

Summary

SQL Mail and the SQL Server Agent are tools that let SQL users integrate SQL Server within the existing server architecture. It does so by informing other SQL users of the status of certain jobs and tasks through the existing MAPI system of a network. Administrators can devote more time to their users' needs. These tools help the administrator worry less about not being informed of scheduled jobs failing or tasks not completing. These tools, along with the other tools available in SQL Server 7.0, help administrators maintain an efficient and dependable database system.

Internet Information Server and Index Server

by Greg Mable

In This Chapter

This chapter takes a look at how SQL Server and two Microsoft products, the Internet Information Server (IIS) and the Index Server, work together to provide a set of services for distributing data over the Internet. You will discover how SQL Server integrates with Active Server pages and how SQL Server's text-searching capability provides full content searching. This means that you can develop a Web site that can search data stored in both SQL Server text fields and various document files, such as Microsoft Word documents. By implementing SQL Server as the database engine for your Web sites along with the Internet Information Server and Index Server, you can establish a set of integrated services for distributing data over the Internet.

IIS and Active Server Pages

Active Server Pages is Microsoft's technology for providing dynamic, data-driven Web applications. ASP lets you develop a Web page that combines HTML text with scripting code. The Internet Information Server supports several scripting languages, and SQL Server fully supports Web pages using Active Server Pages.

Active Server Pages use ActiveX Data Objects as the interface to SQL Server. ADO provides Web applications with access to data from any OLE database source, not only SQL Server. You can develop Web pages that use an ADO connection and write data-access routines using one of the scripting languages supported by IIS. You can then encapsulate these ADO scripts into a set of business objects that can serve as a middle tier between the SQL Server database engine and a Web browser.

SQL Server ships with an example of a Web application that uses ADO to communicate with a SQL Server 7.0 database. The Northwind Inventory Management sample is an online inventory management application that allows users to view the inventory and update product information.

To install the sample Web application, you need a Windows NT Server 4.0 with the Windows NT Option Pack 4.0 installed. Next, create a local directory on the server and copy all the files located on the SQL Server installation CD-ROM from the directory that contains the sample application, which is Mssql7\DevTools\Samples\Ado\Web. Then create a new Web in Internet Information Server 4.0 using the New Web Wizard. This wizard will walk you through the necessary steps to configure a Web site.

Next, using any text editor (such as Notepad), you need to edit the GLOBAL.ASA file and change the server name in the variable ProvStr to match the name of your server. You might also need to modify the include file path to a virtual directory on the Information Server containing the adovbs.inc file.

Then, from IIS 4.0, right-click the folder for the newly created Web site and select Browse. This launches your Web browser and starts the Northwind Inventory Management System application, as shown in Figure 32.1.

FIGURE 32.1

Northwind Inventory Management System sample Web application.

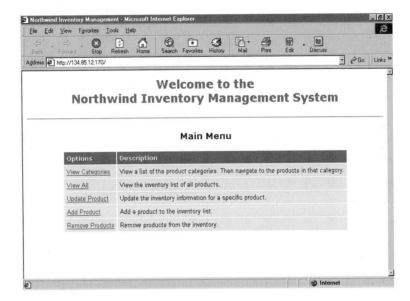

The Northwind Inventory Management System includes a page that lets the user see all the products in the inventory, as shown in Figure 32.2.

FIGURE 32.2

Northwind Products search results page.

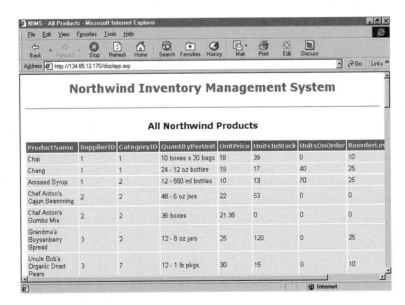

The code to generate that page is based on ADO technology implemented in VBScript. The code sample in Listing 32.1 is an excerpt from the file displayp.asp, which generates the Web page.

LISTING 32.1 SQL QUERY FROM DISPLAYP.ASP TO DISPLAY ALL PRODUCTS

```
'Create recordsets
Set ProductInfo = Server.CreateObject("ADODB.Recordset")
Set CategoryInfo = Server.CreateObject("ADODB.Recordset")

'Create query strings

'Returns products from the Products table for the CategoryID
querystr = "SELECT ProductName, SupplierID, CategoryID,
③QuantityPerUnit, UnitPrice, UnitsInStock," _
③& "UnitsOnOrder, ReorderLevel, Discontinued, ProductID
③FROM Products WHERE CategoryID = " & CategoryID
③& " ORDER BY ProductID"

'Returns the category name associated with CategoryID
querystr2 = "SELECT CategoryName FROM Categories
③WHERE  CategoryID = " & CategoryID

'Returns all products from the Products table
defaultquery = "SELECT ProductName, SupplierID, CategoryID,
③QuantityPerUnit, UnitPrice, UnitsInStock," _
③& "UnitsOnOrder, ReorderLevel, Discontinued, ProductID
③FROM Products"

'Open the Recordsets
IF CategoryID <> "" THEN 'request for products from only one
    ProductInfo.Open querystr, cn
    CategoryInfo.Open querystr2, cn
ELSE 'Retrieve all products in the query
    ProductInfo.Open defaultquery, cn
END IF
%>
```

As you can see, using ADO, you can easily query SQL Server. In this code sample, two recordsets are created. One recordset returns data from the products table, and the other returns data from the categories table. Based on the input from the user, the script executes the appropriate query by opening the recordsets. Once the recordsets have been opened, the data is available to the application. For more information about creating recordsets based on SQL queries, see Appendix D, "Programming Tools and Interfaces." You might also want to check out *Microsoft SQL Server 7 Programming Unleashed* from Sams Publishing for more ADO-related material.

In Listing 32.2, the database records returned from SQL Server are formatted and displayed in an HTML table. The recordsets contain a fields property that stores the value of each field returned in the recordset. The code simply loops through each of the fields in the recordset and displays them in a column on the table.

LISTING 32.2 HTML CODE FROM DISPLAYP.ASP TO DISPLAY ALL PRODUCTS

```
<TABLE CELLPADDING=3 BORDER=0 COLSPAN=8>
    <TR>
<%
   'Output a blank header if this is an Update or Remove display
IF op <> "" THEN
       Response.Write "<TD CLASS=header></TD>"
       IF op = "Remove" THEN 'Create checkboxes to be submitted in %>
           <FORM NAME="RemoveForm" ACTION="remove.asp" METHOD=POST>
<%         END IF
   END IF

   'Output the table headers
   For i = 0 To 8
       Response.Write "<TD CLASS=header>" &
       ③ProductInfo.Fields(i).Name & "</TD>"
   NEXT
%>
    </TR>

<% 'Loop through the recordset to output the table values
    Do While Not ProductInfo.EOF
        Response.Write "<TR>"

        'add a "Remove" checkbox or "Edit" button to the row
        IF op <> "" THEN
            Response.Write "<TD>"
            IF op = "Update" THEN %>
                    <FORM ACTION="update.asp?ProductID=<%=
                    ③ProductInfo.Fields(9)%>" METHOD=POST>
                        <INPUT TYPE=submit NAME=Edit VALUE=<%=op%>>
                    </FORM>
<%          ELSE %>
                    <INPUT TYPE=CHECKBOX NAME=ProductID VALUE=
                    ③<%=ProductInfo.Fields(9)%>>
<%          END IF
            Response.Write "</TD>"
        END IF

        For i = 0 to 8 'Output the field values for the product
            Response.Write "<td>"
            Response.Write ProductInfo.Fields(i).Value
```

continues

LISTING 32.2   CONTINUED

```
        Response.Write "</TD>"
    NEXT

    Response.Write "</TR>"
    ProductInfo.MoveNext
LOOP

'Close the Recordset
ProductInfo.Close %>
```

</TABLE>

You can use the Northwind Inventory Management System to learn how to integrate SQL Server with the Internet Information Server. This sample Web application demonstrates just how easy it is. You will see firsthand how Active Server Pages and ActiveX Data Objects provide a set of interfaces that allow you to build dynamic, data-driven Web applications.

Full-Text Searching and Databases

SQL Server and other relational database management systems have always had the capability to search data stored as text using basic search criteria, but have never really had the capability to search data using more sophisticated forms of search criteria. For example, previous versions of SQL Server cannot handle searches that involve looking up words or phrases in close proximity to one another. To provide this capability, you had to use a third-party product. This usually involved exporting the data from SQL Server and then storing the data in operating system files, which caused the index processing to occur.

Using this two-step process meant that there was no integrated method for a user to combine a full-text query with a SQL query. SQL Server now provides this integration and allows users to create full-text queries against test data in SQL Server, including words and phrases or multiple forms of a word or phrase. The results can always be weighed or given a value as to how close the results are toward meeting the search criteria.

You can use the Full-Text Indexing Wizard to develop full-text indexing on SQL Server text-based columns. The columns of a table can be of any text-based datatype (char, varchar, text, ntext, nchar, or nvarchar). You can group these indexes into catalogs. The Full-Text Indexing Wizard can also create a schedule that automatically determines when the information stored in the full-text catalog is updated.

As shown in Figure 32.3, the Full-Text Indexing Wizard first prompts you for the table to be indexed if you currently have a database highlighted in Enterprise Manager. Otherwise, the wizard prompts you first for the database name. For this example, select the Titles table.

FIGURE 32.3

The Full-Text Indexing Wizard: table selection.

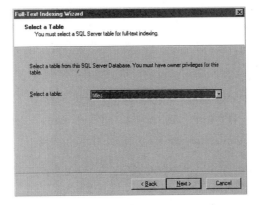

You then specify the unique index on the table so that the wizard can use this index in conjunction with building the text index for the table (see Figure 32.4). For this example, accept the index selected by the wizard (UPKCL_titleidind).

FIGURE 32.4

Unique index selection.

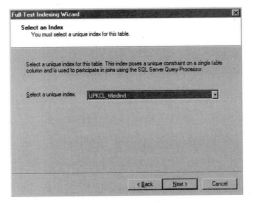

You then specify which columns of the table you want to index, as shown in Figure 32.5. Be aware that the wizard will display all columns of a table instead of only those columns that are capable of full-text indexing. For this example, select the notes and title fields.

32

INTERNET INFORMATION SERVER

FIGURE 32.5

Column selection.

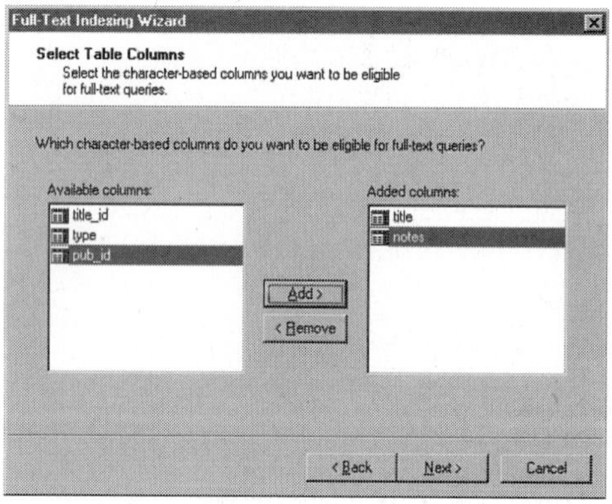

Specify a catalog in which to store the index, as shown in Figure 32.6. This allows you to group several full-text indexes on various tables. You can then manage these indexes as a group and apply updates to them all at once instead of individually. For this example, create a new catalog called `MyCatalog`.

FIGURE 32.6

Cataloging.

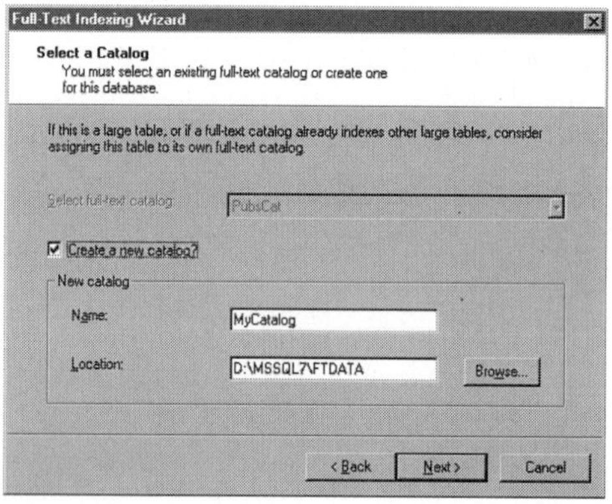

As shown in Figure 32.7, you can specify a schedule to update the indexes automatically. For this example, create a new schedule, give it a name, `MyCatalogSchedule`, set it for a full text-indexing update, and enable it to be executed on a recurring basis every Sunday morning at midnight.

FIGURE 32.7

Update schedule.

Now that you have set up full-text indexing on a table, you are ready to populate the index for the first time. From the Enterprise Manager, you will find an entry in the Full-Text Catalogs object under the Pubs database for the catalog that you just created. If you highlight the entry for `MyCatalog` and bring up its menu by using the right mouse button, one of the options will be to start the population, Full or Incremental. Select the Full option, and the catalog will be built. Because this is such a small catalog, it will only take a few seconds for it to be built.

Once a catalog has been populated, you can issue full-text searches on the columns that have been indexed. You can use the following query in Listing 32.3 as an example and run the query from Enterprise Manager. This query returns all titles that contain the word *cooking* near all forms of the word *computer*.

LISTING 32.3 SQL FULL-TEXT QUERY EXAMPLE

```
Select title, type, notes
From titles
Where CONTAINS(title,'"cooking" NEAR "computer*"')
```

SQL Server uses noise-word lists for the various languages it supports. These lists are stored in the directory \Mssql7\Ftdata\Sqlserver\Config. This directory is created and the noise-word files are installed when you set up SQL Server with the full-text search support. You can edit the noise-word list file for your language to include other noise words. For example, a database administrator at a chemical company might want to add the term *molecule* to the noise-word list.

SQL Server provides Transact-SQL components for full-text querying. These include the predicates CONTAINS and FREETEXT, which can be used in any search condition. You can use the functions CONTAINSTABLE and FREETEXTTABLE in the FROM clause of a SELECT statement. Refer to the SQL Server online help for more information on using these components.

SQL Server also provides some Transact-SQL full-text system stored procedures, such as `sp_fulltext_catalog`, `sp_fulltext_table`, and `sp_fulltext_column`, which are used to define and maintain the indexes.

The Microsoft Search Service is the Windows NT service that provides the capability for full-text indexing. You can configure its properties using the SQL Server Enterprise Manager. As shown in Figure 32.8, you can configure how much system resources are dedicated to full-text indexing.

FIGURE 32.8

The Full-Text Search Service: system resources.

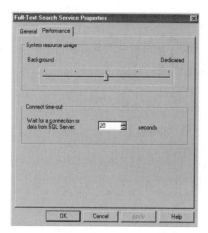

This scale represents the amount of system resources used for full-text indexing. If you set it at Dedicated, the majority of system resources are used. If you set it at Background, other applications that are running have higher priority for the system resources. The default value is 3.

Index Server and Full-Text Searching of Data Files

You can use Microsoft SQL Server 7.0 to support textual queries against data in the file system, as well as SQL Server data. You can use SQL Server's Distributed Query in conjunction with the full-text Transact-SQL components to write such queries that work against the text in the database and in the files, without the need to move the data. This is known as file content searching. For more information about Distributed Queries, see Chapter 26, "Advanced Query Processing."

When performing file content searches, you can specify search criteria that operate on the contents of the file or on any of the file's properties, such as its author. The OLE DB Provider for the Indexing Service supports the capability to search Microsoft Word, Excel, PowerPoint, and HTML files. By using Internet Information Server 4.0 and Index Server 2.0, you can write a query that searches data residing in the database and in the file system.

To test this feature for yourself, you first need to install Internet Information Server 4.0 and Index Server 2.0. Once installed, Index Server automatically scans the directories on Internet Information Server for file content indexing. Create a Microsoft Word file that contains the phrase "cooking with computers is a gas," save the file in one of the directories scanned by Index Server (such as \InetPub\WWWRoot), and then rescan the directory by right-clicking on the directory and selecting Rescan.

Next, you can test to see if Index Server has indexed the Word document you just created. Index Server is installed with a sample query form that you can run from Internet Explorer. (`http://localhost/iissamples/issamples/default.htm` is the URL if you are running the browser on the same machine as Internet Information Server.) As shown in Figure 32.9, you can specify a search criterion to search for the Word document you created.

FIGURE 32.9

The Index Server 2.0 sample query form.

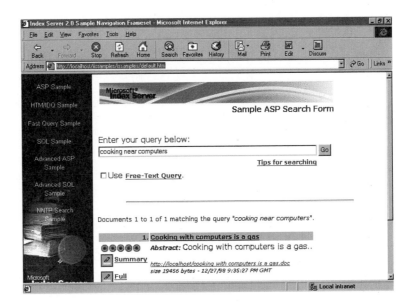

The next step is to link SQL Server with Index Server. You do this by adding Index Server as a linked server using the Enterprise Manager or by running the stored procedure `sp_addlinkedserver`. For more information about adding linked servers, see Chapter 26.

Once you have added Index Server as a linked server, you can execute SQL queries against the data it has indexed. For this example, you can execute the query shown in Listing 32.4 from Enterprise Manager. This query returns the title from the titles table and the document title from the Word document that contains the words *cooking* and *computers*.

LISTING 32.4   SQL FULL-TEXT QUERY OF FILE CONTENT AND DATABASE DATA EXAMPLE

```
Select t.title,q.doctitle
From
titles as t,
openquery(local,'select doctitle from scope() where contains
③(doctitle,''computers and cooking'')')
as q
where contains(t.title,'"computers" and "cooking"')
```

Summary

Microsoft SQL Server 7.0 offers a full set of services for distributing data on the Internet. When using SQL Server with the Internet Information Server, Web developers can create dynamic, data-driven pages using ADO recordsets. When using SQL Server with the Index Server, Web developers can create queries that search for data in both SQL Server and in various document files simultaneously. Combining all these technologies allows you to create a three-tiered, Web-based application.

Microsoft
Transaction Server

by Mark Nippert

IN THIS CHAPTER

The objective of this chapter is to help you understand and maintain Microsoft Transaction Server (MTS), version 2.0. First, I cover the advantages that MTS can offer, and then, I run through several common tasks that you might need to perform.

This chapter has an administrative focus but includes several Visual Basic code listings. These listings are necessary to more fully explain the functionality of MTS. Furthermore, many MTS components are implemented in Visual Basic, so familiarity with the code certainly won't hurt an administrator.

This chapter is example-oriented. Even if you elect not to follow along with the examples, you should be able to apply the techniques to your own tasks.

MTS Overview

Microsoft Transaction Server plays a key role in Microsoft's vision for distributed systems. In a nutshell, the objective of MTS is to take care of many of the functions required to build robust distributed applications that can gracefully handle a large number of requests. Custom software components that are installed under MTS control can take advantage of these MTS features. Figure 33.1 shows a model of system architecture design using MTS.

FIGURE 33.1
System architecture design using MTS.

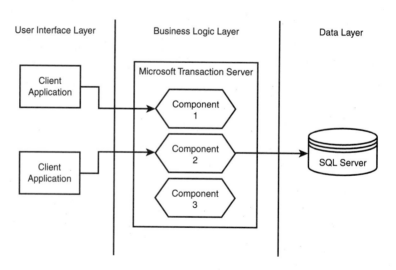

A close working partner of MTS is the Distributed Transaction Coordinator. For more information on MS DTC, refer to Chapter 22, "Transaction Management and Distributed Transactions."

Why Use Transaction Server?

MTS is a complex product, and the techniques for building a distributed system that includes MTS are different from standard coding techniques. As a result, it is important to understand the advantages MTS has to offer so you can decide whether it is worth the extra complexity and maintenance.

Connection Pooling

The connection pooling feature of MTS allows multiple clients or components to share a limited pool of database connections. This saves time and resources that would otherwise be used to open, close, and maintain connections. For more details and examples concerning connection pooling, see "Using Connection Pooling" later in this chapter.

Multiserver Transactions

MTS and DTC can coordinate transactions across multiple back-end databases (see Figure 33.2). This allows the developer to commit or roll back all changes with one statement.

FIGURE 33.2

MTS transactions can enlist multiple back-end databases.

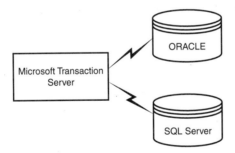

33

MICROSOFT
TRANSACTION
SERVER

Validation

Client applications and users can be validated at the time they call an MTS component. This feature can simplify database administration in an *n*-tier application by moving most security functionality from the database to the middle tier in MTS. For details, see "Configuring Security" later in this chapter.

Flexibility

A common problem in database applications is enforcing business rules at the database level. Developers previously had to enforce business rules in the limited syntax of T-SQL. Developers can now enforce these business rules by using MTS to host components that are written in more flexible languages such as Visual Basic, Visual C++, and Visual J++.

Scalability

Scalability can be thought of as the capacity of a system to handle competing concurrent requests for services. An objective of MTS is to keep a pool of components alive so they can be dynamically allocated to client applications. This technology (object pooling) allows a small pool of objects to serve a large number of client applications.

> **NOTE**
>
> Microsoft's MTS 2.0 help file points out that object pooling is not available in MTS 2.0. However, you can write components to take advantage of object pooling when it is released. For details, look up the IObjectControl interface in the MTS help documentation.

Client Administration

MTS comes with an automatic client setup feature. Using the client setup program, an administrator can readily configure client machines to access components that are hosted on a remote MTS machine.

Setting Up Transaction Server

The setup of MTS 2.0 is straightforward. There are only a couple of items to bear in mind:

- MTS 2.0 comes bundled with the NT Option Pack. The NT Option Pack is available in the Enterprise Edition of Visual Studio 6.0, the Universal MSDN subscription, or from Microsoft's Web site at www.microsoft.com/windows/downloads/contents/wurecommended/s_wuservicepacks/nt4optpk/default.asp.

- MTS 2.0 can be installed on any of Microsoft's 32-bit platforms, just like SQL Server 7.0. Check Microsoft's documentation for restrictions on Windows 95/98 installations of MTS.

- It is safe to install SQL Server 7.0 after installing MTS. In previous versions of SQL Server, you had to reinstall MTS.

Learning the MTS Hierarchy

The objects within MTS are organized into a hierarchy. This hierarchy is managed from the Transaction Server Explorer. Shown in Figure 33.3, the explorer is a snap-in for the Microsoft Management Console.

FIGURE 33.3

Viewing the MTS hierarchy.

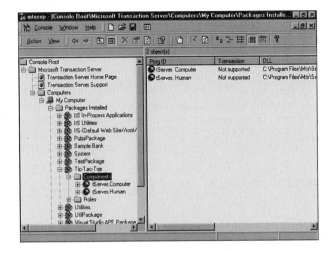

Some of the important items in the MTS hierarchy are described in Table 33.1.

TABLE 33.1 ITEMS IN THE MTS HIERARCHY

Item	Comments
Computers folder	Several computers with MTS can be managed from one console.
Packages Installed folder	Each computer can have several packages installed; all of these packages are contained in the Packages Installed folder.
Package	One package can contain many components. Components within a package share a process, so calls between them are very fast.
Components folder	Each package can contain several components; these components are contained in the Components folder.
Component	A component is the item that actually gets called by outside applications. You can set certain security and transaction support properties at the component level.
Role	A role is the primary security mechanism in MTS. Each package can have its own set of roles defined.

33

MICROSOFT
TRANSACTION
SERVER

Building an MTS Component

In this section, we examine the fundamentals of building components for MTS. There are several important coding techniques for MTS components, but describing these techniques is beyond the scope of this book. Instead, our focus is the pivotal elements of a data access component that allow it to participate in the transactional environment.

You can use several development tools to develop Component Object Model (COM) components for MTS. The examples in this chapter use Visual Basic.

The `ObjectContext`

The `ObjectContext` is the mechanism that MTS components use to access the MTS runtime environment. The `ObjectContext` informs a component about the context within which it is operating. For example, a component can discover the security permissions of the client application through the `ObjectContext`.

The most important function of the `ObjectContext` is to tie together the work of several components into a logical transaction (see Figure 33.4). You can configure components such that if one component aborts, all the other components in the logical transaction will abort as well.

FIGURE 33.4
The
`ObjectContext`
can include
multiple compo-
nents in one logi-
cal transaction.

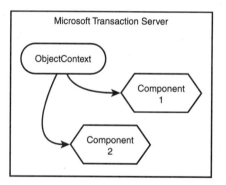

Listing 33.1 shows how a component can obtain a reference to the `ObjectContext` using the `GetObjectContext()` function. The `objContext.SetComplete` statement informs the `ObjectContext` that the method was successful; the `objContext.SetAbort` statement informs the `ObjectContext` that the method was aborted. In order to use the `ObjectContext` in code, you need to have a reference set to the Microsoft Transaction Server Type Library.

LISTING 33.1 USING GetObjectContext(), SetComplete, AND SetAbort IN A
METHOD CALL

```
Public Sub SomeMethod()
       Dim objContext as ObjectContext

     'Get a reference to the MTS Runtime Environment
     Set objContext = GetObjectContext()

      'Trap any errors
      On Error Goto ErrSomeMethod
 'Do Something Useful Here
 'Now Notify the ObjectContext that the method call completed
 'successfully
 objContext.SetComplete
       Exit Function

ErrSomeMethod:
   'Notify the ObjectContext that the method call aborted
   objContext.SetAbort
End Function
```

Methods for Database Activities

Many MTS components include some type of data access functionality. I use data access components here to demonstrate the interaction between MTS and SQL Server 7.0.

The GetAuthors() function in Listing 33.2 gets all the rows from the Authors table in the Pubs database in SQL Server. The function returns these rows in a variant array.

LISTING 33.2 USING AN MTS COMPONENT FOR DATA ACCESS

```
Public Function GetAuthors() as Variant

   Dim cn as rdoConnection
   Dim rsAuthors as rdoResultset
   Dim objContext as ObjectContext

   'Get a reference to the MTS Runtime Environment
   Set objContext = GetObjectContext()

   'Trap any errors
   On Error Goto ErrGetAuthors

   'Set up the Connection
   Set cn = rdoEnvironments(0).OpenConnection("Pubs",
   ③rdDriverNoPrompt, ,"uid=George;pwd=")
```

continues

33

MICROSOFT
TRANSACTION
SERVER

LISTING 33.2   CONTINUED

```
'Get the data and return it in a variant array

Set rsAuthors = cn.OpenResultset("select * from authors",
➂rdOpenForwardOnly, rdConcurReadOnly)
GetAuthors = rsAuthors.GetRows(25)

'Close the recordset
rsAuthors.Close

'Complete the transaction
objContext.SetComplete
Exit Function

ErrGetAuthors:
'Abort the transaction
objContext.SetAbort
End Function
```

The details of the syntax are not important here; simply note the sequence of events in the function:

1. Component obtains a reference to the ObjectContext.

2. Component performs its work.

3. Component either completes or aborts its transaction.

> **TIP**
>
> A component that is hosted by MTS 2.0 cannot have more than 1,024 methods.

Including Other MTS Components

Multiple MTS components can participate in a single logical transaction. If an MTS component needs to call another component, the first component can use the CreateInstance() function. Listing 33.3 illustrates this functionality.

LISTING 33.3   ENLISTING ADDITIONAL COMPONENTS IN A TRANSACTION

```
Public Sub DoSomething()
   Dim objContext as ObjectContext
   Dim objOtherComponent as SomeLib.SomeComponent

   'Get the ObjectContext
   Set objContext = GetObjectContext()
```

```
On Error Goto ErrDoSomething

'Do something useful here.

'Call the other component
Set objOtherComponent = objContext.CreateInstance
③("SomeLib.SomeComponent")
objOtherComponent.DoWork

    objContext.SetComplete
    Exit Sub
ErrDoSomething:
    objContext.SetAbort
End Sub
```

Installing an MTS Component

 In this section, I step through the process of installing a component under MTS control. For this example, I use the PubsDataObject.dll file that comes on the CD-ROM with this book. This file contains components that perform simple data operations on the Pubs database in SQL Server 7.0.

Creating a Package

Before you install a new component in MTS, you'll decide which package you want the component to be a member of. In this case, create a new package:

1. Open the Transaction Server Explorer.

2. Open the My Computer icon and select the Packages Installed folder.

3. Right-click the Packages Installed folder, and select New, Package.

4. Select Create an Empty Package on the Package Wizard screen.

> **NOTE**
>
> The other option on the Package Wizard screen is Install Pre-built Packages. This option can be used to import packages that were created somewhere else and distributed to you.

---

5. Type `PubsPackage` in the Create Empty Package Screen, and click Next.

6. Click Finish on the Set Package Identity screen. This screen is used to specify what user identity the Package will assume while performing its work. In this case, I use the default option of Interactive User.

Adding a Component

At this point, you have a new package with no components installed in it. Now, you need to add the components from the file to the package you just created:

1. Copy the PubsDataObject.dll file from the CD-ROM to a directory on your hard drive.

> **CAUTION**
>
> You must have the following three files registered on you computer before proceeding: rdocurs.dll, msrdo20.dll, and msvbvm50.dll. The PubsDataObject.dll component is dependent on these files. These files are on the CD-ROM accompanying this book.

2. Open PubsPackage icon in Transaction Server Explorer. It should have a Components folder and a Roles folder.

3. Select the Components folder. Right-click the Components folder and select New, Component.

4. Select Install New Components on the Component Wizard screen.

> **NOTE**
>
> The other option on the Component Wizard screen is Import Component(s) That Is Already Registered. The advantage of this option is that you can select which components in a DLL file you want to import. However, there are several important limitations if you elect to import components this way. Microsoft's documentation recommends installing rather than importing components. See the MTS help file for details.

5. Click the Add Files button on the Install Components screen. Select the PubsDataObject.dll file in the dialog box. The Install Components screen should look like Figure 33.5. Note that the Components Found window shows that both the Authors and Titles components were found in the PubsDataObject.dll file.

FIGURE 33.5

Adding components to a package.

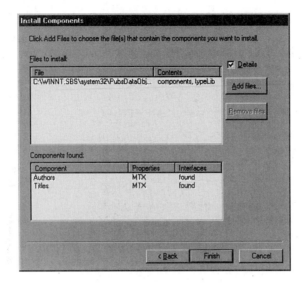

6. Click Finish on the Install Components screen. This action will register the components on your system and install the components under MTS control.

Setting Component Properties

After the components have been installed, you can set properties for these components. In this example, you are going to set the transaction properties for both the components you just installed. Follow these steps for both the PubsDataObject.Authors component and the PubsDataObject.Titles component:

1. Open the Components folder in PubsPackage.

2. Select the component. Right-click the component and select Properties.

3. Select the Transaction tab.

4. Click Requires a Transaction (see Figure 33.6).

5. Click OK.

FIGURE 33.6

*Setting transac-
tion support for a
component.*

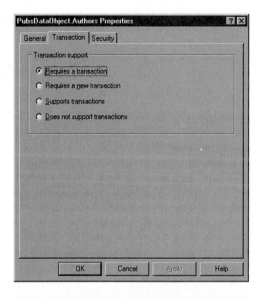

In Visual Basic 6.0, you can set the Transaction Support property during the
development of a component by using the `MTSTransactionMode` property of the
class.

Configuring Security

MTS provides a flexible security model. As with most software products, flexibility can
lead to complexity. This exploration of MTS security includes setting permissions on
components and packages. I also cover the relationship between MTS security and SQL
Server 7.0 security.

MTS security relies on the configuration of users in the NT domain. Users and groups
within an NT domain can be assigned to roles in MTS. These roles are in turn granted
permissions on MTS objects.

Package Security Options

Several steps are necessary to implement security within a package. In this case, use the
PubsPackage package that was described earlier in the chapter:

1. Select the PubsPackage package in the explorer.

2. Right-click the PubsPackage package and select Properties.

3. Click the Security tab.

4. Check the Enable Authorization Checking box, and set the Authentication Level for Calls box to Connect (see Figure 33.7). The other available Authentication levels are Call, Packet, Packet Integrity, and Packet Privacy. See the MTS help documentation for an explanation of Authentication levels.

5. Click OK.

FIGURE 33.7

Setting security options for a package.

33

MICROSOFT TRANSACTION SERVER

Creating Roles

Roles are the entities in MTS to which permissions are assigned. Roles consist of groups or users from an NT domain. Roles are defined on a per-package basis. In other words, each package may have a different set of roles to work with. The following procedure creates a new role and enables that role to use the `PubsDataObject.Authors` component:

1. Select the Roles folder under the PubsPackage package in the Transaction Server Explorer.

2. Right-click the Roles folder, and select New, Role.

3. Type `PubsUsers` in the New Role screen, and click OK.

4. Locate and select the Users folder in the PubsUsers role.

5. Right-click the Users folder and select New, User.

6. In the Add Users and Groups to Role window, click the Show Users button.

7. Select your own Windows NT username in the Names list, and click the Add Button.

8. Click OK.

You have now included your own username in the PubsUsers role of the PubsPackage package. Therefore, any permissions that are assigned to the PubsUsers role will also be assigned to your username.

Setting Role Membership for a Component

Each component within a package can have its own security settings. The Role Membership folder is the mechanism for designating which roles have access to which components. The following example grants the PubsUsers role access to the Authors component but not the Titles component:

1. Open the `PubsDataObject.Authors` component in the Transaction Server Explorer.

2. Select the Role Membership folder.

3. Right-click the Role Membership folder and select New, Role.

4. In the Select Roles window, select the PubsUsers role and click OK (see Figure 33.8).

FIGURE 33.8

Selecting roles for a component.

When you have finished configuring the roles and role membership, the explorer screen should look similar to Figure 33.9. You have added your own username to the PubsUsers role, and you have added the PubsUsers role to the Role Membership folder of the `PubsDataObject.Authors` component.

FIGURE 33.9

*The completed
role configuration
for PubsPackage.*

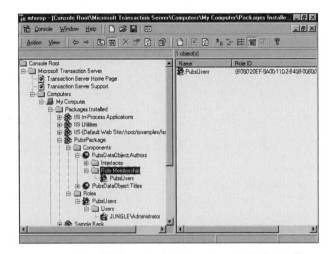

> **TIP**
>
> You should shut down a package after you change its roles or the role member-
> ships of its components. This action will ensure that the new settings take
> effect. To shut down a package, right-click the package and select Shut Down.
> The package will restart itself next time it is called.

33

MICROSOFT
TRANSACTION
SERVER

How Do MTS and SQL Server Security Relate?

There are several ways to combine MTS security and SQL Server 7.0 security. This
section addresses two primary scenarios. The first scenario is when you want to grant
access to the database on a per-user basis, and the second scenario is when you want to
grant access on a per-package basis. Both of these scenarios assume that SQL Server is
using SQL Server and Windows NT security. For a complete discussion of SQL Server
security, see Chapter 10, "Security and User Administration."

Scenario 1—Per User

In this situation, you should build each MTS component to accept database usernames
and passwords as parameters. The component can then use these parameters to open a
connection. To set up this scenario, each user must be given access to the MTS
component through roles, and each user must also have a login for the database.

> **CAUTION**
>
> Using this security scheme could severely limit scalability. You must create a unique connection for each user, which cripples the effectiveness of connection pooling. See "Using Connection Pooling," later in this chapter.

Scenario 2—Per Package

In this scenario, all components in a package call the database under one database login. MTS can validate individual users by checking a component's role membership. Once the users are validated by MTS, the users then perform all database activities under a single database login. This security scheme enables effective use of connection pooling.

Other Security Considerations

There are several other issues to keep in mind regarding MTS security:

- This discussion has only covered declarative security. Programmatic security is also available in MTS. Programmatic security enables an MTS component to determine the authorization of its caller through code.

- It is possible to control who has administrative privileges in MTS. You might want only certain users to be able to make changes to your MTS setup.

- Several different authentication levels are available for MTS components. The examples in this chapter use only the Connect authentication level.

- You must enable Distributed COM (DCOM) security on all client machines that will access a component under MTS control. You can use the dcomcnfg.exe utility to configure the client machines. A full discussion of DCOM security is beyond the scope of this chapter, but the options shown in Figure 33.10 will be adequate for most situations.

FIGURE 33.10

Configuring DCOM security on a client machine.

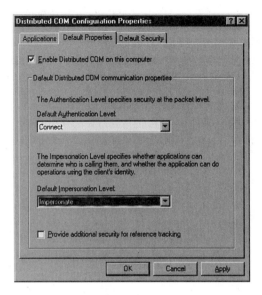

Running an MTS Application

In this section, I step through running a sample MTS application. Several prerequisites are necessary before the test application can be run successfully:

1. Use 32-bit ODBC to create a System DSN named Pubs. This DSN should point to the Pubs database in SQL Server 7.0. For details on ODBC, see Chapter 4, "Client Installation."

2. You should install the PubsDataObject.dll file under MTS control as described in "Installing an MTS Component."

3. You should configure security for the PubsDataObject components as described in "Configuring Security."

4. In SQL Server, set Authentication to SQL Server and Windows NT. Create a login named George that uses SQL Server Authentication and has a blank password. Grant db_datareader access on the Pubs database to George. Also, make sure that the default database for George is Pubs.

5. Ensure DTC is running. Right-click the My Computer icon in MTS Explorer. If the menu lists Start MS DTC as an option, then click it.

6. You must have the VB5 runtime library installed (MSVBVM50.dll). This library is necessary because the sample software was constructed using Visual Basic 5.0.

NOTE

All examples illustrated here were run on a Windows NT Server 4.0 platform.

Now, you're set to get started.

Watching the Ball Spin

 The test application can be found on the CD-ROM accompanying this book. The name of the program is MTSExample.exe. Run the MTSExample.exe program, and then position the MTS Client Example Window and the MTS Explorer as shown in Figure 33.11.

FIGURE 33.11

Running the MTSExample.exe program.

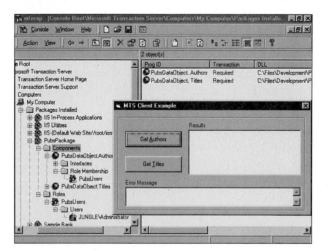

This way, you can see both the test program and the MTS components in the background. Now, you can see what happens. If something unexpected happens, you can refer to the section "Troubleshooting," later in this chapter.

1. Click the Get Authors button on the MTS Client Example screen.

2. A message box informs you that the PubsDataObject.Authors component is spinning.

3. Observe the MTS Explorer in the background to verify that you can see the ball spinning.

4. Click OK; the MTS Client Example displays a list of last names in the Results box.

Here is the key line of code that was executed when you clicked the Get Authors button:

```
Set oAuthors = CreateObject("PubsDataObject.Authors")
```

With this line, the MTSExample program created an instance of the `PubsDataObject.Authors` object in MTS.

Testing Permissions

You can verify the security behavior of MTS by attempting to use both the `PubsDataObject.Authors` component and the `PubsDataObject.Titles` component. At this point, you should have permission to use the Authors component but not the Titles component. The Get Titles button in the MTSExample program uses the Titles component to access SQL Server. Run the MTSExample program and see what happens:

1. Start the MTSExample.exe program.

2. Click the Get Titles button. A message box informs you that the component is spinning in the MTS Explorer. Click OK in the message box.

3. The Error Message box should contain the message `70 Permission Denied`. This indicates that you could not successfully use the methods of the `PubsDataObject.Titles` component.

Can you configure MTS so that the MTSExample program successfully pulls back the list of titles and displays them in the Results box? Give it a try before you go on.

All you need to do is give yourself permission to use the `PubsDataObject.Titles` component. Follow these steps:

1. Open the `PubsDataObject.Titles` component in MTS Explorer.

2. Select the Role Membership folder. Right-click it and select New, Role.

3. Select PubsUsers and click OK.

4. Click the PubsPackage icon. Right-click it and select Shut Down. This action will ensure that the package checks its permission next time it is accessed because the package's process will have to restart.

When you click the Get Titles button in the MTS Client Example program, the titles should load successfully.

Troubleshooting

The sample program in this chapter has many dependencies. This situation is similar to many systems that use MTS. MTS is likely to be in a middle tier in an *n*-tier system, and complex interactions may take place between the MTS software and the software in other tiers. (See Chapter 1, "Evolution of the Client/Server Environment," for details on *n*-tier architecture.) The operating system may even get into the action in terms of governing permissions.

Table 33.2 lists some of the errors you may encounter when running the MTSExample program. Errors in your own system may have similar causes and solutions.

TABLE 33.2 COMMON ERRORS IN THE MTSEXAMPLE PROGRAM

Error Message	Meaning
`429 ActiveX component can't create object`	The MTS component you are trying to use has not been installed correctly. See the section on "Installing an MTS Component."
`70 Permission Denied`	You don't have permission to use the methods of the MTS component. Did you remember to shut down the package after changing MTS permissions?
`13 Type Mismatch`	MTSExample could not pull results from the database. Check the database configuration: Do you have a System DSN named Pubs, a login named George in SQL Server with no password, a default database of Pubs, and read permission on Pubs?

Play with the permissions and configurations in both MTS and SQL Server to see how to cause and fix all three errors. This exercise will more clearly reveal the relationship between SQL Server 7.0 and MTS.

Using Connection Pooling

One of the most useful features of MTS is connection pooling. MTS can hold a connection open for a specified period of time even after a component is finished using the connection. When another component in MTS needs a database connection, MTS already has the connection open and waiting.

Connection pooling will only be effective if many of the database requests occur under the same database login. Note that the database requests can originate from different users as long as they use the same database login. The reason for this restriction is that the database login is a characteristic of a database connection.

If MTS components are written so that they hold open database connections only for a brief time, a limited pool of database connections can serve many client applications. This saves time and server resources and allows a system to scale more gracefully.

Changing the Driver Timeout

After SQL Server 7.0 is installed, you can use ODBC to configure connection pooling. Figure 33.12 shows the Connection Pooling tab of the ODBC Administrator. The important parameter here is the Pool Timeout (in seconds). This parameter tells ODBC how long a connection should be held open in the connection pool after a client application is done with it.

FIGURE 33.12

Changing the connection pooling timeout.

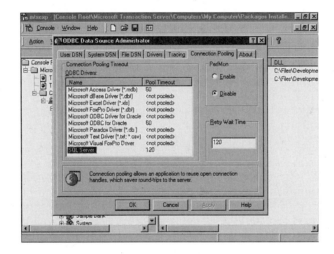

To change the timeout for SQL Server, follow these steps:

1. Open ODBC from the Control Panel. Click the Connection Pooling tab.

2. Double-click SQL Server in the ODBC Drivers box.

3. Select Pool Connections to this driver. The connection pool timeout defaults to 60. For this test, change it to 120. Click OK.

4. Note that the Pool Timeout for SQL Server has changed to 120 in the ODBC Drivers list. Click Apply.

5. Stop and restart the MS SQL Server service. For details on the MS SQL Server service, see Chapter 17, "Running the SQL Server Service Manager."

> **NOTE**
>
> Always remember to restart SQL Server after changing the connection pooling timeout setting in ODBC. This action will enable the changes to take effect.

Verifying Connection Pool Behavior

You can verify the length of the connection pooling timeout setting by using the Current Activity screen in the SQL Server Enterprise Manager. In this example, use the MTSExample program to open a connection to SQL Server and watch the Current Activity window to observe the length of time that the connection remains open:

1. Start the SQL Server Enterprise Manager. Click the SQL Server with the Pubs database.

2. Click the Management folder, open Current Activity, and then click on Process Info.

3. Start the MTSExample program. Click the Get Authors button.

4. When the message box appears, click OK.

5. Switch back to the SQL Server Enterprise Manager. Click Current Activity and then press F5 to refresh the information. Click Process Info. The details pane includes a connection with the login George, as shown in Figure 33.13.

FIGURE 33.13

Monitoring connections in SQL Server's Current Activity pane.

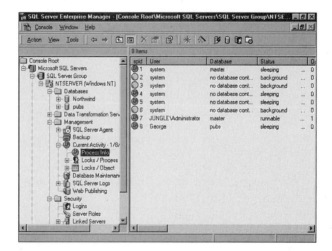

6. Over the next two minutes, repeat step five periodically. The George connection still remains displayed.

7. After two minutes have passed, perform step 5 again. The George connection disappears from the details pane.

You might want to experiment with different connection pooling timeout settings to tune your system performance. A long timeout increases the chance that a connection waits for a would-be client, but the connection uses resources on the server in the meantime.

Summary

Microsoft Transaction Server is likely to be a key member of large software systems. Recent trends towards Web-based, thin-client applications increase the importance of server-side technologies such as MTS. In this chapter, I examined the strengths of MTS, some common administrative tasks, and methods for integrating MTS with SQL Server. If you are planning to build a scalable, robust distributed system, MTS is part of your solution.

33

**MICROSOFT
TRANSACTION
SERVER**

Using the OLAP Server

by Bob Pfeiff

CHAPTER 34

Microsoft's DSS Analysis Server is the server component of Microsoft Decision Support Services (MS DSS), a new business intelligence package that ships with SQL Server 7.0. The DSS Analysis Server provides an easy-to-use, scalable Online Analytic Processing (OLAP) tool. MS DSS also includes the Microsoft Pivot Table Service, a client-side cache and calculation engine for OLAP analysis.

What Is OLAP?

OLAP is part of the data warehouse domain. OLAP falls under the broader scope of Decision Support Systems (DSS) and Executive Information Systems (EIS). In short, it is a collection of methods for looking at huge amounts of data to find interesting patterns and trends for business decision-makers to gain competitive advantages or otherwise optimize business processes.

Many of you are probably venturing into new territory in this chapter. Microsoft has opened a door into an increasingly important and growing segment of the database business. Microsoft DSS will "lower the bar" in terms of ease of use and affordability in the data warehousing business, and combined with the significant raw capacity enhancements in SQL 7.0, DSS will have a major impact on the data warehousing market. There are already indications of this because many of the leading OLAP and statistical analysis software vendors have joined Microsoft's Data Warehousing alliance and are building front-end analysis and presentation tools for Microsoft DSS.

Prepare to step out of the world of Online Transaction Processing (OLTP) systems with relational databases in third normal form. You won't see anything like that in this chapter, although as you delve into the world of data warehousing, you might find yourself thinking of ways to apply its techniques to systems you already work with.

A data warehouse contains all an organization's data and the means to access it to get meaningful information about the organization. A data warehouse can be built top down or bottom up. To build a top-down warehouse, you need to form a complete picture or logical data model for the entire organization—an ambitious and daunting task even for fairly small organizations. This task can be so huge and expensive that it never really gets off the ground. Building a warehouse from the bottom up with a departmental or business-area focus breaks the task of modeling the data into more manageable chunks. Such a departmental approach produces data marts that are subsets of the data warehouse. The bottom-up approach simplifies implementation; it helps get departmental or business-area information to the people who need it, makes it easier to protect sensitive data, and results in better query response times because data marts deal with less data. The potential risk in the data mart approach is that disparity in data-mart implementation can result in a logically disjointed enterprise data warehouse if efforts aren't carefully coordinated across the organization.

The bottom-up approach is an earn-as-you-go means of proceeding, providing tangible results early rather than later. Consequently, the project has a greater chance of long-term survival and success. Microsoft DSS offers an excellent set of tools to build data marts quickly.

OLAP products use a variety of approaches to accomplish their DSS/EIS goals, but underneath all the different implementations lies a dimensional database that is used to build data cubes. Cubes are logical blocks of data that a human can use to look at historical business activity. The basic dimensional schema contains a fact table with detailed facts that are identified by dimensions. Facts are measures of activities; money and quantities are common measures in a dimensional database. Dimensions put the facts in context and include such attributes as units of time, product information, and geographical information, to name a few. Figure 34.1 is a simplified model of a dimensional database and is a basic "star" schema.

FIGURE 34.1

A simple star schema.

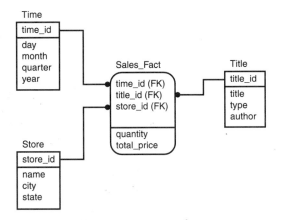

This may look familiar if you are acquainted with the pubs sample database in SQL Server. The fact table (Sales_Fact) in this case contains sales data in the transaction-level of detail. If you want to know the number of books in the computer category ordered on 26th of January in the first quarter of 1998, you can query the Sales_Fact table to sum the qty column where the `time_id` is equal to the `time_id` of that day in the Time table (dimension). It should be obvious that the fact table can be very large because it captures the transaction details for all book sales. Aggregates are calculated from the Sales_Fact table and can be stored in the source database or in an optimized format for quicker access, as you will see later. In this example, you can pre-aggregate data at the month level, eliminating the need to sum the price and qty measures for each day of the month or the months that you're interested in. Such pre-aggregated data can speed up queries but takes time to maintain and consumes more disk space.

34

The dimensions are the paths to the interesting facts; dimension members should be textual and are used as criteria for queries and as row and column headers in query results. Measures chosen using dimensions can be visualized as cubes, as shown in Figure 34.2.

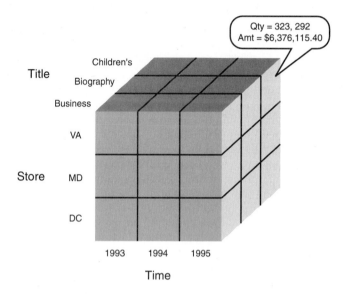

Each cell of the cube contains a fact. The filter criteria and axes of the cube come from the dimension tables. If the measure dollars was chosen from the Sales table, then the cell where the time dimension 1995, the title type dimension Children's, and the geographic dimension VA intersect would contain a dollar amount for children's books sold in Virginia in 1995. Facts should be three things—numeric, continuously valued, and additive—to produce meaningful results over varying spans of time. Dollar amounts and unit quantities are additive; averages of these are not.

Microsoft DSS Analysis Server allows you to build dimensions and cubes from heterogeneous data sources. The DSS Analysis Server can access relational OLTP databases, multidimensional data databases, text data, and any other source that has an OLE DB Provider available. You don't have to move all your data first; just connect to its source. Other approaches that require moving all the data can be more difficult to implement. A single DSS Analysis Server database can be built upon several data sources in a partitioned manner. I provide more detail later in the chapter on specific capabilities.

OLAP Versus OLTP

One of the primary goals of OLAP is increasing data retrieval speed. As you've already seen, the dimensional schema is not a typical normalized relational database; redundant data is stored to facilitate quick retrieval. The data in a dimensional database should be relatively static; in fact, it's not useful for decision support if it changes constantly. The information in a data warehouse is built out of carefully chosen snapshots of business data from OLTP systems. If you capture data at the right times for transfer to the data warehouse, you can quickly make accurate comparisons of important business activities over time.

In an OLTP system, transaction speed is paramount. Data modification operations must be quick, must deal with concurrency, and must provide transactional consistency, so you use a normalized relational database to eliminate data redundancy and minimize the work in the database to process a transaction. An OLTP system is constantly changing; every snapshot of the system, even if taken only a few seconds apart, will be different. Although historical information is certainly available in an OLTP system, it may be impractical to use it for DSS-type analysis. It gets expensive to store old data in an OLTP system, and you might need to reconstruct history dynamically from a series of transactions.

Microsoft DSS Analysis Server supports three OLAP storage methods, providing flexibility to the data warehousing solution and enabling very powerful partitioning and aggregation optimization capabilities that I discuss later in the chapter.

MOLAP

MOLAP stands for dimensional OLAP. MOLAP is an approach in which cubes are built directly from OLTP data sources or from dimensional databases and downloaded to a persistent store.

In Microsoft DSS Analysis Sever, data is downloaded to the server, and details and aggregations are stored in a native Microsoft OLAP format. No zero activity records are stored; for example, if no product A was sold on the 23rd of January, the fact table does not add a row with 0 dollars and 0 units.

The dimension keys in fact tables are compressed, and bitmap indexing is used. A high-speed MOLAP query processor retrieves the data.

ROLAP

Relational OLAP tools use fact data in summary tables in the OLTP data source to speed retrieval. The summary tables are populated by processes in the OLTP system and are not downloaded to the DSS Analysis Server. The summary tables are known as materialized views and contain various levels of aggregation, depending on the options you select when building data cubes with the DSS Analysis Server.

Microsoft DSS Analysis Server builds the summary tables with a column for each dimension and each measure. It indexes each dimension column and creates an additional index on all the dimension columns.

HOLAP

Microsoft DSS Analysis Server also implements a combination of MOLAP and ROLAP called hybrid OLAP. Here, the facts are left in the OLTP data source, and aggregations are stored in the DSS Analysis Server. You use the DSS Analysis Server to boost query performance. This approach helps avoid data duplication, but performance suffers when you query fact data in the OLTP summary tables. The amount of performance degradation depends on the level of aggregation you select.

ROLAP and HOLAP are useful in situations where an organization wants to leverage its investment in relational database technology and existing infrastructure. The summary tables of facts are also accessible in the OLTP system via normal data access methods. Using Microsoft DSS Analysis Server, both ROLAP and HOLAP will require more storage space because they don't use the storage optimizations of the pure MOLAP implementation.

The Data Warehouse Environment

A data warehouse is a collection of many parts. In addition to the obviously necessary source data, the data warehouse must also have a way to transform and move the snapshots of source data to summary tables and static, read-only dimensional structures; have user tools to query the data; and have a metadata layer that stores information about the data and the mechanisms that support the entire system. The environment consists of a data source, load processes, storage, retrieval and use, and the overarching information about the warehouse. Figure 34.3 shows a logical view of the components in a data warehouse.

FIGURE 34.3

The data warehouse environment.

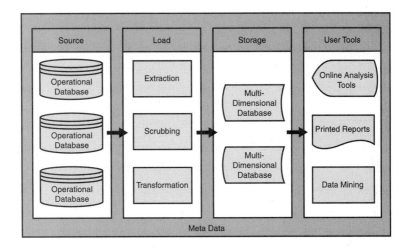

Data Transformation Services

Microsoft Data Transformation Services (DTS) provides a means to move data between sources. Data can be exported, validated and cleaned up, consolidated, transformed, and then imported into the destination. This is a critical link in a data warehouse because raw data, if you will, from OLTP sources is refined for executive-level use.

You can combine column values into a single calculated destination column or divide column values from a single source column into multiple destination columns. You might need to translate values in operational systems. For example, many OLTP systems use product codes that are stored as numeric data. Few people are willing to memorize an entire collection of product codes. An entry of 100235 for a type of shampoo in a product dimension table is useless to a VP for marketing who is interested in how much of that shampoo was sold in California last quarter.

Cleanup and validation of data is critical to its value in the data warehouse also; the old saying "garbage in, garbage out" applies. If data is missing, redundant, or inconsistent, then high-level aggregations can be inaccurate, so you should at least know that these conditions exist. Perhaps the data is rejected for use in the warehouse until the source data can be reconciled. If the shampoo of interest to the VP is called "Shamp" in one database and "Shampoo" in another, then aggregations on either value do not produce complete information about the product.

The DTS Package defines the steps in a transformation workflow. You can execute the steps serially and in combinations of serial, parallel, or conditional. The steps can then be executed through the DTS Data Pump, which is a Component Object Model (COM) compliant OLE DB Service Provider. Microsoft DTS supports any OLE-DB–compliant source or destination.

DTS Packages can be defined in the Microsoft Management Console for registered SQL servers.

> **NOTE**
>
> The SQL 7.0 Books Online has more detailed information on Microsoft DTS that is well worth reading. DTS is installed automatically with SQL Server and SQL Server client utilities on Windows NT, but not on Windows 95/98.

The Repository

Microsoft's Repository is a sharable metadata information store that supports the data warehouse environment by maintaining technical information on data sources and targets, transformations and mapping (such as DTS packages), data cleanup and enhancement rules, and scheduling. Business metadata is stored for end users to facilitate use of the data warehouse. You can also store query and report definitions and documentation in the Repository.

The Repository is based on the Unified Modeling Language (UML) with Microsoft Extensions to provide a common data warehousing infrastructure. Object sharing and reuse is implemented in a visual component manager for Visual Studio.

The Repository is installed by default in the msdb database in the workgroup and enterprise editions of SQL Server. A SQL Server can contain multiple Repositories, but DTS supports only a single Repository database per server in SQL Server Enterprise Manager.

Decision Support Services

Microsoft DSS consists of the DSS Analysis Server and the Pivot Table Service. These tools fit into the storage and user tools areas of the data warehouse environment. They are powerful tools for bridging operational data sources and user views of important trends in data. The DSS Analysis Server can combine heterogeneous data sources across an organization for quick retrieval and analysis of business-significant data. You can set storage options to optimize disk storage requirements instead of query performance. You can use various end-user tools such as Microsoft Excel, Access, English Query, and other third-party tools to access DSS Analysis Server data cubes via the Pivot Table Service.

Figure 34.4 shows where DTS, DSS, and the Repository fit in the data warehouse environment.

FIGURE 34.4

Microsoft Tools in the data warehouse environment.

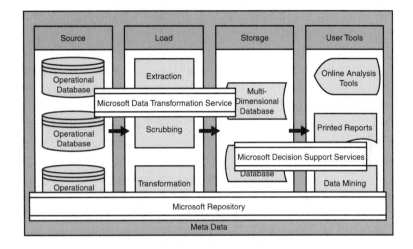

The OLAP Manager

Now, you get into what this chapter is really about. What can the DSS Analysis Server do?

> **NOTE**
>
> Specific installation instructions aren't covered in this chapter, but installing the DSS Analysis Server is straightforward.

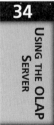

The OLAP Manager is launched from the DSS Analysis Server group in the Start menu, and it will launch the Microsoft Management Console (shown in Figure 34.5), where you'll see a DSS Analysis Servers folder under Console Root. You can add the DSS Analysis Server snap-in to an existing Management Console by selecting Add/Remove Snap-in from the Console menu.

FIGURE **34.5**

*The Microsoft
Management
Console.*

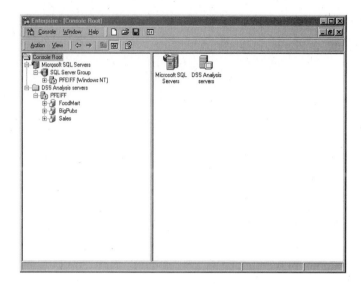

In this case, I opened the Microsoft Management Console from the Start menu in
Windows NT by using Run to execute mmc /a. Then I added the SQL Server Enterprise
Manager and the DSS Analysis Server snap-ins and saved the Management Console
using Save As from the Console menu. The Console is saved as a file with the .MSC
extension. I then created a shortcut to this Management Console file on the desktop so I
have access to SQL Server Enterprise Manager and the OLAP Manager in the same
console.

The OLAP Manager allows you to manage databases, data sources, dimensions, and
cubes for each database. Figure 34.6 shows the database view of the OLAP Manager in
the Management Console. I discuss each piece of an OLAP database in the following
sections.

FIGURE 34.6

Database view in OLAP Manager.

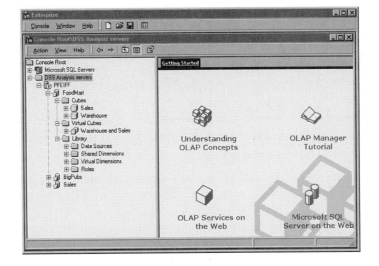

Creating an OLAP Database

An OLAP database is made of data sources, dimensions, cubes and virtual cubes. A data source is simply an ODBC data source set up in the ODBC Administrator found in the Control Panel. Dimensions are constructed of columns from tables that you select that will be used to build and filter data cubes. Cubes are combinations of dimensions whose intersections contain strategically significant measures of business performance, such as quantities and dollar values of sales. Virtual cubes are joins of physical cubes, but they don't use any storage space. Virtual cubes are analogous to views in SQL Server. You can join cubes this way with no more than one dimension in common.

 For the sake of simplicity, these sections will use the FoodMart sample database, which is a Microsoft Access database that installs with the DSS Analysis Server. A FoodMart DSS Analysis Server database is already built; you will create a new database and follow the steps to create the objects you see in the prebuilt database. Later, you will see a less detailed example using the BigPubs database from this book's companion CD-ROM that I believe is a little more interesting to play with.

34

USING THE OLAP
SERVER

> **NOTE**
>
> The following examples use the FoodMart sample included in the DSS Analysis Server.

To create a database, simply right-click Databases under your DSS Analysis Server and choose New Database from the shortcut menu. You get the same menu by clicking Action in the Management Console toolbar if you have Databases selected.

You then see the Database dialog box (see Figure 34.7). Here, you type a name and description for your new database. Type Sales in the text box over the word <New>; add a description if you like. Click OK when you are finished.

FIGURE 34.7

The Database dialog.

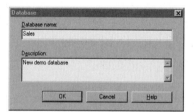

The new database will appear in the tree view. Expand the new database to see the list of objects that you can create in the database. You need a data source before you can create any dimensions or cubes. A data source called FoodMart is already defined, but normally, you would have to configure your data source with the ODBC Administrator in Control Panel.

Adding a Data Source

Expand the Library folder in the Sales database and right-click Data Sources. The Choose New Data Source dialog box opens; again, you can get the same menu by highlighting Data Sources and clicking Action on the Management Console toolbar. You can use an ODBC connection string instead of a defined ODBC data source with the Use connection string option button selected. Open the list under Use data source name and choose FoodMart. You don't need to specify a user ID, password, or database for this connection. Click the Test Connection button; it should report Test completed successfully. Figure 34.8 shows the Data Link Properties dialog.

FIGURE 34.8

The Data Link Properties dialog.

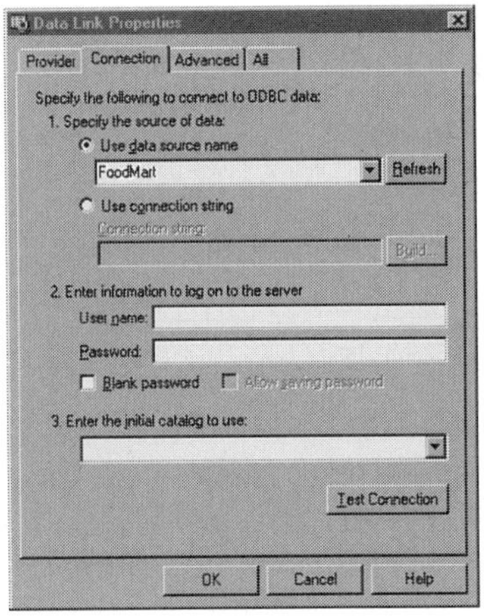

With the Data Link Properties dialog, you can also configure the connection properties and privileges. Click OK when you are finished.

Adding Dimensions

You are ready to start adding dimensions to your database. Dimensions are the building blocks for cubes in the DSS Analysis Server. Start by right-clicking Shared Dimensions in the Sales Database, and then right-click New Dimension and select Wizard to open the Dimension Wizard.

Select the single dimension option button. To keep things simple, the cube you build will be a star schema. You can use snowflake schemas to represent one-to-many relationships within a dimension. Click Next. Notice in the Select the Dimension Table dialog that you can add a new data source and use its tables for dimensions. Expand the FoodMart data source, and select Store; you can browse the first 1,000 rows of data here. Click Next to continue to the Select Dimension Type dialog. Select the Standard dimension option button. Time dimensions are based on transaction-level data and normally come from the fact table, as you will see as you build this cube.

The next dialog lets you define dimension levels. Because you're interested in sales by store, choose store_name and click the arrow to move it to the right pane; add store_state and store_city. Depending on the order you add these, you might get the Level Order message box warning that there are fewer members in a child level. The wizard is checking the hierarchy of the dimension levels. If you click No, the levels will be reordered. It makes sense that the hierarchy is state, city, and store for the purpose of drilling down in detail using the members of this dimension. Click Next to go to the Finishing the Dimension Wizard dialog. Name the dimension `Store` and click Finish.

34

USING THE OLAP SERVER

Now, you're in the Dimension Editor, where the previous steps come together. You can create dimensions directly in this editor by adding tables. You can also process the dimension here.

The upper-left pane has the dimension structure hierarchy. Figure 34.9 shows the Dimension Editor with this dimension built. Close the Dimension Editor.

FIGURE 34.9

The store dimension in the Dimension Editor.

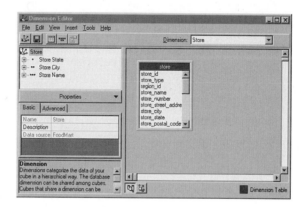

The next piece for this sales example is time. Right-click Shared Dimensions again and select New Dimension. Choose Wizard to open the Dimension Wizard.

Select the single dimension table option and click Next. Select time_by_day from the list of tables in the dialog that opens and click OK. This is a dimension table in the FoodMart dimensional database that you're using. It stores day, week, month, quarter, and other information for a range of dates. These dates are linked to facts by a time_id value. You can look at this data by opening the FoodMart Access database in <drive>:\Program Files\OLAP Services\Samples\FoodMart.MDB. Click Next.

Select the Time dimension option, and the wizard recognizes the column the_date as a date/time column to build the time dimension hierarchy. Click Next. You then select the hierarchy for the time dimension; "Year, Quarter, Month, Day" is the default, which you will use for this exercise. Click Next.

Name the dimension Time and click Finish. The Dimension Editor shows the hierarchy of the dimension. The dimension should look like Figure 34.10.

FIGURE 34.10

The time dimension in the Dimension Editor.

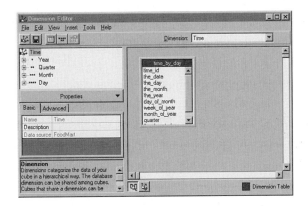

Close the Dimension Editor when you are finished and save it as `Time`. These new dimension definitions are stored in the DSS Analysis Server repository for your Sales database.

Building a Cube

Now that you have some dimensions, you have the building blocks for a cube that will put measures together for analysis, using the dimensions to select the interesting facts. In the OLAP Manager, right-click Cubes in the Sales database and select New Cube and then Wizard from the menu.

The Cube Wizard opens. Click Next on the first dialog, select the sales_fact_1998 table in the Select a Fact Table dialog, and click Next.

You choose the measures to include in the cube in the Define Measures dialog. Add store_sales, store_cost, and unit_sales to the right pane and click Next.

In the Select Cube Dimensions dialog, select Store and Time. Click Next. When the Finishing the Cube Wizard dialog opens, name the cube `Sales by Store` and click Finish.

In the Cube Editor, you should see the sales_fact_1998, the Store, and the Time tables. The relationships between these tables should have been recognized and represented with connecting lines. Figure 34.11 is what you should see. Close the cube.

34

USING THE OLAP SERVER

FIGURE 34.11

*The Sales by
Store cube in the
Cube Editor.*

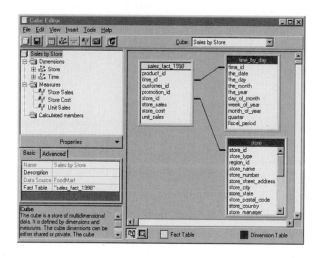

Now you have a definition of the cube stored in the DSS Analysis Server along with the database and dimensions you have already created. The data is stored in files in the Microsoft DSS folder. If you expand each item in the cube in the OLAP Manager, you'll see the measures and dimensions you chose.

This cube hasn't done anything for you yet; it needs to be processed. Here is where you decide on MOLAP, ROLAP, or HOLAP and the degree of aggregation. The cube will be built differently based on these choices.

Processing a Cube

Right-click the Sales by Store cube and select Process from the menu. A message box informs you that the cube has no aggregations designed. As already discussed, pre-aggregation speeds up data retrieval but can consume a lot of disk space and take time to create and maintain. If you choose no, you'll be prompted to build aggregations when you attempt to browse the cube. Click Yes.

The Data Storage and Aggregation Wizard starts and an initial dialog opens; click Next. The next dialog asks you to choose MOLAP, ROLAP, or HOLAP storage. If you choose MOLAP, the DSS Analysis Server will build a multidimensional structure of detail facts, with the granularity of one day based on the Time dimension, other dimensions as you defined, and aggregations to the degree you select. ROLAP will use the fact table you identified in the source database and build new summary tables with dimension and fact data in the source database for aggregations. HOLAP will use the table you identified as the fact table in the source database for the detail facts and build and store the dimensions and aggregations on the DSS Analysis Server. Choose the MOLAP option button and then click Next.

Now, you're in the aggregation design dialog of the wizard. This is a powerful feature of the DSS Analysis Server. Here, you can decide what degree of aggregation you want, based on optimization for retrieval and required disk storage. If a company has line-item sales transaction data for the past 5 years and 250 stores that sell an average of 1,000 items per day, the fact table will have 456,500,000 rows. This is obviously a challenge in terms of disk space by itself without aggregation tables to go along with it. The control that the DSS Analysis Server provides here is important in balancing storage and retrieval speed.

Figure 34.12 is a logical view of the aggregation choices the DSS Analysis Server might make for the Time dimension, based on the level of optimization chosen. The fact table contains the details at the lowest level of granularity. Aggregations are built to optimize roll-up operations so that higher levels of aggregation are easily derived from the existing aggregations to satisfy broader queries. In this case, if a high degree of query optimization weren't possible because of limitations in storage space, the DSS Analysis Server may choose to build aggregates of monthly data only. If a user queried the cube for quarterly, yearly, or multi-year data, those aggregations would be created dynamically from the highest level of pre-aggregated data.

FIGURE 34.12

Logical view of aggregation levels.

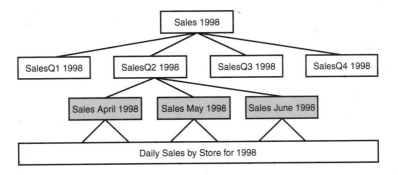

In the Aggregation Design dialog, you get a choice of limiting aggregations by disk space or optimization. You can also run the aggregation designer and watch the graph, stopping the aggregation when you reach a point where you are comfortable. You'll notice that the performance gain may begin to flatten out at a certain point. This relies on the accuracy of the DSS Analysis Server estimates, but there essentially is a point of diminishing returns in using disk space. Going beyond this point gets you increasingly less performance for the space used. Because you can tune individual queries, you might want to cut off aggregations at a point when optimization begins to flatten out and then tune your queries based on observation as the cube is used. Figure 34.13 shows the result of letting the aggregation wizard run out to maximum query optimization.

Figure 34.13

The Data Storage and Aggregation Wizard.

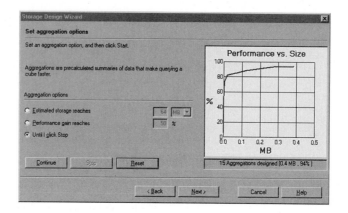

Choose an option; I recommend you experiment a bit just to get a feel for this tool. I set disk space to 0.5MB for this example. Once you choose an option, click Start to design the aggregations. Click Next and then click Finish on the Finish the Data Storage and Aggregation Wizard dialog. You'll be asked to process the aggregations or to save the aggregation design. Choose the Save and Process Aggregations When I Click Finish option, and you will see a progress dialog that shows the SQL statements that the DSS Analysis Server is executing against the source data.

> **Note**
>
> The DSS Analysis Server chooses what aggregations to build. The only user input to this process is selecting the level of query optimization versus the disk space required. MOLAP or HOLAP offers no report or other indication as to what the aggregations are. If you choose ROLAP, however, you can look in the source database at the summary tables created by the DSS Analysis Server.

Now, you have a data cube that can be browsed from the OLAP Manager's Cube Browser with its built-in drill-down features. The Cube Browser isn't a robust end-user analysis tool, and it only exists on the server side. Using the Pivot Table Service, you can write custom client applications using Multidimensional Extensions (MDX) with OLE DB for OLAP or ActiveX Data Objects Multidimensional (ADO MD) or use a number of third-party OLE DB for OLAP-compliant tools to access the cube.

Because you chose MOLAP, the data and indexes for this cube are stored in native DSS Analysis Server files under the Microsoft DSS folder.

Browsing a Data Cube from the OLAP Manager

To browse data in your cube, right-click the new Sales by Store cube in the Sales database and select Browse Data. The Cube Browser opens and presents aggregated data. You'll find data from the dimensions in the display. The Time dimension shows up in the top pane, and you can drill into it by dropping down the list in the combo box and then expanding the categories. Notice that the values in the dimensions are textual and readily understandable. This is the data from the dimension tables you created for the Sales database (see Figure 34.14).

FIGURE 34.14

The Cube Browser.

MeasuresLevel			
+ Store State	Store Sales	Store Cost	Unit Sales
All Store	1,079,147.47	432,565.73	509,987.00
+ BC	98,045.46	39,332.57	46,157.00
+ CA	154,513.49	61,936.33	73,017.00
+ DF	95,526.40	38,292.69	45,223.00
+ Guerrero	49,090.03	19,669.33	23,226.00
+ Jalisco	4,328.87	1,723.23	2,124.00
+ OR	128,598.50	51,512.78	60,612.00
+ Veracruz	52,142.07	20,948.90	24,696.00
+ WA	267,696.43	107,196.00	126,297.00
+ Yucatan	79,063.13	31,659.71	37,143.00
+ Zacatecas	150,143.09	60,294.18	71,502.00

Time — All Time

Double-click a member to drill up or drill down. Drag and drop dimensions to or from the table.   Close   Help

In the Cube Browser, you can drag dimensions and measures around to change the column and row headings, depending on your preference. Double-clicking dimension data drills down into that dimension to lower levels of granularity. For example, drag the Time dimension to the leftmost position of the grid if it isn't already there. The Time dimension values, or members, become the row headers of the grid. Drop down the Store combo box in the top pane and expand All; then, expand CA and click Beverly Hills. This filters the results to show data for stores in Beverly Hills, California. Double-click 1998 in the grid to drill down to more granular time data, then double-click Quarter 3, and then double-click July. Notice that Beverly Hills stores had $1006.15 in sales on July 26. Looking at this data, it appears that Food Mart stores aren't doing too well or that the source data is incomplete because there are many days without any data at all.

The Cube Browser shows you what your cube has in it but also illustrates the utility of a dimensional database. Users can easily "slice and dice" data in meaningful ways. The data can also be "mined" by intelligent applications to find hidden relationships and patterns in the data that could have significant business implications.

34

USING THE OLAP SERVER

The DSS Analysis Server allows you to browse individual dimension data as well. Right-click the Store dimension and select Browse Dimension. The Dimension Browser opens with All; expanding each level gets you to more detailed information as you move down the dimension hierarchy.

OLE DB for OLAP and ADO MD expose the interfaces to do this kind of data browsing, and many leading vendors have used these interfaces to build front-end analysis tools and ActiveX controls. These tools should prove useful for developers of user interfaces in data warehousing and data mart projects.

Modifying a Data Cube

The OLAP Manager makes it easy to modify a cube. In the Sales database, create a new Shared Dimension, selecting the multiple dimension tables option. Add the product_class table and the product table to the dimension. Then, select the product_category column and the product_name column from the list of columns. Name the new dimension Product and save it.

Create another Shared Dimension using the state_province, city, and gender columns of the customer table in that order. A message box will tell you that the number of members in gender is less than the number of members in city; click Yes to preserve this hierarchy. Name this dimension Customer and save it.

Right-click the Sales by Store cube and select Edit.

In the Cube Editor, right-click Dimensions and select Dimension Manager. In the Dimension Manager, add the new Product and Customer dimensions and click OK.

Notice that the product_class table is linked to the fact table via the product table in the cube schema pane of the cube editor. This is where the schema is "snowflaked." In a typical dimensional database, this would represent an additional join to get to the fact data from the product_category dimension, which could adversely affect performance. The DSS Analysis Server builds a single dimension table from the join of these two tables to optimize query performance. If you browse the Product dimension data, it will list products under product category just like any dimension built from a single table.

You can add private dimensions in the Cube Editor. Private dimensions are configured within a cube, are not available to other cubes, and are not defined at the DSS Analysis Server database level. For example, if there is interest in sales based on the number of children in households, just drag the num_children_at_home column from the customer table and drop it on Dimensions in the left pane of the Cube Editor. Notice that the Private Dimensions icon is different from that of the Shared Dimensions.

Calculated members allow you to create new measures and dimension members based on combinations of other measures or dimension members. You can create a measure of net income by subtracting the Store Sales and Store Cost measures. Right-click Calculated Measures and select New Calculated Member (the only choice). The Calculated Member Builder dialog opens (shown in Figure 34.15). Expand Measures and then Measures Level. Highlight Store Sales and click Insert. Click the minus sign, highlight Store Cost, and click Insert. The expression appears in the Value expression pane. Name the member Store Income and click OK.

FIGURE 34.15

The Calculated Member Builder.

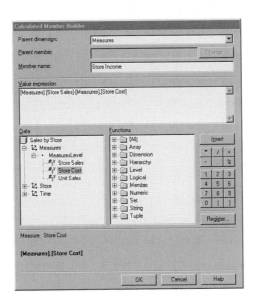

In the Functions pane of the Calculated Member Builder is a list of functions under various categories of DSS Analysis Server objects. These are MDX functions that you can use to build complex OLE DB for OLAP statements that are discussed later in the chapter. The Register button allows you to register other function libraries (DLL files) developed for the DSS Analysis Server that you might want to use.

Figure 34.16 shows the Cube Editor with the new private dimension and calculated member added.

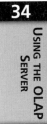

34

USING THE OLAP SERVER

FIGURE 34.16

*Private dimension
and calculated
member added to
the Sales by Store
cube.*

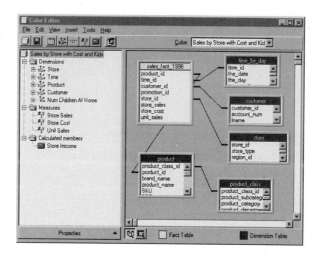

If you try to close the Cube Editor, you'll be warned that existing aggregations will be deleted and the cube will have to be reprocessed; click Cancel. From the File menu, select Save As and name the cube Sales by Store with Cost and Kids.

Right-click the Sales by Store with Cost and Kids cube and select Process. In the Aggregation Wizard, choose ROLAP, choose Estimated percentage of optimization, and set the figure to 20 percent to reduce the amount of processing time. Choose Save and Process Aggregations When I Click Finish at the last dialog. Processing will take several minutes.

> **NOTE**
>
> If you have Microsoft Access installed, you might find it interesting to look at the FoodMart database after creating this new dimensional ROLAP cube. You'll see about 10 new summary tables to support the aggregations created by the DSS Analysis Server. By default, this file installs to <drive>:\Program Files\OLAP Services\Samples\FoodMart.MDB.

Browsing a Multidimensional Cube

The Sales by Store cube had two dimensions, Time and Store. This is relatively easy to navigate. However, the new Sales by Store with Cost and Kids cube has a lot more information to deal with.

Right-click the Sales by Store with Cost and Kids cube and select Browse Data. The top pane has four dimensions in it, all of which can be drilled into finer detail.

Let's try to answer the question, "How much frozen broccoli was sold in 1998 to customers in California with two children?" Figure 34.17 shows the Cube Browser with the results of this query that were obtained by drilling down in the dimensions for Big Time Frozen Broccoli, 1998, 2 children, and CA.

FIGURE 34.17

Browsing a multi-dimensional cube.

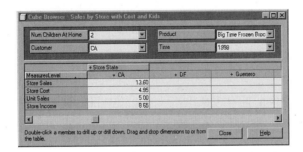

Notice the differences in response time as you rearrange the columns and rows and select details of various levels of granularity. This is because you aggregated some of the data, but some of the aggregations are still being generated on-the-fly and consequently performance suffers.

Query Analysis and Optimization

In the OLAP Manager, you can look at query utilization and performance in a cube. This is another powerful feature in the DSS Analysis Server in that you can look at queries by user, frequency, and execution time to determine how to better optimize aggregations. If a slow-running query is used frequently by many users, or by the CEO, it may be a good candidate for individual tuning. The OLAP Manager allows you to adjust aggregations based on a query to reduce response time.

Right-click the Sales by Store with Cost and Kids cube and select Usage-Based Optimization. A wizard starts and gives you an introduction; click Next. A dialog allows you to filter queries by user, frequency of execution, time frame, and execution time. Select the Queries for the dates check box and After, enter the day prior to the date that you ran the frozen broccoli query, and click Next. You will see a record for each query you ran since the date you entered, the number of times it was executed, and the average execution time in seconds. This is like a SQL trace analysis of your OLAP queries.

Because aggregations already exist, the wizard will ask whether you want to replace them or add new ones. If you replace the existing aggregations, the cube will be reprocessed with this particular query in mind. Select Add New Aggregations to the Existing Ones to simply add aggregations to speed up this query. Click Next. The next dialog is the Aggregation Design Wizard; select the Performance Gain Reaches option and set the value to 30 percent. Notice that the graph starts at the existing aggregations, about .2MB, and moves up from there. Click Next and select Save and Process Aggregations When I Click Finish.

If you re-run the frozen broccoli query, you should see a performance gain. When I did this, the average duration went from 3 seconds for one execution to 1 second for three executions.

Partitioning a Cube

Cube partitioning is another powerful feature of Microsoft DSS Analysis Server. Here, you can deal with individual "slices" of a data cube separately, querying only the relevant data sources. If you partition by dimension, you can perform incremental updates to change that dimension independently of the rest of the cube. Consequently, you only have to reprocess aggregations affected by those changes. This is an excellent feature for scalability.

Start by expanding the Sales by Store with Cost and Kids cube in the Sales database, and then expand Partitions. There is only one that contains all the data for the cube.

Right-click Partitions and select New Partition. The Partition Wizard opens as shown in Figure 34.18. Click Next.

FIGURE 34.18

The Partition Wizard opening dialog.

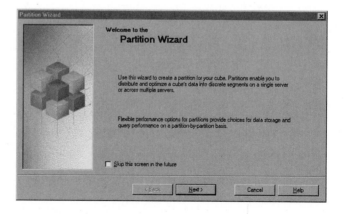

The next dialog is Specify Data Source. Because all the data for the Sales by Store with Cost and Kids cube is in one location (the FoodMart.MDB), you don't need to specify a new data source. The ability to use multiple data sources is a key feature of the DSS Analysis Server because it allows you to access data on clusters of servers, retrieving only what you need from each server to satisfy the request for information. The storage methods can be different on each data source; the only constraint is that the dimensions and facts are logically compatible in the different sources. Click Next.

In the Specify Data Slice dialog, you specify what dimensions you want to partition. Separating the dimensions allows the DSS Analysis Server to query only the data sources that contain the slice of data requested. Select the Product dimension and you will see the members of Product appear in the members pane. Select All to partition the entire dimension and click Next.

In the Finish the Partition Wizard dialog, name the partition Product and choose the Copy the Aggregation Design from an Existing Partition option. Notice the Sales by Store with Cost and Kids partition is the only choice in the combo box because it is the only partition. Leave the Process the Partition When Finished check box unchecked because this processing will take a long time.

If you click the Advanced button, you'll get a dialog that allows you to filter the data in the partition with a WHERE clause and to assign a prefix to the aggregation table names to distinguish them from existing aggregation tables if the ROLAP storage mode is used. Change the Aggregation Prefix to Prod and click OK.

Click Finish in the Finish the Partition Wizard dialog.

The Product partition now appears under Partitions in the Sales by Store with Cost and Kids cube. Right-click the Product partition to see the menu items. Merge combines the aggregations back into the original partition.

With well-designed partitions, a cube can be updated incrementally when it is reprocessed because the partition can be updated independently.

Creating a Virtual Cube

As mentioned before, a virtual cube is a logical join of physical cubes that don't store data themselves. Start by creating a new cube called Stores. Right-click Cubes in the Sales database, select New Cube, and choose Editor.

In the Cube Editor, select Sales_Fact_1998 as the fact table and click OK.

Drag the unit_sales column from the table view in the right pane, and drop it on the Measures folder in the upper-left pane.

In the Cube Editor, add the Stores table using the Insert menu. Drag the store_city column onto Dimensions in the upper-left pane to create a new private dimension. Close the Cube Editor and name the cube `Stores` when prompted.

Right-click the new Stores cube and select Process. Choose the MOLAP option and let the Aggregation Design Wizard build all the aggregations it wants to by choosing the I Click Stop option. Choose Save and Process Aggregations When I Click Finish and then click Finish.

In the Sales database, right-click Virtual Cubes and select New Virtual Cube. The Virtual Cube Wizard starts; all physical cubes in the database are listed. Add Sales by Store and Stores to the pane on the right and click Next. Select the Store Sales measure from the Sales by Store cube and Unit Sales measure from the new Stores cube and click Next. Select the Store City private dimension in the next dialog and click Next. In the Finish the Virtual Cube Wizard dialog, name the cube `StoreVCube` and click Finish.

You can look at the measures and dimensions by expanding the StoreVCube. Right-click StoreVCube and select Process. When processing completes, you can browse the data. Notice that the only value for the Store Sales measure is for the All Store City member of the Store City dimension because the Stores cube only included the Unit Sales measure.

Working with a Relational Database

The examples you've worked to this point have been from a dimensional database that uses a star/snowflake schema.

> **NOTE**
>
> Designing dimensional databases is an art form and requires not only sound dimensional modeling knowledge, but also knowledge of the business processes you're dealing with. There are different schools of thought in data warehousing design approaches. Regardless of which approach you take, having a good understanding of its design techniques is critical to the success of a data warehouse project. Although Microsoft Decision Support Services provides a powerful set of tools to implement data marts, astute execution of design methods is critical to getting the right data, the truly business significant business data, to the end users.

Everything you've done thus far with the DSS Analysis Server can be done against a relational database. I won't provide all the detail I did in the preceding examples, but I'd like to walk through developing the star schema from Figure 34.1 (shown again here in Figure 34.19) using the DSS Analysis Server against a purely relational database.

FIGURE 34.19

The star schema again.

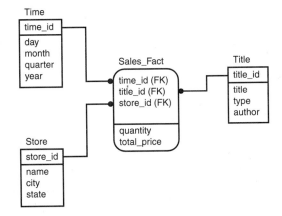

The BigPubs Database

The BigPubs database is available on the companion CD-ROM as it has been in the SQL Server 6.*x* editions of this book. It has the same structure as the Pubs sample database that ships with SQL Server but contains a lot more data. BigPubs is a normalized relational database, unlike the FoodMart database you've been using. The DSS Analysis Server can connect to a relational database and allow you to build dimensions and define measures from it.

> **NOTE**
>
>
> You need to install the BigPubs database from the companion CD-ROM to follow the steps I outline. There are installation scripts and instructions on the CD. You can go through this exercise using the Pubs database, but it has little data in it and isn't as much fun. This example will work with SQL Server 7.0 or 6.5 because the OLAP Services can be installed independently of SQL Server 7.0.

34

USING THE OLAP SERVER

You can emulate the dimensional schema in Figure 34.19 by creating the dimensions and then building a cube in the OLAP Manager.

The fact table in Figure 34.19 has measures of quantity and total_price. Unfortunately, the sales data in the BigPubs database stored in the sales table doesn't contain any price information. To deal with this, create a view in the BigPubs database that includes the sales.qty column and the titles.price column as in the script in Listing 34.1.

LISTING 34.1   SALES_FACT VIEW

```
create view sales_fact
(
title_id,
stor_id,
ord_date,
qty,
amount
)
as
select
    s.title_id,
    s.stor_id,
    s.ord_date,
    s.qty,
    s.qty * convert(smallmoney, isnull(t.price, 0), 1) as amount
from
    sales s
left outer join
    titles t
on
    s.title_id = t.title_id
```

This view will be used as the fact table for the cube you will create in this example.

First, set up an ODBC data source for the BigPubs database with the ODBC Administrator in Control Panel.

Next create a new database in the OLAP Manager—name it whatever you like—and add the data source you just created.

Now, you can set up the dimensions. The Store dimension will get its members from the Stores table in BigPubs, so create a new shared dimension and select Stores as its dimension table. Add state, city, and stor_name in that order to the dimension levels. Save the dimension as Store.

Create the Title dimension using the wizard. Add the titles table. Drag the type and title in that order to get the appropriate hierarchy. Save this dimension as Title.

You create the time dimension using the sales_fact view as the dimension table and selecting the Time Dimension option. Select Year, Quarter, Month, Day for the hierarchy. Save this dimension as `Time`.

Now that you have the dimensions, you can create a cube. Right-click Cubes, select New Cube, and select the sales_fact view as the fact table. Add qty and amount to the Cube Measures pane when you get to it. In this example, I renamed the amount measure to `Total Price`.

Add the Time, Store, and Title dimensions you just created to the cube. You might have to manually link the title_id column in the titles table to the title_id in the sales_fact table; you do this by dragging and dropping from titles to sales_fact in the Cube Editor. Figure 34.20 shows the cube design; save it as `Orders`.

FIGURE 34.20
Cube derived from the BigPubs database.

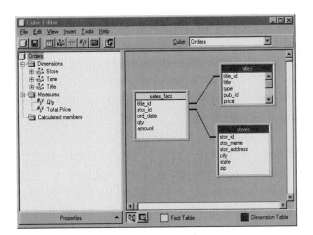

Right-click the cube and process it as HOLAP. Select 80 percent for the Estimated Percentage of Optimization in the Aggregation Designer. It should come up with about 13 aggregations and .6MB of storage required. Process the cube.

Now, you can browse the data. Look at Time–1994, Quarter 1, Store–VA, Centreville, Crown Books Title–Fiction. There were 900 fiction titles with a total value of $8,055.00 ordered by this store for that period, as shown in Figure 34.21.

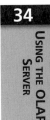

FIGURE 34.21

Orders cube data.

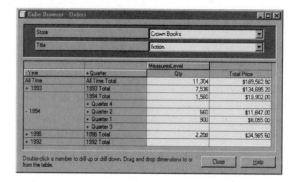

You need the SQL statement in Listing 34.2 to get that single point of data.

LISTING 34.2   SQL EQUIVALENT

```
select
    datepart(yy, sa.ord_date) ord_year,
datepart(qq, sa.ord_date) ord_quarter,
    st.state,
    st.city,
    st.stor_name,
    t.type,
    sa.qty,
    sa.qty * t.price as amount
from
    sales sa
join
    stores st
on
    sa.stor_id = st.stor_id
and
    st.city = 'centreville'
and
    st.state = 'va'
and
    st.stor_name = 'crown books'
join
    titles t
on
    sa.title_id = t.title_id
and
    t.type = 'fiction'
and
    datepart(yy, sa.ord_date)= '1994'
and
    datepart(qq, sa.ord_date) = '1'
```

This statement is not necessarily a terrible thing to write, or terribly slow, but it only gets you a tiny slice of data and the fact table is not very big. The performance of this join would degrade quickly if the fact table grew to millions of rows. Just imagine how much code you'd have to write to provide the functionality of the cube you just produced.

Limitations of a Relational Database

Even using a tool such as the DSS Analysis Server, there are limitations when dealing with a normalized database. As you saw, quantity (qty) was the only measure available in the fact (Sales) table. Using the wizards in the DSS Analysis Server can't get you dollar values to go along with the quantity values because they don't exist in the Sales table. A view solved this problem in the example, but more complicated facts and dimensions may require denormalized tables or a dimensional database in the storage component of the data warehouse to bring information together. Data cleansing and transformation also are major considerations before attempting to present decision-makers with data from OLTP systems.

Getting the Data to Users

Microsoft DSS Analysis Server provides a great deal of flexibility for building scalable OLAP solutions, but how do you present the data to users? The answer lies in the other major component of Microsoft Decision Support Services, the Pivot Table Service. This client-side component delivers much of the functionality of the DSS Analysis Server using the same code base for the dimensional calculation engine, caching, and query processing. The Pivot Table Service manages client/server connections and is the layer for user interfaces to access DSS Analysis Server cubes through the OLE DB for OLAP interface. ActiveX Data Objects Multidimensional (ADO MD) provides an application-level programming interface for development of OLAP applications. Third-party tools and future versions of Microsoft Excel and other Microsoft Office products will use the Pivot Table Service to access cubes.

The Pivot Table Service shares metadata with the DSS Analysis Server, so a request for data on the client causes data and metadata to be downloaded to the client. The Pivot Table Service determines whether requests need to be sent to the server or can be satisfied at the client with downloaded data. If a user requests sales information for the first quarter of 1998 and then later decides to query that data for the first quarter of 1997 for comparison, only the request for 1997 data has to go to the server to get more data because the 1998 data is cached on the client.

Slices of data retrieved to the client computer can also be saved locally for analysis when disconnected from the network. Users can download the data they're interested in and analyze it offline. The Pivot Table Service can also create simple OLAP databases by accessing OLE-DB–compliant data sources.

34

USING THE OLAP SERVER

With the ADO MD interface, developers will be able to access and manipulate objects in a DSS Analysis Server database, enabling Web-based OLAP application development.

Many Independent Software Vendors (ISVs) are working with Microsoft to leverage the rich features of the Decision Support Services and will offer robust user interfaces that can access DSS Analysis Server and Pivot Table Service functionality. Most popular features of OLAP products today such as graphical reports and robust spreadsheet displays should be available when SQL Server 7.0 ships with Decision Support Services. Future versions of Microsoft Office will include the Pivot Table Service to enable built-in analysis in tools such as Excel.

Multidimensional Expressions

The OLE DB for OLAP specification contains Multidimensional Expressions (MDX) syntax that is used to build datasets from cubes. Developers of OLE DB OLAP providers can map MDX syntax to SQL statements or native query languages of other OLAP servers, depending on storage techniques (for example, ROLAP or MOLAP).

MDX statements build datasets using information about cubes from which the data will be read. This includes the number of axes to include, the dimensions on each axis and the level of nesting, the members or member tuples and sort order of each dimension, and the dimension members used to filter, or slice, the data. Tuples are combinations of dimensions such as time and product time that present multidimensional data in a two-dimensional dataset.

The basic parts of an MDX statement are

- Dimension, measure, and axis information in the SELECT clause
- The source cube in the FROM clause
- Dimension slicing in the WHERE clause

Expressions in an MDX statement operate on numbers, strings, members, tuples, and sets. Numbers and strings mean the same thing here as they do in other programming contexts. Members are the values in a dimension and levels are groups of members. If the dimension were time, then a particular year, quarter, or month would be a member, and month values would belong to the month level. Use the dimension browser in the OLAP Manager to view members of a dimension. Sets are collections of tuple elements to further combine facts.

An example of an MDX statement and its results in the MDX sample application that installs with Microsoft DSS are shown in Figure 34.22. You can launch the sample MDX application from the Microsoft Decision Support Services program group.

FIGURE 34.22

An MDX statement and results in the sample MDX application.

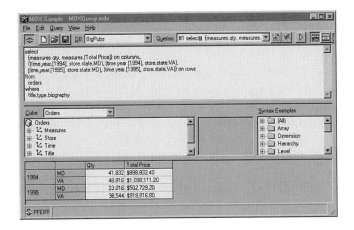

This is a simple MDX statement that shows the basic parts of a working query. In this case, measures are displayed in columns, and Time and Store dimension members make up the axes of this multidimensional query and are displayed in rows. The display of multiple dimensions in rows like this is how the term tuple is used in the context of Microsoft DSS. Finally, the Title dimension slices the data by the biography type. This example uses the Orders cube created from the BigPubs database in the example earlier in the chapter. A number of other examples included in the sample MDX application use the FoodMart sample database.

There is a lot more to the MDX syntax, and a complete discussion of MDX is probably worth a chapter by itself. The OLE DB for OLAP Programmers Reference is available on the Microsoft Web site; it contains detailed information about MDX.

ActiveX Data Objects Multidimensional

ActiveX Data Objects Multidimensional (ADO MD) is an easy-to-use access method for dimensional data via an OLE DB for OLAP provider. You can use ADO MD in Visual Basic, Visual C++, and Visual J++. Like ADO, ADO MD offers a rich application development environment that can be used for multitier client/server and Web application development.

You can retrieve information about a cube, or metadata, and execute MDX statements using ADO MD to create "cellsets" to return interesting data to a user. ADO MD is another subject too broad to cover in any detail in this chapter. Specifications for OLE DB for OLAP and ADO MD are available on the Microsoft Web site.

Summary

Microsoft has introduced some powerful tools with Decision Support Services. This chapter discussed data warehousing terms and architecture and how the DSS Analysis Server fits into the bigger picture. You walked through some specific functionality of the DSS Analysis Server and gained some insight into its power and flexibility. The ease of control of storage methods, degrees of aggregation, cube partitioning, and usage-based optimization are features that make this product a serious data warehousing tool. Microsoft's Decision Support Services will open data warehousing to a large audience of business users and application developers alike. The expense and complexity of undertaking a data warehouse or data mart solution will be significantly reduced, and third-party tools developed for the DSS Analysis Server will provide rich user interfaces to plug in. Microsoft DSS, through the Pivot Table Service, will facilitate data mart publishing via Web sites for quick and easy access by people who need the data. Just remember that even with the great features of these products, you must address significant business and architectural considerations in a data warehouse. You should fully understand dimensional database concepts and the full data warehousing environment before proceeding to implement a data warehouse solution.

Data Transformation Services

by Sharon Bjeletich

IN THIS CHAPTER

Building a Data Warehouse with SQL Server 7.0

The demand for data warehousing has increased recently, as well-established transactional systems can now provide the amount of historical data required to support this technology, and as management starts to understand and appreciate the different levels of business intelligence that database systems can support.

A data warehouse built in SQL Server 7.0 would be by definition a ROLAP (Relational Online Analytical Processing) architecture and might use star and snowflake schemas.

You must perform a great deal of analysis and gather business requirements to ensure that a data warehouse design will be both flexible and scalable and will meet the users' needs. Figure 35.1 shows a simple star schema design based on the Pubs database delivered with SQL Server 7.0 that will be used for the examples in this chapter. Star schemas and other data warehousing terms and concepts are explained more in depth in Chapter 34, "Using the OLAP Server."

FIGURE 35.1

A simple star schema based on the Pubs database.

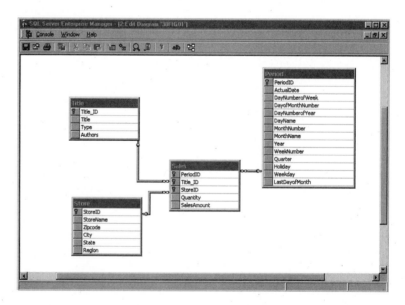

Once you've developed a warehouse design, the hard work of transforming and migrating data begins. Data may come from many places (mainframes, spreadsheets, and so on), and this data must be cleaned up, merged with other data, and transformed to allow insertion into the data warehouse tables. This process can be extremely tedious and time-consuming. In the past, developers used a number of different tools to transform the data and then used either the bulk copy program (bcp) or the SQL Transfer Manager to migrate the data into the database. The new Data Transformation Services consist of three components: the DTS Wizard and DTS Designer, which are both accessed through the Enterprise Manager and let you create these transformation and migration tasks into "packages," and a DTS COM programming interface that you can use within other programming languages to create custom applications. DTS also supports saving transformations for replication.

Running the DTS Wizard

The DTS Wizard is a simple interface to generate DTS packages. However, it is quite powerful and provides an easy but sophisticated way to move data from any OLE-DB, ODBC, or text source to another OLE-DB, ODBC, or text source. You can then transform this data using the tools provided by the wizard or, for more complex transformations, using an ActiveX script written in VBScript or JScript within the wizard. You can also move database schema, but the transfer of all other database objects (indexes, constraints, users, permissions, stored procedures, and so on) is only supported between SQL Server 7.0 servers. This means that DTS does not support transferring database objects between a SQL Server 6.5 and another 6.5 or 7.0 server. Use of the Upgrade Wizard is recommended for this function.

The DTS Wizard (whether an Export or Import is selected) takes the user through four basic steps. The first step is to select the data source; the second is to select the destination. The third step lets you select the migration and transformation type. The options are to copy data with or without the schema, to move data based on a query, or to transfer objects and data between SQL 7.0 servers. The fourth step is where the transformation is determined, and the fifth step is to save, schedule, and replicate the package.

The DTS Wizard provides all of the functionality needed to copy the period data from an Excel spreadsheet to a table in a data warehouse. After you select the source Excel file and define a period table as the destination, you must further specify the transformation because the default transformation does not select the optimal datatypes. Also, the columns that must be converted to bit columns from the numbers in the Excel spreadsheet will not convert automatically. The datatypes are easily changed in the Column Mappings and Transformations dialog (accessed by clicking the ellipsis under the Transform column in the third wizard step). However, you use a scripting language to write the numeric-to-bit conversions. Figure 35.2 shows an example of an ActiveX script written in VBScript to convert these types.

FIGURE 35.2

Sample ActiveX transformation script.

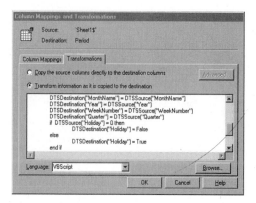

When opened in the DTS Designer window, the package appears as shown in Figure 35.3.

FIGURE 35.3

Period table DTS Package.

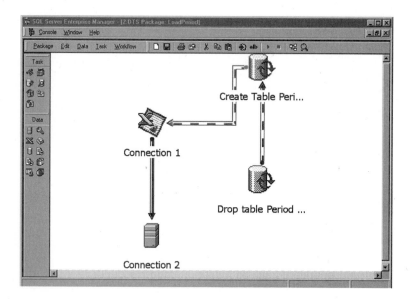

To populate the Title dimension table shown as part of the star schema example described in this chapter, you also need an ActiveX script. The Title dimension table has only one line for all of the authors per Title, but the Pubs database provides for *n* number of authors for a specific title. This means that populating the dimension table requires that you flatten the author rows and concatenate them into one Authors column. This is easy to do with the DTS Wizard and the ActiveX scripting capabilities. Figure 35.4

shows a sample query to retrieve all the Titles that are not currently in the dimension table (allowing these rows to be appended on a scheduled basis).

FIGURE 35.4

Query to retrieve new rows for the Title dimension table.

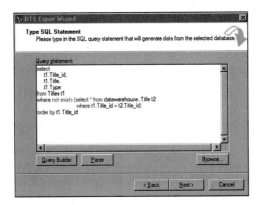

The next step is to transform the author names into one string. The following ActiveX script (in VBScript) uses ADO to query the database in the transformation and then uses the resultset to create the new author list:

```
' Concatenate each title's author into one Authors string

Function Main()

dim strAuthorName

    DTSDestination("title_id") = DTSSource("title_id")
    DTSDestination("title") = DTSSource("title")
    DTSDestination("type") = DTSSource("type")
        DTSGlobalVariables("adoConnection").Value =
        ➥CreateObject("ADODB.Recordset")

    DTSGlobalVariables("adoConnection").Value.Open
    ➥"select rtrim(a.au_fname) + ' ' +
    ➥rtrim(a.au_lname) as AuthorName from authors a join
    ➥titleauthor ta on a.au_id=ta.au_id where
    ➥ta.title_id = '" & DTSSource("title_id") &
    ➥"' order by a.au_lname", "DRIVER={SQL
    ➥Server};Server=.;UID=sa;PWD=;Database=pubs"

    if not DTSGlobalVariables("adoConnection").Value.EOF then
        DTSGlobalVariables("adoConnection").Value.MoveFirst
    end if

    do while not DTSGlobalVariables("adoConnection").Value.EOF

        if strAuthorname = "" then
```

```
            strAuthorname = DTSGlobalVariables
        ➥("adoConnection").Value.Fields("AuthorName")
        else
            strAuthorName = strAuthorName & ", " & DTSGlobalVariables
        ➥("adoConnection").Value.Fields("AuthorName")
        end if
        DTSGlobalVariables("adoConnection").Value.MoveNext
    loop

        DTSGlobalVariables("adoConnection").Value = nothing

    if strAuthorname = "" then strAuthorname = "Unknown Author"
    DTSDestination("Authors") =strAuthorname

    Main = DTSTransformStat_OK
End Function
```

CAUTION

Beware of the new `concat_null_yields_null` session option. When this is set on, a null string concatenated to a non-null string renders the entire string as null. The default for this setting is off.

The results of this transformation are displayed in Figure 35.5.

FIGURE 35.5

Results of the Title dimension transformation.

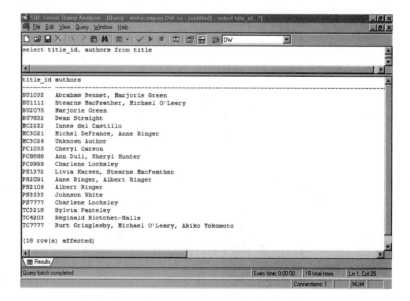

If the DTS package has been saved to SQL Server, it is stored in the sysdtspackages table in the msdb database in binary form, making it difficult to edit directly. However, you can edit it in the DTS Designer. When the Title transformation is opened in Enterprise Manager, you can edit the transformation task by double-clicking the mappings. You can then modify the ActiveX script.

Defining DTS Packages

DTS packages are groups of tasks that performed together in a specific order, result in one or more data transformations and migrations. These packages have versioning and can be encrypted. A package consists of tasks (actions), steps (workflow), and connections (data sources). You can save a DTS package as a COM-structured file, in SQL Server, or in the Microsoft Repository. COM file storage allows for easy usage by multiple users or systems. DTS packages stored in SQL Server are stored as image data, and many packages can quickly bloat the msdb database, impacting performance, maintenance, and backups. Packages saved in the Microsoft Repository (in the msdb database in SQL Server) become part of the metadata, supporting and enhancing an organization's infrastructure. Saving to the Repository also lets you audit all data transformations, including the user information and the date and any errors in package execution. This auditing, referred to as *data lineage*, provides a powerful tool for monitoring the data warehouse loads. The Repository provides the most versatile long-term method of storing DTS packages.

SQL Server 7.0 provides the DTS Designer (run from the Enterprise Manager) to graphically create DTS packages.

Tasks

Tasks are the actions to be taken to accomplish the desired data transformation and migration. A task can execute any SQL statement, send mail, bulk insert data, execute an ActiveX script, or launch an external program.

Steps

Steps are the workflow wrappers for the tasks and are the means for the flow of control. A task step can run alone, parallel to another task step, or sequentially, according to *precedence constraints*. There are three precedence constraints:

- Unconditional. (It does not matter whether the preceding step failed or succeeded.)
- On success. (The preceding step must have been successful for the execution of the next step.)
- On failure.

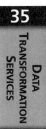

A task without an associated step will not execute. The DTS Designer creates a step for the task by default. However, if you write an external program using the DTS COM interface, you can easily miss the step, and the task will not run.

Workflows have a number of advanced features. You can add a step to a transaction, commit or roll back a transaction at this step on success or failure, close the connection on completion of this step (saving resources), use an ActiveX script for the step execution, or expose the resultset as a data source object (DSO) rowset provider. The last option lets you use the result at this step in another package, either with the OPENROWSET statement or by setting up the package as a linked server. However, once you set this option, the step does not complete, so use it only for a package that is intended to be queried from external sources.

The Data Pump

The DTS data pump is an OLE DB service provider, and a task is an instance of this in-process COM server. It can be considered the workhorse of DTS. The basic collections in a data pump object are the connections, columns (both destination and source), the transformations, and the lookups. The data pump task has only one method, the Execute method. Properties include the ability to set identity inserts, as well as the FastLoad property, which uses non-logged fast bulk copy.

The data pump's main goal is to move and transform data from one source to another. To populate the Sales fact table shown in Figure 35.1, you can use the DTS Designer to create a simple transformation using the Data Pump. In the Designer, you create two connection objects, select them both, and choose Add Transform from the Workflow menu. Figure 35.6 shows the query that you can use as the data source.

FIGURE 35.6

Data source query for Sales fact table.

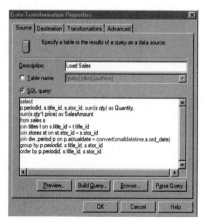

If you add an Execute SQL task from the Task toolbar, you can create a subsequent step to update the statistics on the Sales table on the success of the Load Sales Transform task. Figure 35.7 shows the completed package.

FIGURE 35.7

Package to load the Sales fact table and update statistics.

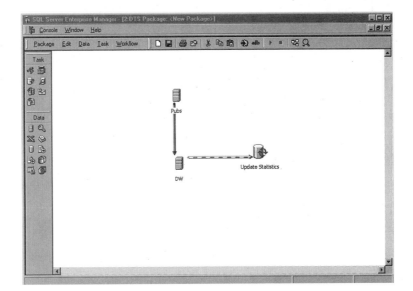

Data-Driven Queries

In real life, loading data warehouse tables tends to be more complex than selecting data, transforming it, and then inserting it into the tables. Data-driven queries provide more flexibility than the Transform task but are row-based, whereas an insert-based data pump task is implemented as one insert statement or as a bulk copy. A data-driven query loops through a resultset, taking actions as determined by conditions defined in an ActiveX script.

Data-driven queries (DDQ) can have up to four queries defined. These are defined as one insert query, one delete query, one update query, and a user-defined query. One query is executed per row in the resultset, depending on the ActiveX script associated with the DDQ.

35

DATA TRANSFORMATION SERVICES

> **NOTE**
>
> Although the queries are named insert, update, delete, and user, queries of these types are not required. You can use any SQL statement. It is preferable to perform inserts with the insert query, but you could actually have three user-defined queries called from the ActiveX script as update, delete, or user queries.

When you need more complex business logic to transform data, a DDQ is also a good candidate. In addition to the four queries that can be executed from the ActiveX script, you can write the row to an error log, skip the row in the insert, or abort the whole task. The action taken for the row by the data pump is determined by the DTSTransform_Stat constant.

You can populate the Store dimension table for the data warehouse in Figure 35.1 with a DDQ. The table in the transactional data does not have region data, but it is required for the data warehouse dimension table. You can find this data using the DTSLookups option. The Store dimension package must be run every night and must delete an existing row for a store, replacing it with the new data. The DDQ looks similar to the Transform task. The source query is shown in Figure 35.8.

FIGURE 35.8

DDQ to load the Store dimension table.

You must create two lookups to support this transformation task: a lookup of the correct region name for a store and a lookup to determine whether a row already exists for a store. You create these lookups in the Options tab. Figure 35.9 shows a parameterized query used for the Region lookup.

FIGURE 35.9

Region lookup query.

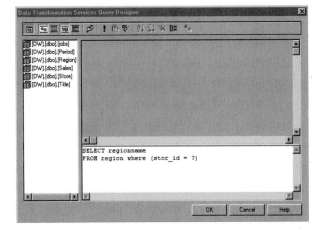

This transformation will use only the insert and delete DDQ queries. Figure 35.10 shows the insert query with the parameter mapping.

FIGURE 35.10

Parameterized DDQ insert query.

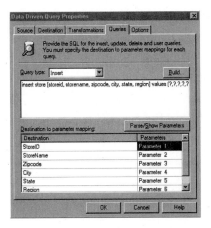

The Transformation tab shows column mapping for convenience only; an ActiveX script is required for a DDQ. You must convert one of the mappings to a script, passing back the desired DTSTransform_Stat for each condition. In the Store DDQ, any row that already exists is deleted; otherwise, the row is inserted. You can use the following VBScript to accomplish this.

```
Function Main()
    if  DTSLookups("StoreLookup").Execute(DTSSource("stor_id"))
    ➡<> "" then
        Main = DTSTransformStat_DeleteQuery
```

```
    else
        DTSDestination("StoreID") =DTSSource("Stor_id")
        DTSDestination("Storename") =DTSSource("Stor_name")
        DTSDestination("Zipcode") =DTSSource("zip")
        DTSDestination("city") =DTSSource("city")
        DTSDestination("State") =DTSSource("State")
        DTSDestination("Region") = DTSLookups("RegionLookup").Execute
        ➥(DTSSource("stor_id"))
        Main = DTSTransformStat_InsertQuery
    end if
End Function
```

Metadata

Metadata is defined as "data about data," and the Microsoft Repository contains the metadata for the server database objects, including packages. You can use the Metadata view in the DTS section of the Enterprise Manager to view database schema and to view the versioning and data lineage of a DTS package. Data lineage determines the source of a piece of data, and you can use DTS packages stored in the Repository to perform this auditing. You can then use the Metadata view to browse the lineage for a package execution, which will show the system name, account name, and date for every execution of a package that has lineage enabled. You enable data lineage in the Advanced options of the Package Properties page. Figure 35.11 shows this property page for the Load Sales package.

FIGURE 35.11

Load Sales package advanced option settings.

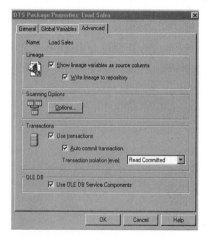

Setting the option to show the lineage variables as source columns will add the DSTLineage_Full and DTSLineage_Short global variables to the DTS package, which can then be mapped to columns that have been added to the destination table. These columns will be populated with the data lineage data whenever the package is run. Figure 35.12 shows the column mappings for the Sales package after two lineage columns (one an integer, the other a unique identifier) have been added to the table.

FIGURE 35.12

Sales package data lineage mapping.

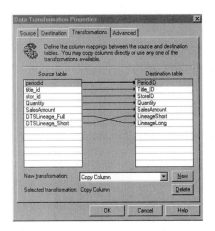

Once you run the package, the lineage columns are populated, and you can use them for data auditing. Browsing the package data in the Metadata view will then show the execution information. Figure 35.13 shows an example of the lineage browse for a package execution.

You can also use the Metadata view to determine the lineage for a lineage column. Entering either the long or short lineage number from a column in the Repository Lineage Lookup section of the Metadata view (shown in Figure 35.14) will return the package metadata (version number, creator, name, and versioning, as well as the system name, account name, and execution time of the package execution that inserted the data).

Summary

The Data Transformation Services add many powerful and versatile (and much needed and welcome) new features to SQL Server. The Metadata and Repository tools will require some careful thought and planning to integrate into existing data warehouses and will provide the foundation for robust ROLAP systems in development. The transformation and migration services will vastly simplify the onerous tasks associated with supporting and populating data warehouses.

35

DATA TRANSFORMATION SERVICES

FIGURE 35.13

Sales package execution lineage.

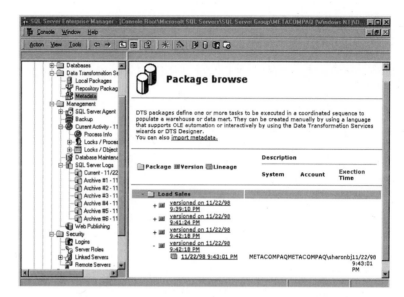

FIGURE 35.14

Repository lineage lookup.

CHAPTER 36

Serving SQL Server Data on the Internet/Intranet

by Greg Mable

IN THIS CHAPTER

In this chapter, you will learn how to serve SQL Server data on the Internet and intranets. You will also learn how to configure SQL Server and SQL Server clients to connect via the Internet. SQL Server 7.0 provides you with a set of tools that you can use to automatically generate Web pages based on data from a table, SQL query, or stored procedure. The SQL Server Web Assistant is a wizard that can guide you through this process. It has been enhanced for SQL Server 7.0 and now supports multiple queries in a single Web page. SQL Server 7.0 also provides support for the replication of data over the Internet using anonymous subscriptions. See Chapter 20, "Replication," for a full discussion on replicating SQL Server data onto the Internet and intranets. The Microsoft Windows TCP/IP Sockets Net-Library has been improved so that it can now work in conjunction with the Microsoft Proxy Server to ensure secure communication over the Internet. This allows a client on the Internet/intranet to connect securely to SQL Server using the MS Proxy Server.

What You Should Know About Client Licensing

Before configuring SQL Server for use in a Web site, you should be aware of the license that you might need to purchase. Keep in mind the distinction between serving the data on the Internet as opposed to an intranet. There is also a distinction between serving SQL Server data in a dynamic Web page versus a static one.

Let's start with the latter distinction. Static Web pages, such as those created with the Web Assistant, do not require users to purchase any special type of license. Even if you schedule the Web page to be updated every hour on the hour using the Web Wizard, it is still a static Web page. The Web page is created before the user accesses it; therefore, it is static. It also does not matter whether the user is on an intranet or the Internet. No special type of licensing is required in this situation.

A dynamic Web page, that is, a Web page created when a user accesses it, does require the user to have a license for SQL Server. For example, a user may open a Web page that dynamically displays a list of recently published books. When the user accesses the page, an application executes, queries SQL Server for a list of recently published books, formats the results, and returns the Web page to the user. This is considered a dynamic page; the page is created when the user accesses it.

This brings us to the next distinction: Internet users versus intranet users. What distinguishes an intranet user from an Internet user? Is it simply a user who connects to a corporate WAN as opposed to the public Internet? Actually, the distinction regards the relationship the user has with your company. An Internet user is any user who connects to the Internet and accesses a dynamic Web page built from SQL Server data but is not employed by your company (or serves in some other role, such as a contractor or vendor).

On the other hand, intranet users are treated like any other SQL Server client; each workstation that accesses a dynamic Web page will need a separate client license. They are treated as though they are connecting to SQL Server directly even though they are accessing a dynamic Web page built by another application and they never really query SQL Server directly. Essentially, then, intranet users are no different from LAN clients.

For Internet users, you can purchase a license that would allow you to serve SQL Server data to an unlimited number of users who access the server from the Internet (and not an intranet).

The SQL Server Internet Connector is a license (and not a methodology or API) that grants you this right. It is required for anyone connecting a Microsoft Internet Information Server or any equivalent third-party Web server to Microsoft SQL Server. It is purchased independent of SQL Server and SQL Server Client Access Licenses and allows an unlimited number of Internet connections to a single SQL Server on a per-processor basis. If the SQL Server is running on a four processor machine, then you need four separate Internet Connector licenses.

Connecting SQL Server to an Intranet or the Internet

You can connect to SQL Server from the Internet using a client application or from one of the built-in tools such as the Query Analyzer. First, you must connect the client and server to the Internet using the TCP/IP or Multiprotocol Net-Libraries. If you use the Multiprotocol Net-Library, you must enable TCP/IP support. For additional security, you can connect to SQL Server through the Microsoft Proxy Server. Microsoft Proxy Server is part of the Windows NT 4.0 option pack and provides secured access to a Windows NT network. By configuring clients to connect to SQL Server through the Proxy Server, you can guard against unauthorized access to SQL Server data and your network. Because Microsoft Proxy Server is integrated with Microsoft Windows NT Server user authentication, you can control access to SQL Server using the built-in Windows NT Security.

You can also configure clients to connect to SQL Server using TCP/IP via a third-party firewall. A firewall is a system that isolates and secures the network from the Internet. To use a firewall, you must configure SQL Server to use TCP/IP as its network protocol and specify a port number for its incoming connections. The firewall system will then forward connections from clients who access this port number to SQL Server.

For additional security, you can also encrypt the data sent over the network between SQL Server and its clients using the Multiprotocol Net-Library. This adds some overhead to SQL Server processing, but the added security may prove worth the slight penalty in performance. You must configure both the client and server to use the Multiprotocol Net-Library.

Using the Web Assistant Wizard

One of the many wizards included with SQL Server 7.0 is the Web Assistant. This wizard allows you to generate an HTML file automatically. You can base your Web page on the contents of a table or the results of a stored procedure. You can generate a Web page automatically whenever the data in the table changes, or you can set a schedule for its refresh interval. When you complete the Web Assistant, it creates a job in the SQL Server Agent. From Enterprise Manager, you can view the job's schedule and associated options.

You can start the Web Assistant by selecting the Wizards option from Enterprise Manager and then selecting Web Assistant from the list of wizards. Keep in mind that any tables or stored procedures that you plan to use must already be created before you run the Web Assistant. The first option that you select is the database; for this example, you can choose pubs.

The next option is to specify a name for the job, as shown in Figure 36.1.

FIGURE 36.1

Specify a job name.

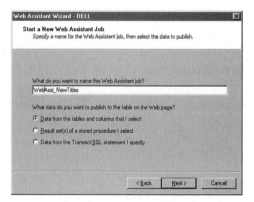

This will be the name of the job that is displayed in the SQL Server Agent. By default, the wizard suggests a name beginning with the name of the database followed by the words Web Page. You might want to refer to Appendix C, "Defining System

Serving SQL Server Data on the Internet/Intranet

CHAPTER 36

829

36

SERVING SQL
SERVER DATA ON
THE INTERNET

Administration and Naming Standards," for suggestions on naming standards. For this example, you can enter WebAsst_NewTitles. You then select the source of the data that you want to publish as a Web page: a table, stored procedure, or SQL query. For this example, select the titles table as the data source, as shown in Figure 36.2. You will create a Web page that will be updated every time a new title appears in the database. This is a type of Web page that often appears on a What's New section of a Web site.

FIGURE 36.2

Specify table and fields.

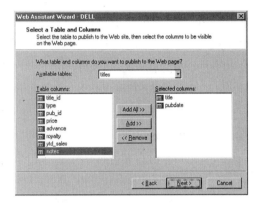

Next, you can choose to display all the rows in the table or a subset of them by specifying a set of criteria. In this example, you can enter the criteria as shown in Figure 36.3. This will display all titles published since the beginning of the year. Later, once you complete the wizard, you can easily change the criteria.

FIGURE 36.3

Specify selection criteria.

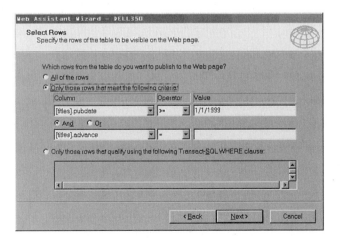

In the next dialog, you specify how often the data should be published. You can schedule the job to run at regular intervals, on demand, as a one-time event, or as in this example, when the data changes as shown in Figure 36.4. Be careful when using this setting, however. If the data changes quite rapidly, SQL Server might unnecessarily generate new Web pages and slow its other processing down.

FIGURE 36.4

Specify a schedule for publication.

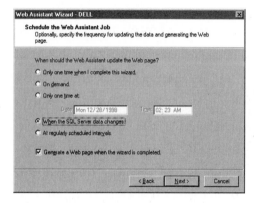

Because you specified that the Web page should be published when the data changes, you specify which table should be monitored for changes. For this example, enter the same table as you specified for the source of data, the titles table, as shown in Figure 36.5. Specify title_id for the column because title_id is a required field.

FIGURE 36.5

Specify a table to monitor.

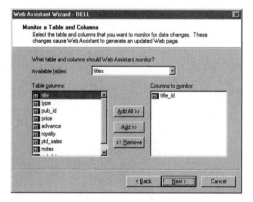

The next step in the Web Assistant is to specify the directory in which to publish the Web page as shown in Figure 36.6. You want to specify a directory that is accessible by the SQL Server account. If you configured SQL Server to run under the local system account, then you need to specify a directory that is local to SQL Server. If you configured SQL Server to run under another account, make sure you specify a directory to which that account has write access. For those cases when you will interact with Internet Information Server, you will specify one of the virtual directories. The default is to publish the page in the HTML subdirectory of the base directory where SQL Server is installed. For this example, specify the IISSamples virtual directory if you have the Internet Information Server installed on the same computer as SQL Server.

FIGURE 36.6

Specify a directory in which to publish.

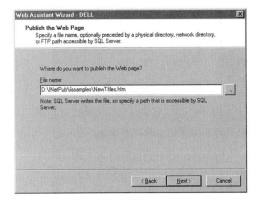

The Web Assistant prompts you to format the Web page using some basic options. You can specify the character set used to display the Web page. This enables you to generate Web pages in any foreign language character set that SQL Server supports. You can also specify a template to use for the page, or you can let the Web Assistant guide you through this process. Templates are HTML files that you can create, which contain placeholders, such as `<%insert_data_here%>`, where you want the query results to be displayed. Templates require a knowledge of how to create HTML files and an understanding of HTML. For this example, let the Web Assistant guide you as shown in Figure 36.7.

FIGURE 36.7

Specify formatting options.

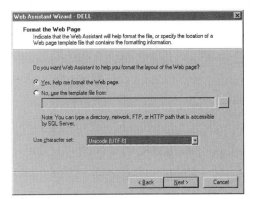

As shown in Figure 36.8, you can specify a title for the Web page and a title and font for the query results table.

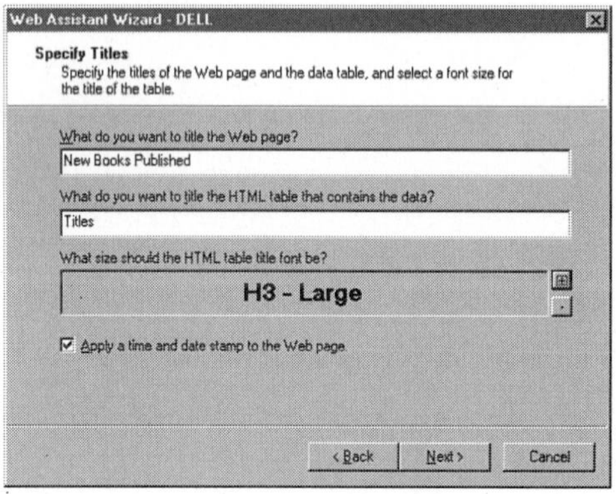

FIGURE 36.8

Specify a title for the Web page and title and font for the table.

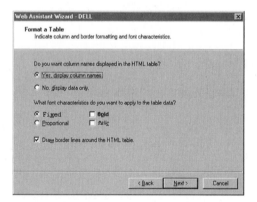

As shown in Figure 36.9, you can specify the format for the query results table.

FIGURE 36.9

Specify a table format.

The next step is to specify any hyperlinks that you want to include on the Web page. Perhaps you want to include a link to your home page (see Figure 36.10). The source of these hyperlinks can be another SQL Server table.

FIGURE 36.10

*Specify
hyperlinks.*

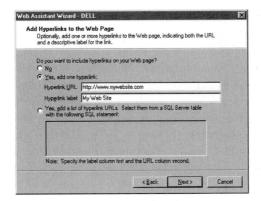

Next, you can specify whether you want to limit the number of rows returned or the number of rows displayed per page, as shown in Figure 36.11. This is useful when you want to ensure that the server does not return more data than you expect or for those occasions when you want to spread the data over several pages instead of a single page. For large resultsets, spreading the data over several pages helps speed up response time.

FIGURE 36.11

Specify row limits.

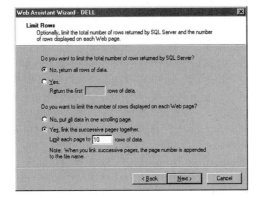

The last step is to review the description of the task that will be created by the Web Assistant and optionally generate a SQL script for the query used to output the data, as shown in Figure 36.12.

FIGURE 36.12

Review your
selections.

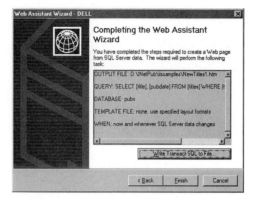

When you click the Finish button, a job is created under the Web Assistant in Enterprise Manager, as shown in Figure 36.13. You can edit the job created by the Web Assistant using Enterprise Manager by right-clicking the job in the Web Assistant and then selecting Properties. You see a dialog from which you can change the output filename or the schedule.

FIGURE 36.13

A job created by
the Web Assistant
Wizard.

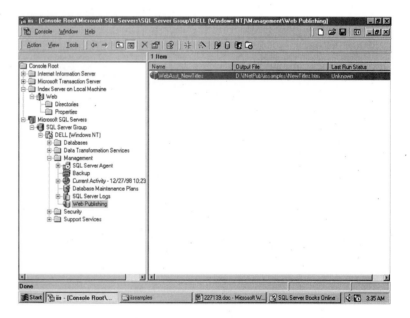

You can test your newly created job by adding a title to the titles table in the pubs database. This will initiate the job and generate a Web page, as shown in Figure 36.14.

FIGURE 36.14

*A Web page gen-
erated by the Web
Assistant Wizard.*

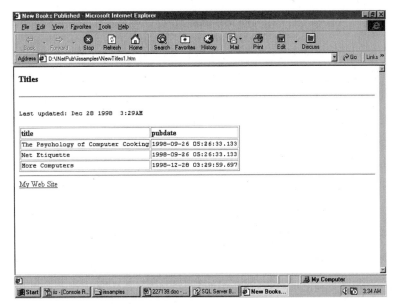

Summary

You can configure Microsoft SQL Server 7.0 and the data clients to access the server
over the Internet. You can configure the server for extra security by implementing the
Microsoft Proxy Server or a third-party firewall. You can add even more security by
encrypting the data as well. SQL Server also provides the Web Assistant Wizard, which
allows you to easily publish SQL Server data on an intranet or the Internet. Be aware that
you might need to purchase a special license, referred to as the Internet Connector, when
serving data from SQL Server using the Information Internet Server or another third-
party server.

Appendixes

PART
VIII

Technical Specifications

APPENDIX A

SQL Server 7.0 was designed to support more effectively both the small- and medium-sized organizations that have been its main customer, but also the larger enterprise organizations. The following tables list the specifications that have changed in SQL Server 7.0.

File Objects

	SQL Server 6.5	*SQL Server 7.0*
Filegroups per database	N/A	256
Files per database	32	32,767
File size (data)	32GB	32TB
File size (log)	32GB	4TB

Database Objects

	SQL Server 6.5	*SQL Server 7.0*
Database size	1TB	1,048,516TB
Bytes per row	1,962	8,060
Columns per base table	250	1,024
Tables per database	2 billion	Limited by number of objects in a database
Bytes per short string column	255	8,000
Identifier length (in characters)	30	128
References per table	31	63
Foreign key table references per table	16	253
Triggers per table	3	Limited by number of objects in a database

Indexes

	SQL Server 6.5	SQL Server 7.0
Unique indexes or constraints per table	249	249 nonclustered and 1 clustered

Transact-SQL

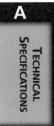

	SQL Server 6.5	SQL Server 7.0
Batch size	128KB	65,536
Tables per select statement	16	256
Columns per insert statement	250	1,024
Columns in GROUP BY, ORDER BY	16	Limited only by number of bytes
SQL string length (batch size)	128KB	128 * TDS packet size

Stored Procedures

	SQL Server 6.5	SQL Server 7.0
Bytes in source text of a stored procedure	65,025	Lesser of batch size or 250MB
Parameters per stored procedure	255	1,024

Configuration

	SQL Server 6.5	*SQL Server 7.0*
Locks per server	2,147,483,647	2,147,483,647 (static) 40% of SQL Server memory (dynamic)
Nested stored procedure levels	16	32
Nested subqueries	16	32
Nested trigger levels	16	32

Troubleshooting

This appendix outlines some of the more common questions you might have when installing and running SQL Server 7.0.

Installation Issues

Q What version of SQL Server 7.0 can I run on Windows 95, Windows 98, or NT Workstation?

A Only the SQL Server 7.0 Desktop Edition can be installed on a Windows 95, Windows 98, or NT Workstation platform. The SQL Server 7.0 Standard Edition runs only on NT Server or NT Enterprise Edition and supports up to four processors. The SQL Server 7.0 Enterprise Edition will run only on NT Enterprise Edition and supports more than four processors, as well as more than 2GB of RAM.

Q Why can't I install named pipes on my Windows 95 or Windows 98 machine?

A SQL Server 7.0 does not support named pipes on a Desktop Edition server on a Windows 95 or Windows 98 machine. You can use named pipes as a client network library to access another server running on Windows NT, however.

Q I am unable to completely uninstall SQL Server 6.5 before installing SQL Server 7.0.

A After deleting all the SQL Server-specific directories, remove all SQL Server-specific entries from the following Registry areas:

```
HKEY_LOCAL_MACHINE\SYSTEM\CurrentControlSet\Services
HKEY_LOCAL_MACHINE\SOFTWARE\Microsoft
```

Q I am unable to install the SQL Server 7.0 server on my Windows 95 or Windows 98 machine. I am receiving exception violations.

A There are a number of areas to check for a Windows 95 or Windows 98 installation that aborts abnormally:

- There have been some problems with installation when the wrong version of the MSVCRT.DLL is on the Windows machine. Replace this DLL with the latest version.

- Ensure that networking is installed and running on the Windows machine.

- There have been some problems with antivirus packages installed on Windows machines interfering with a SQL Server 7.0 installation. Temporarily remove the antivirus software.

Q My installation is aborting with a message indicating that it cannot continue because ODBC is running.

A Reboot your machine and then ensure that you have stopped all services that may be using ODBC, as well as any processes that are currently running (for example, SQL Manager).

Q I have not been able to successfully use the Upgrade Wizard to upgrade my SQL Server 6.5 server to SQL Server 7.0.

A One option to try is to determine whether the SQL Server 6.5 server has a server name registered internally. When a SQL Server 6.5 installation does not create the msdb database, the server name can be missing. Use the sp_addserver system stored procedure to add the server name to the SQL Server 6.5 installation, and then rerun the Upgrade Wizard.

Q I am having trouble connecting with ADO to my new SQL Server 7.0 server.

A There are new ODBC drivers and files delivered on the SQL Server 7.0 CD that you might need on your system to support ADO. You can install them from the SQL Server setup program by selecting a custom installation and then selecting only Client Connectivity.

Operational Issues

B

TROUBLESHOOTING

Q Why can't I see the master or model databases in the SQL Server 7.0 Enterprise Manager?

A In SQL Server 7.0, an attempt was made to prohibit the direct manipulation of the system tables and objects. You can right-click the server name, select Edit SQL Server Registration Properties, and then select the Show System Databases and Objects check box to display these databases.

Q I keep receiving an Error analyzing workload(60) error when running the Query Analyzer Index Tuning Wizard.

A Check that there are no spaces in the database name. This can also cause unexpected problems in other tools.

Q I receive an error indicating that the license for the source and destination connections does not permit the use of DTS to transform data.

A A Standard or Enterprise installation of SQL Server 7.0 that is licensed per server will not allow cross-server operations in some situations. Change the licensing option to per seat, after talking to Microsoft about your licensing agreement.

Q I have code in a stored procedure that concatenates two strings together that worked in SQL Server 6.5 but returns unexpected results in SQL Server 7.0.

A Check that the `concat null yields null` db option has not been set. If this option is set to `True`, the concatenation of strings that include at least one string which evaluates to null will cause the entire concatenation to evaluate to null.

Q Some of my queries seem to move more slowly under SQL Server 7.0 than they did under SQL Server 6.5.

A SQL Server 7.0 creates and caches an execution plan for all queries, not only stored procedures. Although Microsoft indicates that the algorithm for searching the cache for an existing execution plan for a query is optimized, there is still a small overhead for looking for an execution plan, as well as creating a new plan for new queries. (This is similar to the "prepare temporary stored procedures" function used previously by ODBC.) This extra delay might be felt more in organizations with transactional systems that require subsecond performance for queries. In general, queries should run faster under SQL Server 7.0 because of the new join strategies and other enhancements.

Q I am having problems running update queries on a SQL Server 7.0 machine that ran fine on a SQL Server 6.5 machine.

A SQL Server 7.0 does not allow the use of aliases for a column name used in the `set` clause of an update statement. This is quite common when updates to a column in one table are made from a column in another table. Setting the database compatibility setting to `65` with the `sp_dbcmptlevel` system stored procedure will allow the previous behavior that you expect.

Q In the past, I have changed the machine name of the server running SQL Server 6.5 to swap between a hot backup and the production machine. This doesn't work in SQL Server 7.0.

A You cannot change the machine name for a server running SQL Server 7.0. You must uninstall and reinstall SQL Server 7.0.

Q Some of my queries that were expecting a single space for an empty string are no longer working under SQL Server 6.0.

A SQL Server 7.0 returns an empty string as an empty string under the 7.0 compatibility setting.

Q I am getting unexpected results in null comparisons, even though the `ANSI_NULLS` setting is set to `off`.

A In SQL Server 6.5, the `ANSI_NULLS` option is resolved during execution time. In SQL Server 7.0, the option is resolved at the time of the creation of the object. This means that the setting might not be obvious for the execution of a specific object. Developers should take a clear approach to ensuring that the setting is in a known state for object creation.

Q Some of my aggregation queries no longer return results in a sorted order.

A Because of the way that queries which used the group by clause were processed in SQL Server 6.5, the results were returned in sorted order, leading many developers to assume that the order by clause was not required. The ANSI standard does require an order by clause for any ordered resultset, and because SQL Server 7.0 processes these queries in a different manner (including the use of parallelism on some machines), the order cannot be guaranteed. You should always use the order by clause with any request for an ordered resultset.

Q I have a number of stored procedures used as replacements for system stored procedures (for example, a customized sp_who stored procedure). These procedures were created in my production databases in SQL Server 6.5; however, they no longer work in SQL Server 7.0.

A The master database is now searched first for stored procedures that begin with sp_ identifier.

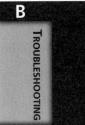

B

TROUBLESHOOTING

Defining System Administration and Naming Standards

by Sharon Bjeletich

IN THIS APPENDIX

This appendix covers two configuration control areas critical for the success of an organization implementing Microsoft SQL Server: the management and maintenance of SQL Server environment standards for the different phases of the software development life cycle and the naming standards used in these environments.

The SQL Server Environment Approach

It is important to attempt to maintain a separate SQL Server environment for each phase in the development, quality control, implementation, and maintenance of a SQL Server installation.

Depending on the organization's resources, the number of different environments may differ, but there should be at least a development environment, a quality control or test environment, and a production environment with clear boundaries between each. An organization may choose to add stress testing, user-acceptance, pre-production, and other environments, which may be considered subsets of a test environment, but this appendix focuses on the development, test, and production environments. Each environment should be on a separate SQL Server.

The Development Environment

A development environment is by definition volatile and should be flexible enough to allow developers to modify database objects and data as needed, as well as start and stop the server as needed. For this reason, the development environment should be on a dedicated SQL Server. Some organizations use a separate database on a production server for a development environment. This is not recommended because the SQL Server engine and the catalog objects that support it (such as master and tempdb) are used in both environments. This basically means that when development is done on the server, the entire server has been demoted to a development server, even though production usage continues.

This section covers three possible scenarios for the development environment:

- Shared database/shared objects and data
- Individual database/individual objects and data
- Shared database/individual objects and data

Shared Database/Shared Objects and Data

In this approach, all developers share the same objects and data. This works well in small development teams with good communication channels and on maintenance projects.

Advantages:

- As all objects are shared, changes are immediately available to all developers, avoiding the difficult process of merging definitions.
- This approach is simple to manage because there are fewer objects and databases to maintain.
- There are reduced storage requirements for only one database and one copy of objects and data.

Disadvantages:

- The natural volatility of the development process causes contention for data, and it can quickly become unfeasible if developers must wait on each other to change data.
- The same can be true of contention for database objects, although this should be less of a problem because architectural changes are normally modeled and are part of a much larger process of impact analysis and change control.

Individual Database/Individual Objects and Data

In the individual database/individual objects and data environment, each developer is assigned a separate database, for which she is the database owner, and has complete control over the database structures and data, which she can change at will. These databases may be on the same SQL Server dedicated to the development environment or on a separate SQL Server. Because SQL Server 7.0 can be installed on a Windows NT workstation, as well as on Windows 95/98, these environments can be completely controlled by the individual developer.

Advantages:

- No developer is dependent on another, and therefore, no contention occurs over data or database structures, providing maximum flexibility.

Disadvantages:

- This approach requires much more space because each developer requires a copy of the database. Some organizations may not be able to support this approach.
- Any changes to the database structures must, at some time, be integrated into the other developer's environments. This task can be time-consuming and generally requires good communication and process control.

C

SYSTEM
ADMINISTRATION
AND NAMING

Shared Database/Individual Objects and Data

In the shared database/individual objects and data environment, developers use the same database but maintain separate objects and data by creating their own objects in the database under their own usernames. The new database roles of db_owner, db_ddladmin, db_datawriter, and db_datareader are applied to the developer username, and any new objects will have the username as object owner.

Because the owner name is not explicitly indicated in the code, it will execute against the developer's object in development and against the production objects in the production environment.

This approach is similar to the individual database/individual objects and data approach but requires less maintenance for the database administrator because there is only one set of databases to administer.

Recommendations

Choosing a development environment depends on the available resources and the particular needs of an organization. Effective communication is essential in all environments, and good process control will help to minimize conflicts.

The Test Environment

The test environment can consist of a number of scenarios, including functional testing, integration testing, user-acceptance testing, performance testing, and pre-production testing.

The Functional Testing Environment

Functional testing ensures that all code functions as expected, and it is usually the first formal quality assurance (QA) test performed by a QA team.

A functional test machine should always be a separate SQL Server from both the development and production machines. It does not need to be configured exactly as the production machine because it is intended to support the test of functionality, not system integration, performance, or user acceptance.

On a test machine, the database administrator as dbo generally creates all objects. Developers should not have any access to this machine, and administrators should run all DDL from a central source control location containing the DDL and installation scripts. Developers need to understand that the DDL for the objects are considered source code and must be under source code control, completely unit tested, and delivered to the QA team. Functional testing tests not only the stored procedures and data in the system, but also the scripts used to install them.

The Performance Testing Environment/Pre-Production Testing Environment

The performance testing and pre-production testing environment should exactly reflect the production environment, including data and logins. Although an organization with limited resources may select to use only a subset of data, this is not recommended because this testing phase is considered the dry run for the final implementation, and all possible problems need to be flushed out at this time. Often, performance issues, blocks, filled transaction logs, and other unanticipated problems may not surface until this point. Although such problems should appear at an earlier point, the performance testing may be the only time that the server environment is exactly the same as the production environment, so in reality, a number of issues tend to arise here.

This server should be built regularly from the production server to ensure that all data and objects are up-to-date. Developers can be given read-only access but should not be able to modify the data or objects in any way.

At this stage, you not only make performance, multiuser, blocking, log space, and other tests, but you also test the installation of all the database objects and data. This is called pre-production testing, and it is the last chance to verify an installation before it is released to production.

The Production Environment

A production environment should be completely separate from the development and test environments, on a separate server, and maintained only by administrators.

> **CAUTION**
>
> There is generally no reason a developer would ever change or have access to a production server as an administrator. Once something is in production, it is under the care and responsibility of the database administrators.

Production servers hold an organization's data and should be regularly maintained and guarded as the valuable assets that they are.

SQL Server Naming Standards

Most professional organizations have a number of standards in place for naming documents, locations, and so on, and the same care should be applied to SQL Server naming standards. These standards should be consistent across the organization because they are an important part of the organizational infrastructure. The use of standards promotes maintainability and can greatly reduce development and support effort and its inherent costs.

The naming standards addressed in this appendix fall into two categories: SQL Server object names and operating system names (files and directories).

Using Indicators

An *indicator* is embedded in the name and is intended to indicate something about that object type. Some organizations require the use of indicators to make an object type apparent to developers (for example, mSaleAmount and vchAddress). Others consider it a waste of space, and a well-named column can indicate enough about the datatype. (A column named CustomerFirstName is obviously a character datatype and one called SaleAmount is a numeric type.) The naming philosophy is something that must be determined by the individual organization and the tools most often used within that organization. How a commonly used tool orders objects may be the deciding factor. If an indicator is used, make it as short and concise as possible.

Using an indicator for the datatype on column and variable names can prevent errors that occur from datatype mismatches, as well as let you avoid constantly referencing a diagram or other document to determine the datatype. Table C.1 lists some common indicators, which normally preface a column or variable name.

TABLE C.1 COMMON DATATYPE INDICATORS

Item	Indicator
Bit	b
Char	ch
Datetime	dt
Decimal	dec
Int	int
Float	f
Money	m
Numeric	num
Tinyint	ti
Varchar	vch

SQL Server Object Names

You should ensure that all names are unambiguous and clearly represent the object. Objects that perform an action (such as stored procedures and triggers) should reflect the type of action. Although names should not be too long, it is best to avoid abbreviation, except for the indicators already discussed. If an abbreviation is required, the most commonly accepted method of abbreviation is to simply remove the vowels. You should avoid using any special characters, including hyphens and underscores for separating words (although there are conflicting views on this). Using capitalization can provide the same separation without the difficulty of the special character. (For example, `ValidateUser` is as clear as `validate_user`.)

> **CAUTION**
>
> Be careful not to use generic nouns for objects names (such as page, time, share, country, and item). Although they are concise and may not be reserved keywords at this time, they may become reserved words in the future.

Column Names

Along with the indicator, the column name should clearly indicate the domain of a column (such as `vchCustomerFirstName` and `vchSupplierFirstname`). It can also be helpful to standardize on a suffix for numeric and character keys. You should use the suffix ID consistently to indicate a numeric key and the suffix code to indicate a character key (as in `SupplierID` and `CountryCode`). You should also choose a standard for the user and date stamp information that many systems require for modifications. (`LastModifiedByUserID`, `LastModifiedByDate`, `ChangedByUserID`, and `ChangedDate` are some examples.)

Stored Procedure Names

A stored procedure name should include a standardized verb to indicate the action performed. You should set a standard for where the verb should fall in the name (a prefix or a suffix). Some suffix examples are `CustomerDataUpdate`, `CustomerDelete`, `CustomerSelect`, and `UserValidate`.

Trigger Names

Triggers names should consist of the table name that the trigger fires against and an abbreviation for the trigger type: `Ins`, `Upd`, or `Del`. Some examples are `CustomerDel`, `CustomerUpd`, and `CustomerIns`.

Index Names

Generally, index names contain only information about the table and the index type, with no information about what columns are included in the index because this can become overly wordy without providing much value. Some examples are `CustomerCU` (clustered unique index on Customer), `CustomerIDX1`, and `CustomerIDX2` (general nonclustered indexes). However, like with all naming standards, there are differing opinions on index naming. The SQL Server 7.0 optimizer now has the capability to use multiple indexes for one query, which means that many administrators will select to create many single-column indexes to support this new feature. In this environment, you might want to support the use of the column name in the index name.

Constraint Names

Primary, foreign, unique, and check constraints should have indicator suffixes. Some examples are `CustomerPK` (primary key), `CustomerFK1`, `CustomerFK2` (foreign keys), `CustomerCK1` (check constraint), and `CustomerUK` or `CustomerAK` (unique constraint indicating a unique or an alternate key).

Operating System Names

You should apply consistency and standards for operating system (OS) names for every SQL Server object, as well as standards for how the scripts for these objects are stored on the source code servers.

Usually, the operating system name should be the same as the object name (unless there is an operating system name size restriction, which would require an abbreviation). Some organizations require that the OS names have extensions that identify the database object (such as `.trg` for trigger scripts, `.vw` for view scripts, and `.tab` for table scripts). SQL Server uses these indicator extensions when it scripts database objects because all of the scripts are generally saved to one directory, requiring a distinguishing extension. If you maintain a standard object directory structure, there is no need for object type filename extensions because the directory name identifies the object type. The most common extension is `.sql`.

Sometimes overlooked in standards creation is the criticality of scripting every database object at its lowest level and storing these scripts in a standard directory structure, under source control. This lets you build servers from scratch from tested common scripts, either in their entirety or in pieces. When a table has become corrupt and must be immediately dropped and recreated during production hours, a tested script that can run without any editing is critical. Creating object scripts at their lowest levels means that there should be an object creation script and an object drop script that create and drop only that object. Therefore, a table would have a create-table script, a drop-table script, and a grant script. Table creation scripts should not have constraints built into them; each constraint should have its own create- and drop-constraint script. In some cases, as with a primary, foreign, or unique constraint, this script would actually be an alter-table-add-constraint and a alter-table-drop-constraint script. You can add or drop a constraint this way without affecting the table and its data.

> **CAUTION**
>
> Do not allow developers to write and edit their database object code on the server itself, using SQL Server Enterprise Manager or the Query Analyzer. This code is not under source control, and these tools are not optimal development editors. Scripts should be created in an editor, kept under source control, and then applied to the server, usually via a batch job of some kind. This ensures the integrity of the code and the server and is simply good programming practice.

Database Object Directory Naming Standards

A central source code server should contain the organization's object scripts, contained in separate object type directories. Figure C.1 suggests a directory hierarchy.

Although this hierarchy might seem overly complex, it allows the most flexibility in a production environment.

Summary

Although you can choose among many schemes, it is well worth the initial effort and time to develop standards. They lower development costs and mistakes and provide an infrastructure and framework for future development.

There are many other areas where you should apply standards that were not covered in this chapter: testing standards, documentation and commenting standards, and application standards. These areas are all critical to a professional information-systems organization and should also be a part of a cohesive approach to database system development and maintenance.

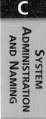

C

SYSTEM
ADMINISTRATION
AND NAMING

Figure C.1

Suggested data-base object directory hierarchy.

```
\servername
   \database
      \create
   \table
      \create
      \drop
      \grants
   \constraints
      \primary
         \create
         \drop
      \foreign
         \create
         \drop
      \unique
         \create
         \drop
   \triggers
      \insert
      \update
      \delete
   \sprocs
      \create
      \drop
      \grants
   \indexes
      \create
      \drop
   \views
      \create
      \drop
      \grants
   \defaults
      \create
      \drop
   \bat
```

Programming Tools and Interfaces

APPENDIX D

This appendix describes the various application programming interfaces (APIs) available with SQL Server. It is intended to give you a brief overview of each API, present the advantages and disadvantages of using one over another, and discuss which of the interfaces play an integral role in Microsoft's future direction.

General Guidelines for Choosing an Interface

As a database administrator, you should know which programming interfaces are available for SQL Server. For example, you might join a team of developers who are working on building a customized program using SQL Server as its back-end database. In this type of environment, you might be asked to assist in deciding which API is best for the type of application being developed. Even if you do not directly write program code using one of the SQL Server APIs, you should know which APIs are available and the advantages and disadvantages of each.

You should also be aware that any third-party product written for SQL Server should have the Windows logo or BackOffice logo. The Windows logo indicates that the products are supported on both Windows NT 4.0 and Windows 95/98 platforms, and those products with BackOffice compliance will run as NT services and support unified logons and TCP/IP among other features. Refer to Microsoft's Web site at http://www.microsoft.com/windows/thirdparty/winlogo/ for Windows compliance and http://www.microsoft.com/backoffice/designed/ for BackOffice compliance.

Table D.1 is a summary of each of the various interfaces available with SQL Server, under which programming language it is available, and whether the API is considered a future direction for Microsoft or part of its legacy code.

TABLE D.1   SQL SERVER API SUPPORT

API	Language	Standard	OLAP Support	SQL Server 7.0 Features
ADO	VB, VC, VJ, VBS, JS	Emerging	Yes	Most
OLE DB	VC	Emerging	Yes	All
RDO	VB, VJ	Current	No	Most
ODBC	VC, VB	Current	No	All
DAO	VB, VC	Current	No	Limited
DB-Library	VB, VC	Legacy	No	Limited

API	Language	Standard	OLAP Support	SQL Server 7.0 Features
VB-SQL OCX	VB	Legacy	No	Limited
Embedded SQL	VC	Legacy	No	Limited

*VB = Visual Basic, VC = Visual C++, VJ = Visual J++, VBS = VBScript, and JS = JavaScript.

ADO

ActiveX Data Objects (ADO) can be considered a wrapper around OLE DB, providing a structured, easy-to-program, and easy-to-use object model—a set of COM interfaces that provide access to many different data sources. You can use ADO to communicate with various OLE-DB–compliant data sources and not just SQL Server. It is recommended as the primary API for accessing data from general-purpose applications. Because ADO is built upon the OLE DB API and is a simplified object model, it reduces development time and the learning curve associated with a new API.

An ADO application communicates with an OLE DB data source using an OLE DB provider. An OLE DB provider is a dynamic link library that uses OLE DB interfaces to access a particular data source. You can use two types of OLE DB providers with SQL Server:

- SQLOLEDB—The SQL Server OLE DB provider that directly maps OLE DB interfaces to SQL Server
- MSDASQL—The OLE DB provider for ODBC that maps OLE DB interfaces to ODBC APIs

The SQL Server OLE DB provider, which is supplied with SQL Server, is the preferred provider to use in ADO applications that access SQL Server. It is a direct mapping of the interface to SQL Server rather than a layer on top of a pre-existing API, such as the MSDASQL with ODBC.

OLE DB

OLE DB is a low-level, COM-based API for accessing data from various data sources. OLE DB is the preferred method for developing SQL Server utilities or applications that require maximum performance. The SQL Server OLE DB provider, SQLOLEDB, is an OLE DB version-2.0–compliant provider. It provides direct access to the SQL Server native protocol, tabular data stream (TDS). With all this power comes a price, however: complexity. It will require more development time, both in terms of the learning curve associated with any new API and the time required to write programs.

SQL-DMO and Namespaces

SQL Distributed Management Objects, SQL-DMO, is a set of COM objects that provide an object model for SQL Server database and replication management. It is implemented as a dual-interface, in-process server. You can develop a SQL-DMO application using an OLE automation controller such as the one in Visual Basic or by developing a COM-based application using C++. SQL-DMO requires the Microsoft SQL Server ODBC driver, version 3.70 or later, which ships with SQL Server 7.0.

SQL Namespace, SQL-NS, is a set of COM interfaces that allows an application to display the user-interface components of the Enterprise Manager. This would allow an application developed in Visual Basic or Visual C++ to display any of the Enterprise Manager's many wizards, property sheets, or dialog boxes. By using SQL Namespace objects, an application developer can take advantage of the already built-in features of SQL Server. For example, an application developer who wants to provide backups of SQL Server databases directly from his application can use SQL Namespace objects to provide this capability rather than code his own.

ODBC and RDO

ODBC is the standard API used to access data stored in relational or ISAM databases. SQL Server supports ODBC as one of its native APIs for developing applications written in Visual C++ and Visual Basic. Applications that communicate with SQL Server using ODBC require more effort than other APIs because it is a low-level interface.

Like ADO, RDO is a set of simplified objects that provide access to ODBC-compliant databases. It requires less effort than ODBC but lacks the speed and degree of control that is available using native ODBC function calls. Applications written in Visual Basic and Visual J++ can use RDO.

For the future use of ODBC, Microsoft recommends that any new applications being developed migrate from using ODBC or RDO to using OLE DB or ADO. OLE DB is the future direction for all data access APIs because it provides the ability to query and retrieve data from such diverse data sources as SQL Server, Microsoft Access, and even Microsoft Excel spreadsheets.

Legacy APIs: DB-Library, ODS, and Embedded SQL

DB-Library is an API that consists of a set of C functions and macros. A subset of this library is available for use with Visual Basic. DB-Library is the original API provided with SQL Server and was its standard API until the advent of ODBC and, now, OLE DB.

> **CAUTION**
>
> DB-Library has not been enhanced beyond the capabilities in SQL Server 6.5. Although all DB-Library applications will still work with SQL Server 7.0, the many new features of SQL Server 7.0 are not available to DB-Library applications. You should consider migrating any DB-Library application to one of the new APIs, such as ADO.

Microsoft Embedded SQL for C allows an application to embed Transact-SQL statements into the C language source code. Embedded SQL for C applications require that the source code be preprocessed by a precompiler. The Embedded SQL precompiler converts embedded Transact-SQL statements into function calls that can be processed by a C compiler. The C compiler then compiles the preprocessed results into an executable program. Embedded SQL is considered a legacy API, and Microsoft suggests using it only when an application has been mandated to maintain strict ANSI SQL standards.

Open Data Services, ODS, is a SQL Server-based API. You can use it to extend the built-in capabilities of SQL Server. The API consists of a set of C/C++ functions and macros that can be used to build extended stored procedures and gateway applications.

Extended stored procedures are dynamic link libraries that add functionality through routines developed in C/C++ (soon in Visual Basic and Visual J++ as well) using the Open Data Services API and the Win32 API. Users can call extended stored procedures in the same way as normal stored procedures. SQL Server contains a number of extended stored procedures, all of which are prefixed with xp. xp_sendmail is a good example of an extended stored procedure. It adds to SQL Server's functionality by allowing you to send email from a Transact-SQL batch.

In previous versions of SQL Server, ODS was the sole means of providing a gateway to non-SQL Server applications from SQL Server. If you were writing an application that stored data in SQL Server and wanted to access another data source stored in a third-party application, then you had to develop a gateway application using ODS. ODS is difficult to program and requires extensive exception handling.

With the advent of SQL Server 7.0's distributed queries feature and the data transformation services, and with the release of the Microsoft Transaction Server, there is less need for ODS. It is advisable that any new gateway applications for SQL Server use one of the component-based technologies. Component-based applications are language independent and are capable of running under MTS, which offers scalability, security, and structured error handling.

INDEX

Get **FREE** books and more...when you register this book online for our Personal Bookshelf Program

http://register.samspublishing.com/

SAMS

Register online and you can sign up for our *FREE Personal Bookshelf Program*...unlimited access to the electronic version of more than 200 complete computer books—immediately! That means you'll have 100,000 pages of valuable information onscreen, at your fingertips!

Plus, you can access product support, including complimentary downloads, technical support files, book-focused links, companion Web sites, author sites, and more!

And you'll be automatically registered to receive a *FREE subscription to a weekly email newsletter* to help you stay current with news, announcements, sample book chapters, and special events, including sweepstakes, contests, and various product giveaways!

We value your comments! Best of all, the entire registration process takes only a few minutes to complete, so go online and get the greatest value going—absolutely FREE!

Don't Miss Out On This Great Opportunity!

Sams is a brand of Macmillan Computer Publishing USA.

For more information, please visit *www.mcp.com*

Other Related Titles

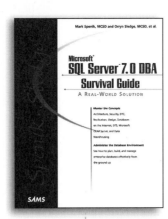

Microsoft SQL Server 7 DBA Survival Guide
Mark Spenik and Orryn Sledge
ISBN: 0-672-31226-3
$49.99 USA/$74.95 CAN

Doing Objects in Visual Basic 6
Deborah Kurata
ISBN: 1-56276-577-9
$49.99 USA/$74.95 CAN

MTS Programming with Visual Basic
Scot Hillier
ISBN: 0-672-31425-8
$29.99 USA/$44.95 CAN

Roger Jennings' Database Developer's Guide with Visual Basic 6
Roger Jennings
ISBN: 0-672-31063-5
$59.99 USA/$89.95 CAN

Building Enterprise Solutions with Visual Studio 6
G.A. Sullivan
ISBN: 0-672-31489-4
$49.99 USA/$74.95 CAN

HTML 4 Unleashed, Second Edition
Rick Darnell
ISBN: 0-672-31347-2
$39.99 USA/$59.95 CAN

The Waite Group's Visual Basic 6 Database How-To
Eric Winemiler
ISBN: 1-57169-152-9
$39.99 USA/$59.95 CAN

COBOL Unleashed
Jon Wessler
ISBN: 0-672-31254-9
$49.99 USA/$74.95 CAN

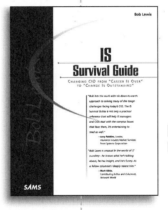

Bob Lewis's IS Survival Guide
Bob Lewis
ISBN: 0-672-31437-1
$24.99 USA/$37.95 CAN

Roger Jennings' Database Workshop: Microsoft Transaction Server 2.0
Stephen Gray and Rick Lievano
ISBN: 0-672-31130-5
$39.99 USA/$59.95 CAN

SAMS

www.samspublishing.com

All prices are subject to change.

What's on the CD-ROM

The companion CD-ROM contains all the authors' source code and samples from the book and many third-party software products.

Windows 95/98/NT 4 Installation Instructions

1. Insert the CD-ROM disc into your CD-ROM drive.
2. From the Windows 95/98/NT 4 desktop, double-click the My Computer icon.
3. Double-click the icon representing your CD-ROM drive.
4. Double-click the icon titled START.EXE to run the installation program.

> **NOTE**
>
> If Windows 95/98/NT 4 is installed on your computer and you have the AutoPlay feature enabled, the START.EXE program starts automatically whenever you insert the disc into your CD-ROM drive.